LITERATURE
AND THE LAW

Editorial Advisors

ASPEN PUBLISHERS

LITERATURE AND THE LAW

Thomas Morawetz

Tapping Reeve Professor of Law and Ethics
University of Connecticut

 Wolters Kluwer

Law & Business

AUSTIN   BOSTON   CHICAGO   NEW YORK   THE NETHERLANDS

Aspen Publishers
Attn: Permissions Department
76 Ninth Avenue, 7th Floor
New York, NY 10011-5201

To contact Customer Care, e-mail customer.care@aspenpublishers.com, call 1-800-234-1660, fax 1-800-901-9075, or mail correspondence to:

Aspen Publishers
Attn: Order Department
PO Box 990
Frederick, MD 21705

Printed in the United States of America.

1 2 3 4 5 6 7 8 9 0

ISBN 978-0-7355-6280-6

Library of Congress Cataloging-in-Publication Data

Morawetz, Thomas, 1942-
Literature and the law/Thomas Morawetz.
    p. cm.
Includes bibliographical references.
ISBN-13: 978-0-7355-6280-6
1. Law and literature. 2. Law in literature. 3. Justice, Administration of, in literature. 4. Literature, Modern–20th century–History and criticism. 5. Literature, Modern–19th century–History and criticism. I. Title.

PN56.L33M67 2007
809'933554—dc22

2007018849

About Wolters Kluwer Law & Business

Wolters Kluwer Law & Business is a leading provider of research information and workflow solutions in key specialty areas. The strengths of the individual brands of Aspen Publishers, CCH, Kluwer Law International and Loislaw are aligned within Wolters Kluwer Law & Business to provide comprehensive, in-depth solutions and expert-authored content for the legal, professional and education markets.

CCH was founded in 1913 and has served more than four generations of business professionals and their clients. The CCH products in the Wolters Kluwer Law & Business group are highly regarded electronic and print resources for legal, securities, antitrust and trade regulation, government contracting, banking, pension, payroll, employment and labor, and healthcare reimbursement and compliance professionals.

Aspen Publishers is a leading information provider for attorneys, business professionals and law students. Written by preeminent authorities, Aspen products offer analytical and practical information in a range of specialty practice areas from securities law and intellectual property to mergers and acquisitions and pension/benefits. Aspen's trusted legal education resources provide professors and students with high-quality, up-to-date and effective resources for successful instruction and study in all areas of the law.

Kluwer Law International supplies the global business community with comprehensive English-language international legal information. Legal practitioners, corporate counsel and business executives around the world rely on the Kluwer Law International journals, loose-leafs, books and electronic products for authoritative information in many areas of international legal practice.

Loislaw is a premier provider of digitized legal content to small law firm practitioners of various specializations. Loislaw provides attorneys with the ability to quickly and efficiently find the necessary legal information they need, when and where they need it, by facilitating access to primary law as well as state-specific law, records, forms and treatises.

Wolters Kluwer Law & Business, a unit of Wolters Kluwer, is headquartered in New York and Riverwoods, Illinois. Wolters Kluwer is a leading multinational publisher and information services company.

for S.E.

Summary of Contents

Contents

ONE
Fiction's Window on Law and Lawyers

TWO
The Meanings of Law

Contents

THREE
Freedom and Crime

FOUR
Criminal Minds

FIVE
Trial and Punishment

Contents

SIX
Finding Meaning

SEVEN
The Law of Literature

Acknowledgments

Many hands contributed to making this book happen. At Aspen Publishers, Carol McGeehan oversaw the acceptance and progress of this project, and I am in her debt. My editor, John Devins, has been the best editor imaginable. He doled out support and insight with perfect sensitivity for our shared aims. I also wish to thank my copyeditor, Troy Froebe, for fine work.

The generous support of the deans at University of Connecticut School of Law made it possible for me to work on this book efficiently and effectively. I am deeply grateful to my good friends, Deans Nell Newton and Jeremy Paul, in countless ways — in particular for a research leave during spring of 2007 and in general for encouragement at every turn.

My student research assistants brought intelligence, interest, and industry to this task. Michael Cummings, Dennis Griffin, and Meredith Long were involved in many aspects, including editing the manuscript, compiling suggested readings, and the onerous job of reviewing proofs. Meredith also solved the difficult job of requesting and processing permissions to reprint materials with skill and aplomb. At earlier stages, Bill Piotrowski helped enormously with my original book proposal and Douglas Heim and Gabe Rosenberg helped with research. I am grateful to all.

I am also indebted to the many students at University of Connecticut School of Law (and elsewhere, including University of San Diego Law School) who took my seminars in law and literature over the past fifteen years and shared their insights. I learned something from each one of them, and many contributed memorably.

The task of preparing stories and articles for insertion into the manuscript requires skill and patience. I am indebted, as ever, to Delia Roy, who directs faculty support services at University of Connecticut School of Law, for her help at many stages. I am also grateful to Joan Wood for indispensable work in manuscript preparation. At our law library, Yan Hong of the library staff and Tom Hemstock, a student assistant, made noteworthy contributions.

Finally and most importantly are those friends who keep us sane by allowing us to share not only ideas but the full panoply of thoughts and feelings. In that regard, my profound thanks go to Scotty Enyart, Herbert Morris, and Elyn Saks.

I would also like to thank the publishers and copyright holders listed here for granting permission to reprint the articles, excerpts, poetry, and stories indicated below.

Allende, Isabel. "The Judge's Wife," from *The Stories of Eva Luna*, pp. 183-193. (Translated from the Spanish by Margaret Sayer Peden). Copyright © 1989 by Isabel Allende. English translation copyright 1991 by Macmillan Publishing Company. Reprinted with permission of Scribner, an imprint of Simon & Schuster Adult Publishing Group.

Balkin, J.M. "Some Realism about Pluralism," 1990 Duke Law Journal 375. Reprinted in part by permission from the Duke Law Journal.

Capek, Karel. "The Clairvoyant," from *Toward the Radical Center*, translated by Norma Comrada, copyright © 1990. Reprinted by permission of The Catbird Press, Publishers.

Christie, Agatha. "Witness for the Prosecution," from *Witness for the Prosecution and Other Stories*, copyright © 1924, 1926, 1929, 1943, 1947, 1948, renewed 1952, 1954, 1957, 1971, 1975 by Agatha Christie Mallowan. Copyright © 1932 by The Curtis Publishing Co. Used by permission of G.P. Putman's Sons, a division of Penguin Group (USA) Inc.

cummings, e.e. "may i feel said he," copyright © 1935, 1963, 1991 by the Trustees for the E.E. Cummings Trust. Copyright © 1978 by George James Firmage, from *Complete Poems: 1904-1962* by e.e. cummings, edited by George J. Firmage. Used by permission of Liveright Publishing Corporation.

Dubus, Andre. "The Intruder," from *Dancing After Hours*, copyright © 1995 by Andre Dubus. Used by permission of Alfred A. Knopf, a division of Random House, Inc.

Emerson, Thomas. "Pornography and the First Amendment: A Reply to Professor MacKinnon," 2 Yale and Law Policy Review 130 (1984). Reprinted by permission of the Yale Law and Policy Review.

Faulkner, William. "Tomorrow," copyright © 1940 and renewed by Estelle Faulkner and Jill Faulkner Summers. Copyright © 1949 by William Faulkner, from *Knight's Gambit*. Used by permission of Random House, Inc.

Fiss, Owen. "State Activism and State Censorship," *The Yale Law Journal*, vol. 100 (1991), pp. 2087-2106. Reprinted by permission of The Yale Law Journal Company and William S. Hein Company.

Gaines, Ernest J. From *A Lesson Before Dying*, copyright © 1993 by Ernest J. Gaines. Used by permission of Alfred A Knopf, a division of Random House, Inc.

Gordimer, Nadine. "Crimes of Conscience," copyright © 1982 by Nadine Gordimer, from *Something Out There*. Used by permission of Viking Penguin, a division of Penguin Group (USA) Inc.

Grey, Thomas C. "The Hermeneutics File," 58 Southern California Law Review 211-236 (1985). Reprinted with the permission of the Southern California Law Review.

Hyland, Richard. "Babel: a she'ur," 11 Cadozo Law Review 1585 (1990). Reprinted by permission of the Cardozo Law Review.

Johnson, Denis. "Dundun," from *Jesus' Son*. Copyright © 1992 by Denis Johnson. Reprinted by permission of Farrar, Straus and Giroux, LLC.

Just, Ward. "About Boston," from *The Congressman Who Loved Flaubert: 21 Stories and Novellas*. Copyright © 1998 by Ward Just. Reprinted by permission of Houghton Mifflin Company. All rights reserved.

Kafka, Franz. "Before the Law," "An Imperial Message," "The New Advocate," "Advocates," "The Problem of Our Laws," and "In the Penal Colony," from *Franz Kafka: The Complete Stories*, edited by Nahum N. Glatzer, copyright © 1946, 1947, 1948, 1949, 1954, 1958, 1971 by Schocken Books. Used by permission of Schocken Books, a division of Random House, Inc.

Lee, Harper. Chapter 20, pp. 212-218 from *To Kill a Mockingbird*. Copyright © 1960 by Harper Lee, renewed 1988 by Harper Lee. Foreword copyright © 1993 by Harper Lee. Reprinted by permission of HarperCollins Publishers.

Miller, Sue. Excerpted from *The Good Mother: A Novel*, pp. 257-280. Copyright © 1986 by Sue Miller. Reprinted by permission of HarperCollins Publishers.

O'Connor, Frank. "Legal Aid," from *The Collected Stories of Frank O'Connor*, copyright © 1981 by Harriet O'Donovan Sheehy, Executrix of the Estate of Frank O'Connor. Used by permission of Alfred A. Knopf, a division of Random House, Inc.

Ozick, Cynthia. "Puttermesser: Her Work History, Her Ancestry, Her Afterlife," from *The Puttermesser Papers*, copyright © 1997 by Cynthia Ozick. Used by permission of Alfred A. Knopf, a division of Random House, Inc.

Roth, Philip. "Eli, the Fanatic," from *Goodbye, Columbus*. Copyright © 1959, renewed 1987 by Philip Roth. Reprinted by permission of Houghton Mifflin Company. All rights reserved.

Salter, James. "American Express." Copyright by James Salter. Reprinted by permission of SLL/Sterling Lord Literistic, Inc.

Smith, Abbe. Excerpts from "Defending Defending," 28 Hofstra Law Review 925 (2000). Reprinted by permission of the Hofstra Law Review.

Ustinov, Peter. "There are 43,200 Seconds in a Day," from *Add a Dash of Pity* (1996), pp. 125-163. (Amherst NY: Prometheus Books.) Copyright © 1958, 1959 by Pavor, S.A. Reprinted with permission of the publisher.

Introduction

Why "Literature and the Law"?

It is natural to think that a course on law and literature is an interesting but optional adjunct to a legal education. To the contrary, I believe it is a valuable and essential element in learning about law. Such courses are proliferating in American law schools and in the literature and legal studies programs of American universities as well.

What makes law and literature courses essential? One is tempted to see them as pleasant diversions, a chance to put aside for a few hours the tax regulations or the Uniform Commercial Code. Faculty members are inclined to see them as irrelevant to their main mission of training practitioners, neither particularly helpful nor harmful. But I believe these attitudes reflect fundamental misunderstandings.

What is a legal education? This question is at once easy and diabolically hard. A legal education turns untrained students into potential lawyers. That's the easy part. But the hard part lies in identifying the characteristics, and not just the skills, that lawyers should have and in deciding how they can be cultivated.

The dark suspicion that lies at the core of jokes about lawyers—and the unjoking mistrust of lawyers as well—is that legal education corrupts those who undergo it, that it dulls one's conscience, dilutes one's sense of principle, and even compromises one's humanity. That is a dire accusation, one that covers a Pandora's box of misgivings about law and lawyers, both plausible and implausible. But one claim that I have always found convincing is that legal education can erode individuality.

What does that mean? Students come to law school with baggage, both literally and figuratively. Each student has a unique personal history, various kinds of knowledge and ignorance, and a collection of social, political, and moral attitudes and opinions. Many of them draw from their first encounters in law classes the conclusion that personal perspectives and values are to be laid aside. Prior successes and prior self-definitions are, they decide, largely irrelevant to the kind of professionalism they are at pains to acquire. The chameleonic ability to identify with any side of any disagreement (and specifically with one's *client's* side, whatever it happens to be) takes precedence over personal conviction and belief. Not every student hears this message the same way, and certainly not every student succumbs to it—but no student will fail to recognize it as part of the induction process.

A student's diminished concern for her own individuality will affect the way she sees others as individuals. It is easy to identify a client only in terms of her legal needs and goals, to define a fellow lawyer by his legal role. Plaintiffs, defendants, judges, rapists, victims, shareholders, trustees—all these terms refer to legal abstractions and to real persons at the same time. The ultimate success of the lawyer may depend on the care she takes to avoid reducing the player to the role he plays in the game.

The most important job, the *essential* job that law and literature courses play is to refocus legal education on the inescapable truth that law is about individuals—their needs, goals, vulnerabilities, and unique characters. The attorney or judge who understands herself as an individual with a special history, trajectory, and set of values is, to that extent, a better attorney or judge. The lawyer who reads statutes and judicial decisions with an eye toward their effects on the interests of individuals is, to that extent, a perceptive interpreter. And the practitioner who sees his client as more than a disgruntled stockholder, or party to a divorce, or defaulting debtor is likely, to that extent, to offer better representation.

Literature—all literature—is at once about individuals and about generalizable bits of experience. Captain Ahab, Hamlet, and Elizabeth Bennett are individuals and they are also symbols. However much or little we see ourselves in them, we extend our experience and our sense of human nature by participating in their lives. Literature is *overtly* about individuals and about their commonalities. Law *covertly* has the same two dimensions. Literature can be the vital corrective in a legal education that allows us to see all of law's facets.

Skills and Insights

Legal writing is rarely held up as a model of transparency; "legalese" is rarely a term of praise. But there are exceptions. Justices Oliver Wendell Holmes, Benjamin Cardozo, and Robert H. Jackson are respected as models of lucid prose. But the fact that their expressive powers are held as exemplary testifies to our normally low expectations about the writing of judges and lawyers.

For the most part, the virtues of good writing and good legal writing coincide. Clarity, immediacy, and lack of ambiguity are essential qualities of good writing in general, and good writing by lawyers in particular. But law students and legal practitioners, along with critics of legal writing, sometimes think otherwise. They are taught to believe that law requires an arsenal of technical terms whose complexity is penetrable only by specialists. They come to believe that wills and contracts, statutes and judicial opinions, court papers and research memoranda must all be written in a special style in which direct, clear, active, and efficient expression is at best a secondary virtue.

That is nonsense. Of course, learning law involves learning crucial terms in each field, e.g., learning the role of consideration and mutual agreement in contract, fault and negligence in torts, *mens rea* and *actus reus* in criminal law. But each term can and should be explainable in an accessible way. The success of a legal text as a means of communication will often depend on its transparency.

The lesson that clear, expressive, and potent communication is achieved in much the same way inside and outside law can be learned effectively by immersing oneself in literature. Fictions and essays, at their best, show how language can be controlled and manipulated to convey meaning and how varied and supple the tools of language are. Reading literature dispels the myth that effective legal writing involves stripping one's prose of style. Language, whether in legal or other contexts, is hardly ever most effective when it is formal and mechanistic. (Of course, certain kinds of documents—wills, contracts, trust agreements, incorporation papers—are exceptions when their only role is to formalize an agreement.) It is not a fault for judicial opinions, legal briefs, or academic articles to reflect the distinctive intelligence and voice of their author.

Lawyers are often required to reconstruct events as stories and present convincing narratives. Works of fiction can show them how that's done. Any client has goals and interests that the lawyer must identify; in doing so, the lawyer must see how his interventions can play a role in the story of the client's life. If litigation is involved, particularly criminal litigation, the lawyer must juggle various stories—the one he reconstructs from available evidence, the one he elicits from witnesses (favorable and adverse), and the one that he conveys to the jury or judge and tries to make his audience believe. The situation at hand may be kaleidoscopic; there may be many truths within one reality with different ways of assigning motives and responsibility.

Every lawyer must wrestle with the problem of truth in narrative. She must ask whether the circumstances of the case can be told honestly in different ways, from different points of view. She must consider at what point she finds herself telling stories that she does not believe. Every litigator struggles with the relationship between the story most favorable to her client and the version that good sense and experience tell her is most plausible. And every jury member, every judge, and every observer of trials and other adjudications struggles with the question of what stories to believe.

Literature—reading it, writing it, interpreting and analyzing it—is the domain of narrative. Every writer, not only of fiction, but of history and biography, is consumed daily with finding and conveying truths in human experience. Reading any narrative precipitates many questions that lawyers in their roles as storytellers must ask. What is the writer's point of view and how did he choose it? What kinds of impressions and truths is the writer trying to convey? Are there alternative ways of looking at these events? Do we have access to the ways in which the actors see themselves?

Values and Choices

Legal positivists pay a great deal of attention to the separateness of questions about the content of law (what the law *is*) and evaluations and criticisms of the content of law (what the law *ought to be*). So much of a law student's time is focused on assimilating what the law is that normative questions about the law's merits and the merits of policies supporting it can be shortchanged. Moreover, a lawyer can easily rationalize *never* addressing such values and norms. One is taught that an important part of lawyering is suspending judgment. Lawyers are trained to see and articulate the conflicting sides of an issue. They are trained as well to put aside their own normative judgments to adopt and promote the interests of clients.

This is something of a paradoxical posture toward values. In their roles as judges or legislators — or even simply as citizens — lawyers are expected to be the conscience of society. Jokes about lawyers are especially harsh insofar as they show lawyers shirking or betraying that role. The paradox can be expressed in terms of serving justice: can one be neutral, ready to take on all causes and interests, and be on the side of justice as well? Too often, law students say that the implicit (or even the explicit) message of legal pedagogy is that the first of these alternatives is dominant and that they learn to put aside their values as distractions and as private matters.

A major point of literature is to wake one's conscience and stir one's sense of justice. Almost any situation worth writing about is morally and psychologically complex. Characters in fiction, like persons in life, may not know what they want, and, when they do know, may often find it beyond their grasp. Their wants and needs will be at odds with the wants and needs of other persons. And, as we as readers enter these situations and conflicts, we sympathize with and support some characters and distance ourselves from others. We wonder what it is about the world, society, persons, and institutions that creates these predicaments, and we think about how we would change things if we could.

Some commentators on law and literature have assumed that the most relevant fictions involve exemplars of moral goodness. That view is too narrow. Literature opens up for us the dimension of values, norms, and feelings, but it does not necessarily tell us how to respond. Plato was openly afraid of the power of literature and its power to seduce and control our attitudes. Ironically, totalitarian governments have often taken the same position, not because literature necessarily inspires good persons to oppose bad governments, but rather because it frees the moral imagination and licenses us to form our own opinions and goals.

The readings in this book raise all kinds of questions—about how lawyers should act; about how law firms shape and limit the lives of lawyers; about how lawyers function in their communities; about the social choices embodied in what the law allows, encourages, and forbids; about how we create institutions to judge others' conduct and punish; and about the place of law in the lives of everyone. And there are broader questions—about the symbolic role of law as a repository of shared goals, as a way of giving the camouflage of legitimacy to power, as the ultimate source of bureaucratic irrationality, or as the sum of our collective social wisdom; about the scope and meaning of free expression in our culture; and about how we find meaning in legal writings, how we agree and disagree when we construe the world of law, and how we deal with disagreement.

The ultimate irony is that some persons turn to law in the belief that it can substitute for personal choice. For them, law represents the settled values and norms of the culture; one can adopt the protective coloration of those norms in preference to struggling for a lifetime to discover and act upon one's own values. In fact, the implicit message of the materials offered here is that understanding law only makes the struggle more imperative and unavoidable.

Topics

This collection of topics and materials has seven chapters, seven distinct topics and sets of issues.

Chapter 1. Fiction's Window on Law and Lawyers

We begin in Chapter 1 by looking at lawyers and lawyering. Everyone, law students included, has opinions about them—about their skills and personalities, their characters and attitudes. We recognize the dangers of generalizing, but we generalize all the same. As one acquires a legal education, one finds some expectations and fears realized; in other ways, one is surprised. In some ways, law is the kind of practice (like medicine, like business, like a sport or a hobby) that only an insider can understand. A layperson can grasp what it is to be a lawyer if he has never been one no more easily than he can understand playing rugby or playing the violin if he has never done so. All the TV shows and novels in the world will not make one an insider. And a good part of what a lawyer learns is the anthropology of law firms and other attorneys' offices. And yet stories can be an excellent surrogate, raising questions that many lawyers often ignore.

In Chapter 1, we look at a series of recent stories about lawyers—who they are, what they do, and how they do it. We have a chance to look behind the stereotypes of the profession to consider what kinds of persons choose to become lawyers. How does legal training and legal practice change their expectations and character? What counts for success in law? What compromises are attorneys or judges likely to have to make? These stories, often with a satiric bite, take us inside law's institutions and ask us to consider how they reflect the classes, hierarchies, and prejudices of society.

Chapter 2. The Meanings of Law

Chapter 2 casts a wider net. Law is more than the world of lawyers and judges. Countless things that we do every day are affected by the fact that we live within a legal system. Driving, buying and selling, what we say and how we say it are all matters that are shaped in one way or another by the existence of law. And, even if we take law and its effects for granted most of the time, we all have attitudes toward it.

Law can represent the vehicle that takes us from barbarity to civilization. It is the backbone of society, the framework that allows communities to function. It allows us to pursue our shared goals in harmony with others. Or it can represent coercive power, rules that constrain our freedom and autonomy and prevent us from achieving some of our goals and desires. In that sense, it stands for public constraints in what might otherwise be the domain of private choice.

Or law can simply stand for a collective attempt to create rational order in the face of the unpredictability and chaos of nature. It can reflect the will to control — through contracts, wills, criminal prohibitions, and countless other means — one's environment and one's relations with others. The political philosopher Hobbes concluded that, without law, we would have "war of all against all." Alternatively, law can be the ultimate vindication of irrationality, a thicket of arbitrary rules and hurdles. Law can be seen as moral, as the home of collective morality, or as the flimsy veil of legitimacy that covers amorality and violence.

Writers as diverse as Herman Melville and Franz Kafka have seen law as paradoxical. Their provocative stories and parables are among the best conversation-starters in literature. Critics, as well as general readers, have spun countless theories about them.

Attitudes to law are much affected by the political and historical circumstances of a particular culture. In Chapter 2, we will look at stories from places as diverse as pre-apartheid South Africa and post-World War II Italy. Each evokes a different set of circumstances and, in turn, a different attitude toward law and lawyers. Some deal with universal themes and experiences, others with historically particular ones.

Chapter 3. Freedom and Crime

In Chapter 3, we consider directly the relation between law and the individual, between social order and personal autonomy. Criminal law deals with prohibitions. It tells us that certain kinds of conduct are so threatening to others and to general welfare that society, through law, must intervene. Individual freedom comes to an end.

Different societies make these determinations in different ways. All agree on certain prohibitions. Hardly anyone in any culture thinks that homicide, theft, or rape is a private matter. But beyond these basic harms, there are many disagreements. A most effective way of raising the question of whether and when criminal law should intervene in persons' lives is through literature. Stories allow us to enter the world of addicts and of those whose lives are closely affected by them. How should law deal with drug addiction? We can get an intimate view of the experience of persons who are severely disabled or terminally ill and ask whether there is a public interest in keeping them alive and whether they can choose to die. Variations in child raising may also become a concern for law when questions about well-being are relevant, even though family life is traditionally a private matter.

In all these contexts, fiction opens doors and eyes. It also allows us to see how attitudes about the balance between public and private concerns have shifted over time, echoing other shifts in political and social attitudes. Abuse within families and euthanasia, for example, have only recently been recognized as matters for public concern.

Chapter 4. Criminal Minds

A different question about the limits of criminal law draws attention to the psychology of crime. Many criminal acts are aberrational, committed in a state of rage, frustration, or derangement. Criminals often have psychological problems; they may have odd, often sociopathic, ways of seeing the acts of others. In criminal law, we are driven to simplify. Legislators, the police, prosecutors, judges, and juries all need simple tests for culpability and guilt. The psychological inquiry is often limited to what the actor intended, what the actor knew, and/or whether reckless conduct was involved.

Common experience, reinforced by the endlessly rich sources of literature, shows how thin the legal picture of psychology—of thought, action, and feeling—really is. The stories in Chapter 4 compel us to look at the complexity of motive, intention, and conflicting feelings and to consider the role of unconscious desires, of habit, and of moral attitudes in potential conflict with law. We will look at the circumstances that lead persons to act harmfully and violently and at the conditions (depression, mental disease, multiple personality syndrome) that complicate and even elude common understanding. Can the law do a better job than it does of accommodating the various modes of human thought and action?

Chapter 5. Trial and Punishment

In Chapter 5, we look more deeply at problems of trial and punishment. It is sometimes said that a lawyer's exclusive responsibility is to her client and that the diligence owed to clients cannot be diluted by other goals or personal values. This principle can often lead to situations in which the most effective strategy—at trial or in negotiations—involves serious social costs and moral consequences. It may be effective, for example, to defend a woman accused of masterminding a criminal conspiracy by drawing on the sexist cliché that women are weak and likely to be under the power of men. The cost of a successful defense may be to reinforce a damaging prejudice. A selection by the novelist, Ernest Gaines, shows us an analogous dilemma facing an attorney who is defending a black youth in the segregated South of the 1930s. Should lawyers be guided by more than the need for the most effective defense? What is society's interest in curtailing bias, and how is it relevant? More generally, how much of the litigator's role is to appeal to a jury's (or judge's) reason and understanding and how much of her role in fact involves triggering irrational beliefs, feelings, and emotions?

Chapter 5 covers questions about punishment as well as trial practice. If there is a general sense that society's interests require punishment to deter crime and reform offenders, there has never been agreement on what forms of punishment are acceptable or effective. It is easy to be seduced into confusing rehabilitation, the goal of turning the criminal into an autonomous person with respect for others, with the goal of enforcing conformity with the majority's values. Kafka's shocking story, *In the Penal Colony*, makes us face the rationality of our own procedures and modes of punishment. The challenge of punishment has, as we will see, inspired many writers to do their most thought-provoking work.

Chapter 6. Finding Meaning

In Chapter 6, we step back from fiction to examine the process of reading and interpreting fictional and legal writings. We will ask the elusive question of how it is that we find meaning in texts. That question, in turn, leads to the question of how we agree and disagree about meaning. Many, but hardly all, terms in legal texts can bear several interpretations. Consider the Constitutional prohibition on cruel and unusual punishment or the requirement of due process. Judges are likely to disagree about the meaning and application of such terms.

Writers who study meaning warn us to avoid a cheap and easy relativism, whereby we argue simply that judges bring their own backgrounds, beliefs, values, and prejudices—and that therefore their disagreements are beyond resolution. In fact, disagreement is the start, not the end, of discourse. Judges bring to the table not only potentially different meanings; they also are parties to a process involving shared methods of analysis and debate. This process allows them to comprehend the reasons and motives behind interpretations other than those they favor. As a result, they can and will give each other reasons to change their minds. Sometimes they will succeed; often they won't.

In the last forty years, scholars in many fields have examined how readers of texts arrive at meaning and discuss it. Within law and literature, those who study judges and their methods of disagreeing among themselves and deciding cases have drawn suggestive analogies to literary analysis. Many articles and books on law and literature compare legal and literary interpretation—how we disagree, how we debate, and how, if at all, we arrive at consensus. This and related studies of meaning go by the Greek label of "hermeneutics." Chapter 6 is an introduction to the hermeneutics of law.

Chapter 7. The Law of Literature

Most of the materials in this book look at law, lawyers, and legal matters from the standpoint of literature. The last chapter, Chapter 7, turns this perspective on its head and looks at literature from the standpoint of law. Freedom of speech is guaranteed by the first amendment of the U.S. Constitution, and free expression has generally been held to be the essence of free speech. Two justifications are usually given for the guarantee of free expression. The narrower one is that free speech makes political progress and democratic rule more likely as agendas are tested in the marketplace of ideas. The more general justification is that, even if the marketplace of ideas works badly, the chance to express, share, and test ideas is an indispensable part of becoming a free and autonomous person.

Certain kinds of expression are said to be outside first amendment protection because they express unacceptable ideas or no ideas at all. Obscenity law has never had a secure footing. Some judges are comfortable putting obscene expressions outside the law because they have no ideational content; others acknowledge the presence of ideas but take on the role of determining which ideas are protected, which not. We will look at the extent to which obscenity can be defined, as well as the larger question of when, if ever, our government can or should be in the business of censoring ideas.

Some writers argue that the diffusion of ideas is significantly limited by the concentration of ownership of the media. By allowing this concentration, the government abets the process by which the marketplace of ideas is constrained. We will look at the merits of this argument and at suggestions that government, through law, take an active role to encourage a diversity of points of view and modes of expression.

The Scope of Law and Literature

The materials in this book show the breadth of law and literature and demonstrate the many ways we can ask and answer questions about law by using literature. It also investigates the law *of* literature, as well as the second-order questions we might have about *how* law and literature are resources for understanding what meaning is.

These topics are just a beginning. We could also look at how literature has affected the course of law. How have our social attitudes to slavery, totalitarianism, exploitation of workers, protection of the environment, and countless other concerns, been changed by essays and fictions? How has literature shaped our political and social consciousness, and thus our law? We could also look at rhetorical devices in law and literature to see what makes language most effective in each domain. In fact, rhetoric has been a study that ties law to literature since the schools of ancient Greece.

However they are traversed, these materials should allow readers to ask again the general questions about law — its purposes, its demands, its limits, and its opportunities — that focused their attention on law in the first place. For non-law students they anticipate in a sophisticated way the subjects of law and its rigors and opportunities.

A Word on Materials and Structure

The materials in the first five chapters are primarily works of fiction. For the most part, they are short stories and occasionally chapters of novels. A few cases and articles are also included. In the last two chapters, articles and some case materials are central. Most of the materials are short; since they are packed with insights and nuances, they reward close attention and exhaustive discussion. Each of the first five chapters can very usefully be supplemented with one or more short novels or plays, and in each case I refer the reader to works that I consider exceptionally relevant (and I offer supporting introductions and discussion points).

I tend to steer away from the most familiar texts in law and literature, works that have been covered extensively elsewhere. *Billy Budd, Bleak House*, and *Crime and Punishment* are obvious examples. Their omission is not meant to slight the works or their importance. But the works are likely to be so familiar to teachers of the course that they can be slipped into the curriculum without substantial new guidance.

Each selection is preceded by a note that introduces the author and discusses the context of the piece. The discussion points that follow draw attention to historical context, legal aspects, psychological and anthropological underpinnings, or other dimensions that may trigger and deepen discussion. They are not intended to identify the "meaning" of the selection; in fact, a major purpose of this book is to dispel the notion that stories and cases simply have a single identifiable point. Debate and multiple points of view are to be expected and encouraged.

LITERATURE AND THE LAW

ONE

Fiction's Window on Law and Lawyers

Fictional lawyers often seem stereotyped. Novels and stories, movies and television are full of good lawyers and bad ones, just as they are even more overstuffed with good cops and bad ones. It's easy to tell them apart, even if there are rare cases in which the good lawyer or cop succumbs to temptation or the bad one reforms. Good lawyers insist on seeking justice and do so steadfastly even when justice is elusive. Bad lawyers — in novels by John Grisham, for example — pursue nothing but their own interests or those of their shadier clients.

The real lives of lawyers are more complicated, both psychologically and morally. Some moral dilemmas are inherent in the profession. As a general matter, lawyers are the agents of the clients. They are expected to identify with the ends of their clients; they offer clients the means to use law's resources. But a client's goals may often conflict with other important social interests and with the lawyer's own preferences for doing good. Thus, the lawyer's professional role may be at cross-purposes with her personal convictions. She can minimize the conflict by choosing clients with discretion, and she can use her influence to shape a client's ends to some extent. And yet conflicts are inevitable.

How do lawyers resolve such conflicts? What are the other psychological perils of law practice? Lawyers believe almost universally that there are emotional and psychological dangers in identifying too closely with a client. While the need to be the client's agent implies that other interests are to be put aside, the lawyer must also establish distance between herself and her client. The understandable result is law can be an isolating profession, rife with constraints on loyalty and confidentiality. Because lawyers circumvent so many conflicts and have to be at once their own masters and their clients' agents, they find ways to rationalize these conflicts by creating professional masks and, in many cases, avoiding introspection.

But introspection is inevitable and indispensable. As a person rather than merely as a professional, the attorney's loyalties are triangulated. Besides his duty of "zealous representation," he also has the same duties that we all have to refrain from harming other persons and to benefit them when he can. Thirdly, but hardly least, he has duties to himself, to be a person of integrity and self-respect, along with duties to his family and friends.

Of course, attorneys run the gamut of personality types — and moral and social dispositions. Some are selfish, others altruistic. Some are reflective, others obtuse. Some, but hardly all, are conscientious. It is important to be cautious when generalizing about any diverse group. But the challenges and conflicts lawyers face are distinctive. The works of fiction in this chapter bring us in touch with a wide range of persons. There is an equally wide spectrum in our authors' points of view toward their characters and, one may infer, toward law. Every work of literature worth examining alludes to something specific and something of more general relevance. In these fictions, specific and idiosyncratic characters face (or avoid) issues that are raised in a particularly acute way for lawyers but that must trouble all of us.

James Salter: American Express

Many lawyers are private corporate lawyers, and many others aspire to that kind of practice. Corporate practice is the most highly paid niche; corporate clients can pay generously to avoid and finesse legal complications. Many law students, for better or worse, aspire to corporate practice without always considering the alternatives, implications, and costs.

In many ways, corporate practice offers a highlighted version of the psychological challenges facing all lawyers. The profession is inherently hierarchic. Because of the special skills and language inherent in law, lawyers often seem to inhabit a realm barely accessible to laypersons. Many lawyers take lightly the injunction to follow their clients' instructions, since they regard themselves as infinitely more knowledgeable about the techniques and available ends than their clients can possibly be. The danger exists that this sense of power and superiority will be carried over to all relationships. While this has obvious costs for the lawyer's friends and family as well as his clients, it also has costs for the lawyer himself. He becomes manipulative and isolated, comfortable only with similar-minded lawyers.

James Salter's "American Express" is a subtle representation of this way of life. Salter himself, who is not a lawyer, is well described by the cliché, a "writer's writer." Over his long career, he has been a careful and slow writer (and a diligent, if not obsessive, rewriter); his writing sparkles as he makes every word count. He packs as much into a paragraph as many writers do in a chapter—and he rewards rereading. He has produced five novels and two books of short stories, as well as travel writings, a seductive memoir (*Burning the Days*), and screenplays, several of them for his long-time friend, Robert Redford.

Salter seems fascinated with the ways individualism may be realized and expressed (or constrained) within institutional constraints. The institution may be the military, as in his first two novels, or the law. Salter's own post-military life has been, by contrast, one of few constraints other than self-imposed ones. "American Express" is part of his 1996 collection, *Dusk and Other Stories*. It is written in a tight, elliptical style that will remind you of a screenplay with rapid, unmarked changes of scene and time. The characterizations and the dialogue are sharp.

❦ American Express ❦

James Salter

It's hard now to think of all the places and nights, Nicola's like a railway car, deep and gleaming, the crowd at the *Un, Deux, Trois,* Billy's. Unknown brilliant faces jammed at the bar. The dark, dramatic eye that blazes for a moment and disappears.

In those days they were living in apartments with funny furniture and on Sundays sleeping until noon. They were in the last rank of the armies of law. Clever junior partners were above them, partners, associates, men in fine suits who had lunch at the Four Seasons. Frank's father went there three or four times a week, or else to the Century Club or the Union where there were men even older than he. Half of the members can't urinate, he used to say, and the other half can't stop.

Alan, on the other hand, was from Cleveland where his father was well known, if not detested. No defendant was too guilty, no case too clear-cut. Once in another part of the state he was defending a murderer, a black man. He knew what the jury was thinking, he knew what he looked like to them. He stood up slowly. It could be they had heard certain things, he began. They may have heard, for instance, that he was a big-time lawyer from the city. They may have heard that he wore three-hundred-dollar suits, that he drove a Cadillac and smoked expensive cigars. He was walking along as if looking for something on the floor. They may have heard that he was Jewish.

He stopped and looked up. Well, he was from the city, he said. He wore three-hundred-dollar suits, he drove a Cadillac, smoked big cigars, and he was Jewish. "Now that we have that settled, let's talk about this case."

Lawyers and sons of lawyers. Days of youth. In the morning in stale darkness the subways shrieked.

"Have you noticed the new girl at the reception desk?"

"What about her?" Frank asked.

They were surrounded by noise like the launch of a rocket. "She's hot," Alan confided.

"How do you know?"

"I know."

"What do you mean, you know?"

"Intuition."

"Int*ui*tion?" Frank said.

"What's wrong?"

"That doesn't count."

Which was what made them inseparable, the hours of work, the lyric, the dreams. As it happened, they never knew the girl at the reception desk with her nearsightedness and wild, full hair. They knew various others, they knew Julie, they knew Catherine, they knew Ames. The best, for nearly two years, was Brenda who had somehow managed to graduate from Marymount and had a walk-through apartment on West Fourth. In a smooth, thin, silver frame was the photograph of her father with his two daughters at the Plaza, Brenda, thirteen, with an odd little smile.

"I wish I'd known you then," Frank told her.

Brenda said, "I bet you do."

It was her voice he liked, the city voice, scornful and warm. They were two of a kind, she liked to say, and in a way it was true. They drank in her favorite places where the owner played the piano and everyone seemed to know her. Still, she counted on him. The city has its incomparable moments—rolling along the wall of the apartment, kissing, bumping like stones. Five in the afternoon, the vanishing light. "No," she was commanding. "No, no, no."

He was kissing her throat. "What are you going to do with that beautiful struma of yours?"

"You won't take me to dinner," she said.

"Sure I will."

"Beautiful what?"

She was like a huge dog, leaping from his arms.

"Come here," he coaxed.

She went into the bathroom and began combing her hair. "Which restaurant are we going to?" she called.

She would give herself but it was mostly unpredictable. She would do anything her mother hadn't done and would live as her mother lived, in the same kind of apartment, in the same soft chairs. Christmas and the envelopes for the doormen, the snow sweeping past the awning, her children coming home from school. She adored her father. She went on a trip to Hawaii with him and sent back postcards, two or three scorching lines in a large, scrawled hand.

It was summer.

"Anybody here?" Frank called.

He rapped on the door which was ajar. He was carrying his jacket, it was hot.

"All right," he said in a loud voice, "come out with your hands over your head. Alan, cover the back."

The party, it seemed, was over. He pushed the door open. There was one lamp on, the room was dark.

"Hey, Bren, are we too late?" he called. She appeared mysteriously in the doorway, barelegged but in heels. "We'd have come earlier but we were working. We couldn't get out of the office. Where is everybody? Where's all the food? Hey, Alan, we're late. There's no food, nothing."

She was leaning against the doorway.

"We tried to get down here," Alan said. "We couldn't get a cab."

Frank had fallen onto the couch. "Bren, don't be mad," he said. "We were working, that's the truth. I should have called. Can you put some music on or something? Is there anything to drink?"

"There's about that much vodka," she finally said.

"Any ice?"

"About two cubes." She pushed off the wall without much enthusiasm. He watched her walk into the kitchen and heard the refrigerator door open.

"So, what do you think, Alan?" he said. "What are you going to do?"

"Me?"

"Where's Louise?" Frank called.

"Asleep," Brenda said.

"Did she really go home?"

"She goes to work in the morning."

"So does Alan."

Brenda came out of the kitchen with the drinks.

"I'm sorry we're late," he said. He was looking in the glass, "Was it a good party?" He stirred the contents with one finger. "This is the ice?"

"Jane Harrah got fired," Brenda said.

"That's too bad. Who is she?"

"She does big campaigns. Ross wants me to take her place."

"Great."

"I'm not sure if I want to," she said lazily.

"Why not?"

"She was sleeping with him."

"And she got fired?"

"Doesn't say much for him, does it?"

"It doesn't say much for her."

"That's just like a man. God."

"What does she look like? Does she look like Louise?"

The smile of the thirteen-year-old came across Brenda's face. "No one looks like Louise," she said. Her voice squeezed the name whose legs Alan dreamed of. "Jane has these thin lips."

"Is that all?"

"Thin-lipped women are always cold."

"Let me see yours," he said.

"Burn up."

"Yours aren't thin. Alan, these aren't thin, are they? Hey, Brenda, don't cover them up."

"Where were you? You weren't really working."

He'd pulled down her hand. "Come on, let them be natural," he said. "They're not thin, they're nice. I just never noticed them before." He leaned back. "Alan, how're you doing? You getting sleepy?"

"I was thinking. How much the city has changed," Alan said.

"In five years?"

"I've been here almost six years."

"Sure, it's changing. They're coming down, we're going up."

Alan was thinking of the vanished Louise who had left him only a jolting ride home through the endless streets. "I know."

That year they sat in the steam room on limp towels, breathing the eucalyptus and talking about Hardmann Roe. They walked to the showers like champions. Their flesh still had firmness. Their haunches were solid and voting.

Hardmann Roe was a small drug company in Connecticut that had strayed slightly outside of its field and found itself suing a large manufacturer for infringement of an obscure patent. The case was highly technical with little chance of success. The opposing lawyers had thrown up a barricade of motions and delays and the case had made its way downwards, to Frik and Frak whose offices were near the copying machines, who had time for such things, and who pondered it amid the hiss of steam. No one else wanted it and this also made it appealing.

So they worked. They were students again, sitting around in polo shirts with their feet on the desk, throwing off hopeless ideas, crumpling wads of paper, staying late in the library and having the words blur in books.

They stayed on through vacations and weekends sometimes sleeping in the office and making coffee long before anyone came to work. After a late dinner they were still talking about it, its complexities, where elements somehow fit in, the sequence of letters, articles in journals, meetings, the limits of meaning. Brenda met a handsome Dutchman who worked for a bank. Alan met Hopie. Still there was this infinite forest, the trunks and vines blocking out the light, the roots of distant things joined. With every month that passed they were deeper into it, less certain of where they had been or if it could end. They had become like the old partners whose existence had been slowly sealed off, fewer calls, fewer consultations, lives that had become lunch. It was known they were swallowed up by the case with knowledge of little else. The opposite was true—no one else understood its details. Three years had passed. The length of time alone made it important. The reputation of the firm, at least in irony, was riding on them.

Two months before the case was to come to trial they quit Weyland, Braun. Frank sat down at the polished table for Sunday lunch. His father was one of the best men in the city. There is a kind of lawyer you trust and who becomes your friend. "What happened?" he wanted to know.

"We're starting our own firm," Frank said.

"What about the case you've been working on? You can't leave them with a litigation you've spent years preparing."

"We're not. We're taking it with us," Frank said.

There was a moment of dreadful silence.

"Taking it with you? You can't. You went to one of the best schools, Frank. They'll sue you. You'll ruin yourself."

"We thought of that."

"Listen to me," his father said.

Everyone said that, his mother, his Uncle Cook, friends. It was worse than ruin, it was dishonor. His father said that.

Hardmann Roe never went to trial, as it turned out. Six weeks later there was a settlement. It was for thirty-eight million, a third of it their fee.

His father had been wrong, which was something you could not hope for. They weren't sued either. That was settled, too. In place of ruin there were new offices overlooking Bryant Park which from above seemed like a garden behind a dark chateau, young clients, opera tickets, dinners in apartments with divorced hostesses, surrendered apartments with books and big, tiled kitchens.

The city was divided, as he had said, into those going up and those coming down, those in crowded restaurants and those on the street, those who waited and those who did not, those with three locks on the door and those rising in an elevator from a lobby with silver mirrors and walnut paneling.

And those like Mrs. Christie who was in the intermediate state though looking assured. She wanted to renegotiate the settlement with her ex-husband. Frank had leafed through the papers. "What do you think?" she asked candidly.

"I think it would be easier for you to get married again."

She was in her fur coat, the dark lining displayed. She gave a little puff of disbelief. "It's not that easy," she said.

He didn't know what it was like, she told him. Not long ago she'd been introduced to someone by a couple she knew very well. "We'll go to dinner," they said, "you'll love him, you're perfect for him, he likes to talk about books."

They arrived at the apartment and the two women immediately went into the kitchen and began cooking. What did she think of him? She'd only had a glimpse, she said, but she liked him very much, his beautiful bald head, his dressing gown. She had begun to plan what she would do with the apartment which had too much blue in it. The man — Warren was his name — was silent all evening. He'd lost his job, her friend explained in the kitchen. Money was no problem, but he was depressed. "He's had a shock," she said. "He likes you." And in fact he'd asked if he could see her again.

"Why don't you come for tea, tomorrow?" he said.

"I could do that," she said. "Of course. I'll be in the neighborhood," she added.

The next day she arrived at four with a bag filled with books, at least a hundred dollars worth which she'd bought as a present. He was in pajamas. There was no tea. He hardly seemed to know who she was or why she was there. She said she remembered she had to meet someone and left the books. Going down in the elevator she felt suddenly sick to her stomach.

"Well," said Frank, "there might be a chance of getting the settlement overturned, Mrs. Christie, but it would mean a lot of expense."

"I see." Her voice was smaller. "Couldn't you do it as one of those things where you got a percentage?"

"Not on this kind of case," he said.

It was dusk. He offered her a drink. She worked her lips, in contemplation, one against the other. "Well, then, what can I do?"

Her life had been made up of disappointments, she told him, looking into her glass, most of them the result of foolishly falling in love. Going out with an older man just because he was wearing a white suit in Nashville which was where she was from. Agreeing to marry George Christie while they were sailing off the coast of Maine. "I don't know where to get the money," she said, "or how."

She glanced up. She found him looking at her, without haste. The lights were coming on in buildings surrounding the park, in the streets, on homeward bound cars. They talked as evening fell. They went out to dinner.

At Christmas that year Alan and his wife broke up. "You're kidding," Frank said. He'd moved into a new place with thick towels and fine carpets. In the foyer was a Biedermeier desk, black, tan, and gold. Across the street was a private school.

Alan was staring out the window which was as cold as the side of a ship. "I don't know what to do," he said in despair. "I don't want to get divorced. I don't want to lose my daughter." Her name was Camille. She was two.

"I know how you feel," Frank said.

"If you had a kid, you'd know."

"Have you seen this?" Frank asked. He held up the alumni magazine. It was the fifteenth anniversary of their graduation. "Know any of these guys?"

Five members of the class had been cited for achievement. Alan recognized two or three of them. "Cummings," he said, "he was a zero—elected to Congress. Oh, God, I don't know what to do."

"Just don't let her take the apartment," Frank said.

Of course, it wasn't that easy. It was easy when it was someone else. Nan Christie had decided, to get married. She brought it up one evening.

"I just don't think so," he finally said.

"You love me, don't you?"

"This isn't a good time ask."

They lay silently. She was staring at something across the room. She was making him uncomfortable.

"It wouldn't work. It's the attraction of opposites," he said.

"We're not opposites."

"I don't mean just you and me. Women fall in love when they get to know you. Men are just the opposite. When they finally know you they're ready to leave."

She got up without saying anything and began gathering her clothes. He watched her dress in silence. There was nothing interesting about it. The funny thing was that he had meant to go on with her.

"I'll get you a cab," he said.

"I used to think that you were intelligent," she said, half to herself. Exhausted, he was searching for a number. "I don't want a cab. I'm going to walk."

"Across the park?"

"Yes." She had an instant glimpse of herself in the next day's paper. She paused at the door for a moment. "Good-bye," she said coolly.

She wrote him a letter which he read several times. *Of all the loves I have known, none has touched me so. Of all the men, no one has given me more.* He showed it to Alan who did not comment.

"Let's go out and have a drink," Frank said.

They walked up Lexington. Frank looked carefree, the scarf around his neck, the open topcoat, the thinning hair. "Well, you know . . ." he managed to say.

They went into a place called Jack's. Light was gleaming from the dark wood and the lines of glasses on narrow shelves. The young bartender stood with his hands on the edge of the bar. "How are you this evening?" he said with a smile. "Nice to see you again."

"Do you know me?" Frank asked.

"You look familiar," the bartender smiled.

"Do I? What's the name of this place, anyway? Remind me not to come in here again."

There were several other people at the bar. The nearest of them carefully looked away. After a while the manager came over. He had emerged from the brown-curtained back, "Anything wrong, sir?" he asked politely.

Frank looked at him. "No," he said, "everything's fine."

"We've had a big day," Alan explained "We're just unwinding."

"We have a dining room upstairs," the manager said. Behind him was an iron staircase winding past framed drawings of dogs — borzois they looked like. "We serve from six to eleven every night."

"I bet you do," Frank said. "Look, your bartender doesn't know me."

"He made a mistake," the manager said.

"He doesn't know me and he never will."

"It's nothing, it's nothing," Alan said, waving his hands.

They sat at a table by the window. "I can't stand these out-of-work actors who think they're everybody's friend," Frank commented.

At dinner they talked about Nan Christie. Alan thought of her silk dresses, her devotion. The trouble, he said after a while, was that he never seemed to meet that kind of woman, the ones who sometimes walked by outside Jack's. The women he met were too human, he complained. Ever since his separation he'd been trying to find the right one . . .

"You shouldn't have any trouble," Frank said. "They're all looking for someone like you."

"They're looking for you."

"They think they are."

Frank paid the check without looking at it. "Once you've been married," Alan was explaining, "you want to be married again."

"I don't trust anyone enough to marry them," Frank said.

"What do you want then?"

"This is all right," Frank said.

Something was missing in him and women had always done anything to find out what it was. They always would. Perhaps it was simpler, Alan thought. Perhaps nothing was missing.

The car, which was a big Renault, a tourer, slowed down and pulled off the *autostrada* with Brenda asleep in back, her mouth a bit open and the daylight gleaming off her cheekbones. It was near Como, they had just crossed, the border police had glanced in at her.

"Come on, Bren, wake up," they said, "we're stopping for coffee."

She came back from the ladies' room with her hair combed and fresh lipstick on. The boy in the white jacket behind the counter was rinsing spoons.

"Hey, Brenda, I forget. Is it *espresso* or *expresso*?" Frank asked her.

"*Espresso,*" she said.

"How do you know?"

"I'm from New York," she said.

"That's right," he remembered. "The Italians don't have an *x*, do they?"

"They don't have a *j* either," Alan said.

"Why is that?"

"They're such careless people," Brenda said. "They just lost them."

It was like old times. She was divorced from Doop or Boos or whoever. Her two little girls were with her mother. She had that quirky smile.

In Paris Frank had taken them to the Crazy Horse. In blackness like velvet the music struck up and six girls in unison kicked their legs in the brilliant light. They wore high heels and a little strapping. The nudity that is immortal. He was leaning on one elbow in the darkness. He glanced at Brenda. "Still studying, eh?" she said.

They were over for three weeks. Frank wasn't sure, maybe they would stay longer, take a house in the south of France or something. Their clients would have to struggle along without them. There comes a time, he said, when you have to get away for a while.

They had breakfast together in hotels with the sound of workmen chipping at the stone of the fountain outside. They listened to the angry woman shouting in the kitchen, drove to little towns, and drank every night. They had separate rooms, like staterooms, like passengers on a fading boat.

At noon the light shifted along the curve of buildings and people were walking far off. A wave of pigeons rose before a trotting dog. The man at the table in front of them had a pair of binoculars and was looking here and there. Two Swedish girls strolled past.

"Now they're turning dark," the man said.

"What is?" said his wife.

"The pigeons."

"Alan," Frank confided.

"What?"

"The pigeons are turning dark."

"That's too bad."

There was silence for a moment.

"Why don't you just take a photograph?" the woman said. "A photograph?"

"Of those women. You're looking at them so much."

He put down the binoculars.

"You know, the curve is so graceful," she said. "It's what makes this square so perfect."

"Isn't the weather glorious?" Frank said in the same tone of voice.

"And the pigeons," Alan said.

"The pigeons, too."

After a while the couple got up and left. The pigeons leapt up for a running child and hissed overhead. "I see you're still playing games," Brenda said. Frank smiled.

"We ought to get together in New York," she said that evening. They were waiting for Alan to come down. She reached across the table to pick up a magazine. "You've never met my kids, have you?" she said.

"No."

"They're terrific kids." She leafed through the pages not paying attention to them. Her forearms were tanned. She was not wearing a wedding band. The first act was over or rather the first five minutes. Now came the plot. "Do you remember those nights at Goldie's?" she said.

"Things were different then, weren't they?"

"Not so different."

"What do you mean?"

She wiggled her bare third finger and glanced at him. Just then Alan appeared. He sat down and looked from one of them to the other. "What's wrong?" he asked. "Did I interrupt something?"

When the time came for her to leave she wanted them to drive to Rome. They could spend a couple of days and she would catch the plane. They weren't going that way, Frank said.

"It's only a three-hour drive."

"I know, but we're going the other way," he said.

"For God's sake. Why won't you drive me?"

"Let's do it," Alan said.

"Go ahead. I'll stay here."

"You should have gone into politics," Brenda said. "You have a real gift."

After she was gone the mood of things changed. They were by themselves. They drove through the sleepy country to the north. The green water slapped as darkness fell on Venice. The lights in some *palazzos* were on. On the curtained upper floors the legs of countesses uncoiled, slithering on the sheets like a serpent.

In Harry's, Frank held up a dense, icy glass and murmured his father's line, "Good night, nurse." He talked to some people at the next table, a German who was manager of a hotel in Düsseldorf and his girlfriend. She'd been looking at him. "Want a taste?" he asked her. It was his second. She drank looking directly at him. "Looks like you finished it," he said.

"Yes, I like to do that."

He smiled. When he was drinking he was strangely calm. In Lugano in the park that time a bird had sat on his shoe.

In the morning across the canal, wide as a river, the buildings of the Giudecca lay in their soft colors, a great sunken barge with roofs and the crowns of hidden trees. The first winds of autumn were blowing, ruffling the water.

Leaving Venice, Frank drove. He couldn't ride in a car unless he was driving. Alan sat back, looking out the window, sunlight falling on the hillsides of antiquity. European days, the silence, the needle floating at a hundred.

In Padua, Alan woke early. The stands were being set up in the market. It was before daylight and cool. A man was laying out boards on the pavement, eight of them like doors to set bags of grain on. He was wearing the jacket from a suit. Searching in the truck he found some small pieces of wood and used them to shim the boards, testing with his foot.

The sky became violet. Under the colonnade the butchers had hung out chickens and roosters, spurred legs bound together. Two men sat trimming artichokes. The blue car of the *carabiniere* lazed past. The bags of rice and dry beans were set out now, the tops folded back like cuffs. A girl in a tailored coat with a scarf around her head called, *"Signore,"* then arrogantly, *"dica!"*

He saw the world afresh, its pavements and architecture, the names that had lasted for a thousand years. It seemed that his life was being clarified, the sediment was drifting down. Across the street in a jeweler's shop a girl was laying things out in the window. She was wearing white gloves and arranging the pieces with care. She glanced up as he stood watching. For a moment their eyes met, separated by the lighted glass. She was holding a lapis lazuli bracelet, the blue of the police car. Emboldened, he formed the silent words, *Quanto costa? Tre cento settante mille,* her lips said. It was eight in the morning when he got back to the hotel. A taxi pulled up and rattled the narrow street. A woman dressed for dinner got out and went inside.

The days passed. In Verona the points of the steeples and then its domes rose from the mist. The white-coated waiters appeared from the kitchen. *Primi, secondi, dolce.* They stopped in Arezzo. Frank came back to the table. He had some postcards. Alan was trying to write to his daughter once a week. He never knew what to say: where they were and what they'd seen. Giotto — what would that mean to her?

They sat in the car. Frank was wearing a soft tweed jacket. It was like cashmere — he'd been shopping in Missoni and everywhere, windbreakers, shoes. Schoolgirls in dark skirts were coming through an arch across the street. After a while one came through alone. She stood as if waiting for someone. Alan was studying the map. He felt the engine start. Very slowly they moved forward. The window glided down.

"*Scusi, signorina,*" he heard Frank say.

She turned. She had pure features and her face was without expression, as if a bird had turned to look, a bird which might suddenly fly away.

Which way, Frank asked her, was the *centro,* the center of town? She looked one way and then the other. "There," she said.

"Are you sure?" he said. He turned his head unhurriedly to look more or less in the direction she was pointing.

"*Si,*" she said.

They were going to Siena, Frank said. There was silence. Did she know which road went to Siena?

She pointed the other way.

"Alan, you want to give her a ride?" he asked.

"What are you talking about?"

Two men in white smocks like doctors were working on the wooden doors of the church. They were up on top of some scaffolding. Frank reached back and opened the rear door.

"Do you want to go for a ride?" he asked. He made a little circular motion with his finger.

They drove through the streets in silence. The radio was playing. Nothing was said. Frank glanced at her in the rearview mirror once or twice. It was at the time of a famous murder in Poland, the killing of a priest. Dusk was falling. The lights were coming on in shop windows and evening papers were in the kiosks. The body of the murdered man lay in a long coffin in the upper right corner of the *Corriere Della Sera.* It was in clean clothes like a worker after a terrible accident.

"Would you like an *aperitivo?*" Frank asked over his shoulder.

"*No,*" she said.

They drove back to the church. He got out for a few minutes with her. His hair was very thin, Alan noticed. Strangely, it made him look younger. They stood talking, then she turned and walked down the street.

"What did you say to her?" Alan asked. He was nervous.

"I asked if she wanted a taxi."

"We're headed for trouble."

"There's not going to be any trouble," Frank said.

His room was on the corner. It was large, with a sitting area near the windows. On the wooden floor there were two worn oriental carpets. On a glass cabinet in the bathroom were his hairbrush, lotions, cologne. The towels were a pale green with the name of the hotel in white. She didn't look at any of that. He had given the *portiere* forty thousand lire. In Italy the laws were very strict. It was nearly the same hour of the afternoon. He kneeled to take off her shoes.

He had drawn the curtains but light came in around them. At one point she seemed to tremble, her body shuddered. "Are you all right?" he said.

She had closed her eyes.

Later, standing, he saw himself in the mirror. He seemed to have thickened around the waist. He turned so that it was less noticeable. He got into bed again but was too hasty. "*Basta,*" she finally said.

They went down later and met Alan in a café. It was hard for him to look at them. He began to talk in a foolish way. What was she studying at school, he asked. For God's sake, Frank said. Well, what did her father do? She didn't understand.

"What work does he do?"

"Furniture," she said.

"He sells it?"

"*Restauro.*"

"In our country, no *restauro,*" Alan explained. He made a gesture. "Throw it away."

"I've got to start running again," Frank decided.

The next day was Saturday. He had the *portiere* call her number and hand him the phone.

"Hello, Eda? It's Frank."

"I know."

"What are you doing?"

He didn't understand her reply.

"We're going to Florence. You want to come to Florence?" he said. There was a silence. "Why don't you come and spend a few days?"

"No," she said.

"Why not?"

In a quieter voice she said, "How do I explain?"

"You can think of something."

At a table across the room children were playing cards while three well-dressed women, their mothers, sat and talked. There were cries of excitement as the cards were thrown down.

"Eda?"

She was still there. "*Si*," she said.

In the hills they were burning leaves. The smoke was invisible but they could smell it as they passed through, like the smell from a restaurant or paper mill. It made Frank suddenly remember childhood and country houses, raking the lawn with his father long ago. The green signs began to say Firenze. It started to rain. The wipers swept silently across the glass. Everything was beautiful and dim.

They had dinner in a restaurant of plain rooms, whitewashed, like vaults in a cellar. She looked very young. She looked like a young dog, the white of her eyes was that pure. She said very little and played with a strip of pink paper that had come off the menu.

In the morning they walked aimlessly. The windows displayed things for women who were older, in their thirties at least, silk dresses, bracelets, scarves. In Fendi's was a beautiful coat, the price beneath in small metal numbers.

"Do you like it?" he asked. "Come on, I'll buy it for you."

He wanted to see the coat in the window, he told them inside.

"For the *signorina?*"

"Yes."

She seemed uncomprehending. Her face was lost in the fur. He touched her cheek through it.

"You know how much that is?" Alan said. "Four million five hundred thousand."

"Do you like it?" Frank asked her.

She wore it continually. She watched the football matches on television in it, her legs curled beneath her. The room was in disorder, they hadn't been out all day.

"What do you say to leaving here?" Alan asked unexpectedly. The announcers were shouting in Italian. "I thought I'd like to see Spoleto."

"Sure. Where is it?" Frank said. He had his hand on her knee and was rubbing it with the barest movement, as one might a dozing cat.

The countryside was flat and misty. They were leaving the past behind them, unwashed glasses, towels on the bathroom floor.

There was a stain on his lapel, Frank noticed in the dining room. He tried to get it off as the headwaiter grated fresh Parmesan over each plate. He dipped the corner of his napkin in water and rubbed the spot. The table was near the doorway, visible from the desk. Eda was fixing an earring.

"Cover it with your napkin," Alan told him.

"Here, get this off, will you?" he asked Eda.

She scratched at it quickly with her fingernail.

"What am I going to do without her?" Frank said.

"What do you mean, without her?"

"So this is Spoleto," he said. The spot was gone. "Let's have some more wine." He called the waiter. "*Senta.* Tell him," he said to Eda.

They laughed and talked about old times, the days when they were getting eight hundred dollars a week and working ten, twelve hours a day. They remembered Weyland and the veins in his nose. The word he always used was "vivid," testimony a bit too vivid, far too vivid, a rather vivid decor.

They left talking loudly. Eda was close between them in her huge coat. "*Alla rovina,*" the clerk at the front desk muttered as they reached the street, "*alle macerie,*" he said, the girl at the switchboard looked over at him, "*alla polvere.*" It was something about rubbish and dust.

The mornings grew cold. In the garden there were leaves piled against the table legs. Alan sat alone in the bar. A waitress, the one with the mole on her lip, came in and began to work the coffee machine. Frank came down. He had an overcoat across his shoulders. In his shirt without a tie he looked like a rich patient in some hospital. He looked like a man who owned a produce business and had been playing cards all night.

"So, what do you think?" Alan said.

Frank sat down. "Beautiful day," he commented. "Maybe we ought to go somewhere."

In the room, perhaps in the entire hotel, their voices were the only sound, irregular and low, like the soft strokes of someone sweeping. One muted sound, then another.

"Where's Eda?"

"She's taking a bath."

"I thought I'd say good-bye to her."

"Why? What's wrong?"

"I think I'm going home."

"What happened?" Frank said.

Alan could see himself in the mirror behind the bar, his sandy hair. He looked pale somehow, nonexistent. "Nothing happened," he said. She had come into the bar and was sitting at the other end of the room. He felt a tightness in his chest. "Europe depresses me."

Frank was looking at him. "Is it Eda?"

"No. I don't know." It seemed terribly quiet. Alan put his hands in his lap. They were trembling.

"Is that all it is? We can share her," Frank said.

"What do you mean?" He was too nervous to say it right. He stole a glance at Eda. She was looking at something outside in the garden.

"Eda," Frank called, "do you want something to drink? *Cosa vuoi?*" He made a motion of glass raised to the mouth. In college he had been a great favorite. Shuford had been shortened to Shuf and then Shoes. He had run in the Penn Relays. His mother could trace her family back for six generations.

"Orange juice," she said.

They sat there talking quietly. That was often the case, Eda had noticed. They talked about business or things in New York.

When they came back to the hotel that night, Frank explained it. She understood in an instant. No. She shook her head. Alan was sitting alone in the bar. He was drinking some kind of sweet liqueur. It wouldn't happen, he knew. It didn't matter anyway. Still, he felt shamed. The hotel above his head, its corridors and quiet rooms, what else were they for?

Frank and Eda came in. He managed to turn to them. She seemed impassive—he could not tell. What was this he was drinking, he finally asked? She didn't understand the question. He saw Frank nod once slightly, as if in agreement. They were like thieves.

In the morning the first light was blue on the window glass. There was the sound of rain. It was leaves blowing in the garden, shifting across the gravel. Alan slipped from the bed to fasten the loose shutter. Below, half hidden in the hedges, a statue gleamed white. The few parked cars shone faintly. She was asleep, the soft, heavy pillow beneath her head. He was afraid to wake her. "Eda," he whispered, "Eda."

Her eyes opened a bit and closed. She was young and could stay asleep. He was afraid to touch her. She was unhappy, he knew, her bare neck, her hair, things he could not see. It would be a while before they were used to it. He didn't know what to do. Apart from that, it was perfect. It was the most natural thing in the world. He would buy her something himself, something beautiful.

In the bathroom he lingered at the window. He was thinking of the first day they had come to work at Weyland, Braun—he and Frank. They would become inseparable. Autumn in the gardens of the Veneto. It vas barely dawn. He would always remember meeting Frank. He couldn't have done these things himself. A young man in a cap suddenly came out of a doorway below. He crossed the driveway and jumped onto a motorbike. The engine started, a faint blur. The headlight appeared and off he went, delivery basket in back. He was going to get the rolls for breakfast. His life was simple. The air was pure and cool. He was part of that great, unchanging order of those who live by wages, whose world is unlit and who do not realize what is above.

Discussion Topics

1. One might easily call "American Express" a symptom of its time and place, New York in the 1980s, rather than a commentary on lawyers. Tom Wolfe's novel, *The Bonfire of the Vanities*, aspired to summarize the ethos of what Wolfe called "the splurge generation." A commentator in *Time* magazine, Myron Magnet, commented that "the point is not that money society has triumphantly driven out all the solid, estimable value, like the shaggy barbarians at the gates of Rome. Rather, the money society has expanded to fill the vacuum left after the institutions that embodied and nourished these values — community, religion, school, university, and especially family — sagged or collapsed or sometimes even self-destructed." In 1979, the sociologist Christopher Lasch wrote an influential book, *The Culture of Narcissism*, suggesting that family and religion had been eclipsed by concern with survival and peace of mind. By 1988, the *New Republic*, in an editorial called "The Culture of Apathy," suggested that peace of mind had in turn been eclipsed by the attractions of sensory pleasure. It concluded that "licentiousness about drugs and sex have put our children at risk" and it criticized liberals who are "so intellectually and psychologically invested in the doctrine of ever-expanding rights — ... the rights of criminals, the rights of pornographers, the rights of everyone to everything — that any suggestion of the baleful consequences of that doctrine appears to them as a threat to the liberal ideal itself."

Is "American Express" simply about the '80s? Keep in mind that the so-called Reagan era is said to have its legacy in the material growth of the '90s and in the rhetoric of the Bush ("W") administration. The ethical issues the story raises may not be mere historical artifacts.

Note also that Salter reminds us that Alan and Frank are "lawyers, sons of lawyers." They are like other professionals and business persons in many ways but still to be seen in light of their profession as well as their culture. What role did lawyers play in the '80s? Were they the midwives of "the money society"? How did the profession itself change in this period, which saw a conspicuous decline in the ranks of public interest lawyers and an unprecedented rise to influence by corporate lawyers?

2. Consider the relationship of Frank and Alan, as well as the relationships of each to his background. Salter tells us about their fathers in very few words. Both were lawyers and lawyers of different kinds. Psychological theories about intergenerational relationships may be helpful in understanding Frank and Alan. Freudian psychoanalytical theory posits the Oedipal hypothesis that sons achieve their male identity by "killing" and replacing their fathers, in fantasy if not reality. A corollary is the notion that sons define themselves in opposition to their fathers' values and dispositions.

Frank's father is, in Wall Street terms, a team player and company man, a senior partner in a corporate firm who belongs to the right clubs. Alan's father, by contrast, is flamboyantly independent and a seeker after spotlights. Frank treats his father's loyalty to his firm with contempt. Alan, the son of a leader, is most comfortable in Frank's shadow.

Generalities and stereotypes have limited usefulness in explaining particular individuals. But Salter uses them as shorthand for making us think about Frank, Alan, and their relationship. The relationships between leaders and followers have become a popular topics for psychological research. Several articles suggest that leaders and followers, being mutually dependent, collaborate in constructing their own view of reality and of their responsibilities. See, for example, Stephen Reicher, "Social Identity and the Dynamics of Leadership," *Leadership Quarterly*, August 2005; Micha Popper, "Leadership as Relationship," *Journal for the Theory of Social Behavior*, 2004. Frank and Alan surely reinforce each other's sense of their place in the world.

3. Individual lawyers and firms are covered by a set of rules called the Model Rules of Professional Conduct. In some cases, violations of the rules can give rise to the disciplining of attorneys and even legal action. Although the Model Rules do not directly address Frank and Alan's conduct with regard to the Hardmann Roe account, a expert on legal ethics says that "the preferable view is that the associate breaches a fiduciary obligation of loyalty to the firm by attempting to persuade existing . . . clients to retain the former associate after his or her withdrawal." (See Charles Wolfram, *Modern Legal Ethics*, 888.) Given the size of the account and the firm's investment in it, Frank's father anticipated quite reasonably that they might be sued.

Many commentators have complained that law has evolved from a profession to a business. Their point is that honor and respect for others are fast disappearing in the conduct of lawyers and firms. Others question the degree to which honor was ever a characteristic of lawyers, and they suggest that single-mindedness and even ruthlessness may benefit clients when lawyers are unrestrained by tacit codes. Richard Wasserstrom's "Roles and Morality" (in David Luban, *The Good Lawyer*, 1984) is widely cited for the view that too often lawyers accept roles "as a shield to moral criticism," claiming that "one's task is to vindicate the claim of one's client, subject only to the proviso that one refrain from violating the law."

4. Salter characterizes Frank and Alan through their relationships with women — Brenda, Mrs. Christie, and Eda. One is a long-term friend; the second has an affair with Frank, and seems roughly his age; the third is an underage girl, a relationship that would be a criminal violation of statutory rape laws in the U.S. In each case, the main connection is with Frank.

We learn much about Brenda, both from the facts of her life and from her own words. How are we to understand their friendship? What sustains it? Frank's affairs with both Nan Christie and Eda have an aspect of prostitution, sexual favors for money. In one case, they are in lieu of legal fees; in the other, they are exchanged for costly gifts. But Nan Christie "decide[s] to get married" — and Frank declines. She responds, angrily ("I used to think that you were intelligent"), but then later writes him a letter saying, "Of all the loves I have known, none has touched me more. Of all the men, no one has given me more."

And yet we know that Frank is cynical, exploitative, and without empathy. How shall we explain Nan Christie? One suggestion is that some women see some men as damaged goods and decide, against all odds, to rehabilitate them. Is this persuasive in this case? No less complicated are the psychological transactions that lead to Eda becoming a pawn, traded by Frank to Alan. The story encourages us to make moral judgments, while making clear their complexity. Alan, Frank, Nan, and Brenda are all part of context in which values are compromised and in which the characters make up their norms as they go along.

5. Frank is preoccupied with the division of the world in those who are going up and those who are going down. Is this the dark side of the American dream of improving oneself, changing one's class, and getting rich? How much does anyone still believe in the dream that upward mobility is one's destiny, that (in words that can seems ironic in many ways) "anyone can become president"? "American Express" may well be the story of what happened to that dream in the '80s. And it ends in Europe, which has (perhaps) never been infected with the dream in its fullest virulence.

Ward Just: About Boston

The lawyer in the next story is in many ways more sympathetic than Alan and Frank. He is a divorce and trusts lawyer with a flourishing career in which he has shown skill, discretion, and integrity. His life, however, is altogether different from what he anticipated when he graduated from law school. And, in mid-life, his attitude to his profession and his circumstances is complicated. Satisfaction and bitterness both play significant roles in his self-understanding. He illustrates well the isolation that is the cost of maintaining independence, the cost of forcing his judgment to rein in his emotions at crucial times.

Like Salter, Ward Just is not a lawyer but a journalist-author. Born in 1935, he has had two distinguished careers. He comes from a family of journalists and was himself a war correspondent for *Newsweek* and head of coverage of the Vietnam war for the *Washington Post*. Since the early seventies, he has published fourteen novels, three books of stories, and a play. Several are set in Washington, D.C., earning him the reputation of one of our smartest writers about politics. Journalism and war are other pre-occupations. As an Illinoisan, he has set a number of his works in Chicago, and he is fascinated by the differences between the culture of New England and the culture of the Midwest. His novels and stories focus more on character than on plot, but his writings have the fluidity and momentum of the most tightly plotted thrillers.

"About Boston" is an early story with a predictably strong sense of place. The narrator embodies the conflicting values and expectations of Chicago and Boston. When we meet him, his career is well-established, and we learn his history through flashbacks.

❧ About Boston ❧

Ward Just

Beth was talking and I was listening. She said, "This was years ago. I was having a little tryst. On a Thursday, in New York, in the afternoon. He telephoned: 'Is it this Thursday or next?' I told him it was never, if he couldn't remember the *week*. Well." She laughed. "It makes your point about letters. Never would've happened if we'd written letters, because you write something and you remember it. Don't you?"

"Usually," I said.

"There isn't a record of anything anymore, it's just telephone calls and bad memory."

"I've got a filing cabinet full of letters," I said, "and most of them are from ten years ago and more. People wrote a lot in the sixties, maybe they wanted a record of what they thought. There was a lot to think about, and it seemed a natural thing to do, write a letter to a friend, what with everything that was going on."

"I wonder if they're afraid," she said.

"No written record? No," I said. "They don't have the time. They won't make the time and there aren't so many surprises now, thanks to the sixties. We're surprised-out. They don't write and they don't read either."

"That one read," she said, referring to the man in the tryst. "He read all the time—history, biography. Sports books, linebackers' memoirs, the strategy of the full-court press." She lowered her voice. "And politics."

"Well," I said. I knew who it was now.

"But he didn't know the week." She lit a cigarette, staring at the match a moment before depositing it, just so, in the ashtray. "You always wrote letters."

I smiled. "A few close friends."

She smiled back. "Where do you think we should begin?"

"Not at the beginning."

"No, you know that as well as I do."

I said, "Probably better."

"Not better," she said.

"I don't know if I'm the man—"

"No," she said firmly. She stared at me across the room, then turned to look out the window. It was dusk, and the dying sun caught the middle windows of the Hancock tower, turning them a brilliant, wavy orange. In profile, with her sharp features and her short black hair, she looked like a schoolgirl. She said, "You're the man, all right. I want you to do it. I'd feel a lot more comfortable, we've known each other so long. Even now, after all this time, we don't have to finish sentences. It'd be hard for me, talking about it to a stranger."

"Sometimes that's easiest," I said.

"Not for me it isn't."

"All right," I said at last. "But if at any time it gets awkward for you—" I was half hoping she'd reconsider. But she waved her hand in a gesture of dismissal, subject closed. She was sitting on the couch in the corner of my office, and now she rose to stand at the window and watch the last of the sun reflected on the windows of the Hancock. A Mondrian among Turners, she called it, its blue mirrors a new physics in the Back Bay. And who cared if in the beginning its windows popped out like so many ill-fitting contact lenses. The Hancock governed everything around it, Boston's past reflected in Boston's future. And it was miraculous that in the cascade of falling glass the casualties were so few.

I watched her: at that angle and in the last of the light her features softened and she was no longer a schoolgirl. I checked my watch, then rang my assistant and said she could lock up; we were through for the day. I fetched a yellow legal pad and a pen and sat in the leather chair, facing Beth. She was at the window, fussing with the cord of the venetian blind. She turned suddenly, with a movement so abrupt that I dropped my pad; the blind dropped with a crash. There had always been something violent and unpredictable in her behavior. But now she only smiled winningly, nodded at the sideboard, and asked for a drink before we got down to business.

I have practiced law in the Back Bay for almost twenty-five years. After Yale I came to Boston with the naive idea of entering politics. The city had a rowdy quality I liked; it reminded me of Chicago, a city of neighborhoods, which wasn't ready for reform. But since I am a lapsed Catholic, neither Irish nor Italian, neither Yankee nor Democrat nor rich, I quickly understood that for me there were no politics in Boston. Chicago is astronomically remote from New England, and it was of no interest to anyone that I had been around politicians most of my life and knew the code. My grandfather had been, briefly, a congressman from the suburbs of Cook County, and I knew how to pull strings. But in Boston my antecedents precluded everything but good-government commit-tees and the United Way.

Beth and I were engaged then, and Boston seemed less daunting than New York, perhaps because she knew it so intimately; it was her town as Chicago was mine. I rented an apartment in the North End and for the first few months we were happy enough, I with my new job and she with her volunteer work at the Mass. General. We broke off the engagement after six months — the usual reasons — and I looked up to find myself behind the lines in enemy territory. I had misjudged Boston's formality and its network of tribal loyalties and had joined Hamlin and White, one of the old State Street firms. I assumed that H,W — as it had been known for a hundred years — was politically connected. An easy error to make, for the firm was counsel to Boston's largest bank and handled the wills and trusts of a number of prominent Brahmin Republicans, and old Hamlin had once been lieutenant governor of Massachusetts. In Chicago that would have spelled political, but in Boston it only spelled probate. There were thirty men in the firm, large for Boston in those days. The six senior men were Hamlin and Hamlin Junior and White III, and Chelm, Warner, and Diuguid. Among the associates were three or four recognizable Mayflower names. The six senior men were all physically large, well over six feet all and in conspicuous good health, by which I mean ruddy complexions and a propensity to roughhouse. They all had full heads of hair, even old Hamlin, who was then eighty. Their talk was full of the jargon of sailing and golf, and in their company I felt the worst sort of provincial rube.

Of course I was an experiment — a balding, unathletic Yale man from Chicago, of middling height, of no particular provenance, and book-smart. I was no one's cousin and no one's ex-roommate. But I was engaged to a Boston girl and I had been first in my class at Yale and the interview with Hamlin Junior had gone well. All of them in the firm spoke in that hard, open-mouthed bray peculiar to

Massachusetts males of the upper classes. The exception was Hamlin Junior, who mumbled. When it was clear, after two years, that their experiment, had failed — or had not, at any event, succeeded brilliantly — it was Hamlin Junior who informed me. He called me into his dark brown office late one afternoon, poured me a sherry, and rambled for half an hour before he got to the point, which was that I was an excellent lawyer mumble mumble damn able litigator mumble mumble but the firm has its own personality, New England salt sort of thing ha-ha mumble sometimes strange to an outsider but it's the way we've always done things mumble question of style and suitability, sometimes tedious but can't be helped wish you the best you're a damn able trial man, and of course you've a place here so long's you want though in fairness I wanted mumble make it known that you wouldn't be in the first foursome as it were mumble mumble. Just one question, I've always wondered: 'S really true that you wanted to go into politics here?

It was my first professional failure, and in my anger and frustration I put it down to simple snobbery. I did not fit into their clubs, and I hated the North Shore and was not adept at games. I was never seen "around" during the winter or on the Cape or the Islands or in Maine in the summer. I spent my vacations in Europe, and most weekends I went to New York, exactly as I did when I *was* at law school in New Haven. New York remains the center of my social life. Also, I was a bachelor. Since the breakup of my engagement, I had become an aggressive bachelor. Beth was bitter and I suspected her of spreading unflattering stories. Of course this was not true, but in my humiliation I believed that it was and that as a consequence the six senior men had me down as homosexual. In addition, I was a hard drinker in a firm of hard drinkers, though unlike them I never had whiskey on my breath in the morning and I never called in sick with Monday grippe. I could never join in the hilarious retelling of locker room misadventures. They drank and joked. I drank and didn't joke.

When I left H,W, I opened an office with another disgruntled provincial — he was from Buffalo, even farther down the scale of things than Chicago — half expecting to fail but determined not to and wondering what on earth I would do and where I would go, now that I'd been drummed out of my chosen city: blackballed. Young litigators are not as a rule peripatetic: you begin in a certain city and remain there; you are a member of the bar, you know the system, you build friendships and clientele and a reputation. Looking back on it, Deshais and I took a terrible risk. But we worked hard and prospered, and now there are twenty lawyers in our firm, which we have perversely designed to resemble a squad of infantry in a World War II propaganda movie: Irish, Italians, Jews, three blacks in the past ten years, one Brahmin, Deshais, and me. Of course we are always quarreling; ours is not a friendly, clubby firm. In 1974, we bought a private house, a handsome brownstone, in the Back Bay, only two blocks from my apartment on Commonwealth Avenue. This is so convenient, such an agreeable way to live—it is my standard explanation to my New York friends who ask why I remain here—that we decided not to expand the firm because it would require a larger building, and all of us love the brownstone, even the younger associates who must commute from Wayland or Milton. Sometimes I think it is the brownstone and the brownstone alone that holds the firm together.

I suppose it is obvious that I have no affection for this spoiled city and its noisy inhabitants. It is an indolent city. It is racist to the bone and in obvious political decline and like any declining city is by turns peevish and arrogant. It is a city without civility or civic spirit, or Jews. The Jews, with their prodigious energies, have tucked themselves away in Brookline, as the old aristocrats, with their memories and trust funds, are on the lam on the North Shore. Remaining are the resentful Irish and the furious blacks. Meanwhile, the tenured theory class issues its pronouncements from the safety of Cambridge, confident that no authority will take serious notice. So the city of Boston closes in on itself, conceited, petulant, idle, and broke.

I observe this from a particular vantage point. To my surprise, I have become a divorce lawyer. The first cases I tried after joining forces with Deshais were complicated divorce actions. They were women referred to me by Hamlin Junior, cases considered—I think he used the word "fraught"—too mumble "fraught" for H,W. In Chicago we used the word "messy," though all this was a long time ago; now they are tidy and without fault. However, then as now there was pulling and hauling over the money. Hamlin Junior admired my trial work and believed me discreet and respectable enough to represent in the first instance his cousin and in the second a dear friend of his wife's. He said that he hoped the matter of the cousin would be handled quietly, meaning without a lengthy trial and without publicity, but that if the case went to trial he wanted her represented by a lawyer ahem who was long off the tee. You know what it is you must do? he asked. I nodded. At that time divorces were purchased; you bought a judge for the afternoon. Happily, the cousin was disposed of in conference, quietly and very expensively for her husband. The success of that case caused Hamlin Junior to send me the second woman, whose disposition was not quite so quiet. Fraught it certainly was, and even more expensive.

I was suddenly inside the bedroom, hearing stories the obverse of those I had heard after hours at H,W. The view from the bedroom was different from the view from the locker room. It was as if a light bulb joke had been turned around and told from the point of view of the bulb. Hundred-watt Mazda shocks WASP couple! I discovered that I had a way with women in trouble. That is precisely because I do not pretend to understand them, as a number of my colleagues insist that they "understand women." But I do listen. I listen very carefully, and then I ask questions and listen again. Then they ask me questions and I am still listening hard, and when I offer my answers they are brief and as precise as I can make them. And I never, never overpromise. No woman has ever rebuked me with "But you *said,* and now you've broken your word."

The cousin and the wife's friend were satisfied and told Hamlin Junior, who said nothing to his colleagues. He seemed to regard me as the new chic restaurant in town, undiscovered and therefore underpriced; it would become popular soon enough, but meanwhile the food would continue excellent and the service attentive and the bill modest. For years he referred clients and friends to me, and I always accepted them even when they were routine cases and I had to trim my fees. And when Hamlin Junior died, I went to his funeral, and was not at all startled to see so many familiar female faces crowding the pews.

My divorce business was the beginning, and there was a collateral benefit — no, bonanza. I learned how money flows in Boston, and where; which were the rivers and which were the tributaries and which were the underground streams. Over the years, I have examined hundreds of trusts and discovered a multiformity of hidden assets, liquid and solid, floating and stationary, lettered and numbered, above ground and below. The trusts are of breathtaking ingenuity, the product of the flintiest minds in Massachusetts, and of course facilitated over the years by a willing legislature. And what has fascinated me from the beginning is this: the trust that was originally devised to avoid taxes or to punish a recalcitrant child or to siphon income or to "protect" an unworldly widow or to reach beyond the grave to control the direction of a business or a fortune or a marriage can fall apart when faced with the circumstances of the present, an aggrieved client, and a determined attorney.

This is not the sort of legal practice I planned, but it is what I have. Much of what I have discovered in divorce proceedings I have replicated in my trust work, adding a twist here and there to avoid unraveling by someone like me, sometime in the future. Wills and trusts are now a substantial part of my business, since I have access to the flintiest minds in Massachusetts. Turn, and turn about. However, it is a risible anomaly of the upper classes of Boston that the estates have grown smaller and the trusts absurdly complex — Alcatraz to hold juvenile delinquents.

So one way and another I am in the business of guaranteeing the future. A trust, like a marriage, is a way of getting a purchase on the future. That is what I tell my clients, especially the women; women have a faith in the future that men, as a rule, do not. I am careful to tell my clients that although that is the objective, it almost never works; or it does not work in the way they intend it to work. It is all too difficult, reading the past, without trying to read the future as well. It is my view that men, at least, understand this, having, as a rule, a sense of irony and proportion. At any event, this is my seat at the Boston opera. It is lucrative and fascinating work. There was no compelling reason, therefore, not to listen to the complaint of Beth Earle Doran Greer, my former fiancée.

She said quietly, "It's finished."

I said nothing.

She described their last year together, the two vacations and the month at Edgartown, happy for the most part. They had one child, a boy, now at boarding school. It had been a durable marriage, fifteen years; the first one had lasted less than a year, and she had assumed that, despite various troubles, this one would endure. Then last Wednesday he said he was leaving her and his lawyer would be in touch.

"Has he?"

"No," she said.

"Who is he?"

She named a State Street lawyer whom I knew by reputation. He was an excellent lawyer. I was silent again, waiting for her to continue.

"Frank didn't say anything more than that!"

"Do you know where he is?"

"I think he's at the farm." I waited again, letting the expression on my face do the work. There were two questions. Is he alone? Do you want him back? She said again, "It's finished." Then, the answer to the other question: "There is no one else." I looked at her, my face in neutral. She said, "Hard as that may be to understand."

Not believe, *understand;* a pointed distinction. I nodded, taking her at her word. It was hard, her husband was a great bon vivant.

"That's what he says, and I believe him. His sister called me to say that there isn't anybody else, but I didn't need her to tell me. Believe me, I know the signs. There isn't a sign I don't know and can't see a mile away, and he doesn't show any of them. Five years ago—that was something else. But she's married and not around anymore, and that's over and done with. And besides, if there was someone else he'd tell me. It'd be like him."

I nodded again and made a show of writing on my pad.

"And there isn't anyone else with me either!"

"Well," I said, and smiled.

"Is it a first?"

I laughed quietly. "Not a first," I said. "Maybe a second."

She laughed, and lit a cigarette. "You were afraid it would be another cliché, she would be twenty and just out of Radcliffe. Meanwhile, I would've taken up with the garage mechanic or the gamekeeper. Or Frank's best friend; they tell me that's chic now." She looked at me sideways and clucked, "You know me better than that. Clichés aren't my style."

I said, "I never knew you at all!"

"Yes, you did," she said quickly. I said nothing. "You always listened; in those days you were a very good listener. And you're a good listener now."

"The secret of my success," I said. But I knew my smile was getting thinner.

"The mouthpiece who listens," she said. "That's what Nora told me when she was singing your praises. Really, she did go on. Do they fall in love with you, like you're supposed to do with a psychiatrist?"

Nora was a client I'd represented in an action several years before, a referral from Hamlin Junior. She was a great friend of Beth's but a difficult woman and an impossible client. I said, "No."

"It was a pretty good marriage," she said after a moment's pause. "You'd think, fifteen years ..." I leaned forward, listening. Presently, in order to focus the conversation, I would ask the first important question: What is it that you want me to do now? For the moment, though, I wanted to hear more. I have never regarded myself as a marriage counselor, but it is always wise to know the emotional state of your client. So far, Beth seemed admirably rational and composed, almost cold-blooded. I wondered if she had ever consulted a psychiatrist, then decided she probably hadn't. There was something impersonal about her locution "like you're supposed to." She said abruptly, "How did you get into this work? It's so unlike you. Remember the stories you told me about your grandfather and his friend? The relationship they had, and how that was the kind of lawyer you wanted to be?"

I remembered all right, but I was surprised that she did. My grandfather and I were very close, and when I was a youngster we lunched together every Saturday. My father drove me to the old man's office, in an unincorporated area of Cook County, near Blue Island. I'd take the elevator to the fourth floor, the building dark and silent on Saturday morning. My grandfather was always courteous and formal, treating me as he would treat an important adult. On Saturday mornings my grandfather met with Tom. Tom was his lawyer. I was too young to know exactly what they were talking about, though as I look back on it, their conversation was in a private language. There was a "matter" that needed "handling," or "a man"—perhaps "sound," perhaps "a screwball"—who had to be "turned." Often there was a sum of money involved—three, four, fi' thousand dollars. These questions would be discussed sparely, long pauses between sentences. Then, as a signal that the conversation was near its end, my grandfather would say, "Now this is what I want to do," and his voice would fall. Tom would lean close to the old man, listening hard; I never saw him make a note. Then: "Now you figure out how I can do it." And Tom would nod, thinking, his face disappearing into the collar of his enormous camel-hair coat. He never removed the coat, and he sat with his gray fedora in both hands, between his knees, turning it like the steering wheel of a car. When he finished thinking, he would rise and approach me and gravely shake hands. Then he would offer me a piece of licorice from the strand he kept in his coat, the candy furry with camel hair. He pressed it on me until accepted. I can remember him saying good-bye to my grandfather and, halting at the door, smiling slightly and winking. Tom would exit whistling, and more often than not my grandfather would make a telephone call, perhaps two, speaking inaudibly into the receiver. Finally, rumbling in his basso profundo, he would make the ritual call to the Chicago Athletic Club to reserve his usual table for two, "myself and my young associate."

In those days children were not allowed in the men's bar, so we ate in the main dining room, a huge chamber with high ceilings and a spectacular view of the lakefront. We sat at a table by the window, and on a clear day we could see Gary and Michigan City to the southeast. Long-hulled ore boats were smudges on the horizon. Once, during the war, we saw a pocket aircraft carrier, a training vessel for navy pilots stationed at Great Lakes. The old man would wave his hand in the direction of the lake and speak of the Midwest as an ancient must have spoken of the Fertile Crescent: the center of the world, a homogeneous, God-fearing, hardworking *region*, its interior position protecting it from its numerous enemies. With a sweep of his hand he signified the noble lake and the curtain of smoke that hung over Gary's furnaces, thundering even on Saturdays. Industry, he'd say, *heavy* industry working at one hundred percent of capacity. Chicagoland, foundry to the world. His business was politics, he said; and his politics was business. "We can't let them take it away from us, all this . . ."

When the old man died, Tom was his principal pallbearer. It was a large funeral; the governor was present with his suite, along with a score or more of lesser politicians. Tom was dry-eyed, but I knew he was grieving. At the end of it he came over to me and shook my hand, solemnly as always, and said, "Your grandfather was one of the finest men who ever lived, a great friend, a great Republican, a great American, and a great client." I thought that an extraordinary inventory and was about to say so when he gripped my arm and exclaimed, "You ever need help of any kind, you come to me. That man and I . . ." He pointed at my grandfather's casket, still aboveground under its green canopy, then tucked his chin into the camel hair. "We've been through the mill, fought every day of our lives. I don't know what will happen without him." He waved dispiritedly at the gravestones around us, stones as far as the eye could see, and lowered his voice so that I had to bend close to hear. "The world won't be the same without him," Tom said. "The Midwest's going to hell."

Tom died a few years later, without my having had a chance to take him up on his offer. But from my earliest days in that fourth-floor office I knew I would be a lawyer. I wanted to be Tom to someone great, and prevent the world from going to hell. Tom was a man who listened carefully to a complex problem, sifting and weighing possibilities. Then, settled and secure in his own mind, he figured a way to get from here to there. It was only an idiosyncrasy of our legal system that the route was never a straight line.

"I mean," she said brightly, leaning forward on the couch, "listening to a bunch of hysterical women with their busted marriages, that wasn't what I expected at all."

"They are not always hysterical," I said, "and some of them are men."

"And you never married," she said.

That was not true, but I let it pass.

"No," she said, rapping her knuckles on the coffee table. "You *were* married. I heard that a long time ago. I heard that you were married, a whirlwind romance in Europe, but then it broke up right away."

"That's right," said.

"She was French."

"English," I said.

"And there were no children."

"No," I said. We were silent while I walked to the sideboard, made a drink for myself, and refilled hers.

"Do you remember how we used to talk, that place on Hanover Street we used to go to, all that pasta and grappa? I practiced my Italian on them. Always the last ones out the door, running down Hanover Street to that awful place you had on—where was it?"

"North Street," I said.

"North Street. We'd get to dinner and then we'd go to your place and you'd take me back to Newton in your red Chevrolet. Three, four o'clock in the morning. I don't know how you got any work done, the hours we kept."

I nodded, remembering.

"And of course, when I heard you'd been sacked at H,W, I didn't know what to think, except that it was for the best." She paused. "Which I could've told you if you'd asked." I handed her the highball and sat down, resuming my lawyerly posture, legs crossed, the pad in my lap. "Do you ever think about your grandfather? Or what would've happened if you'd gone back to Chicago instead of following me here? Whether you'd gone into politics, like him?"

"I didn't follow you," I said. "We came together. It was where we intended to live, together."

"Whatever." She took a long swallow of her drink. "Chicago's such a different place from Boston, all that prairie. Boston's close and settled and old, so charming." I listened, tapping the pencil on my legal pad. It was dark now. At night the city seemed less close and settled. The cars in the street outside were bumper to bumper, honking. There was a snarl at the intersection, one car double-parked and another stalled. A car door slammed and there were angry shouts. She looked at me, smiling. "I don't want anything particular from him."

I made a note on my pad.

"I have plenty of money; so does he. Isn't that the modern way? No punitive damages?" She hesitated. "So there won't be any great opportunity to delve into the assets. And Frank's trust. Or mine."

I ignored that. "Of course there's little Frank."

She looked at me with the hint of a malicious grin. "How did you know his name?"

"Because I follow your every movement," I said, with as much sarcasm as I could muster. "For Christ's sake, Beth. I don't know how I know his name. People like Frank Greer always name their children after themselves."

"Don't get belligerent," she said. "A more devoted father —" she began and then broke off.

"Yes," I said.

" — he's devoted to little Frank." She hesitated, staring out the window for a long mount. She was holding her glass with both hands, in her lap. She said, "What was the name of that man, your grandfather's lawyer?"

"Tom," I said.

"God, yes," she said laughing lightly. "Tom, one of those sturdy Midwestern names."

I think." I said evenly, "I think Tom is a fairly common name. I think it is common even in Boston."

She laughed again, hugely amused. "God, yes, it's common."

I glared at her, not at all surprised that she remembered which buttons worked and which didn't. Beth had an elephant's memory for any man's soft spots. Why Tom was one of mine was not easily explained; Beth would have one explanation, I another. But of course she remembered. My background was always a source of tension between us, no doubt because my own attitude was ambiguous. She found my grandfather and Tom . . . quaint. They were colorful provincials, far from her Boston milieu, and she condescended to them exactly as certain English condescend to Australians.

"It's a riot," she said.

"So," I said quietly, glancing at my watch. "What is it that you want me to do now?"

"A quick, clean divorce," she said. "Joint custody for little Frank, though it's understood he lives with me. Nothing changes hands, we leave with what we brought, status quo ante. I take my pictures, he takes his shotguns. Except, naturally, the house in Beverly. It's mine anyway, though for convenience it's in both our names. He understands that."

"What about the farm?"

"We split that, fifty-fifty."

"Uh-huh," I said.

"Is it always this easy?"

"We don't know how easy it'll be," I said carefully. "Until I talk to his lawyer. Maybe it won't be easy at all. It depends on what he thinks his grievances are."

"He hasn't got any."

"Well," I said.

"So it'll be easy," she said, beginning to cry.

We had agreed to go to dinner after meeting in my office. I proposed the Ritz; she countered with a French restaurant I had never heard of. She insisted, Boylston Street nouvelle cuisine, and I acceded, not without complaint. I told her about a client, a newspaperman who came to me every six years for his divorce. The newspaperman said that the nouvelle cuisine reminded him of the nouveau journalism—a colorful plate, agreeably subtle, wonderfully presented with inspired combinations, and underdone. The portions were small, every dish had a separate sauce, and you were hungry when you finished. A triumph of style over substance.

She listened patiently, distracted.

I was trying to make her laugh. "But I can get a New York strip here, which they'll call an entrecôte, and there isn't a lot you can do to ruin a steak. Though they will try."

"You haven't changed," she said bleakly.

"Yes, I have," I said. "In the old days I would've been as excited about this place as you are. I'd know the names of the specialties of the house and of the chef. In the old days I was as al dente as the veggies. But not anymore." I glanced sourly around the room. The colors were pastel, various tints of yellow, even to a limp jonquil in the center of each table, all of it illuminated by candles thin as pencils and a dozen wee chandeliers overhead. It was very feminine and not crowded; expensive restaurants rarely were in Boston now; the money was running out.

"I'm sorry about the tears," she said.

I said, "Don't be."

"I knew I was going to bawl when I made that remark about Tom and you reacted."

"Yes," I said. I'd known it too.

"It made me sad. It reminded me of when we were breaking up and all the arguments we had."

I smiled gamely. "I was al dente then, and I broke easily." I knew what she was leading up to, and I didn't want it. When the waiter arrived I ordered whiskey for us both, waiting for the little superior sneer and feeling vaguely disappointed when he smiled pleasantly and flounced off. I started to tell her a story but she cut me off, as I knew she would.

"It reminded me of that ghastly dinner and how awful everything was afterward."

I muttered something noncommittal, but the expression on her face told me she wanted more, so I said it was over and forgotten, part of the buried past, et cetera. Like hell. We had argued about the restaurant that night, as we had tonight, except I won and we went to the Union Oyster House. My parents were in town, my father ostensibly on business; in fact they were in Boston to meet Beth. The dinner did not go well from the beginning; the restaurant was crowded and the service indifferent. My parents didn't seem to care, but Beth was irritated — "The Union Oyster Tourist Trap" — and that in turn put me on edge, or perhaps it was the other way around. Halfway through dinner, I suspect in an effort to salvage things, my father shyly handed Beth a wrapped package. It was a bracelet he had selected himself; even my mother didn't know about it. It was so unlike him, and such a sweet gesture, tears jumped to my eyes. Even before she opened it, I knew it would not be right. Beth had a particular taste in jewelry and as a consequence rarely wore any. I hoped she could disguise her feelings, but as it happened she giggled. And did not put the bracelet on, but hurried it into her purse after leaning over the table and kissing my father. He did not fail to notice the bracelet rushed out of sight.

Probably he didn't miss the giggle, either. In the manner of families, after a suitable silent interval my father and I commenced to quarrel. On the surface it was a quarrel about businessmen and professional men, but actually it had to do with the merits of the East and the merits of the Midwest and my father's knowledge that I had rejected the values of his region. The Midwest asserted its claims early, and if you had a restless nature you left. It forced you to leave; there were no halfway measures in the heartland, at that time a province as surely as Franche-Comté or Castile, an interior region pressed by the culture of the coasts, defensive, suspicious, and claustrophobic. When I left I tried to explain to him that a New Yorker's restlessness or ambition could take him to Washington as a Bostonian's could take him to New York, the one city representing power and the other money. No Midwesterner, making the momentous decision to leave home, would go from Chicago to Cleveland or from Minneapolis to Kansas City. These places are around the corner from one another. The Midwest is the same wherever you go, the towns larger or smaller but the culture identical. Leaving the Midwest, one perforce rejects the Midwest and its values; its sense of inferiority — so I felt then — prevented any return. In some way it had failed. What sound reason could there be for leaving God's country, the very soul of the nation, to live and work on the cluttered margins? It had failed you and you had failed it, whoring after glitter. My father's chivalry did not allow him to blame "that girl" publicly, but I knew that privately he did. Too much — too much Boston, too much money, too determined, too self-possessed. He hated to think that his son — flesh of my flesh, blood of my blood! — could be led out of Chicagoland by a woman. The image I imagine it brought to his mind was of an ox dumbly plodding down a road, supervised by a young woman lightly flicking its withers with a stick. That ghastly dinner!

"The thing is." She smiled wanly, back in the present now, that is, her own life, and what she had made of it. "It's so — *tiresome.* I know the marriage is over, it's probably been finished for years. But starting over again. I don't want to start over again. I haven't the energy." She sighed. "He's said for years that he's got to find himself. He's forty-eight years old and he's lost and now he wants to be found. And I'm sure he will be."

"Usually it's the other way around," I said. "These days, it's the women who want to find themselves. Or get lost, one or the other."

"Frank has a feminine side." I nodded, thinking of Frank Greer as a pastel. Frank in lime green and white, cool and pretty as a gin and tonic. "But the point isn't Frank," Beth said. "It's me. I don't want to start over again. I started over again once and that didn't work and then I started over again and it was fun for a while and then it was a routine, like everything else. I like the routine. And I was younger then."

I did not quite follow that, so I said, "I know."

"Liar," she said. "How could you? You've never been married."

"Beth," I said.

She looked at me irritably. "That doesn't count. You've got to be married for at least five years before it's a marriage. And there have to be children, or at least a child. Otherwise it's just shacking up and you can get out of it as easily and painlessly as you got into it, which from the sound of yours was pretty easy and painless."

She looked away while the waiter set down our drinks and, with a flourish, the menus.

"How long ago was it?"

"Almost twenty years ago," I said.

"Where is she now?"

I shrugged. I had no idea. When she left me she went back to London. I heard she had a job there; then, a few years ago, I heard she was living in France, married, with children. Then I heard that she was no longer in France but somewhere else on the Continent, unmarried now.

"That's what I mean," she said. "You don't even know where she *is*."

"Well," I said. "She knows where I am."

"What was her name?"

"Rachel," I said.

Beth thought a moment. "Was she Jewish?"

"Yes," I said.

Beth made a little sound, but did not comment. The amused look on her face said that my father must have found Rachel even more unsuitable than Beth. As it happened, she was right, but it had nothing to do with Rachel's Jewishness. She was a foreigner with pronounced political opinions. "And you like living alone," Beth said.

"At first I hated it," I said. "But I like it now and I can't imagine living any other way. It's what I do, live alone. You get married, I don't. Everyone I know gets married and almost everyone I know gets divorced."

"Well, you see it from the outside."

"It's close enough," I said.

"Yes, but it's not *real*." She glanced left into Boylston Street. It was snowing, and only a few pedestrians were about, bending into the wind. She shivered when she looked at the stiff-legged pedestrians, their movements so spiritless and numb against the concrete of the sidewalk, the sight bleaker still by contrast with the pale monochrome and the fragrance of the restaurant. Outside was a dark, malicious, European winter, Prague perhaps, or Moscow. "We might've made it," she said tentatively, still looking out the window.

I said nothing. She was dead wrong about that.

She sat with her chin in her hand, staring into the blowing snow. "But we were so different, and you were so bad."

The waiter was hovering and I turned to ask him the specialties of the day. They were a tiny bird en croute, a fish soufflé, and a vegetable ensemble. Beth was silent, inspecting the menu; she had slipped on a pair of half-glasses for this chore. I ordered a dozen oysters and an entrecôte, medium well. I knew that if I ordered it medium well I had a fair chance of getting it medium rare. Then I ordered a baked potato and a Caesar salad and another drink. The waiter caught something in my tone and courteously suggested that medium well was excessive. I said all right, if he would promise a true medium rare. Beth ordered a fish I never heard of and called for the wine list. The waiter seemed much happier dealing with Beth than with me. They conferred over the wine list for a few moments, and then he left.

She said, "You're always so defensive."

"I don't like these places, I told you that." heard the Boston whine in my voice and retreated a step. "The waiter's OK."

"You never did like them," she said. "But at least *before* . . . " She shook her head, exasperated.

"Before, what?" I asked.

"At least you were a provincial, there was an excuse."

I pulled at my drink, irritated. But when I saw her smiling slyly I had to laugh. Nothing had changed, though we had not seen each other in fifteen years and had not spoken in twenty. The occasion fifteen years ago was a wedding reception. I saw her standing in a corner talking to Frank Greer. She was recently divorced from Doran. I was about to approach to say hello; then I saw the expression on her face and withdrew. She and Greer were in another world, oblivious of the uproar around them, and I recognized the expression: it was the one I thought was reserved for me. Now, looking at her across the restaurant table, it was as if we had never been apart, as if our attitudes were frozen in aspic. We were still like a divided legislature, forever arguing over the economy, social policy, the defense budget, and the cuisine in the Senate dining room. The same arguments, conducted in the same terms; the same old struggle for control of our future. Her prejudice, my pride.

"You have to tell me one thing." She turned to inspect the bottle the waiter presented, raising her head so she could see through the half-glasses. She touched the label of the wine with her fingernails and said yes, it was fine, excellent really, and then, turning, her head still raised, she assured me that I would find it drinkable, since it came from a splendid little château vineyard near the Wisconsin Dells. The waiter looked at her dubiously and asked whether he should open it now and put it on ice, and she said yes, of course, she wanted it so cold she'd need her mittens to pour it. I was laughing and thinking how attractive she was, a woman whose humor improved with age, if she would just let up a little on the other. Also, I was waiting for the "one thing" I would have to tell her.

I said, "You're a damn funny woman."

"I have good material," she said.

"Not always," I replied.

"The one thing," she said, "that I can't figure out. Never could figure out. Why did you stay here? This isn't your kind of town at all, never was. It's so circumspect, and sure of itself. I'm surprised you didn't go back to Chicago after you were canned by H,W."

"I like collapsing civilizations," I said. "I'm a connoisseur of collapse and systems breakdown and bankruptcy—moral, ethical, and financial. So Boston is perfect." I thought of the town where I grew up, so secure and prosperous then, so down-at-heel now, the foundry old, exhausted, incidental, and off the subject. We lived in Chicago's muscular shadow and were thankful for it, before the world went to hell. "And I wasn't about to be run out of town by people like that," I added truculently.

"So it was spite," she said.

"Not spite," I said equably. "Inertia."

"And you're still spending weekends in New York?"

I nodded. Not as often now as in the past, though. "Weird life you lead," she said.

I said, "What's so weird about it?"

"Weekdays here, weekends in New York. And you still have your flat near the brownstone, the same one?"

I looked at her with feigned surprise. "How did you know about my flat?"

"For God's sake," she said. "Nora's a friend of mine."

It was never easy to score a point on Beth Earle. I said, "I've had it for almost twenty years. And I'll have it for twenty more. It's my Panama Canal. I bought it, I paid for it, it's mine, and I intend to keep it."

She shook her head, smiling ruefully. She said that she had lived in half a dozen houses over the years and remembered each one down to the smallest detail: the color of the tile in the bathroom and the shape of the clothes closet in the bedroom. She and Doran had lived in Provincetown for a year, and then had moved to Gloucester. That was when Doran was trying to paint. Then, after

Doran, she lived alone in Marblehead. When she was married to Frank Greer they went to New York, then returned to Boston; he owned an apartment on Beacon Hill. They lived alone there for two years, and then moved to Beverly — her idea; she was tired of the city. She counted these places on her fingers. "Six," she said. "And all this time, you've been in the same place in the Back Bay." She was leaning across the table, and now she looked up. The waiter placed a small salad in front of her and the oysters in front of me. The oysters were Cotuits. She signaled for the wine and said that "Monsieur" would taste. She told the waiter I was a distinguished gourmet, much sought after as a taster, and that my wine cellar in Michigan City was the envy of the region. She gave the impression that the restaurant was lucky to have me as a patron. The waiter shot me a sharp look and poured the wine into my glass. I pronounced it fine. Actually, I said it was "swell," and then, gargling heartily, "dandy." I gave Beth one of the oysters and insisted that she eat it the way it was meant to be eaten, naked out of the shell, without catsup or horseradish. She sucked it up, and leaned across the table once again. "Don't you miss them, the arguments? The struggle, always rubbing off someone else? The fights, the friction — ?" I laughed loudly. "Miss them to death," I said.

* * *

We finished the bottle of white and ordered a bottle of red; she said she preferred red with fish. I suspected that that was a concession to my entrecôte, which at any event was rare and bloody. She continued to press, gently at first, then with vehemence. She was trying to work out her life and thought that somehow I was a clue to it. At last she demanded that I describe my days in Boston. She wanted to know how I live, the details, "the quotidian." I was reluctant to do this, having lived privately for so many years. Also, there was very little to describe. I had fallen into the bachelor habit of total predictability. Except to travel to the airport and the courts, I seldom left the Back Bay. My terrain was bordered by the Public Garden and the Ritz, Storrow Drive, Newbury Street, the brownstone where I worked, and Commonwealth Avenue where I lived. I walked to work, lunched at the Ritz, took a stroll in the Garden, returned to the brownstone, and at seven or so went home. People I knew tended to live in the Back Bay or on the Hill, so if I went out in the evening I walked. Each year it became easier not to leave the apartment; I needed an exceptional reason to do so. I liked my work and worked hard at it.

She listened avidly, but did not comment. The waiter came to clear the table and offer dessert. We declined, ordering coffee and cognac.

"What kind of car do you have?" she asked suddenly.

I said I didn't own one.

"What kind of car does she own?"

I looked at her: Who?

"Your secretary," she said. "I hear you have a relationship with your secretary."

"She's been my assistant for a very long time," I said.

"Her car," Beth said.

I said, "A Mercedes."

"Well," she said.

"Well, what?"

"Well, nothing," she said. "Except so do I."

"Two cheers for the Krauts," I said.

"Is she a nice woman?"

I laughed. "Yes," I said. "Very. And very able."

"She approves of the arrangement."

"Beth," I said.

Beth said, "I wonder what she gets out of it."

"She won't ever have to get divorced," I said. "That's one thing she gets out of it."

"Was she the woman in the outer office?"

"Probably," I said.

Beth was silent a moment, toying with her coffee cup. There was only one other couple left in the restaurant, and they were preparing to leave. "You were always secretive," she said.

"You were not exactly an open book."

She ignored that. "It's not an attractive trait, being secretive. It leaves you wide open."

For what? I wondered. I looked at her closely, uncertain whether it was she talking or the wine. We were both tight, but her voice had an edge that had not been there before. I poured more coffee, wondering whether I should ask the question that had been in my mind for the past hour. I knew I would not like the answer, whatever it was, but I was curious. Being with her again, I began to remember things I had not thought of in years; it was as if the two decades were no greater distance than the width of the table, and I had only to lean across the space and take her hand to be twenty-five again. The evening had already been very unsettling and strange; no reason, I thought, not to make it stranger still.

I said quietly, "How was I so bad?"

"You never let go," she said. "You just hung on for dear life."

"Right," I said. I had no idea what she was talking about.

"Our plans," she began.

"Depended on me letting go?"

She shrugged. "You tried to fit in and you never did."

"In Boston," I said.

She moved her head, yes and no; apparently the point was a subtle one. "I didn't want to come back here and you insisted. I was depending on you to take me away, or at least make an independent life. You never understood that I had always been on the outs with my family."

I stifled an urge to object. I had never wanted to come to Boston. It was where she lived. It was her town, not mine. Glorious Boston, cradle of the Revolution. I had no intrinsic interest in Boston; I only wanted to leave the Midwest. Boston was as good a city as any, and she lived there.

"You were such a damn good *listener*." She bit the word off, as if it were an obscenity. "Better than you are now, and you're pretty good now. Not so good at talking, though. You listened so well a woman forgot that you never talked yourself, never let on what it was *that was on your mind*. Not one of your strong points, talking."

"Beth," I said evenly. She waited, but I said nothing more; there was nothing more to say anyhow, and I knew the silence would irritate her.

"And it was obvious it would never work; we never got grounded here. And it was obvious you never would, you could never let go of your damn prairie *complexe d'infériorité*. And as a result you were" — she sought the correct word — *"louche."*

"I am not Andre Malraux," I said. "What the hell does that mean?"

"It means secretive," she said. "And something more. Furtive."

"Thanks," I said.

"It's a mystery to me why I'm still here. Not so great a mystery as you, but mystery enough. You had to lead the way, though, and you didn't. And I knew H,W was a mistake."

"It was your uncle who suggested it," I said.

"After you asked him," she said.

"At your urging," I said.

"When it looked like you wouldn't land anything and I was tired of the griping."

"You were the one who was nervous," I said.

"I didn't care where we lived," she said. "That was the point you never got." Her voice rose, and I saw the waiter turn and say something to the maitre d'. The other couple had left and we were alone in the restaurant. Outside, a police car sped by, its lights blazing, but without sirens. The officer in the passenger seat was white-haired and fat, and he was smoking a cigar. It had stopped snowing but the wind was fierce, blowing debris and rattling windows. The police car had disappeared. I motioned to the waiter for the check. But Beth was far from finished.

"So I married Doran."

"And I didn't marry anybody."

"You married Rachel."

"According to you, Rachel doesn't count."

"Neither did Doran."

The waiter brought the check and I automatically reached for my wallet. She said loudly, "No," and I looked at her, momentarily confused. I had forgotten it was her treat. I had become so absorbed in the past; always when we had been together, I had paid, and it seemed cheap of me to let her pay now. But that was what she wanted and I had agreed to it. She had the check in her hand and was inspecting it for errors. Then, satisfied, she pushed it aside along with a credit card. She exhaled softly and turned to look out the window.

She said quietly, talking to the window, "Do you think it will be easy?"

"I don't know," I said.

"Please," she said. She said it hesitantly, as if the word were unfamiliar. "Just tell me what you think. I won't hold you to it if you're wrong."

"His lawyer," I began.

"Please," she said again, more forcefully.

"You're asking me for assurances that I can't give. I don't know."

"Just a guess," she said. "In your line of work you must make guesses all the time. Make one now, between us. Between friends?"

"Well, then," I said. "No."

"The first one was easy?"

"Maybe this will be too," I said.

"But you don't think so."

"No," I said. I knew Frank Greer.

She said, "You're a peach." She put on her glasses.

I did not reply to that.

"I mean it," she said.

Apparently she did, for she looked at me and smiled warmly. "I have disrupted your life."

I shook my head no.

"Yes, I have. That's what I do sometimes, disrupt the lives of men."

There was so much to say to that, and so little to be gained. I lit a cigarette, listening.

With a quick movement she pushed the half-glasses over her forehead and into her hair, all business. "Get in touch with him tomorrow. Can you do that?"

"Sure," I said.

"And let me know what he says, right away?"

"Yes," I said.

"I don't think it's going to be so tough."

"I hope you're right," I said.

"But I've always been an optimist where men are concerned."

I smiled and touched her hand. I looked at her closely, remembering her as a young woman; I knew her now and I knew her then, but there was nothing in between. That was undiscovered territory. I saw the difficulties ahead. They were big as mountains, Annapurna-size difficulties, a long slog at high altitudes, defending Beth. I took my hand away and said, "You can bail out any time you want if this gets difficult or awkward. I know it isn't easy. I can put you in touch with any one of a dozen—" She stared at me for a long moment. In the candlelight her face seemed to flush. Suddenly I knew she was murderously angry.

"I think you're right," she said.

"Look," I began.

"Reluctant lawyers are worse than useless." She took off her glasses and put them in her purse. When she snapped the purse shut it sounded like a pistol shot.

"I'll call you tomorrow," I said. I knew that I had handled it badly, but there was no retreat now.

She stood up and the waiter swung into position, helping her with her chair and bowing prettily from the waist.

Outside on Boylston Street the wind was still blowing, and the street was empty except for two cabs at the curb. We stood a moment on the sidewalk, not speaking. She stood with her head turned away, and I thought for a moment she was crying. But when she turned her head I saw the set of her jaw. She was too angry to cry. She began to walk up the street, and I followed. The wind off the Atlantic was vicious. I thought of it as originating in Scotland or Scandinavia, but of course that was wrong. Didn't the wind blow from west to east? This one probably originated in the upper Midwest or Canada. It had a prairie feel to it. We both walked unsteadily with our heads tucked into our coat collars. I thought of Tom and his camel-hair coat. At Arlington Street she stopped and fumbled for her keys, and then resumed the march. A beggar was at our heels, asking for money. I turned, apprehensive, but he was a sweet-faced drunk. I gave him a dollar and he ambled off. Her car was parked across the street from the Ritz, a green Mercedes convertible with her initials in gold on the door. The car gleamed in the harsh white light of the streetlamps. She stooped to unlock the door, and when she opened it the smell of leather, warm and inviting, spilled into the frigid street. I held the door for her, but she did not get in. She stood looking at me, her face expressionless. She started to say something, but changed her mind. She threw her purse into the back seat and the next thing I knew I was reeling backward, then slipping on an icy patch and falling. Her fist had come out of nowhere and caught me under the right eye. Sprawled on the sidewalk, speechless, I watched her get into the car and drive away. The smell of leather remained in my vicinity.

The doorman at the Ritz had seen all of it, and now he hurried across Arlington Street. He helped me up, muttering and fussing, but despite his best intentions he could not help smiling. He kept his face half turned away so I would not see. Of course he knew me; I was a regular in the bar and the café.

Damn woman, I said. She could go ten with Marvin Hagler.

He thought it all right then to laugh.

Not like the old days, I said.

Packed quite a punch, did she, sir? Ha-ha.

I leaned against the iron fence and collected my wits. Anything broken? he asked.

I didn't think so. I moved my legs and arms, touched my eye. It was tender but there was no blood. I knew I would have a shiner and wondered how I would explain that at the office.

Let's get you into the bar, he said. A brandy.

No. I shook my head painfully and reached for my wallet. The doorman waited, his face slightly averted as before. I found a five, then thought better of it and gave him a twenty. He didn't have to be told that twenty dollars bought silence. He tucked the money away in his vest and tipped his hat, frowning solicitously.

You wait here one minute, he said. I'll fetch a cab.

No need, I replied. Prefer to walk. I live nearby.

I know, he said, looking at me doubtfully. Then, noticing he had customers under the hotel canopy, he hurried back across the street. I watched him go, assuring the people with a casual wave of his hand that the disturbance was a private matter, minor and entirely under control.

I moved away too, conscious of being watched and realizing that I was very tight. I was breathing hard and could smell my cognac breath. I felt my eye beginning to puff and I knew that I would have bruises on my backside. I decided to take a long way home and walked through the iron gate into the Garden. There was no one about, but the place was filthy, papers blowing everywhere and ashcans stuffed to overflowing. The flurries had left a residue of gray snow. I passed a potato-faced George Washington on horseback on my way along the path to the statue facing Marlborough Street. This was my favorite. Atop the column a physician cradled an unconscious patient, "to commemorate the discovery that the inhaling of ether causes insensibility to pain. First proved to the world at the Mass. General Hospital." It was a pretty little

Victorian sculpture. On the plinth someone had scrawled UP THE
I.R.A. in red paint.

I exited at the Beacon Street side. A cab paused, but I waved him
on. I labored painfully down Beacon to Clarendon and over to
Commonwealth, my shoes scuffing little shards of blue glass,
hard and bright as diamonds; this was window glass from the automobiles vandalized nightly. While I waited at the light a large
American sedan pulled up next to me, its fender grazing my leg,
two men and a woman staring menacingly out the side windows.
I took a step backward, and the sedan sped through the red light,
trailing rock music and laughter. Tires squealed as the car accelerated, wheeling right on Newbury.

My flat was only a few blocks away. I walked down the deserted
mall, my eyes up and watchful. Leafless trees leaned over the walk-
way, their twisted branches grotesque against the night sky.
I walked carefully, for there was ice and dog shit everywhere.
The old-fashioned streetlights, truly handsome in daytime were
useless now. It was all so familiar; I had walked down this mall
every day for twenty years. Twenty years ago, when there was no
danger after dark, Rachel and I took long strolls on summer evenings trying to reach an understanding, and failing. I remembered
her musical voice and her accent; when she was distressed she
spoke rapidly, but always with perfect diction. I looked up, searching for my living room window. I was light-headed now and stum-
bling, but I knew I was close. The Hancock was to my left, as big as a
mountain and as sheer, looming like some futuristic religious icon
over the low, crabbed sprawl of the Back Bay. I leaned against a tree,
out of breath. There was only a little way now; I could see the light
in the window. My right eye was almost closed, and my vision
blurred. The wind bit into my face, sending huge tears running
down my cheeks. I hunched my shoulders against the wind and
struggled on, through the empty streets of the city I hated so.

Discussion Topics

1. Unlike "American Express," "About Boston" is written in the first
person. Often, but not always, first person narratives make it easy to identify with the protagonist. Authors can also use this strategy in a paradoxical
way; knowing the character's thoughts and feelings, we may come to
feel alienated from him. Which way does this work in Just's story? Note
that our loyalties may be divided: Beth and the narrator practically demand
that we take sides.

2. Put aside the question of first-person narrative and focus on the main conflict. Beth's meeting with the narrator is volatile in part because of hidden agendas. Of all the divorce lawyers in Boston, she settles on her former fiancé. Their meeting becomes, inevitably, the occasion for reliving their past. Our judgments about each of them — and it is hard to refrain from judgment — are based on past and present events. We judge Beth not only by her present expectations but by what we know about her from the early years. When we look at the narrator, we may accept or not Beth's fault-finding.

The narrator's response to Beth is governed in part by the strictures of good lawyering. Lawyers are well-advised not to raise false expectations or to identify too closely with a client's goals. And their job requires some emotional distancing. If these considerations weigh against the narrator taking Beth's case, the apparent straight-forwardness of the legal case (at least as Beth sees it) weighs on the other side. In judging the narrator, it is important to keep in mind that what might seem coldness is in part at least the nature of the professional role. Notwithstanding this, the story can be a Rorschach test for the reader's sympathies.

3. Boston plays a special role in America's history, just as it plays one in this story. The narrator's unequivocal hatred for Boston raises two questions. Is his dislike justified? Why has he lived his professional life in a place he so despises?

In the 1970s and 1980s Boston became a symbol of civil unrest — of white resistance to busing and school integration and of strife over community activism. Along with other northeastern cities, it suffered from "white flight," the abandonment of the inner urban core by people of means. Economic and geographic divisions reinforced each other; gaps widened. As Just points out, tension developed as well between old money and new money. National corporations invested in the city and built their own kinds of skyscrapers ("a Mondrian among Turners") in an architecture that fought with a city dedicated to tradition and perhaps ossified by time.

In this context, it is not clear what the narrator hated most. Was it the dead hand of old families, represented by the trust practice of Hamlin and White? Was it the arena of conflict that Boston had become? Or was it more personal, his failure to realize his aspirations and values in a world that shared little with Chicago?

It would have been easy to leave Boston and begin a practice elsewhere. What held him? His firm was increasingly well-established, and perhaps inertia kept him in place. Perhaps tenacity — perverse tenacity? masochism? — kept him from giving up his fight to subdue what seemed an alien culture. Is his hatred of Boston deep and well-founded, or is it something of a pose?

4. The narrator's goals were clear when he graduated from Yale Law. What he achieves differs significantly from his plans and hopes.

What counts as success? It is easy to assume that success is a matter of achieving what one sets out to do. By that unforgiving standard, his life fails. But his practice is largely satisfying, beneficial to others, and well-regarded. It is a neat fit with his innate skills and allows him to do rewarding (and well-rewarded) work.

His personal life has also taken unexpected turns. He planned to marry Beth, but in the end he has had no lasting marriage. And yet he is hardly monastic. His pleasures remain, for the most part, in New York while his work is in Boston. Is the disjunction between success and failure too simple or ambiguous a measure? Or is this life one in which a verdict is clear?

5. The story ends in violence. Beth's assault is a catalyst both for the events in the story and for our feelings about the characters. Until the final round, Beth and the narrator are feeling their way, never completely evasive but never quite candid. Their meeting and dinner mix vestiges of intimacy and familiarity with the constraints of professionalism and mutual respect. It turns into an explosive blend. We are tempted to assign fault, but we are likely to disagree as we do so.

Cynthia Ozick: Puttermesser: Her Work History, Her Ancestry, Her Afterlife

There are hints about the sociology of law, or at least the sociology of lawyers, in the first two stories. The main characters in each case leave their first law firms to establish new ones, thus creating environments congenial to themselves. The protagonist of the next story, Ruth Puttermesser, also leaves her first firm. His professional situation is described with sharp irony in part because it reflects a transitional period for the two minorities she represents. She is both a woman and a Jew. She is also a unique character who combines logic and rigor in her legal work with a rich fantasy life.

Puttermesser creator, Cynthia Ozick (born 1928), has been a prolific writer of criticism and fiction throughout her long career. Born to Russian emigrés, she has been a New Yorker since birth (with a brief break at the Ohio State University for her master's degree in English, with a thesis on Henry James). Ozick has published novels, stories, parables, novellas, and many articles of literary criticism. She has won many fellowships and prizes.

Feminism, Jewish culture, and antisemitism are frequent themes in her work. She has said often that, as a child, she was told by her rabbi that "a girl doesn't have to study" and was called a killer of Christ by neighborhood children.

"Puttermesser" is one of her most celebrated stories, one that lets her explore her distinctive interests in women's lives and Jewish lives with a cold bath of irony. Ruth Puttermesser begins her career as an associate with a "blue-blooded Wall Street firm" which, as Ozick tells us, treated her with benevolence "because benevolence was theirs to dispense."

Ozick returned to Puttermesser and wrote four more stories about her "work history [and] afterlife." The five stories were published as a novel, *The Puttermesser Papers.* In due course, Ruth becomes mayor of New York City through supernatural interventions and eventually ends up (after her death) having adventures in Paradise. It's hardly the normal trajectory of a lawyer's life.

❧ Puttermesser: Her Work History, Her Ancestry, Her Afterlife ❧

Cynthia Ozick

Puttermesser was thirty-four, a lawyer. She was also something of a feminist, not crazy, but she resented having "Miss" put in front of her name; she thought it pointedly discriminatory, she wanted to be a lawyer among lawyers. Though she was no virgin she lived alone, but idiosyncratically — in the Bronx, on the Grand Concourse, among other people's decaying old parents. Her own had moved to Miami Beach; in furry slippers left over from high school she roamed the same endlessly mazy apartment she had grown up in, her aging piano sheets still on top of the upright with the teacher's X marks on them showing up to where she should practice. Puttermesser always pushed a little ahead of the actual assignment; in school, too. Her teachers told her mother she was "highly motivated," "achievement oriented." Also she had "scholastic drive." Her mother wrote all these things down in a notebook, kept it always, and took it with her to Florida in case she should die there. Puttermesser had a younger sister who was also highly motivated, but she had married an Indian, a Parsee chemist, and gone to live in Calcutta. Already the sister had four children and seven saris of various fabrics.

Puttermesser went on studying. In law school they called her a grind, a competitive-compulsive, an egomaniac out for aggrandizement. But ego was no part of it; she was looking to solve something, she did not know what. At the back of the linen closet she found a stack of her father's old shirt cardboards (her mother was provident, stingy: in kitchen drawers Puttermesser still discovered folded squares of used ancient waxed paper, million-creased into whiteness, cheese-smelling, nesting small unidentifiable wormlets); so behind the riser pipe in the bathroom Puttermesser kept weeks' worth of Sunday *Times* crossword puzzles stapled to these laundry boards and worked on them indiscriminately. She played chess against herself, and was always victor over the color she had decided to identify with. She organized tort cases on index cards. It was not that she intended to remember everything: situations — it was her tendency to call intellectual problems "situations" — slipped into her mind like butter into a bottle.

A letter came from her mother in Florida:

> Dear Ruth,
> I know you won't believe this but I swear it's true the other day Daddy was walking on the Avenue and who should he run into but Mrs. Zaretsky, the thin one from Burnside not the stout one from Davidson, you remember her Joel? Well he's divorced now no children thank God so he's free as a bird as they say his ex- the poor thing couldn't conceive. *He* had tests he's O.K. He's only an accountant not good enough for you because God knows I never forget the day you made Law Review but you should come down just to see what a tender type he grew up into. Every tragedy has its good side Mrs. Zaretsky says he comes down now practically whenever she calls him long distance. Daddy said to Mrs. Zaretsky well, an accountant, you didn't overeducate your son anyhow, with daughters it's different. But don't take this to heart honey Daddy is as proud as I am of your achievements. Why don't you write we didn't hear from you too long busy is busy but parents are parents.

Puttermesser had a Jewish face and a modicum of American distrust of it. She resembled no poster she had ever seen: with a Negroid passion she hated the Breck shampoo girl, so blond and bland and pale-mouthed; she boycotted Breck because of the golden-haired posters, all crudely idealized, an American wet dream, in the subway. Puttermesser's hair came in bouncing scallops — layered waves from scalp to tip, like imbricated roofing tile. It was nearly black and had a way of sometimes sticking straight out. Her nose had thick, well-haired, uneven nostrils, the right one noticeably wider than the other. Her eyes were small, the lashes short, invisible. She had the median Mongol lid — one of those Jewish faces with a vaguely Oriental cast. With all this, it was a fact she was not bad-looking. She had a good skin with, so far, few lines or pits or signs of looseness-to-come. Her jaw was pleasing — a baby jowl appeared only when she put her head deep in a book.

In bed she studied Hebrew grammar. The permutations of the triple-lettered root elated her. How was it possible that a whole language, hence a whole literature, a civilization even, should rest on the pure presence of three letters of the alphabet? The Hebrew verb, a stunning mechanism: three letters, whichever fated three, could command all possibility simply by a change in their pronunciation, or the addition of a wing-letter fore and aft. Every conceivable utterance blossomed from this trinity. It seemed to her not so much a language for expression as a code for the world's design, indissoluble, predetermined, translucent. The idea of the grammar of Hebrew turned Puttermesser's brain into a palace, a sort of Vatican; inside its corridors she walked from one resplendent triptych to another.

She wrote her mother a letter refusing to come to Florida to look over the divorced accountant's tenderness. She explained her life again; she explained it by indirection. She wrote:

> I have a cynical apperception of power, due no doubt to my current job. You probably haven't heard of the Office for Visas and Registration, OVIR for short. It's located, on Ogaryova Street, in Moscow, U.S.S.R. I could enumerate for you a few of the innumerable bureaucratic atrocities of OVIR, not that anyone knows them all. But I could give you a list of the names of all those criminals, down to the women clerks, Yefimova, Korolova, Akulova, Arkhipova, Izrailova, all of them on Kolpachni Street in an office headed by Zolotukhin, the assistant to Colonel Smyrnov, who's under Ovchinikov, who is second in command to General Viryein, only Viryein and Ovchinikov aren't on Kolpachni Street, they're the ones in the head office — the M.V.D., Internal Affairs Ministry — on Ogaryova Street. Some day all the Soviet Jews will come out of the spider's clutches of these people, and be free. Please explain to Daddy that this is one of the highest priorities of my life at this time in my personal history. Do you really think a Joel Zaretsky can share such a vision?

Immediately after law school, Puttermesser entered the firm of Midland, Reid & Cockleberry. It was a blueblood Wall Street firm, and Puttermesser, hired for her brains and ingratiating (read: immigrant-like) industry, was put into a back office to hunt up all-fours cases for the men up front. Though a Jew and a woman, she felt little discrimination: the back office was chiefly the repository of unmitigated drudgery and therefore of usable youth. Often enough it kept its lights burning till three in the morning. It was right that the Top Rung of law school should earn you the Bottom of the Ladder in the actual world of all fours. The wonderful thing was the fact of the Ladder itself. And though she was the only woman, Puttermesser was not the only Jew. Three Jews a year joined the back precincts of Midland, Reid (four the year Puttermesser came, which meant they thought "woman" more than "Jew" at the sight of her). Three Jews a year left — not the same three. Lunchtime was difficult. Most of the young men went to one or two athletic clubs nearby to "work out"; Puttermesser ate from a paper bag at her desk, along with the other Jews, and this was strange: the young male Jews appeared to be as committed to the squash courts as the others. Alas, the athletic clubs would not have them, and this too was preternatural — the young Jews were indistinguishable from the others. They bought the same suits from the same tailors, wore precisely the same shirts and shoes, were careful to avoid tie clips and to be barbered a good deal shorter than the wild men of the streets, though a bit longer than the prigs in the banks.

Puttermesser remembered what Anatole France said of Dreyfus: that he was the same type as the officers who condemned him. "In their shoes he would have condemned himself."

Only their accents fell short of being identical: the "a" a shade too far into the nose, the "i" with its telltale elongation, had long ago spread from Brooklyn to Great Neck, from Puttermesser's Bronx to Scarsdale. These two influential vowels had the uncanny faculty of disqualifying them for promotion. The squash players, meanwhile, moved out of the back offices into the front offices. One or two of them were groomed — curried, fed sugar, led out by the muzzle — for partnership: were called out to lunch with thin and easeful clients, spent an afternoon in the dining room of one of the big sleek banks, and, in short, developed the creamy cheeks and bland habits of the always-comfortable.

The Jews, by contrast, grew more anxious, hissed together meanly among the urinals (Puttermesser, in the ladies' room next door, could hear malcontent rumblings in the connecting plumbing), became perfectionist and uncasual, quibbled bitterly, with stabbing forefingers, over principles, and all in all began to look and act less like superannuated college athletes and more like Jews. Then they left. They left of their own choice; no one shut them out.

Puttermesser left too, weary of so much chivalry — the partners in particular were excessively gracious to her, and treated her like a fellow-aristocrat. Puttermesser supposed this was because *she* did not say "a" in her nose or elongate her "i," and above all she did not dentalize her "t," "d," or "l," keeping them all back against the upper palate. Long ago her speech had been "standardized" by the drilling of fanatical teachers, elocutionary missionaries hired out of the Midwest by Puttermesser's prize high school, until almost all the regionalism was drained out; except for the pace of her syllables, which had a New York deliberateness, Puttermesser could have come from anywhere. She was every bit as American as her grandfather in his captain's hat. From Castle Garden to blue New England mists, her father's father, hat-and-neckwear peddler to Yankees! In Puttermesser's veins Providence, Rhode Island, beat richly. It seemed to her the partners felt this.

Then she remembered that Dreyfus spoke perfect French, and was the perfect Frenchman.

For farewell she was taken out to a public restaurant — the clubs the partners belonged to (they explained) did not allow women — and apologized to her.

"We're sorry to lose you," one said, and the other said, "No one for you in this outfit for under the canvas, hah?"

"The canvas?" Puttermesser said.

"Wedding canopy," said the partner, with a wink. "Or do they make them out of sheepskin—I forget."

"An interesting custom. I hear you people break the dishes at a wedding too," said the second partner.

An anthropological meal. They explored the rites of her tribe. She had not known she was strange to them. Their beautiful manners were the cautiousness you adopt when you visit the interior: Dr. Livingstone, I presume? They shook hands and wished her luck, and at that moment, so close to their faces with those moist smile ruts flowing from the sides of their wafer-like noses punctured by narrow, even nostrils, Puttermesser was astonished into noticing how strange *they* were—so many luncheon Martinis inside their bellies, and such beautiful manners even while drunk, and, important though they were, insignificant though she was, the fine ceremonial fact of their having brought her to this carpeted place. Their eyes were blue. Their necks were clean. How closely they were shaven!—like men who grew no hair at all. Yet hairs curled inside their ears. They let her take away all her memo pads with her name printed on them. She was impressed by their courtesy, their benevolence, through which they always got their way. She had given them three years of meticulous anonymous research, deep deep nights going after precedents, dates, lost issues, faded faint politics; for their sakes she had yielded up those howling morning headaches and half a dioptre's worth of sight in both eyes. Brilliant students make good aides. They were pleased though not regretful. She was replaceable: a clever black had been hired only that morning. The palace they led her to at the end of it all was theirs by divine right: in which they believed, on which they acted. They were benevolent because benevolence was theirs to dispense.

She went to work for the Department of Receipts and Disbursements. Her title was Assistant Corporation Counsel—it had no meaning, it was part of the subspeech on which bureaucracy relies. Of the many who held this title most were Italians and Jews, and again Puttermesser was the only woman. In this great City office there were no ceremonies and no manners: gross shouts, ignorant clerks, slovenliness, litter on the floors, grit stuck all over antiquated books. The ladies' room reeked: the women urinated standing up, and hot urine splashed on the toilet seats and onto the muddy tiles.

The successive heads of this department were called Commissioners. They were all political appointees—scavengers after spoils. Puttermesser herself was not quite a civil servant and not quite *not* a civil servant—one of those amphibious creatures hanging between base contempt and bare decency; but she soon felt the ignominy of belonging to that mean swarm of City employees rooted bleakly in cells inside the honeycomb of the Municipal Building. It was a monstrous place, gray everywhere, abundantly tunnelled, with multitudes of corridors and stairs and shafts, a kind of swollen doom through which the bickering of small-voiced officials whinnied. At the same time there were always curious farm sounds — in the summer the steady cricket of the air-conditioning, in the winter the gnash and croak of old radiators. Nevertheless the windows were broad and high and stupendously filled with light; they looked out on the whole lower island of Manhattan, revealed as an island, down to the Battery, all crusted over with the dried lava of shape and shape: rectangle over square, and square over spire. At noon the dark gongs of St. Andrew's boomed their wild and stately strokes.

To Puttermesser all this meant she had come down in the world. Here she was not even a curiosity. No one noticed a Jew. Unlike the partners at Midland, Reid, the Commissioners did not travel out among their subjects and were rarely seen. Instead they were like shut-up kings in a tower, and suffered from rumors.

But Puttermesser discovered that in City life all rumors are true. Putative turncoats are genuine turncoats. All whispered knifings have happened: officials reputed to be about to topple, topple. So far Puttermesser had lasted through two elections, seeing the powerful become powerless and the formerly powerless inflate themselves overnight, like gigantic winds, to suck out the victory of the short run. When one Administration was razed, for the moment custom seemed leveled with it, everything that smelled of "before," of "the old way" — but only at first. The early fits of innovation subsided, and gradually the old way of doing things crept back, covering everything over, like grass, as if the building and its workers were together some inexorable vegetable organism with its own laws of subsistence. The civil servants were grass. Nothing destroyed them, they were stronger than the pavement, they were stronger than time. The Administration might turn on its hinge, throwing out one lot of patronage eaters and gathering in the new lot: the work went on. They might put in fresh carpeting in the new Deputy's office, or a private toilet in the new Commissioner's, and change the clerks' light bulbs to a lower wattage, and design an extravagant new colophon for a useless old document — they might do anything they liked: the work went on as before. The organism breathed, it comprehended itself.

So there was nothing for the Commissioner to do, and he knew it, and the organism knew it. For a very great salary the Commissioner shut his door and cleaned his nails behind it with one of the shining tools of a fancy Swiss knife, and had a secretary who was rude to everyone, and made dozens of telephone calls every day.

The current one was a rich and foolish playboy who had given the Mayor money for his campaign. All the high officials of every department were either men who had given the Mayor money or else courtiers who had humiliated themselves for him in the political clubhouse—mainly by flattering the clubhouse boss, who before any election was already a secret mayor and dictated the patronage lists. But the current Commissioner owed nothing to the boss because he had given the Mayor money and was the Mayor's own appointee; and anyhow he would have little to do with the boss because he had little to do with any Italian. The boss was a gentlemanly Neapolitan named Fiore, the chairman of the board of a bank; but still, he was only an Italian, and the Commissioner cared chiefly for blue-eyed bankers. He used his telephone to make luncheon appointments with them, and sometimes tennis. He himself was a blue-eyed Guggenheim, a German Jew, but not one of the grand philanthropic Guggenheims. The name was a cunning coincidence (cut down from Guggenheimer), and he was rich enough to be taken for one of the real Guggenheims, who thought him an upstart and disowned him. Grandeur demands discreetness; he was so discreetly disowned that no one knew it, not even the Rockefeller he had met at Choate.

This Commissioner was a handsome, timid man, still young, and good at boating; on weekends he wore sneakers and cultivated the friendship of the dynasties—Sulzbergers and Warburgs, who let him eat with them but warned their daughters against him. He had dropped out of two colleges and finally graduated from the third by getting a term-paper factory to plagiarize his reports. He was harmless and simple-minded, still devoted to his brainy late father, and frightened to death of news conferences. He understood nothing: art appreciation had been his best subject (he was attracted to Renaissance nudes), economics his worst. If someone asked, "How much does the City invest every day?" or "Is there any Constitutional bar against revenue from commuters?" or "What is your opinion about taxing exempt properties?" his pulse would catch in his throat, making his nose run, and he had to say he was pressed for time and would let them have the answers from his Deputy in charge of the Treasury. Sometimes he would even call on Puttermesser for an answer.

Now if this were an optimistic portrait, exactly here is where Puttermesser's emotional life would begin to grind itself into evidence. Her biography would proceed romantically, the rich young Commissioner of the Department of Receipts and

Disbursements would fall in love with her. She would convert him to intelligence and to the cause of Soviet Jewry. He would abandon boating and the pursuit of bluebloods. Puttermesser would end her work history abruptly and move on to a bower in a fine suburb.

This is not to be. Puttermesser will always be an employee in the Municipal Building. She will always behold Brooklyn Bridge through its windows; also sunsets of high glory, bringing her religious pangs. She will not marry. Perhaps she will undertake a long-term affair with Vogel, the Deputy in charge of the Treasury; perhaps not.

The difficulty with Puttermesser is that she is loyal to certain environments.

Puttermesser, while working in the Municipal Building, had a luxuriant dream, a dream of *gan eydn* — a term and notion handed on from her great-uncle Zindel, a former shammes in a shul that had been torn down. In this reconstituted Garden of which is to say in the World to Come, Puttermesser, who was not afflicted with quotidian uncertainty in the Present World, had even more certainty of her aims. With her weakness for fudge (others of her age, class, and character had advanced to Martinis, at least to ginger ale; Puttermesser still drank ice cream with cola, despised mints as too tingly, eschewed salty liver canapes, hunted down chocolate babies, Kraft caramels, Mary Janes, Milky Ways, peanut brittle, and immediately afterward furiously brushed her teeth, scrubbing off guilt) — with all this nasty self-indulgence, she was nevertheless very thin and unironic. Or: to postulate an afterlife was her single irony — a game in the head not unlike a melting fudge cube held against the upper palate.

There, at any rate, Puttermesser would sit, in Eden, under a middle-sized tree, in the solid blaze of an infinite heart-of-summer July, green, green, green everywhere, green above and green below, herself gleaming and made glorious by sweat, every itch annihilated, fecundity dismissed. And there Puttermesser would, as she imagined it, *take in.* Ready to her left hand, the box of fudge (rather like the fudge sold to the lower school by the eighth-grade cooking class in P.S. 74, The Bronx, circa 1942); ready to her right hand, a borrowed steeple of library books: for into Eden the Crotona Park Branch has ascended intact, sans librarians and fines, but with its delectable terrestrial binding-glue fragrances unevaporated.

Here Puttermesser sits. Day after celestial day, perfection of desire upon perfection of contemplation, into the exaltations of an uninterrupted forever, she eats fudge in human shape (once known — no use covering this up — as nigger babies), or fudge in square shapes (and in Eden there is no tooth decay); and she reads. Puttermesser reads and reads. Her eyes in Paradise are unfatigued.

And if she still does not know what it is she wants to solve, she has only to read on. The Crotona Park Branch is as paradisal here as it was on earth. She reads anthropology, zoology, physical chemistry, philosophy (in the green air of heaven Kant and Nietzsche together fall into crystal splinters). The New Books section is peerless: she will learn about the linkages of genes, about quarks, about primate sign language, theories of the origins of the races, religions of ancient civilizations, what Stonehenge meant. Puttermesser will read Non-Fiction into eternity; and there is still time for Fiction! Eden is equipped above all with timelessness, so Puttermesser will read at last all of Balzac, all of Dickens, all of Turgenev and Dostoevski (her mortal self has already read all of Tolstoy and George Eliot); at last Puttermesser will read *Kristin Lavransdatter* and the stupendous trilogy of Dmitri Merezhkovski, she will read *The Magic Mountain* and the whole "Faerie Queene" and every line of *The Ring and the Book,* she will read a biography of Beatrix Potter and one of Walter Scott in many entrancing volumes and one of Lytton Strachey, at last, at last! In Eden insatiable Puttermesser will be nourished, if not glutted. She will study Roman law, the more arcane varieties of higher mathematics, the nuclear composition of the stars, what happened to the Monophysites, Chinese history, Russian, and Icelandic.

But meanwhile, still alive, not yet translated upward, her days given over to the shadow reign of a playboy Commissioner, Puttermesser was learning only Hebrew.

Twice a week, at night (it seemed), she went to Uncle Zindel for a lesson. Where the bus ran through peeling neighborhoods the trolley tracks sometimes shone up through a broken smother of asphalt, like weeds wanting renewal. From childhood Puttermesser remembered how trolley days were better days: in summer the cars banged along, self-contained little carnivals, with open wire-mesh sides sucking in hot winds, the passengers serenely jogging on the seats. Not so this bus, closed like a capsule against the slum.

The old man, Zindel the Stingy, hung on to life among the cooking smells of Spanish-speaking blacks. Puttermesser walked up three flights of steps and leaned against the crooked door, waiting for the former shammes with his little sack. Each evening Zindel brought up a single egg from the Cuban grocery. He boiled it while Puttermesser sat with her primer.

"You should go downtown" the shammes said, "where they got regular language factories. Berlitz. N.Y.U. They even got an *ulpan,* like in Israel."

"You're good enough" Puttermesser said. "You know everything they know."

"And something more also. Why you don't live downtown, on the East Side, fancy?"

"The rent is too much, I inherited your stinginess."

"And such a name. A nice young fellow meets such a name, he laughs. You should change it to something different, lovely, nice. Shapiro, Levine. Cohen, Goldweiss, Blumenthal. I don't say make it *different,* who needs Adams, who needs McKee, I say make it a name not a joke. Your father gave you a bad present with it. For a young girl, Butterknife!"

"I'll change it to Margarine-messer."

"Never mind the ha-ha. My father, what was your great-greatgrandfather, didn't allow a knife to the table Friday night. When it came to *kiddush*—*knifes* off! All knifes! On Sabbath an instrument, a blade? On Sabbath a weapon? A point? An edge? What makes bleeding among mankind? What makes war? Knifes! No knifes! Off! A clean table! And something else you'll notice. By us we got only *messer,* you follow? By them they got sword, they got lance, they got halberd. Go to the dictionary, I went once. So help me, what don't one of them knights carry? Look up in the book, you'll see halberd, you'll see cutlass, pike, rapier, foil, ten dozen more. By us a pike is a fish. Not to mention what nowadays they got—bayonet stuck on the gun, who knows what else the poor soldier got to carry in the pocket. Maybe a dagger same as a pirate. But by us—what we got? A *messer! Puttermesser,* you slice off a piece butter, you cut to live, not to kill. A name of honor, you follow? Still, for a young girl—"

"Uncle Zindel, I'm past thirty."

Uncle Zindel blinked lids like insect's wings, translucent. He saw her voyaging, voyaging. The wings of his eyes shadowed the Galilee. They moved over the Tomb of the Patriarchs. A tear for the tears of Mother Rachel rode on his nose. "Your mother knows you're going? Alone on an airplane, such a young girl? You wrote her?"

"I wrote her, Uncle Zindel. I'm not flying."

"By sea is also danger. What Mama figures, in Miami who is there? The dead and dying. In Israel you'll meet someone. You'll marry, you'll settle there. What's the difference, these days, modern times, quick travel?"

Uncle Zindel's egg was ready, hard-boiled. The shammes tapped it and the shell came off raggedly. Puttermesser consulted the alphabet: *aleph, beys, gimel;* she was not going to Israel, she had business in the Municipal Building. Uncle Zindel, chewing, began finally to teach: "First see how a *gimel* and which way a *zayen.* Twins, but one kicks a leg left, one right. You got to practice the difference. If legs don't work, think pregnant bellies. Mrs. *Zayen* pregnant in one direction, Mrs. *Gimel* in the other. Together they give birth to *gez*, which means what you cut off. A night for knifes! Listen, going home from here you should be extra careful tonight. Martinez, the upstairs not the next door, her daughter they mugged and they took."

The shammes chewed, and under his jaws Puttermesser's head bent, practicing the bellies of the holy letters.

Stop. Stop, stop! Puttermesser's biographer, stop! Disengage, please. Though it is true that biographies are invented, not recorded, here you invent too much. A symbol is allowed, but not a whole scene: do not accommodate too obsequiously to Puttermesser's romance. Having not much imagination, she is literal with what she has. Uncle Zindel lies under the earth of Staten Island. Puttermesser has never had a conversation with him; he died four years before her birth. He is all legend: Zindel the Stingy, who even in *gan eydn* rather than eat will store apples until they rot. Zindel the Unripe. Why must Puttermesser fall into so poignant a fever over the cracked phrases of a shammes of a torn-down shul?

(The shul was not torn down, neither was it abandoned. It disintegrated. Crumb by crumb it vanished. Stones took some of the windows. There were no pews, only wooden folding chairs. Little by little these turned into sticks. The prayer books began to flake: the bindings flaked, the glue came unstuck in small brown flakes, the leaves grew brittle and flaked into confetti. The congregation too began to flake off — the women first, wife after wife after wife, each one a pearl and a consolation, until there they stand, the widowers, frail, gazing, palsy-struck. Alone and in terror. Golden Agers, Senior Citizens! And finally they too flake away, the shammes among them. The shul becomes a wisp, a straw, a feather, a hair.)

But Puttermesser must claim an ancestor. She demands connection — surely a Jew must own a past. Poor Puttermesser has found herself in the world without a past. Her mother was born into the din of Madison Street and was taken up to the hullabaloo of Harlem at an early age. Her father is nearly a Yankee: his father gave up peddling to captain a dry-goods store in Providence, Rhode Island. In summer he sold captain's hats, and wore one in all his photographs. Of the world that was, there *is* only this single grain of memory: that once an old man, Puttermesser's mother's uncle, kept his pants up with a rope belt, was called Zindel, lived without a wife, ate frugally, knew the holy letters, died with thorny English a wilderness between his gums. To him Puttermesser sings, America is a blank, and Uncle Zindel is all her ancestry. Unironic, unimaginative, her plain but stringent mind strains beyond the parents — what did they have? Only day-by-day in their lives, coffee in the morning, washing underwear, occasionally a trip to the beach. Blank. What did they know? Everything from the movies; something — scraps — from the newspaper. Blank.

Behind the parents, beyond and before them, things teem. In old photographs of the Jewish East Side, Puttermesser sees the teeming. She sees a long coat. She sees a woman pressing onions from a pushcart. She sees a tiny child with a finger in its mouth who will become a judge.

Past the judge, beyond and behind him, something more is teeming. But this Puttermesser cannot see. The towns, the little towns. Zindel born into a flat-roofed house a modest distance from a stream.

What can Puttermesser do? She began life as a child of an anti-Semite. Her father would not eat kosher meat — it was, he said, too tough. He had no superstitions. He wore the mother down, she went to the regular meat market at last.

The scene with Uncle Zindel did not occur. How Puttermesser loved the voice of Zindel in the scene that did not occur!

(He is under the ground. The cemetery is a teeming city of toy skyscrapers shouldering each other. Born into a wooden house, Zindel now has a flat stone roof. Who buried him? Strangers from the *landsmanshaft* society. Who said a word for him? No one. Who remembers him now?)

Puttermesser does not remember Uncle Zindel; Puttermesser's mother does not remember him. A name in the dead grandmother's mouth. Her parents have no ancestry. Therefore Puttermesser rejoices in the cadences of Uncle Zindel's voice above the Cuban grocery. Uncle Zindel, when alive, distrusted the building of Tel Aviv because he was practical, Messiah was not imminent. But now, in the scene that did not occur, how naturally he supposes Puttermesser will journey to a sliver of earth in the Middle East, surrounded by knives, missiles, bazookas!

The scene with Uncle Zindel did not occur. It could not occur because, though Puttermesser dares to posit her ancestry, we may not. Puttermesser is not to be examined as an artifact but as an essence. Who made her? No one cares. Puttermesser is henceforth to be presented as given. Put her back into Receipts and Disbursements, among office Jews and patronage collectors. While winter dusk blackens the Brooklyn Bridge, let us hear her opinion about the taxation of exempt properties. The bridge is not the harp Hart Crane said it was in his poem. Its staves are prison bars. The women clerks, Yefimova, Korolova, Akulova, Arkhipova, Izrailova, are on Kolpachni Street, but the vainglorious General Viryein is not. He is on Ogaryova Street. Joel Zaretsky's ex-wife is barren. The Commissioner puts on his tennis sneakers. He telephones. Mr. Fiore, the courtly secret mayor behind the Mayor, also telephones. Hey! Puttermesser's biographer! What will you do with her now?

Discussion Topics

1. Ozick's style can be unsettling. She seems to offer a straight narrative, one in which we can distinguish reality (the artificial reality of the story) from fantasy (the fantasies of Puttermesser, not Ozick). But she tricks us. The Hebrew lessons with Uncle Zindel are presented as reality, but we are ultimatey told that they are in fact Ruth's fantasies. So we must be on our guard; we are on notice that we cannot trust everything she says.

We are in for more disorientation. We are told that "Puttermesser dares to posit her ancestry" so "we may not. Puttermesser is not to be examined as an artifact but as an essence. Who made her? No one cares." A character in a work of fiction is, of course, an artifact. By contrast, a living person, who constructs her life from day to day, may properly be called an essence or a "given." And we *do* care, do we not, who made her, namely Ozick. So these comments are all quite puzzling.

What seems to be going on here is that Ozick is emancipating her character. "If you want to posit your own life through fantasy, I'm washing my hands of you. You're on your own." These moves will be intriguing to readers of critical theory and bewildering to most others. So-called postmodern writers draw attention to the limits of a writer's authority and autonomy. The reader reconstructs a text by interpreting meaning, and the work is, so it is claimed, the product of collaboration between writer and reader. To the extent that readers bring different backgrounds and expectations, the work itself becomes different. And, because the ideal or objective reader is a mirage, there is no single master interpretation of a work.

Just as a work of art can mean different things to different readers so can a life. A biographer faces some of the same problems as a writer of fiction, and different biographers can find order and meaning in a particular life in radically different ways. There is unlikely to be a purely objective answer to "Who's right?" And just as the author of fiction may see his work (and his intentions) in ways that differ from the interpretations of most readers — whereby the author seems to be just one of many readers of his story — so too the person who has lived a life may not be authoritative or definitive in determining its meaning. Moreover, the line between facts and interpretations may be elusive. Aside from certain parameters, such as date of birth, death, and marriage, the apparent facts of life may be endlessly subject to interpretation and debate. (Did they really have a bad marriage? Did he really suffer from depression?)

Ozick, as a literary critic, has all of these theories in mind. She relishes a character who is herself a fantasist. And she toys with her readers, conceding how much her control over the story is, on the one hand, at the mercy of readers, and, on the other, at the mercy of her difficult protagonist.

2. What is the difference between fantasy and imagination? Ozick tells us repeatedly that Puttermesser is unironic and without imagination.

("Not having much imagination, she is literal with what she has.") And yet she is a first-class fantasist. Arguably imagination is creative. The products of imagination are likely to get a reaction from others, to be intellectually or emotionally engaging. Puttermesser's fantasies are banal and down-to-earth. She reads books and eats chocolates. She has Hebrew lessons and realistic conversations with a dead relative. In ordinary usage, however, we tend to equate fantasy and imagination — and Ozick is at pains to point out the difference.

3. How is Puttermesser seen by her law school classmates, professors, or fellow lawyers? She is said to be a "grind." She is certainly efficient and competent, even exemplary as an attorney. Does our knowledge of inner life change that assessment? Perhaps it would be a mistake to see a fissure or incompatibility between her inner life and her professional one. Her fantasies and eccentricities detract not at all from her skills and her aptitude for and enjoyment of law. She is a problem-solver. Her fascination with crossword puzzles is of a piece with her career choice of law.

We are surprised by the inner life of someone else because we are so rarely given access to another person's fantasies and private habits. Writers about lawyering consider whether private dimensions can wither and fade, whether the role can swallow the person and the lawyer can become a husk. That's one hypothesis about lawyers who seem soulless. Another is that the roles of law provide remarkably effective camouflage for the hidden private life.

A related point is that lawyers are neither trained nor disposed to be introspective (although there are many exceptions). Puttermesser herself is not inclined to self-examination. She has activities and fantasies, attitudes and responses, but she hardly reflects on why she has them. She has a disengaged and healthy self-confidence that allows her to see her departure from Midland Reid (properly) as in no way a personal failure, and she adjusts smoothly to new circumstances at the Department of Receipts and Disbursements.

4. It is said that the makeup of the legal profession has changed greatly in the last forty years, that firms and the profession as a whole are increasingly diverse and reflective of society's racial and gender mix. Admissions committees at law schools and hiring committees at firms have been attentive to diversity. Is the hiring and promotion policy at Midland Reid therefore an anachronism?

A cynic would say that diversity was also at the core of Midland's hiring practice. Blacks, women, and Jews were sought after and hired as associates. At the level of promotion, Midland's partners might argue, prejudice plays no role but the firm's future does. Thus, the firm's success is assured only by promoting "rainmakers," those junior members of the firm who are likely to insure social and political continuity with the firm's established client base and to attract more of the same.

We are told that "the more things change, the more they stay the same." Ozick, through Puttermesser's eyes, gives looks at the social anthropology of law firms. How easily can these factors be changed — and how much will exists to do so? Whether the makeup and attitudes of the profession have indeed changed remains a controversial issue. In March, 2003, *Fordham Law Review* devoted a symposium to it. The number of women and minority lawyers who achieve partnerships in major firms remains small.

5. Ozick's story can also be seen as Puttermesser's quest to belong to a tradition. Her family has largely disclaimed its Jewish heritage. In her fantasies, Puttermesser restores her links to Hebrew and her religious ancestors. Law represents a different kind of tradition, and Puttermesser gravitates to it precisely because, like much of Judaism, it represents a history of rational problem solving. But Midland's traditions are not hers and not ones that she is in a position to assimilate. The Office of Receipts and Disbursements is hardly the home of a legal tradition, and yet Puttermesser's search is for something more abstract. To what extent can faith in the law complement faith in religion or one's ethnic heritage, and to what extent can they be complementary?

Karel Capek: The Clairvoyant

Criminal prosecutors are often tempted to push hard against ethical constraints. Their job, as it is defined in the American system, is to convince juries of the defendants' guilt beyond a reasonable doubt. The defense wins as long as the jury is not unanimously persuaded. Although prosecutors, like the other participants at trial, ostensibly seek justice, their arena is one of combat and their reputation rests on their record of victories. For better or worse, prosecutors are often feared and sometimes demonized.

Karel Capek's story, "The Clairvoyant," is about a prosecutor and his methods of litigating. The author is one of the most intriguing figures in twentieth century east European literature. Among other things, Capek (and his brother, Josef) gave us the term "robot." He wrote science fiction before the genre existed. He wrote humorously and sometimes chillingly about the implications of modern science — about artificial intelligence, atomic bombs, and evolution. *War with the Newts*, one of his best-loved books, concerns an invasion by intelligent salamanders.

In his later work, political warnings are a constant theme. He was far-seeing about the rise of totalitarian government and the power of corporations. He wrote in many genres: plays, fairy tales, novels, stories, and thrillers. During the first Czech republic (1918-1938) he was closely associated with the liberal and widely respected president, T. S. Masaryk.

❖ The Clairvoyant ❖

Karel Capek

"You know, Mr. DA," Mr. Janowitz declared, "I'm not an easy person to fool; after all, I'm not a Jew for nothing, right? But what this fellow does is simply beyond belief. It isn't just graphology, it's — I don't know what. Here's how it works: you give him some- one's handwriting in an unsealed envelope; he never even looks at the writing, just pokes his fingers inside the envelope and feels the handwriting, all over; and all the while his face is twisting as if he were in pain. And before very long, he starts telling you about the nature of the writer, but he does it in such a way that — well, you'd be dumbfounded. He pegs the writer perfectly, down to the last detail. I gave him an envelope with a letter from old Weinberg in it; he had Weinberg figured out in no time, diabetes, even his planned bankruptcy. What do you say to that?"

"Nothing," the DA said drily. "Maybe he knows old Weinberg."

"But he never once looked at the handwriting," Mr. Janowitz protested. "He says every person's handwriting has its own aura, and he says that you can feel it, clearly and precisely. He says it's purely a physical phenomenon, like radio. This isn't some kind of swindle, Mr. DA; this Prince Karadagh doesn't make a penny from it. He's supposed to be from a very old family in Baku, according to what this Russian told me. But I'll tell you what, come see for your- self; he'll be here this evening. You must come."

"Listen, Mr. Janowitz," the DA said, "this is all very nice, but I only believe fifty per cent of what foreigners say, especially when I don't know how they make their living; I believe Russians even less, and fakirs less than that; but when on top of everything else the man's a prince, then I don't believe one word of it. Where did you say he learned this? Ah yes, in Persia. Forget it, Mr. Janowitz; the whole Orient's a fraud."

"But Mr. DA," Mr. Janowitz protested, "this young fellow explains it all scientifically; no magic tricks, no mysterious powers, I'm telling you, strictly scientific method."

"Then he's an even bigger phony," the DA admonished him. "Mr. Janowitz, I'm surprised at you; you've managed to live your entire life without strictly scientific methods, and here you are embracing them wholesale. Look, if there were something to it, it would have been known a long time ago, right?"

"Well," Mr. Janowitz replied, a little shaken, "but when I saw with my own eyes how he guessed everything about old Weinberg! Now there's genius for you. I'll tell you what, Mr. DA, come and have a look for yourself; if it's a hoax, you'll know it, that's your specialty, sir; nobody can put one over on you, Mr. DA."

"Hardly," the DA said modestly. "All right, I'll come, Mr. Janowitz, but only to keep an eye on your phenomenon's fingers. It's a shame that people are so gullible. But you mustn't tell him who I am; wait, I'll bring along some handwriting in an envelope for him, something special. Count on it, friend, I'll prove he's a phony."

You should understand that the district attorney (or, more accurately: chief public prosecutor Dr. Klapka) would, in his next court proceeding, be trying the case against Hugo Müller, who was charged with premeditated murder. Mr. Hugo Müller, millionaire industrialist, had been accused of insuring his younger brother Ota for a large sum of money and then drowning him in the lake at a summer resort; in addition to this he also had been under suspicion, during the previous year, of dispatching his lover, but of course that had not been proven. In short, it was a major trial, one to which the district attorney wanted to devote particular attention; and he had labored over the trial documents with all the persistence and acumen that had made him a most formidable prosecutor. The case was not clear; the district attorney would have given God-knows-what for one particle of direct evidence; but as things stood, he would have to rely more on his winning way with words if the jury were to award him a rope for Mr. Müller; you must understand that, for prosecutors, this is a point of honor.

Mr. Janowitz was a bit flustered that evening. "Dr. Klapka," he announced in muffled tones, "this is Prince Karadagh; well, let's get started."

The district attorney cast probing eyes on this exotic creature; he was a young and slender man with eyeglasses, the face of a Tibetan monk and delicate, thievish hands. Fancy-pants quack, the district attorney decided.

"Mr. Karadagh," Mr. Janowitz jabbered, "over here by this little table. There's some mineral water already there. Please, switch on that little floor lamp; we'll turn off the overhead light so it won't disturb you. There. Please, gentlemen, there should be silence. Mr. — eh, Mr. Klapka here brought some handwriting of some sort; if Mr. Karadagh would be so good as to — "

The district attorney cleared his throat briefly and seated himself so as to best observe the clairvoyant. "Here is the handwriting," he said, and he took an unsealed envelope from his breast pocket. "If I may — "

"Thank you," the clairvoyant said impassively. He took hold of the envelope and, with eyes closed, turned it over in his fingers. Suddenly he shuddered, twisting his head. "Curious," he muttered and bolted a sip of water. He then inserted his slim fingers into the envelope and suddenly stopped; it seemed as if his pale yellow face turned paler still.

There was such a silence in the room that a slight rattling could be heard from Mr. Janowitz, for Mr. Janowitz suffered from goiter.

The thin lips of Prince Karadagh trembled and contorted as if his fingers were clenching a red-hot iron, and sweat broke out on his forehead. "I cannot endure this," he hissed in a tight voice; he extracted his fingers from the envelope, rubbed them with a hand-kerchief and quickly moved them back and forth over the table-cloth, as one sharpens a knife, after which he once again sipped agitatedly from his glass of water and then cautiously took the envelope between his fingers.

"The man who wrote this," he began in a parched voice, "the man who wrote this . . . There is great strength here, but a — (obviously he was searching for a word) strength which lies there, waiting. This lying in wait is terrible," he cried out and dropped the envelope on the table. "I would not want this man as my enemy!"

"Why?" the district attorney could not refrain from asking. "Is he guilty of something?"

"Don't question me," the clairvoyant said. "Every question gives a hint. I only know that he could be guilty of anything at all, of great and terrible deeds. There is astonishing determination here . . . for success . . . for money . . . This man would not scruple over the life of a fellow creature. No, this is not an ordinary criminal; a tiger also is not a criminal; a tiger is a great lord. This man would not be capable of low trickery, but he thinks of himself as ruling over human lives. When he is on the prowl, he sees people only as prey. Therefore he kills them."

"Beyond good and evil," the district attorney murmured with unmistakable approval.

"Those are only words," Prince Karadagh said. "No one is beyond good and evil. This man has his own strict concept of moral-ity; he is in debt to no one, he does not steal, he does not lie; if he kills, it is as if he checkmated in a game of chess. It is his game, but he plays it correctly." The clairvoyant wrinkled his brow in concen-tration. "I don't know what it is. I see a large lake and a motor boat on it."

"And what else?" the district attorney burst out, scarcely breathing.

"There is nothing else to see; it is completely obscure. It is so strangely obscure compared with that brutal and ruthless determi-nation to bring down his prey. But there is no passion in it, only intellect. Absolute intellectual reasoning in every detail. As if he were resolving some technical problem or mental exercise. No, this man feels no remorse for anything. He is so confident of himself, so self-assured; he has no fear even of his own conscience. I have the impression of a man who looks down on all from above; he is conceited in the extreme and self-congratulatory; it pleases him that people fear him." The clairvoyant sipped his water. "But he is also a hypocrite. At heart, an opportunist who would like to astound the world by his actions — Enough. I am tired. I do not like this man."

"Listen, Janowitz," the district attorney flung out excitedly, "he is truly astonishing, this clairvoyant of yours. What he described is a perfect likeness. A strong and ruthless man who views people only as prey; the perfect player in his own game; a brain who systematically, intellectually plans his moves and feels no remorse for anything; a gentleman yet also an opportunist. Mr. Janowitz, this Karadagh pinpointed him one hundred per cent!"

"You don't say!" said the flattered Mr. Janowitz. "Didn't I tell you? That was a letter from Schliefen, the textile man from Liberec, right?"

"It most certainly was not," exclaimed the district attorney. "Mr. Janowitz, it was a letter from a murderer."

"Imagine that," Mr. Janowitz marveled, "and I thought it was Schliefen; he's a real crook, that Schliefen."

"No. It was a letter from Hugo Müller, fratricide. Do you remember how that clairvoyant talked about a boat on a lake? Müller threw his brother from that boat into the water."

"Imagine that," Mr. Janowitz said, astonished. "You see? That is a fabulous talent, Mr. District Attorney!"

"Unquestionably," the district attorney declared. "The way he grasped Müller's true nature and the motives behind his actions, Mr. Janowitz, is simply phenomenal. Not even I could have hit the mark with Müller precisely. And this clairvoyant found it out by feeling a few lines of Müller's handwriting — Mr. Janowitz, there's something to this; there must be some sort of special aura or something in people's handwriting."

"What did I tell you?" Mr. Janowitz said triumphantly. "If you would be so kind, Mr. District Attorney, I've never seen the handwriting of a murderer."

"With pleasure," Mr. District Attorney said, and he took the envelope from his pocket. "It's an interesting letter, besides," he added, removing the paper from the envelope, and suddenly his face changed color. "I . . . Mr. Janowitz," he blurted out, somewhat uncertainly, "this letter is a court document; it is . . . I'm not allowed to show it to you. Please forgive me."

Before long, the district attorney was hurrying homeward, not even noticing that it was raining. I'm an ass, he told himself bitterly, I'm a fool, how could that have happened to me? I'm an idiot! That in my hurry I grabbed not Müller's letter but my own handwriting, my notes on the trial, I shoved them in that envelope! I'm an imbecile! So that was my handwriting! Thanks very much! Watch out, you swindler, I'll be lying in wait for you!

But otherwise, the district attorney reflected, all in all, for the most part, what the clairvoyant had said wasn't too bad. Great strength; astonishing determination, if you please; I'm not capable of low trickery; I have my own strict concept of morality — As a matter of fact that is quite flattering. That I regret nothing? Thank God, I have no reason to: I merely discharge my obligations. And as for intellectual reasoning, that's also true. But as for being a hypocrite, he's mistaken. It's still nothing but a hoax.

Suddenly he paused. It stands to reason, he told himself, what that clairvoyant said can be applied to anyone at all! These are only generalities, nothing more. Everyone's a bit of a hypocrite and an opportunist. That's the whole trick: to speak in such a way that anybody could be identified. That's it, the district attorney decided, and opening his umbrella, he proceeded home at his normal energetic pace.

"My God!" groaned the presiding judge, stripping off his gown, "seven o'clock already; it did drag on again! When the district attorney spoke for two hours — but, dear colleague, he won it; to get the rope on such weak evidence, I'd call that success. Well, you never know with a jury. But he spoke skillfully," the presiding judge granted, washing his hands. "Mainly in the way he dealt with Müller's character, that was a full-fledged portrait; you know, the monstrous, inhuman nature of a murderer — it left you positively shaken. Remember how he said: This is no ordinary criminal; he isn't capable of low trickery, he neither lies nor steals; and if he murders a man, he does it as calmly as checkmating in a game of chess. He does not kill from passion, but from cold intellectual reasoning, as if he were resolving some technical problem or mental exercise. It was very well spoken, my friend. And something else: When he is on the prowl, he sees his fellow creatures only as prey — you know, that business about the tiger was perhaps a little theatrical, but the jury liked it."

"Or," the associate judge added, "the way he said: Clearly this murderer regrets nothing; he is so confident of himself, so self-assured — he has no fear even of his own conscience."

"Or then again," the presiding judge continued, wiping his hands with a towel, "the psychological observation that he is a hypocrite and an opportunist who would like to astound the world by his actions —

"This Klapka, though," the associate judge said appreciatively. "He's a dangerous adversary."

"Hugo Müller found guilty by twelve votes," the presiding judge marveled, "who would have thought it! Klapka got him after all. For him, it's like a hunt or a game of chess. He is totally consumed by his cases — My friend, I wouldn't want to have him as my enemy."

"He likes it," the associate judge replied, "when people fear him."

"A touch complacent, that's him," the presiding judge said thoughtfully. "But he has astonishing determination . . . chiefly for success. A great strength, friend, but — " The appropriate words failed him. "Well, let's go have dinner."

Discussion Topics

1. Some philosophers of law say that it exists to legitimize certain forms of power that otherwise would be seen as intolerably predatory and destructive. It is easy to imagine examples. A legislature might pass a law that allows the state to take away property or incarcerate someone under mere suspicion; in the absence of the law and done by a private individual, that would be theft and kidnaping.

Prosecutors have the power to curtail freedom and even to end lives, or at least they are part of a process in which their persuasive powers can bring about these results. Does Capek imply that the cunning that makes for a supreme criminal is the same as the cunning that makes for a successful prosecutor? Is his implication that the law channels predatory instincts into roles that have the cover of respectability and even necessity?

2. Prosecutors in the U.S., like all other practitioners of law from attorneys to judges, are covered by the ABA Model Rules, in particular, rule 3.8 (Special Responsibilities of a Prosecutor). In addition, the ABA has put forth Standards of Criminal Justice Regarding the Prosecution Function and many states have adopted them. Standard 3-5.8 (Argument to the Jury) provides the following:

> (a) In the closing argument to the jury, the prosecutor may argue all reasonable inferences from evidence in the record. The prosecutor should not intentionally misstate the evidence or mislead the jury as to the inferences it may draw.
>
> (b) The prosecutor should not express his or her personal belief or opinion as to the truth or falsity of any testimony or evidence or the guilt of the defendant.
>
> (c) The prosecutor should not make arguments calculated to appeal to the prejudices of the jury.

(d) The prosecutor should refrain from argument which would divert the jury from its duty to decide the case on the evidence.

If these rules had been part of Czech legal practice, would Public Prosecutor Klapka have been in compliance? Consider both the letter of the rules and their spirit. One may also question whether the rules state a rarely attained ideal and whether prosecutors routinely violate the underlying implicit sense of fair play.

3. The meaning of the story hinges on the question whether Prince Karadagh is truly clairvoyant or a fraud. Has he, by touching the written words of the district attorney, seen deeply into his character? And has Klapka, in his argument to the court, proved the validity of that insight?

The description is ethically and philosophically complex. In his philosophical writings, Nietzsche wrote about the "overman," the superior person who is "beyond good and evil." Such a person is seen as ruthless by others and sees himself as outside moral boundaries because he represents a higher aspiration that is beyond the common collective imagination. Ayn Rand, the novelist and philosopher widely read by adolescents, conjures up a version of the Nietzschean ideal by presenting heroes with a sense of personal destiny and special gifts. Her suggestion is that these qualities put them beyond any responsibility to or for others. But the broad consensus of moral philosophy suggests that concern and respect for others is an essential aspect of the well-lived and ethical life, and that its absence can be pathological.

Colm Tóibín: *The Heather Blazing**

For the last decade, Colm Tóibín has been a fast-rising star of Irish literature. He has published five novels, several books of travel writing, and critical essays. *The Master*, his recent novel about episodes in the life of Henry James, brought him international attention and landed on many lists of the year's best books. *The Heather Blazing*, his second novel, introduces us to an Irish high court judge, Eamon Redmond, as he approaches retirement and decides his last major cases. Redmond's life is told in flashbacks; we gain intimate knowledge of his motherless childhood with his schoolteacher father, his early apprenticeship in Irish politics, and his uneasy relationships with his wife and children.

The Heather Blazing is, above all, a study of inhibition and constraint. In his legal judgments, Redmond adheres to what he sees as the strict application of law, uncolored by empathic or moral concerns. He refuses

---

*Strongly recommended additional reading: This novel does not appear in this volume and must be purchased separately.

to grant the petition for reinstatement for a sixteen-year-old girl who had been expelled from a convent school after becoming pregnant. "As he worked on the judgment, he realized more than ever that he had no strong moral views, that he had ceased to believe in anything. But he was careful in writing the judgment not to make this clear" (page 90).

In his personal life, there are similar strains. His wife, Carmel, who seems devoted to him, tells him, "You've always been so distant, so far away from everybody. It is hard to know you, you let me see so little of you. . . . You don't love any of us" (page 156). His daughter also has a child out of wedlock; he shows little sympathy or interest in her situation and seems mildly indifferent, mildly angry at his social activist son.

But Redmond is far from simple. Some readers see *The Heather Blazing* as a story of redemption, self-discovery, and a reawakened sense of intimacy. Others see Redmond as a victim of circumstances. They are moved by the effects of losing his mother and other close relatives and having to assume some responsibility at a early age for his father. The novel raises such issues as the following:

(a) To what extent is one responsible for the person one becomes? What is the relationship between explaining how one's character is shaped and excusing or justifying actions? A basic premise of law is that actions cannot be excused simply because they can be understood, that in general we assume responsibility for ourselves regardless of histories. Both moral and legal judgments depend on some assumption of responsibility. Even if Tóibín gives us insight into Redmond's genesis, it is not clear that our understanding exempts him from criticism.

(b) To what extent is isolation part of every judge's destiny? It is taken for granted that judges can be compromised, in the eyes of onlookers if not in fact, by close contact with lawyers and others who are (actual or potential) parties to their cases. Impartiality requires distance. Personal ties and interests can distort judgment. Just as lawyers are expected to maintain the confidences of their clients even from their most intimate family members, judges are expected to shoulder the burden of deciding cases without help or solace from spouses or friends. Is Redmond blameless for keeping his own counsel or is his apparent coldness a personal and idiosyncratic problem?

(c) It is hardly obvious that a person who conscientiously abstains from intense feelings and close ties is the best person to make judgments that affect the lives of others. Two questions are closely connected here. One is whether legal judgment is largely a matter of rational thought divorced from emotions. Since Plato, we are accustomed to compartmentalize reasoning and feeling — to see thinking and feeling as opposed and to conclude that feelings can subvert reason. While it is certainly true that strong emotions can drive persons to do irrational things, one might conclude that an absence of feeling can also produce irrational decisions and actions. On this view, thought and feeling, especially about decisions that affect the course of people's lives, may be complementary.

None of this, of course, gives us a formula for judicial decision. But it does suggest that Redmond's emotional and moral austerity may be a handicap rather than an asset.

(d) Even while lawyers have suffered in public esteem, judges retain respect and dignity. The reader, just like Redmond's associates and neighbors, is likely to accord him deference as a high court judge. Is this attitude warranted? *The Heather Blazing* doesn't take a position on this, but there are clues to the trajectory of Redmond's career. In Ireland, as in the U.S., judges are appointed by politicians. One may reasonably infer that politicians everywhere favor appointees with whose politics they are comfortable. Redmond begins his public life by giving a political speech and is elected early to public office. As a prosecutor, he is comfortable following the agenda of his political supporters. If there is not enough evidence to call him a political hack, there is also little evidence of extraordinary legal or judicial skills.

(e) We must be careful not to assume that Irish high court judges are just like the American Supreme Court. The Catholic church has historically had influence on Irish law, but most commentators agree that law is becoming more secular. Changes in the law during the 1990s concerned the rights of illegitimate children, divorce, homosexuality, and blasphemy. These matters are discussed in Christine James, "Cead Mile Failte? Ireland Welcomes Divorce," 8 *Duke Journal of Comparative and International Law* 175 (1997); and Kathryn O'Brien, "Ireland's Secular Revolution: The Waning Influence of the Catholic Church and the Future of Ireland's Blasphemy Law," 18 *Connecticut Journal of International Law* 395 (2002).

A discussion and critique of the growth of secular judicial activism in recent Irish jurisprudence is the subject of David Gwynn Morgan's book, *A Judgment Too Far: Judicial Activism and the Constitution*, 2001. As applied to *The Heather Blazing,* these studies allow the inference that Redmond would have had latitude to accommodate moral and secular concerns in his judgments had he so chosen.

Albert Camus: *The Fall**

Albert Camus was the second youngest recipient of the Nobel prize in literature when he received it in 1957 at the age of 44. His literary corpus was small: three short novels, two books of philosophical thoughts, a few plays, and a book of short stories, but he was one of the most visible and influential

---

*Strongly recommended additional reading: This novel does not appear in this volume and must be purchased separately.

writers of his time. He was born into poverty in Algeria and worked his way through the University of Algiers. He quickly became an influential journalist and founded a theater troupe. During the Occupation, he edited *Combat*, a leading underground newspaper. In 1960, at the height of his fame and productivity, he died suddenly in a car crash at the age of 46.

Although he disclaimed the label, Camus was associated with the philosophy of existentialism. After World War II, many observers concluded that the religious, moral, and social values of the western world had failed to control the barbarous and predatory elements of human nature and political life. Existentialism was the expression of this sense of bankruptcy. Camus coined the notion, the "absurd," to refer to the frustration of the human impulse to find the meaning of life in institutions — religious, political, social — that transcend individuals, institutions that had betrayed human trust. The response to the absurd cannot be, he argued, despair but rather the willingness to affirm and go forward with one's aims in face of the recognition that one will likely fail. He used the mythical metaphor of the story of Sisyphus, who persists in rolling a boulder up an incline notwithstanding the certain knowledge that the boulder will roll back down and he will have to start again.

The Fall is the story of an attorney in Paris who faces a crisis of self-definition. His life and law practice seem exemplary; he seeks out the neediest clients, presents a heroic posture in court, and wins wide acclaim. But, as he tells us, self-esteem is his ruling passion, not his clients' welfare. And any evidence that his control over events is incomplete devastates him. The novel itself is his own narrative whereby, over a series of nightly encounters with a fellow lawyer (the reader?), he describes his eventual retreat to Amsterdam (where the narratives occur) as a "judge-penitent," a person who does penance for his life by telling it endlessly to others, by sitting in self-judgment.

What makes *The Fall* seductive for many readers is the voice of the narrator. He is deeply cynical, certain of our isolation from others and of the ways in which we use others for our own selfish purposes. But he is also a voice of wry wit, erudition, and self-deprecation. He blames himself for having every failing that he can possibly find in others. The book is unsettling because of the narrator's urgency and intensity, and because his aims remain unclear until the end.

Some of the most provocative discussion points in *The Fall* are likely to be the following:

(a) There is inevitably a paradox in being a lawyer. The job is to serve oneself by serving others. In helping clients attain their own ends, one builds a career and often lives quite well. In theory, the personal benefits are a by-product, an incidental result, of the services one performs. In fact, a lawyer is almost always mindful of the tangible material results of her work and such intangible benefits as reputation and self-esteem. Every lawyer must in some cases finesse the inevitable conflicts between her interests and those of clients. Jean-Baptiste Clamence, the narrator of *The Fall*, cannot escape his self-regard.

(b) Readers are often troubled by whether Clamence is a kind of solipsistic monster or a version of everyman. Does he simply strip away and do without the illusions that most of us use to see ourselves as caring for others and others as caring for us, or is his self-absorption a kind of pathology? Clamence refers frequently to his "passion for heights," his need to distance himself from others by figuratively standing above them and feeling superior. He says he feels comfortable on small islands. Is there a paradox inherent in all of us such that we think both that no man is (or wants to be) an island (because we need others) and every man is an island (because we are ultimately answerable to ourselves)? If so, is the profession of lawyers a paradigmatic example of this clash?

(c) A recurrent theme of the book is judging. Clamence says that we all passionately fear and avoid being judged, that we cannot avoid judging ourselves, and that we sit in judgment of others all the time. In comparison with the judging that goes on everyday, the Last Judgment is insignificant. Is he right? To what extent is law a domain in which judgment is central, and to what extent are lawyers persons who are called upon to judge their clients (and their opponents), to judge their own performance, and to be judged by others in turn?

(d) At the end of *The Fall* Clamence suggests to his interlocutor that his purpose has not been to submit his autobiography or judge himself, but to create a story made of fact and fiction designed to turn his listener into a judge-penitent, to prompt a similar kind of self-examination. Is introspection the main aim of the story? Lawyers are not often introspective — and one of Camus' aims may be to identify and use that failing.

(5) How does *The Fall* echo the themes of existentialism? Clamence examines his life and makes choices accordingly, but the reader remains uncertain whether that life is being affirmed or held in limbo. The Sisyphean figure must ultimately look outward and make choices to take action in the world, to use her freedom, whether or not there can be success. But Clamence is the negation of such choice; he counsels self-awareness but is finally paralyzed by the possibility of action.

◖ Further Reading

Three bodies of writing cast light on the lives and circumstances of lawyers.

(1) The first and most immediate of these is not made up of fiction. Rather, the last forty years have produced serious self-examination on the

part of the legal profession. This is a legacy of the Watergate scandals, a governmental and national crisis that was seen as the work of lawyers. Since the 1970s, law schools have required courses on legal ethics and professional responsibility. For the most part, these courses have also embraced the psychology and sociology of lawyering. A significant and unprecedented number of books and articles have examined the transformation of law from — as commentators often conclude — a profession to a business. The psychological tensions and costs of lawyering are significant concerns.

Four of the most important books are *The Practice of Justice* by William Simon (Harvard University Press, 1998), *A Nation Under Lawyers* by Mary Ann Glendon (Farrar, Straus, and Giroux, 1994), *The Lost Lawyer* by Anthony Kronman (Belknap/Harvard, 1993), and *Lawyers and Justice* by David Luban (Princeton University Press, 1988). Each book gives a thorough grounding in the responsibilities and practical tensions of legal representation. Kronman and Luban bring philosophical sophistication in looking at the underlying ethical dilemmas. Glendon's book is more distinctively sociological, and Simon's brings an intensive focus on different dimensions of practice.

Many of the best articles are brought together by Professor Luban in *The Good Lawyer: Lawyers' Roles and Lawyers' Ethics* (Rowman and Allanheld, 1983). Richard Wasserstrom's "Roles and Morality" and Bernard Williams' "Professional Morality and its Dispositions" make indispensable distinctions. It goes without saying that the postures taken by the characters in the stories in chapter 1 are illustrations of the circumstances explored in these books and articles.

There is a strong collection of articles discussing how prosecutors are seen in popular culture and in literature at 34 *University of Toledo Law Review* 749 (2003).

(2) Several disparate works of fiction cast light on the minds and choices of lawyers in ways that expand the focus of chapter 1. Two eloquent portraits of the lawyer as idealist and social reformer are Jerome Lawrence's play *Inherit the Wind* (about Clarence Darrow's and William Jennings Bryan's titanic battle in the Scopes trial) and Harper Lee's familiar book on the struggle against racism, *To Kill a Mockingbird*. Both works allow us to consider how lawyers can identify themselves with social causes on a grand scale. The scope of their lives and achievements contrasts with the comparatively modest aspirations and roles of the characters in chapter 1.

Two works that explore the conscience of lawyers in contrasting ways are Ivan Klima's modern Czech novel, *Judge on Trial*, and William Shakespeare's dark and unclassifiable play, *Measure for Measure*. Klima looks at the pressures on the conscience and independence of a judge in a totalitarian regime. His decisions are complicated by personal ties; his attempts to achieve his ideals are compromised by internal as well as external dilemmas. No such inhibitions limit Angelo, the temporary legal administrator of Vienna in Shakespeare's play, whose strict (and twisted) enforcement of the laws is guided by sadism and his thirst for power. These two works show, on the one hand, how lawyers and judges are corrupted when unbounded power lies elsewhere, and on the other hand how unlimited legal power, entrusted to an insecure and malevolent agent, can result in total personal corruption.

The novelist and Wall Street attorney, Louis Auchincloss, has spent a lifetime writing novels and stories, many of which are shrewd descriptions of corporate practice, its dilemmas, challenges, and temptations. They are a diverse set of windows on the varieties of lawyering that coexist within the apparent homogeneity of large firm practice.

(3) Legal biographies and autobiographies are a reservoir of insights into the lives of lawyers. Unfortunately, relatively few biographies or autobiographies have as their subjects "ordinary lawyers," those whose lives echo the stories in this chapter. Most biographies concern lawyers who have become notable and famous as judges or litigators or, on the other hand, notorious for their involvement in specific cases. Biographies of lawyers often force us to create the psychological subtext for ourselves.

Among the most interestingly crafted and psychologically attuned biographies are Linda Greenhouse's recent *Becoming Justice Blackmun*, G. Edward White's *Justice Oliver Wendell Holmes: Law and the Inner Self*, and Andrew Kauffman's *Cardozo*. An inspiring if not particularly self-questioning autobiography is William Kunstler's *My Life as a Radical Lawyer*.

TWO

The Meanings of Law

None of us has ever lived without law. But what does it mean to live under law? Often the things that are most familiar are hardest to grasp. Life, love, pain, beauty, friendship, harm are essential parameters of each person's existence — and yet philosophers have struggled for more than 2,000 years to understand and explain what they are and what they mean.

Law is ubiquitous because it seems to be needed for social order, and social order is necessary if life is to be relatively secure and predictable, if we are to make plans of any kind and have a good chance of carrying them out. The English legal philosopher H.L.A. Hart pointed out that we might not need law if we were benign and considerate without limit, if we put the interests of others ahead of our own. Or we might not need it if we were as unself-conscious as animals, or if we had no desires and goals. But given the universal ambition and vulnerability of human beings, some imposed order is inevitable when persons move from isolation to community.

Legal philosophers have struggled to identify the *essence* of law. Positivists have pointed out its relation to power; law emanates from those who have power and claim authority and is enforced by persons with power over community members at large. Natural law theorists (sometimes called "naturalists," even though that term has many meanings) have tended to see law as the expression of shared goals, of the pooled interests of all. In this chapter, we will not pursue the intriguing and unending search in the philosophy of law for a comprehensive account of the nature and conditions for law. Instead we will look at the meanings — rational, emotional, conscious, unconscious — law has acquired in the light of experience. We will look at law as a metaphor and symbol. In this sense, writers of fiction stand in for all of us. When they use law symbolically, they echo the fact that for everyone law is a symbol as well as a fact of life.

Reason and unreason. It is natural to associate law with reason. Nature can be random and unpredictable; the spontaneous acts of persons can also be random, governed by feelings and momentary desires. Law, it may be thought, exists to transform disorder into order. It uses reason to pool the interests of society, especially the most basic interests of survival and the opportunity to flourish, and sets in place rules that regulate conduct and tame the worst aspects of human nature. Thus, nature and reason exist as opposites, and law is one of the tools by which reason controls nature.

But it is equally easy to see law as pervaded by unreason. The rules of law may reflect nothing but the will and fantasies of those who happen to have the power to lay them down and enforce them. The order that results may be worse than the randomness of nature; it may involve slavery and systematic exploitation and cruelty. Even when the rules of law are relatively benign, the procedures used by various institutions of law may be incomprehensible and interminable. The system, created perhaps in good will, may be paralyzed by irrational complexity and pointless formalities.

Morality and immorality. Law and morality have always had a close but uneasy coexistence. Both are systems of constraint and judgment about conduct. Law constrains by using the organized force of the state; morality constrains through informal methods of disapproval and exclusion. Both involve judgment; while judgments of illegality and immorality may overlap, they certainly do not coincide. We can all easily name legal offenses that do not violate morality, and vice versa.

Nonetheless, the most important ways in which one person can harm another are recognized by both law and morality. The most important kinds of harms covered by criminal prohibitions — killings, rape, theft — are also condemned by morality. Breaking an agreement, creating a nuisance, failing to take responsibility for causing an accident are all instances of legal and moral wrongs.

There is also a holistic sense which associates law and morality. The tradition of natural law claims to uncover and justify ultimate laws of human association that allow individuals to flourish and the community to achieve its collective aims. These laws represent the highest social morality. In a religious framework they are called the laws of God, and the laws of human societies are said to be measured against natural law and to aspire to it as a goal.

Law can, in this sense, symbolize a moral ideal. But, as the contrast between laws of God and laws of men implies, the ideal can easily be subverted. It is not hard to imagine a legal system that turns morality on its head, one that embodies harms and cruelties that are hardly imaginable in nature, atrocities that only the human imagination makes possible. The historical destiny of the twentieth century was to realize such systems of law.

There is a healthy tradition of dystopian novels, works of fiction that take their lessons from history, especially mid-twentieth-century history, and show how legal and social systems can be dehumanizing. In that sense, law becomes the antithesis of morality, a symbol of the most terrible things we can do to one another.

Nature and the unnatural. The distinction between law and morality intersects with the distinction between nature and the unnatural. Some observers claim that both law and morality represent what is best about human nature. Morality exists to reinforce the most positive intentions and to suppress our destructive impulses. According to this model, human nature is a moral battleground between our good and bad selves. The institutions of morality and of law are the informal and formal ways in which our good selves are given the upper hand.

This picture of human nature may be criticized as naive and primitive. ("Surely human nature is more complex than this.") But the notion of warring impulses has deep roots, perhaps ineradicable ones, in most religions, in much philosophy, in Freudian psychology, and throughout our culture. The implications of this notion are, however, that law and morality are *both* natural and unnatural. If our more selfish and destructive selves are more basic, more true, then the attempt to rein them in stands in the way of nature. If, on the other hand, our more noble selves are as much part of our natural endowment as any other aspect, then law and morality grow smoothly out of human nature.

In other words, do the requirements of living harmoniously with others enhance our nature or frustrate it? The question may be unanswerable, in part because discovering and defining human nature is the endless job of cultural history. And the process of scrutinizing ourselves may inevitably have the result of changing human nature. We may not be stable targets of investigation. None of this, however, stands in the way of using law as a symbol both of our high nature and of mandates that can be dangerously unnatural.

Universality and particularity. When we think about biology and physics, we take for granted that laws of nature are universal. When we talk about human nature, we are less certain about its universality. We aspire to find psychological laws, but we often have to treat them as culturally relative. The separation of good and bad selves is not so much a scientific as an esthetic and social hypothesis — and even that hypothesis is configured differently in each culture.

Legal systems, unlike laws of nature, are likely to be particular rather than universal. Tort law, property law, business law, and constitutional law are notoriously different and hard to reconcile between systems. Conflicts of law is a major legal specialty. And yet we also find that criminal law is remarkably similar across systems, and scholars in international law work to articulate universal systems of human rights. Thus, we have particular laws coexisting with laws that transcend particularity.

Law can be understood both in terms of universal rules and particular ones. Obviously, this distinction echoes the one between natural law and positive law, and it is a distant cousin of the one between moral laws and laws that may have nothing to do with morality.

***

Writers rarely use law to symbolize one thing. It is a multipurpose symbol that reflects the many roles that law plays in each life. The role of law in the stories that follow is never simple, always debatable.

Law, Equality, Class

Herman Melville: The Paradise of Bachelors and The Tartarus of Maids

Herman Melville's father and brother practiced law. He was also the son-in-law of Lemuel Shaw, chief justice of the state supreme court and one of the prominent judges in nineteenth-century Massachusetts. One does not, however, immediately associate law with his stories or his life.

Melville's writings can be sorted into three periods. The early novels, such as *Typee* and *Omoo*, had exotic settings, were classifiable as tropical romances, and were notably popular. The main works of his middle period were also novels of the sea, but they had much greater complexity and presented readers with significant challenges. *Redburn* and *Moby Dick* were not major successes in their day. The latter is widely seen as precipitating Melville's decline as a writer of widely read fiction. In later life, Melville produced such works as *Pierre, or the Ambiguities* and *The Confidence-Man*, books that are puzzles, books whose meaning remains hotly debated by critics and scholars.

There is a intrinsic beauty to Melville's writing. Sentence by sentence, he has both grace and irony. Difficulties arise not in enjoying his prose but in stepping back and judging the whole. "The Paradise of Bachelors and the Tartarus of Maids" is one of his least known works. It reads more like a travel memoir than a story. There is barely a plot, even if the structure involves the adventures of a seed-merchant from Massachusetts as he travels in England and his own state.

Law may seem to be peripheral to the two-part story. But Melville sees law as an essential part of social structure; his subtle critique of social structure is at the same time a critique of law. It will be evident that law is a tool of social segregation, one that exacerbates class and gender separations.

❊ The Paradise of Bachelors ❊

Herman Melville

It lies not far from Temple-Bar.

Going to it, by the usual way, is like stealing from a heated plain into some cool, deep glen, shady among harboring hills.

Sick with the din and soiled with the mud of Fleet Street—where the Benedick tradesmen are hurrying by, with ledger-lines ruled along their brows, thinking upon rise of bread and fall of babies—you adroitly turn a mystic corner—not a street—glide down a dim, monastic way, flanked by dark, sedate, and solemn piles, and still wending on, give the whole care-worn world the slip, and, disentangled, stand beneath the quiet cloisters of the Paradise of Bachelors.

Sweet are the oases in Sahara; charming the isle-groves of August prairies; delectable pure faith amidst a thousand perfidies: but sweeter, still more charming, most delectable, the dreamy Paradise of Bachelors, found in the stony heart of stunning London.

In mild meditation pace the cloisters; take your pleasure, sip your leisure, in the garden waterward; go linger in the ancient library; go worship in the sculptured chapel: but little have you seen, just nothing do you know, not the sweet kernel have you tasted, till you dine among the banded Bachelors, and see their convivial eyes and glasses sparkle. Not dine in bustling commons, during term-time, in the hall; but tranquilly, by private hint, at a private table; some fine Templar's hospitably invited guest.

Templar? That's a romantic name. Let me see. Brian de Bois Guilbert was a Templar, I believe. Do we understand you to insinuate that those famous Templars still survive in modern London? May the ring of their armed heels be heard, and the rattle of their shields, as in mailed prayer the monk-knights kneel before the consecrated Host? Surely a monk-knight were a curious sight picking his way along the Strand, his gleaming corselet and snowy surcoat spattered by an omnibus. Long-bearded, too, according to his order's rule; his face fuzzy as a pard's; how would the grim ghost look among the crop-haired, close-shaven citizens? We know indeed—sad history recounts it—that a moral blight tainted at last this sacred Brotherhood. Though no sworded foe might outskill them in the fence, yet the worm of luxury crawled beneath their guard, gnawing the core of knightly troth, nibbling the monastic vow, till at last the monk's austerity relaxed to wassailing, and the sworn knights-bachelors grew to be but hypocrites and rakes.

But for all this, quite unprepared were we to learn that Knights-Templars (if at all in being) were so entirely secularized as to be reduced from carving out immortal fame in glorious battling for the Holy Land, to the carving of roast-mutton at a dinner-board. Like Anacreon, do these degenerate Templars now think it sweeter far to fall in banquet than in war? Or, indeed, how can there be any survival of that famous order? Templars in modern London! Templars in their red-cross mantles smoking cigars at the Divan! Templars crowded in a railway train, till, stacked with steel helmet, spear, and shield, the whole train looks like one elongated locomotive!

No. The genuine Templar is long since departed. Go view the wondrous tombs in the Temple Church; see there the rigidly-haughty forms stretched out, with crossed arms upon their stilly hearts, in everlasting and undreaming rest. Like the years before the flood, the bold Knights-Templars are no more. Nevertheless, the name remains, and the nominal society, and the ancient grounds, and some of the ancient edifices. But the iron heel is changed to a boot of patent-leather; the long two-handed sword to a one-handed quill; the monk-giver of gratuitous ghostly counsel now counsels for a fee; the defender of the sarcophagus (if in good practice with his weapon) now has more than one case to defend; the vowed opener and clearer of all highways leading to the Holy Sepulchre, now has it in particular charge to check, to clog, to hinder, and embarrass all the courts and avenues of Law; the knight-combatant of the Saracen, breasting spear-points at Acre, now fights law-points in Westminster Hall. The helmet is a wig. Struck by Time's enchanter's wand, the Templar is to-day a Lawyer.

But, like many others tumbled from proud glory's height — like the apple, hard on the bough but mellow on the ground — the Templar's fall has but made him all the finer fellow.

I dare say those old warrior-priests were but gruff and grouty at the best; cased in Birmingham hardware, how could their crimped arms give yours or mine a hearty shake? Their proud, ambitious, monkish souls clasped shut, like horn-book missals; their very faces clapped in bomb-shells; what sort of genial men were these? But best of comrades, most affable of hosts, capital diner is the modern Templar. His wit and wine are both of sparkling brands.

The church and cloisters, courts and vaults, lanes and passages, banquet-halls, refectories, libraries, terraces, gardens, broad walks, domicils, and dessert-rooms, covering a very large space of ground, and all grouped in central neighborhood, and quite sequestered from the old city's surrounding din; and every thing about the place being kept in most bachelor-like particularity, no part of London offers to a quiet wight so agreeable a refuge.

The Temple is, indeed, a city by itself. A city with all the best appurtenances, as the above enumeration shows. A city with a park to it, and flower-beds, and a river-side — the Thames flowing by as openly, in one part, as by Eden's primal garden flowed the mild Euphrates. In what is now the Temple Garden the old Crusaders used to exercise their steeds and lances; the modern Templars now lounge on the benches beneath the trees, and, switching their patent-leather boots, in gay discourse exercise at repartee.

Long lines of stately portraits in the banquet-halls, show what great men of mark — famous nobles, judges, and Lord Chancellors — have in their time been Templars. But all Templars are not known to universal fame; though, if the having warm hearts and warmer welcomes, full minds and fuller cellars, and giving good advice and glorious dinners, spiced with rare divertisements of fun and fancy, merit immortal mention, set down, ye muses, the names of R. F. C. and his imperial brother.

Though to be a Templar, in the one true sense, you must needs be a lawyer, or a student at the law, and be ceremoniously enrolled as member of the order, yet as many such, though Templars, do not reside within the Temple's precincts, though they may have their offices there, just so, on the other hand, there are many residents of the hoary old domicils who are not admitted Templars. If being, say, a lounging gentleman and bachelor, or a quiet, unmarried, literary man, charmed with the soft seclusion of the spot, you much desire to pitch your shady tent among the rest in this serene encampment, then you must make some special friend among the order, and procure him to rent, in his name but at your charge, whatever vacant chamber you may find to suit.

Thus, I suppose, did Dr. Johnson, that nominal Benedick and widower but virtual bachelor, when for a space he resided here. So, too, did that undoubted bachelor and rare good soul, Charles Lamb. And hundreds more, of sterling spirits, Brethren of the Order of Celibacy, from time to time have dined, and slept, and tabernacled here. Indeed, the place is all a honeycomb of offices and domicils. Like any cheese, it is quite perforated through and through in all directions with the snug cells of bachelors. Dear, delightful spot! Ah! when I bethink me of the sweet hours there passed, enjoying such genial hospitalities beneath those time-honored roofs, my heart only finds due utterance through poetry; and, with a sigh, I softly sing, "Carry me back to old Virginny!"

Such then, at large, is the Paradise of Bachelors. And such I found it one pleasant afternoon in the smiling month of May, when, sallying from my hotel in Trafalgar Square, I went to keep my dinner-appointment with that fine Barrister, Bachelor, and Bencher, R. F. C. (he is the first and second, and should be the third; I hereby nominate him), whose card I kept fast pinched between my gloved forefinger and thumb, and every now and then snatched still another look at the pleasant address inscribed beneath the name, "No. —, Elm Court, Temple."

At the core he was a right bluff, care-free, right comfortable, and most companionable Englishman. If on a first acquaintance he seemed reserved, quite icy in his air—patience; this Champagne will thaw. And if it never do, better frozen Champagne than liquid vinegar.

There were nine gentlemen, all bachelors, at the dinner. One was from "No. —, King's Bench Walk, Temple;" a second, third, and fourth, and fifth, from various courts or passages christened with some similarly rich resounding syllables. It was indeed a sort of Senate of the Bachelors, sent to this dinner from widely-scattered districts, to represent the general celibacy of the Temple. Nay it was, by representation, a Grand Parliament of the best Bachelors in universal London; several of those present being from distant quarters of the town, noted immemorial seats of lawyers and unmarried men—Lincoln's Inn, Furnival's Inn; and one gentleman, upon whom I looked with a sort of collateral awe, hailed from the spot where Lord Verulam once abode a bachelor—Gray's Inn.

The apartment was well up toward heaven. I know not how many strange old stairs I climbed to get to it. But a good dinner, with famous company, should be well earned. No doubt our host had his dining-room so high with a view to secure the prior exercise necessary to the due relishing and digesting of it.

The furniture was wonderfully unpretending, old, and snug. No new shining mahogany, sticky with undried varnish; no uncomfortably luxurious ottomans, and sofas too fine to use, vexed you in this sedate apartment. It is a thing which every sensible American should learn from every sensible Englishman, that glare and glitter, gimcracks and gewgaws, are not indispensable to domestic solacement. The American Benedick snatches, down-town, a tough chop in a gilded show-box; the English bachelor leisurely dines at home on that incomparable South Down of his, off a plain deal board.

The ceiling of the room was low. Who wants to dine under the dome of St. Peter's? High ceilings! If that is your demand, and the higher the better, and you be so very tall, then go dine out with the topping giraffe in the open air.

In good time the nine gentlemen sat down to nine covers, and soon were fairly under way.

If I remember right, ox-tail soup inaugurated the affair. Of a rich russet hue, its agreeable flavor dissipated my first confounding of its main ingredient with teamster's gads and the raw-hides of ushers. (By way of interlude, we here drank a little claret.) Neptune's was the next tribute rendered—turbot coming second; snow-white, flaky, and just gelatinous enough, not too turtleish in its unctuousness.

(At this point we refreshed ourselves with a glass of sherry.) After these light skirmishers had vanished, the heavy artillery of the feast marched in, led by that well-known English generalissimo, roast beef. For aids-de-camp we had a saddle of mutton, a fat turkey, a chicken-pie, and endless other savory things; while for avant-couriers came nine silver flagons of humming ale. This heavy ordnance having departed on the track of the light skirmishers, a picked brigade of game-fowl encamped upon the board, their camp-fires lit by the ruddiest of decanters.

Tarts and puddings followed, with innumerable niceties; then cheese and crackers. (By way of ceremony, simply, only to keep up good old fashions, we here each drank a glass of good old port.)

The cloth was now removed; and like Blucher's army coming in at the death on the field of Waterloo, in marched a fresh detachment of bottles, dusty with their hurried march.

All these manoeuvrings of the forces were superintended by a surprising old field-marshal (I can not school myself to call him by the inglorious name of waiter), with snowy hair and napkin, and a head like Socrates. Amidst all the hilarity of the feast, intent on important business, he disdained to smile. Venerable man!

I have above endeavored to give some slight schedule of the general plan of operations. But any one knows that a good, genial dinner is a sort of pell-mell, indiscriminate affair, quite baffling to detail in all particulars. Thus, I spoke of taking a glass of claret, and a glass of sherry, and a glass of port, and a mug of ale — all at certain specific periods and times. But those were merely the state bumpers, so to speak. Innumerable impromptu glasses were drained between the periods of those grand imposing ones.

The nine bachelors seemed to have the most tender concern for each other's health. All the time, in flowing wine, they most earnestly expressed their sincerest wishes for the entire well-being and lasting hygiene of the gentlemen on the right and on the left. I noticed that when one of these kind bachelors desired a little more wine (just for his stomach's sake, like Timothy), he would not help himself to it unless some other bachelor would join him. It seemed held something indelicate, selfish, and unfraternal, to be seen taking a lonely, unparticipated glass. Meantime, as the wine ran apace, the spirits of the company grew more and more to perfect genialness and unconstraint. They related all sorts of pleasant stories. Choice experiences in their private lives were now brought out, like choice brands of Moselle or Rhenish, only kept for particular company. One told us how mellowly he lived when a student at Oxford; with various spicy anecdotes of most frank-hearted noble lords, his liberal companions. Another bachelor, a gray-headed man, with a sunny face, who, by his own account, embraced every opportunity of leisure to cross over into the Low Countries, on sudden tours of inspection of the fine old Flemish architecture there — this learned, white-haired, sunny-faced old bachelor, excelled in his descriptions of the elaborate splendors of those old guild-halls, town-halls, and stadthold-houses, to be seen in the land of the ancient Flemings. A third was a great frequenter of the British Museum, and knew all about scores of wonderful antiquities, of Oriental manuscripts, and costly books without a duplicate. A fourth had lately returned from a trip to Old Granada, and, of course, was full of Saracenic scenery. A fifth had a funny case in law to tell. A sixth was erudite in wines. A seventh had a strange characteristic anecdote of the private life of the Iron Duke, never printed, and never before announced in any public or private company. An eighth had lately been amusing his evenings, now and then, with translating a comic poem of Pulci's. He quoted for us the more amusing passages.

And so the evening slipped along, the hours told, not by a water-clock, like King Alfred's, but a wine-chronometer. Meantime the table seemed a sort of Epsom Heath; a regular ring, where the decanters galloped round. For fear one decanter should not with sufficient speed reach his destination, another was sent express after him to hurry him; and then a third to hurry the second; and so on with a fourth and fifth. And throughout all this nothing loud, nothing unmannerly, nothing turbulent. I am quite sure, from the scrupulous gravity and austerity of his air, that had Socrates, the field-marshal, perceived aught of indecorum in the company he served, he would have forthwith departed without giving warning. I afterward learned that, during the repast, an invalid bachelor in an adjoining chamber enjoyed his first sound refreshing slumber in three long, weary weeks.

It was the very perfection of quiet absorption of good living, good drinking, good feeling, and good talk. We were a band of brothers. Comfort — fraternal, household comfort, was the grand trait of the affair. Also, you could plainly see that these easy-hearted men had no wives or children to give an anxious thought. Almost all of them were travelers, too; for bachelors alone can travel freely, and without any twinges of their consciences touching desertion of the fire-side.

The thing called pain, the bugbear styled trouble — those two legends seemed preposterous to their bachelor imaginations. How could men of liberal sense, ripe scholarship in the world, and capacious philosophical and convivial understandings — how could they suffer themselves to be imposed upon by such monkish fables? Pain! Trouble! As well talk of Catholic miracles. No such thing. — Pass the sherry, Sir. — Pooh, pooh! Can't be! — The port, Sir, if you please. Nonsense; don't tell me so. — The decanter stops with you, Sir, I believe.

And so it went.

Not long after the cloth was drawn our host glanced significantly upon Socrates, who, solemnly stepping to a stand, returned with an immense convolved horn, a regular Jericho horn, mounted with polished silver, and otherwise chased and curiously enriched; not omitting two life-like goat's heads, with four more horns of solid silver, projecting from opposite sides of the mouth of the noble main horn.

Not having heard that our host was a performer on the bugle, I was surprised to see him lift this horn from the table, as if he were about to blow an inspiring blast. But I was relieved from this, and set quite right as touching the purposes of the horn, by his now inserting his thumb and forefinger into its mouth; whereupon a slight aroma was stirred up, and my nostrils were greeted with the smell of some choice Rappee. It was a mull of snuff. It went the rounds. Capital idea this, thought I, of taking snuff about this juncture. This goodly fashion must be introduced among my countrymen at home, further ruminated I.

The remarkable decorum of the nine bachelors — a decorum not to be affected by any quantity of wine — a decorum unassailable by any degree of mirthfulness — this was again set in a forcible light to me, by now observing that, though they took snuff very freely, yet not a man so far violated the proprieties, or so far molested the invalid bachelor in the adjoining room as to indulge himself in a sneeze. The snuff was snuffed silently, as if it had been some fine innoxious powder brushed off the wings of butterflies.

But fine though they be, bachelors' dinners, like bachelors' lives, can not endure forever. The time came for breaking up. One by one the bachelors took their hats, and two by two, and arm-in-arm they descended, still conversing, to the flagging of the court; some going to their neighboring chambers to turn over the Decameron ere retiring for the night; some to smoke a cigar, promenading in the garden on the cool river-side; some to make for the street, call a hack, and be driven snugly to their distant lodgings.

I was the last lingerer.

"Well," said my smiling host, "what do you think of the Temple here, and the sort of life we bachelors make out to live in it?"

"Sir," said I, with a burst of admiring candor — "Sir, this is the very Paradise of Bachelors!"

❈ The Tartarus of Maids ❈

It lies not far from Woedolor Mountain in New England. Turning to the east, right out from among bright farms and sunny meadows, nodding in early June with odorous grasses, you enter ascendingly among bleak hills. These gradually close in upon a dusky pass, which, from the violent Gulf Stream of air unceasingly driving between its cloven walls of haggard rock, as well as from the tradition of a crazy spinster's hut having long ago stood somewhere hereabouts, is called the Mad Maid's Bellows'-pipe.

Winding along at the bottom of the gorge is a dangerously narrow wheel-road, occupying the bed of a former torrent. Following this road to its highest point, you stand as within a Dantean gateway. From the steepness of the walls here, their strangely ebon hue, and the sudden contraction of the gorge, this particular point is called the Black Notch. The ravine now expandingly descends into a great, purple, hopper-shaped hollow, far sunk among many Plutonian, shaggy-wooded mountains. By the country people this hollow is called the Devil's Dungeon. Sounds of torrents fall on all sides upon the ear. These rapid waters unite at last in one turbid brick-colored stream, boiling through a flume among enormous boulders. They call this strange-colored torrent Blood River. Gaining a dark precipice it wheels suddenly to the west, and makes one maniac spring of sixty feet into the arms of a stunted wood of gray-haired pines, between which it thence eddies on its further way down to the invisible lowlands.

Conspicuously crowning a rocky bluff high to one side, at the cataract's verge, is the ruin of an old saw-mill, built in those primitive times when vast pines and hemlocks superabounded throughout the neighboring region. The blackmossed bulk of those immense, rough-hewn, and spike-knotted logs, here and there tumbled all together, in long abandonment and decay, or left in solitary, perilous projection over the cataract's gloomy brink, impart to this rude wooden ruin not only much of the aspect of one of rough-quarried stone, but also a sort of feudal, Rhineland, and Thurmberg look, derived from the pinnacled wildness of the neighboring scenery.

Not far from the bottom of the Dungeon stands a large white-washed building, relieved, like some great white sepulchre, against the sullen background of mountain-side firs, and other hardy evergreens, inaccessibly rising in grim terraces for some two thousand feet.

The building is a paper-mill.

Having embarked on a large scale in the seedsman's business (so extensively and broadcast, indeed, that at length my seeds were distributed through all the Eastern and Northern States, and even fell into the far soil of Missouri and the Carolinas), the demand for paper at my place became so great, that the expenditure soon amounted to a most important item in the general account. It need hardly be hinted how paper comes into use with seedsmen, as envelopes. These are mostly made of yellowish paper, folded square; and when filled, are all but flat, and being stamped, and superscribed with the nature of the seeds contained, assume not a little the appearance of business-letters ready for the mail. Of these small envelopes I used an incredible quantity — several hundreds of thousands in a year. For a time I had purchased my paper from the wholesale dealers in a neighboring town. For economy's sake, and partly for the adventure of the trip, I now resolved to cross the mountains, some sixty miles, and order my future paper at the Devil's Dungeon paper-mill.

The sleighing being uncommonly fine toward the end of January, and promising to hold so for no small period, in spite of the bitter cold I started one gray Friday noon in my pung, well fitted with buffalo and wolf robes; and, spending one night on the road, next noon came in sight of Woedolor Mountain.

The far summit fairly smoked with frost; white vapors curled up from its white-wooded top, as from a chimney. The intense congelation made the whole country look like one petrifaction. The steel shoes of my pung craunched and gritted over the vitreous, chippy snow, as if it had been broken glass. The forests here and there skirting the route, feeling the same all-stiffening influence, their inmost fibres penetrated with the cold, strangely groaned — not in the swaying branches merely, but likewise in the vertical trunk — as the fitful gusts remorselessly swept through them. Brittle with excessive frost, many colossal tough-grained maples, snapped in twain like pipe-stems, cumbered the unfeeling earth.

Flaked all over with frozen sweat, white as a milky ram, his nostrils at each breath sending forth two horn-shaped shoots of heated respiration, Black, my good horse, but six years old, started at a sudden turn, where, right across the track — not ten minutes fallen — an old distorted hemlock lay, darkly undulatory as an anaconda.

Gaining the Bellows'-pipe, the violent blast, dead from behind, all but shoved my high-backed pung up-hill. The gust shrieked through the shivered pass, as if laden with lost spirits bound to the unhappy world. Ere gaining the summit, Black, my horse, as if exasperated by the cutting wind, slung out with his strong hind legs, tore the light pung straight up-hill, and sweeping grazingly through the narrow notch, sped downward madly past the ruined saw-mill. Into the Devil's Dungeon horse and cataract rushed together.

With might and main, quitting my seat and robes, and standing backward, with one foot braced against the dashboard, I rasped and churned the bit, and stopped him just in time to avoid collision, at a turn, with the bleak nozzle of a rock, couchant like a lion in the way—a road-side rock.

At first I could not discover the paper-mill.

The whole hollow gleamed with the white, except, here and there, where a pinnacle of granite showed one windswept angle bare. The mountains stood pinned in shrouds—a pass of Alpine corpses. Where stands the mill? Suddenly a whirling, humming sound broke upon my ear. I looked, and there, like an arrested avalanche, lay the large whitewashed factory. It was subordinately surrounded by a cluster of other and smaller buildings, some of which, from their cheap, blank air, great length, gregarious windows, and comfortless expression, no doubt were boarding-houses of the operatives. A snow-white hamlet amidst the snows. Various rude, irregular squares and courts resulted from the somewhat picturesque clusterings of these buildings, owing to the broken, rocky nature of the ground, which forbade all method in their relative arrangement. Several narrow lanes and alleys, too, partly blocked with snow fallen from the roof, cut up the hamlet in all directions.

When, turning from the traveled highway, jingling with bells of numerous farmers—who, availing themselves of the fine sleighing, were dragging their wood to market—and frequently diversified with swift cutters dashing from inn to inn of the scattered villages—when, I say, turning from that bustling main-road, I by degrees wound into the Mad Maid's Bellows'-pipe, and saw the grim Black Notch beyond, then something latent, as well as something obvious in the time and scene, strangely brought back to my mind my first sight of dark and grimy Temple-Bar. And when Black, my horse, went darting through the Notch, perilously grazing its rocky wall, I remembered being in a runaway London omnibus, which in much the same sort of style, though by no means at an equal rate, dashed through the ancient arch of Wren. Though the two objects did by no means completely correspond, yet this partial inadequacy but served to tinge the similitude not less with the vividness than the disorder of a dream. So that, when upon reining up at the protruding rock I at last caught sight of the quaint groupings of the factory-buildings, and with the traveled highway and the Notch behind, found myself all alone, silently and privily stealing through deep-cloven passages into this sequestered spot, and saw the long, high-gabled main factory edifice, with a rude tower—for hoisting heavy boxes—at one end, standing among its crowded outbuildings and boarding-houses, as the Temple Church amidst the surrounding offices and dormitories, and when the marvelous retirement of this mysterious mountain nook fastened its whole spell upon me, then, what memory lacked, all tributary imagination furnished, and I said to myself, "This is the very counterpart of the Paradise of Bachelors, but snowed upon, and frost-painted to a sepulchre."

Dismounting, and warily picking my way down the dangerous declivity — horse and man both sliding now and then upon the icy ledges — at length I drove, or the blast drove me, into the largest square, before one side of the main edifice. Piercingly and shrilly the shotted blast blew by the corner; and redly and demoniacally boiled Blood River at one side. A long wood-pile, of many scores of cords, all glittering in mail of crusted ice, stood crosswise in the square. A row of horse-posts, their north sides plastered with adhesive snow, flanked the factory wall. The bleak frost packed and paved the square as with some ringing metal.

The inverted similitude recurred — "The sweet, tranquil Temple garden, with the Thames bordering its green beds," strangely meditated I.

But where are the gay bachelors?

Then, as I and my horse stood shivering in the wind-spray, a girl ran from a neighboring dormitory door, and throwing her thin apron over her bare head, made for the opposite building.

"One moment, my girl; is there no shed hereabouts which I may drive into?"

Pausing, she turned upon me a face pale with work, and blue with cold; an eye supernatural with unrelated misery.

"Nay," faltered I, "I mistook you. Go on; I want nothing."

Leading my horse close to the door from which she had come, I knocked. Another pale, blue girl appeared, shivering in the doorway as, to prevent the blast, she jealously held the door ajar.

"Nay, I mistake again. In God's name shut the door. But hold, is there no man about?"

That moment a dark-complexioned well-wrapped personage passed, making for the factory door, and spying him coming, the girl rapidly closed the other one.

"Is there no horse-shed here, Sir?"

"Yonder, to the wood-shed," he replied, and disappeared inside the factory.

With much ado I managed to wedge in horse and pung between the scattered piles of wood all sawn and split. Then, blanketing my horse, and piling my buffalo on the blanket's top, and tucking in its edges well around the breast-band and breeching, so that the wind might not strip him bare, I tied him fast, and ran lamely for the factory door, stiff with frost, and cumbered with my driver's dread-naught.

Immediately I found myself standing in a spacious place, intolerably lighted by long rows of windows, focusing inward the snowy scene without.

At rows of blank-looking counters sat rows of blank-looking girls, with blank, white folders in their blank hands, all blankly folding blank paper.

In one corner stood some huge frame of ponderous iron, with a vertical thing like a piston periodically rising and falling upon a heavy wooden block. Before it—its tame minister—stood a tall girl, feeding the iron animal with half-quires of rose-hued note paper, which, at every downward dab of the piston-like machine, received in the corner the impress of a wreath of roses. I looked from the rosy paper to the pallid cheek, but said nothing.

Seated before a long apparatus, strung with long, slender strings like any harp, another girl was feeding it with foolscap sheets, which, so soon as they curiously traveled from her on the cords, were withdrawn at the opposite end of the machine by a second girl. They came to the first girl blank; they went to the second girl ruled.

I looked upon the first girl's brow, and saw it was young and fair; I looked upon the second girl's brow, and saw it was ruled and wrinkled. Then, as I still looked, the two—for some small variety to the monotony—changed places; and where had stood the young, fair brow, now stood the ruled and wrinkled one.

Perched high upon a narrow platform, and still higher upon a high stool crowning it, sat another figure serving some other iron animal; while below the platform sat her mate in some sort of reciprocal attendance.

Not a syllable was breathed. Nothing was heard but the low, steady, overruling hum of the iron animals. The human voice was banished from the spot. Machinery—that vaunted slave of humanity—here stood menially served by human beings, who served mutely and cringingly as the slave serves the Sultan. The girls did not so much seem accessory wheels to the general machinery as mere cogs to the wheels.

All this scene around me was instantaneously taken in at one sweeping glance—even before I had proceeded to unwind the heavy fur tippet from around my neck. But as soon as this fell from me the dark-complexioned man, standing close by, raised a sudden cry, and seizing my arm, dragged me out into the open air, and without pausing for a word instantly caught up some congealed snow and began rubbing both my cheeks.

"Two white spots like the whites of your eyes," he said; "man, your cheeks are frozen."

"That may well be," muttered I; " 'tis some wonder the frost of the Devil's Dungeon strikes in no deeper. Rub away."

Soon a horrible, tearing pain caught at my reviving cheeks. Two gaunt blood-hounds, one on each side, seemed mumbling them. I seemed Actaeon.

Presently, when all was over, I re-entered the factory, made known my business, concluded it satisfactorily, and then begged to be conducted throughout the place to view it.

"Cupid is the boy for that," said the dark-complexioned man. "Cupid!" and by this odd fancy-name calling a dimpled, red-cheeked, spirited-looking, forward little fellow, who was rather impudently, I thought, gliding about among the passive-looking girls — like a gold fish through hueless waves — yet doing nothing in particular that I could see, the man bade him lead the stranger through the edifice.

"Come first and see the water-wheel," said this lively lad, with the air of boyishly-brisk importance.

Quitting the folding-room, we crossed some damp, cold boards, and stood beneath a great wet shed, incessantly showering with foam, like the green barnacled bow of some East Indiaman in a gale. Round and round here went the enormous revolutions of the dark colossal water-wheel, grim with its one immutable purpose.

"This sets our whole machinery a-going, Sir; in every part of all these buildings; where the girls work and all."

I looked, and saw that the turbid waters of Blood River had not changed their hue by coming under the use of man.

"You make only blank paper; no printing of any sort, I suppose? All blank paper, don't you?"

"Certainly; what else should a paper-factory make?"

The lad here looked at me as if suspicious of my commonsense.

"Oh, to be sure!" said I, confused and stammering; "it only struck me as so strange that red waters should turn out pale thee — paper, I mean."

He took me up a wet and rickety stair to a great light room, furnished with no visible thing but rude, manger-like receptacles running all round its sides; and up to these mangers, like so many mares haltered to the rack, stood rows of girls. Before each was vertically thrust up a long, glittering scythe, immovably fixed at bottom to the manger-edge. The curve of the scythe, and its having no snath to it, made it look exactly like a sword. To and fro, across the sharp edge, the girls forever dragged long strips of rags, washed white, picked from baskets at one side; thus ripping asunder every seam, and converting the tatters almost into lint. The air swam with the fine, poisonous particles, which from all sides darted, subtilely, as motes in sun-beams, into the lungs.

"This is the rag-room," coughed the boy.

"You find it rather stifling here," coughed I, in answer, "but the girls don't cough."

"Oh, they are used to it."

"Where do you get such hosts of rags?" picking up a handful from a basket.

"Some from the country round about; some from far over sea — Leghorn and London."

"'Tis not unlikely, then," murmured I, "that among these heaps of rags there may be some old shirts, gathered from the dormitories of the Paradise of Bachelors. But the buttons are all dropped off. Pray, my lad, do you ever find any bachelor's buttons hereabouts?"

"None grow in this part of the country. The Devil's Dungeon is no place for flowers."

"Oh! you mean the flowers so called — the Bachelor's Buttons?"

"And was not that what you asked about? Or did you mean the gold bosom-buttons of our boss, Old Bach, as our whispering girls all call him?"

"The man, then, I saw below is a bachelor, is he?"

"Oh, yes, he's a Bach."

"The edges of those swords, they are turned outward from the girls, if I see right; but their rags and fingers fly so, I can not distinctly see."

"Turned outward."

Yes, murmured I to myself; I see it now; turned outward; and each erected sword is so borne, edge-outward, before each girl. If my reading fails me not, just so, of old, condemned state-prisoners went from the hall of judgment to their doom: an officer before, bearing a sword, its edge turned outward, in significance of their fatal sentence. So, through consumptive pallors of this blank, raggy life, go these white girls to death.

"Those scythes look very sharp," again turning toward the boy.

"Yes; they have to keep them so. Look!"

That moment two of the girls, dropping their rags, plied each a whet-stone up and down the sword-blade. My unaccustomed blood curdled at the sharp shriek of the tormented steel.

Their own executioners; themselves whetting the very swords that slay them; meditated I.

"What makes those girls so sheet-white, my lad?"

"Why" — with a roguish twinkle, pure ignorant drollery, not knowing heartlessness — "I suppose the handling of such white bits of sheets all the time makes them so sheety."

"Let us leave the rag-room now, my lad."

More tragical and more inscrutably mysterious than any mystic sight, human or machine, throughout the factory, was the strange innocence of cruel-heartedness in this usage-hardened boy.

"And now," said he, cheerily, "I suppose you want to see our great machine, which cost us twelve thousand dollars only last autumn. That's the machine that makes the paper, too. This way, Sir."

Following him, I crossed a large, bespattered place, with two great round vats in it, full of a white, wet, woolly-looking stuff, not unlike the albuminous part of an egg, soft-boiled.

"There," said Cupid, tapping the vats carelessly, "these are the first beginnings of the paper; this white pulp you see. Look how it swims bubbling round and round, moved by the paddle here. From hence it pours from both vats into that one common channel yonder, and so goes, mixed up and leisurely, to the great machine. And now for that."

He led me into a room, stifling with a strange, blood-like, abdominal heat, as if here, true enough, were being finally developed the germinous particles lately seen.

Before me, rolled out like some long Eastern manuscript, lay stretched one continuous length of iron frame-work — multitudinous and mystical, with all sorts of rollers, wheels, and cylinders, in slowly-measured and unceasing motion.

"Here first comes the pulp now," said Cupid, pointing to the nighest end of the machine. "See; first it pours out and spreads itself upon this wide, sloping board; and then look — slides, thin and quivering beneath the first roller there. Follow on now, and see it as it slides from under that to the next cylinder. There; see how it has become just a very little less pulpy now. One step more, and it grows still more to some slight consistence. Still another cylinder, and it is so knitted — though as yet mere dragon-fly wing — that it forms an air-bridge here, like a suspended cobweb, between two more separated rollers; and flowing over the last one, and under again, and doubling about there out of sight for a minute among all those mixed cylinders you indistinctly see, it reappears here, looking now at last a little less like pulp and more like paper, but still quite delicate and defective yet awhile. But — a little further onward, Sir, if you please — here now, at this further point, it puts on something of a real look, as if it might turn out to be something you might possibly handle in the end. But it's not yet done, Sir. Good way to travel yet, and plenty more of cylinders must roll it."

"Bless my soul!" said I, amazed at the elongation, interminable convolutions, and deliberate slowness of the machine; "it must take a long time for the pulp to pass from end to end, and come out paper."

"Oh! not so long," smiled the precocious lad, with a superior and patronizing air; "only nine minutes. But look; you may try it for yourself. Have you a bit of paper? Ah! here's a bit on the floor. Now mark that with any word you please, and let me dab it on here, and we'll see how long before it comes out at the other end."

"Well, let me see," said I, taking out my pencil; "come, I'll mark it with your name."

Bidding me take out my watch, Cupid adroitly dropped the inscribed slip on an exposed part of the incipient mass.

Instantly my eye marked the second-hand on my dial-plate. Slowly I followed the slip, inch by inch; sometimes pausing for full half a minute as it disappeared beneath inscrutable groups of the lower cylinders, but only gradually to emerge again; and so, on, and on, and on — inch by inch; now in open sight, sliding along like a freckle on the quivering sheet; and then again wholly vanished; and so, on, and on, and on — inch by inch; all the time the main sheet growing more and more to final firmness — when, suddenly, I saw a sort of paper-fall, not wholly unlike a water-fall; a scissory sound smote my ear, as of some cord being snapped; and down dropped an unfolded sheet of perfect foolscap, with my "Cupid" half faded out of it, and still moist and warm.

My travels were at an end, for here was the end of the machine.

"Well, how long was it?" said Cupid.

"Nine minutes to a second," replied I, watch in hand.

"I told you so."

For a moment a curious emotion filled me, not wholly unlike that which one might experience at the fulfillment of some mysterious prophecy. But how absurd, thought I again; the thing is a mere machine, the essence of which is unvarying punctuality and precision.

Previously absorbed by the wheels and cylinders, my attention was now directed to a sad-looking woman standing by.

"That is rather an elderly person so silently tending the machine-end here. She would not seem wholly used to it either."

"Oh," knowingly whispered Cupid, through the din, "she only came last week. She was a nurse formerly. But the business is poor in these parts, and she's left it. But look at the paper she is piling there."

"Ay, foolscap," handling the piles of moist, warm sheets, which continually were being delivered into the woman's waiting hands. "Don't you turn out any thing but foolscap at this machine?"

"Oh, sometimes, but not often, we turn out finer work, cream-laid and royal sheets, we call them. But foolscap being in chief demand, we turn out foolscap most."

It was very curious. Looking at that blank paper continually dropping, dropping, dropping, my mind ran on in wonderings of those strange uses to which those thousand sheets eventually would be put. All sorts of writings would be writ on those now vacant things — sermons, lawyers' briefs, physicians' prescriptions, love-letters, marriage certificates, bills of divorce, registers of births, death-warrants, and so on, without end. Then, recurring back to them as they here lay all blank, I could not but bethink me of that celebrated comparison of John Locke, who, in demonstration of his theory that man had no innate ideas, compared the human mind at birth to a sheet of blank paper; something destined to be scribbled on, but what sort of characters no soul might tell.

Pacing slowly to and fro along the involved machine, still humming with its play, I was struck as well by the inevitability as the evolvement-power in all its motions.

"Does that thin cobweb there," said I, pointing to the sheet in its more imperfect stage, "does that never tear or break? It is marvelous fragile, and yet this machine it passes through is so mighty."

"It never is known to tear a hair's point."

"Does it never stop — get clogged?"

"No. It *must* go. The machinery makes it go just *so*; just that very way, and at that very pace you there plainly see it go. The pulp can't help going."

Something of awe now stole over me, as I gazed upon this inflexible iron animal. Always, more or less, machinery of this ponderous, elaborate sort strikes, in some moods, strange dread into the human heart, as some living, panting Behemoth might. But what made the thing I saw so specially terrible to me was the metallic necessity, the unbudging fatality which governed it. Though, here and there, I could not follow the thin, gauzy vail of pulp in the course of its more mysterious or entirely invisible advance, yet it was indubitable that, at those points where it eluded me, it still marched on in unvarying docility to the autocratic cunning of the machine. A fascination fastened on me. I stood spell-bound and wandering in my soul. Before my eyes — there, passing in slow procession along the wheeling cylinders, I seemed to see, glued to the pallid incipience of the pulp, the yet more pallid faces of all the pallid girls I had eyed that heavy day. Slowly, mournfully, beseechingly, yet unresistingly, they gleamed along, their agony dimly outlined on the imperfect paper, like the print of the tormented face on the handkerchief of Saint Veronica.

"Halloa! the heat of the room is too much for you," cried Cupid, staring at me.

"No — I am rather chill, if any thing."

"Come out, Sir — out — out," and, with the protecting air of a careful father, the precocious lad hurried me outside.

In a few moments, feeling revived a little, I went into the folding-room — the first room I had entered, and where the desk for transacting business stood, surrounded by the blank counters and blank girls engaged at them.

"Cupid here has led me a strange tour," said I to the dark-complexioned man before mentioned, whom I had ere this discovered not only to be an old bachelor, but also the principal proprietor. "Yours is a most wonderful factory. Your great machine is a miracle of inscrutable intricacy."

"Yes, all our visitors think it so. But we don't have many. We are in a very out-of-the-way corner here. Few inhabitants, too. Most of our girls come from far-off villages."

"The girls," echoed I, glancing round at their silent forms. "Why is it, Sir, that in most factories, female operatives, of whatever age, are indiscriminately called girls, never women?"

"Oh! as to that — why, I suppose, the fact of their being generally unmarried — that's the reason, I should think. But it never struck me before. For our factory here, we will not have married women; they are apt to be off-and-on too much. We want none but steady workers: twelve hours to the day, day after day, through the three hundred and sixty-five days, excepting Sundays, Thanksgiving, and Fast-days. That's our rule. And so, having no married women, what females we have are rightly enough called girls."

"Then these are all maids," said I, while some pained homage to their pale virginity made me involuntarily bow.

"All maids."

Again the strange emotion filled me.

"Your cheeks look whitish yet, Sir," said the man, gazing at me narrowly. "You must be careful going home. Do they pain you at all now? It's a bad sign, if they do."

"No doubt, Sir," answered I, "when once I have got out of the Devil's Dungeon, I shall feel them mending."

"Ah, yes; the winter air in valleys, or gorges, or any sunken place, is far colder and more bitter than elsewhere. You would hardly believe it now, but it is colder here than at the top of Woedolor Mountain."

"I dare say it is, Sir. But time presses me; I must depart."

With that, remuffling myself in dread-naught and tippet, thrusting my hands into my huge seal-skin mittens, I sallied out into the nipping air, and found poor Black, my horse, all cringing and doubled up with the cold.

Soon, wrapped in furs and meditations, I ascended from the Devil's Dungeon.

At the Black Notch I paused, and once more bethought me of Temple-Bar. Then, shooting through the pass, all alone with inscrutable nature, I exclaimed — Oh! Paradise of Bachelors! and oh! Tartarus of Maids!

Discussion Topics

1. What is the narrator's attitude to his visit to the bachelors' apartment in the Inns of Court? Can one assume that Melville's attitude is the same as the narrator? The evidence is mixed. On one hand, the comparison of the modern "templars" with the historic knights templar seems full of irony. Risk and heroism are no longer part of modern lives. And yet the narrator points out that the original knights themselves declined and were corrupted. Moreover, he does not seriously question whether the modern bachelors, like the knights, are dedicated to a higher cause than their own comfort and pleasure. We see them at play but not at work.

It is possible to find ironic disapproval in Melville's description of the bachelors' dinner. If one does, is that a reflection of what we bring as readers who are skeptical of privilege or is it a genuine reflection of Melville's attitude? The details of the dinner merit analysis. Melville is at pains to point out the mutual good will of the diners; their indulgences never become license, and they never get out of hand. Can one criticize their materialism? Or have they simply achieved an admirably high degree of sophistication and civility?

2. The first part of story is sometimes printed alone. The juxtaposition of the two parts is clearly important and must lead one to rethink Melville's intent in "Paradise." While it is possible to take the first part at face value as description, the second part is packed with symbols that force us to look at the symbolic dimensions of the whole.

Consider the various contrasts between the first and second parts. Most obviously, one is about a community of men, the other about a community of women. One has an urban setting in the old world; the other describes a rural place in the new world. The first is about professions that have been around forever; the second is about modern business and the dislocations forced by economic development. In the first, the colors of one's imagination are rich and muted; in the second, the colors are stark — black, white, and red. One has warmth; the other is chilling to the bone.

How does Melville expect us to respond to this contrast between the lives of unmarried men and the plight of unmarried women? The men speak; the women are silent. The men have blood coursing through them; the women have been bled to near death; they are ashen, and the water in the mill is blood-red.

One may question how much it matters that the men are lawyers. If Melville is pointing to a radical injustice, is law to blame? Is there a legal remedy to the situation that Melville describes?

3. Alfred Konefsky, a legal historian, recently published "The Accidental Legal Historian: Herman Melville and the History of American Law" (52 *Buffalo Law Review* 1179 (2004)). He points out that Melville's work "offers us a unique lens into his time — a way of understanding how law actually functioned to shape or constrain social relations and to resolve moral dilemmas." Konefsky goes on to suggest that American culture according to Melville was one "in which hierarchy predominated, power and authority were abused, and justice was compromised with terrible consequences . . . for individual Americans."

In these respects, Melville appears to have differed from most legal historians who took for granted that "dependent/heirarchical relations were gradually replaced [in nineteenth century America] by free, equal relations in which independent legal actors flourished by asserting their individual rights unrestrained by abuses of authority or power." Konefsky points out that, by contrast, Melville believed "either that legally dependent relationships still dominated American life, or that assertions of individual freedoms provided a mask for a dependency devoid of bonds of mutual obligation."

"Paradise . . . Tartarus . . ." presents two extreme poles of a social hierarchy. Consider the interdependency of these two realms and what keeps each secure in its place. Can law be blamed merely for inaction—or is it a constituent instrument by which the hierarchy comes into being?

Herman Melville: Bartleby, the Scrivener

"Bartleby, the Scrivener" is a perplexing work. At one level it offers a perspective on the operation of a small law office in mid-nineteenth-century New York City and the attitudes of a moderately successful attorney with limited ambitions. But Bartleby, who enters as an employee, disturbs both the routine of the office and the state of mind of attorney-narrator. He escapes the grasp of both law and reason—and his symbolic function has been debated by critics for more than a hundred years.

❧ Bartleby, The Scrivener ❧

Herman Melville

I am a rather elderly man. The nature of my avocations, for the last thirty years, has brought me into more than ordinary contact with what would seem an interesting and somewhat singular set of men, of whom, as yet, nothing, that I know of, has ever been written—I mean, the law-copyists, or scriveners. I have known very many of them, professionally and privately and, if I pleased, could relate divers histories, at which good-natured gentlemen might smile, and sentimental souls might weep. But I waive the biographies of all other scriveners, for a few passages in the life of Bartleby, who was a scrivener, the strangest I ever saw, or heard of. While, of other law-copyists, I might write the complete life, of Bartleby nothing of that sort can be done. I believe that no materials exist, for a full and satisfactory biography of this man. It is an irreparable loss to literature. Bartleby was one of those beings of whom nothing is ascertainable, except from the original sources, and, in his case, those are very small. What my own astonished eyes saw of Bartleby, that is all I know of him, except, indeed, one vague report, which will appear in the sequel.

Ere introducing the scrivener, as he first appeared to me, it is fit I make some mention of myself, my employees, my business, my chambers, and general surroundings; because some such description is indispensable to an adequate understanding of the chief character about to be presented. Imprimis: I am a man who, from his youth upwards, has been filled with a profound conviction that the easiest way of life is the best. Hence, though I belong to a profession proverbially energetic and nervous, even to turbulence, at times, yet nothing of that sort have I ever suffered to invade my peace. I am one of those unambitious lawyers who never addresses a jury, or in any way draws down public applause; but, in the cool tranquillity of a snug retreat, do a snug business among rich men's bonds, and mortgages, and title-deeds. All who know me, consider me an eminently safe man. The late John Jacob Astor, a personage little given to poetic enthusiasm, had no hesitation in pronouncing my first grand point to be prudence; my next, method. I do not speak it in vanity, but simply record the fact, that I was not unemployed in my profession by the late John Jacob Astor; a name which, I admit, I love to repeat; for it hath a rounded and orbicular sound to it, and rings like unto bullion. I will freely add, that I was not insensible to the late John Jacob Astor's good opinion.

Some time prior to the period of which this little history begins, my avocations had been largely increased. The good old office, now extinct in the State of New York, of a Master in Chancery, had been conferred upon me. It was not a very arduous office, but very pleasantly remunerative. I seldom lose my temper; much more seldom indulge in dangerous indignation at wrongs and outrages; but, I must be permitted to be rash here, and declare, that I consider the sudden and violent abrogation of the office of Master in Chancery, by the new Constitution, as a — premature act; inasmuch as I had counted upon a life-lease of the profits, whereas I only received those of a few short years. But this is by the way.

My chambers were up stairs, at No. — Wall Street. At one end, they looked upon the white wall of the interior of a spacious sky-light shaft, penetrating the building from top to bottom.

This view might have been considered rather tame than otherwise, deficient in what landscape painters call "life." But, if so, the view from the other end of my chambers offered, at least, a contrast, if nothing more. In that direction, my windows commanded an unobstructed view of a lofty brick wall, black by age and everlasting shade; which wall required no spy-glass to bring out its lurking beauties, but, for the benefit of all near-sighted spectators, was pushed up to within ten feet of my window panes. Owing to the great height of the surrounding buildings, and my chambers being on the second floor, the interval between this wall and mine not a little resembled a huge square cistern.

At the period just preceding the advent of Bartleby, I had two persons as copyists in my employment, and a promising lad as an office-boy. First, Turkey; second, Nippers; third, Ginger Nut. These may seem names, the like of which are not usually found in the Directory. In truth, they were nicknames, mutually conferred upon each other by my three clerks, and were deemed expressive of their respective persons or characters. Turkey was a short, pursy Englishman, of about my own age—that is, somewhere not far from sixty. In the morning, one might say, his face was of a fine florid hue, but after twelve o'clock, meridian—his dinner hour—it blazed like a grate full of Christmas coals; and continued blazing—but, as it were, with a gradual wane—till six o'clock, P.M., or thereabouts; after which, I saw no more of the proprietor of the face, which, gaining its meridian with the sun, seemed to set with it, to rise, culminate, and decline the following day, with the like regularity and undiminished glory. There are many singular coincidences I have known in the course of my life, not the least among which was the fact, that, exactly when Turkey displayed his fullest beams from his red and radiant countenance, just then, too, at that critical moment, began the daily period when I considered his business capacities as seriously disturbed for the remainder of the twenty-four hours. Not that he was absolutely idle, or averse to business, then; far from it. The difficulty was, he was apt to be altogether too energetic. There was a strange, inflamed, flurried, flighty recklessness of activity about him. He would be incautious in dipping his pen into his inkstand. All his blots upon my documents were dropped there after twelve o'clock, meridian. Indeed, not only would he be reckless, and sadly given to making blots in the afternoon, but, some days, he went further, and was rather noisy. At such times, too, his face flamed with augmented blazonry, as if cannel coal had been heaped on anthracite. He made an unpleasant racket with his chair; spilled his sand-box; in mending his pens, impatiently split them all to pieces, and threw them on the floor in a sudden passion; stood up, and leaned over his table, boxing his papers about in a most indecorous manner, very sad to behold in an elderly man like him. Nevertheless, as he was in many ways a most valuable person to me, and all the time before twelve o'clock, meridian, was the quickest, steadiest creature, too, accomplishing a great deal of work in a style not easily to be matched — for these reasons, I was willing to overlook his eccentricities, though, indeed, occasionally, I remonstrated with him. I did this very gently, however, because, though the civilest, nay, the blandest and most reverential of men in the morning, yet, in the afternoon, he was disposed, upon provocation, to be slightly rash with his tongue — in fact, insolent. Now, valuing his morning services as I did, and resolved not to lose them — yet, at the same time, made uncomfortable by his inflamed ways after twelve o'clock — and being a man of peace, unwilling by my admonitions to call forth unseemly retorts from him, I took upon me, one Saturday noon (he was always worse on Saturdays) to hint to him, very kindly, that, perhaps, now that he was growing old, it might be well to abridge his labors; in short, he need not come to my chambers after twelve o'clock, but, dinner over, had best go home to his lodgings, and rest himself till tea-time. But no; he insisted upon his afternoon devotions. His countenance became intolerably fervid, as he oratorically assured me — gesticulating with a long ruler at the other end of the room — that if his services in the morning were useful, how indispensable, then, in the afternoon?

"With submission, sir," said Turkey, on this occasion, "I consider myself your right-hand man. In the morning I but marshal and deploy my columns; but in the afternoon I put myself at their head, and gallantly charge the foe, thus" — and he made a violent thrust with the ruler.

"But the blots, Turkey," intimated I.

"True; but, with submission, sir, behold these hairs! I am getting old. Surely, sir, a blot or two of a warm afternoon is not to be severely urged against gray hairs. Old age — even if it blot the page — is honorable. With submission, sir, we *both* are getting old."

This appeal to my fellow-feeling was hardly to be resisted. At all events I saw that go he would not. So, I made up my mind to let him stay, resolving, nevertheless, to see to it that, during the afternoon, he had to do with my less important papers.

Nippers, the second on my list, was a whiskered, sallow, and, upon the whole, rather piratical-looking young man, of about five and twenty. I always deemed him the victim of two evil powers — ambition and indigestion. The ambition was evinced by a certain impatience of the duties of a mere copyist, an unwarrantable usurpation of strictly professional affairs, such as the original drawing up of legal documents. The indigestion seemed betoken in an occasional nervous testiness and grinning irritability, causing the teeth to audibly grind together over mistakes committed in copying; unnecessary maledictions, hissed, rather than spoken, in the heat of business; and especially by a continual discontent with the height of the table where he worked. Though of a very ingenious mechanical turn, Nippers could never get this table to suit him. He put chips under it, blocks of various sorts, bits of pasteboard, and at last went so far as to attempt an exquisite adjustment, by final pieces of folded blotting-paper. But no invention would answer. If, for the sake of easing his back, he brought the table lid at a sharp angle well up towards his chin, and wrote there like a man using the steep roof of a Dutch house for his desk, then he declared that it stopped the circulation in his arms. If now he lowered the table to his waistbands, and stooped over it in writing, then there was a sore aching in his back. In short, the truth of the matter was, Nippers knew not what he wanted. Or, if he wanted anything, it was to be rid of a scrivener's table altogether. Among the manifestations of his diseased ambition was a fondness he had for receiving visits from certain ambiguous-looking fellows in seedy coats, whom he called his clients. Indeed, I was aware that not only was he, at times, considerable of a ward-politician, but he occasionally did a little business at the Justices' courts, and was not unknown on the steps of the Tombs. I have good reason to believe, however, that one individual who called upon him at my chambers, and who, with a grand air, he insisted was his client, was no other than a dun, and the alleged title-deed, a bill. But, with all his failings, and the annoyances he caused me, Nippers, like his compatriot Turkey, was a very useful man to me; wrote a neat, swift hand; and, when he chose, was not deficient in a gentlemanly sort of way; and so, incidentally, reflected credit upon my chambers. Whereas, with respect to Turkey, I had much ado to keep him from being a reproach to me. His clothes were apt to look oily, and smell of eating-houses. He wore his pantaloons very loose and baggy in summer. His coats were execrable; his hat not to be handled. But while the hat was a thing of indifference to me, inasmuch as his natural civility and deference, as a dependent Englishman, always led him to doff it the moment he entered the room, yet his coat was another matter. Concerning his coats, I reasoned with him; but with no effect. The truth was, I suppose, that a man with so small an income could not afford to sport such a lustrous face and a lustrous coat at one and the same time. As Nippers once observed, Turkey's money went chiefly for red ink. One winter day, I presented Turkey with a highly respectable-looking coat of my own — a padded gray coat, of a most comfortable warmth, and which buttoned straight up from the knee to the neck. I thought Turkey would appreciate the favor, and abate his rashness and obstreperousness of afternoons. But no; I verily believe that buttoning himself up in so downy and blanket-like a coat had a pernicious effect upon him — upon the same principle that too much oats are bad for horses. In fact, precisely as a rash, restive horse is said to feel his oats, so Turkey felt his coat. It made him insolent. He was a man whom prosperity harmed.

Though, concerning the self-indulgent habits of Turkey, I had my own private surmises, yet, touching Nippers, I was well persuaded that, whatever might be his faults in other respects, he was, at least, a temperate young man. But, indeed, nature herself seemed to have been his vintner, and, at his birth, charged him so thoroughly with an irritable, brandy-like disposition, that all subsequent potations were needless. When I consider how, amid the stillness of my chambers, Nippers would sometimes impatiently rise from his seat, and stooping over his table, spread his arms wide apart, seize the whole desk, and move it, and jerk it, with a grim, grinding motion on the floor, as if the table were a perverse voluntary agent, intent on thwarting and vexing him, I plainly perceive that, for Nippers, brandy-and-water were altogether superfluous.

It was fortunate for me that, owing to its peculiar cause — indigestion — the irritability and consequent nervousness of Nippers were mainly observable in the morning, while in the afternoon he was comparatively mild. So that, Turkey's paroxysms only coming on about twelve o'clock, I never had to do with their eccentricities at one time. Their fits relieved each other, like guards. When Nipper's was on, Turkey's was off; and vice versa. This was a good natural arrangement, under the circumstances.

Ginger Nut, the third on my list, was a lad, some twelve years old. His father was a car-man, ambitious of seeing his son on the bench instead of a cart, before he died. So he sent him to my office, as student at law, errand-boy, cleaner and sweeper, at the rate of one dollar a week. He had a little desk to himself, but he did not use it much. Upon inspection, the drawer exhibited a great array of the shells of various sorts of nuts. Indeed, to this quick-witted youth, the whole noble science of the law was contained in a nut-shell. Not the least among the employments of Ginger Nut, as well as one which he discharged with the most alacrity, was his duty as cake and apple purveyor for Turkey and Nippers. Copying law-papers being proverbially a dry, husky sort of business, my two scriveners were fain to moisten their mouths very often with Spitzenbergs, to be had at the numerous stalls nigh the Custom House and Post Office. Also, they sent Ginger Nut very frequently for that peculiar cake — small, flat, round, and very spicy — after which he had been named by them. Of a cold morning, when business was but dull, Turkey would gobble up scores of these cakes, as if they were mere wafers — indeed, they sell them at the rate of six or eight for a penny — the scrape of his pen blending with the crunching of the crisp particles in his mouth. Of all the fiery afternoon blunders and flurried rashnesses of Turkey, was his once moistening a ginger-cake between his lips, and clapping it on to a mortgage, for a seal. I came within an ace of dismissing him then. But he mollified me by making an oriental bow, and saying —

"With submission, sir, it was generous of me to find you in stationery on my own account."

Now my original business — that of a conveyancer and title hunter, and drawer-up of recondite documents of all sorts — was considerably increased by receiving the master's office. There was now great work for scriveners. Not only must I push the clerks already with me, but I must have additional help.

In answer to my advertisement, a motionless young man one morning stood upon my office threshold, the door being open, for it was summer. I can see that figure now — pallidly neat, pitiably respectable, incurably forlorn! It was Bartleby.

After a few words touching his qualifications, I engaged him, glad to have among my corps of copyists a man of so singularly sedate an aspect, which I thought might operate beneficially upon the flighty temper of Turkey, and the fiery one of Nippers.

I should have stated before that ground glass folding-doors divided my premises into two parts, one of which was occupied by my scriveners, the other by myself. According to my humor, I threw open these doors, or closed them. I resolved to assign Bartleby a corner by the folding-doors, but on my side of them, so as to have this quiet man within easy call, in case any trifling thing was to be done. I placed his desk close up to a small side window in that part of the room, a window which originally had afforded a lateral view of certain grimy back-yards and bricks, but which, owing to subsequent erections, commanded at present no view at all, though it gave some light. Within three feet of the panes was a wall, and the light came down from far above, between two lofty buildings, as from a very small opening in a dome. Still further to a satisfactory arrangement, I procured a high green folding screen, which might entirely isolate Bartleby from my sight, though not remove him from my voice. And thus, in a manner, privacy and society were conjoined.

At first, Bartleby did an extraordinary quantity of writing. As if long famishing for something to copy, he seemed to gorge himself on my documents. There was no pause for digestion. He ran a day and night line, copying by sun-light and by candlelight. I should have been quite delighted with his application, had he been cheerfully industrious. But he wrote on silently, palely, mechanically.

It is, of course, an indispensable part of a scrivener's business to verify the accuracy of his copy, word by word. Where there are two or more scriveners in an office, they assist each other in this examination, one reading from the copy the other holding the original. It is a very dull, wearisome, and lethargic affair. I can readily imagine that, to some sanguine temperaments, it would be altogether intolerable. For example, I cannot credit that the mettle-some poet, Byron, would have contentedly sat down with Bartleby to examine a law document of say five hundred pages, closely written in a crimpy hand.

Now and then, in the haste of business, it had been my habit to assist in comparing some brief document myself, calling Turkey or Nippers for this purpose. One object I had, in placing Bartleby so handy to me behind the screen, was, to avail myself of his services on such trivial occasions. It was on the third day I think, of his being with me, and before any necessity had arisen for having his own writing examined, that, being much hurried to complete a small affair I had in hand, I abruptly called to Bartleby. In my haste and natural expectancy of instant compliance, I sat with my head bent over the original on my desk, and my right hand sideways, and somewhat nervously extended with the copy, so that, immediately upon emerging from his retreat, Bartleby might snatch it and pro-ceed to business without the least delay.

In this very attitude did I sit when I called to him, rapidly stating what it was I wanted him to do — namely, to examine a small paper with me. Imagine my surprise, nay, my consternation, when, without moving from his privacy, Bartleby, in a singularly mild, firm voice, replied, "I would prefer not to."

I sat awhile in perfect silence, rallying my stunned faculties. Immediately it occurred to me that my ears had deceived me, or Bartleby had entirely misunderstood my meaning. I repeated my request in the clearest tone I could assume; but in quite as clear a one came the previous reply, "I would prefer not to."

"Prefer not to," echoed I, rising in high excitement, and crossing the room with a stride. "What do you mean? Are you moonstruck? I want you to help me compare this sheet here — take it," and I thrust it towards him.

"I would prefer not to," said he.

I looked at him steadfastly. His face was leanly composed, his gray eye dimly calm. Not a wrinkle of agitation rippled him. Had there been the least uneasiness, anger, impatience or impertinence in his manner; in other words, had there been any thing ordinarily human about him, doubtless I should have violently dismissed him from the premises. But as it was, I should have as soon thought of turning my pale plaster-of-paris bust of Cicero out of doors. I stood gazing at him awhile, as he went on with his own writing, and then reseated myself at my desk. This is very strange, thought I. What had one best do? But my business hurried me. I concluded to forget the matter for the present, reserving it for my future leisure. So calling Nippers from the other room, the paper was speedily examined.

A few days after this, Bartleby concluded four lengthy documents, being quadruplicates of a week's testimony taken before me in my High Court of Chancery. It became necessary to examine them. It was an important suit, and great accuracy was imperative. Having all things arranged, I called Turkey, Nippers, and Ginger Nut, from the next room, meaning to place the four copies in the hands of my four clerks, while I should read from the original. Accordingly, Turkey, Nippers, and Ginger Nut had taken their seats in a row, each with his document in his hand, when I called to Bartleby to join this interesting group.

"Bartleby! quick, I am waiting."

I heard a slow scrape of his chair legs on the uncarpeted floor, and soon he appeared standing at the entrance of his hermitage.

"What is wanted?" said he, mildly.

"The copies, the copies," said I hurriedly. "We are going to examine them. There"—and I held towards him the fourth-quadruplicate.

"I would prefer not to," he said, and gently disappeared behind the screen.

For a few moments I was turned into a pillar of salt, standing at the head of my seated column of clerks. Recovering myself, I advanced towards the screen, and demanded the reason for such extraordinary conduct.

"*Why* do you refuse?"

"I would prefer not to."

With any other man I should have flown outright into a dreadful passion, scorned all further words, and thrust him ignominiously from my presence. But there was something about Bartleby that not only strangely disarmed me, but, in a wonderful manner, touched and disconcerted me. I began to reason with him.

"These are your own copies we are about to examine. It is labor saving to you, because one examination will answer for your four papers. It is common usage. Every copyist is bound to help examine his copy. Is it not so? Will you not speak? Answer!"

"I prefer not to," he replied in a flutelike tone. It seemed to me that, while I had been addressing him, he carefully revolved every statement that I made; fully comprehended the meaning; could not gainsay the irresistible conclusion; but, at the same time, some paramount consideration prevailed with him to reply as he did.

"You are decided, then, not to comply with my request—a request made according to common usage and common sense?"

He briefly gave me to understand, that on that point my judgment was sound. Yes: his decision was irreversible.

It is not seldom the case that, when a man is browbeaten in some unprecedented and violently unreasonable way, he begins to stagger in his own plainest faith. He begins, as it were, vaguely to surmise that, wonderful as it may be, all the justice and all the reason is on the other side. Accordingly, if any disinterested persons are present, he turns to them for some reinforcement of his own faltering mind.

"Turkey," said I, "what do you think of this? Am I not right?"

"With submission, sir," said Turkey, in his blandest tone, "I think that you are."

"Nippers," said I, "what do *you* think of it?"

"I think I should kick him out of the office."

(The reader, of nice perceptions, will here perceive that, it being morning, Turkey's answer is couched in polite and tranquil terms, but Nippers replies in ill-tempered ones. Or, to repeat a previous sentence, Nippers's ugly mood was on duty, and Turkey's off.)

"Ginger Nut," said I, willing to enlist the smallest suffrage in my behalf, "what do *you* think of it?"

"I think, sir, he's a little *luny*," replied Ginger Nut, with a grin.

"You hear what they say," said I, turning towards the screen, "come forth and do your duty."

But he vouchsafed no reply. I pondered a moment in sore perplexity. But once more business hurried me. I determined again to postpone the consideration of this dilemma to my future leisure. With a little trouble we made out to examine the papers without Bartleby, though at every page or two Turkey deferentially dropped his opinion, that this proceeding was quite out of the common; while Nippers, twitching in his chair with a dyspeptic nervousness, ground out, between his set teeth, occasional hissing maledictions against the stubborn oaf behind the screen. And for his (Nippers's) part, this was the first and the last time he would do another man's business without pay.

Meanwhile Bartleby sat in his hermitage, oblivious to everything but his own peculiar business there.

Some days passed, the scrivener being employed upon another lengthy work. His late remarkable conduct led me to regard his ways narrowly. I observed that he never went to dinner; indeed, that he never went anywhere. As yet I had never, of my personal knowledge, known him to be outside of my office. He was a perpetual sentry in the corner. At about eleven o'clock though, in the morning, I noticed that Ginger Nut would advance toward the opening in Bartleby's screen, as if silently beckoned thither by a gesture invisible to me where I sat. The boy would then leave the office, jingling a few pence, and reappear with a handful of ginger-nuts, which he delivered in the hermitage, receiving two of the cakes for his trouble.

He lives, then, on ginger-nuts, thought I; never eats a dinner, properly speaking; he must be a vegetarian, then; but no! he never eats even vegetables, he eats nothing but ginger-nuts. My mind then ran on in reveries concerning the probable effects upon the human constitution of living entirely on ginger-nuts. Ginger-nuts are so called, because they contain ginger as one of their peculiar constituents, and the final flavoring one. Now, what was ginger? A hot, spicy thing. Was Bartleby hot and spicy? Not at all. Ginger, then, had no effect upon Bartleby. Probably he preferred it should have none.

Nothing so aggravates an earnest person as a passive resistance. If the individual so resisted be of a not inhumane temper, and the resisting one perfectly harmless in his passivity, then, in the better moods of the former, he will endeavor charitably to construe to his imagination what proves impossible to be solved by his judgment. Even so, for the most part, I regarded Bartleby and his ways. Poor fellow! thought I, he means no mischief; it is plain he intends no insolence; his aspect sufficiently evinces that his eccentricities are involuntary. He is useful to me. I can get along with him. If I turn him away, the chances are he will fall in with some less-indulgent employer, and then he will be rudely treated, and perhaps driven forth miserably to starve. Yes. Here I can cheaply purchase a delicious self-approval. To befriend Bartleby; to humor him in his strange willfulness, will cost me little or nothing, while I lay up in my soul what will eventually prove a sweet morsel for my conscience. But this mood was not invariable with me. The passiveness of Bartleby sometimes irritated me. I felt strangely goaded on to encounter him in new opposition — to elicit some angry spark from him answerable to my own. But, indeed, I might as well have essayed to strike fire with my knuckles against a bit of Windsor soap. But one afternoon the evil impulse in me mastered me, and the following little scene ensued:

"Bartleby," said I, "when those papers are all copied, I will compare them with you."

"I would prefer not to."

"How? Surely you do not mean to persist in that mulish vagary?"

No answer.

I threw open the folding-doors near by, and, turning upon Turkey and Nippers, exclaimed:

"Bartleby a second time says, he won't examine his papers. What do you think of it, Turkey?"

It was afternoon, be it remembered. Turkey sat glowing like a brass boiler; his bald head steaming; his hands reeling among his blotted papers.

"Think of it?" roared Turkey; "I think I'll just step behind his screen, and black his eyes for him!"

So saying, Turkey rose to his feet and threw his arms into a pugilistic position. He was hurrying away to make good his promise, when I detained him, alarmed at the effect of incautiously rousing Turkey's combativeness after dinner.

"Sit down, Turkey;" said I, "and hear what Nippers has to say. What do you think of it, Nippers? Would I not be justified in immediately dismissing Bartleby?"

"Excuse me, that is for you to decide, sir. I think his conduct quite unusual, and, indeed, unjust, as regards Turkey and myself. But it may only be a passing whim."

"Ah," exclaimed I, "you have strangely changed your mind, then—you speak very gently of him now."

"All beer," cried Turkey; "gentleness is effects of beer— Nippers and I dined together to-day. You see how gentle *I* am, sir. Shall I go and black his eyes?"

"You refer to Bartleby, I suppose. No, not to-day, Turkey," I replied; "pray, put up your fists."

I closed the doors, and again advanced towards Bartleby. I felt additional incentives tempting me to my fate. I burned to be rebelled against again. I remembered that Bartleby never left the office.

"Bartleby," said I, "Ginger Nut is away; just step around to the Post Office, won't you? (it was but a three minutes' walk), and see if there is anything for me."

"I would prefer not to."

"You *will* not?"

"I *prefer* not."

I staggered to my desk, and sat there in a deep study. My blind inveteracy returned. Was there any other thing in which I could procure myself to be ignominiously repulsed by this lean, penniless wight?—my hired clerk? What added thing is there, perfectly reasonable, that he will be sure to refuse to do?

"Bartleby!"

No answer.

"Bartleby," in a louder tone.

No answer.

"Bartleby," I roared.

Like a very ghost, agreeable to the laws of magical invocation, at the third summons, he appeared at the entrance of his hermitage.

"Go to the next room, and tell Nippers to come to me."

"I prefer not to," he respectfully and slowly said, and mildly disappeared.

"Very good, Bartleby," said I, in a quiet sort of serenely-severe self-possessed tone, intimating the unalterable purpose of some terrible retribution very close at hand. At the moment I half intended something of the kind. But upon the whole, as it was drawing towards my dinner-hour, I thought it best to put on my hat and walk home for the day, suffering much from perplexity and distress of mind.

Shall I acknowledge it? The conclusion of this whole business was, that it soon became a fixed fact of my chambers, that a pale young scrivener, by the name of Bartleby, had a desk there; that he copied for me at the usual rate of four cents a folio (one hundred words); but he was permanently exempt from examining the work done by him, that duty being transferred to Turkey and Nippers, out of compliment, doubtless, to their superior acuteness; more-over, said Bartleby was never, on any account, to be dispatched on the most trivial errand of any sort; and that even if entreated to take upon him such a matter, it was generally understood that he would "prefer not to" — in other words, that he would refuse point-blank.

As days passed on, I became considerably reconciled to Bartleby. His steadiness, his freedom from all dissipation, his inces-sant industry (except when he chose to throw himself into a standing revery behind his screen), his great stillness, his unalter-ableness of demeanor under all circumstances, made him a valuable acquisition. One prime thing was this — *he was always there* — first in the morning, continually through the day, and the last at night. I had a singular confidence in his honesty. I felt my most precious papers perfectly safe in his hands. Sometimes, to be sure, I could not, for the very soul of me, avoid falling into sudden spasmodic passions with him. For it was exceeding difficult to bear in mind all the time those strange peculiarities, privileges, and unheard of exemptions, forming the tacit stipulations on Bartleby's part under which he remained in my office. Now and then, in the eagerness of dispatching pressing business, I would inadvertently summon Bartleby, in a short, rapid tone, to put his finger, say, on the incipient tie of a bit of red tape with which I was about compressing some papers. Of course, from behind the screen the usual answer, "I prefer not to," was sure to come; and then, how could a human creature, with the common infirmities of our nature, refrain from bitterly exclaiming upon such perverseness — such unreasonableness. However, every added repulse of this sort which I received only tended to lessen the probability of my repeating the inadvertence.

Here it must be said, that according to the custom of most legal gentlemen occupying chambers in densely-populated law buildings, there were several keys to my door. One was kept by a woman residing in the attic, which person weekly scrubbed and daily swept and dusted my apartments. Another was kept by Turkey for convenience sake. The third I sometimes carried in my own pocket. The fourth I knew not who had.

Now, one Sunday morning I happened to go to Trinity Church, to hear a celebrated preacher, and finding myself rather early on the ground I thought I would walk around to my chambers for a while. Luckily, I had my key with me; but upon applying it to the lock, I found it resisted by something inserted from the inside. Quite surprised, I called out; when to my consternation a key was turned from within; and thrusting his lean visage at me, and holding the door ajar, the apparition of Bartleby appeared, in his shirt sleeves, and otherwise in a strangely tattered deshabille, saying quietly that he was sorry, but he was deeply engaged just then, and — preferred not admitting me at present. In a brief word or two, he moreover added, that perhaps I had better walk around the block two or three times, and by that time he would probably have concluded his affairs.

Now, the utterly unsurmised appearance of Bartleby, tenanting my law-chambers of a Sunday morning, with his cadaverously gentlemanly nonchalance, yet withal firm and self-possessed, had such a strange effect upon me, that incontinently I slunk away from my own door, and did as desired. But not without sundry twinges of impotent rebellion against the mild effrontery of this unaccountable scrivener. Indeed, it was his wonderful mildness chiefly, which not only disarmed me, but unmanned me as it were. For I consider that one, for the time, is a sort of unmanned when he tranquilly permits his hired clerk to dictate to him, and order him away from his own premises. Furthermore, I was full of uneasiness as to what Bartleby could possibly be doing in my office in his shirt sleeves, and in an otherwise dismantled condition of a Sunday morning. Was anything amiss going on? Nay, that was out of the question. It was not to be thought of for a moment that Bartleby was an immoral person. But what could he be doing there? — copying? Nay again, whatever might be his eccentricities, Bartleby was an eminently decorous person. He would be the last man to sit down to his desk in any state approaching to nudity. Besides, it was Sunday; and there was something about Bartleby that forbade the supposition that he would by any secular occupation violate the properties of the day.

Nevertheless, my mind was not pacified; and full of a restless curiosity, at last I returned to the door. Without hindrance I inserted my key, opened it, and entered. Bartleby was not to be seen. I looked round anxiously, peeped behind his screen; but it was very plain that he was gone. Upon more closely examining the place, I surmised that for an indefinite period Bartleby must have ate, dressed, and slept in my office, and that, too without plate, mirror, or bed. The cushioned seat of a rickety old sofa in one corner bore the faint impress of a lean, reclining form. Rolled away under his desk, I found a blanket; under the empty grate, a blacking box and brush; on a chair, a tin basin, with soap and a ragged towel; in a newspaper a few crumbs of ginger-nuts and a morsel of cheese. Yes, thought I, it is evident enough that Bartleby has been making his home here, keeping bachelor's hall all by himself. Immediately then the thought came sweeping across me, what miserable friendlessness and loneliness are here revealed! His poverty is great; but his solitude, how horrible! Think of it. Of a Sunday, Wall Street is deserted as Petra; and every night of every day it is an emptiness. This building, too, which of weekdays hums with industry and life, at nightfall echoes with sheer vacancy, and all through Sunday is forlorn. And here Bartleby makes his home; sole spectator of a solitude which he has seen all populous—a sort of innocent and transformed Marius brooding among the ruins of Carthage!

For the first time in my life a feeling of over-powering stinging melancholy seized me. Before, I had never experienced aught but a not unpleasing sadness. The bond of a common humanity now drew me irresistibly to gloom. A fraternal melancholy! For both I and Bartleby were sons of Adam. I remembered the bright silks and sparkling faces I had seen that day, in gala trim, swanlike sailing down the Mississippi of Broadway; and I contrasted them with the pallid copyist, and thought to myself, All, happiness courts the light, so we deem the world is gay; but misery hides aloof, so we deem that misery there is none. These sad fancyings—chimeras, doubtless, of a sick and silly brain—led on to other and more special thoughts, concerning the eccentricities of Bartleby. Presentiments of strange discoveries hovered round me. The scrivener's pale form appeared to me laid out, among uncaring strangers, in its shivering winding sheet.

Suddenly I was attracted by Bartleby's closed desk, the key in open sight left in the lock.

I mean no mischief, seek the gratification of no heartless curiosity, thought I; besides, the desk is mine, and its contents, too, so I will make bold to look within. Everything was methodically arranged, the papers smoothly placed. The pigeon holes were deep, and removing the files of documents, I groped into their recesses. Presently I felt something there, and dragged it out. It was an old bandanna handkerchief, heavy and knotted. I opened it, and saw it was a savings bank.

I now recalled all the quiet mysteries which I had noted in the man. I remembered that he never spoke but to answer; that, though at intervals he had considerable time to himself, yet I had never seen him reading — no, not even a newspaper; that for long periods he would stand looking out, at his pale window behind the screen, upon the dead brick wall; I was quite sure he never visited any refectory or eating house; while his pale face clearly indicated that he never drank beer like Turkey, or tea and coffee even, like other men; that he never went anywhere in particular that I could learn; never went out for a walk, unless, indeed, that was the case at present; that he had declined telling who he was, or whence he came, or whether he had any relatives in the world; that though so thin and pale, he never complained of ill health. And more than all, I remembered a certain unconscious air of pallid — how shall I call it? — of pallid haughtiness, say, or rather an austere reserve about him, which had positively awed me into my tame compliance with his eccentricities, when I had feared to ask him to do the slightest incidental thing for me, even though I might know, from his long-continued motionlessness, that behind his screen he must be standing in one of those dead-wall reveries of his.

Revolving all these things, and coupling them with the recently discovered fact, that he made my office his constant abiding place and home, and not forgetful of his morbid moodiness; revolving all these things, a prudential feeling began to steal over me. My first emotions had been those of pure melancholy and sincerest pity; but just in proportion as the forlornness of Bartleby grew and grew to my imagination, did that same melancholy merge into fear, that pity into repulsion. So true it is, and so terrible, too, that up to a certain point the thought or sight of misery enlists our best affections; but, in certain special cases, beyond that point it does not. They err who would assert that invariably this is owing to the inherent selfishness of the human heart. It rather proceeds from a certain hopelessness of remedying excessive and organic ill. To a sensitive being, pity is not seldom pain. And when at last it is perceived that such pity cannot lead to effectual succor, common sense bids the soul be rid of it. What I saw that morning persuaded me that the scrivener was the victim of innate and incurable disorder. I might give alms to his body; but his body did not pain him; it was his soul that suffered, and his soul I could not reach.

I did not accomplish the purpose of going to Trinity Church that morning. Somehow, the things I had seen disqualified me for the time from church-going. I walked homeward, thinking what I would do with Bartleby. Finally, I resolved upon this — I would put certain calm questions to him the next morning, touching his history, etc., and if he declined to answer them openly and unreservedly (and I supposed he would prefer not), then to give him a twenty dollar bill over and above whatever I might owe him, and tell him his services were no longer required; but that if in any other way I could assist him, I would be happy to do so, especially if he desired to return to his native place, wherever that might be, I would willingly help to defray the expenses. Moreover, if, after reaching home, he found himself at any time in want of aid, a letter from him would be sure of a reply.

The next morning came.

"Bartleby," said I, gently calling to him behind his screen.

No reply.

"Bartleby," said I, in a still gentler tone, "come here; I am not going to ask you to do anything you would prefer not to do — I simply wish to speak to you."

Upon this he noiselessly slid into view.

"Will you tell me, Bartleby, where you were born?"

"I would prefer not to."

"Will you tell me *anything* about yourself?"

"I would prefer not to."

"But what reasonable objection can you have to speak to me? I feel friendly towards you."

He did not look at me while I spoke, but kept his glance fixed upon my bust of Cicero, which, as I then sat, was directly behind me, some six inches above my head.

"What is your answer, Bartleby," said I, after waiting a considerable time for a reply, during which his countenance remained immovable, only there was the faintest conceivable tremor of the white attenuated mouth.

"At present I prefer to give no answer," he said, and retired into his hermitage.

It was rather weak in me I confess, but his manner, on this occasion, nettled me. Not only did there seem to lurk in it a certain calm disdain, but his perverseness seemed ungrateful, considering the undeniable good usage and indulgence he had received from me.

Again I sat ruminating what I should do. Mortified as I was at his behavior, and resolved as I had been to dismiss him when I entered my office, nevertheless I strangely felt something superstitious knocking at my heart, and forbidding me to carry out my purpose, and denouncing me for a villain if I dared to breathe one bitter word against this forlornest of mankind. At last, familiarly, drawing my chair behind his screen, I sat down and said: "Bartleby, never mind, then, about revealing your history; but let me entreat you, as a friend, to comply as far as may be with the usages of this office. Say now, you will help to examine papers to-morrow or next day: in short, say now, that in a day or two you will begin to be a little reasonable: — say so, Bartleby."

"At present I would prefer not to be a little reasonable," was his mildly cadaverous reply.

Just then the folding-doors opened, and Nippers approached. He seemed suffering from an unusually bad night's rest, induced by severer indigestion than common. He overheard those final words of Bartleby.

"*Prefer not*, eh?" gritted Nippers — "I'd *prefer* him, if I were you, sir," addressing me — "I'd *prefer* him; I'd give him, preferences, the stubborn mule! What is it, sir, pray, that he *prefers* not to do now?"

Bartleby moved not a limb.

"Mr. Nippers," said I, "I'd prefer that you withdraw for the present."

Somehow, of late, I had got into the way of involuntarily using this word "prefer" upon all sorts of not exactly suitable occasions. And I trembled to think that my contact with the scrivener had already and seriously affected me in a mental way. And what further and deeper aberration might it not yet produce? This apprehension had not been without efficacy in determining me to summary measures.

As Nippers, looking very sour and sulky, was departing, Turkey blandly and deferentially approached.

"With submission, sir," said he, "yesterday I was thinking about Bartleby here, and I think that if he would but prefer to take a quart of good ale every day, it would do much towards mending him, and enabling him to assist in examining his papers."

"So you have got the word, too," said I slightly excited.

"With submission, what word, sir." asked Turkey, respectfully crowding himself into the contracted space behind the screen, and by so doing, making me jostle the scrivener. "What word, sir?"

"I would prefer to be left alone here," said Bartleby, as if offended at being mobbed in his privacy.

"*That's* the word, Turkey," said I — "*that's* it."

"Oh, *prefer*? oh yes — queer word. I never use it myself. But, sir, as I was saying, if he would but prefer —"

"Turkey," interrupted I, "you will please withdraw."

"Oh, certainly, sir, if you prefer that I should."

As he opened the folding-door to retire, Nippers at his desk caught a glimpse of me, and asked whether I would prefer to have a certain paper copied on blue paper or white. He did not in the least roguishly accent the word prefer. It was plain that it involuntarily rolled from his tongue. I thought to myself, surely I must get rid of a demented man, who already has in some degree turned the tongues, if not the heads of myself and clerks. But I thought it prudent not to break the dismission at once.

The next day I noticed that Bartleby did nothing but stand at his window in his dead-wall revery. Upon asking him why he did not write, he said that he had decided upon doing no more writing.

"Why, how now? what next?" exclaimed I, "do no more writing?"

"No more."

"And what is the reason?"

"Do you not see the reason for yourself," he indifferently replied.

I looked steadfastly at him, and perceived that his eyes looked dull and glazed. Instantly it occurred to me, that his unexampled diligence in copying by his dim window for the first few weeks of his stay with me might have temporarily impaired his vision.

I was touched. I said something in condolence with him. I hinted that of course he did wisely in abstaining from writing for a while; and urged him to embrace the opportunity of taking wholesome exercise in the open air. This, however, he did not do. A few days after this, my other clerks being absent, and being in a great hurry to dispatch certain letters by the mail, I thought that, having nothing else earthly to do, Bartleby would surely be less inflexible than usual, and carry these letters to the post-office. But he blankly declined. So, much to my inconvenience, I went myself.

Still added days went by. Whether Bartleby's eyes improved or not, I could not say. To all appearance, I thought they did. But when I asked him if they did, he vouchsafed no answer. At all events, he would do no copying. At last, in reply to my urgings, he informed me that he had permanently given up copying.

"What!" exclaimed I; "suppose your eyes should get entirely well—better than ever before—would you not copy then?"

"I have given up copying," he answered, and slid aside.

He remained as ever, a fixture in my chamber. Nay—if that were possible—he became still more of a fixture than before. What was to be done? He would do nothing in the office; why should he stay there? In plain fact, he had now become a millstone to me, not only useless as a necklace, but afflictive to bear. Yet I was sorry for him. I speak less than truth when I say that, on his own account, he occasioned me uneasiness. If he would but have named a single relative or friend, I would instantly have written, and urged their taking the poor fellow away to some convenient retreat. But he seemed alone, absolutely alone in the universe. A bit of wreck in the mid Atlantic. At length, necessities connected with my business tyrannized over all other considerations. Decently as I could, I told Bartleby that in six days time he must unconditionally leave the office. I warned him to take measures, in the interval, for procuring some other abode. I offered to assist him in this endeavor, if he himself would but take the first step towards a removal. "And when you finally quit me, Bartleby," added I, "I shall see that you go not away entirely unprovided. Six days from this hour, remember."

At the expiration of that period, I peeped behind the screen, and lo! Bartleby was there.

I buttoned up my coat, balanced myself; advanced slowly toward him, touched his shoulder, and said, "The time has come; you must quit this place; I am sorry for you; here is money; but you must go."

"I would prefer not," he replied, with his back still toward me.

"You *must*."

He remained silent.

Now I had an unbounded confidence in this man's common honesty. He had frequently restored to me sixpences and shillings carelessly dropped upon the floor, for I am apt to be very reckless in such shirt-button affairs. The proceeding, then, which followed will not be deemed extraordinary.

"Bartleby," said I, "I owe you twelve dollars on account; here are thirty-two; the odd twenty are yours—Will you take it?" and I handed the bills towards him.

But he made no motion.

"I will leave them here, then," putting them under a weight on the table. Then taking my hat and cane and going to the door, I tranquilly turned and added—"After you have removed your things from these offices, Bartleby, you will of course lock the door—since every one is now gone for the day but you—and if you please, slip your key underneath the mat, so that I may have it in the morning. I shall not see you again; so good-by to you. If, hereafter, in your new place of abode, I can be of any service to you, do not fail to advise me by letter. Good-by, Bartleby, and fare you well."

But he answered not a word; like the last column of some ruined temple, he remained standing mute and solitary in the middle of the otherwise deserted room.

As I walked home in a pensive mood, my vanity got the better of my pity. I could not but highly plume myself on my masterly management in getting rid of Bartleby. Masterly I call it, and such it must appear to any dispassionate thinker. The beauty of my procedure seemed to consist in its perfect quietness. There was no vulgar bullying, no bravado of any sort, no choleric hectoring, and striding to and fro across the apartment, jerking out vehement commands for Bartleby to bundle himself off with his beggarly traps. Nothing of the kind. Without loudly bidding Bartleby depart—as an inferior genius might have done—I *assumed* the ground that depart he must; and upon that assumption built all I had to say.

The more I thought over my procedure, the more I was charmed with it. Nevertheless, next morning, upon awakening, I had my doubts—I had somehow slept off the fumes of vanity. One of the coolest and wisest hours a man has, is just after he awakes in the morning. My procedure seemed as sagacious as ever—but only in theory. How it would prove in practice—there was the rub. It was truly a beautiful thought to have assumed Bartleby's departure; but, after all, that assumption was simply my own, and none of Bartleby's. The great point was, not whether I had assumed that he would quit me, but whether he would prefer so to do. He was more a man of preferences than assumptions.

After breakfast, I walked down town, arguing the probabilities *pro* and *con*. One moment I thought it would prove a miserable failure, and Bartleby would be found all alive at my office as usual; the next moment it seemed certain that I should find his chair empty. And so I kept veering about. At the corner of Broadway and Canal Street, I saw quite an excited group of people standing in earnest conversation.

"I'll take odds he doesn't," said a voice as I passed.

"Doesn't go?—done!" said I, "put up your money."

I was instinctively putting my hand in my pocket to produce my own, when I remembered that this was an election day. The words I had overheard bore no reference to Bartleby, but to the success or non-success of some candidate for the mayoralty. In my intent frame of mind, I had, as it were, imagined that all Broadway shared in my excitement, and were debating the same question with me. I passed on, very thankful that the uproar of the street screened my momentary absent-mindedness.

As I had intended, I was earlier than usual at my office door. I stood listening for a moment. All was still. He must be gone. I tried the knob. The door was locked. Yes, my procedure had worked to a charm; he indeed must be vanished. Yet a certain melancholy mixed with this: I was almost sorry for my brilliant success. I was fumbling under the door mat for the key, which Bartleby was to have left there for me, when accidentally my knee knocked against a panel, producing a summoning sound, and in response a voice came to me from within—"Not yet; I am occupied."

It was Bartleby.

I was thunderstruck. For an instant I stood like the man who, pipe in mouth, was killed one cloudless afternoon long ago in Virginia, by summer lightning; at his own warm open window he was killed, and remained leaning out there upon the dreamy afternoon, till some one touched him, when he fell.

"Not gone!" I murmured at last. But again obeying that wondrous ascendancy which the inscrutable scrivener had over me, and from which ascendancy, for all my chafing, I could not completely escape, I slowly went down stairs and out into the street, and while walking round the block, considered what I should next do in this unheard-of perplexity. Turn the man out by an actual thrusting I could not; to drive him away by calling him hard names would not do; calling in the police was an unpleasant idea; and yet, permit him to enjoy his cadaverous triumph over me — this, too, I could not think of. What was to be done? or, if nothing could be done, was there anything further that I could assume in the matter? Yes, as before I had prospectively assumed that Bartleby would depart, so now I might retrospectively assume that departed he was. In the legitimate carrying out of this assumption, I might enter my office in a great hurry, and pretending not to see Bartleby at all, walk straight against him as if he were air. Such a proceeding would in a singular degree have the appearance of a home-thrust. It was hardly possible that Bartleby could withstand such an application of the doctrine of assumptions. But upon second thoughts the success of the plan seemed rather dubious. I resolved to argue the matter over with him again.

"Bartleby," said I, entering the office, with a quietly severe expression, "I am seriously displeased. I am pained, Bartleby. I had thought better of you. I had imagined you of such a gentlemanly organization, that in any delicate dilemma a slight hint would suffice — in short, an assumption. But it appears I am deceived. Why," I added, unaffectedly starting, "you have not even touched that money yet," pointing to it, just where I had left it the evening previous.

He answered nothing.

"Will you, or will you not, quit me?" I now demanded in a sudden passion, advancing close to him.

"I would prefer *not* to quit you," he replied, gently emphasizing the I.

"What earthly right have you to stay here? Do you pay any rent? Do you pay my taxes? Or is this property yours?"

He answered nothing.

"Are you ready to go on and write now? Are your eyes re-covered? Could you copy a small paper for me this morning? or help examine a few lines? or step round to the post-office? In a word, will you do anything at all, to give a coloring to your refusal to depart the premises?"

He silently retired into his hermitage.

I was now in such a state of nervous resentment that I thought it but prudent to check myself at present from further demonstrations. Bartleby and I were alone. I remembered the tragedy of the unfortunate Adams and the still more unfortunate Colt in the solitary office of the latter; and how poor Colt, being dreadfully incensed by Adams, and imprudently permitting himself to get wildly excited, was at unawares hurried into his fatal act—an act which certainly no man could possibly deplore more than the actor himself. Often it had occurred to me in my pondering upon the subject, that had that altercation taken place in the public street, or at a private residence, it would not have terminated as it did. It was the circumstance of being alone in a solitary office, up stairs, of a building entirely unhallowed by humanizing domestic associations—an uncarpeted office, doubtless, of a dusty, haggard sort of appearance—this it must have been, which greatly helped to enhance the irritable desperation of the hapless Colt.

But when this old Adam of resentment rose in me and tempted me concerning Bartleby, I grappled him and threw him. How? Why, simply by recalling the divine injunction: "A new commandment give I unto you, that ye love one another." Yes, this it was that saved me. Aside from higher considerations, charity often operates as a vastly wise and prudent principle—a great safeguard to its possessor. Men have committed murder for jealousy's sake, and anger's sake, and hatred's sake, and selfishness' sake, and spiritual pride's sake; but no man, that ever I heard of, ever committed a diabolical murder for sweet charity's sake. Mere self-interest, then, if no better motive can be enlisted, should, especially with high-tempered men, prompt all beings to charity and philanthropy. At any rate, upon the occasion in question, I strove to drown my exasperated feelings towards the scrivener by benevolently construing his conduct. Poor fellow, poor fellow! thought I, he don't mean anything; and besides, he has seen hard times, and ought to be indulged.

I endeavored, also, immediately to occupy myself, and at the same time to comfort my despondency. I tried to fancy, that in the course of the morning, at such time as might prove agreeable to him, Bartleby, of his own free accord, would emerge from his hermitage and take up some decided line of march in the direction of the door. But no. Half-past twelve o'clock came; Turkey began to glow in the face, overturn his inkstand, and become generally obstreperous; Nippers abated down into quietude and courtesy; Ginger Nut munched his noon apple; and Bartleby remained standing at his window in one of his profoundest dead-wall reveries. Will it be credited? Ought I to acknowledge it? That afternoon I left the office without saying one further word to him.

Some days now passed, during which, at leisure intervals I looked a little into "Edwards on the Will," and "Priestly on Necessity." Under the circumstances, those books induced a salutary feeling. Gradually I slid into the persuasion that these troubles of mine, touching the scrivener, had been all predestinated from eternity, and Bartleby was billeted upon me for some mysterious purpose of an allwise Providence, which it was not for a mere mortal like me to fathom. Yes, Bartleby, stay there behind your screen, thought I; I shall persecute you no more; you are harmless and noiseless as any of these old chairs; in short, I never feel so private as when I know you are here. At last I see it, I feel it; I penetrate to the predestinated purpose of my life. I am content. Others may have loftier parts to enact; but my mission in this world, Bartleby, is to furnish you with office-room for such period as you may see fit to remain.

I believe that this wise and blessed frame of mind would have continued with me, had it not been for the unsolicited and uncharitable remarks obtruded upon me by my professional friends who visited the rooms. But thus it often is, that the constant friction of illiberal minds wears out at last the best resolves of the more generous. Though to be sure, when I reflected upon it, it was not strange that people entering my office should be struck by the peculiar aspect of the unaccountable Bartleby, and so be tempted to throw out some sinister observations concerning him. Sometimes an attorney, having business with me, and calling at my office, and finding no one but the scrivener there, would undertake to obtain some sort of precise information from him touching my whereabouts; but without heeding his idle talk, Bartleby would remain standing immovable in the middle of the room. So after contemplating him in that position for a time, the attorney would depart, no wiser than he came.

Also, when a Reference was going on, and the room full of lawyers and witnesses, and business driving fast, some deeply-occupied legal gentleman present, seeing Bartleby wholly unemployed, would request him to run round to his (the legal gentleman's) office and fetch some papers for him. Thereupon, Bartleby would tranquilly decline, and yet remain idle as before. Then the lawyer would give a great stare, and turn to me. And what could I say? At last I was made aware that all through the circle of my professional acquaintance, a whisper of wonder was running round, having references to the strange creature I kept at my office. This worried me very much. And as the idea came upon me of his possibly turning out a long-lived man, and keep occupying my chambers, and denying my authority; and perplexing my visitors; and scandalizing my professional reputation; and casting a general gloom over the premises; keeping soul and body together to the last upon his savings (for doubtless he spent but half a dime a day), and in the end perhaps outlive me, and claim possession of my office by right of his perpetual occupancy: as all these dark anticipations crowded upon me more and more, and my friends continually intruded their relentless remarks upon the apparition in my room; a great change was wrought in me. I resolved to gather all my faculties together, and forever rid me of this intolerable incubus.

Ere revolving any complicated project, however, adapted to this end, I first simply suggested to Bartleby the propriety of his permanent departure. In a calm and serious tone, I commended the idea to his careful and mature consideration, but, having taken three days to meditate upon it, he apprised me, that his original determination remained the same; in short, that he still preferred to abide with me.

What shall I do? I now said to myself, buttoning up my coat to the last button. What shall I do? what ought I to do? what does conscience say I *should* do with this man, or, rather, ghost. Rid myself of him, I must; go, he shall. But how? You will not thrust him, the poor, pale, passive mortal—you will not thrust such a helpless creature out of your door? you will not dishonor yourself by such cruelty? No, I will not, I cannot do that. Rather would I let him live and die here, and then mason up his remains in the wall. What, then, will you do? For all your coaxing, he will not budge. Bribes he leaves under your own paper-weight on your table; in short, it is quite plain that he prefers to cling to you.

Then something severe, something unusual must be done. What! surely you will not have him collared by a constable, and commit his innocent pallor to the common jail? And upon what ground could you procure such a thing to be done?—a vagrant, is he? What! he a vagrant, a wanderer, who refuses to budge? It is because he will not be a vagrant, then, that you seek to count him as a vagrant. That is too absurd. No visible means of support: there I have him. Wrong again: for indubitably he *does* support himself, and that is the only unanswerable proof that any man can show of his possessing the means so to do. No more, then. Since he will not quit me, I must quit him. I will change my offices; I will move elsewhere, and give him fair notice, that if I find him on my new premises I will then proceed against him as a common trespasser.

Acting accordingly, next day I thus addressed him: "I find these chambers too far from the City Hall; the air is unwholesome. In a word, I propose to remove my offices next week, and shall no longer require your services. I tell you this now, in order that you may seek another place."

He made no reply, and nothing more was said.

On the appointed day I engaged carts and men, proceeded to my chambers, and, having but little furniture, everything was removed in a few hours. Throughout, the scrivener remained standing behind the screen, which I directed to be removed the last thing. It was withdrawn; and, being folded up like a huge folio, left him the motionless occupant of a naked room. I stood in the entry watching him a moment, while something from within me upbraided me.

I re-entered, with my hand in my pocket — and — and my heart in my mouth.

"Good-by, Bartleby; I am going — good-by, and God some way bless you; and take that," slipping something in his hand. But it dropped upon the floor, and then — strange to say — I tore myself from him whom I had so longed to be rid of.

Established in my new quarters, for a day or two I kept the door locked, and started at every footfall in the passages. When I returned to my rooms, after any little absence, I would pause at the threshold for an instant, and attentively listen, ere applying my key. But these fears were needless. Bartleby never came nigh me.

I thought all was going well, when a perturbed-looking stranger visited me, inquiring whether I was the person who had recently occupied rooms at No. — Wall Street.

Full of forebodings, I replied that I was.

"Then, sir," said the stranger, who proved a lawyer, "you are responsible for the man you left there. He refuses to do any copying; he refuses to do anything; he says he prefers not to; and he refuses to quit the premises."

"I am very sorry, sir," said I, with assumed tranquillity, but an inward tremor, "but, really, the man you allude to is nothing to me — he is no relation or apprentice of mine, that you should hold me responsible for him."

"In mercy's name, who is he?"

"I certainly cannot inform you. I know nothing about him. Formerly I employed him as a copyist; but he has done nothing for me now for some time past."

"I shall settle him, then — good morning, sir."

Several days passed, and I heard nothing more; and, though I often felt a charitable prompting to call at the place and see poor Bartleby, yet a certain squeamishness, of I know not what, withheld me.

All is over with him, by this time, thought I, at last, when, through another week, no further intelligence reached me. But, coming to my room the day after, I found several persons waiting at my door in a high state of nervous excitement.

"That's the man — here he comes," cried the foremost one, whom I recognized as the lawyer who had previously called upon me alone.

"You must take him away, sir, at once," cried a portly person among them, advancing upon me, and whom I knew to be the landlord of No. — Wall Street. "These gentlemen, my tenants, cannot stand it any longer; Mr. B——," pointing to the lawyer, "has turned him out of his room, and he now persists in haunting the building generally, sitting upon the banisters of the stairs by day, and sleeping in the entry by night. Everybody is concerned; clients are leaving the offices; some fears are entertained of a mob; something you must do, and that without delay."

Aghast at this torrent, I fell back before it, and would fain have locked myself in my new quarters. In vain I persisted that Bartleby was nothing to me—no more than to any one else. In vain—I was the last person known to have anything to do with him, and they held me to the terrible account. Fearful, then, of being exposed in the papers (as one person present obscurely threatened), I considered the matter, and, at length, said, that if the lawyer would give me a confidential interview with the scrivener, in his (the lawyer's) own room, I would, that afternoon, strive my best to rid them of the nuisance they complained of.

Going up stairs to my old haunt, there was Bartleby silently sitting upon the banister at the landing.

"What are you doing here, Bartleby?" said I.

"Sitting upon the banister," he mildly replied.

I motioned him into the lawyer's room, who then left us.

"Bartleby," said I, "are you aware that you are the cause of great tribulation to me, by persisting in occupying the entry after being dismissed from the office?"

No answer.

"Now one of two things must take place. Either you must do something, or something must be done to you. Now what sort of business would you like to engage in? Would you like to reengage in copying for some one?"

"No; I would prefer not to make any change."

"Would you like a clerkship in a dry-goods store?"

"There is too much confinement about that. No, I would not like a clerkship; but I am not particular."

"Too much confinement," I cried, "why you keep yourself confined all the time!"

"I would prefer not to take a clerkship," he rejoined, as if to settle that little item at once.

"How would a bar-tender's business suit you? There is no trying of the eye-sight in that."

"I would not like it at all; though, as I said before, I am not particular."

His unwonted wordiness inspirited me. I returned to the charge.

"Well, then, would you like to travel through the country collecting bills for the merchants? That would improve your health."

"No, I would prefer to be doing something else."

"How, then, would going as a companion to Europe, to entertain some young gentleman with your conversation—how would that suit you?"

"Not at all. It does not strike me that there is anything definite about that. I like to be stationary. But I am not particular."

"Stationary you shall be, then," I cried, now losing all patience, and, for the first time in all my exasperating connection with him, fairly flying into a passion. "If you do not go away from these premises before night, I shall feel bound—indeed, I *am* bound—to—to—to quit the premises myself!" I rather absurdly concluded, knowing not with what possible threat to try to frighten his immobility into compliance. Despairing of all further efforts, I was precipitately leaving him, when a final thought occurred to me—one which had not been wholly unindulged before.

"Bartleby," said I, in the kindest tone I could assume under such exciting circumstances, "will you go home with me now—not to my office, but my dwelling—and remain there till we can conclude upon some convenient arrangement for you at our leisure? Come, let us start now, right away."

"No: at present I would prefer not to make any change at all."

I answered nothing; but, effectually dodging every one by the suddenness and rapidity of my flight, rushed from the building, ran up Wall Street towards Broadway, and jumping into the first omnibus, was soon removed from pursuit. As soon as tranquillity returned, I distinctly perceived that I had now done all that I possibly could, both in respect to the demands of the landlord and his tenants, and with regard to my own desire and sense of duty, to benefit Bartleby, and shield him from rude persecution. I now strove to be entirely care-free and quiescent; and my conscience justified me in the attempt; though, indeed, it was not so successful as I could have wished. So fearful was I of being again hunted out by the incensed landlord and his exasperated tenants, that, surrendering my business to Nippers, for a few days, I drove about the upper part of the town and through the suburbs, in my rockaway; crossed over to Jersey City and Hoboken, and paid fugitive visits to Manhattan-ville and Astoria. In fact, I almost lived in my rockaway for the time.

When again I entered my office, lo, a note from the landlord lay upon the desk. I opened it with trembling hands. It informed me that the writer had sent to the police, and had Bartleby removed to the Tombs as a vagrant. Moreover, since I knew more about him than any one else, he wished me to appear at that place, and make a suitable statement of the facts. These tidings had a conflicting effect upon me. At first I was indignant; but, at last, almost approved. The landlord's energetic, summary disposition, had led him to adopt a procedure which I do not think I would have decided upon myself; and yet, as a last resort, under such peculiar circumstances, it seemed the only plan.

As I afterwards learned, the poor scrivener, when told that he must be conducted to the Tombs, offered not the slightest obstacle, but, in his pale, unmoving way, silently acquiesced.

Some of the compassionate and curious bystanders joined the party; and headed by one of the constables arm in arm with Bartleby, the silent procession filed its way through all the noise, and heat, and joy of the roaring thoroughfares at noon.

The same day I received the note, I went to the Tombs, or, to speak more properly, the Halls of Justice. Seeking the right officer, I stated the purpose of my call, and was informed that the individual I described was, indeed, within. I then assured the functionary that Bartleby was a perfectly honest man, and greatly to be compassionated, however, unaccountably eccentric. I narrated all I knew, and closed by suggesting the idea of letting him remain in as indulgent confinement as possible, till something less harsh might be done — though, indeed, I hardly knew what. At all events, if nothing else could be decided upon, the alms-house must receive him. I then begged to have an interview.

Being under no disgraceful charge, and quite serene and harmless in all his ways, they had permitted him freely to wander about the prison, and, especially, in the inclosed grass-platted yards thereof. And so I found him there, standing all alone in the quietest of the yards, his face towards a high wall, while all around, from the narrow slits of the jail windows, I thought I saw peering out upon him the eyes of murderers and thieves.

"Bartleby!"

"I know you," he said, without looking round — "and I want nothing to say to you."

"It was not I that brought you here, Bartleby," said I, keenly pained at his implied suspicion. "And to you, this should not be so vile a place. Nothing reproachful attaches to you by being here. And see, it is not so sad a place as one might think. Look, there is the sky, and here is the grass."

"I know where I am," he replied, but would say nothing more, and so I left him.

As I entered the corridor again, a broad meat-like man, in an apron, accosted me, and, jerking his thumb over his shoulder, said — "Is that your friend?"

"Yes."

"Does he want to starve? If he does, let him live on the prison fare, that's all."

"Who are you?" asked I, not knowing what to make of such an unofficially speaking person in such a place.

"I am the grub-man. Such gentlemen as have friends here, hire me to provide them with something good to eat."

"Is this so?" said I, turning to the turnkey.

He said it was.

"Well, then," said I, slipping some silver into the grub-man's hands (for so they called him), "I want you to give particular attention to my friend there; let him have the best dinner you can get. And you must be as polite to him as possible."

"Introduce me, will you?" said the grub-man, looking at me with an expression which seemed to say he was all impatience for an opportunity to give a specimen of his breeding.

Thinking it would prove of benefit to the scrivener, I acquiesced; and, asking the grub-man his name, went up with him to Bartleby.

"Bartleby, this is a friend; you will find him very useful to you."

"Your sarvant, sir, your sarvant," said the grub-man, making a low salutation behind his apron. "Hope you find it pleasant her, sir; nice grounds — cool apartments — hope you'll stay with us sometime — try to make it agreeable. What will you have for dinner to-day?"

"I prefer not to dine to-day;" said Bartleby, turning away. "It would disagree with me; I am unused to dinners." So saying, he slowly moved to the other side of the inclosure, and took up a position fronting the dead-wall.

"How's this?" said the grub-man, addressing me with a stare of astonishment. "He's odd, ain't he?"

"I think he is a little deranged," said I, sadly.

"Deranged? deranged is it? Well, now, upon my word, I thought that friend of yourn was a gentleman forger; they are always pale and genteel-like, them forgers. I can't help pity 'em — can't help it, sir. Did you know Monroe Edwards?" he added, touchingly, and paused. Then, laying his hand piteously on my shoulder, sighed, "he died of consumption at Sing-Sing. So you weren't acquainted with Monroe?"

"No, I was never socially acquainted with any forgers. But I cannot stop longer. Look to my friend yonder. You will not lose by it. I will see you again."

Some few days after this, I again obtained admission to the Tombs, and went through the corridors in quest of Bartleby; but without finding him.

"I saw him coming from his cell not long ago," said a turnkey, "may be he's gone to loiter in the yards."

So I went in that direction.

"Are you looking for the silent man?" said another turnkey, passing me. "Yonder he lies — sleeping in the yard there. 'Tis not twenty minutes since I saw him lie down."

The yard was entirely quiet. It was not accessible to the common prisoners. The surrounding walls, of amazing thickness, kept off all sounds behind them. The Egyptian character of the masonry weighed upon me with its gloom. But a soft imprisoned turf grew under foot. The heart of the eternal pyramids, it seemed, wherein, by some strange magic, through the clefts, grass-seed, dropped by birds, had sprung.

Strangely huddled at the base of the wall, his knees drawn up, and lying on his side, his head touching the cold stones, I saw the wasted Bartleby. But nothing stirred. I paused; then went close up to him; stooped over, and saw that his dim eyes were open; otherwise he seemed profoundly sleeping. Something prompted me to touch him. I felt his hand, when a tingling shiver ran up my arm and down my spine to my feet.

The round face of the grub-man peered upon me now. "His dinner is ready. Won't he dine to-day, either? Or does he live without dining?"

"Lives without dining," said I, and closed the eyes.

"Eh! — He's asleep, ain't he?"

"With kings and counselors," murmured I.

There would seem little need for proceeding further in this history. Imagination will readily supply the meagre recital of poor Bartleby's interment. But, ere parting with the reader, let me say, that if this little narrative has sufficiently interested him, to awaken curiosity as to who Bartleby was, and what manner of life he led prior to the present narrator's making his acquaintance, I can only reply, that in such curiosity I fully share, but am wholly unable to gratify it. Yet here I hardly know whether I should divulge one little item of rumor, which came to my ear a few months after the scrivener's decease. Upon what basis it rested, I could never ascertain; and hence, how true it is I cannot now tell. But, inasmuch as this vague report has not been without a certain suggestive interest to me, however sad, it may prove the same with some others; and so I will briefly mention it. The report was this: that Bartleby had been a subordinate clerk in the Dead Letter Office at Washington, from which he had been suddenly removed by a change in the administration. When I think over this rumor, hardly can I express the emotions which seize me. Dead letters! does it not sound like dead men? Conceive a man by nature and misfortune prone to a pallid hopelessness, can any business seem more fitted to heighten it than that of continually handling these dead letters, and assorting them for the flames? For by the cart-load they are annually burned. Sometimes from out the folded paper the pale clerk takes a ring — the finger it was meant for, perhaps, moulders in the grave; a bank-note sent in swiftest charity—he whom it would relieve, nor eats nor hungers any more; pardon for those who died despairing; hope for those who died unhoping; good tidings for those who died stifled by unrelieved calamities. On errands of life, these letters speed to death.

Ah, Bartleby! Ah, humanity!

Discussion Topics

1. The fact that "Bartleby ..." is widely read in high schools and colleges does not mean it is widely understood. Critics offer a smorgasbord of interpretations. Here are some possibilities.

   a. A simple one and unsatisfying one is that Bartleby is crazy, or at least suicidally depressive. No modern reader can quite avoid thinking this. But the story would hardly have the fascination it does if that were all.

   b. All of us have goals that we pursue with our best efforts, and all of us meet immovable objects that we cannot affect. This happens in relations with others as it does in impersonal contexts. For the narrator, Bartleby represents that kind of frustration. All efforts leave him untouched.

   c. A point somewhat different from (b) is that we all have experiences that we cannot begin to *comprehend*. Having an effect in these situations is beside the point. We cannot even fathom or explain what is happening. Certainly this too reflects what the narrator feels about Bartleby.

   d. The law in particular claims to be a tool for organizing and controlling experience. The narrator is an experienced practitioner of the law. But none of his special skills begins to equip him to handle Bartleby. Does Bartleby reflect the limits of law?

   All of these theories are easily supported by the events of the story. But in the face of each and all of them, it remains a puzzle.

2. At an important juncture in developing his theories of psychology, Freud claimed that there were two conflicting impulses in human experience and motivation, the impulse to live and flourish (*eros*) and the anti-life impulse to destroy oneself (*thanatos*). Everything we do is the resolution of these conflicting forces, and our lives are an unending effort to ward off the death instinct, the impulse to self-destruction.

Consider Bartleby's employment in the dead letter office. Can it be argued that Melville anticipates Freud and that Bartleby is the embodiment of the death instinct? He wills his own self-annihilation. He "prefers not" to do any of things that would give his life meaning, that would change his fate. Paradoxically, this even extends to refraining from *actively* taking his own life. Only passive suicide is possible.

The last lines of the story convey that we are all like Bartleby, that death in the end overcomes us all.

3. Why do Turkey and Nippers begin to mimic Bartleby? Is there a bit of Bartleby that seeps into all of them? Are they beginning to express their own "preferences"? Notwithstanding other theories (above), is Bartleby's expression of his preferences a kind of freedom? Is he autonomous in a way to which the other characters aspire but can hardly imagine?

4. In his introductory remarks to a law and literature symposium at University of New Mexico Law School (31 *New Mexico Law Review* 67 (2001)), Scott Turow, the lawyer and novelist, cited "Bartleby" as a favorite work. Turow sees the story as an attempt by Melville to ridicule his father-in-law's efforts, as Massachusetts chief justice, to put forward a rule of negligence whereby a tort plaintiff may not prevail unless he can show he acted with reasonable care. For Turow, we have a "disquieting sense that justice has not been done when this harmless, inoffensive man [Bartleby] ends up dead in the New York Tombs." Melville, according to Turow, questions whether we can "ever do justice in the individual case" if we fail "to understand each other's motives."

5. Alfred Konefsky, in the article cited above, concludes that Bartleby is challenging the traditional hierarchy and employment relationship between lawyers and their workers. "The lawyer has made the mistake of assuming that a workplace functioned in a predictable, ordered way. Bartleby apparently prefers not to believe that the office ought to function in any particular way. As a result, the lawyer is forced to concede Bartleby's success in reversing the traditional hierarchy and dependence; he is now aware that he is once 'again obeying the wondrous ascendancy which the inscrutable scrivener had over me'."

Other critics have also seen Bartleby as having a social and political agenda in challenging the lawyer. In other words, Marxist readings of the story are not unknown. Do you find this political kind of reading plausible?

6. It is possible to look back on law practice in Melville's time with nostalgia for its predictability and ease or with distress at its dullness. Consider the aspects of law practice reflected in Bartleby in comparison with the roughly contemporary pictures offered in the first chapter readings by Salter, Ozick, and Just.

Guiseppe di Lampedusa: Joy and the Law

Literary history is full of major/minor writers who were at odds with their time and place. Guiseppe Tomasi di Lampedusa (1896-1957) was a Sicilian landowner and aristocrat who was torn between the ideals of life in the various city-states that existed before the unification of Italy and life among free-thinking cosmopolitan intellectuals of Europe and especially England. He is best known for his monumental and internationally popular novel, *The Leopard (Il Gattopardo)*, published two years after his death from lung cancer. An international success, *The Leopard* became a well-reviewed movie in 1963. The novel covers the fate of Italy's aristocracy between 1860 and 1910; its critique of the unification movement is seen both as a veiled account of his own family and as a symbolic response to Mussolini's nationalist-fascist movement.

Di Lampedusa wrote little during his life, publishing only three essays. His life was that of wealthy aristocrat and gentleman farmer. He spent much of his life abroad. Among his posthumous publications are a few short stories. "Joy and the Law," which is said to be widely read in Italian secondary schools, is atypical of his writings, concerned not with the aristocracy or large social movements but with a working-class accountant and his family. Again, law seems initially to be tangential to the story. But, again, if law is seen as implicit in the creation and maintenance of social structure and social class, the story turns out to be significantly about law.

❧ Joy and the Law ❧

Guiseppe di Lampedusa

When he got into the bus he irritated everyone.

The briefcase crammed with other people's business, the enormous parcel which made his left arm stick out, the grey velvet scarf, the umbrella on the point of opening, all made it difficult for him to produce his return ticket. He was forced to put his parcel on the ticket collector's bench, setting off an avalanche of small coins; as he tried to bend down to pick them up, he provoked protests from those who stood behind him, who feared that because of his dallying their coats would be caught in the automatic doors. At last he managed to squeeze into the row of people clinging to the handles in the gangway. He was slight of build, but his bundles gave him the cubic capacity of a nun in seven habits. As the bus slid through the chaos of the traffic, his inconvenient bulk spread resentment from front to rear of the coach. He stepped on people's feet, they trod on his; he invited rebuke, and when he heard the word cornuto from the rear of the bus alluding to his presumed marital disgrace, his sense of honor compelled him to turn his head in that direction and make his exhausted eyes assume what he imagined to be a threatening expression.

The bus, meanwhile, was passing through streets where rustic baroque fronts hid a wretched hinterland which emerged at each street corner in the yellow light of eighty-year-old shops.

At his stop he rang the bell, descended, tripped over the umbrella, and found himself alone at last on his square meter of disconnected footpath. He hastened to make sure that he still had his plastic wallet. And then he was free to relish his bliss.

Enclosed in that wallet were 37,245 lire — the "thirteenth monthly salary" received as a Christmas bonus an hour before. This sum meant the removal of several thorns from his flesh: the obligations to his landlord, all the more pressing because his was a controlled rent and he owed two quarters; and to the ever-punctual installment collector for the short lapin coat ("It suits you better than a long coat, my dear — it makes you look slimmer"); the dirty looks from the fishmonger and the greengrocer. Those four bank notes of high denomination also eased the fear of the next electricity bill, the pained glances at the children's shoes, and the anxious watching of the gas cylinder's flickering flame; they did not represent opulence, certainly, but did give that breathing space in distress which is the true joy of the poor; a couple of thousand lire might survive for a while, before being eaten up in the resplendence of a Christmas dinner.

However, he had known too many "thirteenths" to attribute the euphoria which now enveloped him to the ephemeral exhilaration they could produce. He was filled with a rosy feeling, as rosy as the wrapping on the sweet burden that was making his left arm numb. The feeling sprang from the seven-kilo Christmas cake, the panettone that he had brought home from the office. He had no passion for the mixture — as highly guaranteed as it was questionable — of flour, sugar, dried eggs and raisins. At heart he did not care for it at all. But seven kilos of luxury food all at once! A limited but vast abundance in a household where provisions came in hectograms and half-liters! A famous product in a larder devoted to third-rate items! What a joy for Maria! What a riot for the children who for two weeks would explore the unknown Wild West of an afternoon snack!

These, however, were the joys of others, the material joys of vanilla essence and colored cardboard; of panettone, in sum. His personal joy was different—a spiritual bliss based on pride and loving affection; yes, spiritual!

When, a few hours before, the baronet who was managing director of his firm had distributed pay envelopes and Christmas wishes with the overbearing affability of the pompous old man that he was, he also announced that the seven-kilo panettone, which had come with the compliments of the big firm that produced it, would be awarded to the most deserving employee; and he asked his dear colleagues democratically (that was the word he had actually used) to choose the lucky man then and there.

The panettone had stood on the middle of the desk, heavy, hermetically sealed, "laden with good omens" as the same baronet, dressed in Fascist uniform, would have said in Mussolini's phrase twenty years before. There was laughing and whispering among the employees; and then everyone, the managing director first, shouted his name. A great satisfaction; a guarantee that he would keep his job—in short, a triumph. Nothing that followed could lessen the tonic effect; neither the three hundred lire that he had to pay in the coffee bar below, treating his friends in the twofold dusk of a squally sunset and dim neon lights, nor the weight of his trophy, nor the unpleasant comments in the bus—nothing; not even the lightning flash from the depths of his consciousness that it had all been an act of rather condescending pity from his fellow-employees: he was really too poor to permit the weed of pride to sprout where it had no business to appear.

He turned toward home across a decrepit street to which the bombardments of fifteen years previously had given the finishing touches, and finally reached the grim little square in the depths of which the ghostly edifice in which he lived stood tucked away.

He heartily greeted Cosimo, the porter, who despised him because he knew that his salary was lower than his own. Nine steps, three steps, nine steps: the floor where Cavaliere Tizio lived. Pooh! He did have a Fiat 1100, true enough, but he also had an old, ugly and dissolute wife. Nine steps, three steps—a slip almost made him fall—nine steps: young Sempronio's apartment; worse still!—a bone-idle lad, mad on Lambrettas and Vespas, whose hall was still unfurnished. Nine steps, three steps, nine steps: his own apartment, the little abode of a beloved, honest and honored man, a prize-winner, a book-keeper beyond compare.

He opened the door and entered the narrow hall, already filled with the heavy smell of onion soup. He placed the weighty parcel, the briefcase loaded with other people's affairs, and his muffler on a little locker the size of a hamper. His voice rang out: "Maria! Come quickly! Come and see—what a beauty!"

His wife came out of the kitchen in a blue housecoat spotted with grime from saucepans; her little hands, still red from washing up, rested on a belly deformed by pregnancies. The children with their slimy noses crowded around the rose-colored sight and squealed without daring to touch it.

"Oh good! Did you bring your pay back? I haven't a single lira left."

"Here it is, dear. I'll only keep the small change—245 lire. But look at this grace of God here!"

Maria had been pretty; until a few years previously she had had a cheeky little face and whimsical eyes. But the wrangles with the shopkeepers had made her voice grow harsh, the poor food had ruined her complexion, the incessant peering into a future clouded with problems had spent the luster of her eyes. Only the soul of a saint survived within her, inflexible and bereft of tenderness; deep-seated virtue expressing itself in rebukes and restrictions; and in addition a repressed but persistent pride of class because she was the granddaughter of a big hatter in one of the main streets, and despised the origins of her Girolamo—whom she adored as a silly but beloved child—because they were inferior to her own.

Indifferently her eyes ran over the gilded cardboard box. "That's fine. Tomorrow we'll send it to Signor Risma, the solicitor; we're under such an obligation to him!"

Two years previously this solicitor had given him a complicated book-keeping job to do, and over and above paying for it, had invited both of them to lunch in his abstract-and-metal apartment. The clerk had suffered acutely from the shoes bought specially for the occasion. And he and his Maria, his Andrea, his Saverio, his little Josephine were now to give up the only seam of abundance they had hit in many, many years, for that lawyer who had everything.

He ran to the kitchen, grabbed a knife, and rushed to cut the gold string that a deft working girl in Milan had beautifully tied around the wrapping paper; but a reddened hand wearily touched his shoulder. "Girolamo, don't behave like a child—you know we have to repay Risma's kindness."

The law had spoken: the law laid down by unblemished hat-shop owners.

"But dear, this is a prize, an award of merit, a token of esteem!"

"Don't say that. Nice people, those colleagues of yours, with their tender feelings! It was alms-giving, Giro, nothing but alms-giving." She called him by his old pet name, and smiled at him with eyes that only for him still held traces of the old spell. "Tomorrow

I'll buy a little panettone, just big enough for us, and four of those twisted red candles from Standa's — that'll make a fine feast!"

The next day he bought an undistinguished miniature panettone, and not four but two of the astonishing candles; through a delivery agency, at a cost of another two hundred lire, he forwarded the mammoth cake to the solicitor Risma.

After Christmas he had to buy a third panettone which, disguised by slicing, he took to his colleagues who were teasing him because they hadn't been offered a morsel of the sumptuous trophy.

A smoke screen enveloped the fate of the original cake. He went to the Lightning Delivery Agency to make enquiries. With disdain he was shown the receipts book which the solicitor's manservant had signed upside down. However, just after Twelfth Night a visiting card arrived "with sincerest thanks and best wishes."

Honor was saved.

Discussion Topics

1. The only lawyer in the story is Signor Risma, who is offstage. The law that di Lampedusa has in mind, the law that rules the life of Girolamo and Maria, is not the legal code but the code of honor. Short as it is, the story has a complex message about how a sense of honor has shaped the family and its expectations. Consider the attitude that Maria takes toward her social responsibilities and her place in society. How does that attitude affect her life, her husband, her children? Why does she cling to this sense of honor? What would her life and the life of those around her be like without it?

2. Irony is a major element of the story, as is gentle humor. Di Lampedusa does not see Girolamo as quite the fool that others do, but he is still hapless. Maria's adherence to honor ironically keeps the family from experiencing some of the joys that might come with a less stringent set of rules. But the trade-off might, in this context, be a loss for her of self-respect and self-image.

3. We saw that Melville is implicitly concerned with social class and hierarchy. Social gradations are also much on di Lampedusa's mind. The gap between Risma and Girolamo's family is such that Maria sees the lawyer's home and life much as the ancient Greeks might have seen the gods on Mount Olympus. Does the legal profession cultivate this kind of exclusivity and thrive on social precedence? On the other hand, do lawyers have a social responsibility to create an egalitarian society?

Law, Reason, Meaning

Franz Kafka: Before the Law

Franz Kafka (1883-1924) is one of the towering figures of twentieth-century literature. He grew up in Prague in a middle-class German-speaking Jewish family. He is famous for living a tortured life of anxiety and self-doubt; his lifelong battle with tuberculosis, from which he died, was complicated by psychogenic symptoms of many kinds. His overbearing father was an inescapable presence, and his struggles over his personal commitments to women have become legendary.

Kafka received his degree as Doctor of Law from Charles University (Prague) in l906. He eventually settled into long-term employment with the Workers' Accident Insurance Institute for the Kingdom of Bohemia. His day job allowed him to write fiction — most of which he was unwilling to publish. At his death, he instructed Max Brod, his lifelong friend and executor, to destroy his unpublished manuscripts. The rest, as one says, is history. Brod disregarded this wish and Kafka's works, including the novels *The Castle* and *The Trial*, have become among the most influential writings in twentieth-century literature.

Among Kafka's stories are several parables about law. Their meaning is elusive, even if it is evident that they present law obsessively as central to individual lives. Law, for Kafka, is closely tied to our self-understanding and our pursuit of life's meaning. Each parable admits of many interpretations; each is an opportunity to stretch your imagination and exercise interpretive skills.

❦ Before the Law ❦

Franz Kafka

Before the Law stands a doorkeeper. To this doorkeeper there comes a man from the country and prays for admittance to the Law. But the doorkeeper says that he cannot grant admittance at the moment." The man thinks it over and then asks if he will be allowed in later. "It is possible," says the doorkeeper, "but not at the moment." Since the gate stands open, as usual, and the doorkeeper steps to one side, the man stoops to peer through the gateway into the interior. Observing that, the doorkeeper laughs and says: "If you are so drawn to it, just try to go in despite my veto. But take note: I am powerful. And I am only the least of the doorkeepers. From hall to hall there is one doorkeeper after another, each more powerful than the last. The third doorkeeper is already so terrible that even I cannot bear to look at him." These are difficulties the man from the country has not expected; the Law, he thinks, should surely be accessible at all times and to everyone, but as he now takes a closer look at the doorkeeper in his fur coat, with his big sharp nose and long, thin, black Tartar beard, he decides that it is better to wait until he gets permission to enter. The doorkeeper gives him a stool and lets him sit down at one side of the door. There he sits for days and years. He makes many attempts to be admitted, and wearies the doorkeeper by his importunity. The doorkeeper frequently has little interviews with him, asking him questions about his home and many other things, but the questions are put indifferently, as great lords put them, and always finish with the statement that he cannot be let in yet. The man, who has furnished himself with many things for his journey, sacrifices all he has, however valuable, to bribe the doorkeeper. The doorkeeper accepts everything, but always with the remark: "I am only taking it to keep you from thinking you may have omitted anything." During these many years the man fixes his attention almost continuously on the doorkeeper. He forgets the other doorkeepers, and this first one seems to him the sole obstacle preventing access to the Law. He curses his bad luck, in his early years boldly and loudly; later, as he grows old, he only grumbles to himself. He becomes childish, and since in his yearlong contemplation of the doorkeeper he has come to know even the fleas in his fur collar, he begs the fleas as well to help him and to change the doorkeeper's mind. At length his eyesight begins to fail, and he does not know whether the world is really darker or whether his eyes are only deceiving him. Yet in his darkness he is now aware of a radiance that streams inextinguishably from the gateway of the Law. Now he has not very long to live. Before he dies, all his experiences in these long years gather themselves in his head to one point, a question he has not yet asked the doorkeeper. He waves him nearer, since he can no longer raise his stiffening body. The doorkeeper has to bend low toward him, for the difference in height between them has altered much to the man's disadvantage. "What do you want to know now?" asks the doorkeeper; "you are insatiable!" "Everyone strives to reach the Law," says the man, "so how does it happen that for all these many years no one but myself has ever begged for admittance?" The doorkeeper recognizes that the man has reached his end, and, to let his failing senses catch the words, roars in his ear: "No one else could ever be admitted here, since this gate was made only for you. I am now going to shut it."

Discussion Topics

1. What are the aims of "the man from the country"? What does "admittance to the Law" mean to him? Not surprisingly, one's first thought might be that he is trying to be admitted to the bar or that he is trying to win a case but that the complexities of law defy him.

A parable typically suggests a universal truth. But trying and failing to become a member of the bar is clearly not the plight of most attorneys, nor do most claimants spend their lives pursuing one discrete cause. Moreover, if we look at other details, the notion that the door and the doorkeeper exist only for this man and the strong suggestion that his project is doomed *ab initio*, we may move to a broader interpretation.

The story forces us to consider what project or quest can be the dominant, all-consuming project of a person's life. To raise the question is to invite religious and philosophical notions about the unity and meaning of life. If that is Kafka's aim, why does he use "law" to symbolize that search? And how does he think such a search must conclude?

2. The details of the story are seductive. Note that there is not one door, but a series. And yet the man from the country cannot even gain admittance to the first. Note that the doorkeeper teases him with the prospect of passing through and that he imagines himself coming close. A short work such as this underlines the fact that no detail of a work of fiction is entirely accidental, that we can always ask why the author, why Kafka, chose to tell us *this*.

Franz Kafka: An Imperial Message

The following story is usually printed with "Before the Law" and complements it in its content.

❧ An Imperial Message ❧

Franz Kafka

The emperor, so a parable runs, has sent a message to you, the humble subject, the insignificant shadow cowering in the remotest distance before the imperial sun; the Emperor from his death bed has sent a message to you alone. He has commanded the messenger to kneel down by the bed, and has whispered the message to him; so much store did he lay on it that he ordered the messenger to whisper it back into his ear again. Then by a nod of the head he has confirmed that it is right. Yes, before the assembled spectators of his death—all the obstructing walls have been broken down, and on the spacious and loftily mounting open staircases stand in a ring the great princes of the Empire — before all these he has delivered his message. The messenger immediately sets out on his journey; a powerful, an indefatigable man; now pushing with his right arm, now with his left, he cleaves a way for himself through the throng; if he encounters resistance he points to his breast, where the symbol of the sun glitters; the way is made easier for him than it would be for any other man. But the multitudes are so vast; their numbers have no end. If he could reach the open fields how fast he would fly, and soon doubtless you would hear the welcome hammering of his fists on your door. But instead how vainly does he wear out his strength; still he is only making his way through the chambers of the innermost palace; never will he get to the end of them; and if he succeeded in that nothing would be gained; he must next fight his way down the stair; and if he succeeded in that nothing would be gained; the courts would still have to be crossed; and after the courts the second outer palace; and once more stairs and courts; and once more another palace; and so on for thousands of years; and if at last he should burst through the outermost gate — but never, never can that happen — the imperial capital would lie before him, the center of the world, crammed to bursting with its own sediment. Nobody could fight his way through here even with a message from a dead man. But you sit at your window when evening falls and dream it to yourself.

Discussion Topics

1. If one takes "An Imperial Message" as a complement to "Before the Law," it is plausible to conclude that the message that the man in country awaits in vain is the message that emperor is trying to send. The supplicant is on the outside trying to get in; the message is on the inside, and no courier is strong and fast enough to carry it outside.

Does "Imperial Message" help explain why the man in the country cannot achieve success — or does it confuse us all the more? What might the contents of the message be?

2. Both stories make tantalizing references to space and power. In both we are dealing with metaphors for infinity, the infinite series of doors and the infinite distances the messenger must cover. And in both cases we are dealing with limits to power, the powerlessness of the man in the country is mirrored by the powerlessness of the emperor to convey his message. This is ironic, of course, because the emperor is as powerful as a person can be.

3. At the end, we learn that the "message from a dead man" cannot possibly be delivered. But, waiting for it, you "dream it to yourself." Is the message ultimately conveyed even if the messenger fails to deliver it? Or is the dream a mere dream, a fantasy of self-deception?

Franz Kafka: Advocates

The following story has a dream-like structure in its rapid shifts of venue and attitude.

❧ Advocates ❧

Franz Kafka

I was not at all certain whether I had any advocates, I could not find out anything definite about it, every face was unfriendly, most people who came toward me and whom I kept meeting in the corridors looked like fat old women, they had huge blue-and-white striped aprons covering their entire bodies, kept stroking their stomachs and swaying awkwardly to and fro. I could not even find out whether we were in a law court. Some faces spoke for it, others against. What reminded me of a law court more than all the details was a droning noise which could be heard incessantly in the distance; one could not tell from which direction it came, it filled every room to such an extent that one had to assume it came from everywhere, or, what seemed more likely, that just the place where one happened to be standing was the very place where the droning originated, but this was probably an illusion, for it came from a distance. These corridors, narrow and austerely vaulted, turning in gradual curves with high, sparsely decorated doors, seemed to have been created specially for profound silence; they were the corridors of a museum or a library. Yet if it were not a law court why was I searching for an advocate here? Because I was searching for an advocate everywhere; he is needed everywhere, if anything less in court than elsewhere, for a court, one assumes, passes judgment according to the law. If one were to assume that this was being done unfairly or frivolously, then life would not be possible; one must have confidence that the court allows the majesty of the law its full scope, for this is its sole duty. Within the law all is accusation, advocacy, and verdict; any interference by an individual here would be a crime. It is different, however, in the case of the verdict itself; this is based on inquiries being made here and there, from relatives and strangers, from friends and enemies, in the family and public life, in town and village — in short, everywhere. Here it is most necessary to have advocates, advocates galore, the best possible advocates, one next to the other, a living wall, for advocates are by nature hard to set in motion; the plaintiffs, however, those sly foxes, those slinking weasels, those little mice, they slip through the tiniest gaps, scuttle through the legs of the advocates. So look out! That's why I am here, I'm collecting advocates. But I have not found any as yet, only those old women keep on coming and going; if I were not on my search it would put me to sleep. I'm not in the right place — alas, I cannot rid myself of the feeling that I'm not in the right place. I ought to be in a place where all kinds of people meet, from various parts of the country, from every class, every profession, of all ages; I ought to have an opportunity of choosing carefully out of a crowd those who are kind, those who are able, and those who have an eye for me. Perhaps the most suitable place for this would be a huge fairground; instead of which I am hanging about in these corridors where only these old women are to be seen, and not even many of them, and always the same ones, and even those few will not let themselves be cornered, despite their slowness; they slip away from me, float about like rain clouds, and are completely absorbed by unknown activities. Why is it then that I run headlong into a house without reading the sign over the door, promptly find myself in these corridors, and settle here with such obstinacy that I cannot even remember ever having been in front of the house, ever having run up the stairs! But back I cannot go, this waste of time, this admission of having been on the wrong track would be unbearable for me. What? Run downstairs in this brief, hurried life accompanied as it is by that impatient droning? Impossible. The time allotted to you is so short that if you lose one second you have already lost your whole life, for it is no longer, it is always just as long as the time you lose. So if you have started out on a walk, continue it whatever happens; you can only gain, you run no risk, in the end you may fall over a precipice perhaps, but had you turned back after the first steps and run downstairs you would have fallen at once — and not perhaps, but for certain. So if you find nothing in the corridors open the doors, if you find nothing behind these doors there are more floors, and if you find nothing up there, don't worry, just leap up another flight of stairs. As long as you don't stop climbing, the stairs won't end, under your climbing feet they will go on growing upwards.

Discussion Topics

1. "Advocates" is nightmare-like insofar as nothing is stable and the narrator is in constant confusion. In the end, he tells us that he cannot possibly run backwards, but must run endlessly up the stairs, flights of stairs that multiply endlessly. In a sense, this parallels our lives: we must go forward and we cannot go back in time and space to relive and remake our choices.

2. Counterintuitively, the narrator says that advocates are needed "less in court than elsewhere, for a court, one assumes, passes judgment according to the law." In this sense the law seems to be a refuge of predictability and procedure while the rest of life carries no assurance of substantive or procedural fairness. He refers to "the verdict itself," for which advocates are "most necessary." The verdict is unclear. Is it a legal verdict, the verdict of public opinion, or even the final judgment on one's life?

3. The narrator concludes that a fairground rather than a law court would be the best place to find an advocate. And he offers clues about the kinds of advocates that would be best. What roles in what situations would such advocates play?

Franz Kafka: The New Advocate

"The New Advocate" is best seen as a joke, which does not mean that it is trivial or without debatable meaning.

❧ The New Advocate ❧

Franz Kafka

We have a new advocate, Dr. Bucephalus. There is little in his appearance to remind you that he was once Alexander of Macedon's battle charger. Of course, if you know his story, you are aware of something. But even a simple usher whom I saw the other day on the front steps of the Law Courts, a man with the professional appraisal of the regular small bettor at a racecourse, was running an admiring eye over the advocate as he mounted the marble steps with a high action that made them ring beneath his feet.

In general the Bar approves the admission of Bucephalus. With astonishing insight people tell themselves that, modern society being what it is, Bucephalus is in a difficult position, and therefore, considering also his importance in the history of the world, he deserves at least a friendly reception. Nowadays—it cannot be denied—there is no Alexander the Great. There are plenty of men who know how to murder people; the skill needed to reach over a banqueting table and pink a friend with a lance is not lacking; and for many Macedonia is too confining, so that they curse Philip, the father—but no one, no one at all, can blaze a trail to India. Even in his day the gates of India were beyond reach, yet the King's sword pointed the way to them. Today the gates have receded to remoter and loftier places; no one points the way; many carry swords, but only to brandish them, and the eye that tries to follow them is confused.

So perhaps it is really best to do as Bucephalus has done and absorb oneself in law books. In the quiet lamplight, his flanks unhampered by the thighs of a rider, free and far from the clamor of battle, he reads and turns the pages of our ancient tomes.

Discussion Topics

1. The horse of Alexander the Great has become a lawyer. (Is Kafka suggesting that law schools may have discriminated against four-footed applicants?) Just as Melville advised us that the knights templar with their heroic missions across continents have become lawyers with local missions in court, so too Bucephalus has shifted from helping Alexander blaze "a trail to India" to "turn[ing] the pages of ancient tomes" in the law library. Is there equivalence between the new role and the old one?

2. The key to the parable may be, "Nowadays — it cannot be denied — there is no Alexander the Great." To be sure, Kafka reminds us, Alexander murdered people and our contemporaries retain that ability. But Alexander was capable of carrying out great deeds that shaped human history. He murdered only in the service of world-historical goals.

The notion of a past and lost era of greatness is a common theme. We often think that the Founders wrote the Constitution with a kind of vision and insight which no longer exists. In fact, every era and every field of endeavor is haunted by the great figures of its past and the self-doubt that accompanies comparisons with them. If Kafka was aware of this, are his references to Alexander ironic?

Franz Kafka: The Problem of Our Laws

The following brief story reflects a series of attitudes toward law that define a range of philosophical possibilities. It is one of the richest and least known of Kafka's parables.

❖ The Problem of Our Laws ❖

Franz Kafka

Our laws are not generally known; they are kept secret by the small group of nobles who rule us. We are convinced that these ancient laws are scrupulously administered; nevertheless it is an extremely painful thing to be ruled by laws that one does not know. I am not thinking of possible discrepancies that may arise in the interpretation of the laws, or of the disadvantages involved when only a few and not the whole people are allowed to have a say in their interpretation. These disadvantages are perhaps of no great importance. For the laws are very ancient; their interpretation has been the work of centuries, and has itself doubtless acquired the status of law; and though there is still a possible freedom of interpretation left, it has now become very restricted. Moreover the nobles have obviously no cause to be influenced in their interpretation by personal interests inimical to us, for the laws were made to the advantage of the nobles from the very beginning, they themselves stand above the laws, and that seems to be why the laws were entrusted exclusively into their hands. Of course, there is wisdom in that — who doubts the wisdom of the ancient laws? — but also hardship for us; probably that is unavoidable.

The very existence of these laws, however, is at most a matter of presumption. There is a tradition that they exist and that they are a mystery confided to the nobility, but it is not and cannot be more than a mere tradition sanctioned by age, for the essence of a secret code is that it should remain a mystery. Some of us among the people have attentively scrutinized the doings of the nobility since the earliest times and possess records made by our forefathers — records which we have conscientiously continued — and claim to recognize amid the countless number of facts certain main tendencies which permit of this or that historical formulation; but when in accordance with these scrupulously tested and logically ordered conclusions we seek to adjust ourselves somewhat for the present or the future, everything becomes uncertain, and our work seems only an intellectual game, for perhaps these laws that we are trying to unravel do not exist at all. There is a small party who are actually of this opinion and who try to show that, if any law exists, it can only be this: The Law is whatever the nobles do. This party see everywhere only the arbitrary acts of the nobility, and reject the popular tradition, which according to them possesses only certain trifling and incidental advantages that do not offset its heavy drawbacks, for it gives the people a false, deceptive, and overconfident security in confronting coming events. This cannot be gainsaid, but the overwhelming majority of our people account for it by the fact that the tradition is far from complete and must be more fully inquired into, that the material available, prodigious as it looks, is still too meager, and that several centuries will have to pass before it becomes really adequate. This view, so comfortless as far as the present is concerned, is lightened only by the belief that a time will eventually come when the tradition and our research into it will jointly reach their conclusion, and as it were gain a breathing space, when everything will have become clear, the law will belong to the people, and the nobility will vanish. This is not maintained in any spirit of hatred against the nobility; not at all, and by no one. We are more inclined to hate ourselves, because we have not yet shown ourselves worthy of being entrusted with the laws. And that is the real reason why the party who believe that there is no law have remained so few — although their doctrine is in certain ways so attractive, for it unequivocally recognizes the nobility and its right to go on existing.

Actually one can express the problem only in a sort of paradox: Any party that would repudiate not only all belief in the laws, but the nobility as well, would have the whole people behind it; yet no such party can come into existence, for nobody would dare to repudiate the nobility. We live on this razor's edge. A writer once summed the matter up in this way: The sole visible and indubitable law that is imposed upon us is the nobility, and must we ourselves deprive ourselves of that one law?

Discussion Topics

1. Of all Kafka's parables, this one is unambiguously about law, looking at it literally as well as symbolically. In a mere three paragraphs, Kafka gestures toward ways in which legal philosophers have talked about law over the history of jurisprudence. One school of thought maintains that law is the repository of our collective wisdom about social organization and shared goals. The law must be interpreted by the experts and is inaccessible, because of its complexity and historicity, to ordinary people. The nobles are the natural custodians of the law since they presided over its creation, and (one thinks) they have no special interest in influencing its interpretation.

This hierarchical notion can be challenged by a second school of thought that questions both the trustworthiness of the "nobles" and the very existence of the law. These scholars argue that references to the law's mandate are simply camouflage for a system in which those in power do whatever they want. Justice Holmes famously said that law is whatever the judges say it is.

A third theory is that the values implicit in law can only make themselves manifest over time. A Marxist twist on this notion is that "we have not yet shown ourselves worth of being entrusted with the laws."

2. In each of the parables, irony is never far from the surface. Consider the ways in which irony colors the ways Kafka describes the "problem of our laws." Which sense of the nature of law most likely reflects his own?

Law and Justice

Isabel Allende: The Judge's Wife

Isabel Allende has achieved critical recognition along with popular success. Born in 1942, she remains a prolific novelist and memoirist. Her family has been prominent in Chilean politics and public affairs. Her father was Chile's ambassador to Peru; her uncle, Salvador Allende, was president of Chile in the early 1970s and was overthrown in a violent right-wing coup in 1973. Since then, she has spent much of her life in exile in South America and Europe. She has had U.S. citizenship since 2003 and lives with her current husband, Willie Gordon, in San Rafael, California.

History, feminism, and romantic myth play significant parts in her novels, and they are all evident in "The Judge's Wife." Judge Hidalgo is a narrow and harsh interpreter of law; his young wife, Casilda, brings joy and harmony to his life and represents a juncture of emotion, reason, and social purpose. She transcends the expectations of others and the narrow agendas of the men in her world—Hidalgo the judge and Vidal the outlaw—but she can only do so through self-sacrifice.

❧ The Judge's Wife ❧
Isabel Allende

Nicolas Vidal always knew he would lose his head over a woman. So it was foretold on the day of his birth, and later confirmed by the Turkish woman in the corner shop the one time he allowed her to read his fortune in the coffee grounds. Little did he imagine though that it would be on account of Casilda, Judge Hidalgo's wife. It was on her wedding day that he first glimpsed her. He was not impressed, preferring his women dark-haired and brazen. This ethereal slip of a girl in her wedding gown, eyes filled with wonder, and fingers obviously unskilled in the art of rousing a man to pleasure, seemed to him almost ugly. Mindful of his destiny, he had always been wary of any emotional contact with women, hardening his heart and restricting himself to the briefest of encounters whenever the demands of manhood needed satisfying. Casilda, however, appeared so insubstantial, so distant, that he cast aside all precaution and, when the fateful moment arrived, forgot the prediction that usually weighted in all his decisions. From the roof of the bank, where he was crouching with two of his men, Nicolas Vidal peered down at this young lady from the capital. She had a dozen equally pale and dainty relatives with her, who spent the whole of the ceremony fanning themselves with an air of utter bewilderment, then departed straight away, never to return. Along with everyone else in the town, Vidal was convinced the young bride would not withstand the climate, and that within a few months the old women would be dressing her up again, this time for her funeral. Even if she did survive the heat and the dust that filtered in through every pore to lodge itself in the soul, she would be bound to succumb to the fussy habits of her confirmed bachelor of a husband. Judge Hidalgo was twice her age, and had slept alone for so many years he didn't have the slightest notion of how to go about pleasing a woman. The severity and stubbornness with which he executed the law even at the expense of justice had made him feared throughout the province. He refused to apply any common sense in the exercise of his profession, and was equally harsh in his condemnation of the theft of a chicken as of a premeditated murder. He dressed formally in black, and, despite the all-pervading dust in this god-forsaken town, his boots always shone with beeswax. A man such as he was never meant to be a husband, and yet not only did the gloomy wedding-day prophecies remain unfulfilled, but Casilda emerged happy and smiling from three pregnancies in rapid succession. Every Sunday at noon she would go to mass with her husband, cool and collected beneath her Spanish mantilla, seemingly untouched by our pitiless summer, as wan and frail-looking as on the day of her arrival: a perfect example of delicacy and refinement. Her loudest words were a soft-spoken greeting; her most expressive gesture was a graceful nod of the head. She was such an airy, diaphanous creature that a moment's carelessness might mean she disappeared altogether. So slight an impression did she make that the changes noticeable in the Judge were all the more remarkable. Though outwardly he remained the same—he still dressed as black as a crow and was as stiff-necked and brusque as ever—his judgments in court altered dramatically. To general amazement, he found the youngster who robbed the Turkish shopkeeper innocent, on the grounds that she had been selling him short for years, and the money he had taken could therefore be seen as compensation. He also refused to punish an adulterous wife, arguing that since her husband himself kept a mistress he did not have the moral authority to demand fidelity. Word in the town had it that the Judge was transformed the minute he crossed the threshold at home: that he flung off his gloomy apparel, rollicked with his children, chuckled as he sat Casilda on his lap. Though no one ever succeeded in confirming these rumours, his wife got the credit for his new-found kindness, and her reputation grew accordingly. None of this was of the slightest interest to Nicolas Vidal, who as a wanted man was sure there would be no mercy shown him the day he was brought in chains before the Judge. He paid no heed to the talk about Dona Casilda, and the rare occasions he glimpsed her from afar only confirmed his first impression of her as a lifeless ghost.

Born thirty years earlier in a windowless room in the town's only brothel, Vidal was the son of Juana the Forlorn and an unknown father. The world had no place for him. His mother knew it, and so tried to wrench him from her womb with sprigs of parsley, candle butts, douches of ashes and other violent purgatives, but the child clung to life. Once, years later, Juana was looking at her mysterious son and realized that, while all her infallible methods of aborting might have failed to dislodge him, they had none the less tempered his soul to the hardness of iron. As soon as he came into the world, he was lifted in the air by the midwife who examined him by the light of an oil-lamp. She saw he had four nipples.

"Poor creature: he'll lose his head over a woman," she predicted, drawing on her wealth of experience.

Her words rested on the boy like a deformity. Perhaps a woman's love would have made his existence less wretched. To atone for all her attempts to kill him before birth, his mother chose him a beautiful first name, and an imposing family name picked at random. But the lofty name of Nicolas Vidal was no protection against the fateful cast of his destiny. His face was scarred from knife fights before he reached his teens, so it came as no surprise to decent folk that he ended up a bandit. By the age of twenty, he had become the leader of a band of desperadoes. The habit of violence toughened his sinews. The solitude he was condemned to for fear of falling prey to a woman lent his face a doleful expression. As soon as they say him, everyone in the town knew from his eyes, clouded by tears, he would never allow to fall, that he was the son of Juana the Forlorn. Whenever there was an outcry after a crime had been committed in the region, the police set out with dogs to track him down, but after scouring the hills invariably returned empty-handed. In all honesty they preferred it that way, because they could never have fought him. His gang gained such a fearsome reputation that the surrounding villages and estates paid to keep them away. This money would have been plenty for his men, but Nicolas Vidal kept them constantly on horseback in a whirlwind of death and destruction so they would not lose their taste for battle. Nobody dared take them on. More than once, Judge Hidalgo had asked the government to send troops to reinforce the police, but after several useless forays the soldiers returned to their barracks and Nicolas Vidal's gang to their exploits. On one occasion only did Vidal come close to falling into the hands of justice, and then he was saved by his hardened heart.

Weary of seeing the laws flouted, Judge Hidalgo resolved to forget his scruples and set a trap for the outlaw. He realized that to defend justice he was committing an injustice, but chose the lesser of two evils. The only bait he could find was Juana the For-lorn, as she was Vidal's sole known relative. He had her dragged from the brothel where by now, since no clients were willing to pay for her exhausted charms, she scrubbed floors and cleaned out the lavatories. He put her in a specially made cage which was set up in the middle of the Plaza de Armas, with only a jug of water to meet her needs.

"As soon as the water's finished, she'll start to squawk. Then her son will come running, and I'll be waiting for him with the sol-diers," Judge Hidalgo said.

News of this torture, unheard of since the days of slavery, reached Nicolas Vidal's ears shortly before his mother drank the last of the water. His men watched as he received the report in silence, without so much as a flicker of emotion on his blank lone wolf's face, or a pause in the sharpening of his dagger blade on a leather strap. Though for many years he had had no contact with Juana, and retained few happy childhood memories, this was a question of honour. No man can accept such an insult, his gang reasoned as they got guns and horses ready to rush into the ambush and, if need be, lay down their lives. Their chief showed no sign of being in a hurry. As the hours went by tension mounted in the camp. The perspiring, impatient men stared at each other, not daring to speak. Fretful, they caressed the butts of their revolvers and their horses' manes, or busied themselves coiling their lassos. Night fell. Nicolas Vidal was the only one in the camp who slept. At dawn, opinions were divided. Some of the men reckoned he was even more heartless than they had ever imagined, while others maintained their leader was planning a spectacular ruse to free his mother. The one thing that never crossed any of their minds was that his courage might have failed him, for he had always proved he had more than enough to spare. By noon, they could bear the suspense no longer, and went to ask him what he planned to do.

"I'm not going to fall into his trap like an idiot," he said.

"What about your mother?"

"We'll see who's got more balls, the Judge or me," Nicolas Vidal coolly replied.

By the third day, Juana the Forlorn's cries for water had ceased. She lay curled on the cage floor, with wildly staring eyes and swollen lips, moaning softly whenever she regained consciousness, and the rest of the time dreaming she was in hell. Four armed guards stood watch to make sure nobody brought her water. Her groans penetrated the entire town, filtering through closed shutters or being carried by the wind through the cracks in doors. They got stuck in corners, where dogs worried at them, and passed them on in their howls to the newly born, so that whoever heard them was driven to distraction. The Judge couldn't prevent a steady stream of people filing through the square to show their sympathy for the old woman, and was powerless to stop the prostitutes going on a sympathy strike just as the miners' fortnight holiday was beginning. That Saturday, the streets were thronged with lusty workmen desperate to unload their savings, who now found nothing in town apart from the spectacle of the cage and this universal wailing carried mouth to mouth down from the river to the coast road. The priest headed a group of Catholic ladies to plead with Judge Hidalgo for Christian mercy and to beg him to spare the poor old innocent woman such a frightful death, but the man of the law bolted his door and refused to listen to them. It was then they decided to turn to Dona Casilda.

The Judge's wife received them in her shady living room. She listened to their pleas looking, as always, bashfully down at the floor. Her husband had not been home for three days, having locked himself in his office to wait for Nicolas Vidal to fall into his trap. Without so much as glancing out of the window, she was aware of what was going on, for Juana's long-drawn-out agony had forced its way even into the vast rooms of her residence. Dona Casilda waited until her visitors had left, dressed her children in their Sunday best, tied a black ribbon round their arms as a token of mourning, then strode out with them in the direction of the square. She carried a food hamper and a bottle of fresh water for Juana the Forlorn. When the guards spotted her turning the corner, they realized what she was up to, but they had strict orders, and barred her way with their rifles. When, watched now by a small crowd, she persisted, they grabbed her by the arms. Her children began to cry.

Judge Hidalgo sat in his office overlooking the square. He was the only person in the town who had not stuffed wax in his ears, because his mind was intent on the ambush and he was straining to catch the sound of horses' hoofs, the signal for action. For three long days and nights he put up with Juana's groans and the insults of the townspeople gathered outside the courtroom, but when he heard his own children start to wail he knew he had reached the bounds of his endurance. Vanquished, he walked out of the office with his three days' beard, his eyes bloodshot from keeping watch, and the weight of a thousand years on his back. He crossed the street, turned into the square and came face to face with his wife. They gazed at each other sadly. In seven years, this was the first time she had gone against him, and she had chosen to do so in front of the whole town. Easing the hamper and the bottle from Casilda's grasp, Judge Hidalgo himself opened the cage to release the prisoner.

"Didn't I tell you he wouldn't have the balls?" laughed Nicolas Vidal when the news reached him.

His laughter turned sour the next day, when he heard that Juana the Forlorn had hanged herself from the chandelier in the brothel where she had spent her life, overwhelmed by the shame of her only son leaving her to fester in a cage in the middle of the Plaza de Armas.

"That Judge's hour has come," said Vidal.

He planned to take the Judge by surprise, put him to a horrible death, then dump him in the accursed cage for all to see. The Turkish shopkeeper sent him word that the Hidalgo family had left that same night for a seaside resort to rid themselves of the bitter taste of defeat.

The Judge learned he was being pursued when he stopped to rest at a wayside inn. There was little protection for him there until an army patrol could arrive, but he had a few hours' start, and his motor car could outrun the gang's horses. He calculated he could make it to the next town and summon help there. He ordered his wife and children into the car, put his foot down on the accelerator and sped off along the road. He ought to have arrived with time to spare, but it had been ordained that Nicolas Vidal was that day to meet the woman who would lead him to his doom.

Overburdened by the sleepless nights, the townspeople's hostility, the blow to his pride and the stress of this race to save his family, Judge Hidalgo's heart gave a massive jolt, then split like a pomegranate. The car ran out of control, turned several somersaults and finally came to a halt in the ditch. It took Dona Casilda some minutes to work out what had happened. Her husband's advancing years had often led her to think what it would be like to be left a widow, yet she had never imagined he would leave her at the mercy of his enemies. She wasted little time dwelling on her situation, knowing she must act at once to get her children to safety. When she gazed around her, she almost burst into tears. There was no sign of life in the vast plain baked by a scorching sun, only barren cliffs beneath an unbounded sky bleached colourless by the fierce light. A second look revealed the dark shadow of a passage or cave on a distant slope, so she ran towards it with two children in her arms and the third clutching her skirts.

One by one she carried her children up the cliff. The cave was a natural one, typical of many in the region. She peered inside to be certain it wasn't the den of some wild animal, sat her children against its back wall, then, dry-eyed, kissed them goodbye.

"The troops will come to find you a few hours from now. Until then, don't for any reason whatsoever come out of here, even if you hear me screaming—do you understand?"

Their mother gave one final glance at the terrified children clinging to each other, then clambered back down to the road. She reached the car, closed her husband's eyes, smoothed back her hair and settled down to wait. She had no idea how many men were in Nicolas Vidal's gang, but prayed there were a lot of them so it would take them all the more time to have their way with her. She gathered strength pondering on how long it would take her to die if she determined to do it as slowly as possible. She willed herself to be desirable, luscious, to create more work for them and thus gain time for her children.

Casilda did not have long to wait. She soon saw a cloud of dust on the horizon and heard the gallop of horses' hoofs. She clenched her teeth. Then, to her astonishment, she saw there was only one rider, who stopped a few yards from her, gun at the ready. By the scar on his face she recognized Nicolas Vidal, who had set out all alone in pursuit of Judge Hidalgo, as this was a private matter between the two men. The Judge's wife understood she was going to have to endure something far worse than a lingering death.

A quick glance at her husband was enough to convince Vidal that the Judge was safely out of his reach in the peaceful sleep of death. But there was his wife, a shimmering presence in the plain's glare. He leapt from his horse and strode over to her. She did not flinch or lower her gaze, and to his amazement he realized that for the first time in his life another person was facing him without fear. For several seconds that stretched to eternity, they sized each other up, trying to gauge the other's strength, and their own powers of resistance. It gradually dawned on both of them that they were up against a formidable opponent. He lowered his gun. She smiled.

Casilda won each moment of the ensuing hours. To all the wiles of seduction known since the beginning of time she added new ones born of necessity to bring this man to the heights of rapture. Not only did she work on his body like an artist, stimulating his every fibre to pleasure, but she brought all the delicacy of her spirit into play on her side. Both knew their lives were at stake, and this added a new and terrifying dimension to their meeting. Nicolas Vidal had fled from love since birth, and knew nothing of intimacy, tenderness, secret laughter, the riot of the senses, the joy of shared passion. Each minute brought the detachment of troops and the noose that much nearer, but he gladly accepted this in return for her prodigious gifts. Casilda was a passive, demure, timid woman who had been married to an austere old man in front of whom she had never dared appear naked. Not once during that unforgettable afternoon did she forget that her aim was to win time for her children, and yet at some point, marvelling at her own possibilities, she gave herself completely, and felt something akin to gratitude towards him. That was why, when she heard the soldiers in the distance, she begged him to flee to the hills. Instead, Nicolas Vidal chose to fold her in a last embrace, thus fulfilling the prophecy that had sealed his fate from the start.

Discussion Topics

1. Casilda is a symbolic figure. But what precisely does she symbolize? She has power to change others, but her power is limited. She tempers and humanizes her husband, Judge Hildalgo, but his treatment of Juana the Forlorn shows that he is unreformed. Is she the spirit of justice? Is she the voice of femininity?

The psychologist Carol Gilligan is associated with the theory that men and women reason differently in moral and personal situations. Women, according to Gilligan, give greater attention to responsibility for others and care; men focus on maintaining and defending hierarchies. As a consequence, women may achieve beneficial change while men are frozen in postures of command and subordination. Note that both Hidalgo and Vidal are unable to resolve their conflict until Casilda intervenes.

2. Law has sometimes been said to be an instrument of legitimated violence and coercion. In that sense, the harsh judge or "hanging judge" is not an aberration but a manifestation of law's basic spirit. From that point of view, Hidalgo and Vidal are equals in opposition, although the former carries the imprimatur of legality. Both are tyrants, both violent. Is this a fair judgment about law or is it only the view that could be held by an outsider to the law, by a self-justifying "outlaw"?

3. The last moments of the story are complex. A plain reading is that Casilda sacrifices herself, allows herself to be raped by Vidal in order to detain him and insure his capture. But we are also told that Casilda, "a passive, demure, timid woman" finally "marveling at her own possibilities, . . . gave herself completely, and felt something akin to gratitude towards him." And she urges him to flee. The life of Casilda as an instrument of justice is here complicated by the life of Casilda as a woman of finally realized passion. How do these narratives—the story of law enforcement and the story of emotions—intersect?

4. A number of scholars have written about the romance of the outlaw, a theme that has particular resonance in Latin American literature. Martha Grace Duncan, in her book, *Romantic Outlaws, Beloved Prisons* (1996) suggests that we romanticize outlaws to fight the fear of leading ordinary lives and of "recognizing our ultimate solitude and our mortal condition." Critics have seen her book as evidence that literature can illuminate our attitudes toward crime and law, attitudes that are explicit in our cultural experience but only implicit when we deal with law.

Law and Injustice

Nadine Gordimer: Crimes of Conscience

Nadine Gordimer was the 1991 recipient of the Nobel Prize in literature. By then, she had accumulated a bibliography of over twenty-five novels and volumes of stories, most of them about the psychological and moral costs of apartheid in her home country, South Africa. Born in 1923, she grew up in a wealthy family in Transvaal; her mother was British, her father was a Jewish jeweler from Latvia. Her early and continued international fame as a writer protected her from persecution by South Africa's apartheid government. She was a persistent, outspoken, and visible critic of its policies.

In an early novel (*Occasion for Loving*), Gordimer says that "all claims of natural feeling are over-ridden alike by a line in a statute book that takes no account of humanness, that recognizes neither love nor respect nor jealousy nor rivalry nor compassion nor hate—nor any human attitude where there are black and white together." Her work explores the consequences of an unjust legal regime, the ways it corrupts and distorts personal relations and self-perception. In the post-apartheid era, she continues to examine the price of reconciliation. "Crimes of Conscience" is a fine and typical example of her interests.

❧ Crimes of Conscience ❧

Nadine Gordimer

Apparently they noticed each other at the same moment, coming down the steps of the Supreme Court on the third day of the trial. By then casual spectators who come for a look at the accused—to see for themselves who will risk prison walls round their bodies for ideas in their heads—have satisfied curiosity; only those who have some special interest attend day after day. He could have been a journalist; or an aide to the representative of one of the Western powers who "observe" political trials in countries problematic for foreign policy and subject to human rights lobbying back in Western Europe and America. He wore a corduroy suit of unfamiliar cut. But when he spoke it was clear he was, like her, someone at home — he had the accent, and the casual, colloquial turn of phrase. "What a session! I don't know . . . After two hours of that . . . , feel like I'm caught in a roll of sticky tape . . . unreal . . ."

There was no mistaking her. She was a young woman whose cultivated gentleness of expression and shabby homespun style of dress, in the context in which she was encountered, suggested not transcendental mediation centre or environmental concern group or design studio, but a sign of identification with the humanity of those who had nothing and risked themselves. Her only adornment, a necklace of ostrich-shell discs stacked along a thread, moved tight at the base of her throat tendons as she smiled and agreed. "Lawyers work like that . . . I've noticed. The first few days, it's a matter of people trying each to confuse the other side."

Later in the week, they had coffee together during the court's lunch adjournment. He expressed some naive impressions of the trial, but as if fully aware of gullibility. Why did the State call witnesses who came right out and said the regime oppressed their spirits and frustrated their normal ambitions? Surely that kind of testimony favoured the Defence, when the issue was a crime of conscience? She shook fine hair, ripply as a mohair rug. "Just wait. Just wait. That's to establish credibility. To prove their involvement with the accused, their intimate knowledge of what the accused said and did, to *inculpate* the accused in what the Defence's going to deny. Don't you see?"

"Now I see." He smiled to himself. "When I was here before, I didn't take much interest in political things . . . activist politics, I suppose you'd call it? It's only since I've been back from overseas . . ."

She asked conversationally what was expected of her: how long had he been away?

"Nearly five years. Advertising then computers . . ." The dying-out of the sentence suggested the lack of interest in which these careers had petered. "Two years ago I just felt I wanted to come back. I couldn't give myself a real reason. I've been doing the same sort of work here — actually, I ran a course at the business school of a university, this year — and I'm slowly beginning to find out *why* I wanted to. To come back. It seems it's something to do with things like *this*."

She had a face that showed her mind following another's; eyebrows and mouth expressed quiet understanding.

"I imagine all this sounds rather feeble to you. I don't suppose you're someone who stands on the sidelines."

Her thin, knobbly little hands were like tools laid upon the formica counter of the coffee bar. In a moment of absence from their capability, they fiddled with the sugar sachets while she answered. "What makes you think that?"

"You seem to know so much. As if you'd been through it yourself . . . Or maybe . . . you're a law student?"

"Me? Good lord, no." After one or two swallows of coffee, she offered a friendly response. "I work for a correspondence college."

"Teacher."

Smiling again: "Teaching people I never see."

"That doesn't fit too well. You look the kind of person who's more involved."

For the first time, polite interest changed, warmed. "That's what you missed, in London? Not being involved . . . ?"

At that meeting he gave her a name, and she told him hers.

The name was Derek Felterman. It was his real name. He *had* spent five years in London; he *had* worked in an advertising company and then studied computer science at an appropriate institution, and it was in London that he was recruited by someone from the Embassy who wasn't a diplomat but a representative of the internal security section of State security in his native country. Nobody knows how secret police recognize likely candidates; it is as mysterious as sexing chickens. But if the definitive characteristic sought is there to be recognized, the recruiting agent will see it, no matter how deeply the individual may hide his likely candidacy from himself.

He was not employed to infiltrate refugee circles plotting abroad. It was decided that he would come home "clean," and begin work in the political backwater of a coastal town, on a university campus. Then he was sent north to the mining and industrial centre of the country, told to get himself an ordinary commercial job without campus connections, and, as a new face, seek contacts wherever the information his employers wanted was likely to be let slip — left-wing cultural gatherings, poster-waving protest groups, the public gallery at political trials. His employers trusted him to know how to ingratiate himself; that was one of the qualities he had been fancied for, as a woman might fancy him for some other characteristic over which he had no volition — the way one corner of his mouth curled when he smiled, or the brown gloss of his eyes.

He, in turn, had quickly recognized her — first as a type, and then, the third day, when he went away from the court for verification of her in police files, as the girl who had gone secretly to visit a woman friend who was under House Arrest, and subsequently had served a three-month jail sentence for refusing to testify in a case brought against the woman for breaking her isolation ban. Aly, she had called herself. Alison Jane Ross. There was no direct connection to be found between Alison Jane Ross's interest in the present trial and the individuals on trial; but from the point of view of his avocation this did not exclude her possible involvement with a master organization or back-up group involved in continuing action of the subversive kind the charges named. Felterman literally moved in to friendship with her, carrying a heavy case of books and a portable grill. He had asked if she would come to see a play with him on Saturday night. Alas, she was moving house that Saturday; perhaps he'd like to come and help, instead? The suggestion was added, tongue-in-cheek at her own presumption. He was there on time. Her family of friends, introduced by diminutives of their names, provided a combined service of old combi, springless station-wagon, take-away food and affectionate energy to fuel and accomplish the move from a flat to a tiny house with an ancient palm tree filling a square of garden, grating its dried fronds in the wind with the sound of a giant insect rubbing its legs together. To the night-song of that creature they made love for the first time a month later. Although all the Robs, Jimbos and Ricks, as well as the Jojos, Bets and Lils, kissed and hugged their friend Aly, there seemed to be no lover about who had therefore been supplanted. On the particular, delicate path of intimacy along which she drew him or that he laid out before her, there was room only for the two of them. At the beginning of ease between them, even before they were lovers, she had come of herself to the stage of mentioning that experience of going to prison, but she talked of it always in banal surface terms — how the blankets smelled of disinfectant and the Chief Wardress's cat used to do the inspection round with its mistress. Now she did not ask him about other women, although he was moved, occasionally, in some involuntary warm welling-up complementary to that other tide — of sexual pleasure spent — to confess by the indirection of an anecdote, past affairs, women who had had their time and place. When the right moment came naturally to her, she told without shame, resentment or vanity that she had just spent a year "on her own" as something she felt she needed after living for three years with someone who, in the end, went back to his wife. Lately there had been one or two brief affairs — "Sometimes — don't you find — an old friend suddenly becomes something else . . . just for a little while, as if a face is turned to another angle . . . ? And next day, it's the same old one again. Nothing's changed."

"Friends are the most important thing for you, aren't they? I mean, everybody has friends, but you . . . You'd really do *anything*. For your friends. Wouldn't you?"

There seemed to come from her reaction rather than his words a reference to the three months she had spent in prison. She lifted the curly pelmet of hair from her forehead and the freckles faded against a flush colouring beneath: "And they for me."

"It's not just a matter of friendship, either — of course, I see that. Comrades — a band of brothers . . ."

She saw him as a child staring through a window at others playing. She leant over and took up his hand, kissed him with the kind of caress they had not exchanged before, on each eyelid.

Nevertheless her friends were a little neglected in favour of him. He would have liked to have been taken into the group more closely, but it is normal for two people involved in a passionate love affair to draw apart from others for a while. It would have looked unnatural to press to behave otherwise. It was also understood between them that Felterman didn't have much more than acquaintances to neglect; five years abroad and then two in the coastal town accounted for that. He revived for her pleasures she had left behind as a schoolgirl: took her water-skiing and climbing. They went to see indigenous people's theatre together, part of a course in the politics of culture she was giving him not by correspondence, without being aware of what she was doing and without giving it any such pompous name. She was not to be persuaded to go to a disco-theque, but one of the valuable contacts he did have with her group of friends of different races and colours was an assumption that he would be with her at their parties, where she out-danced him, having been taught by blacks how to use her body to music. She was wild and nearly lovely, in this transformation, from where he drank and watched her and her associates at play. Every now and then she would come back to him: an offering, along with the food and drink she carried. As months went by, he was beginning to distinguish certain patterns in her friendships; these were extended beyond his life with her into proscribed places and among people restricted by law from contact, like the woman for whom she had gone to prison. Slowly she gained the confidence to introduce him to risk, never discussing but evidently always sensitively trying to gauge how much he really wanted to find out if "why he wanted to come back" had to do with "things like this."

It was more and more difficult to leave her, even for one night, going out late, alone under the dry, chill agitation of the old palm tree, rustling through its files. But although he knew his place had been made for him to live in the cottage with her, he had to go back to his flat that was hardly more than an office, now, unoccupied except for the chair and dusty table at which he sat down to write his reports: he could hardly write them in the house he shared with her.

She spoke often of her time in prison. She herself was the one to find openings for the subject. But even now, when they lay in one another's arms, out of reach, undiscoverable to any investigation, out of scrutiny, she did not seem able to tell of the experience what there really was in her being, necessary to be told: why she risked, for whom and what she was committed. She seemed to be waiting passionately to be given the words, the key. From him.

It was a password he did not have. It was a code that was not supplied him.

And then one night it came to him; he found a code of his own; that night he had to speak. "I've been spying on you."

Her face drew into a moment of concentration akin to the animal world, where a threatened creature can turn into a ball of spikes or take on a fearsome aspect of blown-up muscle and defensive garishness.

The moment left her face instantly as it had taken her. He had turned away before it as a man does with a gun in his back.

She shuffled across the bed on her haunches and took his head in her hands, holding him.

Discussion Topics

1. Is Derek as much a victim of the legal regime as Alison or is he the villain of the story? Does it matter, in judging him, whether he is apolitical or whether he believes strongly that the government's survival is important and that its policies are justified? We can only judge him through his actions, and they allow a limited set of inferences. The story raises the question of the comparative morality of various kinds of spying-through-intimacy. Is it worse to spy by using love and intimacy as a strategy, worse, say, than using friendship or mere acquaintance?

2. Gordimer leaves us in some doubt about Alison's sophistication or naivete. We are not certain that she has any suspicion, but she is cautious with Derek as she has to be with everyone. Our attitude toward her is inevitably affected by our attitude toward apartheid. Note how difficult it is, in a politically charged story, to judge the characters apart from their politics.

3. It is important to recall how many regimes in the twentieth century survived by having vast armies of internal civilian spies reporting on the activities of their fellow citizens. As totalitarian regimes flourished for a while in Germany, Russia, China, Cambodia and elsewhere, writers like Eugene Zamiatin, George Orwell, and Aldous Huxley focused on dystopias in their novels. Control of the indigenous population through information and manipulation was the constant theme of their inventions. Even if the most flagrantly unfree societies have failed, one can consider how the experience of totalitarianism and its transitory successes have affected our understanding of human nature and accustomed us to inroads on our privacy. Would Derek, Alison, and their relationship be conceivable in any other context?

4. The end of the story is open and puzzling. What are the intentions behind Derek's confession and what is its effect? Is it naive to think that love conquers politics? Inevitably, we want to write the next scene, to know whether Alison shares her secrets, whether Derek continues to write his reports.

Law and the Adversarial Relationship

Frank O'Connor: Legal Aid

The man who wrote as Frank O'Connor was born Michael O'Donovan in 1903 to a poor family (an alcoholic father, a mother who supported the family with menial work) in Cork, Ireland. His family drama was a familiar one. His love for books antagonized his father but was fostered and encouraged by his mother. His pseudonym was based on his mother's maiden name. He became secretary to James Joyce and a colleague of W.B. Yeats, and in time became director of the Abbey Theater. Unlike Joyce, he remained Irish to the core, even though his wife was American and he taught at American universities. He died in Ireland in 1966. Best known for his short stories, he also wrote well-regarded novels, plays, and poems.

"Legal Aid" shows off O'Connor's sly humor. It reflects the universal expectation that law — or at least lawyers — thrive on adversity. Attorneys benefit when others suffer, when others are at war. In "Legal Aid," litigation is fanned to a flame, almost. As in many of the other stories, law exists not to improve life but to complicate it and intensify its problems.

❈ Legal Aid ❈

Frank O'Connor

Delia Carty came of a very respectable family. It was going as maid to the O'Gradys of Pouladuff that ruined her. That whole family was slightly touched. The old man, a national teacher, was hardly ever at home, and the daughters weren't much better. When they weren't away visiting, they had people visiting them, and it was nothing to Delia to come in late at night and find one of them plastered round some young fellow on the sofa.

That sort of thing isn't good for any young girl. Like mistress like maid; inside six months she was smoking, and within a year she was carrying on with one Tom Flynn, a farmer's son. Her father, a respectable, hard-working man, knew nothing about it, for he would have realized that she was no match for one of the Flynns, and even if Tom's father, Ned, had known, he would never have thought it possible that any laborer's daughter could imagine herself a match for Tom.

Not, God knows, that Tom was any great catch. He was a big uncouth galoot who was certain that love-making, like drink, was one of the simple pleasures his father tried to deprive him of, out of spite. He used to call at the house while the O'Gradys were away, and there would be Delia in one of Eileen O'Grady's frocks and with Eileen O'Grady's lipstick and powder on, doing the lady over the tea thing in the parlor. Throwing a glance over his shoulder in case anyone might spot him, Tom would heave himself onto the sofa with his boots over the end.

"Begod, I love sofas," he would say with simple pleasure.

"Put a cushion behind you," Delia would say.

"Oh, begod," Tom would say, making himself comfortable, "if ever I have a house of my own 'tis unknown what sofas and cushions I'll have. Them teachers must get great money. What the hell do they go away at all for?"

Delia loved making the tea and handing it out like a real lady, but you couldn't catch Tom out like that.

"Ah, what do I want tay for?" he would say with a doubtful glance at the cup. "Haven't you any whiskey? Ould O'Grady must have gallons of it. . . . Leave it there on the table. Why the hell don't they have proper mugs with handles a man could get a grip on? Is that taypot silver? Pity I'm not a teacher!"

It was only natural for Delia to show him the bedrooms and the dressing-tables with the three mirrors, the way you could see yourself from all sides, but Tom, his hands under his head, threw himself with incredulous delight on the low double bed and cried: "Springs! Begod, 'tis like a car!"

What the springs gave rise to was entirely the O'Gradys' fault since no one but themselves would have left a house in a lonesome part to a girl of nineteen to mind. The only surprising thing was that it lasted two years without Delia showing any signs of it. It probably took Tom that time to find the right way.

But when he did he got into a terrible state. It was hardly in him to believe that a harmless poor devil like himself whom no one ever bothered his head about could achieve such unprecedented results on one girl, but when he understood it he knew only too well what the result of it would be. His father would first beat hell out of him and then throw him out and leave the farm to his nephews. There being no hope of conciliating his father, Tom turned his attention to God, who, though supposed to share Ned Flynn's views about fellows and girls, had some nature in Him. Tom stopped seeing Delia, to persuade God that he was reforming and to show that anyway it wasn't his fault. Left alone he could be a decent, good-living young fellow, but the Carty girl was a forward, deceitful hussy who had led him on instead of putting him off the way any well-bred girl would do. Between lipstick, sofas, and tay in the parlor, Tom put it up to God that it was a great wonder she hadn't got him into worse trouble.

Delia had to tell her mother, and Mrs. Carty went to Father Corcoran to see could he induce Tom to marry her. Father Corcoran was a tall, testy old man who, even at the age of sixty-five, couldn't make out for the life of him what young fellows saw in girls, but if he didn't know much about lovers he knew a lot about farmers.

"Wisha, Mrs. Carty," he said crankily, "how could I get him to marry her? Wouldn't you have a bit of sense? Some little financial arrangement, maybe, so that she could leave the parish and not be a cause of scandal—I might be able to do that."

He interviewed Ned Flynn, who by this time had got Tom's version of the story and knew financial arrangements were going to be the order of the day unless he could put a stop to them. Ned was a man of over six foot with a bald brow and a smooth unlined face as though he never had a care except his general concern for the welfare of humanity which made him look so abnormally thoughtful. Even Tom's conduct hadn't brought a wrinkle to his brow.

"I don't know, father," he said, stroking his bald brow with a dieaway air, "I don't know what you could do at all."

"Wisha, Mr. Flynn," said the priest who, when it came to the pinch, had more nature than twenty Flynns, "wouldn't you do the handsome thing and let him marry her before it goes any farther?"

"I don't see how much farther it could go, father," said Ned.

"It could become a scandal."

"I'm afraid 'tis that already, father."

"And after all," said Father Corcoran, forcing himself to put in a good word for one of the unfortunate sex whose very existence was a mystery to him, "is she any worse than the rest of the girls that are going? Bad is the best of them, from what I see, and Delia is a great deal better than most."

"That's not my information at all, father," said Ned, looking like "The Heart Bowed Down."

"That's a very serious statement, Mr. Flynn," said Father Corcoran, giving him a challenging look.

"It can be proved, father," said Ned gloomily. "Of course I'm not denying the boy was foolish, but the cleverest can be caught."

"You astonish me, Mr. Flynn," said Father Corcoran who was beginning to realize that he wasn't even going to get a subscription. "Of course I can't contradict you, but 'twill cause a terrible scandal."

"I'm as sorry for that as you are, father," said Ned, "but I have my son's future to think of."

Then, of course, the fun began. Foolish to the last, the O'Gradys wanted to keep Delia on till it was pointed out to them that Mr. O'Grady would be bound to get the blame. After this, her father had to be told. Dick Carty knew exactly what became a devoted father, and he beat Delia till he had to be hauled off her by the neighbors. He was a man who loved to sit in his garden reading his paper; now he felt he owed it to himself not to be seen enjoying himself, so instead he sat over the fire and brooded. The more he brooded the angrier he became. But seeing that, with the best will in the world, he could not beat Delia every time he got angry, he turned his attention to the Flynns. Ned Flynn, that contemptible bosthoon, had slighted one of the Cartys in a parish where they had lived for hundreds of years with unblemished reputations; the Flynns, as everyone knew, being mere upstarts and outsiders without a date on their gravestones before 1850 — nobodies!

He brought Delia to see Jackie Canty, the solicitor in town. Jackie was a little jenny-ass of a man with thin lips, a pointed nose, and a pince-nez that wouldn't stop in place, and he listened with grave enjoyment to the story of Delia's misconduct. "And what happened then, please?" he asked in his shrill singsong, looking at the floor and trying hard not to burst out into a giggle of delight. "The devils!" he thought. "The devils!" It was as close as Jackie was ever likely to get to the facts of life, an opportunity not to be missed.

"Anything in writing?" he sang, looking at her over the pince-nez. "Any letters? Any documents?"

"Only a couple of notes I burned," said Delia, who thought him a very queer man, and no wonder.

"Pity!" Jackie said with an admiring smile. "A smart man! Oh, a very smart man!"

"Ah, 'tisn't that at all," said Delia uncomfortably, "only he had no occasion for writing."

"Ah, Miss Carty," cried Jackie in great indignation, looking at her challengingly through the specs while his voice took on a steely ring, "a gentleman in love always finds plenty of occasion for writing. He's a smart man; your father might succeed in an action for seduction, but if 'tis defended 'twill be a dirty case."

"Mr. Canty," said her father solemnly, "I don't mind how dirty it is so long as I get justice." He stood up, a powerful man of six feet, and held up his clenched fist. "Justice is what I want," he said dramatically. "That's the sort I am. I keep myself to myself and mind my own business, but give me a cut, and I'll fight in a bag, tied up!"

"Don't forget that Ned Flynn has the money, Dick," wailed Jackie.

"Mr. Canty," said Dick with a dignity verging on pathos, "you know me?"

"I do, Dick, I do."

"I'm living in this neighborhood, man and boy, fifty years, and I owe nobody a ha'penny. If it took me ten years, breaking stones by the road, I'd pay it back, every penny."

"I know, Dick, I know," moaned Jackie. "But there's other things as well. There's your daughter's reputation. Do you know what they'll do? They'll go into court and swear someone else was the father!"

"Tom could never say that," Delia cried despairingly. "The tongue would rot in his mouth!"

Jackie had no patience at all with this chit of a girl, telling him his business. He sat back with a weary air, his arm over the back of his chair.

"That statement has no foundation," he said icily. "There is no record of any such things happening a witness. If there was, the inhabitants of Ireland would have considerably less to say for themselves. You would be surprised the things respectable people will say in the witness box. Rot in their mouths indeed! Ah, dear me, no. With documents, of course, it would be different, but it is only our word against theirs. Can it be proved that you weren't knocking round with any other man at this time, Miss Carty?"

"Indeed, I was doing nothing of the sort," Delia said indignantly "I swear to God I wasn't, Mr. Canty. I hardly spoke to a fellow the whole time, only when Tom and myself might have a row and I'd go out with Timmy Martin!"

"Timmy Martin!" Canty cried dramatically, pointing an accusing finger at her. "There is their man!"

"But Tom did the same with Betty Daly," cried Delia on the point of tears, "and he only did it to spite me. I swear there was nothing else in it, Mr. Canty, nor he never accused me of it."

"Mark my words," chanted Jackie with a mournful smile, "he'll make up for lost time now."

In this he showed considerably more foresight than Delia gave him credit for. After the baby was born and the action begun, Tom and his father went to town to see their solicitor, Peter Humphreys. Peter, who knew all he wanted to know about the facts of life, liked the case much less than Jackie. A crosseyed, full-blooded man who had made his money when law was about land, not love, he thought it a terrible comedown. Besides, he didn't think it nice to be listening to such things.

"And so, according to you, Timmy Martin is the father?" he asked Tom.

"Oh, I'm not swearing he is," said Tom earnestly, giving himself a heave in his chair and crossing his legs. "How the hell could I? All I am saying is that I wasn't the only one, and what's more she boasted about it. Boasted about it, begod!" he added with a look of astonishment at such female depravity.

"Before witnesses?" asked Peter, his eyes doing a double cross with hopelessness.

"As to that," replied Tom with great solemnity, looking over his shoulder for an open window he could spit through, "I couldn't swear."

"But you understood her to mean Timmy Martin?"

"I'm not accusing Timmy Martin at all," said Tom in great alarm, seeing how the processes of law were tending to involve him in a row with the Martins, who were a turbulent family with ways of getting their own back unknown to any law. "Timmy Martin is one man she used to be round with. It might be Timmy Martin or it might be someone else, or what's more," he added with the look of a man who has had a sudden revelation, "it might be more than one." He looked from Peter to his father and back again to see what effect the revelation was having, but like other revelations it didn't seem to be going down too well. "Begod," he said giving himself another heave, "it might be any God's number . . . But, as to that," he added cautiously, "I wouldn't like to swear."

"Nor indeed, Tom," said his solicitor with a great effort at politeness, "no one would advise you. You'll want a good counsel."

"Begod, I suppose I will," said Tom with astonished resignation before the idea that there might be people in the world bad enough to doubt his word.

There was great excitement in the village when it became known that the Flynns were having the Roarer Cooper as counsel. Even as a first-class variety turn Cooper could always command attention, and everyone knew that the rights and wrongs of the case would be relegated to their proper position while the little matter of Eileen O'Grady's best frock received the attention it deserved.

On the day of the hearing the court was crowded. Tom and his father were sitting at the back with Peter Humphreys, waiting for Cooper, while Delia and her father were talking to Jackie Canty and their own counsel, Ivers. He was a well-built young man with a high brow, black hair, and half-closed, red-tinged sleepy eyes. He talked in a bland drawl.

"You're not worrying, are you?" he asked Delia kindly. "Don't be a bit afraid ... I suppose there's no chance of them settling, Jackie?"

"Musha, what chance would there be?" Canty asked scoldingly. "Don't you know yourself what sort they are?"

"I'll have a word with Cooper myself," said Ivers. "Dan isn't as bad as he looks." He went to talk to a coarse-looking man in wig and gown who had just come in. To say he wasn't as bad as he looked was no great compliment. He had a face that was almost a square, with a big jaw and blue eyes in wicked little slits that made deep dents across his cheekbones.

"What about settling this case of ours, Dan?" Ivers asked gently.

Cooper didn't even return his look; apparently he was not responsive to charm.

"Did you ever know me to settle when I could fight?" he growled.

"Not when you could fight your match," Ivers said, without taking offense. "You don't consider that poor girl your match?"

"We'll soon see what sort of girl she is," replied Cooper complacently as his eyes fell on the Flynns. "Tell me," he whispered, "what did she see in my client?"

"What you saw yourself when you were her age, I suppose," said Ivers. "You don't mean there wasn't a girl in a tobacconist's shop that you thought came down from Heaven with the purpose of consoling you?"

"She had nothing in writing," Cooper replied gravely. "And, unlike your client, I never saw double."

"You don't believe that yarn, do you?"

"That's one of the things I'm going to inquire into."

"I can save you the trouble. She was too fond of him."

"Hah!" snorted Cooper as though this were a good joke. "And I suppose that's why she wants the cash."

"The girl doesn't care if she never got a penny. Don't you know yourself what's behind it? A respectable father. Two respectable fathers! The trouble about marriage in this country, Dan Cooper, is that the fathers always insist on doing the courting."

"Hah!" grunted Cooper, rather more uncertain of himself. "Show me this paragon of the female sex, Ivers."

"There in the brown hat beside Canty," said Ivers without looking round. "Come on, you old devil, and stop trying to pretend you're Buffalo Bill. It's enough going through what she had to go through. I don't want her to go through any more."

"And why in God's name do you come to me?" Cooper asked in sudden indignation. "What the hell do you take me for? A Society for Protecting Fallen Women? Why didn't the priest make him marry her?"

"When the Catholic Church can make a farmer marry a laborer's daughter the Kingdom of God will be at hand," said Ivers. "I'm surprised at you, Dan Cooper, not knowing better at your age."

"And what are the neighbors doing here if she has nothing to hide?"

"Who said she had nothing to hide?" Ivers asked lightly, throwing in his hand. "Haven't you daughters of your own? You know she played the fine lady in the O'Gradys' frocks. If 'tis any information to you she wore their jewelry as well."

"Ivers, you're a young man of great plausibility," said Cooper, "but you can spare your charm on me. I have my client's interests to consider. Did she sleep with the other fellow?"

"She did not."

"Do you believe that?"

"As I believe my own mother."

"The faith that moves mountains," Cooper said despondently. "How much are ye asking?"

"Two hundred and fifty," replied Ivers, shaky for the first time.

"Merciful God Almighty!" moaned Cooper, turning his eyes to the ceiling. "As if any responsible Irish court would put that price on a girl's virtue. Still, it might be as well. I'll see what I can do."

He moved ponderously across the court and with two big arms outstretched like wings shepherded out the Flynns.

"Two hundred and fifty pounds?" gasped Ned, going white. "Where in God's name would I get that money?"

"My dear Mr. Flynn," Cooper said with coarse amiability "that's only half the yearly allowance his Lordship makes the young lady that obliges him, and she's not a patch on that girl in court. After a lifetime of experience I can assure you that for two years' fornication with a fine girl like that you won't pay a penny less than five hundred."

Peter Humphreys's eyes almost grew straight with the shock of such reckless slander on a blameless judge. He didn't know what had come over the Roarer. But that wasn't the worst. When the settlement was announced and the Flynns were leaving he went up to them again.

"You can believe me when I say you did the right thing, Mr. Flynn," he said. "I never like cases involving good-looking girls. Gentlemen of his Lordship's age are terribly susceptible. But tell me, why wouldn't your son marry her now as he's about it?"

"Marry her?" echoed Ned, who hadn't yet got over the shock of having to pay two hundred and fifty pounds and costs for a little matter he could have compounded for with Father Corcoran for fifty. "A thing like that!"

"With two hundred and fifty pounds, man?" snarled Cooper. " 'Tisn't every day you'll pick up a daughter-in-law with that . . . What do you say to the girl yourself?" he asked Tom.

"Oh, begod, the girl is all right," said Tom.

Tom looked different. It was partly relief that he wouldn't have to perjure himself, partly astonishment at seeing his father so swiftly overthrown. His face said: "The world is wide."

"Ah, Mr. Flynn, Mr. Flynn," whispered Cooper scornfully, "sure you're not such a fool as to let all that good money out of the family?"

Leaving Ned gasping, he went on to where Dick Carty, aglow with pride and malice, was receiving congratulations. There were no congratulations for Delia who was standing near him. She felt a big paw on her arm and looked up to see the Roarer.

"Are you still fond of that boy?" he whispered.

"I have reason to be, haven't I?" she retorted bitterly.

"You have," he replied with no great sympathy. "The best. I got you that money so that you could marry him if you wanted to. Do you want to?"

Her eyes filled with tears as she thought of the poor broken china of an idol that was being offered her now.

"Once a fool, always a fool," she said, sullenly.

"You're no fool at all, girl," he said, giving her arm an encouraging squeeze. "You might make a man of him yet. I don't know what the law in this country is coming to. Get him away to hell out of this till I find Michael Ivers and get him to talk to your father."

The two lawyers made the match themselves at Johnny Desmond's pub, and Johnny said it was like nothing in the world so much as a mission, with the Roarer roaring and threatening hellfire on all concerned, and Michael Ivers piping away about the joys of Heaven. Johnny said it was the most instructive evening he ever had. Ivers was always recognized as a weak man so the marriage did him no great harm, but of course it was a terrible comedown for a true Roarer, and Cooper's reputation has never been the same since then.

Discussion Topics

1. Does law offer any opportunities for helping the Cartys and the Flynns resolve their problems — or are lawyers only interested in exploiting them? Is this a general problem with law? A pervasive aspect of law is that it turns many situations into adversarial contests. It is sometimes difficult to know when a problem is genuinely adversarial and when conflict results from misunderstandings, posturings, and so on. Often, the parties have difficulty identifying their own interests and the means to achieve them. It would seem to be the job of lawyers to help them do this, but perhaps this may be more an ideal than reality.

2. Note at the end of the story that the "Roarer"'s reputation never recovered from his intervention in this case. What does this tell us about what some writers have called the "role morality" of legal practice? One may distinguish three positions, one whereby the lawyer's moral role is best described as solving the situation in the best interest of all parties ("lawyer for the situation"), the second whereby the lawyer's role is to serve her client regardless of the effects on others, and the third whereby the lawyer does what the client may misguidedly want as long as the lawyer benefits (in terms of reputation or finances). "Legal Aid" explores these possibilities; it also points out the consequences for the Roarer of choosing the first.

✍ Further Reading

(1) Perhaps the best-known and most compelling description of law taking on a life of its own, severed from its rule of serving human needs, is the opening chapter of Charles Dickens's monumental novel, *Bleak House*. In Dickens' London, the language, procedures, formalities, attitudes, and expectations bound up with law have created a world in which persons are ensnared without recourse or hope. Law pursues its own ends with no reference to the rational or emotional needs or expectations of persons. As a result, the internal pursuit of order and subservience to rules is the ultimate form of unreason.

A modern and complementary portrayal of law with a malign life of its own is William Gaddis's comic novel, *A Frolic of His Own*. Like Dickens, Gaddis is impressed with the ways in which law has the capacity to swallow up and transform individuals and their goals. To say, as many critics do, that this is Gaddis's most accessible novel, is hardly to say that it is easy.

(2) The connections between law and power are well-illustrated by dystopian novels. In the most familiar novels of this genre — Aldous Huxley's *Brave New World*, George Orwell's *1984*, and Eugene Zamiatin's

We—law is the tool of totalitarian repression. The power of law is complemented by sophisticated psychological techniques for internalizing obedience and suppressing individuality. Any focus on justice and rights disappears as law and the will of the state assume a shared identity. Ray Bradbury's *Fahrenheit 451* also describes a world in which comformist thought is the norm and ideas are aggressively discouraged.

(3) A much more positive role for law as the vehicle of fair results and as a place for benign ingenuity is a central theme of William Shakespeare's *The Merchant of Venice*. The play is designed to turn our opinion of law on its head. Initially, Shylock relies on the commercial law of Venice to enforce a formally required but cruelly unfair debt. Portia, using her legal sophistication, shows how the law can be used to secure an equitable outcome. Law in service to idealism is also the driving force behind Robert Bolt's play about Sir Thomas More, *A Man for All Seasons*. Bolt's theme is the role of law as a bulwark against the will of tyrants.

(4) A darker view of the uses of law and its limitations pervades *Billy Budd* by Herman Melville. In this short novel, legal rules serve vindictiveness and envy—and stand opposed to goodness and spontaneity. Interestingly, Shakespeare, Bolt, and Melville can all be seen as exploring law's limits. For Shakespeare, law supports good causes only when it is wielded by a clever lawyer. For Bolt, law is its own reward, and the victims of power find justice only in the world beyond this one. And for Melville, goodness alone, without the argumentative skills to resist persecution, will not avail in the face of law.

The plays of Henrik Ibsen, mostly notably *An Enemy of the People* and *The Wild Duck*, also show that naive idealism is unlikely to prevail against the shrewd and self-interested uses of law by those with power. He implies that the interests of society (and individuals) are often subverted by the institutions that interpret and apply law.

(5) Finally, the notion of law as a symbol is rooted deeply in the ideological conflict between the social philosophers, Thomas Hobbes and Jean-Jacques Rousseau. Hobbes (*Leviathan* and other works) is famous for arguing that law and the state are absolutely essential to control the innate antagonistic dispositions of persons. Once rules are in place, and only then, human society can flourish. Life without the state and law is necessarily "nasty, brutish, and short." Rousseau (*The Social Contract* and other works) by contrast saw the natural state of persons as benign and cooperative. For him, the state and law tended to enslave persons. "Man is born free, and everywhere he is in chains."

THREE

Freedom and Crime

Law puts limits on freedom. Where there is law, some behavior is non-optional. Rules prohibit homicide, theft, rape, and countless other acts that some persons are inclined to commit. Criminal law is the principal arena for such prohibitions but hardly the only one. Tort law, contract law, corporate law, and many other areas put burdens and exact prices for acting in certain ways that damage the interests of others.

In fact, the relation between law and freedom is hardly clear. A common and justifiable belief is that law makes freedom possible. Thomas Hobbes defined a state of nature as war or all against all. It is plausible to argue one has very little freedom when one is at war with everyone else. The state, through law, makes possible the freedom to act with the security of pursuing some goals without interference. But the decision of the state about which actions to allow and protect and which actions to prohibit is in some ways a delicate and controversial one. In liberal political theory, a basic premise is that freedom (or liberty) should be protected unless the exercise of freedom compromises the freedom of others. The goal of law should be to secure equal freedom for all. Crimes in general are the most extreme interferences with others' freedom.

These are noble principles and aspirations, and they are hard to translate into practice. Almost everything we do has some effect on other persons and changes the context in which they make their own decisions. Life is a matter of negotiated (or forced) compromises with the interests and desires of those around us. A radically different conception of freedom from the one above holds that true freedom exists only in a state of anarchy. Every state, that is, every monopoly of power in the form of government and law, erodes the freedom of the individual and shifts control to established authority. This view reflects Jean-Jacques Rousseau's sentiment that "men are born free, but everywhere they are in chains."

The first view of freedom, the notion that authority and organized society make freedom possible rather than that they inevitably destroy it, has generally prevailed in political theory. In every society, the distinction between what is private and what is public involves delicate negotiation. Some areas of criminal law are relatively uncontroversial. As we saw, the use of freedom to deprive others of freedom by force and violence cannot be a realistic option. Every society, therefore, prohibits homicide, rape, and assault. The choice of taking another's property by force or stealth is also a general threat to welfare. The basic elements of criminal law, and the basic necessary infringements of public order on private choice, are thus more or less given.

But we quickly arrive at hard questions about law. It is customary to say that the easy questions involve harm. John Stuart Mill gave us the resilient principle that law has to interfere, and liberty has to yield, when individuals choose to harm others. Immediately, we have two questions. What is the scope of harm? And should criminal law limit itself to interpersonal harm? The first question has become more difficult as we have refined our understanding of human psychology. It is one thing to prohibit physical assaults; it is something else to make law the guardian of hurt feelings and damaged psyches. Can we allow free expression and, at the same time, protect persons from the significant psychological harm implicit in everyday life?

The second question is, in fact, answered in the negative. Criminal law has never limited itself to harm. The moral convictions of legislators, ostensibly reflecting the moral sense of the community, have in every culture produced laws against offensive behavior that is not obviously harmful. A common example is the prohibition on nudity or offensive dress ("lascivious carriage"). Other historical examples demonstrate how seriously moral values change with time and, in historical perspective, some prohibitions seem inexcusable. For most of our history, miscegenation was prohibited. And we are still struggling over the legal consequences of consensual homosexual acts between adults.

To be sure, arguments can always be constructed in the attempt to show that any particular kind of behavior is harmful, not merely offensive (to some). But such arguments must always be tested by plausibility. Controversial examples of categories that straddle the distinction between harm and offense include laws against prostitution and adult pornography.

Criminal law is also used paternalistically, to protect persons from harm that they may do to themselves. Familiar paternalistic laws are drug prohibitions, seat belt laws, and laws against aiding a suicide. The rationale for paternalistic laws is complex. One argument is that certain goals or objects are ones that no rational or reasonable person would seek. Thus, such laws arguably do not interfere with important freedoms. Another argument is that certain conditions impede reasonable judgment and lead to self-destructive acts. A decision made in deep depression or in response to a severe drug addiction is arguably not a genuine decision freely made. Yet another argument is that some laws infringe freedom minimally and produce significant gains (seat belt law, for example).

The first two arguments for paternalistic laws raise further questions. Who decides what goals a rational person would seek? Would a rational person engage in sadomasochistic behavior? Would a rational person climb a mountain with a historical fatality rate among climbers of 75 percent? Would a rational person donate half her liver to a stranger? We are each the captives of our own history, disposition, and imagination when we decide what a rational person might do. Similarly, the question of what conditions make decisions irrational (or at least not choices worthy of respect) is tough. Most persons do not have a default state of normal mood and emotion; our attitudes and feelings are different at different times, and the decisions we make differ accordingly. Of course, some conditions involve such impairment that we need to be protected from ourselves, but what those conditions are and what interventions are warranted is hardly transparent.

Thus, criminal law generally prohibits conduct not simply to prevent harm but also because of offense and for paternalistic reasons. But should it do so? Each of these criteria for criminalization is part of the problem of distinguishing public from private matters and of defining the notion of meaningful freedom and autonomy. In addition to the core crimes involving serious and indelible harm, criminal codes reflect many other decisions about the periphery of law. The stories (and poems and plays) in this chapter offer a chance to debate the scope of the public interest in private lives. We will look at such matters as date rape and the public monitoring of dating conduct, child abuse and the scope of freedom to raise one's child as one wishes, suicide and the decision to end one's life, drug addiction and the freedoms exercised by members of the drug subculture, and finally the choices of communities to shape themselves by limiting the kinds of activities that they will allow. The chapter also involves an ongoing invitation to construct and analyze analogous situations for yourself.

Dating and Date Rape

e.e. cummings: may i feel said he

e.e. cummings (1894-1962), was one of the most popular poets of the early and middle twentieth century. He studiously used lower-case letters and experimented with unusual punctuation and eccentric placement of words on the page. It has been customary to write his name accordingly, but ironically he did not approve of this usage. He was also a painter, playwright, and essayist, and he was part of the World War I generation of

Americans (as a soldier, as well) that spent time in Paris in the 1920s and was generally regarded as the avant-garde. In contrast to his style, the sentiments in his poems are usually conventional and accessible.

cummings is not a political poet, and he refers to law rarely in his work. The following poem illuminates changing social preoccupations. While it seems very likely that cummings did not have sexual violations and legal remedies in mind while writing it, one can easily transpose them to the situation at hand. When one does so, one sees the complexity of applying rape law to situations, like date rape, in which the parties know and partially trust each other and in which their communications and intentions are affected by conflicting desires and perhaps also by intoxication.

❧ may i feel said he ❧

e.e. cummings

may i feel said he
(i'll squeal said she
just once said he)
it's fun said she

(may i touch said he
how much said she
a lot said he)
why not said she

(let's go said he
not too far said she
what's too far said he
where you are said she)

may i stay said he
(which way said she
like this said he
if you kiss said she

may i move said he
is it love said she)
if you're willing said he
(but you're killing said she

but it's life said he
but your wife said she
now said he)
ow said she

(tiptop said he
don't stop said she
oh no said he)
go slow said she

(come? said he
ummm said she)
you're divine! said he
(you are Mine said she)

Discussion Topics

1. In the last forty years, many matters that had long been considered private have become public issues. The feminist movement has contributed to this trend by focusing on the situation of women in the middle of the twentieth century. In the workplace and at home, women were second-class citizens who were expected to defer their interests to those of men. Most high-paying and high-prestige jobs were not (or were barely) available to women; spousal abuse was a dark secret publicly denied.

The change in social attitude and social practice has been enormous. One does not have to be a feminist to agree women acquiesced in suppressing their aims quite generally in the 1950s. Scholars and social activists vary in judging how much more needs to be done, but the fruits of egalitarianism are evident. This has meant, of course, that government and law have entered into the erstwhile privacy of the workplace and the home to an unprecedented extent.

It was long assumed that rape law was concerned with stranger-rape. Relations among dating partners and between husband and wife involved private negotiations. This has changed dramatically. Wives are no longer assumed to be available-at-will sexually as a corollary of the marriage contract. And forcible (and therefore impermissible) sex is seen as a familiar occurrence in dating.

The question remains how much and in what ways the law should oversee dating. The situation in cummings' poem illustrates what might be regarded as a typical encounter.

2. Opinions vary with regard to the public role. On one hand, some feminists argue that consent for intercourse must always be manifest and transparent. The aggressive partner who initiates intercourse must be able to prove that consent occurred. The model here is contractual. On the other hand, some observers claim that the back-and-forth interaction between dating partners defies all formulas. The psychology of each partner is complex. Men may believe that the male role requires them to make overtures and that women who decline or are ambivalent are doing so because of female role expectations and not because of lack of desire or will. Each player has all kinds of ambivalence, perhaps, and each brings his or her own personal idiosyncracies. Often, the ability of each partner to make and carry out clear decisions is compromised by drink or drugs.

Given the complexity of each dating relationship, how should the relevant rape law be written? Should the aggressive partner be expected to prove consent? If so, what kind of evidence will do? Should date rape law be reserved for the most coercive and deceptive situations, e.g., those in which the victims are drugged?

3. How do the interests and motives of "he" and "she" emerge in cummings' poem? Proponents of the view that "no" means "no" might find evidence that "she" clearly refused ("what's too far said he, where you are said she"). Others might emphasize the playfulness and ambiguity of each player's comments.

4. Do the comments in cummings' poem reflect a difference between men and women with regard to the expectations they bring to dating? It is said that men have short-term expectations, wanting sex, while women are looking for long-term commitment ("you're divine! said he, (you are Mine said she)"). Note that the "M" is the only capital letter in the poem (except for the first letter). Are these expectations still prevalent in male and female psychology — at least as reflected in popular culture? Are they stereotypes that have changed and whose value is now weak?

5. Many sociologists believe that dating patterns have changed in a permanent way. High school and college students socialize with groups of friends and pair off less than in the past. Sex, when it happens, is more casual and tends to occur by mutual agreement. Men and women exercise care equally. Stereotypes reflect the conventions of the past and not today's reality. Does this description fit the world you inhabit? If so, what consequences does it have for the law of rape? Note that, in the world described above, privacy still has a place but with a new configuration.

6. The Supreme Court of Pennsylvania has been a leader in applying indecent assault and deviate sexual intercourse laws to situations in which acquaintance rape is alleged. (See *Commonwealth v. Fischer*, 721 A.2d 1111, and *Commonwealth v. Berkowitz*, 641 A.2d 1161.) The court's cases demonstrate sensitivity to distinguishing the element of consent from that of force and to identifying various kinds of force or coercion. They also illustrate the difficulties of reconstructing private events that were seen differently by the parties who participated.

Child Abuse

Sue Miller: *The Good Mother*

In the last thirty years, child abuse has become a highly visible social problem. Debates rage over what constitutes abuse, about whether abuse is over- or under-reported, and about whether unconventional methods of child care can be confused with abuse. As more and more couples divorce and as custody becomes an ever more public matter, the choices made in child rearing have public as well as personal consequences.

The Good Mother, a novel by Sue Miller, is the story of Anna, a divorced mother with a four-year-old daughter, who is in danger of losing custody. The author immersed herself in family law while writing the book, and she acknowledges her legal consultants. The chapter reprinted here shows the beginning of Anna's legal battle and explores its implications for her love affair with Leo, an artist with whom she lives.

Sue Miller has published steadily since her first novel, *The Good Mother*, appeared in 1986. Born in 1943 and graduated from Radcliffe College in 1964, she spent a couple of decades teaching, working in day care, and writing under fellowships while being a single parent. The changing situation of women in contemporary America remains her focus.

❧ *from* The Good Mother ❧

Sue Miller

When I called my lawyer on Monday, he was reassuring. This kind of thing happened all the time, he said. Threats about custody, they were like a post-divorce sport. It would probably turn out that Brian was negotiating for something—less money, more time, something like that—and was introducing the issue of custody as a red herring, just to soften me up.

"What I'd do if I were you," he said, "is just go on about my business.

"You planning to go down there on Friday? Go on down there. My guess is no one'll say anything about any of this. The name of the game is intimidation."

"So you wouldn't worry about it?" I asked. I hadn't told him about Leo, and I was glad it seemed that now I wouldn't have to.

"I sure as hell wouldn't," he said. "In these kind of situations, don't worry about a thing till you're holding the papers in your hand. You get some kind of papers, then you call me back and we'll worry together. That's what I'm here for."

He was a heavyset, avuncular man, balding and oddly graceful in small things. I had met him only once, during the divorce proceedings, when I went downtown to his office to review the agreement with him. He had urged a few changes, had acted frustrated by my unresponsiveness. "You're not really getting your money's worth out of me," he'd said, shaking his big head. And I'd felt almost apologetic that I didn't want more from Brian.

He had come with me out to the elevator when I left, and as I watched him walk away, I was struck by his gait, something dainty and controlled in it, as though before he put on all the weight he'd been a dancer, an athlete.

I told Leo that Muth thought it was all right, didn't think we should worry.

"You told him about the thing with Molly," he said.

"No, but he said that it was most likely just a threat, anyway, that Brian would turn out to be working out something else, like less money or something."

"But you didn't tell him what happened," he persisted.

"Do you want to call him back?" I burst out. "I don't think we need to worry about it."

He looked at me. I'd been awake and dressed long before he'd gotten up, and had called the lawyer promptly at eight-thirty. We hadn't touched or kissed this morning. We'd moved around the kitchen getting our separate breakfasts, doing our separate chores, like an old married couple sunk deep in habitual solitude, but without that sense of comfort or familiarity.

"No, fine," he said. He was sitting at the table, wearing the same clothes he'd been wearing when we made love the night before. His white skin was puffy around his eyes.

"Whatever you say."

"I say let's forget it," I said angrily.

"I hope we can."

On Wednesday morning, I was sitting alone in the living room in my nightgown — Leo was still asleep — when the guy came with the papers. As soon as the doorbell rang I knew what it was. I felt as though I'd gone through it already. I stood in the hallway and watched him below me slowly mounting the twisting stairway, as though he were a memory. I felt as distanced from the coming event as one does from a dream; but curious too: whose face would he wear? what words would he say?

He looked up at me from the landing below. "You Anna Dunlop?" he asked. He was young, wore a maroon jacket that read Cambridge 1977 Babe Ruth All Stars on its breast. On the arm that held out the envelope, the same gold script spelled Bud.

"Dunlap," I said.

He looked at the envelope as he moved up towards me. "Oh, right," he said, and grinned sheepishly. He was homely, with crusts of acne clustered beardlike around his mouth and chin. He held the envelope out. "This is for you," he said.

"Many thanks." I took it.

He shrugged, and immediately started down the stairs, moving backwards for the first few steps. "It's a job," he said. "What can I tell you." When he'd rounded the second landing and was more or less out of sight, he started taking the stairs two and three at a time, thundering down them like a child released from some social constraint.

I shut the door and walked down the dark hallway to the kitchen, tearing open the envelope as I went. I set it down for a moment to dial the telephone, but even as it began to ring, I was reading. The words on the papers before me also seemed familiar, but shocking. They leapt up: complaint for modification of agreement . . . motion for temporary custody . . . sexual irregularities with minor child . . . I didn't want to see more. I folded the papers and put them back into the jagged envelope. The secretary was telling me that Muth hadn't arrived at the office yet. She took my number in a chirping, efficient voice.

I got another cup of coffee when I'd hung up, and took it out onto the back porch. I sat on the wooden chair there. After he had begun to spend his nights with us, Leo brought his galvanized tub over for Molly to use as a pool on the back porch. Now it leaned, empty and rimed with white, against the brown clapboards. Next to it was a milk crate full of plastic bottles and cups, tubes, toy boats, all the things she played with in the water.

Across the yard, my neighbor moved in her window, waved. I lifted my cup in response, as though it were just another day.

The phone shrilled. It was Muth. As I talked to him, I heard Leo groan, could imagine him stretching, in my room.

I told Muth that Brian had sent papers, that I had received them earlier this morning.

"Aha," he said. "Well, I was wrong. Down to business, huh?"

"I guess so," I said.

"Well, can you tell me, Mrs. Dunlap, I mean, is it clear from what he says, on what grounds he's making the motion? Or do you wanna read it to me, or what?" I heard Leo get up, his bare feet approaching the kitchen. I turned my body away from the open doorway.

"Sexual irregularities, he says."

"Sexual irregularities?"

"Yes," I said. Leo's steps had paused at the door.

"With who?" Muth asked.

"My lover," I said. "The man I've been seeing." Leo was motionless behind me.

"Aha," Muth said, and waited. I said nothing. Then: "Well, you wanna tell me where this is coming from, Mrs. Dunlap? I mean is this coming out of left field, or where?"

"Not exactly." My voice was low, my shoulders hunched away from the doorway.

"So you mean, this guy had some kind of contact, some kind of sexual contact, with, ah, the kid. With Molly?"

"Yes, in a certain sense, yes. Or it could be construed that way, yes." I heard Leo turn, pad away toward the bathroom.

"Aha," he said. And waited again. But I couldn't answer right away. I heard Leo down the hall, the rush of water, the singing of the pipes. I felt ashamed. You let it happen, Brian had said. It seemed as palpable a failure to me as the long swollen scratch on her dirty cheek at Sammy Brower's house.

"I'd like to come in and talk to you," I said finally.

"Yes," he said. "Yes, it's clear that that's what we'd better do. The sooner the better, I'd say. And, ah, can you bring your friend? He's going to have to, most likely, be included in all this. You know, there'll be a hearing, et cetera. You know, as a matter of fact, Mrs. Dunlap, maybe you could check these papers and see if there's a date, a date you're supposed to show up. Did you check for that?"

"No," I said.

"Well, you wanna do that now?" he asked.

"Sure," I said. I set the phone down, took the papers out again, leafed through them. There it was — August seventeenth. I picked the phone up. "It's here," I said.

"What do we get?" he asked. "A week, ten days?"

"It's Friday," I said. "A week from Friday."

"Aha," he said. "Well, I'll tell you, then, I'll give you to my secretary, and ask her to set you up pronto. I think I might have a space even today. Tomorrow for sure. We ought to get going on this, you know, figure out what angle we're going to take, that kinda jazz, pretty soon. As soon as possible, actually."

"Yes," I said, and he clicked off. After a moment, the secretary's flutey voice came on the line. Mr. Muth had time late in the morning tomorrow, she said. Was eleven-thirty all right? I agreed. She told me Mr. Muth wanted to be certain both of us were coming.

There was no problem, I told her. We'd both be there.

When Leo emerged from his shower, I was dressed, back in the kitchen, washing up. He stood in the doorway again and watched me, gripping a towel around his waist, his drooping curls raining silver drops on his shoulders. I looked at him. "That was my lawyer on the phone," I said.

"I wondered." He pulled the towel to the side, held it tighter at his hip. He would never have worn it before. It was like the sign of our mutual fall from grace; but I was, for the moment, glad not to see him naked.

"I got the papers today," I told him.

"Oh," he said. His face asked me how bad it was. "It's real then."

"It is," I said. I tried to keep my voice determined and cheerful.

He shook his head. "Jesus, Anna. I know you know it, but . . . I'm sorry."

He stepped towards me, into the kitchen, but I raised my hand.

"I don't see this as your fault," I said. "I don't want you to tell me that."

And I turned back to the counter, making big circles with the pink sponge. "Muth can see us tomorrow," I said.

"Did he say anything?"

"About what?"

"Well, about what would happen. About whether this was . . . about getting Molly back."

"Not really. I didn't really talk to him in much detail."

"But you told him what happened?"

I looked at him. "Roughly, yes, but not in any detail."

He turned, as though he were going to leave the room. His arched footprints left a quickly fading steamy print on the linoleum, like the breath of his feet. At the door he stopped and said, without looking at me, "I'd like to be able to talk about this stuff, Anna. It's like you keep wishing it will go away if we don't discuss it. That's hard for me. It doesn't help me. Or anything."

I shook my head. "And I don't want to talk about it," I said. "I don't see how that would help. It's done. I don't blame you. That's not what it's about. But it's just that I feel like I'm holding on by a thread here, plus I've still got stuff I have to do at work. To keep going. These fucking rats."

I shrugged. "I just need to do this my way, I think. But I am sorry, I really am sorry, if it makes it worse for you."

"That's not it. It's not that I'm feeling sorry for myself. I . . . Jesus. That would be pretty self-indulgent. I just . . ." He looked at me. "I don't want to lose you."

"That's not the issue, is it?" I asked. "Your losing me?" And I turned away. In a moment I sensed, rather than heard, that he'd left the room. When I went to find him a few minutes later, to say I was sorry, he was gone. I imagined him swinging down the hall barefoot, partly dressed, as quickly and silently as he had in the spring when he'd wanted to get out before Molly heard him.

Leo wore a jacket and tie to Muth's office the next day. He'd had to borrow them from a friend, since he didn't own either. The jacket was a little tight, and Leo's cuffs, his big hands, stuck out. He looked like a farmboy visiting in town.

"That's very sweet of you," I said. "Wearing that." We were driving down Storrow Drive in light midmorning traffic. Summer school students lay reading, sunbathing on the green banks of the river. He looked at me quickly to be sure I was sincere. When he saw that I was, he thanked me. It struck me suddenly that much of our conversation for the last several days had been just this polite — apologies, thanks, careful backing away from demands or questions. Each of us was behaving as though the other was fragile, easily damaged. Nothing was natural between us. We hadn't made love since Sunday night, the night Leo returned; and as I remembered all that, it seemed to me that I had known, even as we did it, that it marked the end of something. Now we lay in the same bed together each night, sometimes touching each other lightly, without passion, before we turned away and sought sleep. But sex seemed unthinkable.

So did sleeping alone though. It was as though neither of us wanted to face himself. Even the night before, when I'd gone to his house just to apologize after I'd finished up at the lab, when I was sure each of us would want to be alone, we were unable to find a way to separate.

"I don't need to stay," I'd said, standing in his doorway. "I just came to say I was sorry for being so sharp this morning."

"No, no, that's O.K.," he said. "I understand. Come on in. I mean, I'd like you to stay." He stood back to make room for my entrance, then hesitated. "Unless you want to be alone or something." We looked at each other a moment. The thought of being alone terrified me.

"I'll stay," I said, and instantly felt how much I didn't want to, how much I had wanted to be alone. But I was already crossing his threshold.

I would hurt his feelings if I left, it was too late. And so we slept together another night with our backs curved towards each other, just as Brian and I had done in the last stages of our marriage.

In the morning, I'd gone home to change my clothes, then driven back over to Leo's to pick him up. He was waiting for me on the corner by his building, and I almost drove past him, he looked so unfamiliar in his costume. In the car, I kept looking over at him as I drove, but he seemed unconscious of me, lost in his own nervousness. His hands drummed on his knees. Once or twice he popped his knuckles.

We parked in an expensive lot downtown, and then, because we were early for the appointment with Muth, we stopped for coffee. The cafeteria was dim, functional, with small formica tables.

The people around us were a curious combination of bums and businessmen. They seemed completely at home in one another's company. It was we who were out of place in this world—both wearing uniforms that seemed uncomfortable on us. My dress was a little too fancy, not secretarial enough. And when I saw the businessmen, dark and tailored, I realized that Leo looked worse in his attempt at respectability than he would have if he'd just worn a T-shirt and jeans. There was something that appeared nearly psychopathic to me abruptly, in the ill-fitting disguise. I sat across from him, sipping the burnt-tasting coffee and talking about what Muth was like, and I wanted to reach over and loosen the tie, wanted to ask him to take the jacket off. But I couldn't. He'd done it for me, to help me get Molly back.

Upstairs, when Muth approached us across the carpeted expanse of the firm's outer offices, I watched his face carefully for signs of his response to Leo; but it was unreadable, pleasant as ever. He was in shirtsleeves, rolled up, and a tie. He shook Leo's hand and mine as though we were perfectly respectable people.

In his office, he arranged the chairs for us, making small talk in his rambling way about the Red Sox. Once he'd got us settled, he sat down behind his desk, and asked me for the papers. I handed the torn envelope across to him. Leo and I sat in silence for three or four minutes while he read through them, neither of us looking at the other. I was intensely conscious of Leo though, of his restless shifting in his chair. I hoped he wouldn't be rude if Muth probed too deep.

Muth's face, bent over his desk, fell into a somber frowning paunchiness. Once or twice he ran his hand over his balding head. But when be looked up, he was neutral, boyishly middle-aged again.

"Well," he said. "The news is not good, I guess."

I found myself smiling politely, making some agreeable answer. Leo stared at me.

"I think what would help me right now," Muth said, extracting a pencil from a jar of them on his desk, "is to find out exactly what you think it is that's got Mr. Dunlap so fired up here. I think the phrase he uses is sexual irregularities, and I think you said on the phone, Mrs. Dunlap, that there had been some kind of contact between Mr. Cutter and . . . ah, Molly. That right?"

"Yes," I said. I nodded.

"Well, that's what I need to get straight then. Just what it was, when it happened, how often, that kind of thing." He looked up, expectantly, pleasantly.

"Once," Leo said.

"Once," he repeated, and wrote something down. He smiled at Leo. "Can you, ah, can you fill me in on it a bit, Mr. Cutter?"

I looked at Leo. He shifted forward in his chair, and without looking over at me, he started talking. As he began, I thought, Why, he's practiced this.

"It was sometime in June when it happened. Anna had left Molly and me alone for the evening. She was at the lab or something, I don't remember what, but she was supposed to get back in time to tuck Molly in. Molly and I had gone out to get ice cream. I'd given her a bath" — Muth's pencil whispered quickly on the page — "gotten her into her pj's, all that stuff. It was hot. I'd been working all day. Molly was in her room, playing, and she sounded happy, so I figured I'd take a shower. I told her I was going to, so she'd know where to find me, if she needed me." Leo's hands had been folded in his lap at first. Now, as he relaxed a little, they came to life, helped him tell the story.

"I, you know, got in the shower, and after a while, she came into the bathroom, started talking to me. It was like she just wanted company. She was just talking about this and that, the stories she'd picked out for her mother to read to her, some stuff that happened to her at day care. She was just sitting on the toilet seat, talking, the way she sometimes did."

"She'd come in before when you were in the shower?" Muth asked. He didn't look up.

"Me, or her mother, yeah. She liked the company."

Muth nodded.

"When I pushed the curtain back and started drying off, I noticed Molly was staring at me, at my" — there was the slightest hesitation as Leo chose the word — "penis. But she'd seen me naked before, I didn't think much of it. I was fooling around, you know, dancing."

"Dancing," Muth repeated.

"Yeah. I was dancing and singing actually." Leo's voice had begun to sound angry. I leaned forward. He looked up at me, then moved uncomfortably in his chair. When he spoke again, his voice was calm. "Singing 'Singin' in the Rain.' She liked that." He shrugged. "And then I finished, and I was just drying off, and she said, out of the blue, 'That's your penis?'" He cleared his throat. "You know, she was learning that stuff, those words. She had a book that talked about it, and they did the body parts at day care. Her mother — Anna — had talked about it some too, telling her the names of stuff." He shrugged again. "So I said yeah. She was, she was standing up, she'd gotten closer to the tub. I was, actually, a little uncomfortable about it. But I'd seen how relaxed Anna was about it all, and I didn't want to screw that up or anything. So I tried to seem natural, not cover up or anything.

"But then she said, 'Can I touch it?'"

Muth looked up sharply at Leo, his pencil still on the yellow pad.

"I honestly didn't think about it for more than a second. I just said sure. And, um, she did. She . . . held it for a second. And just the contact, I guess. The contact, and I think, the kind of . . . weirdness of the situation made me . . . that is, I started to get an erection. And I said, 'That's enough, Molly,' and I turned away. I put the towel on. She made some other comment, some question about my . . . about it getting big. And I told her that sometimes happened with men. And I went and got dressed." He looked at Muth, as if awaiting judgment.

"And that was that?" Muth asked.

"Yes. Pretty much." He paused. Then: "She did talk about it some more that night. She seemed a little anxious about it actually. She talked about the facts of life. Of sex. You know, she knew the purpose of an erection in a vague sense. She knew, sort of, what it was for, and I think it confused her. That I had one. So I tried to explain. I'm not sure how well I did."

"Aha," Muth said. "And did you discuss this with Mrs. Dunlap?"

"No." He shifted in his chair.

"Why not?"

"I was . . . To tell the truth, I was embarrassed. And I thought I'd handled it O.K. Or as well as anyone could've. So I didn't see that it was a problem."

"Aha," Muth said. Then he looked at Leo. "Can I just ask you, Mr., ah, Cutter, why you didn't just say no to the child. You said it made you uncomfortable. Why didn't you just tell her she couldn't touch you?"

"I didn't think that's what Anna — Mrs. Dunlap — would have wanted me to do."

"You didn't think Mrs. Dunlap would have wanted you to?" Suddenly Muth seemed lawyer like to me, in a way he never had before. I could imagine him being mean in a courtroom.

"No," Leo said. "I thought she'd want me to be as relaxed, as natural with Molly, as she was. About her body and that kind of thing." Muth made a note, then looked up again.

"So you might say you misunderstood the rules."

Leo shrugged. "I thought I understood them."

There was a long pause. Then Muth said, "I think when the time comes, Mr. Cutter, it'd be better for Mrs. Dunlap in the situation we've got here, if you just said you misunderstood them."

After a moment Leo inclined his head slightly, stiffly.

Muth began to talk to me. He asked me what the rules were; how much Leo and I were naked around Molly; whether she'd been in bed with us; how much she knew about the facts of life. He asked me to describe the book I'd read to her, to describe the pictures in it. (They were cartoon figures, cheerful, dumpy, humorous.) He said he'd like me to bring the book in next time I came, that it might be helpful, depending on what Molly had said to Brian. He asked me how long Leo and I had been involved, how long he'd been spending nights at our house, how much Molly understood of our relationship, how often Leo had been alone with Molly. He took notes throughout, and sometimes as he wrote, his face took on the same frowning cast it had had when he bent over the papers from Brian; but whenever he lifted it to me and Leo, it was bland and open as a curious baby's.

Mostly I talked, though occasionally Leo offered an observation. Muth asked about how things had been when I'd been married to Brian, what his attitudes about sex had been, whether the patterns in the house had changed a lot since then, whether Molly had seemed at all disturbed by those changes. When finally he seemed to be running out of questions, I asked him what he thought would happen, what he thought Brian's chances were.

He shook his head. "This kind of thing is tough to call, Mrs. Dunlap. A lot depends on what Molly said, on how bothered she seems to be about it. But these judges, you know, they're by and large conservative. They don't like to hear anything about sexual stuff with kids." I sensed Leo moving slightly in his chair. "You know," Muth gestured with his slender fingers open, "they hear terrible stuff all the time. After a while, they lump everything like that together in their minds."

"What if," I cleared my throat. "What if I said I wouldn't see Leo anymore. Would that make a difference?"

I could feel Leo snap to alertness, his eyes on me. My mouth parched. But Muth knew only strategy, seemed unconscious of anything that passed between us. He was already shaking his head.

"They hear it all the time. You can try it, for sure, but they don't believe it anyway. A promise, to them, is what someone is willing to say to get a kid back. Period."

The silence in the room was now explosive. Muth, unperturbed, looked from Leo to me. "O.K., then," he said. "If it's all right with you, Mr. Cutter, I'd like to talk to Mrs. Dunlap alone for a few minutes." He stood, Leo stood. "If you could just wait outside. . . ." He crossed to the door and opened it for Leo. "It was good to talk with you," Muth said, extending his hand. Leo reached out and shook it. "I appreciate your honesty."

Leo made a murmuring noise. Then without looking back at me, he left.

Even watching his stiff back out of the room, I was so focused on what all this meant for Molly, for Molly and me, that I didn't realize I could have managed not to ask my question in front of Leo by waiting only a few minutes longer. At the time, hurting him, alienating him, seemed inevitable, part of the price I had to pay.

Muth sat down. His tone was confidential. He invited me to share any doubts, any observations about aberrant behavior in Leo. I told him I had no doubts about him, that Leo had, except in this instance, behaved with Molly as I would have wanted him to.

"So it was just in this case that he misunderstood you?"

I waited a moment before I answered. "Yes," I said, feeling that I was betraying Leo as much by my agreement with Muth now, as I had by my question in front of him earlier.

Muth went on to talk about my work schedule, about how much Molly had seen Brian since the divorce, about how much she'd seen of him when we were still married, about who was taking care of Molly in Washington while Brian and Brenda worked. Three or four times he circled back around to Leo again, what I knew of his background, his sexual history before me. I tried to sound firm and confident, determined to try not to betray him any more than I felt I already had.

Finally he leaned back and tossed his pencil onto the pad.

"Okay," he said. "Now I think the approach here is gonna be to down-pedal all this stuff about permissiveness. You know and I know that it's probably healthier for a kid to be pretty much open about this sexual stuff, right?"

I nodded.

"But what we're not gonna do here is, we're not gonna try to educate the judge about it, O.K.? Because that's not gonna work, right?"

I nodded.

"What we're gonna focus on is how happy she was, how much time you spent with her, how responsible you were. How Mr. Dunlap's a bit of a workaholic, how his wife has the same kind of job, how the choice is really between a loving mother and a paid babysitter. O.K.? Let them ask the stuff about this sexual thing with Cutter. It's gotta come out. But we're not gonna defend it or tie it in with the idea of sexual openness or anything. It's just gonna be a mistake he made. Got it?"

I nodded, ashamed. You, Brian's voice said, you let it happen.

"Now, let me tell you what I think we oughta do," Muth said. "See if you agree with me."

"O.K.," I said.

"I think that with what we've got here, our best chance is gonna be an expert, a shrink. See, you and Mr. Cutter both are clearly, you know, you come off, well—articulate, concerned with her, with Molly. With a guardian, a psychiatrist appointed by the court, you could talk, you know, the way you have with me here, and I think that would be our best shot. With their training, they look beyond just the bare facts. They're there to pick up, you know"—his hand circled in the air—"attitudes, feelings. My sense is, if we go with that, if I make a motion that we get a shrink to make a recommendation, that within a very short time he'd see what I've seen here: it was a mistake, it was, basically, Cutter's mistake, it's not about to happen again, right?"

"Right," I said.

"So, then he recommends she stays with you; and the judge, they give a lot of credence to that. I think . . . well, that's what I'd suggest anyway."

"That sounds reasonable to me," I said. And then, not to seem too passive, "Are there alternative strategies?"

He shook his head. "Not that readily come to mind. You have anything on the father?"

"What do you mean?"

"Well, like this." He gestured at the papers. "You know, like what he's got on you. Has he done anything you can point to where it's clearly bad judgment, incompetence?"

"Not really. He's very busy, as I've said. He always had trouble finding time for her."

"Sure, yeah, we'll use that, but in itself that's not enough."

"No, I really don't have anything."

"So," he said, and lifted his big shoulders. "Let's go with the shrink?"

"Yes," I said.

"Even with him though, I'd downpedal the specifics. But you could tell him, I mean he might be very interested that Mr. Dunlap was what you might say, uptight about sexual stuff. And it wouldn't hurt if you could remember, like, a scene where, if he might have frightened Molly a little with that strictness or something. But it will just be a more relaxed context, if you know what I mean. Less concerned with exactly what happened and more concerned with why, and that's to our advantage. You understand?"

I nodded. He came forward in his chair, leaned towards me.

"'Cause what happened, on the face of it, isn't good." He shook his head. "I mean, I can understand how it happened, you can understand how it happened, but I can also tell you how their attorney's going to present it, and it's not going to sound good." He shifted back again. "You know, there's a certain way of looking at this stuff—and I hate to tell you, but it's how a lot of the world sees it—and what we've got there is a guy, a guy kind of down and out, no regular job"—he raised his hand as I stirred, letting me know he knew it wasn't so. I was again struck by his hand's delicacy, the fingers that curved in slightly like a dancer's—"left alone with a kid, cavorting around in front of her, encouraging contact, aroused by her touch. They may suggest a lot worse, too, and he'll be the only one to deny it. You see what I mean. And depending on the judge, on how much he's able to imagine another context for that behavior, that'll be how it goes. That and the recommendation of the family service officer. So that's one thing potentially in your favor. That and Mr. Dunlap's pattern of fathering."

"And how soon will all this happen? When?"

He shrugged. "First there's this hearing, right?"

I nodded.

"O.K. The procedure there is we all make these motions, and then probably we get sent to the F.S.O."

"The F.S.O.?"

"Yeah, the family service officer. It'll be like an interview. It's usually a woman, a social worker, you know, young, bright. She'll sort of assess things, make sure this guardian deal with the shrink seems appropriate, work out the details. So, we oughta find out then, by Friday, a lot of stuff: approximately when you'll all see the shrink—and the kid will too, Molly, and the father—and maybe even, I think I'll push for it, a court date set."

"And that's when it'll get decided? The court date?"

"Right, the trial. Depending on how long it takes to see the shrink, that could be a couple of months. Maybe less. And that will take a couple of days, the trial. You know, you'll testify, your ex-husband will, the shrink, the whole thing."

"And is it true that I can't see Molly until then?"

"No way," he shook his head. "No. It's not true. Chances are your ex-husband will get temporary custody—he's moving for that, till the trial, you know, and that's pretty typical. But we'll fix you up with visitation, don't you worry. No," he said, and grinned, "he's just making points telling you that, showing everybody how seriously he takes all this. We'll have no trouble getting you visitation once he's done proving that."

We sat for a moment. He cleared his throat. "Now, about money," he said.

For a moment I didn't understand him, thought he was referring to some part of the financial arrangement between me and Brian. Brian had paid him for the divorce, so I'd never thought of a fee as part of this transaction.

"Oh," I said, and I couldn't keep the surprise out of my voice. "Of course."

"The retainer'll be twenty-five hundred. And it might be, I suppose, another thousand or so in the end."

I hoped my face wasn't registering the shock that I felt, the sharp sense of my idiocy. "I'm sorry, I don't know this, but when do I pay you?" I tried to keep my voice smooth, the question academic.

"Yesterday," he said, and grinned.

I looked quickly down at my hands. When I thought I had control of my face, I looked up at him and tried smiling back. "I'll have to make it tomorrow or the next day."

He nodded. "I understand," he said. "I won't say 'I told you so' about your divorce agreement, but I understand." He rose, and I did too. "But I will need it before the court date," he said, and he crossed to the door.

"You'll have it," I said, my mind already racing through my possibilities, turning down one dead-end corridor after another.

He walked me back to the reception area. Leo sat in one of the boxy upholstered chairs, and I was startled again at how the ill-fitting jacket robbed him of all his grace and poise. He seemed a liability, sitting there, and I felt a pulse of rage at him. I stood a little distant as Muth shook hands with him again.

We rode in silence in opposite corners of the carpeted elevator. Two women stood in front of us by the doors. One of them was talking about what sounded like her divorce. "My lawyer keeps saying 'Now, we're not out to punish anyone here, we just want what's right,' but I don't think he understands. I don't care what's right, I want to fucking punish the guy."

Her friend shook her head. "Sure you do. After what he's put you through?"

The doors opened. We crossed the marble lobby, stepped outside.

Muth's office, the reception room, the elevator, had all been windowless, lit by overhead spots. I was startled to see the sunshine, feel the light summer air push my dress against me. We walked the short block to the parking lot, and I paid the attendant. I was aware of the rigidity of Leo's presence, of his anger; but I was, in a serious way, preoccupied. And so I was startled, when I got into the car next to him and shut my door, that after a moment of inert silence, he violently struggled out of the jacket and threw it against the dashboard. Then he tore at the tie and pulled it off. He caught his collar yanking at it, and the button at the neck of the shirt pulled off, ripping the cloth, and ricocheting with a sharp snap off the windshield. We sat locked together among all the empty cars, the sound of Leo's panting rage filling the space between us, and I wondered how we'd get through the next ten days, two weeks, without damaging each other. In my several seconds of terror, when I thought he might be going to hurt me, what I had felt for Leo was a cold, welling hate.

Discussion Topics

1. Before addressing the particular event that becomes the crux of the custody litigation, it is useful to reflect on Anna's convictions about and methods of parenting. Social conventions change rapidly in this area, and the received wisdom about the psychology of young children changes accordingly. The 1960s and early '70s, formative years for Sue Miller (and for the author of this book), were times of social experimentation. Much was said about the dangers of psychological repression; the free and unconstrained expression of emotion was seen as a means of achieving healthy growth. Some psychologists, but hardly a majority, remarked about America's social taboos about the body and its functions and considered them harmful. To this day, much greater outrage follows the display of Janet Jackson's breast on television than follows most reports of homicidal violence. This can easily seem very odd.

In any event, Anna clearly believed that Molly, her daughter, would be helped and not harmed by early and comfortable familiarity with bodies. This belief was more common, perhaps, thirty years ago than it is today. To what extent is raising Molly Anna's prerogative? At what point and for what reasons should it become a matter of public concern? Note that the line has shifted in the last thirty years. On the one hand, we allow parents to home-school their children (and generally to influence how they are taught) more than we did thirty years ago. On the other hand, we watch for signs of child abuse and give children and guardians newly independent roles in monitoring rights. Thus, matters that were public have become private and once-private matters have become public.

2. Clearly Molly's encounter with Leo gets out of his control. Is it something he should have foreseen? How blameworthy is he? Our answer to these questions will depend on what we consider the likely effects on Molly. Is the event itself likely to harm her? Is it something she is likely to remember, or something that will have unconscious ramifications? Even experts on child psychology will differ about these questions, but we all have deep (if not necessarily reliable) instincts about them.

If the incident becomes a crux of a custody battle, it will gain much greater importance in Molly's imagination and life than it would otherwise have. If one concludes that that event will harm Molly, it is important to distinguish the consequences of the acts themselves from the consequences they have when manipulated by the actors and institutions of law.

3. It becomes clear that Anna will have to choose between Molly and Leo. The novel makes clear that this choice is costly. Leo brings comfort, love, and ease to Anna, conditions that were absent in her marriage to Molly's father. The choice, in this context, seems inevitable: she will try to keep Molly even if it means the end of her affair.

Note that the choice is largely forced on her by the operation of law. Law and lawyers have made custody an adversarial game in which each party tries to blacken and demonize the other. Molly's father gives every indication that he wants to play the game. An obvious question is whether anyone but lawyers profits from this state of affairs. A prolonged battle is hardly in Molly's interest and is likely to hurt Anna and Leo.

Consider why and how family lawyers justify this process. It is said that the interests of the child will best be revealed to the court when every possible negative factor is uncovered. Therefore, the partisans on each side should have an incentive to discover such facts. A problem, of course, is that facts require interpretation. The shower incident is not merely a fact but an opportunity for interpretation. Are judges in a position to make the wisest interpretations of the dark facts presented to them and to arrive at the wisest decisions?

4. Some commentators consider family law not only inherently conservative but also inherently hypocritical. On this view, it not only falls back on stereotypes of good parenting and good marriage that are out of touch with modern world. It also declines to follow what it really knows to be true because it must pay lip service to homilies and conventional beliefs. In other words, the justification that family law follows the received wisdom of the ages rather than the fads of contemporary psychology faces the criticism that the received "wisdom" was never wisdom at all and that, however little we know now, we still know more than we did in the past.

Bring this down to earth. Is a couple made up of a man and a woman inherently better at parenting than a same sex couple? Should parents try to stay together "for the sake of the children" even if the marriage is loveless and full of animosity? We all know there are conventional answers to these questions and the law, perhaps more in this area than in others, is reluctant to experiment. But is reliance on conventions the best policy for those most affected — or does it just hide and perpetuate mistakes?

5. Muth, Anna's lawyer, reflects the conventional character of family law when he says that he must not try to "educate" the judge. Consider whether he is acting in Anna's best interests and clarifying the practices of law for her. Is he simply the midwife of the bad consequences that the custody battle will have for Anna? Can he control the effects and circumstances more than he does? Or is he a model of sound lawyering?

Suicide and Euthanasia

Brian Clark: *Whose Life Is It Anyway?*

Born in 1932, Brian Clark has been a steady presence on the British stage. Thirteen of his plays have been produced, but few have crossed the

Atlantic. By far his best known play is *Whose Life Is It Anyway?* (1978, produced in the U.S. in 1981), which was made into a popular film with Richard Dreyfuss.

Whose Life taps into one of the most sensitive topics in law and ethics, the right to terminate one's own life. The ethical and legal posture of Western culture, both secular and religious, has been that such a right does not exist. Christianity and Judaism see suicide as an affront to God. The morality of America and Europe has typically understood personal autonomy as extending to the development, exploitation, and enjoyment of life, not to its termination.

And yet many philosophers and political theorists argue that the most important right is that right to choose to live and that all other rights are founded on it. They point out that no one is in a better position to decide that value of one's life than oneself. But the view that one should be able to determine whether one's life is worth living conflicts with the assumed axiom that life is *inherently* worth living.

Clark's play focuses on a thirty-something sculptor, Ken Harrison, whose spinal cord has been severely injured in a car accident and who has become a quadriplegic. Ken can remain alive only with constant care for the rest of his life. Without such care, his body would quickly poison itself. He wants to end medical care, thus ending his life; his doctors oppose his decision.

❧ Whose Life Is It Anyway? ❧

Brian Clark

(*First Act*)

SISTER. A visitor for you, Mr. Harrison.

HILL. Good afternoon, Mr. Harrison.

KEN. Good afternoon.

HILL. You're looking very much better.

(SISTER has placed a chair by the bed.)

KEN. It's the nursing you know.

SISTER. I'm glad you realize it, Mr. Harrison.

KEN. Oh, I do, Sister, I do.

SISTER. I'll leave you gentlemen now.

HILL. Thank you, Sister. (She goes out.) You really do look better.

KEN. Yes. I'm as well now as I shall ever be.

HILL (unzipping his briefcase). I've brought all the papers. Things are moving along very satisfactorily now and . . .

KEN. I don't want to talk about the accident.

HILL. I understand it must be very distressing . . .

KEN. No, no. It's not that. I didn't get you alone about the compensation.

HILL. Oh . . . Sister said on the phone . . .

KEN. Yes, I know. Could you come away from the door? Look, do you work for yourself? I mean, you don't work for an insurance company or something, do you?

HILL. No. I'm in practice as a solicitor, but I . . .

KEN. Then there's no reason why you couldn't represent me generally . . . apart from this compensation thing.

HILL. Certainly, if there's anything I can do . . .

KEN. There is.

HILL. Yes?

KEN. Get me out of here.

HILL. I don't understand, Mr. Harrison.

KEN. It's quite simple. I can't exist outside the hospital, so they've got to keep me here if they want to keep me alive and they seem intent on doing that. I've decided that I don't want to stay in the hospital any longer.

HILL. But surely they wouldn't keep you here longer than necessary?

KEN. I'm almost completely paralyzed and I always will be. I shall never be discharged by the hospital. I have coolly and calmly thought it out and I have decided that I would rather not go on. I therefore want to be discharged to die.

HILL. And you want me to represent you?

KEN. Yes. Tough.

HILL. And what is the hospital's attitude?

KEN. They don't know about it yet. Even tougher.

HILL. This is an enormous step.

KEN. Mr. Hill, with all respect, I know that our hospitals are wonderful. I know that many people have succeeded in making good lives with appalling handicaps. I'm happy for them and respect and admire them. But each man must make his own decision. And mine is to die quietly and with as much dignity as I can muster and I need your help.

HILL. Do you realize what you're asking me to do?

KEN. I realize. I'm not asking that you make any decision about my life and death, merely that you represent me and my views to the hospital.

HILL. Yes, well, the first thing is to see the Doctor. What is his name?

KEN. Dr. Emerson.

HILL. I'll try and see him now and come back to you.

KEN. Then you'll represent me?

HILL. Mr. Harrison, I'll let you know my decision after I've seen Dr. Emerson.

KEN. All right, but you'll come back to tell me yourself, even if he convinces you he's right?

HILL. Yes, I'll come back.

(CROSS FADE on the sluice room. NURSE SADLER and JOHN are talking.)

JOHN. So why not?
NURSE. It's just that I'm so busy . . .
JOHN. All work and no play . . . makes for a boring day.
NURSE. Anyway, I hardly know you.
JOHN. Right. That's why I want to take you out . . . to find out what goes on behind those blue eyes . . .
NURSE. At present, there's just lists of bones and organs, all getting themselves jumbled up.
JOHN. Because you're working too hard.
NURSE. Ask me next week.
JOHN. Okay. It's a deal.
NURSE. Right!
JOHN. And I'll ask you this afternoon as well.

(CROSS FADE on DR. EMERSON's room.)

DR. EMERSON. Mr. Hill? Sister just rang through.
HILL. Dr. Emerson? (They shake hands.)
DR. EMERSON. You've been seeing Mr. Harrison?
HILL. Yes.
DR. EMERSON. Tragic case . . . I hope you'll be able to get enough money for him to ease his mind.
HILL. Dr. Emerson. It's not about that I wanted to see you. I thought I was coming about that, but Mr. Harrison wishes to retain me to represent him on quite another matter.
DR. EMERSON. Oh?
HILL. Yes, he wants to be discharged.
DR. EMERSON. That's impossible.
HILL. Why?
DR. EMERSON. To put it bluntly, he would die if we did that.
HILL. He knows that. It's what he wants.
DR. EMERSON. And you are asking me to kill my patient?
HILL. I am representing Mr. Harrison's wishes to you and asking for your reaction.
DR. EMERSON. Well, you've had it. It's impossible. Now if that's really all you came about . . .
HILL. Dr. Emerson, you can, of course, dismiss me like that if you choose to, but I would hardly think it serves anyone's interests, least of all Mr. Harrison's.
DR. EMERSON. I am trying to save Mr. Harrison's life. There is no need to remind me of my duty to my patient, Mr. Hill.

HILL. Or mine to my client, Dr. Emerson.

DR. EMERSON. Are you telling me that you have accepted the job of coming to me to urge a course of action that will lose your client his life?

HILL. I hadn't accepted it . . . no . . . I told Mr. Harrison I would talk to you first. Now I have and I begin to see why he thought it necessary to be represented.

DR. EMERSON. All right . . . Let's start again. Now tell me what you want to know.

HILL. Mr. Harrison wishes to be discharged from the hospital. Will you please make the necessary arrangements?

DR. EMERSON. No.

HILL. May I ask why not?

DR. EMERSON. Because Mr. Harrison is incapable of living outside the hospital and it is my duty as a doctor to preserve life.

HILL. I take it that Mr. Harrison is a voluntary patient here.

DR. EMERSON. Of course.

HILL. Then I fail to see the legal basis for your refusal.

DR. EMERSON. Can't you understand that Mr. Harrison is suffering from depression? He is incapable of making a rational decision about his life and death.

HILL. Are you maintaining that Mr. Harrison is mentally unbalanced?

DR. EMERSON. Yes.

HILL. Would you have any objection to my bringing in a psychiatrist for a second opinion?

DR. EMERSON. Of course not, but why not ask the consultant psychiatrist here? I'm sure he will be able to convince you.

HILL. Has he examined Mr. Harrison?

DR. EMERSON. No, but that can be quickly arranged.

HILL. That's very kind of you, Dr. Emerson, but I'm sure you'll understand if I ask for my own—whose opinion you are not sure of before he examines the patient.

DR. EMERSON. Good afternoon, Mr. Hill.

HILL. Good afternoon. (MR. HILL takes up his briefcase and leaves.)

DR. EMERSON (picks up the phone). Could you find out where Dr. Travers is, please? I want to see him urgently, and put me through to the hospital secretary, please. Well, put me through when he's free.

(CROSS FADE on KEN's room. The door opens and MR. HILL comes in.)

KEN. Well, how was it on Olympus?

HILL. Cloudy.

KEN. No joy then?

HILL. Dr. Emerson does not wish to discharge you.

KEN. Surprise, surprise. So what do we do now?

HILL. Mr. Harrison, I will be perfectly plain. Dr. Emerson claims that you are not in a sufficiently healthy mental state to make a rational decision, especially one of this seriousness and finality. Now my position is, I am not competent to decide whether or not he is right.

KEN. So how will you decide?

HILL. I should like to have you examined by an independent psychiatrist and I will accept his view of the case and advise you accordingly.

KEN. Fair enough. Will Dr. Emerson agree?

HILL. He has already. I ought to warn you that Dr. Emerson is likely to take steps to have you admitted here as a person needing treatment under the Mental Health Act of 1959. This means that he can keep you here and give you what treatment he thinks fit.

KEN. Can he do that?

HILL. He probably can.

KEN. Haven't I any say in this?

HILL. Oh, yes. He will need another signature and that doctor will have to be convinced that you ought compulsorily to be detained. Even if he agrees, we can appeal.

KEN. Let's get on with it, then.

HILL. One thing at a time. First, you remember, our own psychiatrist.

KEN. Wheel him in.

HILL. I'll be in touch soon then.

KEN. Oh, before you go. Yesterday I refused to take a tranquillizer and Dr. Emerson came and gave me an injection. It made me pretty dopey. If I was like that when the psychiatrist came, he'd lock me up for life!

HILL. I'll mention it to him. Goodbye for now then.

KEN. Goodbye.

(CROSS FADE on DR. EMERSON's office. DR. EMERSON is writing. DR. TRAVERS knocks on his door and looks in.)

DR. EMERSON. Can you find me Dr. Scott, please? (He puts the phone down.)

DR. TRAVERS. You wanted to see me?

DR. EMERSON. Ah, yes. If you can spare a moment.

DR. TRAVERS. What's the problem?

DR. EMERSON. Nasty one really. I have a road accident case paralyzed from the neck down. He's naturally very depressed and wants to discharge himself. But with a neurogenic bladder and all the rest of it, he couldn't last a week out of here. I need time to get him used to the idea.

DR. TRAVERS. How long ago was the accident?

DR. EMERSON. Six months.

DR. TRAVERS. A long time.

DR. EMERSON. Yes, well there were other injuries, but we've just about got him physically stabilized. The trouble is that he's got himself a solicitor and if I am to keep him here, I'll have to admit him compulsorily under the Mental Health Act. I wondered if you'd see him.

DR. TRAVERS. I'll see him of course, but my signature won't help you.

DR. EMERSON. Why not? You're the psychiatrist, aren't you?

DR. TRAVERS. Yes, but under the Act, you need two signatures and only one can come from a practitioner of the hospital where the patient is to be kept.

DR. EMERSON. Bloody hell!

DR. TRAVERS. Not to worry. I take it you regard this as an emergency.

DR. EMERSON. Of course I do.

DR. TRAVERS. Well, sign the application and then you've got three days to get another signature.

DR. EMERSON. There'll be no problem about that surely?

DR. TRAVERS. Depends upon whether he's clinically depressed or not.

DR. EMERSON. You haven't understood. He's suicidal. He's determined to kill himself.

DR. TRAVERS. I could name you several psychiatrists who wouldn't take that as evidence of insanity.

DR. EMERSON. Well, I could name several psychiatrists who are evidence of insanity. I've had a lot of experience in this kind of case. I'm sure, absolutely sure, I can win him around, given time — a few months . . .

DR. TRAVERS. I understand, Michael.

DR. EMERSON. . . . So you'll look at him, will you? And get another chap in?

DR. TRAVERS. Yes, I'll do that.

DR. EMERSON (twinkling). And . . . do me a favor, will you? Try and find an old codger like me, who believes in something better than suicide.

DR. TRAVERS (grinning). There's a chap at Ellertree . . . a very staunch Catholic, I believe. Would that suit you?

DR. EMERSON. By Jesus — sounds just the man!

DR. TRAVERS. I'll see his notes and drop in on him.

DR. EMERSON. Thank you very much, Paul. I'm very grateful — and Harrison will be, too.

(DR. SCOTT comes in the room.)

DR. SCOTT. Oh, sorry.
DR. TRAVERS. It's all right . . . I'm just off . . . I'll see him then, Michael, this afternoon.

(DR. TRAVERS leaves. DR. SCOTT looks at DR. EMERSON questioningly.)

DR. SCOTT. You wanted me?
DR. EMERSON. Ah, yes. Harrison's decided to discharge himself.
DR. SCOTT. Oh, no, but I'm not surprised.
DR. EMERSON. So, Travers is seeing him now.
DR. SCOTT. Dr. Travers won't make him change his mind.
DR. EMERSON. I am committing him under Section 26.
DR. SCOTT. Oh, will Dr. Travers sign it?
DR. EMERSON. Evidently if I do, he can't, but he knows a chap over in Ellertree who probably will.
DR. SCOTT. I see.
DR. EMERSON. I have no choice, do you see, Clare? He's got himself a solicitor. It's the only way I can keep him here.
DR. SCOTT. Are you sure you should?
DR. EMERSON. Of course. No question.
DR. SCOTT. It's his life.
DR. EMERSON. But my responsibility.
DR. SCOTT. Only if he's incapable of making his own decision.
DR. EMERSON. But he isn't capable. I refuse to believe that a man with a mind as quick as his, a man with enormous mental resources, would calmly choose suicide.
DR. SCOTT. But he has done just that.
DR. EMERSON. And, therefore, I say he is unbalanced.
DR. SCOTT. But surely a wish to die is not necessarily a symptom of insanity? A man might want to die for perfectly sane reasons.
DR. EMERSON. No, Clare, a doctor cannot accept the choice for death; he's committed to life. When a patient is brought into my unit, he's in a bad way. I don't stand about thinking whether or not it's worth saving his life, I haven't the time for doubts. I get in there, do whatever I can to save life. I'm a doctor, not a judge.
DR. SCOTT. I hope you will forgive me, sir, for saying this, but I think that is just how you are behaving — as a judge.
DR. EMERSON. You must, of course, say what you think — but I am the responsible person here.

DR. SCOTT. I know that, sir. (She makes to go.)

DR. EMERSON. I'm sure it's not necessary for me to say this but I'd rather there was no question of misunderstanding later ... Mr. Harrison is now physically stable. There is no reason why he should die; if he should die suddenly, I would think it necessary to order a post-mortem and to act on whatever was found.

DR. SCOTT. ... Mr. Harrison is your patient, sir.

DR. EMERSON (smiling). Of course, of course. You make that sound a fate worse than death.

DR. SCOTT. Perhaps for him it is. (She goes out.)

(CROSS FADE on KEN's room. DR. TRAVERS comes in.)

DR. TRAVERS. Mr. Harrison?

KEN. That's right.

DR. TRAVERS. Dr. Travers.

KEN. Are you a psychiatrist?

DR. TRAVERS. Yes.

KEN. For or against me ... Or does that sound like paranoia?

DR. TRAVERS. You'd hardly expect me to make an instant diagnosis.

KEN. Did Dr. Emerson send you?

DR. TRAVERS. I work here, in the hospital.

KEN. Ah.

DR. TRAVERS. Would you describe yourself as suffering from paranoia?

KEN. No.

DR. TRAVERS. What would you say paranoia was?

KEN. Difficult. It depends on the person. A man whose feelings of security are tied to his own sense of what is right and can brook no denial. If he were, say, a sculptor, then we would describe his mental condition as paranoia. If, on the other hand, he was a doctor, we would describe it as professionalism.

DR. TRAVERS (laughing). You don't like doctors!

KEN. Do you like patients?

DR. TRAVERS. Some.

KEN. I like some doctors.

DR. TRAVERS. What's wrong with doctors then?

KEN. Speaking generally, I suppose that as a profession, you've not learnt that the level of awareness of the population has risen dramatically; that black magic is no longer much use and that people can and want to understand what's wrong with them and many of them can make decisions about their own lives.

DR. TRAVERS. What they need is information.

KEN. Of course, but as a rule, doctors dole out information like a kosher butcher gives out pork sausages.

DR. TRAVERS. That's fair. But you'd agree that patients need medical knowledge to make good decisions?

KEN. I would. Look at me, for example. I'm a sculptor, an airy-fairy artist, with no real hard knowledge and no capability to understand anything about my body. You're a doctor but I think I would hold my own with a competition in anatomy with you.

DR. TRAVERS. It's a long time since I did any anatomy.

KEN. Of course. Whereas I was teaching it every day up to six months ago. It wouldn't be fair.

DR. TRAVERS. Your knowledge of anatomy may be excellent, but what's your neurology like, or your dermatology, endocrinology, urology and so on.

KEN. Lousy, and insofar as these bear on my case, I should be grateful for information so that I can make a proper decision. But it is my decision. If you came to my studio to buy something, and look at all my work, and you say: 'I want that bronze' and I say to you: 'Look, you don't know anything about sculpture. The proportion of that is all wrong, the texture is boring and it should have been made in wood anyway. You are having the marble!' You'd think I was nuts. If you were sensible you'd ask for my professional opinion but if you were a mature adult, you'd reserve the right to choose for yourself.

DR. TRAVERS. But we're not talking about a piece of sculpture to decorate a room, but about your life.

KEN. That's right, Doctor. My life.

DR. TRAVERS. But your obvious intelligence weakens your case. I'm not saying that you would find life easy but you do have resources that an unintelligent person doesn't have.

KEN. That sounds like Catch 22. If you're clever and sane enough to put up an invincible case for suicide, it demonstrates you ought not to die. (DR. TRAVERS moves the stool near the bed.) That's a disturbing tidiness compulsion you've got there.

DR. TRAVERS. I was an only child; enough of me. Have you any relationships outside the hospital? . . . You're not married, I see.

KEN. No, thank God.

DR. TRAVERS. A girl friend?

KEN. A fiancee actually. I asked her not to visit me any more. About a fortnight ago.

DR. TRAVERS. She must have been upset.

KEN. Better that than a lifetime's sacrifice.

DR. TRAVERS. She wanted to . . . stay with you then?

KEN. Oh yes . . . Had it all worked out . . . But she's a young, healthy woman. She wants babies — real ones. Not ones that never will learn to walk.

DR. TRAVERS. But if that's what she really wants.

KEN. Oh, come on, Doctor. If that's what she really wants, there's plenty of other cripples who want help. I told her to go to release her, I hope, from the guilt she would feel if she did what she really wanted to.

DR. TRAVERS. That's very generous.

KEN. Balls. Really, Doctor, I did it for me. It would destroy my self-respect if I allowed myself to become the object with which people can safely exploit their masochist tendencies.

DR. TRAVERS. That's putting it very strongly.

KEN. Yes. Too strong. But you are beginning to sound like the chaplain. He was in here the other day. He seemed to think I should be quite happy to be God's chosen vessel into which people could pour their compassion ... That it was all right being a cripple because it made other folk feel good when they helped me.

DR. TRAVERS. What about your parents?

KEN. Working class folk — they live in Scotland. I thought it would break my mother — I always thought of my father as a very tough egg. But it was the other way round. My father can only think with his hands. He used to stand around here — completely at a loss. My mother would sit there — just understanding. She knows what suffering's about. They were here a week ago — I got rid of my father for a while and told my mother what I was going to do. She looked at me for a minute. There were tears in her eyes. She said, 'Aye lad, it's thy life ... don't worry about your dad — I'll get him over it.' ... She stood up and I said: 'What about you?' 'What about me?' she said, 'Do you think life's so precious to me, I'm frightened of dying?' ... I'd like to think I was my mother's son.

DR. TRAVERS. Yes, well, we shall have to see.

KEN. What about? You mean you haven't made up your mind?

DR. TRAVERS. I shall have to do some tests.

KEN. What tests for Christ's sake? I can tell you now, my time over a hundred metres is lousy.

DR. TRAVERS. You seem very angry.

KEN. Of course I'm angry ... No, no ... I'm ... Yes, I am angry. (Breathing.) But I am trying to hold it in because you'll just write me off as in a manic phase of a manic depressive cycle.

DR. TRAVERS. You are very free with psychiatric jargon.

KEN. Oh, well then, you'll be able to say I'm an obsessive hypochondriac. (Breathing.)

DR. TRAVERS. I certainly wouldn't do that, Mr. Harrison.

KEN. Can't you see what a trap I am in? Can anyone prove that they are sane? Could you?

DR. TRAVERS. I'll come and see you again.

KEN. No, don't come and see me again, because every time you come, I'll get more and more angry, and more and more upset and depressed. And eventually you will destroy my mind.

DR. TRAVERS. I'm sorry if I upset you, Mr. Harrison.

(DR. TRAVERS replaces the stool and exits. He crosses to the SISTER's office. Enter DR. SCOTT and MR. HILL.)

DR. SCOTT. I hate the idea. It's against all my training and instincts.

HILL. Mine, too. But in this case, we're not dealing with euthanasia, are we?

DR. SCOTT. Something very close.

HILL. No. Something very far away. Suicide.

DR. SCOTT. Thank you for a lovely meal.

HILL. Not at all, I am glad you accepted. Tell me, what would you think, or rather feel, if there was a miracle and Ken Harrison was granted the use of his arms for just one minute and he used them to grab a bottle of sleeping tablets and swallowed the lot?

DR. SCOTT. It's irrational but . . . I'd be very . . . relieved.

HILL. It wouldn't go against your instincts? You wouldn't feel it was a wasted life and fight with stomach pumps and all that?

DR. SCOTT. No . . . not if it was my decision.

HILL. You might even be sure there was a bottle of tablets handy and you not there.

DR. SCOTT. You make it harder and harder . . . but yes, I might do that . . .

HILL. Yes. Perhaps we ought to make suicide respectable again. Whenever anyone kills himself there's a whole legal rigmarole to go through — investigations, inquests and so on — and it all seems designed to find someone or something to blame. Can you ever recall a coroner saying something like: 'We've heard all the evidence of how John Smith was facing literally insuperable odds and he made a courageous decision. I record a verdict of a noble death'?

DR. SCOTT. No . . . It's been a . . . very pleasant evening.

HILL. Thank you. For me, too.

DR. SCOTT. I don't know if I've helped you, though.

HILL. You have. I've made up my mind.

DR. SCOTT. You'll help him?

HILL. Yes. I hope you're not sorry.

DR. SCOTT. I'm pleased.

HILL. I'm sure it is morally wrong for anyone to try to hand the responsibility for their death to anyone else. And it's wrong to accept that responsibility, but Ken isn't trying to do that.

DR. SCOTT. I'm glad you've made up your mind . . . Goodnight. (They stop.)

HILL. I hope I see you again.

DR. SCOTT. I'm on the phone . . . Goodnight.

HILL. Goodnight.

(They exit. NURSE SADLER goes into KEN's room with a meal.)

KEN. You still on duty?

NURSE. We're very short-staffed ... (She prepares to feed KEN with a spoon.) It looks good tonight ... Minced beef.

KEN. Excellent ... and what wine shall we order then? How about a '48 claret. Yes, I think so ... Send for the wine waiter.

NURSE. You are a fool, Mr. Harrison.

KEN. Is there any reason why I shouldn't have wine?

NURSE. I don't know. I'll ask Sister if you like ...

KEN. After all, the hospital seems determined to depress my consciousness. But they'd probably think it's immoral if I enjoy it. (NURSE SADLER gives him a spoonful of mince.) It's a bit salty.

NURSE. Do you want some water?

KEN. That would be good. Very nice ... Not too full of body. Chateau Ogston Reservoir, I think, with just a cheeky little hint of Jeyes fluid from the sterilizer.

NURSE. We use Milton.

KEN. Oh dear ... you'd better add to my notes. The final catastrophe. Mr. Harrison's palate is failing; rush up the emergency taste resuscitation unit. (In a phoney American accent.) Nurse, give me orange ... No response ... Quick the lemon ... God! Not a flicker. We're on the tightrope ... Nurse pass the ultimate ... Quick, there's no time to lose ... Pass the hospital mince. That would bring people back from the dead. Don't tell Emerson that or he'll try it. I don't want any more of that.

(NURSE SADLER exits. DR. SCOTT comes in.)

KEN. Sister.

DR. SCOTT. No, it's me. Still awake?

KEN. Yes.

DR. SCOTT. It's late.

KEN. What time is it?

DR. SCOTT. Half past eleven.

KEN. The Night Sister said I could have the light for half an hour. I couldn't sleep. I wanted to think.

DR. SCOTT. Yes.

KEN. You look lovely.

DR. SCOTT. Thank you.

KEN. Have you been out?

DR. SCOTT. For a meal.

KEN. Nice. Good company?

DR. SCOTT. You're fishing.

KEN. That's right.

DR. SCOTT. Yes, it was good company.

KEN. A colleague?

DR. SCOTT. No. Actually it was Philip Hill, your solicitor.

KEN. Well, well, well . . . The randy old devil. He didn't take long to get cracking, did he?

DR. SCOTT. It was just a dinner.

KEN. I know I engaged him to act for me. I didn't realize he would see his duties so comprehensively.

DR. SCOTT. It was just a dinner!

KEN. Well, I hope my surrogate self behaved myself.

DR. SCOTT. You were a perfect gentleman.

KEN. Mm . . . then perhaps I'd better engage another surrogate.

DR. SCOTT. Do you mind really?

KEN. No. Unless you convinced him that Emerson was right.

DR. SCOTT. I didn't try.

KEN. Thank you.

DR. SCOTT. I think you are enjoying all this.

KEN. I suppose I am in a way. For the first time in six months I feel like a human being again.

DR. SCOTT. Yes. (A pause.) Isn't that the whole point, Ken?

KEN. You called me Ken.

DR. SCOTT. Do you mind?

KEN. Oh! No, I liked it. I'll just chalk it up as another credit for today.

DR. SCOTT. I was saying, isn't that just the point; isn't that what this fight has shown you? That you are a human being again. You're not fighting for death. I don't think you want to win.

KEN. That was what I had to think about.

DR. SCOTT. And have you . . . changed your mind?

KEN. No. I know I'm enjoying the fight and I had to be sure that I wanted to win, really get what I'm fighting for, and not just doing it to convince myself I'm still alive.

DR. SCOTT. And are you sure?

KEN. Yes, quite sure; for me life is over. I want it recognized because I can't do the things that I want to do. That means I can't say the things I want to say. Is that a better end? You understand, don't you?

(NURSE SADLER comes in with a feeding cup.)

NURSE. I didn't know you were here, Doctor.

DR. SCOTT. Yes, I'm just going.

KEN. See what I mean, Doctor. Here is my substitute mum, with her porcelain pap. This isn't for me.

DR. SCOTT. No . . .

KEN. So tomorrow, on with the fight!

DR. SCOTT. Goodnight . . . and good luck.

(FADE.)

(*Second Act*)

KERSHAW. So our psychiatrist is prepared to state that Harrison is sane.

HILL. Yes, he was sure. I'll have his written report tomorrow. He said he could understand the hospital fighting to save their patient from himself, but no matter how much he sympathized with them and how much he wished he could get Harrison to change his mind, nevertheless, he was sane and knew exactly what he was doing and why he was doing it.

KERSHAW. And you say that the hospital is holding him under Section 26?

HILL. Yes, they rang me this morning. They got another chap in from Ellertree to sign it as well as Emerson.

KERSHAW. Hm . . . Tricky. There's no precedent for this, you know. Fascinating.

HILL. Yes.

KERSHAW. And you're sure in your mind he knows what he's doing?

HILL. Yes.

KERSHAW. Well. Let's see him, shall we?

HILL. Here's the Sister's office.

KERSHAW. Is she your standard gorgon?

HILL. Only on the outside. But under that iron surface beats a heart of stainless steel. (They go into SISTER's office.)

HILL. Good morning, Sister.

SISTER. Morning, Mr. Hill.

HILL. This is a colleague, Mr. Kershaw.

SISTER. Good morning.

KERSHAW. Good morning.

HILL. Is it alright to see Mr. Harrison?

SISTER. Have you asked Dr. Emerson?

HILL. Oh yes, before we came.

SISTER. I see . . .

HILL. You can check with him . . .

SISTER. . . . I don't think that's necessary . . . However, I'm afraid I shall have to ask you if I can stay with Mr. Harrison while you interview him.

HILL. Why?

SISTER. We are very worried about Mr. Harrison's mental condition as you know. Twice recently he has . . . got excited . . . and his breathing function has not been able to cope with the extra demands. Dr. Emerson has ordered that at any time Mr. Harrison is subjected to stress, someone must be there as a precaution.

HILL. . . . I see. (He glances at MR. KERSHAW, who shrugs.) Very well.

SISTER. This way, gentlemen. (They go into KEN's room.)

HILL. Good morning, Mr. Harrison.

KEN. Morning.

HILL. I've brought along Mr. Kershaw. He is the barrister who is advising us.

KERSHAW. Good morning, Mr. Harrison.

HILL. Your doctor has insisted that Sister remains with us — to see you don't get too excited.

KEN. Oh! Sister, you know very well that your very presence always excites me tremendously. It must be the white apron and black stockings. A perfect mixture of mother and mistress. (SISTER grins a little sheepishly and takes a seat at the head of the bed. KEN strains his head to look at her. SISTER turns back the covers.) Sister, what are you doing! Oh. Just for a minute there, Sister . . . (SISTER takes his pulse.)

HILL. . . . Well . . .

SISTER. Just a moment, Mr. Hill . . . (She finishes taking the pulse.) Very well.

KEN. So, Mr. Kershaw, what is your advice?

(MR. KERSHAW pauses. MR. HILL makes to speak, but MR. KERSHAW stops him with a barely perceptible shake of the head. A longer pause.)

KERSHAW. . . . If you succeed in your aim you will be dead within a week.

KEN. I know.

KERSHAW. . . . I am informed that without a catheter the toxic substance will build up in your bloodstream and you will be slowly poisoned by your own blood.

KEN (smiles). . . . You should have brought along a tape-recorder. That speech would be much more dramatic with sound effects!

KERSHAW (relaxing and smiling). I had to be sure you know what you are doing.

KEN. I know.

KERSHAW. And you have no doubt whatsoever; no slightest reservations? . . .

KEN. None at all.

KERSHAW. Let's look at the possibilities. You are now being held under the Mental Health Act Section 26, which means they can keep you here and give you any treatment they believe you need. Under the law we can appeal to a tribunal.

KEN. How long will that take?

KERSHAW. Up to a year.

KEN. A year! A year! Oh God, can't it be quicker than that?

KERSHAW. It might be quicker, but it could be a year.

KEN. Jesus Christ! I really would be crazy in a year.

KERSHAW. That's the procedure.

KEN. I couldn't stay like this for another year, I couldn't.

HILL. We could always try habeas corpus.

KERSHAW. That would depend if we could find someone.

KEN. Habeas corpus? What's that? I thought it was something to do with criminals.

KERSHAW. Well, it usually is, Mr. Harrison. Briefly, it's against the law to deprive anyone of their liberty without proper cause. If anyone is so deprived, they or a friend can apply for a writ of habeas corpus, which is the Latin for 'you may have the body.'

KEN. Particularly apt in my case.

KERSHAW. The people who are doing the detaining have to produce the . . . person, before the judge and if they can't give a good enough reason for keeping him, the judge will order that he be released.

KEN. It sounds as if it will take as long as that tribunal you were talking about.

KERSHAW. No. Habeas corpus is one of the very few legal processes that move very fast. We can approach any judge at any time even when the courts aren't sitting and he will see that it's heard straight away — in a day or so usually.

HILL. If you could find a judge to hear it.

KEN. Why shouldn't a judge hear it.

KERSHAW. Habeas corpus itself is fairly rare. This would be rarer.

KEN. Will I have to go to court?

KERSHAW. I doubt it. The hearing can be in court or in private, in the Judge's Chambers as we say. The best thing to do in this case is for Mr. Hill and me to find a judge, issue the writ, then we'll get together with the hospital's barrister and we'll approach the judge together and suggest we hold the subsequent hearing here.

KEN. In this room?

KERSHAW. I expect the judge will agree. If he ordered you to be produced in court and anything happened to you, it would be a classical case of prejudging the issue.

KEN. I wouldn't mind.

KERSHAW. But the judge would feel rather foolish. I should think it would be in a few days.

KEN. Thank you. It'll be an unusual case for you — making a plea for the defendant's death.

KERSHAW. I'll be honest with you. It's a case I could bear to lose.

KEN. If you do — it's a life sentence for me.

KERSHAW. Well, we shall see. Good morning, Mr. Harrison. (They go out with the SISTER. They pause at the SISTER's office.)
HILL. Thank you very much, Sister . . . I'm very sorry about all this. I do realize it must be upsetting for you.
SISTER. Not at all, Mr. Hill. As I have a stainless steel heart, it's easy to keep it sterilized of emotion. Good morning.

(She goes into her room. HILL and KERSHAW go out.)

(CROSS FADE on KEN's room. JOHN and NURSE SADLER are setting chairs for the hearing. JOHN begins to sing 'Dry Bones.')

NURSE. John!
JOHN. What's the matter? (NURSE SADLER is confused.)
NURSE. Nothing of course . . . silly . . . (KEN picks up the vibes between the two.)
KEN. Hello, hello . . . What have we here? Don't tell me that Cupid has donned his antiseptic gown and is flying the corridors of the hospital, shooting his hypodermic syringes into maidens' hearts . . .
NURSE. No!
KEN. John?
JOHN. Honestly, your honor, I'm not guilty. I was just walking down the corridor when I was struck dumb by the beauty of this nurse.
NURSE. Don't be an idiot, John . . . We need an extra chair . . . Can you go and find one, please?
JOHN. Your wishes, oh queen, are my command. (He bows and goes out.)
NURSE. He is a fool.
KEN. He isn't. He's been bloody good to me. Have you been out with him? . . . It's none of my business, of course.
NURSE. We went to a club of his last night . . . He plays in a band, you know.
KEN. Yes, I know.
NURSE. They're really good. They should go a long way . . . Still, I shouldn't be going on like this.
KEN. Why not? . . . Because I'm paralyzed? Because I can't go dancing?
NURSE. Well . . .
KEN. The other day I was low and said to John, who was shaving me, I was useless, what could I do? I served no purpose and all the rest of the whining miseries. John set about finding things I could do. He said, first, because I could move my head from side to side (KEN does so.) I could be a tennis umpire; then as my head was going, I could knock a pendulum from side to side and keep a clock

going. Then he said I could be a child-minder and because kids were always doing what they shouldn't, I could be perpetually shaking my head. He went on and on getting more and more fantastic—like radar scanners. I laughed so much that the Sister had to rush in and give me oxygen.

NURSE. He is funny.

KEN. He's more than that. He's free!

NURSE. Free?

KEN. Free of guilt. Most everybody here feels guilt about me— including you. That's why you didn't want to tell me what a fantastic time you had dancing. So everybody makes me feel worse because I make them feel guilty. But not John. He's sorry for me but he knows bloody well it isn't his fault. He's a tonic.

(JOHN comes back carrying SISTER's armchair.)

NURSE. John! Did Sister say you could have that chair?

JOHN. She wasn't there . . .

NURSE. She'll kill you; no-one ever sits in her chair.

JOHN. Why? Is it contaminated or something? I just thought that if the poor old Judge had to sit here listening to that miserable bugger moaning on about wanting to die, the least we could do was to make him comfortable.

KEN (laughing to NURSE SADLER). See?

(JOHN sits in the chair and assumes a grave face.)

JOHN. Now, this is a very serious case. The two charges are proved . . . Firstly, this hospital has been found guilty of using drugs to make people happy. That's terrible. Next and most surprising of all, this hospital, in spite of all their efforts to the contrary, are keeping people alive! We can't have that. (Footsteps outside.)

NURSE. Sister's coming! (JOHN jumps up and stands between the chair and the door. SISTER comes in and as she approaches the bed with her back to the chair. JOHN slips out of the room.)

KEN. Well now, we have some very important visitors today, Sister.

SISTER. Indeed we have.

KEN. Will you be here?

SISTER. No.

KEN. I feel a bit like a traitor.

SISTER. . . . We all do what we've got to.

KEN. That's right, but not all of us do it as well as you, Sister.

SISTER (quickly). ...Thank you. (She moves quickly to go. DR. SCOTT comes in.)

DR. SCOTT. Good morning, Sister.

SISTER (brightly). Good morning. (She goes quickly without noticing the chair. DR. SCOTT watches her go.)

KEN. I've upset her, I'm afraid.

DR. SCOTT. You shouldn't do that. She is a marvelous Sister. You ought to see some of the others.

KEN. That's what I told her.

DR. SCOTT. Oh, I see. Well, I should think that's just about the one way past her defenses. How are you this morning?

KEN. Fine.

DR. SCOTT. And you're going ahead with it?

KEN. Of course.

DR. SCOTT. Of course.

KEN. I haven't had any tablets, yesterday or today.

DR. SCOTT. No.

KEN. Thank you.

DR. SCOTT. Thank the Judge. He ordered it.

KEN. Ah!

(DR. EMERSON comes in.)

DR. EMERSON. Good morning, Mr. Harrison.

KEN. Morning, Doctor.

DR. EMERSON. There's still time.

KEN. No, I want to go on with it ... unless you'll discharge me.

DR. EMERSON. I'm afraid I can't do that. The Judge and lawyers are conferring. I thought I'd just pop along and see if you were alright. We've made arrangements for the witnesses to wait in the Sister's office. I am one, so I should be grateful if you would remain here, with Mr. Harrison.

DR. SCOTT. Of course.

DR. EMERSON. Well, I don't want to meet the Judge before I have to. I wish you the best of luck, Mr. Harrison, so that we'll be able to carry on treating you.

KEN (smiling). Thank you for your good wishes. (DR. EMERSON nods and goes out.)

DR. SCOTT. If I didn't know you I'd say he was the most obstinate man I've ever met. (As DR. EMERSON makes for his office, MR. HILL comes down the corridor.)

HILL. Good morning.

DR. EMERSON. Morning. (MR. HILL stops and calls after DR. EMERSON.)

HILL. Oh, Dr. Emerson.

DR. EMERSON. Yes?

HILL. I don't know. I just want to say how sorry I am that you have been forced into such a . . . distasteful situation.

DR. EMERSON. It's not over yet, Mr. Hill. I have every confidence that the law is not such an ass that it will force me to watch a patient of mine die unnecessarily.

HILL. We are just as confident that the law is not such an ass that it will allow anyone arbitrary power.

DR. EMERSON. My power isn't arbitrary; I've earned it with knowledge and skill and it's also subject to the laws of nature.

HILL. And to the laws of the state.

DR. EMERSON. If the state is so foolish as to believe it is competent to judge a purely professional issue.

HILL. It's always doing that. Half the civil cases in the calendar arise because someone is challenging a professional's opinion.

DR. EMERSON. I don't know about other professions but I do know this one, medicine, is being seriously threatened because of the intervention of law. Patients are becoming so litigious that doctors will soon be afraid to offer any opinion or take any action at all.

HILL. Then they will be sued for negligence.

DR. EMERSON. We can't win.

HILL. Everybody wins. You wouldn't like to find yourself powerless in the hands of, say, a lawyer or a . . . bureaucrat. I wouldn't like to find myself powerless in the hands of a doctor.

DR. EMERSON. You make me sound as if I were some sort of Dracula . . .

HILL. No. I for one certainly don't doubt your good faith but in spite of that I wouldn't like to place anyone above the law.

DR. EMERSON. I don't want to be above the law; I just want to be under laws that take full account of professional opinion.

HILL. I'm sure it will do that, Dr. Emerson. The question is, whose professional opinion?

DR. EMERSON. We shall see.

(MR. ANDREW EDEN, the hospital's barrister, and MR. HILL and MR. KERSHAW comes into KEN's room.)

HILL. Morning, Mr. Harrison. This is Mr. Eden who will be representing the hospital.

KEN. Hello.

(They settle themselves into the chairs. The SISTER enters with the JUDGE.)

SISTER. Mr. Justice Millhouse.

JUDGE. Mr. Kenneth Harrison?

KEN. Yes, my Lord.

JUDGE. This is an informal hearing which I want to keep as brief as possible. You are, I take it, Dr. Scott?

DR. SCOTT. Yes, my Lord.

JUDGE. I should be grateful, Doctor, if you would interrupt the proceedings at any time you think it necessary.

DR. SCOTT. Yes, my Lord.

JUDGE. I have decided in consultation with Mr. Kershaw and Mr. Hill that we shall proceed thus. I will hear a statement from Dr. Michael Emerson as to why he believes Mr. Harrison is legally detained, and then a statement from Dr. Richard Barr, who will support the application. We have decided not to subject Mr. Harrison to examination and cross-examination. KEN. But I . . .

JUDGE (sharply). Just a moment, Mr. Harrison. If, as appears likely, there remains genuine doubt as to the main issue, I shall question Mr. Harrison myself. Dr. Scott, I wonder if you would ask Dr. Emerson to come in.

DR. SCOTT. Yes, my Lord. (She goes out.) Would you come in now, sir.

(SISTER and DR. EMERSON come into KEN's room.)

JUDGE. Dr. Emerson, I would like you take the oath. (The JUDGE hands DR. EMERSON a card with the oath written on it.)

DR. EMERSON. I swear the evidence that I give shall be the truth, the whole truth and nothing but the truth.

JUDGE. Stand over there, please. (The JUDGE nods to MR. EDEN.)

EDEN. You are Dr. Michael Emerson?

DR. EMERSON. I am.

EDEN. And what is your position here?

DR. EMERSON. I am a consultant physician and in charge of the intensive care unit.

EDEN. Dr. Emerson, would you please give a brief account of your treatment of this patient.

DR. EMERSON (referring to notes). Mr. Harrison was admitted here on the afternoon of October 9th, as an emergency following a road accident. He was suffering from a fractured left tibia and right tibia and fibia, a fractured pelvis, four fractured ribs, one of which had punctured the lung, and dislocated fourth vertebra, which had ruptured the spinal cord. He was extensively bruised and had minor lacerations. He was deeply unconscious and remained so for thirty hours. As a result of treatment, all the broken bones and ruptured tissue have healed with the exception of a severed spinal cord and this, together with a mental trauma, is now all that remains of the initial injury.

EDEN. Precisely, Doctor. Let us deal with those last two points. The spinal cord. Will there be any further improvement in that?

DR. EMERSON. In the present state of medical knowledge, I would think not.

EDEN. And the mental trauma you spoke of?

DR. EMERSON. It's impossible to injure the body to the extent that Mr. Harrison did and not affect the mind. It is common in these cases that depression and the tendency to make wrong decisions goes on for months, even years.

EDEN. And in your view Mr. Harrison is suffering from such a depression?

DR. EMERSON. Yes.

EDEN. Thank you, Doctor.

JUDGE. Mr. Kershaw?

KERSHAW. Doctor. Is there any objective way you could demonstrate this trauma? Are there, for example, the results of any tests, or any measurements you can take to show it to us?

DR. EMERSON. No.

KERSHAW. Then how do you distinguish between a medical syndrome and a sane, even justified, depression?

DR. EMERSON. By using my thirty years' experience as a physician, dealing with both types.

KERSHAW. No more questions, my Lord.

JUDGE. Mr. Eden, do you wish to re-examine?

EDEN. No, my Lord.

JUDGE. Thank you, Doctor. Would you ask Dr. Barr if he would step in please? (DR. EMERSON goes out.)

DR. EMERSON. It's you now, Barr.

(SISTER brings DR. BARR into KEN's room.)

SISTER. Dr. Barr.

JUDGE. Dr. Barr, will you take the oath please. (He does so.) Mr. Kershaw.

KERSHAW. You are Dr. Richard Barr?

DR. BARR. I am.

KERSHAW. And what position do you hold?

DR. BARR. I am a consultant psychiatrist at Norwood Park Hospital.

KERSHAW. That is primarily a mental hospital, is it not?

DR. BARR. It is.

KERSHAW. Then you must see a large number of patients suffering from depressive illness.

DR. BARR. I do, yes.

KERSHAW. You have examined Mr. Harrison?

DR. BARR. I have, yes.

KERSHAW. Would you say that he was suffering from such an illness?

DR. BARR. No, I would not.

KERSHAW. Are you quite sure, Doctor?

DR. BARR. Yes, I am.

KERSHAW. The court has heard evidence that Mr. Harrison is depressed. Would you dispute that?

DR. BARR. No, but depression is not necessarily an illness. I would say that Mr. Harrison's depression is reactive rather than endogenous. That is to say, he is reacting in a perfectly rational way to a very bad situation.

KERSHAW. Thank you, Dr. Barr.

JUDGE. Dr. Eden?

EDEN. Dr. Barr. Are there any objective results that you could produce to prove Mr. Harrison is capable?

DR. BARR. There are clinical symptoms of endogenous depression, of course, disturbed sleep patterns, loss of appetite, lassitude, but even if they were present, they would be masked by the physical condition.

EDEN. So how can you be sure this is in fact just a reactive depression?

DR. BARR. Just by experience, that's all, and by discovering when I talk to him that he has a remarkably incisive mind and is perfectly capable of understanding his position and of deciding what to do about it.

EDEN. One last thing, Doctor; do you think Mr. Harrison has made the right decision?

KERSHAW (quickly). Is that really relevant, my Lord? After all.

JUDGE. Not really.

DR. BARR. I should like to answer it though.

JUDGE. Very well.

DR. BARR. No, I thought he made the wrong decision. (To KEN.) Sorry.

EDEN. No more questions, my Lord.

JUDGE. Do you wish to re-examine, Mr. Kershaw?

KERSHAW. No, thank you, my Lord.

JUDGE. That will be all, Dr. Barr. (DR. BARR goes out. The JUDGE stands.)

JUDGE. Do you feel like answering some questions?

KEN. Of course.

JUDGE. Thank you.

KEN. You are too kind.

JUDGE. Not at all.

KEN. I mean it. I'd prefer it if you were a hanging judge.

JUDGE. There aren't any any more.

KEN. Society is now much more sensitive and humane?

JUDGE. You could put it that way.

KEN. I'll settle for that.

JUDGE. I would like you to take the oath. Dr. Scott, his right hand, please. (KEN takes the oath.) The consultant physician here has given evidence that you are not capable of making a rational decision.

KEN. He's wrong.

JUDGE. When then do you think he came to that opinion?

KEN. He's a good doctor and won't let a patient die if he can help it.

JUDGE. He found that you were suffering from acute depression.

KEN. Is that surprising? I am almost totally paralyzed. I'd be insane if I weren't depressed.

JUDGE. But there is a difference between being unhappy and being depressed in the medical sense.

KEN. I would have thought that my psychiatrist answered that point.

JUDGE. But, surely, wishing to die must be strong evidence that the depression has moved beyond a mere unhappiness into a medical realm?

KEN. I don't wish to die.

JUDGE. Then what is this case all about?

KEN. Nor do I wish to live at any price. Of course I want to live but as far as I am concerned, I'm dead already. I merely require the doctors to recognize the fact. I cannot accept this condition constitutes life in any real sense at all.

JUDGE. Certainly, you're alive legally.

KEN. I think I could challenge even that.

JUDGE. How?

KEN. Any reasonable definition of life must include the idea of its being self-supporting. I seem to remember something in the papers—when all the heart transplant controversy was on—about it being all right to take someone's heart if they require constant attention from respirators and so on to keep them alive.

JUDGE. There also has to be absolutely no brain activity at all. Yours is certainly working.

KEN. It is and sanely.

JUDGE. That is the question to be decided.

KEN. My Lord, I am not asking anyone to kill me. I am only asking to be discharged from this hospital.

JUDGE. It comes to the same thing.

KEN. Then that proves my point; not just the fact that I will spend the rest of my life in the hospital, but that while I am here, everything is geared just to keeping my brain active, with no real possibility of it every being able to direct anything. As far as I can see, that is an act of deliberate cruelty.

JUDGE. Surely, it would be more cruel if society let people die, when it could, with some effort, keep them alive.

KEN. No, not more cruel, just as cruel.

JUDGE. Then why should the hospital let you die — if it is just as cruel?

KEN. The cruelty doesn't reside in saving someone or allowing them to die. It resides in the fact that the choice is removed from the man concerned.

JUDGE. But a man who is very desperately depressed is not capable of making a reasonable choice.

KEN. As you said, my Lord, that is the question to be decided.

JUDGE. All right. You tell me why it is a reasonable choice that you decided to die.

KEN. It is a question of dignity. Look at me here. I can do nothing, not even the basic primitive functions. I cannot even urinate, I have a permanent catheter attached to me. Every few days my bowels are washed out. Every few hours two nurses have to turn me over or I would rot away from bedsores. Only my brain functions unimpaired but even that is futile because I can't act on any conclusions it comes to. This hearing proves that. Will you please listen.

JUDGE. I am listening.

KEN. I choose to acknowledge the fact that I am in fact dead and I find the hospital's persistent effort to maintain this shadow of life an indignity and it's inhumane.

JUDGE. But wouldn't you agree that many people with appalling physical handicaps have overcome them and lived essentially creative, dignified lives?

KEN. Yes, I would, but the dignity starts with their choice. If I choose to live, it would be appalling if society killed me. If I choose to die, it is equally appalling if society keeps me alive.

JUDGE. I cannot accept that it is undignified for society to devote resources to keeping someone alive. Surely it enhances that society.

KEN. It is not undignified if the man wants to stay alive, but I must restate that the dignity starts with his choice. Without it, it is degrading because technology has taken over from human will. My Lord, if I cannot be a man, I do not wish to be a medical achievement. I'm fine . . . I am fine.

JUDGE. It's alright. I have no more questions. (The JUDGE stands up and walks to the window. He thinks a moment.) This is a most unusual case. Before I make a judgement I want to state that I believe all the parties have acted in good faith. I propose to consider this for a moment. The law on this is fairly clear. A deliberate decision to embark on a course of action that will lead inevitably to death is not ipso facto evidence of insanity. If it were, society would have to reward many men with a dishonorable burial rather than a posthumous medal for gallantry. On the other hand, we do have to bear in mind that Mr. Harrison has suffered massive physical injuries and it is possible that his mind is affected. Any judge in his career will have met men who are without doubt insane in the meaning of the Act and yet appear in the witness box to be rational. We must, in this case, be most careful not to allow Mr. Harrison's obvious wit and intelligence to blind us to the fact that he could be suffering from a depressive illness . . . and so we have to face the disturbing fact of the divided evidence . . . and bear in mind that, however much we may sympathize with Mr. Harrison in his cogently argued case to be allowed to die, the law instructs us to ignore it if it is the product of a disturbed or clinically depressed mind . . . However, I am satisfied that Mr. Harrison is a brave and cool man who is in complete control of his mental faculties and I shall therefore make an order for him to be set free. (A pause. The JUDGE walks over to KEN.) Well, you got your hanging judge!

KEN. I think not, my Lord. Thank you. (The JUDGE nods and smiles.)

JUDGE. Goodbye. (He turns and goes. He meets DR. EMERSON in the SISTER's room. While he talks to him everyone else, except DR. SCOTT, comes out.)

JUDGE. Ah, Dr. Emerson.

DR. EMERSON. My Lord?

JUDGE. I'm afraid you'll have to release your patient.

DR. EMERSON. I see.

JUDGE. I'm sorry. I understand how you must feel.

DR. EMERSON. Thank you.

JUDGE. If ever I have to have a road accident, I hope it's in this town and I finish up here.

DR. EMERSON. Thank you again.

JUDGE. Goodbye. (He walks down the corridor. DR. EMERSON stands a moment then slowly goes back to the room. KEN is looking out of the window. DR. SCOTT is sitting by the bed.)

DR. EMERSON. Where will you go?

KEN. I'll get a room somewhere.

DR. EMERSON. There's no need.

KEN. Don't let's.

DR. EMERSON. We'll stop treatment, remove the drips. Stop feeding you if you like. You'll be unconscious in three days, dead in six at most.

KEN. There'll be no last minute resuscitation?
DR. EMERSON. Only with your express permission.
KEN. That's very kind; why are you doing it?
DR. EMERSON. Simple! You might change your mind.

(KEN smiles and shakes his head.)

KEN. Thanks. I won't change my mind, but I'd like to stay.

(DR. EMERSON nods and goes. DR. SCOTT stands and moves to the door.)

KEN. You were right, you know. He really is a most obstinate man! (DR. SCOTT turns and moves to KEN as if to kiss him.) Oh, don't, but thank you.

(DR. SCOTT smiles weakly and goes out. The Lights are held for a long moment, and then snap out.)

Discussion Topics

1. Modern medicine is based on the assumption that lives are to be preserved at all cost. This has produced situations in which terminal patients are kept alive when there is no hope of recovery or improvement. They are often in constant pain and, it is said, they become medical objects without the usual marks of personal dignity. Foreign countries and at least one American state (Oregon) have formalized "death with dignity" procedures. Oregon's law permits doctors to prescribe lethal amounts of barbiturates for terminally ill patients (and *only* terminally ill patients).

Patients themselves may, in most hospital settings, choose "do not resuscitate" options which prevent doctors from using the most extreme measures to preserve inevitably dying bodies. And in many settings, doctors tacitly withhold treatments that have no chance of improving such patient's conditions.

If we have thought deeply about the right to die for those who are dying imminently, we have not extended the discussion to those who are not dying. And Ken Harrison is clearly not dying. With familiar medical procedures, his life can extend indefinitely. If we say that he has the right to die, we do so on one of two grounds. The narrower ground is that anyone whose life is severely impaired, who is perhaps incapacitated, may choose to end his life. Or we may say that any person has the right to judge whether

her life is worth living and to implement such a decision. The next two notes explore these possibilities, but it is important to keep in mind which of these two arguments you favor with regard to Ken (if, indeed, you side with him).

2. If able-bodied persons with normal skills may not choose to die, what degree of incapacity gives rise to that option? Note that there is something peculiar about this question. It presupposes that normal lives are worth living, and it asks us to determine a line or a set of criteria beyond which the value of life may legitimately be doubted. The result of such an answer would be to tell some individuals, "Your life is clearly worth living," and to tell others, "For you, we're not so sure."

Of course, however we draw the line, we leave the ultimate choice to the patient. We are saying, "Because of your incapacity, your decision will be both understandable and respected." We are determining a threshold for considering such choices. What might such a threshold be? In Ken's case, his paralysis rules out his main means of livelihood, sculpting, and the esthetic perspective by which he has lived his life. One possible standard, therefore, would be to allow the choice to die to those whose main talents and activities can no longer be carried out. Another standard would be impairment of the general ability to carry on daily life.

Let's focus on two objections to the attempt to define such a standard. The first is that the questions have no objective answer. Does the sudden onset of blindness impair one's ability to carry on daily life? It certainly requires reorientation. But blind people have daily lives as well. Does even Ken's impairment keep him from experiencing daily life? There are many, many things he cannot do, but many that he can. He can see, think, read, eat, and so on. It is hard to see, therefore, that the question of whether daily life is *sufficiently* impaired can be answered by anyone but the patient.

A second objection is that any attempt to answer the question underestimates the resilience or at least the unpredictability of human experience. If we take note of the obvious fact that Ken will not be able to sculpt, we cannot tell—and it very likely that *he* cannot tell, how his interests will shift in the future.

3. One might take a simpler and more radical approach and say that all persons, regardless of impairment or not, have the right to choose to die. The underlying assumption is clearly a robust notion of free will. People know what they want, for the most part, and should be able to decide and act accordingly. But is this so? It is easy to develop a counter argument. It might be said that most of us most of the time are under the influence of unconscious wishes, desires, and fears. We like to pretend that we are autonomous deciders, but autonomy is a shallow notion that covers up complex psychological determinants. Can we ever know that we will not regret any particular decision? Can we know that we are "in our right mind" at any particular time?

Dr. Emerson suggests that Ken is depressed. Depression can be one of the more common and determinable factors in eroding free will and making our decisions suspect. The evidence in the play is perhaps ambiguous. On one hand, Ken seems articulate and clear-headed in looking at his situation. It is hard to imagine less emotionalism and more cold, hard rationality. On the other hand, his cold irony is so extreme that it may readily be seen as a mask for desperation. Is he keeping himself too rigidly in control?

Thus, even if we take the extreme position, that any person has the right to choose to die if the decision is autonomous and freely made, we must admit that autonomy and free will are endlessly debatable. Should the teenager whose girlfriend has just slept with his best friend be able to choose to die? Should the soldier suffering psychological distress after a term in Iraq be left to his own devices and his own suicidal decision?

4. Aside from the issues raised the play, the question arises whether Clark's sympathies lie on one side or the other. Does he dispose us to side with Ken (and Justice Millhouse) and against Dr. Emerson? It seems hard to come away from the play without favoring Ken and taking his argument seriously. Is this, in other words, a didactic play that is essentially argumentative — with an axe to grind?

5. If we return to the distinction between public and private matters, what gives us (and the state and its laws) a public interest in the preservation of life? Of course, we have an interest in prohibiting homicide. But the interest goes beyond that to preventing suicide. Perhaps we presume that most suicidal decisions are irrational or coerced. But it is not clear why that should make a difference. We make other irrational or coerced decisions all the time without state interference. So we are left with two questions. One is whether indeed the presumption would be correct. The second is why these particular decisions are public matters — and may be public matters even when it is clear that neither irrationality nor coercion is present.

6. In 1998, the journal *Medicine and Law* published several incisive articles on the subject of physician-assisted suicide. A symposium on the subject may be found in volume 17.

Drug Culture

Denis Johnson: Dundun

Some writers lead dull, pedestrian lives. Denis Johnson (born 1949 in Munich, Germany) is not one of them. His life has given him material for several literary careers. He grew up in Tokyo, Manila, and Washington.

He has been married several times, and has a long history of drug and alcohol use. His best-known work, a book of short stories called *Jesus' Son*, was written while he was in California recovering from an extended bout of malaria, contracted in the Philippines at a low point in his life. He now lives in Idaho with his third wife. He began as a poet and has published five volumes of poetry, but he is most famous for his seven novels. He has recently written a number of plays and is resident playwright at the Intersection for the Arts in San Francisco.

"Dundun" is one of the stories in *Jesus' Son*, which was made into an award-winning movie in 1992. Like most of Johnson's work, it is about the subculture of drugs, drinking, and prostitution. Its focus is the consciousness of persons whose lives are dominated by drugs, whose sense of survival and mutual obligations is deeply affected and distorted by their constant intoxication.

❧ Dundun ❧

Denis Johnson

I went out to the farmhouse where Dundun lived to get some pharmaceutical opium from him, but I was out of luck.

He greeted me as he was coming out into the front yard to go to the pump, wearing new cowboy boots and a leather vest, with his flannel shirt hanging out over his jeans. He was chewing on a piece of gum.

"McInnes isn't feeling too good today. I just shot him."

"You mean killed him?"

"I didn't mean to."

"Is he really dead?"

"No. He's sitting down."

"But he's alive."

"Oh, sure, he's alive. He's sitting down now in the back room."

Dundun went on over to the pump and started working the handle.

I went around the house and in through the back. The room just through the back door smelled of dogs and babies. Beatle stood in the opposite doorway. She watched me come in. Leaning against the wall was Blue, smoking a cigarette and scratching her chin thoughtfully. Jack Hotel was over at an old desk, setting fire to a pipe the bowl of which was wrapped in tinfoil.

When they saw it was only me, the three of them resumed looking at McInnes, who sat on the couch all alone, with his left hand resting gently on his belly.

"Dundun shot him?" I asked.

"Somebody shot somebody," Hotel said.

Dundun came in behind me carrying some water in a china cup and a bottle of beer and said to McInnes: "Here."

"I don't want that," McInnes said.

"Okay. Well, here, then." Dundun offered him the rest of his beer.

"No thanks."

I was worried. "Aren't you taking him to the hospital or anything?"

"Good idea," Beatle said sarcastically.

"We started to," Hotel explained, "but we ran into the corner of the shed out there."

I looked out the side window. This was Tim Bishop's farm. Tim Bishop's Plymouth, I saw, which was a very nice old grey-and-red sedan, had sideswiped the shed and replaced one of the corner posts, so that the post lay on the ground and the car now held up the shed's roof.

"The front windshield is in millions of bits," Hotel said.

"How'd you end up way over there?"

"Everything was completely out of hand," Hotel said.

"Where's Tim, anyway?"

"He's not here," Beatle said.

Hotel passed me the pipe. It was hashish, but it was pretty well burned up already.

"How you doing?" Dundun asked McInnes. "I can feel it right here. It's just stuck in the muscle."

Dundun said, "It's not bad. The cap didn't explode right, I think."

"It misfired."

"It misfired a little bit, yeah."

Hotel asked me, "Would you take him to the hospital in your car?"

"Okay," I said.

"I'm coming, too," Dundun said.

"Have you got any of the opium left?" I asked him.

"No," he said. "That was a birthday present. I used it all up."

"When's your birthday?" I asked him.

"Today."

"You shouldn't have used it all up before your birthday, then," I told him angrily.

But I was happy about this chance to be of use. I wanted to be the one who saw it through and got McInnes to the doctor without a wreck. People would talk about it, and I hoped I would be liked.

In the car were Dundun, McInnes, and myself.

This was Dundun's twenty-first birthday. I'd met him in the Johnson County facility during the only few days I'd ever spent in jail, around the time of my eighteenth Thanksgiving. I was the older of us by a month or two. As for McInnes, he'd been around forever, and in fact, I, myself, was married to one of his old girlfriends.

We took off as fast as I could go without bouncing the shooting victim around too heavily.

Dundun said, "What about the brakes? You get them working?"

"The emergency brake does. That's enough."

"What about the radio?" Dundun punched the button, and the radio came on making an emission like a meat grinder.

He turned it off and then on, and now it burbled like a machine that polishes stones all night. "How about you?" I asked McInnes. "Are you comfortable?"

"What do you think?" McInnes said.

It was a long straight road through dry fields as far as a person could see. You'd think the sky didn't have any air in it, and the earth was made of paper. Rather than moving, we were just getting smaller and smaller.

What can be said about those fields? There were blackbirds circling above their own shadows, and beneath them the cows stood around smelling one another's butts. Dundun spat his gum out the window while digging in his shirt pocket for his Winstons. He lit a Winston with a match. That was all there was to say.

"We'll never get off this road," I said.

"What a lousy birthday," Dundun said.

McInnes was white and sick, holding himself tenderly. I'd seen him like that once or twice even when he hadn't been shot. He had a bad case of hepatitis that often gave him a lot of pain.

"Do you promise not to tell them anything?" Dundun was talking to McInnes.

"I don't think he hears you," I said.

"Tell them it was an accident, okay?" McInnes said nothing for a long moment. Finally he said, "Okay."

"Promise?" Dundun said.

But McInnes said nothing. Because he was dead.

Dundun looked at me with tears in his eyes. "What do you say?"

"What do you mean, what do I say? Do you think I'm here because I know all about this stuff?"

"He's dead."

"All right. I know he's dead."

"Throw him out of the car."

"Damn right throw him out of the car," I said. "I'm not taking him anywhere now."

For a moment I fell asleep, right while I was driving. I had a dream in which I was trying to tell someone something and they kept interrupting, a dream about frustration.

"I'm glad he's dead," I told Dundun. "He's the one who started everybody calling me Fuck-head."

Dundun said, "Don't let it get you down." We whizzed along down through the skeleton remnants of Iowa.

"I wouldn't mind working as a hit man," Dundun said.

Glaciers had crushed this region in the time before history. There'd been a drought for years, and a bronze fog of dust stood over the plains. The soybean crop was dead again, and the failed, wilted cornstalks were laid out on the ground like rows of underthings. Most of the farmers didn't even plant anymore. All the false visions had been erased. It felt like the moment before the Savior comes. And the Savior did come, but we had to wait a long time.

Dundun tortured Jack Hotel at the lake outside of Denver. He did this to get information about a stolen item, a stereo belonging to Dundun's girlfriend, or perhaps to his sister. Later, Dundun beat a man almost to death with a tire iron right on the street in Austin, Texas, for which he'll also someday have to answer, but now he is, I think, in the state prison in Colorado.

Will you believe me when I tell you there was kindness in his heart? His left hand didn't know what his right hand was doing. It was only that certain important connections had been burned through. If I opened up your head and ran a hot soldering iron around in your brain, I might turn you into someone like that.

Discussion Topics

1. The government's so-called "war on drugs" has been going for as long as many of us can remember, going on without any real prospect of victory. Some of the basic statistics are puzzling. The incidence of drug use has been relatively stable over the last fifty years with occasional peaks and valleys, but the percentage of persons incarcerated for drug crimes has increased exponentially. An enormous part of the crime-fighting effort in this country has been devoted to drug-related crimes.

Unlike most crimes, addiction is at the heart of the issue. If consumers did not crave drugs, the business of producing and selling them would dry up. To be sure, a significant part of drug sales involve recreational users who are not addicts. But the connection between drugs and criminality is in large part a matter of feeding the needs of addicts — a matter of the desperateness of their need, of the consequent high profits to be made from them, and of the ruthless business practices used to control markets for drugs.

Most sociologists and psychologists agree that we are not using all relevant resources to face the problem of addiction. We do not do enough to prevent people from becoming addicts and to help addicts overcome addiction. For many experts, the problem is a medical and social one rather than a problem for law. In terms of your general intuitive understanding, consider how you think resources should be used.

The possible legalization of drugs, perhaps all drugs, remains a politically charged issue with many untested hypotheses. Little is known about how legalization would affect consumption and addiction and about how our systems of prevention and treatment would be reconfigured. Many observers find lessons in the experience of the Netherlands in decriminalizing most drug consumption.

2. "Dundun" implicitly asks whether there is a role for public intervention in the community Johnson explores. However dysfunctional they may be, should Dundun, McInnes, Hotel, Beatle, and their friends be allowed the life they have chosen? Are they exercising autonomous choice in a meaningful way, and do their choices deserve our respect? Part of Johnson's agenda is to uncover the dignity at the core of these troubled lives. At the very least, he is taking them on their own terms. Recall that, in considering the Clark play, we considered whether there is a right of self-destruction. Do the habitués of this drug community have such a right and are they exercising it?

3. For the most part, we assume that those who commit crimes have understandable beliefs, feelings, and attitudes and that it is part of the jury's job to figure them out. It may be said that at a certain point people drift so far away from so-called normal responses and emotions that they have created their own world. This creates conceptual as well as practical problems with regard to applying criminal law to them.

Consider the attitudes toward intentional or reckless homicide displayed in "Dundun." In shooting McInnes, was Dundun acting recklessly, that is, with awareness that he was creating a high degree of risk of death? To ask the question is to impose a set of "normal" expectations that Dundun and his friends hardly satisfy.

Does this mean that, if they present a problem that needs to addressed, we should use other resources than criminal law to address it?

Controlling One's Community

Philip Roth: Eli the Fanatic

Not all public interventions in private lives are responses to violence — rape, child abuse, drug-induced mayhem, or suicide. In many cases, communities choose to regulate themselves to maintain a particular way of life. They may zone out certain kinds of business, may impose esthetic limitations, and may control the kinds of housing they provide. There are limitations on this power. For example, a community cannot limit the race of its members.

Much elective zoning is legal. There remains the ethical and normative question whether such rules impinge unfairly on the rights of individuals. In Philip Roth's story, "Eli the Fanatic," community rules in a Long Island suburb outlaw using residential property for any business, such as a school. A Jewish orthodox elementary school, a yeshiva, is set up by a group of recent refugees from Germany. The story takes place soon after World War II.

Philip Roth has often written about Jewish life in America during his long and distinguished career. There are autobiographical elements in many of his more than thirty novels. Most have been received enthusiastically by critics. In a recent poll of writers determining the best novels of the second half of the twentieth century, Roth had six of his novels among the twenty-two listed; no other writer had more than two. But there is a significant generation gap. Readers over forty tend to know him well, but he has hardly any audience among younger groups.

❧ Eli the Fanatic ❧

Philip Roth

Leo Tzuref stepped out from back of a white column to welcome Eli Peck. Eli jumped back, surprised; then they shook hands and Tzuref gestured him into the sagging old mansion. At the door Eli turned, and down the slope of lawn, past the jungle of hedges, beyond the dark, untrampled horse path, he saw the street lights blink on in Woodenton. The stores along Coach House Road tossed up a burst of yellow — it came to Eli as a secret signal from his townsmen: "Tell this Tzuref where we stand, Eli. This is a modern community, Eli, we have our families, we pay taxes . . ." Eli, burdened by the message, gave Tzuref a dumb, weary stare.

"You must work a full day," Tzuref said, steering the attorney and his briefcase into the chilly hall.

Eli's heels made a racket on the cracked marble floor, and he spoke above it. "It's the commuting that's killing," he said, and entered the dim room Tzuref waved open for him. "Three hours a day . . . I came right from the train." He dwindled down into a harp-backed chair. He expected it would be deeper than it was and consequently jarred himself on the sharp bones of his seat. It woke him, this shiver of the behind, to his business. Tzuref, a bald shaggy-browed man who looked as if he'd once been very fat, sat back of an empty desk, halfway hidden, as though he were settled on the floor. Everything around him was empty. There were no books in the bookshelves, no rugs on the floor, no draperies in the big casement windows. As Eli began to speak Tzuref got up and swung a window back on one noisy hinge. "May and it's like August," he said, and with his back to Eli, he revealed the black circle on the back of his head. The crown of his head was missing! He returned through the dimness — the lamps had no bulbs — and Eli realized all he'd seen was a skullcap. Tzuref struck a match and lit a candle, just as the half-dying shouts of children at play rolled in through the open window. It was as though Tzuref had opened it so Eli could hear them.

"Aah, now," he said. "I received your letter."

Eli poised, waiting for Tzuref to swish open a drawer and remove the letter from his file. Instead the old man leaned forward onto his stomach, worked his hand into his pants pocket, and withdrew what appeared to be a week-old handkerchief. He uncrumpled it; he unfolded it; he ironed it on the desk with the side of his hand. "So," he said.

Eli pointed to the grimy sheet which he'd gone over word-by-word with his partners, Lewis and McDonnell. "I expected an answer," Eli said. "It's a week."

"It was so important, Mr. Peck, I knew you would come."

Some children ran under the open window and their mysterious babble — not mysterious to Tzuref, who smiled — entered the room like a third person. Their noise caught up against Eli's flesh and he was unable to restrain a shudder. He wished he had gone home, showered and eaten dinner, before calling on Tzuref. He was not feeling as professional as usual — the place was too dim, it was too late. But down in Woodenton they would be waiting, his clients and neighbors. He spoke for the Jews of Woodenton, not just himself and his wife.

"You understood?" Eli said.

"It's not hard."

"It's a matter of zoning . . ." and when Tzuref did not answer, but only drummed his fingers on his lips, Eli said, "We didn't make the laws . . ."

"You respect them."

"They protect us . . . the community."

"The law is the law," Tzuref said.

"Exactly!" Eli had the urge to rise and walk about the room.

"And then of course" — Tzuref made a pair of scales in the air with his hands — "The law is not the law. When is the law that is the law not the law?" He jiggled the scales. "And vice versa."

"Simply," Eli said sharply. "You can't have a boarding school in a residential area." He would not allow Tzuref to cloud the issue with issues. "We thought it better to tell you before any action is undertaken."

"But a house in a residential area?"

"Yes. That's what residential means." The DP's English was perhaps not as good as it seemed at first. Tzuref spoke slowly, but till then Eli had mistaken it for craft — or even wisdom. "Residence means home," he added.

"So this is my residence."

"But the children?"

"It is their residence."

"Seventeen children?"

"Eighteen," Tzuref said.

"But you teach them here."

"The Talmud. That's illegal?"

"That makes it school."

Tzuref hung the scales again, tipping slowly the balance.

"Look, Mr. Tzuref, in America we call such a place a boarding school."

"Where they teach the Talmud?"

"Where they teach period. You are the headmaster, they are the students."

Tzuref placed his scales on the desk. "Mr. Peck," he said, "I don't believe it..." but he did not seem to be referring to anything Eli had said.

"Mr. Tzuref, that is the law. I came to ask what you intend to do."

"What I must do?"

"I hope they are the same."

"They are." Tzuref brought his stomach into the desk. "We stay." He smiled. "We are tired. The headmaster is tired. The students are tired."

Eli rose and lifted his briefcase. It felt so heavy packed with the grievances, vengeances, and schemes of his clients. There were days when he carried it like a feather — in Tzuref's office it weighed a ton.

"Goodbye, Mr. Tzuref."

"Sholom," Tzuref said.

Eli opened the door to the office and walked carefully down the dark tomb of a corridor to the door. He stepped out on the porch and, leaning against a pillar, looked down across the lawn to the children at play. Their voices whooped and rose and dropped as they chased each other round the old house. The dusk made the children's game look like a tribal dance. Eli straightened up, started off the porch, and suddenly the dance was ended. A long piercing scream trailed after. It was the first time in his life anyone had run at the sight of him. Keeping his eyes on the lights of Woodenton, he headed down the path.

And then, seated on a bench beneath a tree, Eli saw him. At first it seemed only a deep hollow of blackness — then the figure emerged. Eli recognized him from the description. There he was, wearing the hat, that hat which was the very cause of Eli's mission, the source of Woodenton's upset. The town's lights flashed their message once again: "Get the one with the hat. What a nerve, what a nerve . . ."

Eli started towards the man. Perhaps he was less stubborn than Tzuref, more reasonable. After all, it was the law. But when he was close enough to call out, he didn't. He was stopped by the sight of the black coat that fell down below the man's knees, and the hands which held each other in his lap. By the round-topped, wide-brimmed Talmudic hat, pushed onto the back of his head. And by the beard, which hid his neck and was so soft and thin it fluttered away and back again with each heavy breath he took. He was asleep, his sidelocks curled loose on his cheeks. His face was no older than Eli's.

Eli hurried towards the lights.

The note on the kitchen table unsettled him. Scribblings on bits of paper had made history this past week. This one, however, was unsigned. "Sweetie," it said, "I went to sleep. I had a sort of Oedipal experience with the baby today. Call Ted Heller."

She had left him a cold soggy dinner in the refrigerator. He hated cold soggy dinners, but would take one gladly in place of Miriam's presence. He was ruffled, and she never helped that, not with her infernal analytic powers. He loved her when life was proceeding smoothly — and that was when she loved him. But sometimes Eli found being a lawyer surrounded him like quicksand — he couldn't get his breath. Too often he wished he were pleading for the other side; though if he were on the other side, then he'd wish he were on the side he was. The trouble was that sometimes the law didn't seem to be the answer, law didn't seem to have anything to do with what was aggravating everybody. And that, of course, made him feel foolish and unnecessary . . . Though that was not the situation here — the townsmen had a case. But not exactly, and if Miriam were awake to see Eli's upset, she would set about explaining his distress to him, understanding him, forgiving him, so as to get things back to Normal, for Normal was where they loved one another. The difficulty with Miriam's efforts was they only upset him more; not only did they explain little to him about himself or his predicament, but they convinced him of her weakness. Neither Eli nor Miriam, it turned out, was terribly strong. Twice before he'd faced this fact, and on both occasions had found solace in what his neighbors forgivingly referred to as "a nervous breakdown."

Eli ate his dinner with his briefcase beside him. Halfway through, he gave in to himself, removed Tzuref's notes, and put them on the table, beside Miriam's. From time to time he flipped through the notes, which had been carried into town by the one in the black hat. The first note, the incendiary:

> *To whom it may concern:*
> *Please give this gentleman the following: Boys shoes with rubber heels and soles.*
>
> *5 prs size 6c*
> *3 prs size 5c*
> *3 prs size 5b*
> *2 prs size 4a*
> *3 prs size 4c*
> *1 pr size 7b*
> *1 pr size 7c*
>
> *Total 18 prs. boys shoes. This gentleman has a check already signed. Please fill in correct amount.*
> L. TZUREF, *Director, Yeshivah of Woodenton, N.Y. (5/8/48)*

"Eli, a regular greenhorn," Ted Heller had said. "He didn't say a word. Just handed me the note and stood there, like in the Bronx the old guys who used to come around selling Hebrew trinkets."

"A Yeshivah!" Artie Berg had said. "Eli, in Woodenton, a Yeshivah! If I want to live in Brownsville, Eli, I'll live in Brownsville."

"Eli," Harry Shaw speaking now, "the old Puddington place. Old man Puddington'll roll over in his grave. Eli, when I left the city, Eli, I didn't plan the city should come to me."

Note number two:

> *Dear Grocer:*
> *Please give this gentleman ten pounds of sugar. Charge it to our account, Yeshivah of Woodenton, NY — which we will now open with you and expect a bill each month. The gentleman will be in to see you once or twice a week.*
> L. TZUREF, *Director (5/10/48)*
> *P.S. Do you carry kosher meat?*

"He walked right by my window, the greenie," Ted had said, "and he nodded, Eli. He's my friend now."

"Eli," Artie Berg had said, "he handed the damn thing to a clerk at Stop & Shop — and in that hat yet!"

"Eli," Harry Shaw again, "it's not funny. Someday, Eli, it's going to be hundred little kids with little yamalkahs chanting their

Hebrew lessons in Coach House Road, and then it's not going to strike you funny."

"Eli, what goes on up there — my kids hear strange sounds."

"Eli, this is a modern community."

"Eli, we pay taxes."

"Eli."

"Eli!"

At first it was only another townsman crying in his ear; but when he turned he saw Miriam, standing in the doorway, behind her belly.

"Eli, sweetheart, how was it?"

"He said no."

"Did you see the other one?" she asked.

"Sleeping, under a tree."

"Did you let him know how people feel?"

"He was sleeping."

"Why didn't you wake him up? Eli, this isn't an everyday thing."

"He was tired!"

"Don't shout, please," Miriam said.

"Don't shout. I'm pregnant. The baby is heavy." Eli found he was getting angry at nothing she'd said yet; it was what she was going to say.

"He's a very heavy baby the doctor says," Miriam told him.

"Then sit down and make my dinner." Now he found himself angry about her not being present at the dinner which he'd just been relieved that she wasn't present at. It was as though he had a raw nerve for a tail, that he kept stepping on. At last Miriam herself stepped on it.

"Eli, you're upset. I understand."

"You don't understand."

She left the room. From the stairs she called, "I do, sweetheart."

It was a trap! He would grow angry knowing she would be "understanding." She would in turn grow more understanding seeing his anger. He would in turn grow angrier . . . The phone rang.

"Hello," Eli said.

"Eli, Ted. So?"

"So nothing."

"Who is Tzuref? He's an American guy?"

"No. A DP. German."

"And the kids?"

"DP's too. He teaches them."

"What? What subjects?" Ted asked.

"I don't know."

"And the guy with the hat, you saw the guy with the hat?"

"Yes. He was sleeping."

"Eli, he sleeps with the hat?"

"He sleeps with the hat."

"Goddam fanatics," Ted said. "This is the twentieth century, Eli. Now it's the guy with the hat. Pretty soon all the little Yeshivah boys'll be spilling down into town."

"Next thing they'll be after our daughters."

"Michele and Debbie wouldn't look at them."

"Then," Eli mumbled, "you've got nothing to worry about, Teddie," and he hung up.

In a moment the phone rang. "Eli? We got cut off. We've got nothing to worry about? You worked it out?"

"I have to see him again tomorrow. We can work something out."

"That's fine, Eli. I'll call Artie and Harry."

Eli hung up.

"I thought you said nothing worked out." It was Miriam.

"I did."

"Then why did you tell Ted something worked out?"

"It did."

"Eli, maybe you should get a little more therapy."

"That's enough of that, Miriam."

"You can't function as a lawyer by being neurotic. That's no answer."

"You're ingenious, Miriam."

She turned, frowning, and took her heavy baby to bed.

The phone rang.

"Eli, Artie. Ted called. You worked it out? No trouble?"

"Yes."

"When are they going?"

"Leave it to me, will you, Artie? I'm tired. I'm going to sleep."

In bed Eli kissed his wife's belly and laid his head upon it to think. He laid it lightly, for she was that day entering the second week of her ninth month. Still, when she slept, it was a good place to rest, to rise and fall with her breathing and figure things out.

"If that guy would take off that crazy hat. I know it, what eats them. If he'd take off that crazy hat everything would be all right."

"What?" Miriam said.

"I'm talking to the baby."

Miriam pushed herself up in bed. "Eli, please, baby, shouldn't you maybe stop in to see Dr. Eckman, just for a little conversation?"

"I'm fine."

"Oh, sweetie!" she said, and put her head back on the pillow.

"You know what your mother brought to this marriage—a sling chair and a goddam New School enthusiasm for Sigmund Freud."

Miriam feigned sleep, he could tell by the breathing.

"I'm telling the kid the truth, aren't I, Miriam? A sling chair, three months to go on a New Yorker subscription, and An Introduction to Psychoanalysis. Isn't that right?"

"Eli, must you be aggressive?"

"That's all you worry about, is your insides. You stand in front of the mirror all day and look at yourself being pregnant."

"Pregnant mothers have a relationship with the fetus that fathers can't understand."

"Relationship my ass. What is my liver doing now? What is my small intestine doing now? Is my island of Lagerhans on the blink?"

"Don't be jealous of a little fetus, Eli."

"I'm jealous of your island of Lagerhans!"

"Eli, I can't argue with you when I know it's not me you're really angry with. Don't you see, sweetie, you're angry with yourself."

"You and Eckman."

"Maybe he could help, Eli."

"Maybe he could help you. You're practically lovers as it is."

"You're being hostile again," Miriam said.

"What do you care—it's only me I'm being hostile towards."

"Eli, we're going to have a beautiful baby, and I'm going to have a perfectly simple delivery, and you're going to make a fine father, and there's absolutely no reason to be obsessed with whatever is on your mind. All we have to worry about—" she smiled at him " —is a name."

Eli got out of bed and slid into his slippers. "We'll name the kid Eckman if it's a boy and Eckman if it's a girl."

"Eckman Peck sounds terrible."

"He'll have to live with it," Eli said, and he went down to his study where the latch on his briefcase glinted in the moonlight that came through the window.

He removed the Tzuref notes and read through them all again. It unnerved him to think of all the flashy reasons his wife could come up with for his reading and rereading the notes. "Eli, why are you so preoccupied with Tzuref?" "Eli, stop getting involved. Why do you think you're getting involved, Eli?" Sooner or later, everybody's wife finds their weak spot. His goddam luck he had to be neurotic! Why couldn't he have been born with a short leg.

He removed the cover from his typewriter, hating Miriam for the edge she had. All the time he wrote the letter, he could hear what she would be saying about his not being able to let the matter drop. Well, her trouble was that she wasn't able to face the matter. But he could hear her answer already: clearly, he was guilty of "a reaction formation." Still, all the fancy phrases didn't fool Eli: all she wanted really was for Eli to send Tzuref and family on their way, so that the community's temper would quiet, and the calm circumstances of their domestic happiness return. All she wanted were order and love in her private world. Was she so wrong? Let the world bat its brains out—in Woodenton there should be peace. He wrote the letter anyway:

Dear Mr. Tzuref:
Our meeting this evening seems to me inconclusive. I don't think there's any reason for us not to be able to come up with some sort of compromise that will satisfy the Jewish community of Woodenton and the Yeshivah and yourself. It seems to me that what most disturbs my neighbors are the visits to town by the gentleman in the black hat, suit, etc. Woodenton is a progressive suburban community whose members, both Jewish and Gentile, are anxious that their families live in comfort and beauty and serenity. This is, after all, the twentieth century, and we do not think it too much to ask that the members of our community dress in a manner appropriate to the time and place.

Woodenton, as you may not know, has long been the home of well-to-do Protestants. It is only since the war that Jews have been able to buy property here, and for Jews and Gentiles to live beside each other in amity. For this adjustment to be made, both Jews and Gentiles alike have had to give up some of their more extreme practices in order not to threaten or offend the other. Certainly such amity is to be desired. Perhaps if such conditions had existed in prewar Europe, the persecution of the Jewish people, of which you and those 18 children have been victims, could not have been carried out with such success—in fact, might not have been carried out at all.

Therefore, Mr. Tzuref, will you accept the following conditions? If you can, we will see fit not to carry out legal action against the Yeshivah for failure to comply with township Zoning ordinances No. 18 and No. 23. The conditions are simply:

1. The religious, educational, and social activities of the Yeshivah of Woodenton will be confined to the Yeshivah grounds.

2. Yeshivah personnel are welcomed in the streets and stores of Woodenton provided they are attired in clothing usually associated with American life in the 20th century.

If these conditions are met, we see no reason why the Yeshivah of Woodenton cannot live peacefully and satisfactorily with the Jews of Woodenton—as the Jews of Woodenton have come to live with the Gentiles of Woodenton. I would appreciate an immediate reply.
Sincerely, ELI PECK, Attorney

Two days later Eli received his immediate reply:

Mr. Peck:
The suit the gentleman wears is all he's got.
Sincerely, Leo Tzuref, Headmaster

Once again, as Eli swung around the dark trees and onto the lawn, the children fled. He reached out with his briefcase as if to stop them, but they were gone so fast all he saw moving was a flock of skullcaps.

"Come, come ..." a voice called from the porch. Tzuref appeared from behind a pillar. Did he live behind those pillars? Was he just watching the children at play? Either way, when Eli appeared, Tzuref was ready, with no forewarning.

"Hello," Eli said.

"Sholom."

"I didn't mean to frighten them."

"They're scared, so they run."

"I didn't do anything."

Tzuref shrugged. The little movement seemed to Eli strong as an accusation. What he didn't get at home, he got here.

Inside the house they took their seats. Though it was lighter than a few evenings before, a bulb or two would have helped. Eli had to hold his briefcase towards the window for the last gleamings. He removed Tzuref's letter from a manila folder. Tzuref removed Eli's letter from his pants pocket. Eli removed the carbon of his own letter from another manila folder. Tzuref removed Eli's first letter from his back pocket. Eli removed the carbon from his briefcase. Tzuref raised his palms. "... It's all I've got ..."

Those upraised palms, the mocking tone — another accusation. It was a crime to keep carbons! Everybody had an edge on him — Eli could do no right.

"I offered a compromise, Mr. Tzuref. You refused."

"Refused, Mr. Peck? What is, is."

"The man could get a new suit."

"That's all he's got."

"So you told me," Eli said.

"So I told you, so you know."

"It's not an insurmountable obstacle, Mr. Tzuref. We have stores."

"For that too?"

"On Route 12, a Robert Hall — "

"To take away the one thing a man's got?"

"Not take away, replace."

"But I tell you he has nothing. Nothing. You have that word in English? Nicht? Gornisht?"

"Yes, Mr. Tzuref, we have the word."

"A mother and a father?" Tzuref said. "No. A wife? No. A baby? A little ten-month-old baby? No! A village full of friends? A synagogue where you knew the feel of every seat under your pants? Where with your eyes closed you could smell the cloth of the

Torah?" Tzuref pushed out of his chair, stirring a breeze that swept Eli's letter to the floor. At the window he leaned out, and looked, beyond Woodenton. When he turned he was shaking a finger at Eli. "And a medical experiment they performed on him yet! That leaves nothing, Mr. Peck. Absolutely nothing!"

"I misunderstood."

"No news reached Woodenton?"

"About the suit, Mr. Tzuref. I thought he couldn't afford another."

"He can't."

They were right where they'd begun. "Mr. Tzuref!" Eli demanded. "Here?" He smacked his hand to his billfold.

"Exactly!" Tzuref said, smacking his own breast.

"Then we'll buy him one!" Eli crossed to the window and taking Tzuref by the shoulders, pronounced each word slowly. "We-will-pay-for-it. All right?"

"Pay? What, diamonds!"

Eli raised a hand to his inside pocket, then let it drop. Oh stupid! Tzuref, father to eighteen, had smacked not what lay under his coat, but deeper, under the ribs.

"Oh . . ." Eli said. He moved away along the wall. "The suit is all he's got then."

"You got my letter," Tzuref said.

Eli stayed back in the shadow, and Tzuref turned to his chair. He swished Eli's letter from the floor, and held it up. "You say too much . . . all this reasoning . . . all these conditions."

"What can I do?"

"You have the word 'suffer' in English?"

"We have the word suffer. We have the word law too."

"Stop with the law! You have the word suffer. Then try it. It's a little thing."

"They won't," Eli said.

"But you, Mr. Peck, how about you?"

"I am them, they are me, Mr. Tzuref."

"Aach! You are us, we are you!"

Eli shook and shook his head. In the dark he suddenly felt that Tzuref might put him under a spell. "Mr. Tzuref, a little light?"

Tzuref lit what tallow was left in the holders. Eli was afraid to ask if they couldn't afford electricity. Maybe candles were all they had left.

"Mr. Peck, who made the law, may I ask you that?"

"The people."

"No."

"Yes."

"Before the people."

"No one. Before the people there was no law." Eli didn't care for the conversation, but with only candlelight, he was being lulled into it.

"Wrong," Tzuref said.

"We make the law, Mr. Tzuref. It is our community. These are my neighbors. I am their attorney. They pay me. Without law there is chaos."

"What you call law, I call shame. The heart, Mr. Peck, the heart is law! God!" he announced.

"Look, Mr. Tzuref, I didn't come here to talk metaphysics. People use the law, it's a flexible thing. They protect what they value, their property, their well-being, their happiness—"

"Happiness? They hide their shame. And you, Mr. Peck, you are shameless?"

"We do it," Eli said, wearily, "for our children. This is the twentieth century . . ."

"For the goyim maybe. For me the fifty-eighth." He pointed at Eli. "That is too old for shame."

Eli felt squashed. Everybody in the world had evil reasons for his actions. Everybody! With reasons so cheap, who buys bulbs. "Enough wisdom, Mr. Tzuref. Please. I'm exhausted."

"'Who isn't?" Tzuref said.

He picked Eli's papers from his desk and reached up with them. "What do you intend for us to do?"

"What you must," Eli said. "I made the offer."

"So he must give up his suit?"

"Tzuref, Tzuref, leave me be with that suit! I'm not the only lawyer in the world. I'll drop the case, and you'll get somebody who won't talk compromise. Then you'll have no home, no children, nothing. Only a lousy black suit! Sacrifice what you want. I know what I would do."

To that Tzuref made no answer, but only handed Eli his letters. "It's not me, Mr. Tzuref, it's them."

"They are you."

"No," Eli intoned, "I am me. They are them. You are you."

"You talk about leaves and branches. I'm dealing with under the dirt."

"Mr. Tzuref, you're driving me crazy with Talmudic wisdom. This is that, that is the other thing. Give me a straight answer."

"Only for straight questions."

"Oh, God!"

Eli returned to his chair and plunged his belongings into his case. "Then, that's all," he said angrily.

Tzuref gave him the shrug.

"Remember, Tzuref, you called this down on yourself."

"I did?"

Eli refused to be his victim again. Double-talk proved nothing.

"Goodbye," he said.

But as he opened the door leading to the hall, he heard Tzuref. "And your wife, how is she?"

"Fine, just fine." Eli kept going.

"And the baby is due when, any day?"

Eli turned. "That's right."

"Well," Tzuref said, rising. "Good luck."

"You know?"

Tzuref pointed out the window — then, with his hands, he drew upon himself a beard, a hat, a long, long coat. When his fingers formed the hem they touched the floor. "He shops two, three times a week, he gets to know them."

"He talks to them?"

"He sees them."

"And he can tell which is my wife?"

"They shop at the same stores. He says she is beautiful. She has a kind face. A woman capable of love . . . though who can be sure."

"He talks about us, to you?" demanded Eli.

"You talk about us, to her?"

"Goodbye, Mr. Tzuref."

Tzuref said, "Sholom. And good luck — I know what it is to have children. Sholom," Tzuref whispered, and with the whisper the candles went out. But the instant before, the flames leaped into Tzuref's eyes, and Eli saw it was not luck Tzuref wished him at all.

Outside the door, Eli waited. Down the lawn the children were holding hands and whirling around in a circle. At first he did not move. But he could not hide in the shadows all night. Slowly he began to slip along the front of the house. Under his hands he felt where bricks were out. He moved in the shadows until he reached the side. And then, clutching his briefcase to his chest, he broke across the darkest spots of the lawn. He aimed for a distant glade of woods, and when he reached it he did not stop, but ran through until he was so dizzied that the trees seemed to be running beside him, fleeing not towards Woodenton but away. His lungs were nearly ripping their seams as he burst into the yellow glow of the Gulf station at the edge of town.

"Eli, I had pains today. Where were you?"

"I went to Tzuref."

"Why didn't you call? I was worried."

He tossed his hat past the sofa and onto the floor. "Where are my winter suits?"

"In the hall closet. Eli, it's May."

"I need a strong suit." He left the room, Miriam behind him.

"Eli, talk to me. Sit down. Have dinner. Eli, what are you doing? You're going to get moth balls all over the carpet."

He peered out from the hall closet. Then he peered in again — there was a zipping noise, and suddenly he swept a greenish tweed suit before his wife's eyes.

"Eli, I love you in that suit. But not now. Have something to eat. I made dinner tonight — I'll warm it."

"You've got a box big enough for this suit?"

"I got a Bonwit's box, the other day. Eli, why?"

"Miriam, you see me doing something, let me do it."

"You haven't eaten."

"I'm *doing* something." He started up the stairs to the bedroom.

"Eli, would you please tell me what it is you want, and why?"

He turned and looked down at her. "Suppose this time you give me the reasons before I tell you what I'm doing. It'll probably work out the same anyway."

"Eli, I want to help."

"It doesn't concern you."

"But I want to help you," Miriam said.

"Just be quiet, then."

"But you're upset," she said, and she followed him up the stairs, heavily, breathing for two.

"Eli, what now?"

"A shirt." He yanked open all the drawers of their new teak dresser. He extracted a shirt.

"Eli, batiste? With a tweed suit?" she inquired.

He was at the closet now, on his knees. "Where are my cordovans?"

"Eli, why are you doing this so compulsively? You look like you have to do something."

"Oh, Miriam, you're supersubtle."

"Eli, stop this and talk to me. Stop it or I'll call Dr. Eckman."

Eli was kicking off the shoes he was wearing. "Where's the Bonwit box?"

"Eli, do you want me to have the baby right here!"

Eli walked over and sat down on the bed. He was draped not only with his own clothing, but also with the greenish tweed suit, the batiste shirt, and under each arm a shoe. He raised his arms and let the shoes drop onto the bed. Then he undid his necktie with one hand and his teeth and added that to the booty.

"Underwear," he said. "He'll need underwear."

"Who!"

He was slipping out of his socks.

Miriam kneeled down and helped him ease his left foot out of the sock. She sat with it on the floor. "Eli, just lie back. Please."

Freedom and Crime

"Plaza 9-3103."

"What?"

"Eckman's number," he said. "It'll save you the trouble."

"Eli—"

"You've got that goddam tender 'You need help' look in your eyes, Miriam, don't tell me you don't."

"I don't."

"I'm not flipping," Eli said.

"I know, Eli."

"Last time I sat in the bottom of the closet and chewed on my bedroom slippers. That's what I did."

"I know."

"And I'm not doing that. This is not a nervous breakdown, Miriam, let's get that straight."

"Okay," Miriam said. She kissed the foot she held. Then, softly, she asked, "What are you doing?"

"Getting clothes for the guy in the hat. Don't tell me why, Miriam. Just let me do it."

"That's all?" she asked.

"That's all."

"You're not leaving?"

"No."

"Sometimes I think it gets too much for you, and you'll just leave."

"What gets too much?"

"I don't know, Eli. Something gets too much. Whenever everything's peaceful for a long time, and things are nice and pleasant, and we're expecting to be even happier. Like now. It's as if you don't think we deserve to be happy."

"Damn it, Miriam! I'm giving this guy a new suit, is that all right? From now on he comes into Woodenton like everybody else, is that all right with you?"

"And Tzuref moves?"

"I don't even know if he'll take the suit, Miriam! What do you have to bring up moving!"

"Eli, I didn't bring up moving. Everybody did. That's what everybody wants. Why make everybody *unhappy*. It's even a law, Eli."

"Don't tell me what's the law."

"All right, sweetie. I'll get the box."

"I'll get the box. Where is it?"

"In the basement."

When he came up from the basement, he found all the clothes neatly folded and squared away on the sofa: shirt, tie, shoes, socks, underwear, belt, and an old gray flannel suit. His wife sat on the end of the sofa, looking like an anchored balloon.

"Where's the green suit?" he said.

"Eli, it's your loveliest suit. It's my favorite suit. Whenever I think of you, Eli, it's in that suit."

"Get it out."

"Eli, it's a Brooks Brothers suit. You say yourself how much you love it."

"Get it out."

"But the gray flannel's more practical. For shopping."

"Get it out."

"You go overboard, Eli. That's your trouble. You won't do anything in moderation. That's how people destroy themselves."

"I do everything in moderation. That's my trouble. The suit's in the closet again?"

She nodded, and began to fill up with tears. "Why does it have to be your suit? Who are you even to decide to give a suit? What about the others?" She was crying openly, and holding her belly. "Eli, I'm going to have a baby. Do we need all this?" and she swept the clothes off the sofa to the floor.

At the closet Eli removed the green suit. "It's a J. Press," he said, looking at the lining.

"I hope to hell he's happy with it!" Miriam said, sobbing.

A half hour later the box was packed. The cord he'd found in the kitchen cabinet couldn't keep the outfit from popping through. The trouble was there was too much: the gray suit and the green suit, an oxford shirt as well as the batiste. But let him have two suits! Let him have three, four, if only this damn silliness would stop! And a hat—of course! God, he'd almost forgotten the hat. He took the stairs two at a time and in Miriam's closet yanked a hatbox from the top shelf. Scattering hat and tissue paper to the floor, he returned downstairs, where he packed away the hat he'd worn that day. Then he looked at his wife, who lay outstretched on the floor before the fireplace. For the third time in as many minutes she was saying, "Eli, this is the real thing."

"Where?"

"Right under the baby's head, like somebody's squeezing oranges."

Now that he'd stopped to listen he was stupefied. He said, "But you have two more weeks . . ." Somehow he'd really been expecting it was to go on not just another two weeks, but another nine months. This led him to suspect, suddenly, that his wife was feigning pain so as to get his mind off delivering the suit. And just as suddenly he resented himself for having such a thought. God, what had he become! He'd been an unending bastard towards her since this Tzuref business had come up—just when her pregnancy must have been most burdensome. He'd allowed her no access to him, but still, he was sure, for good reasons: she might tempt him out of his confusion with her easy answers. He could be tempted all right, it was why he fought so hard. But now a sweep of love came over him at the thought of her contracting womb, and his child. And yet he would not indicate it to her. Under such splendid marital conditions, who knows but she might extract some promise from him about his concern with the school on the hill.

Having packed his second bag of the evening, Eli sped his wife to Woodenton Memorial. There she proceeded not to have her baby, but to lie hour after hour through the night having at first oranges, then bowling balls, then basketballs, squeezed back of her pelvis. Eli sat in the waiting room, under the shattering African glare of a dozen rows of fluorescent bulbs, composing a letter to Tzuref.

> *Dear Mr. Tzuref*
> *The clothes in this box are for the gentleman in the hat. In a life of sacrifice what is one more? But in a life of no sacrifices even one is impossible. Do you see what I'm saying, Mr. Tzuref? I am not a Nazi who would drive eighteen children, who are probably frightened at the sight of a firefly, into homelessness. But if you want a home here, you must accept what we have to offer. The world is the world, Mr. Tzuref. As you would say, what is, is. All we say to this man is change your clothes. Enclosed are two suits and two shirts, and everything else he'll need, including a new hat.*
> *When he needs new clothes let me know.*
> *We await his appearance in Woodenton, as we await friendly relations with the Yeshivah of Woodenton.*

He signed his name and slid the note under a bursting flap and into the box. Then he went to the phone at the end of the room and dialed Ted Heller's number.

"Hello."

"Shirley, it's Eli."

"Eli, we've been calling all night. The lights are on in your place, but nobody answers. We thought it was burglars."

"Miriam's having the baby."

"At home?" Shirley said. "Oh, Eli, what a fun idea!"

"Shirley, let me speak to Ted."

After the ear-shaking clatter of the phone whacking the floor, Eli heard footsteps, breathing, throat-clearing, then Ted. "A boy or a girl?"

"Nothing yet."

"You've given Shirley the bug, Eli. Now she's going to have *our* next one at home."

"Good."

"That's a terrific way to bring the family together, Eli."

"Look, Ted, I've settled with Tzuref."

"When are they going?"

"They're not exactly going, Teddie. I settled it — you won't even know they're there."

"A guy dressed like 1000 B.C. and I won't know it? What are you thinking about, pal?"

"He's changing his clothes."

"Yeah, to what? Another funeral suit?"

"Tzuref promised me, Ted. Next time he comes to town, he comes dressed like you and me."

"What! Somebody's kidding somebody, Eli."

Eli's voice shot up. "If he says he'll do it, he'll do it!"

"And, Eli," Ted asked, "he said it?"

"He said it." It cost him a sudden headache, this invention.

"And suppose he doesn't change, Eli. Just suppose. I mean that might happen, Eli. This might just be some kind of stall or something."

"No," Eli assured him.

The other end was quiet a moment. "Look, Eli," Ted said, finally, "he changes. Okay? All right? But they're still up there, aren't they? That doesn't change."

"The point is you won't know it."

Patiently Ted said, "Is this what we asked of you, Eli? When we put our faith and trust in you, is that what we were asking? We weren't concerned that this guy should become a Beau Brummel, Eli, believe me. We just don't think this is the community for them. And, Eli, we isn't me. The Jewish members of the community appointed me, Artie, and Harry to see what could be done. And we appointed you. And what's happened?"

Eli heard himself say, "What happened, happened."

"Eli, you're talking in crossword puzzles."

"My wife's having a baby," Eli explained, defensively.

"I realize that, Eli. But this is a matter of zoning, isn't it? Isn't that what we discovered? You don't abide by the ordinance, you go. I mean I can't raise mountain goats, say, in my backyard — "

"This isn't so simple, Ted. People are involved — "

"People? Eli, we've been through this and through this. We're not just dealing with people — these are religious fanatics is what they are. Dressing like that. What I'd really like to find out is what goes on up there. I'm getting more and more skeptical, Eli, and I'm not afraid to admit it. It smells like a lot of hocus-pocus abracadabra stuff to me. Guys like Harry, you know, they think and they think and they're afraid to admit what they're thinking. I'll tell you. Look, I don't even know about this Sunday school business. Sundays I drive my oldest kid all the way to Scarsdale to learn Bible stories . . . and you know what she comes up with? This Abraham in the Bible was going to kill his own kid for a sacrifice. She gets nightmares from it, for God's sake! You call that religion? Today a guy like that they'd lock him up. This is an age of science, Eli. I size people's feet with an X-ray machine, for God's sake. They've disproved all that stuff, Eli, and I refuse to sit by and watch it happening on my own front lawn."

"Nothing's happening on your front lawn, Teddie. You're exaggerating, nobody's sacrificing their kid."

"You're damn right, Eli—I'm not sacrificing mine. You'll see when you have your own what it's like. All the place is, is a hideaway for people who can't face life. It's a matter of needs. They have all these superstitions, and why do you think? Because they can't face the world, because they can't take their place in society. That's no environment to bring kids up in, Eli."

"Look, Ted, see it from another angle. We can convert them," Eli said, with half a heart.

"What, make a bunch of Catholics out of them? Look, Eli—pal, there's a good healthy relationship in this town because it's modern Jews and Protestants. That's the point, isn't it, Eli? Let's not kid each other, I'm not Harry. The way things are now are fine—like human beings. There's going to be no pogroms in Woodenton. Right? 'Cause there's no fanatics, no crazy people—" Eli winced, and closed his eyes a second—"just people who respect each other, and leave each other be. Common sense is the ruling thing, Eli. I'm for common sense. Moderation."

"Exactly, exactly, Ted. I agree, but common sense, maybe, says make this guy change his clothes. Then maybe—"

"Common sense says that? Common sense says to me they go and find a nice place somewhere else, Eli. New York is the biggest city in the world, it's only 30 miles away—why don't they go there?"

"Ted, give them a chance. Introduce them to common sense."

"Eli, you're dealing with fanatics. Do they display common sense? Talking a dead language, that makes sense? Making a big thing out of suffering, so you're going oy-oy-oy all your life, that's common sense? Look, Eli, we've been through all this. I don't know if you know—but there's talk that Life magazine is sending a guy out to the Yeshivah for a story. With pictures."

"Look, Teddie, you're letting your imagination get inflamed. I don't think Life's interested."

"But I'm interested, Eli. And we thought you were supposed to be."

"I am," Eli said, "I am. Let him just change the clothes, Ted. Let's see what happens."

"They live in the medieval ages, Eli — it's some superstition, some rule."

"Let's just see," Eli pleaded.

"Eli, every day — "

"One more day," Eli said. "If he doesn't change in one more day. . . ."

"What?"

"Then I get an injunction first thing Monday. That's that."

"Look, Eli — it's not up to me. Let me call Harry — "

"You're the spokesman, Teddie. I'm all wrapped up here with Miriam having a baby. Just give me the day — them the day."

"All right, Eli. I want to be fair. But tomorrow, that's all. Tomorrow's the judgment day, Eli, I'm telling you."

"I hear trumpets," Eli said, and hung up. He was shaking inside — Teddie's voice seemed to have separated his bones at the joints. He was still in the phone booth when the nurse came to tell him that Mrs. Peck would positively not be delivered of a child until the morning. He was to go home and get some rest, he looked like he was having the baby. The nurse winked and left.

But Eli did not go home. He carried the Bonwit box out into the street with him and put it in the car. The night was soft and starry, and he began to drive the streets of Woodenton. Square cool windows, apricot-colored, were all one could see beyond the long lawns that fronted the homes of the townsmen. The stars polished the permanent baggage carriers atop the station wagons in the driveways. He drove slowly, up, down, around. Only his tires could be heard taking the gentle curves in the road.

What peace. What incredible peace. Have children ever been so safe in their beds? Parents — Eli wondered — so full in their stomachs? Water so warm in its boilers? Never. Never in Rome, never in Greece. Never even did walled cities have it so good! No wonder then they would keep things just as they were. Here, after all, were peace and safety — what civilization had been working toward for centuries. For all his jerkiness, that was all Ted Heller was asking for, peace and safety. It was what his parents had asked for in the Bronx, and his grandparents in Poland, and theirs in Russia or Austria, or wherever else they'd fled to or from. It was what Miriam was asking for. And now they had it — the world was at last a place for families, even Jewish families. After all these centuries, maybe there just had to be this communal toughness — or numbness — to protect such a blessing. Maybe that was the trouble with the Jews all along — too soft. Sure, to live takes guts . . . Eli was thinking as he drove on beyond the train station, and parked his car at the darkened Gulf station. He stepped out, carrying the box.

At the top of the hill one window trembled with light. What was Tzuref doing up there in that office? Killing babies — probably not. But studying a language no one understood? Practicing customs with origins long forgotten? Suffering sufferings already suffered once too often? Teddie was right — why keep it up! However, if a man chose to be stubborn, then he couldn't expect to survive. The world is give-and-take. What sense to sit and brood over a suit. Eli would give him one last chance.

He stopped at the top. No one was around. He walked slowly up the lawn, setting each foot into the grass, listening to the shh shhh shhhh his shoes made as they bent the wetness into the sod. He looked around. Here was nothing. Nothing! An old decaying house — and a suit.

On the porch he slid behind a pillar. He felt someone was watching him. But only the stars gleamed down. And at his feet, off and away, Woodenton glowed up. He set his package on the step of the great front door.

Inside the cover of the box he felt to see if his letter was still there. When he touched it, he pushed it deeper into the green suit, which his fingers still remembered from winter. He should have included some light bulbs. Then he slid back by the pillar again, and this time there was something on the lawn. It was the second sight he had of him. He was facing Woodenton and barely moving across the open space towards the trees. His right fist was beating his chest. And then Eli heard a sound rising with each knock on the chest. What a moan! It could raise hair, stop hearts, water eyes. And it did all three to Eli, plus more. Some feeling crept into him for whose deepness he could find no word. It was strange. He listened — it did not hurt to hear this moan. But he wondered if it hurt to make it. And so, with only stars to hear, he tried. And it did hurt. Not the bumblebee of noise that turned at the back of his throat and winged out his nostrils. What hurt buzzed down. It stung and stung inside him, and in turn the moan sharpened. It became a scream, louder, a song, a crazy song that whined through the pillars and blew out to the grass, until the strange hatted creature on the lawn turned and threw his arms wide, and looked in the night like a scarecrow.

Eli ran, and when he reached the car the pain was only a bloody scratch across his neck where a branch had whipped back as he fled the greenie's arms.

The following day his son was born. But not till one in the afternoon, and by then a great deal had happened.

First, at nine-thirty the phone rang. Eli leaped from the sofa — where he'd dropped the night before — and picked it screaming from the cradle. He could practically smell the hospital as he shouted into the phone, "Hello, yes!"

"Eli, it's Ted. Eli, he did it. He just walked by the store. I was opening the door, Eli, and I turned around and I swear I thought it was you. But it was him. He still walks like he did, but the clothes, Eli, the clothes."

"Who?"

"The greenie. He has on man's regular clothes. And the suit, it's a beauty."

The suit barreled back into Eli's consciousness, pushing all else aside. "What color suit?"

"Green. He's just strolling in the green suit like it's a holiday. Eli, is it a Jewish holiday?"

"Where is he now?"

"He's walking straight up Coach House Road, in this damn tweed job. Eli, it worked. You were right."

"We'll see."

"What next?"

"We'll see."

He took off the underwear in which he'd slept and went into the kitchen where he turned the light under the coffee. When it began to perk he held his head over the pot so it would steam loose the knot back of his eyes. It still hadn't when the phone rang.

"Eli, Ted again. Eli, the guy's walking up and down every street in town. Really, he's on a tour or something. Artie called me, Herb called me. Now Shirley calls that he just walked by our house. Eli, go out on the porch you'll see."

Eli went to the window and peered out. He couldn't see past the bend in the road, and there was no one in sight.

"Eli?" He heard Ted from where he dangled over the telephone table. He dropped the phone into the hook, as a few last words floated up to him — "Eli you saw him?" He threw on the pants and shirt he'd worn the night before and walked barefoot on to his front lawn. And sure enough, his apparition appeared around the bend: in a brown hat a little too far down on his head, a green suit too far back on the shoulders, an unbuttoned-down button-down shirt, a tie knotted so as to leave a two-inch tail, trousers that cascaded onto his shoes — he was shorter than that black hat had made him seem. And moving the clothes was that walk that was not a walk, the tiny-stepped shlumpy gait. He came round the bend, and for all his strangeness — it clung to his whiskers, signaled itself in his locomotion — he looked as if he belonged. Eccentric, maybe, but he belonged. He made no moan, nor did he invite Eli with wide-flung arms. But he did stop when he saw him. He stopped and put a hand to his hat. When he felt for its top, his hand went up too high. Then it found the level and fiddled with the brim. The fingers fiddled, fumbled, and when they'd finally made their greeting, they traveled down the fellow's face and in an instant seemed to have touched each one of his features. They dabbed the eyes, ran the length of the nose, swept over the hairy lip, until they found their home in the hair that hid a little of his collar. To Eli the fingers said, *I have a face, I have a face at least.* Then his hand came through the beard and when it stopped at his chest it was like a pointer — and the eyes asked a question as tides of water shifted over them. *The face is all right, I can keep it?* Such a look was in those eyes that Eli was still seeing them when he turned his head away. They were the hearts of his jonquils, that only last week had appeared — they were the leaves on his birch, the bulbs in his coach lamp, the droppings on his lawn: those eyes were the eyes in his head. They were his, he had made them. He turned and went into his house and when he peeked out the side of the window, between shade and molding, the green suit was gone.

The phone rang.

"Eli, Shirley."

"I saw him, Shirley," and he hung up.

He sat frozen for a long time. The sun moved around the windows. The coffee steam smelled up the house. The phone began to ring, stopped, began again. The mailman came, the cleaner, the bakery man, the gardener, the ice cream man, the League of Women Voters lady. A Negro woman spreading some strange gospel calling for the revision of the Food and Drug Act knocked at the front, rapped the windows, and finally scraped a half-dozen pamphlets under the back door. But Eli only sat, without underwear, in last night's suit. He answered no one.

Given his condition, it was strange that the trip and crash at the back door reached his inner ear. But in an instant he seemed to melt down into the crevices of the chair, then to splash up and out to where the clatter had been. At the door he waited. It was silent, but for a fluttering of damp little leaves on the trees. When he finally opened the door, there was no one there. He'd expected to see green, green, green, big as the doorway, topped by his hat, waiting for him with those eyes. But there was no one out there, except for the Bonwit's box which lay bulging at his feet. No string tied it and the top rode high on the bottom.

The coward! He couldn't do it! He couldn't!

The very glee of that idea pumped fuel to his legs. He tore out across his back lawn, past his new spray of forsythia, to catch a glimpse of the bearded one fleeing naked through yards, over hedges and fences, to the safety of his hermitage. In the distance a pile of pink and white stones — which Harriet Knudson had painted the previous day — tricked him. "Run," he shouted to the rocks, "Run, you . . ." but he caught his error before anyone else did, and though he peered and craned there was no hint anywhere of a man about his own size, with white, white, terribly white skin (how white must be the skin of his body!) in cowardly retreat. He came slowly, curiously, back to the door. And while the trees shimmered in the light wind, he removed the top from the box. The shock at first was the shock of having daylight turned off all at once. Inside the box was an eclipse. But black soon sorted from black, and shortly there was the glassy black of lining, the coarse black of trousers, the dead black of fraying threads, and in the center the mountain of black: the hat. He picked the box from the doorstep and carried it inside. For the first time in his life he *smelled* the color of blackness: a little stale, a little sour, a little old, but nothing that could overwhelm you. Still, he held the package at arm's length and deposited it on the dining room table.

Twenty rooms on a hill and they store their old clothes with me! What am I supposed to do with them? Give them to charity? That's where they came from. He picked up the hat by the edges and looked inside. The crown was smooth as an egg, the brim practically threadbare. There is nothing else to do with a hat in one's hands but put it on, so Eli dropped the thing on his head. He opened the door to the hall closet and looked at himself in the full-length mirror. The hat gave him bags under the eyes. Or perhaps he had not slept well. He pushed the brim lower till a shadow touched his lips. Now the bags under his eyes had inflated to become his face. Before the mirror he unbuttoned his shirt, unzipped his trousers, and then, shedding his clothes, he studied what he was. What a silly disappointment to see yourself naked in a hat. Especially in that hat. He sighed, but could not rid himself of the great weakness that suddenly set on his muscles and joints, beneath the terrible weight of the stranger's strange hat.

He returned to the dining room table and emptied the box of its contents: jacket, trousers, and vest (it smelled deeper than blackness). And under it all, sticking between the shoes that looked chopped and bitten, came the first gleam of white. A little fringed serape, a gray piece of semi-underwear, was crumpled at the bottom, its thready border twisted into itself. Eli removed it and let it hang free. What is it? For warmth? To wear beneath underwear in the event of a chest cold? He held it to his nose but it did not smell from Vick's or mustard plaster. It was something special, some Jewish thing. Special food, special language, special prayers, why not special BVD's? So fearful was he that he would be tempted back into wearing his traditional clothes — reasoned Eli — that he had carried and buried in Woodenton everything, including the special underwear. For that was how Eli now understood the box of clothes. The greenie was saying, Here, I give up. I refuse even to be tempted. We surrender. And that was how Eli continued to understand it until he found he'd slipped the white fringy surrender flag over his hat and felt it clinging to his chest. And now, looking at himself in the mirror, he was momentarily uncertain as to who was tempting who into what. Why did the greenie leave his clothes? Was it even the greenie? Then who was it? And why? But, Eli, for Christ's sake, in an age of science things don't happen like that. Even the goddam pigs take drugs.

Regardless of who was the source of the temptation, what was its end, not to mention its beginning, Eli, some moments later, stood draped in black, with a little white underneath, before the full-length mirror. He had to pull down on the trousers so they would not show the hollow of his ankle. The greenie, didn't he wear socks? Or had he forgotten them? The mystery was solved when Eli mustered enough courage to investigate the trouser pockets. He had expected some damp awful thing to happen to his fingers should he slip them down and out of sight—but when at last he jammed bravely down he came up with a khaki army sock in each hand. As he slipped them over his toes, he invented a genesis: a G.I.'s present in 1945. Plus everything else lost between 1938 and 1945, he had also lost his socks. Not that he had lost the socks, but that he'd had to stoop to accepting these, made Eli almost cry. To calm himself he walked out the back door and stood looking at his lawn.

On the Knudson back lawn, Harriet Knudson was giving her stones a second coat of pink. She looked up just as Eli stepped out. Eli shot back in again and pressed himself against the back door. When he peeked between the curtain all he saw were paint bucket, brush, and rocks scattered on the Knudsons' pink-spattered grass. The phone rang. Who was it—Harriet Knudson? Eli, there's a Jew at your door. That's me. Nonsense, Eli, I saw him with my own eyes. That's me, I saw you too, painting your rocks pink. Eli, you're having a nervous breakdown again. Jimmy, Eli's having a nervous breakdown again. Eli, this is Jimmy, hear you're having a little breakdown, anything I can do, boy? Eli, this is Ted, Shirley says you need help. Eli, this is Artie, you need help. Eli, Harry, you need help you need help . . . The phone rattled its last and died.

"God helps them who help themselves," intoned Eli, and once again he stepped out the door. This time he walked to the center of his lawn and in full sight of the trees, the grass, the birds, and the sun, revealed that it was he, Eli, in the costume. But nature had nothing to say to him, and so stealthily he made his way to the hedge separating his property from the field beyond and he cut his way through, losing his hat twice in the underbrush. Then, clamping the hat to his head, he began to run, the threaded tassels jumping across his heart. He ran through the weeds and wild flowers, until on the old road that skirted the town he slowed up. He was walking when he approached the Gulf station from the back. He supported himself on a huge tireless truck rim, and among tubes, rusted engines, dozens of topless oil cans, he rested. With a kind of brainless cunning, he readied himself for the last mile of his journey.

"How are you, Pop?" It was the garage attendant, rubbing his greasy hands on his overalls, and hunting among the cans.

Eli's stomach lurched and he pulled the big black coat round his neck.

"Nice day," the attendant said and started around to the front.

"Sholom," Eli whispered and zoomed off towards the hill.

The sun was directly overhead when Eli reached the top. He had come by way of the woods, where it was cooler, but still he was perspiring beneath his new suit. The hat had no sweatband and the cloth clutched his head. The children were playing. The children were always playing, as if it was that alone that Tzuref had to teach them. In their shorts, they revealed such thin legs that beneath one could see the joints swiveling as they ran. Eli waited for them to disappear around a corner before he came into the open. But something would not let him wait—his green suit. It was on the porch, wrapped around the bearded fellow, who was painting the base of a pillar. His arm went up and down, up and down, and the pillar glowed like white fire. The very sight of him popped Eli out of the woods onto the lawn. He did not turn back, though his insides did. He walked up the lawn, but the children played on; tipping the black hat, he mumbled, "Shhh shhhh," and they hardly seemed to notice.

At last he smelled paint.

He waited for the man to turn to him. He only painted. Eli felt suddenly that if he could pull the black hat down over his eyes, over his chest and belly and legs, if he could shut out all light, then a moment later he would be home in bed. But the hat wouldn't go past his forehead. He couldn't kid himself—he was there. No one he could think of had forced him to do this.

The greenie's arm flailed up and down on the pillar. Eli breathed loudly, cleared his throat, but the greenie wouldn't make life easier for him. At last, Eli had to say "Hello."

The arm swished up and down; it stopped—two fingers went out after a brush hair stuck to the pillar.

"Good day," Eli said.

The hair came away; the swishing resumed.

"Sholom," Eli whispered and the fellow turned.

The recognition took some time. He looked at what Eli wore. Up close, Eli looked at what he wore. And then Eli had the strange notion that he was two people. Or that he was one person wearing two suits. The greenie looked to be suffering from a similar confusion. They stared long at one another. Eli's heart shivered, and his brain was momentarily in such a mixed-up condition that his hands went out to button down the collar of his shirt that somebody else was wearing. What a mess! The greenie flung his arms over his face.

"What's the matter . . ." Eli said. The fellow had picked up his bucket and brush and was running away. Eli ran after him.

"I wasn't going to hit . . ." Eli called. "Stop . . ." Eli caught up and grabbed his sleeve. Once again, the greenie's hands flew up to his face. This time, in the violence, white paint spattered both of them.

"I only want to . . ." But in that outfit Eli didn't really know what he wanted. "To talk . . ." he said finally. "For you to look at me. Please, just look at me . . ."

The hands stayed put, as paint rolled off the brush onto the cuff of Eli's green suit.

"Please . . . please," Eli said, but he did not know what to do. "Say something, speak *English*," he pleaded.

The fellow pulled back against the wall, back, back, as though some arm would finally reach out and yank him to safety. He refused to uncover his face.

"Look," Eli said, pointing to himself. "It's your suit. I'll take care of it."

No answer—only a little shaking under the hands, which led Eli to speak as gently as he knew how.

"We'll . . . we'll moth-proof it. There's a button missing"—Eli pointed—"I'll have it fixed. I'll have a zipper put in . . . Please, please—just look at me . . ." He was talking to himself, and yet how could he stop? Nothing he said made any sense—that alone made his heart swell. Yet somehow babbling on, he might babble something that would make things easier between them. "Look . . ." He reached inside his shirt to pull the frills of underwear into the light. "I'm wearing the special underwear, even . . . Please," he said, "please, please, please" he sang, as if it were some sacred word. "Oh, please . . ."

Nothing twitched under the tweed suit—and if the eyes watered, or twinkled, or hated, he couldn't tell. It was driving him crazy. He had dressed like a fool, and for what? For this? He reached up and yanked the hands away.

"There!" he said—and in that first instant all he saw of the greenie's face were two white droplets stuck to each cheek.

"Tell me —" Eli clutched his hands down to his sides — "Tell me, what can I do for you, I'll do it . . ."

Stiffly, the greenie stood there, sporting his two white tears.

"Whatever I can do . . . Look, look, what I've done already." He grabbed his black hat and shook it in the man's face.

And in exchange, the greenie gave him an answer. He raised one hand to his chest, and then jammed it, finger first, towards the horizon. And with what a pained look! As though the air were full of razors! Eli followed the finger and saw beyond the knuckle, out past the nail, Woodenton.

"What do you want?" Eli said. "I'll bring it!"

Suddenly the greenie made a run for it. But then he stopped, wheeled, and jabbed that finger at the air again. It pointed the same way. Then he was gone.

And then, all alone, Eli had the revelation. He did not question his understanding, the substance or the source. But with a strange, dreamy elation, he started away.

On Coach House Road, they were double-parked. The Mayor's wife pushed a grocery cart full of dog food from Stop N' Shop to her station wagon. The President of the Lions Club, a napkin around his neck, was jamming pennies into the meter in front of the Bit-in-Teeth Restaurant. Ted Heller caught the sun as it glazed off the new Byzantine mosaic entrance to his shoe shop. In pinkened jeans, Mrs. Jimmy Knudson was leaving Halloway's Hardware, a paint bucket in each hand. Roger's Beauty Shoppe had its doors open — women's heads in silver bullets far as the eye could see. Over by the barbershop the pole spun, and Artie Berg's youngest sat on a red horse, having his hair cut; his mother flipped through Look, smiling: the greenie had changed his clothes.

And into this street, which seemed paved with chromium, came Eli Peck. It was not enough, he knew, to walk up one side of the street. That was not enough. Instead he walked ten paces up one side, then on an angle, crossed to the other side, where he walked ten more paces, and crossed back. Horns blew, traffic jerked, as Eli made his way up Coach House Road. He spun a moan high up in his nose as he walked. Outside no one could hear him, but he felt it vibrate the cartilage at the bridge of his nose.

Things slowed around him. The sun stopped rippling on spokes and hubcaps. It glowed steadily as everyone put on brakes to look at the man in black. They always paused and gaped, whenever he entered the town. Then in a minute, or two, or three, a light would change, a baby squawk, and the flow continue. Now, though lights changed, no one moved.

"He shaved his beard," Eric the barber said.

"Who?" asked Linda Berg.

"The . . . the guy in the suit. From the place there."

Linda looked out the window.

"It's Uncle Eli," little Kevin Berg said, spitting hair.

"Oh, God," Linda said, "Eli's having a nervous breakdown."

"A nervous breakdown!" Ted Heller said, but not immediately. Immediately he had said "Hoooly . . ."

Shortly, everybody in Coach House Road was aware that Eli Peck, the nervous young attorney with the pretty wife, was having a breakdown. Everybody except Eli Peck. He knew what he did was not insane, though he felt every inch of its strangeness. He felt those black clothes as if they were the skin of his skin — the give and pull as they got used to where he bulged and buckled. And he felt eyes, every eye on Coach House Road. He saw headlights screech to within an inch of him, and stop. He saw mouths: first the bottom jaw slides forward, then the tongue hits the teeth, the lips explode, a little thunder in the throat, and they've said it: Eli Peck Eli Peck Eli Peck Eli Peck. He began to walk slowly, shifting his weight down and forward with each syllable: E-li-Peck-E-li-Peck-E-li-Peck. Heavily he trod, and as his neighbors uttered each syllable of his name, he felt each syllable shaking all his bones. He knew who he was down to his marrow — they were telling him. Eli Peck. He wanted them to say it a thousand times, a million times, he would walk forever in that black suit, as adults whispered of his strangeness and children made "Shame . . . shame" with their fingers.

"It's going to be all right, pal . . ." Ted Heller was motioning to Eli from his doorway. "C'mon, pal, it's going to be all right . . ."

Eli saw him, past the brim of his hat. Ted did not move from his doorway, but leaned forward and spoke with his hand over his mouth. Behind him, three customers peered through the doorway. "Eli, it's Ted, remember Ted . . ."

Eli crossed the street and found he was heading directly towards Harriet Knudson. He lifted his neck so she could see his whole face.

He saw her forehead melt down to her lashes. "Good morning, Mr. Peck."

"Sholom," Eli said, and crossed the street where he saw the President of the Lions.

"Twice before . . ." he heard someone say, and then he crossed again, mounted the curb, and was before the bakery, where a delivery man charged past with a tray of powdered cakes twirling above him. "Pardon me, Father," he said, and scooted into his truck. But he could not move it. Eli Peck had stopped traffic.

He passed the Rivoli Theater, Beekman Cleaners, Harris' Westinghouse, the Unitarian Church, and soon he was passing only trees. At Ireland Road he turned right and started through

Woodenton's winding streets. Baby carriages stopped whizzing and creaked—"Isn't that . . ." Gardeners held their clipping. Children stepped from the sidewalk and tried the curb. And Eli greeted no one, but raised his face to all. He wished passionately that he had white tears to show them . . . And not till he reached his own front lawn, saw his house, his shutters, his new jonquils, did he remember his wife. And the child that must have been born to him. And it was then and there he had the awful moment. He could go inside and put on his clothes and go to his wife in the hospital. It was not irrevocable, even the walk wasn't. In Woodenton memories are long but fury short. Apathy works like forgiveness. Besides, when you've flipped, you've flipped—it's Mother Nature.

What gave Eli the awful moment was that he turned away. He knew exactly what he could do but he chose not to. To go inside would be to go halfway. There was more . . . So he turned and walked towards the hospital and all the time he quaked an eighth of an inch beneath his skin to think that perhaps he'd chosen the crazy way. To think that he'd chosen to be crazy! But if you chose to be crazy, then you weren't crazy. It's when you didn't choose. No, he wasn't flipping. He had a child to see.

"Name?"

"Peck."

"Fourth floor." He was given a little blue card.

In the elevator everybody stared. Eli watched his black shoes rise four floors.

"Four."

He tipped his hat, but knew he couldn't take it off.

"Peck," he said. He showed the card.

"Congratulations," the nurse said, ". . . the grandfather?"

"The father. Which room?"

She led him to 412. "A joke on the Mrs.?" she said, but he slipped in the door without her.

"Miriam?"

"Yes?"

"Eli."

She rolled her white face towards her husband. "Oh, Eli . . . Oh, Eli."

He raised his arms. "What could I do?"

"You have a son. They called all morning."

"I came to see him."

"Like *that*!" she whispered harshly. "Eli, you can't go around like that."

"I have a son. I want to see him."

"Eli, why are you doing this to me!" Red seeped back into her lips. "He's not your fault," she explained. "Oh, Eli, sweetheart, why do you feel guilty about everything. Eli, change your clothes. I forgive you."

"Stop forgiving me. Stop understanding me."

"But I love you."

"That's something else."

"But, sweetie, you don't have to dress like that. You didn't do anything. You don't have to feel guilty because . . . because everything's all right. Eli, can't you see that?"

"Miriam, enough reasons. Where's my son?"

"Oh, please, Eli, don't flip now. I need you now. Is that why you're flipping—because I need you?"

"In your selfish way, Miriam, you're very generous. I want my son."

"Don't flip now. I'm afraid, now that he's out." She was beginning to whimper. "I don't know if I love him, now that he's out. When I look in the mirror, Eli, he won't be there . . . Eli, Eli, you look like you're going to your own funeral. Please, can't you leave well enough alone? Can't we just have a family?"

"No."

In the corridor he asked the nurse to lead him to his son. The nurse walked on one side of him, Ted Heller on the other.

"Eli, do you want some help? I thought you might want some help."

"No."

Ted whispered something to the nurse; then to Eli he whispered, "Should you be walking around like this?"

"Yes."

In his ear Ted said, "You'll . . . you'll frighten the kid."

"There," the nurse said. She pointed to a bassinet in the second row and looked, puzzled, to Ted. "Do I go in?" Eli said.

"No," the nurse said. "She'll roll him over." She rapped on the enclosure full of babies. "Peck," she mouthed to the nurse on the inside.

Ted tapped Eli's arm. "You're not thinking of doing something you'll be sorry for . . . are you, Eli? Eli—I mean you know you're still Eli, don't you?"

In the enclosure, Eli saw a bassinet had been wheeled before the square window.

"Oh, Christ . . ." Ted said. "You don't have this Bible stuff on the brain—" And suddenly he said, "You wait, pal." He started down the corridor, his heels tapping rapidly.

Eli felt relieved—he leaned forward. In the basket was what he'd come to see. Well, now that he was here, what did he think he was going to say to it? I'm your father, Eli, the Flipper? I am wearing a black hat, suit, and fancy underwear, all borrowed from a friend?

How could he admit to this reddened ball — *his* reddened ball — the worst of all: that Eckman would shortly convince him he wanted to take off the whole business. He couldn't admit it! He wouldn't do it!

Past his hat brim, from the corner of his eye, he saw Ted had stopped in a doorway at the end of the corridor. Two interns stood there smoking, listening to Ted. Eli ignored it.

No, even Eckman wouldn't make him take it off! No! He'd wear it, if he chose to. He'd make the kid wear it! Sure! Cut it down when the time came. A smelly hand-me-down, whether the kid liked it or not!

Only Teddie's heels clacked; the interns wore rubber soles — for they were there, beside him, unexpectedly. Their white suits smelled, but not like Eli's.

"Eli," Ted said, softly, "visiting time's up, pal."

"How are you feeling, Mr. Peck? First child upsets everyone. . . ."

He'd just pay no attention; nevertheless, he began to perspire, thickly, and his hat crown clutched his hair.

"Excuse me — Mr. Peck . . ." It was a new rich bass voice. "Excuse me, rabbi, but you're wanted . . . in the temple." A hand took his elbow, firmly; then another hand, the other elbow. Where they grabbed, his tendons went taut.

"Okay, rabbi. Okay okay okay okay okay okay. . . ." He listened; it was a very soothing word, that okay. "Okay okay everything's going to be okay." His feet seemed to have left the ground some, as he glided away from the window, the bassinet, the babies. "Okay easy does it everything's all right all right — "

But he rose, suddenly, as though up out of a dream, and flailing his arms, screamed: "I'm the father!"

But the window disappeared. In a moment they tore off his jacket — it gave so easily, in one yank. Then a needle slid under his skin. The drug calmed his soul, but did not touch it down where the blackness had reached.

Discussion Topics

1. Religious life in the U.S. and Jewish religious life in particular have changed in the last fifty years since Roth's story was written. Religious fundamentalism and orthodoxy have become more familiar and widespread. Many people who were not observant in the 1960s and '70s took greater interest in their cultural, ethnic, and religious roots as they grew older. And many younger people around the country are raised in strict religious households. Fifty years ago, atheism and agnosticism were widely discussed and many people self-identified with these positions. This is not to say that they have declined in adherence, but they have certainly declined as topics of discourse.

The orthodox community in Roth's story might have seemed much stranger and more threatening to Roth's characters than it might to our contemporaries. Also, they may have had more of a stake in their non-observance than today's Jews might have. It is also significant that, given the remarkable persecution of Jews in World War II, these secular Jews might well be ambivalent about being Jewish (and perhaps unconscious of their ambivalence). They may identify with the plight of Jews but at the same time blame and abhor the fate of having been born into a group that has just been so seriously victimized.

2. Eli the lawyer dramatizes in his person the ambivalence of the Jew. His allegiances are in the secular community — and so, it seems, are his convictions. And yet by the story's end he has assumed the clothing (and the persona?) of the "greenie." Roth's intentions here are hardly transparent, and it would not be wrong to find several levels of irony. Has Eli now discovered his true identity or has he suffered, as his wife is convinced, another nervous breakdown? Is his conversion likely to last and sustain him? Has he earned it? Does he even know, in the way the members of the yeshiva know, what it entails?

3. It may be wise not to see the story as a simple parable of light and darkness, of the good refugees and the evil townspeople. As we have already seen, Eli's conversion may not be simply a matter of discovering truth and light. Another matter is the conduct of Tzuref, who runs the yeshiva. To be sure, he is engaged in admirable work and has suffered. But he flaunts his suffering. One may infer that he sees his suffering, and the suffering of European Jews in general, as giving him special entitlements to ignore the rules of others.

This is a claim that arises in many contexts. Reparations for past injustices are a valid topic of discussion with regard to Native Americans and African-Americans. It seems cold-hearted and self-serving to say that past suffering should be ignored. But that's simply the start of the conversation. The law, if it is to be fair, must generally treat victims and non-victims alike. Exceptions must be rare and carefully considered. No one has a clear answer to the question of what special benefits (or rectification) the victim is owed.

4. Eli takes on his task as a *lawyer*, as legal representative for his friends. As such, he has a special obligation to act in their interest and in light of their expressed wishes. He also has an obligation to inform them truthfully about the progress of their case. Consider the extent to which Eli departs from these norms. Consider also what his options might have been—and whether he should have continued to act on behalf of the friends.

5. *Ginsberg v. Yeshiva of Far Rockaway,* 325 N.E.2d 876 (1975), is a leading case on exclusionary zoning, one which involves the status of a Jewish school.

✆ Further Reading

(1) Discussions of crime and criminalization can rarely be divorced from discussions of poverty, social class, and downward mobility. A number of landmark novels and stories demonstrate the ways in which lives that become economically and socially marginal are lives for which criminality becomes a trap. John Steinbeck's *The Grapes of Wrath* is the great novel of the American depression of the 1930s—of the migration west and the economic decline of proud families. It is also the story of Tom Joad's fall into crime. Richard Wright's story, "The Man Who Saw the Flood," in the collection *Nine Men* documents the decline of a black sharecropper dealing with the aftereffects of a flood in circumstances of social injustice.

Historically, women faced with poverty and limited opportunities have often been lured into prostitution. Edith Wharton's *The House of Mirth* and Stephen Crane's *Maggie* are both sympathetic accounts of what used to be called "fallen women." Both works lead us to question the social and moral roles of the crime of prostitution—and perhaps to sympathize with the feminist account of its origins and purpose.

(2) Criminal law has often been used in the name of religious goals masquerading as secular social goals. Arthur Miller's play, *The Crucible,* vividly shows the corrupting psychological effects of hysteria over witch-craft along with the political uses to which hysteria can be put. A religious agenda also colors the legal conflict in the play, *Inherit the Wind,* by Jerome Lawrence. Based on the Scopes "monkey trial" of the 1920s, it concerns a teacher charged with the crime of teaching evolution.

In contemporary legal and political debate, the decriminalization of abortion similarly implicates religious opinion under the color of morality and politics. John Irving's *The Cider House Rules* is the story of the life and times of an abortionist.

(3) Hidden assumptions about homogeneity are sometimes built into our attitudes toward criminalization. We ignore the fact that behaviors are seen in disparate ways in subcultures. William Faulkner's novel, *Sanctuary,* mimics a thriller as it depicts a violent rural society. The subculture of addicts, the subject of "Dundun," is also effectively sketched in "Where

I'm Calling From," by Raymond Carver in his collection, *Cathedral.* The attitudes and lives of countercultures of the 1960s and '70s were the life-long subject of Hunter Thompson, Jr. *Fear and Loathing in Las Vegas* and *Hell's Angels* are among his most evocative nonfiction works.

(4) Perhaps the greatest challenge for those who would define crime and the line the divides private rights from public intervention is the explanation of crimes not just against individuals but against humanity. In this sense, criminality is not simply what a state chooses to outlaw on the basis of criteria that it tries to make clear. Rather, a standard of atrociousness is presumed to exist and demand enforcement notwithstanding the choices of particular governments and their legislatures. The screenplay for the film *Judgment at Nuremberg* explores this notion in the context of the trial of the architects of Nazi Germany. Even more relevant and valuable is the concluding address of the chief prosecutor at those trials, Supreme Court Justice Robert Jackson.

Treason is a related concern. Perhaps the best novel that explores this issues is E.L. Doctorow's *The Book of Daniel*, based on the treason trials of Julius and Ethel Rosenberg in the 1950s.

FOUR

Criminal Minds

When we look at crime, we are as much concerned with why the defendant acted as we with what she did. If we learn that the defendant shot her husband to death, it matters whether she shot him in self-defense while he was abusing her or whether she shot him in his sleep after taking out a two million dollar insurance policy on him. If we learn that she ran into and killed a bicyclist, it matters whether she was driving carefully and slowly through opaque fog, whether she was driving erratically and fast after having had ten vodka tonics, or whether she pointed the car directly at the victim and accelerated as she ran him over.

These circumstances are all clues to her state of mind — her awareness, her thoughts, and her emotions. Students taking criminal law learn to look for two elements in every instance of a possible criminal act. One is called, unsurprisingly, the criminal act (or, in Latin, *actus reus*); the other is the criminal state of mind (*mens rea*).

Take the example of the crime that all legal systems take most seriously, homicide. The importance of homicide reflects a virtually universal moral sentiment that taking another person's life is the ultimate harm. But within the class of homicides one immediately needs to distinguish the very worst kinds from those in which the culpability is qualified. Criminal law almost always defines *intentional* killings as worse than *unintentional* killings. Usually this is reflected in the difference between the terms "murder" and "manslaughter"; an intentional killing is presumptively murder; an unintentional one is presumptively the less serious crime of manslaughter.

But there are many exceptions. An intentional killing may be committed out of sudden anger that has an understandable and reasonable cause; one may kill a business associate on discovering that he has systematically lied and cheated, destroying the worth of the shared partnership. In such cases, criminal law recognizes mitigation in terms of understandable cases of "extreme emotional distress," and such a case may be treated as manslaughter. Also, one may have an intentional killing is that altogether justified and not subject to criminal prosecution; acting in self-defense is a familiar example.

On the other hand, compare two unintentional killings. The first is caused by a driver who has drunk too much and, while speeding, notices too little about his surroundings. He fails to see a jogger and runs her over. The second occurs in the context of abuse and is caused by a father who regularly beats his adolescent children, sometimes causing medical emergencies. The second example involves torture. In the eyes of criminal law, a resulting death may well involve aggravating conditions; intuitively it seems as serious as intentional killing. Accordingly, the worst unintended killings can be murder.

The terms of criminal law thus give us a grid that we can impose on situations to classify the appropriate legal response. The response itself is complex because it involves decisions made at many levels. Police investigators know what kind of evidence is relevant and assemble the elements of the case. Prosecutors decide what charge best fits the evidence and can be proved. The judge oversees this process and can second-guess whether the charge is appropriate. And of course the jury decides guilt and innocence.

Terms such as "intention" and "recklessness" inhabit a realm that involves both ordinary language and ordinary experience, on the other hand, and the technical usages and narratives of law, on the other. The question whether lawyers use the term "intention" in the same way everyday citizens do in conversation is a hard question. When judges and lawyers communicate with juries, when journalists and broadcasters discuss the law, it is taken for granted that "intention" has its common meaning. But it also has a special meaning. If someone acts purely out of habit, acts unthinkingly, the act may still be intentional in the eyes of law. Suppose a hospital employee routinely fails to separate dangerous waste products from other waste and places it all in a public dump. This has become habitual over several years. If she knows that the materials have risk, her acts in the eyes of law are intentional.

In other words, criminal law, in the interest of managing and organizing infinitely diverse situations, puts us on a narrow diet of terms. Acts are intentional or unintentional; law shuns a gray area. Acts are reckless or they are blamelessly accidental; there is no in-between. This slim diet is not just a matter of terms but a matter of the underlying psychological picture of human nature. We all know that every situation can be distinguished from every other one in countless ways. Law deals with this problem by making many distinctions legally irrelevant.

Nonetheless, both lawyers and laypersons know that every situation of criminal conduct is psychologically complex beyond the distinctions marked by intention and recklessness. We all engage in different kinds of denial and self-delusion. Many of our motives and intentions are unconscious; we tell ourselves that we are doing one thing when we should know that we are doing another. The stories that we tell ourselves about others' actions and about the likely consequences of our own actions are often illusory.

If the coherence and manageability of law depends on putting these psychological phenomena aside, it can only succeed part way. The works of fiction in this chapter gives us the chance to see whether and where the simplified picture of psychology in criminal law breaks down. They let us take what we all know from life, that all actions are complicated and hard to explain and that violent acts are especially so, and apply it to the neat and lucid categories that criminal law needs to operate smoothly.

If we reflect on some of the stories in chapters 1 through 3 we can see many examples. In Just's "About Boston," why does Beth assault the narrator? Is it an "intentional" act mitigated by "emotional distress" or a situation more complicated than those terms can capture? In Melville's "Bartleby," how can we explain the actions of Bartleby himself or the lawyer/narrator (who is surely more transparent than Bartleby)? In Allende's "The Judge's Wife," what best explains the judge's cruel treatment of Juana the Forlorn and Casilda's choices at the story's end? Where do intentions start and stop? How much of a person's actions are predetermined by her history and circumstances?

Among the questions that we will look at with care are questions about character and unconscious aims. The attitudes expressed in a violent act toward another person invariably have a history. We often call a person's history of responses and attitudes a matter of character. But law tends paradoxically to treat the individual act and its intentionality in a vacuum without regard to character; character and individual history are matters of evidence only when they are closely related to the act at hand.

The law also pretends that we act on our intentions without significant distortion by unconscious thoughts and motives. The first two stories we will consider, the short novel *The Stranger* by Albert Camus and the story "The Intruder" by Andre Dubus, raise questions about the extent to which we are the authors, acting intentionally, of our own conduct.

Two stories that follow raise questions about motives and their relevance. It is generally said that motives are irrelevant in criminal law. If the accused killed his victim deliberately, the crime is murder regardless of whether the motive is inheritance, long-stoked desires for revenge, or jealousy. If one intends to steal a loaf of bread, the crime is petty theft whether one wants to resell the bread or relieve one's own hunger. Criminal codes make no mention of motive. But in fact we do not separate the ideas of motive and purpose quite so distinctly that we can say purposes are relevant but motives are not. If one acts in self-defense, staying alive and intact is often one's motive as well as one's purpose. If one acts harmfully to bring about a greater good (a situation which may give rise to the defense of necessity), the good result is one's motive.

When, if ever, is taking the law in one's own hands morally justified? Are there situations in which vigilante actions are justified? These questions come up in O. Henry's startling story, "A Departmental Case." A related but different motive is honor. The notion of honor can seem obsolete, reminding us of codes that governed medieval knights or "gentlemen and ladies" at a time when societies had a rigid class structure. But de Maupassant's story, "The Assassin," shows how notions of honor can still color our judgments about criminal responsibility.

In all these instances, common sense tells us that criminal law deals with a simplified model of human behavior. It makes legally irrelevant certain factors that we generally regard as significant to explain behavior and evaluate it morally. Perhaps the most extreme simplification comes when we consider rationality and irrationality. We are not in the habit of labeling most acts rational or not. We use the term for the most part in special cases. We act rationally when we engage in means-ends planning and choose means that are likely to achieve our ends. The ends themselves may also be evaluated as rational or not: an end that is incompatible with the other ends of our life is prima facie not a rational one.

By this test of rationality, most of us most of the time are far from what economists call "rational maximizers." We have the extra dessert even though we have the goal of losing weight; we procrastinate even though the test or the publisher's deadline is imminent. But criminal law tends to assume that most behavior is rational and, more importantly, that most persons are rational. Even though we know that the most forgiving observer would say that our lives are patterns of rational and irrational acts, in the eyes of law we are rational persons. And if we are rational persons as far as law in concerned, our individual acts are rational as well.

Under the cover of this assumption, as we have seen, unconscious intentions and purposes have no place. We are all conscious planners. Moreover, a strict distinction is maintained between the rational majority, which is held to responsibility for all its acts, and the insane. Rationality in this sense and sanity are seen as the same thing. Under the assumption that we are rational and sane, we are fully responsible as the authors of our acts *unless* we can meet the strict and narrow test of insanity.

The last reading in this chapter, R.L. Stevenson's short novel, *Dr. Jekyll and Mr. Hyde,* gives us a chance to explore the limits of responsibility and sanity. In the well-known story, Jekyll takes a chemical agent that allows a different personality, Hyde, to emerge. He begins to live as two different people with different appearances, dispositions, and desires. We will compare his situation with the plight of those who suffer multiple personality disorder. But more generally we will look at the borders of responsibility. For those who are emotionally, developmentally, and psychologically compromised, what is the scope of responsibility? And how should our moral responses affect the law?

Awareness, Character, and Responsibility

Albert Camus: *The Stranger**

Before he wrote *The Fall* (see chapter 1), Albert Camus gained a worldwide reputation with his first and widely acclaimed book, *The Stranger*. This is the first-person narrative of a young, disaffected office worker who, midway through the story, shoots to death an Arab man on the beach. He is tried, convicted, and sentenced to death. The circumstances of the killing are both clear and mysterious. They are clear insofar as we are kept in intimate touch with the protagonist's (Meursault's) awareness. We know the minutiae of his thoughts and feelings. At the same time, his killing of the Arab is almost gratuitous and barely motivated. We know that he and a friend are being stalked by the Arab (and his friends) and there is an earlier confrontation. But there is no clear threat to Meursault or anyone else at the moment he kills. Distraction and indifference seem to play as much a role as any clear motive.

The Stranger offers a challenge to familiar categories of homicide. Trying to apply the notions of intention, acting with knowledge and deliberation, creating risk, accident, inadvertence, and self-defense stretches and perhaps defeats our lawyerly understanding of these concepts.

In discussing *The Stranger*, the following points are likely to be of use:

(a) Is Meursault a version of everyman or is he pathological in his lack of affect, his indifference to events and feelings? One might argue that true feelings and social expectations are generally at odds and that, when we meet social expectations, we are often acting hypocritically by manufacturing artificial emotions. Meursault shows little grief at his mother's funeral. One might protest that grief cannot be produced on demand and that a general expectation of timely weeping and lamentation is the stuff of cheap fiction and not life. One can also say, however, that he is peculiarly and disturbingly cold. Similarly, his willingness to marry Marie, even though he is dispassionate and says he does not think he loves her, may or may not show pathology.

(b) Do events before the fatal confrontation on the beach make clear that he is morally corrupt and that the descriptions of his character offered by the prosecution have sound bases? The prosecution struggles to explain his actions in the light of his apparent character. One might argue that, in every case, prosecutors must build a case that is consistent with guilt and that therefore they must always bring out dark aspects of character. Do the

---

*Strongly recommended reading: This novel does not appear in this volume and must be purchased separately. It is not indispensable, but it is a superb introduction to the fissures between the complexity of human motivation and psychology and the strictures imposed by criminal law's picture of human behavior.

events that the prosecution offers form a coherent and relevant picture of Meursault's character? A true one?

(c) Imagine yourself a jury-member at Meursault's trial. What would be your verdict? Does your decision change if your evidence is not limited to the prosecution's case but if you have read *The Stranger* and had access to Meursault's mind?

(d) In the last section of the novel, Meursault discovers the value of freedom, of a life that is indeterminate and that one makes for oneself. This discovery is a central tenet of the philosophy of existentialism. Although Camus disclaimed the title of "existentialist," he is seen as one of the most influential proponents of the view that the value of life lies in one's choices and efforts rather than one's successes. One cannot capitulate to the agendas of religious, political, and social institutions unreflectively, but must appropriate them through choice and will. *The Stranger* is the seed of this idea.

The Unconscious

Andre Dubus: The Intruder

Stories sometimes give warning when they are not to be taken at face value. "Bartleby" and Kafka's parables sound the alarm that we are to look beyond conventional narrative and ask what the characters symbolize and why the story takes the odd shape it does. But other stories can seem straightforward. The events seem fully explained by what we are told, and the circumstances of the story are easily imagined and easily believed. But that transparency can be an illusion. Not always, but more often than we may suppose, authors expect us to dig beneath the surface and offer clues about a subterranean text that complements the obvious one.

"The Intruder" begins by telling us what a rich and active fantasy life Kenneth has. We know that his thoughts work on several levels. He seems to know what is true and what is fiction. But is he capable of self-delusion? The author, Andre Dubus, seems to warn us early to keep track not only of reality but also of Kenneth's fantasies and, one may assume, his unconscious.

Dubus, who died in 1999 at the age of 63, was a prolific writer of short stories and essays. Although he was little known by general readers, critics and fans much respect his work. Originally from Louisiana, he divided his life between the South and New England, for the most part teaching creative writing at small colleges. At the age of fifty, he was paralyzed and almost killed when he was struck by a car while helping strangers who were themselves stranded by an accident. In his last books, he writes movingly about the tragedies of his life.

❧ The Intruder ❧

Andre Dubus

Because Kenneth Girard loved his parents and his sister and because he could not tell them why he went to the woods, his first moments there were always uncomfortable ones, as if he had left the house to commit a sin. But he was thirteen and he could not say that he was going to sit on a hill and wait for the silence and trees and sky to close in on him, wait until they all became a part of him and thought and memory ceased and the voices began. He could only say that he was going for a walk and, since there was so much more to say, he felt cowardly and deceitful and more lonely than before.

He could not say that on the hill he became great, that he had saved a beautiful girl from a river (the voice then had been gentle and serious and she had loved him), or that he had ridden into town, his clothes dusty, his black hat pulled low over his sunburned face, and an hour later had ridden away with four fresh notches on the butt of his six-gun, or that with the count three-and-two and the bases loaded, he had driven the ball so far and high that the outfielders did not even move, or that he had waded through surf and sprinted over sand, firing his Tommy gun and shouting to his soldiers behind him.

Now he was capturing a farmhouse. In the late movie the night before, the farmhouse had been very important, though no one ever said why, and sitting there in the summer dusk, he watched the backs of his soldiers as they advanced through the woods below him and crossed the clear, shallow creek and climbed the hill that he faced. Occasionally he lifted his twenty-two-caliber rifle and fired at a rusty tin can across the creek, the can becoming a Nazi face in a window as he squeezed the trigger and the voices filled him: You got him, Captain. You got him. For half an hour he sat and fired at the can, and anyone who might have seen him could never know that he was doing anything else, that he had been wounded in the shoulder and lost half his men but had captured the farmhouse.

Kenneth looked up through the trees, which were darker green now. While he had been watching his battle, the earth, too, had become darker, shadowed, with patches of late sun on the grass and brown fallen pine needles. He stood up, then looked down at the creek, and across it, at the hill on the other side. His soldiers were gone. He was hungry, and he turned and walked back through the woods.

Then he remembered that his mother and father were going to a party in town that night and he would be alone with Connie.

He liked being alone, but, even more, he liked being alone with his sister. She was nearly seventeen; her skin was fair, her cheeks colored, and she had long black hair that came down to her shoulders; on the right side of her face, a wave of it reached the corner of her eye. She was the most beautiful girl he knew. She was also the only person with whom, for his entire life, he had been nearly perfectly at ease. He could be silent with her or he could say whatever occurred to him and he never had to think about it first to assure himself that it was not foolish or, worse, uninteresting.

Leaving the woods, he climbed the last gentle slope and entered the house. He leaned his rifle in a corner of his room, which faced the quiet blacktop road, and went to the bathroom and washed his hands. Standing at the lavatory, he looked into the mirror. He suddenly felt as if he had told a lie. He was looking at his face and, as he did several times each day, telling himself, without words, that it was a handsome face. His skin was fair, as Connie's was, and he had color in his cheeks; but his hair, carefully parted and combed, was more brown than black. He believed that Connie thought he was exactly like her, that he was talkative and well liked. But she never saw him with his classmates. He felt that he was deceiving her.

He left the house and went into the outdoor kitchen and sat on a bench at the long, uncovered table and folded his arms on it.

"Did you kill anything?" Connie said.

"Tin cans."

His father turned from the stove with a skillet of white perch in his hand.

"They're good ones," he said.

"Mine are the best," Kenneth said.

"You didn't catch but two."

"They're the best."

His mother put a plate in front of him, then opened a can of beer and sat beside him. He sat quietly watching his father at the stove. Then he looked at his mother's hand holding the beer can. There were veins and several freckles on the back of it. Farther up her forearm was a small yellow bruise; the flesh at her elbow was wrinkled. He looked at her face. People said that he and Connie looked like her, so he supposed it was true, but he could not see the resemblance.

"Daddy and I are going to the Gossetts' tonight," she said.

"I know."

"I wrote the phone number down," his father said. "It's under the phone."

"Okay."

His father was not tall either, but his shoulders were broad. Kenneth wondered if his would be like that when he grew older. His father was the only one in the family who tanned in the sun.

"And *please*, Connie," his mother said, "will you go to sleep at a reasonable hour? It's hard enough to get you up for Mass when you've had a good night's sleep."

"Why don't we go into town for the evening Mass?"

"No. I don't like it hanging over my head all day."

"All right. When will y'all be home?"

"About two. And that doesn't mean read in bed till then. You need your sleep."

"We'll go to bed early," Connie said.

His father served fried perch and hush puppies onto their plates and they had French bread and catsup and Tabasco sauce and iced tea. After dinner, his father read the newspaper and his mother read a Reader's Digest condensation, then they showered and dressed, and at seven-thirty, they left. He and Connie followed them to the door. Connie kissed them; then he did. His mother and father looked happy, and he felt good about that.

"We'll be back about two," his mother said. "Keep the doors locked."

"Definitely," Connie said. "And we'll bar the windows."

"Well, you never know. Y'all be good. G'night."

"Hold down the fort, son," his father said.

"I will."

Then they were gone, the screen door slamming behind them, and Connie left the sunporch, but he stood at the door, listening to the car starting and watching its headlights as it backed down the trail through the yard, then turned into the road and drove away. Still he did not move. He loved the nights at the camp when they were left alone. At home, there was a disturbing climate about their evenings alone, for distant voices of boys in the neighborhood reminded him that he was not alone entirely by choice. Here, there were no sounds.

He latched the screen and went into the living room. Connie was sitting in the rocking chair near the fireplace, smoking a cigarette. She looked at him; then flicked ashes into an ashtray on her lap.

"Now don't you tell on me."

"I didn't know you did that."

"Please don't tell. Daddy would skin me alive."

"I won't."

He could not watch her. He looked around the room for a book.

"Douglas is coming tonight," she said.

"Oh." He picked up the Reader's Digest book and pretended to look at it. "Y'all going to watch TV?" he said.

"Not if you want to."

"It doesn't matter."

"You watch it. You like Saturday nights."

She looked as if she had been smoking for a long time, all during the summer and possibly the school year, too, for months or even a year without his knowing it. He was hurt. He laid down the book.

"Think I'll go outside for a while," he said.

He went onto the sunporch and out the door and walked down the sloping car trail that led to the road. He stopped at the gate, which was open, and leaned on it. Forgetting Connie, he looked over his shoulder at the camp, thinking that he would never tire of it. They had been there for six weeks, since early June, his father coming on Friday evenings and leaving early Monday mornings, driving sixty miles to their home in southern Louisiana. Kenneth fished during the day, swam with Connie in the creeks, read novels about baseball, and watched the major league games on television. He thought winter at the camp was better, though. They came on weekends and hunted squirrels, and there was a fireplace.

He looked down the road. The closest camp was half a mile away, on the opposite side of the road, and he could see its yellow-lighted windows through the trees. *That's the house. Quiet now. We'll sneak through the woods and get the guard, then charge the house. Come on.* Leaning against the gate, he stared into the trees across the road and saw himself leading his soldiers through the woods. They reached the guard. His back was turned and Kenneth crawled close to him, then stood up and slapped a hand over the guard's mouth and stabbed him in the back. They rushed the house and Kenneth reached the door first and kicked it open. The general looked up from his desk, then tried to get his pistol from his holster. Kenneth shot him with his Tommy gun. *Grab those papers, men. Let's get out of here.* They got the papers and ran outside and Kenneth stopped to throw a hand grenade through the door. He reached the woods before it exploded.

He turned from the gate and walked toward the house, looking around him at the dark pines. He entered the sunporch and latched the screen; then he smelled chocolate, and he went to the kitchen. Connie was stirring a pot of fudge on the stove. She had changed to a fresh pale blue shirt, the tails of it hanging almost to the bottom of her white shorts.

"It'll be a while," she said.

He nodded, watching her hand and the spoon. He thought of Douglas coming and began to feel nervous.

"What time's Douglas coming?"

"Any minute now. Let me know if you hear his car."

"All right."

He went to his room and picked up his rifle; then he saw the magazine on the chest of drawers and he leaned the rifle in the corner again. Suddenly his mouth was dry. He got the magazine and quickly turned the pages until he found her; she was stepping out of the surf on the French Riviera, laughing, as if the man with her had just said something funny. She was blond and very tan and she wore a bikini. The photograph was in color. For several moments he looked at it; then he got the rifle and cleaning kit and sat in the rocking chair in the living room, with the rifle across his lap. He put a patch on the cleaning rod and dipped it in bore cleaner and pushed it down the barrel, the handle of the rod clanging against the muzzle. He worked slowly, pausing often to listen for Douglas's car, because he wanted to be cleaning the rifle when Douglas came. Because Douglas was a tackle on the high school football team in the town, and Kenneth had never been on a football team, and never would be.

The football players made him more uncomfortable than the others. They walked into the living room and firmly shook his father's hand, then his hand, beginning to talk as soon as they entered, and they sat and waited for Connie, their talking never ceasing, their big chests and shoulders leaned forward, their faces slowly turning as they looked at each picture on the wall, at the designs on the rug, at the furniture, passing over Kenneth as if he were another chair, filling the room with a feeling of strength and self-confidence that defeated him, paralyzing his tongue and even his mind, so that he merely sat in thoughtless anxiety, hoping they would not speak to him, hoping especially that they would not ask: *You play football?* Two of them had, and he never forgot it. He had answered with a mute, affirming nod.

He had always been shy and, because of it, he had stayed on the periphery of sports for as long as he could remember. When his teachers forced him to play, he spent an anxious hour trying not to become involved, praying in right field that no balls would come his way, lingering on the outside of the huddle so that no one would look up and see his face and decide to throw him a pass on the next play.

But he found that there was one thing he could do and he did it alone, or with his father: he could shoot and he could hunt. He felt that shooting was the only thing that had ever been easy for him. Schoolwork was, too, but he considered that a curse.

He was not disturbed by the boys who were not athletes, unless, for some reason, they were confident anyway. While they sat and waited for Connie, he was cheerful and teasing, and they seemed to like him. The girls were best. He walked into the living room and they stopped their talking and laughing and all of them greeted him and sometimes they said: "Connie, he's so cute," or "I wish you were three years older," and he said: "Me, too," and tried to be witty and usually was.

He heard a car outside.

"Douglas is here," he called.

Connie came through the living room, one hand arranging the wave of hair near her right eye, and went into the sunporch. Slowly, Kenneth wiped the rifle with an oily rag. He heard Douglas's loud voice and laughter and heavy footsteps on the sunporch; then they came into the living room. Kenneth raised his face.

"Hi," he said.

"How's it going?"

"All right."

Douglas Bakewell was not tall. He had blond hair, cut so short on top that you could see his scalp, and a reddish face, and sunburned arms, covered with bleached hair. A polo shirt fit tightly over his chest and shoulders and biceps.

"Whatcha got there?" Douglas said.

"Twenty-two."

"Let's see."

"Better dry it."

He briskly wiped it with a dry cloth and handed it to Douglas. Quickly, Douglas worked the bolt, aimed at the ceiling, and pulled the trigger.

"Nice trigger," he said.

He held it in front of his waist and looked at it, then gave it to Kenneth.

"Well, girl," he said, turning to Connie, "where's the beer?"

"Sit down, and I'll get you one."

She went to the kitchen. Douglas sat on the couch and, Kenneth picked up his cleaning kit and, not looking at Douglas, walked into his bedroom. He stayed there until Connie returned from the kitchen; then he went into the living room. They were sitting on the couch. Connie was smoking again. Kenneth kept walking toward the sunporch.

"I'll let you know when the fudge is ready," Connie said.

"All right."

On the sunporch, he turned on the television and sat in front of it. He watched ten minutes of a Western before he was relaxed again, before he settled in his chair, oblivious to the quiet talking in the living room, his mind beginning to wander happily as a gunfighter in dark clothes moved across the screen.

By the time the fudge was ready, he was watching a detective story, and when Connie called him, he said: "Okay, in a minute," but did not move, and finally she came to the sunporch with a saucer of fudge and set it on a small table beside his chair.

"When that's over, you better go to bed," she said.

"I'm not sleepy."

"You know what Mother said."

"*You're* staying up."

"Course I am. I'm also a little older than you."

"I want to see the late show."

"No!"

"Yes, I am."

"I'll tell Daddy."

"He doesn't care."

"I'll tell him you wouldn't listen to me."

"I'll tell him you smoke."

"Oh, I could *wring* your neck!"

She went to the living room. He tried to concentrate on the Western, but it was ruined. The late show came on and he had seen it several months before and did not want to see it again, but he would not go to bed. He watched absently. Then he had to urinate. He got up and went into the living room, walking quickly, only glancing at them once, but when he did, Connie smiled and, with her voice friendly again, said: "What is it?"

He stopped and looked at her.

"*Red River.*"

He smiled.

"I already saw it," he said.

"You watching it again?"

"Maybe so."

"Okay."

He went to the bathroom and when he came back, they were gone. He went to the sunporch. Connie and Douglas were standing near the back door. The television was turned off. Kenneth wondered if Connie had seen *Red River*. If she had not, he could tell her what had happened during the part she missed. Douglas was whispering to Connie, his face close to hers. Then he looked at Kenneth.

"Night," he said.

"G'night," Kenneth said.

He was gone. Kenneth picked up the saucer his fudge had been on and took it to the kitchen and put it in the sink. He heard Douglas's car backing down the trail, and he went to the sunporch, but Connie was not there, so he went to the bathroom door and said: "You seen *Red River*?"

"Yes."

"You taking a bath?"

"Just washing my face. I'm going to bed."

He stood quietly for a moment. Then he went into the living room and got a magazine and sat in the rocking chair, looking at the people in the advertisements. Connie came in, wearing a robe. She leaned over his chair and he looked up and she kissed him.

"Good night," she said.

"G'night."

"You going to bed soon?"

"In a minute."

She got her cigarettes and an ashtray from the coffee table and went to her room and closed the door. After a while, he heard her getting into bed.

He looked at half the magazine, then laid it on the floor. Being awake in a house where everyone else was sleeping made him lonely. He went to the sunporch and latched the screen, then closed the door and locked it. He left the light on but turned out the one in the living room. Then he went to his room and took off everything but his shorts. He was about to turn out the light when he looked at the chest of drawers and saw the magazine. He hesitated. Then he picked it up and found the girl and looked at the exposed tops of her breasts and at her navel and below it. Suddenly he closed the magazine and raised his eyes to the ceiling, then closed them and said three Hail Mary's. Without looking at it, he picked up the magazine and took it to the living room, and went back to his bedroom and lay on his belly on the floor and started doing push-ups. He had no trouble with the first eight; then they became harder, and by the fifteenth he was breathing fast and his whole body was trembling as he pushed himself up from the floor. He did one more, then stood up and turned out the light and got into bed.

His room extended forward of the rest of the house, so that, from his bed, he could look through the window to his left and see the living room and Connie's bedroom. He rolled on his back and pulled the sheet up to his chest. He could hear crickets outside his window

He flexed his right arm and felt the bicep. It seemed firmer than it had in June, when he started doing pushups every night. He closed his eyes and began the Lord's Prayer and got as far as *Thy kingdom come* before he heard it.

Now it was not the crickets that he heard. He heard his own breathing and the bedsprings as his body tensed; then he heard it again, somewhere in front of the house: a cracking twig, a rustle of dried leaves, a foot on hard earth. Slowly, he rolled on his left side and looked out the window. He waited to be sure, but he did not have to; then he waited to decide what he would do, and he did not have to wait for that either, because he already knew, and he looked at the far corner of the room where his rifle was, though he could not see it, and he looked out the window again, staring at the windows of the living room and Connie's room, forcing himself to keep his eyes there, as if it would be all right if the prowler did not come into his vision, did not come close to the house; but listening to the slow footsteps, Kenneth knew that he would.

Get up. Get up and get the rifle. If you don't do it now, he might come to this window and look in and then it'll be too late.

For a moment, he did not breathe. Then, slowly, stopping at each sound of the bedsprings, he rolled out of bed and crouched on the floor beneath the window. He did not move. He listened to his breathing, for there was no other sound, not even crickets, and he began to tremble, thinking the prowler might be standing above him, looking through his window at the empty bed. He held his breath. Then he heard the footsteps again, in front of the house, closer now, and he thought: *He's by the pines in front of Connie's room.* He crawled away from the window, thinking of a large, bearded man standing in the pine trees thirty yards from Connie's room, studying the house and deciding which window to use; then he stood up and walked on tiptoes to the chest of drawers and moved his hand over the top of it until he touched the handful of bullets, his fingers quickly closing on them, and he picked up the rifle and took out the magazine and loaded it, then inserted it again and laid the extra bullets on the chest of drawers. Now he had to work the bolt. He pulled it up and back and eased it forward again.

Staying close to the wall, he tiptoed back to the window, stopping at the edge of it, afraid to look out and see a face looking in. He heard nothing. He looked through the windows in the opposite wall, thinking that if the prowler had heard him getting the rifle, he could have run back to the road, back to wherever he had come from, or he could still be hiding in the pines, or he could have circled to the rear of the house to hide again and listen, but there was no way of knowing, and he would have to stand in the room, listening, until his father came home. He thought of going to wake Connie, but he was afraid to move. Then he heard him again, near the pines, coming toward the house. He kneeled and pressed his shoulder against the wall, moving his face slightly, just enough to look out the screen and see the prowler walking toward Connie's window, stopping there and looking over his shoulder at the front yard and the road, then reaching out and touching the screen.

Kenneth rose and moved away from the wall, standing close to his bed now; he aimed through the screen, found the side of the man's head, then fired. A scream filled the house, the yard, his mind, and he thought at first it was the prowler, who was lying on the ground now, but it was a high, shrieking scream; it was Connie, and he ran into the living room, but she was already on the sun-porch, unlocking the back door, not screaming now, but crying, pulling open the wooden door and hitting the screen with both hands, then stopping to unlatch it, and he yelled: "Connie!"

She turned, her hair swinging around her cheek.

"Get away from me!"

Then she ran outside, the screen door slamming, the shriek starting again, a long, high wail, ending in front of the house with "*Douglas, Douglas, Douglas!*" Then he knew.

Afterward, it seemed that the events of a year had occurred in an hour, and, to Kenneth, even that hour seemed to have a quality of neither speed nor slowness, but a kind of suspension, as if time were not passing at all. He remembered somehow calling his father and crying into the phone: "I shot Douglas Bakewell," and because of the crying, his father kept saying: "What's that, son? What did you say?" and then he lay facedown on his bed and cried, thinking of Connie outside with Douglas, hearing her sometimes when his own sounds lulled, and sometimes thinking of Connie inside with Douglas, if he had not shot him. He remembered the siren when it was far away and their voices as they brought Connie into the house. The doctor had come first, then his mother and father, then the sheriff; but, remembering, it was as if they had all come at once, for there was always a soothing or questioning face over his bed. He remembered the footsteps and hushed voices as they carried the body past his window, while his mother sat on the bed and stroked his forehead and cheek. He would never forget that.

Now the doctor and sheriff were gone and it seemed terribly late, almost sunrise. His father came into the room, carrying a glass of water, and sat on the bed.

"Take this," he said. "It'll make you sleep."

Kenneth sat up and took the pill from his father's palm and placed it on his tongue, then drank the water. He lay on his back and looked at his father's face. Then he began to cry.

"I thought it was a prowler," he said.

"It was, son. A prowler. We've told you that."

"But Connie went out there and she stayed all that time and she kept saying '*Douglas*' over and over; I heard her—"

"She wasn't out there with *him*. She was just out in the yard. She was in shock. She meant she wanted Douglas to be there with her. To help."

"No, *no*. It was *him*."

"It was a prowler. You did right. There's no telling what he might have done."

Kenneth looked away.

"He was going in her room," he said. "That's why she went to bed early. So I'd go to bed."

"It was a prowler," his father said.

Now Kenneth was sleepy. He closed his eyes and the night ran together in his mind and he remembered the rifle in the corner and thought: *I'll throw it in the creek tomorrow. I never want to see it again.* He would be asleep soon. He saw himself standing on the hill and throwing his rifle into the creek; then the creek became an ocean, and he stood on a high cliff and for a moment he was a mighty angel, throwing all guns and cruelty and sex and tears into the sea.

Discussion Topics

1. Does this story have a hidden subtext? Is the story simply about a tragic mistake whereby Kenneth takes Douglas for an intruder? If so, why does Dubus draw our attention to Kenneth's fantasies and his sexual insecurities at the age of puberty?

Consider whether Kenneth had good reason to suspect that the intruder was Douglas, even to know. A psychiatrist might say he repressed that knowledge, that he rationalized the situation by fantasizing that he was protecting Connie against an intruder. On this theory, his knowledge was unconscious. Was it fully unconscious? Are there any grounds for thinking he killed Douglas intentionally?

These questions force us to address Kenneth's attitude to Connie and her boyfriends. Consider what his feelings were and whether it goes too far to think that he had unacknowledged incestuous feelings toward her. Even if we make such assumptions, how abnormal or pathological does this make him? According to psychoanalytic theory, such fantasies toward siblings might be normal and expected. That is not to say, of course, that it is normal to act out such fantasies or to entertain them consciously with intensity or passion.

2. If we assume that Kenneth in some way knew that his victim was Douglas, has he committed murder, an intentional killing? Can or should the legal system intervene? Is there any point in investigating the case with the possibility of bringing charges?

It seems likely that an investigation would yield nothing and that a jury could never be convinced beyond a reasonable doubt that Kenneth knew the intruder was Douglas. Note, however, that with a slight change, the story would have a different posture. Suppose a passerby noticed that there was a full moon, that Douglas stood up in full view, and that Kenneth looked straight at him for several seconds before firing.

3. If no legal action is taken, what should be done with Kenneth? It seems likely he will have some counseling even if his claims about the intruding stranger are never questioned. If we do have such suspicions, should he be treated differently? On one hand, one might ask whether he is a danger to himself or others. On the other, one might say that his act was an aberration and that he will "grow out" of the problems of adolescence. If you were his psychiatrist, how would you treat him?

4. It seems likely that most persons who commit violent acts have many fantasies and unrealistic thoughts. For the most part, the criminal process treats them as irrelevant except for a showing of insanity. (This statement needs to be qualified: for example, baseless assumptions that one is acting in self-defense may be the basis for mitigation and may support a defense of mistake.) In particular, it is likely that rapists commit their violence because of unconscious ways in which they regard themselves and their sexuality and that they choose their victims because of unconscious anger. Attitudes toward race, class, gender, and ethnicity — often unconscious — probably play a significant role in other kinds of violent crimes.

Unconscious fantasies can, from a moral standpoint, seem mitigating, aggravating, or neither. If we know that the offender was severely abused and neglected as a child, we might see the fantasies drawn from that experience as limiting her responsibility. If we know that unconscious racist fantasies lead a killer to seek out certain kinds of victims, that may lead us to condemn him more seriously. But, from the standpoint of criminal law, what is unconscious is said to be irrelevant. (Of course, when conscious racism or ethnic bias is present, the law often does take note.)

Vigilante Justice

O. Henry: A Departmental Case

In movies, on TV, and in novels, we often empathize with those who take the law into their own hands. Once a character is certified as a good person with a dependable sense of right, wrong, and justice, we are thrilled when he or she is unleashed to bring justice about as efficiently as possible. The procedures of the legal system can work too slowly and bring bad results. It is a common belief that procedural safeguards embodied in the rights of defendants can lead to the release of dangerous and violent felons. Extralegal measures are needed to correct the problem.

Of course, many movies and shows argue the opposite. Vigilantes are often carried away by emotion and act on their mistakes. Vigilante justice can be indiscriminate mob violence. Safeguards to prevent this are indispensable in a civilized society, and many works of fiction as well as experience itself illustrate this.

In a sense, there is a conflict between head and heart. Our heads tell us that justice must have its formalities and procedures notwithstanding their costs. But we respond emotionally to those who vindicate the good without constraint. Perhaps we are most comfortable when the conflict is minimized because it occurs in settings where settled government does not yet exist (the Old West) or where it is irredeemably corrupted (the context of many superhero comic book stories).

O. Henry sets the story below in Texas in transition. Law enforcement is in the hands of reliable and modern institutions, but the protagonist, Luke Standifer, a hero of the Old West, is reluctant to give up his ways. The author himself, born in North Carolina, lived in Austin, Texas between 1882 and 1898, when he began serving time for bank embezzlement. While in prison, William Sydney Porter (1862-1910) began writing short stories under the name, O. Henry. After his release in 1901, he moved to New York, the setting of most of his stories. Porter died from alcoholism in 1910. His pen name has become synonymous with the device of a surprise ending.

❧ A Departmental Case ❧

O. Henry

In Texas you may travel a thousand miles in a straight line. If your course is a crooked one, it is likely that both the distance and your rate of speed may be vastly increased. Clouds there sail serenely against the wind. The whippoorwill delivers its disconsolate cry with the notes exactly reversed from those of the Northern brother. Given a drought and a subsequently lively rain, and lo! from a glazed and stony soil will spring in a single night blossomed lilies, miraculously fair. Tom Green County was once the standard of measurement. I have forgotten how many New Jerseys and Rhode Islands it was that could have been stowed away and lost in its chaparral. But the legislative axe has slashed Tom Green into a handful of counties hardly larger than European kingdoms. The legislature convenes at Austin, near the center of the state; and, while the representative from Rio Grande country is gathering his palm leaf fan and his linen duster to set out for the capital, the Pan-handle solon winds his muffler above his well-buttoned overcoat and kicks the snow from his well-greased boots ready for the same journey. All this merely to hint that the big ex-republic of the Southwest forms a sizable star on the flag; and to prepare for the corollary that things sometimes happen there uncut to pattern and unfettered by metes and bounds.

The Commissioner of Insurance, Statistics, and History of the State of Texas was an official of no very great or very small importance. The past tense is used, for now he is Commissioner of Insurance alone. Statistics and history are no longer proper nouns in the government records.

In the year 188–, the governor appointed Luke Coonrod Standifer to be the head of this department. Standifer was then fifty-five years of age, and a Texan to the core. His father had been one of the state's earliest settlers and pioneers. Standifer himself had served the commonwealth as Indian fighter, soldier, ranger, and legislator. Much learning he did not claim, but he had drunk pretty deep of the spring of experience.

If other grounds were less abundant, Texas should be well up in the lists of glory as the grateful republic. For both as republic and state, it has busily heaped honors and solid rewards upon its sons who rescued it from the wilderness.

Wherefore and therefore, Luke Coonrod Standifer, son of Ezra Standifer, ex-Texas ranger, simon-pure democrat, and lucky dweller in an unrepresented portion of the politico-geographical map, was appointed Commissioner of Insurance, Statistics, and History.

Standifer accepted the honor, with some doubt as to the nature of the office he was to fill and his capacity for filling it—but he accepted, and by wire. He immediately set out from the little country town where he maintained (and was scarcely maintained by) a somnolent and unfruitful office of surveying and map-drawing. Before departing, he had looked under the I's, S's, and H's in the "Encyclopaedia Britannica" what information and preparation toward his official duties that those weighty volumes afforded.

A few weeks of incumbency diminished the new commissioner's awe of the great and important office he had been called upon to conduct. An increasing familiarity with its workings soon restored him to his accustomed placid course of life. In his office was an old spectacled clerk—a consecrated, informed, able machine, who held his desk regardless of changes of administrative heads. Old Kauffman instructed his new chief gradually in the knowledge of the department without seeming to do so, and kept the wheels revolving without the slip of a cog.

Indeed, the Department of Insurance, Statistics, and History carried no great heft of the burden of state. Its main work was the regulating of the business done in the state by foreign insurance companies, and the letter of the law was its guide. As for statistics — well, you wrote letters to county officers, and scissored other people's reports, and each year you got out a report of your own about the corn crop and the cotton crop and pecans and pigs and black and white population, and a great many columns of figures headed "bushels" and "acres" and "square miles," etc.—and there you were. History? The branch was purely a receptive one. Old ladies interested in the science bothered you some with long reports of proceedings of their historical societies. Some twenty or thirty people would write you each year that they had secured Sam Houston's pocket-knife or Santa Ana's whisky-flask or Davy Crockett's rifle—all absolutely authenticated—and demanded legislative appropriation to purchase. Most of the work in the history branch went into pigeonholes.

One sizzling August afternoon the commissioner reclined in his office chair, with his feet upon the long, official table covered with green billiard cloth. The commissioner was smoking a cigar, and dreamily regarding the quivering landscape framed by the window that looked upon the treeless capitol grounds. Perhaps he was thinking of the rough and ready life he had led, of the old days of breathless adventure and movement, of the comrades who now trod other paths or had ceased to tread any, of the changes civilization and peace had brought, and, maybe, complacently, of the snug and comfortable camp pitched for him under the dome of the capitol of the state that had not forgotten his services.

The business of the department was lax. Insurance was easy. Statistics were not in demand. History was dead. Old Kauffman, the efficient and perpetual clerk, had requested an infrequent half-holiday, incited to the unusual dissipation by the joy of having successfully twisted the tail of a Connecticut insurance company that was trying to do business contrary to the edicts of the great Lone Star State.

The office was very still. A few subdued noises trickled in through the open door from the other departments—a dull tinkling crash from the treasurer's office adjoining, as a clerk tossed a bag of silver to the floor of the vault—the vague intermittent clatter of a dilatory typewriter—a dull tapping from the state geologist's quarters as if some woodpecker had flown in to bore for his prey in the cool of the massive building—and then a faint rustle, and the light shuffling of the well-worn shoes along the hall, the sounds ceasing at the door toward which the commissioner's lethargic back was presented. Following this, the sound of a gentle voice speaking words unintelligible to the commissioner's somewhat dormant comprehension, but giving evidence of bewilderment and hesitation.

The voice was feminine; the commissioner was of the race of cavaliers who make salaam before the trail of a skirt without considering the quality of its cloth.

There stood in the door a faded woman, one of the numerous sisterhood of the unhappy. She was dressed all in black—poverty's perpetual mourning for lost joys. Her face had the contours of twenty and the lines of forty. She may have lived that intervening score of years in a twelve-month. There was about her yet an aurum of indignant, unappeased, protesting youth that shone faintly through the premature veil of unearned decline.

"I beg your pardon, ma'am," said the commissioner, gaining his feet to the accompaniment of a great creaking and sliding of his chair.

"Are you the governor, sir?" asked the vision of melancholy.

The commissioner hesitated at the end of his best bow, with his hand in the bosom of his double-breasted "frock." Truth at last conquered.

"Well, no, ma'am. I am not the governor. I have the honor to be Commissioner of Insurance, Statistics, and History. Is there anything, ma'am, I can do for you? Won't you have a chair, ma'am?"

The lady subsided into the chair handed her, probably from purely physical reasons. She wielded a cheap fan—last token of gentility to be abandoned. Her clothing seemed to indicate a reduction almost to extreme poverty. She looked at the man who was not the governor, and saw kindliness and simplicity and a rugged, unadorned courtliness emanating from a countenance tanned, and toughened by forty years of outdoor life. Also, she saw that his eyes were clear and strong and blue. Just as they had been when he used them to skim the horizon for raiding Kiowas and Sioux. His mouth was as set and firm as it had been on that day when he bearded the old Lion Sam Houston himself, and defied him during that season when secession was the theme. Now, in bearing and dress, Luke Coonrod Standifer endeavored to do credit to the important arts and sciences of Insurance, Statistics, and History. He had abandoned the careless dress of his country home. Now, his broad-brimmed black slouch hat, and his long-tailed "frock" made him not the least imposing of the official family, even if his office was reckoned to stand at the tail of the list.

"You wanted to see the governor, ma'am?" asked the commissioner, with a deferential manner he always used toward the fair sex.

"I hardly know," said the lady, hesitatingly. "I suppose so." And then, suddenly drawn by the sympathetic look of the other, she poured forth the story of her need.

It was a story so common that the public has come to look at its monotony instead of its pity. The old tale of an unhappy married life—made so by a brutal, conscienceless husband, a robber, a spendthrift, amoral, coward, and a bully, who failed to provide even the means of the barest existence. Yes, he had come down in the scale so low as to strike her. It happened only the day before — there was the bruise on one temple — she had offended his highness by asking for a little money to live on. And yet she must needs, womanlike, append a plea for her tyrant — he was drinking; he had rarely abused her thus when sober.

"I thought," mourned this pale sister of sorrow, "that maybe the state might be willing to give me some relief. I've heard of such things being done for the families of old settlers. I've heard tell that the state used to give land to the men who fought for it against Mexico, and settled up the country, and helped drive out the Indians. My father did all of that, and he never received anything. He never would take it. I thought the governor would be the one to see, and that's why I came. If Father was entitled to anything, they might let it come to me."

"It's possible, ma'am," said Standifer, "that such might be the case. But 'most all the veterans and settlers got their land certificates issued and located long ago. Still, we can look that up in the land office and be sure. Your father's name, now, was . . ."

"Amos Colvin, sir."

"Good Lord!" exclaimed Standifer, rising and unbuttoning his tight coat, excitedly. "Are you Amos Colvin's daughter? Why, ma'am, Amos Colvin and me were thicker than two hoss thieves for more than ten years! We fought Kiowas, drove cattle, and ran-gered side by side nearly all over Texas. I remember seeing you once before now. You were a kid, about seven, a-riding a little yellow pony up and down. Amos and me stopped at your home for a little grub when we were trailing that band of Mexican cattle thieves down through Karnes and Bee. Great tarantulas! and you're Amos Colvin's little girl! Did you ever hear your father mention Luke Standifer — just kind of casually — as if he'd met me once or twice?"

A little pale smile flitted across the lady's white face.

"It seems to me," she said, "that I don't remember hearing him talk about much else. Every day there was some story he had to tell about what he and you had done. Mighty near the last thing I heard him tell was about the time when the Indians wounded him, and you crawled out to him through the grass, with a canteen of water while they — ."

"Yes, yes — well — oh, that wasn't anything," said Standifer, "hemming" loudly and buttoning his coat again briskly. "And now, ma'am, who was the infernal skunk — I beg your pardon, ma'am — who was the gentleman you married?"

"Benton Sharp."

The commissioner plumped down again into his chair with a groan.

This gentle, sad little woman in the rusty black gown, the daughter of his oldest friend, the wife of Benton Sharp! Benton Sharp, one of the most noted "bad" men in that part of the state — a man who had been a cattle thief, an outlaw, a desperado, and was now a gambler, a swaggering bully, who plied his trade in the larger frontier towns, relying upon his record and the quickness of his gun play to maintain his supremacy. Seldom did anyone take the risk of going "up against" Benton Sharp. Even the law officers were content to let him make his own terms of peace. Sharp was a ready and an accurate shot, and as lucky as a brand-new penny at coming clear of scrapes. Standifer wondered how this pillaging eagle ever came to be mated with Amos Colvin's little dove and expressed his wonder.

Mrs. Sharp sighed.

"You see, Mr. Standifer, we didn't know anything about him, and he can be very pleasant and kind when he wants to. We lived down in the little town of Goliad. Benton came riding down that way and stopped there a while. I reckon I was some better looking then than I am now. He was good to me for a whole year after we were married. He insured his life for me for five thousand dollars. But for the last six months he has done everything but kill me. I often wish he had done that, too. He got out of money for a while, and abused me shamefully for not having anything he could spend. Then Father died and left me the little home in Goliad. My husband made me sell that and turned me out into the world. I've barely been able to live, for I'm not strong enough to work. Lately, I heard he was making money in San Antonio, so I went there, and found him, and asked for a little help. This," touching the livid bruise on her temple, "is what he gave me. So I came on to Austin to see the governor. I once heard Father say that there was some land or a pension coming to him from the state that he never would ask for."

Luke Standifer rose to his feet, and pushed his chair back. He looked rather perplexedly around the big office with its handsome furniture.

"It's a long trail to follow," he said, slowly, "trying to get back dues from the government. There's red tape and lawyers and rulings and evidences and courts to keep you waiting. I'm not certain," continued the commissioner, with a profoundly meditative frown, "whether this department that I'm the boss of has any jurisdiction or not. It's only Insurance, Statistics, and History, ma'am, and it don't sound as if it would cover the case. But sometimes a saddle blanket can be made to stretch. You keep your seat, just for a few minutes, ma'am, till I step into the next room and see about it."

The state treasurer was seated within his massive, complicated railings, reading a newspaper. Business for the day was about over. The clerks lolled at their desks, awaiting the closing hour. The Commissioner of Insurance, Statistics, and History entered, and leaned in at the window.

The treasurer, a little, brisk old man, with snow-white moustache and beard, jumped up youthfully and came forward to greet Standifer. They were friends of old.

"Uncle Frank," said the commissioner, using the familiar name by which the historic treasurer was addressed by every Texan, "how much money have you got on hand?"

The treasurer named the sum of the last balance down to the odd cents — something more than a million dollars.

The commissioner whistled lowly, and his eyes grew hopefully bright.

"You know, or else you've heard of, Amos Colvin, Uncle Frank?"

"Knew him well," said the treasurer, promptly. "A good man. A valuable citizen. One of the settlers in the Southwest."

"His daughter," said Standifer, "is sitting in my office. She's penniless. She's married to Benton Sharp, a coyote and a murderer. He's reduced her to want and broken her heart. Her father helped build up this state, and it's the state's turn to help his child. A couple of thousand dollars will buy back her home and let her live in peace. The State of Texas can't afford to refuse it. Give me the money, Uncle Frank, and I'll give it to her right away. We'll fix up the red-tape business afterward."

The treasurer looked a little bewildered.

"Why, Standifer," he said, "you know I can't pay a cent out of the treasury without a warrant from the comptroller. I can't disburse a dollar without a voucher to show for it."

The commissioner betrayed a slight impatience.

"I'll give you a voucher," he declared. "What's this job they've given me for? Am I just a knot on a mesquite stump? Can't my office stand for it? Charge it up to Insurance and the other two sideshows. Don't Statistics show that Amos Colvin came to this state when it was in the hands of Greasers and rattlesnakes and Comanches, and fought day and night to make a white man's country of it? Don't they show that Amos Colvin's daughter is brought to ruin by a villain who's trying to pull down what you and I and old Texans shed our blood to build up? Don't History show that the Lone Star State never yet failed to grant relief to the suffering and oppressed children of the men who made her the grandest commonwealth in the Union? If Statistics and History don't bear out the claim of Amos Colvin's child I'll ask the next legislature to abolish my office. Come, now, Uncle Frank, let her have the money. I'll sign the papers officially, if you say so; and then if the governor or the comptroller, or the janitor or anybody else makes a kick, by the Lord I'll refer the matter to the people and see if they won't indorse the act."

The treasurer looked sympathetic but shocked. The commissioner's voice had grown louder as he rounded off the sentences that, however praiseworthy they might be in sentiment, reflected somewhat upon the capacity of the head of a more or less important department of state. The clerks were beginning to listen.

"Now, Standifer," said the treasurer, soothingly, "you know I'd like to help in this matter, but stop and think a moment, please. Every cent in the treasury is expended only by appropriation made by the legislature, and drawn out by checks issued by the comptroller. I can't control the use of a cent of it. Neither can you. Your department isn't disbursive — it isn't even administrative — it's purely clerical. The only way for the lady to obtain relief is to petition the legislature, and — ."

"To the devil with the legislature," said Standifer, turning away.

The treasurer called him back.

"I'd be glad, Standifer, to contribute a hundred dollars personally toward the immediate expenses of Colvin's daughter." He reached for his pocketbook.

"Never mind, Uncle Frank," said the commissioner, in a softer tone. "There's no need of that. She hasn't asked for anything of that sort yet. Besides, her case is in my hands. I see now what a little ragtag, bob-tail, gotch-eared department I've been put in charge of. It seems to be about as important as an almanac or a hotel register. But while I'm running it, it won't turn away any daughters of Amos Colvin without stretching its jurisdiction to cover, if possible. You want to keep your eye on the Department of Insurance, Statistics, and History."

The commissioner returned to his office, looking thoughtful. He opened and closed an inkstand on his desk many times with extreme and undue attention before he spoke. "Why don't you get a divorce?" he asked, suddenly.

"I haven't the money to pay for it," answered the lady.

"Just at present," announced the commissioner, in a formal tone, "the powers of my department appear to be considerably stringhalted. Statistics seem to be overdrawn at the bank, and History isn't good for a square meal. But you've come to the right place, ma'am. The department will see you through. Where did you say your husband is, ma'am?"

"He was in San Antonio yesterday. He is living there now."

Suddenly the commissioner abandoned his official air. He took the faded little woman's hands in his, and spoke in the old voice he used on the trail and around campfires.

"Your name's Amanda, isn't it?"

"Yes, sir."

"I thought so. I've heard your dad say it often enough. Well, Amanda, here's your father's best friend, the head of a big office in the state government, that's going to help you out of your troubles. And here's the old bush-whacker and cowpuncher that your father has helped out of scrapes time and time again wants to ask you a question. Amanda, have you got enough money to run you for the next two or three days?"

Mrs. Sharp's white face flushed the least bit.

"Plenty, sir — for a few days."

"All right, then, ma'am. Now you go back where you are stopping here, and you come to the office again the day after tomorrow at four o'clock in the afternoon. Very likely by that time there will be something definite to report to you." The commissioner hesitated, and looked a trifle embarrassed. "You said your husband had insured his life for $5,000. Do you know whether the premiums have been kept paid upon it or not?"

"He paid for a whole year in advance about five months ago," said Mrs. Sharp. "I have the policy and receipts in my trunk."

"Oh, that's all right, then," said Standifer. "It's best to look after things of that sort. Some day they may come in handy."

Mrs. Sharp departed, and soon afterward Luke Standifer went down to the little hotel where he boarded and looked up the railroad time-table in the daily paper. Half an hour later he removed his coat and vest, and strapped a peculiarly constructed pistol holster across his shoulder, leaving the receptacle close under his left armpit. Into the holster he shoved a short-barreled .44-calibre revolver. Putting on his clothes again, he strolled down to the station and caught the five-twenty afternoon train for San Antonio.

The San Antonio Express of the following morning contained this sensational piece of news:

BENTON SHARP MEETS HIS MATCH

THE MOST NOTED DESPERADO IN SOUTHWEST TEXAS SHOT TO DEATH IN THE GOLD FRONT RESTAURANT — PROMINENT STATE OFFICIAL SUCCESSFULLY DEFENDS HIMSELF AGAINST THE NOTED BULLY — MAGNIFICENT EXHIBITION OF QUICK GUN PLAY.

Last night about eleven o'clock Benton Sharp, with two other men, entered the Gold Front Restaurant and seated themselves at a table. Sharp had been drinking, and was loud and boisterous, as he always was when under the influence of liquor. Five minutes after the party was seated a tall, well-dressed, elderly gentleman entered the restaurant. Few present recognized the Honorable Luke Standifer, the recently appointed Commissioner of Insurance, Statistics, and History.

Going over to the same side where Sharp was, Mr. Standifer prepared to take a seat at the next table. In hanging his hat upon one of the hooks along the wall he let it fall upon Sharp's head. Sharp turned, being in an especially ugly humor, and cursed the other roundly. Mr. Standifer apologized calmly for the accident, but Sharp continued his vituperations. Mr. Standifer was observed to draw near and speak a few sentences to the desperado in so low a tone that no one else caught the words. Sharp sprang up, wild with rage. In the meantime, Mr. Standifer had stepped some yards away, and was standing quietly with his arms folded across the breast of his loosely hanging coat.

With that impetuous and deadly rapidity that made Sharp so dreaded, he reached for the gun he always carried in his hip pocket—a movement that has preceded the death of at least a dozen men at his hands. Quick as the motion was, the bystanders assert that it was met by the most beautiful exhibition of lightning gun-pulling ever witnessed in the Southwest. As Sharp's pistol was being raised—and the act was really quicker than the eye could follow—a glittering .44 appeared as if by some conjuring trick in the right hand of Mr. Standifer, who, without a perceptible movement of his arm, shot Benton Sharp through the heart. It seems that the new Commissioner of Insurance, Statistics, and History has been an old-time Indian fighter and ranger for many years, which accounts for the happy knack he has of handling a .44.

It is not believed that Mr. Standifer will be put to any inconvenience beyond a necessary formal hearing to-day, as all the witnesses who were present unite in declaring that the deed was done in self-defense.

When Mrs. Sharp appeared at the office of the commissioner, according to appointment, she found that gentleman calmly eating a golden russet apple. He greeted her without embarrassment and without hesitation at approaching the subject that was the topic of the day.

"I had to do it, ma'am," he said, simply, "or get it myself. Mr. Kauffman," he added, turning to the old clerk, "please look up the records of the Security Life Insurance Company and see if they are all right."

"No need to look," grunted Kauffman, who had everything in his head. "It's all O.K. They pay all losses within ten days."

Mrs. Sharp soon rose to depart. She had arranged to remain in town until the policy was paid. The commissioner did not detain her. She was a woman, and he did not know just what to say to her at present. Rest and time would bring her what she needed.

But, as she was leaving, Luke Standifer indulged himself in an official remark:

"The Department of Insurance, Statistics, and History, ma'am, has done the best it could with your case. 'Twas a case hard to cover according to red tape. Statistics failed, and History missed fire, but, if I may be permitted to say it, we came out particularly strong on Insurance."

Discussion Topics

1. Did Luke Standifer do "the right thing"? Are we troubled by the death of Benton Sharp? For that matter, how troubled are we by the fate of the victims of vigilantes such as Batman or Dirty Harry?

One thing that the three "heroes" have in common is that they are characters in fiction. And in fiction, the author is in a sense all-powerful. Among other powers, the author can shape the moral universe. While we are often drawn to complex or ambiguous characters, we also like to be able to know the bad and identify with the good. The victims of vigilante justice in fiction are rarely morally complex. Does O. Henry have anything good to say about Sharp other than that he is a good shot?

We are disposed at times to cheer for vigilantes in the real world, for example, the bystander who shoots dead the serial killer just as he is released from jail "on a technicality." And increasingly the most complex international events are described in the same morally black-and-white terms as characters in Batman. Wars are portrayed as contests between good and evil; world leaders and their governments are said to be part of an "axis of evil." It becomes easy to borrow and transpose comic-book fiction's focus on ends and the dismissal of means and procedures in this light.

The problem with this transposition is that, while fiction has an author who controls the moral temperature, reality has no such author. The extremist story of moral absolutes can be told by each side. Every party is free to make up its own moral justification for violence. Thus, we must be cautious in two ways. We must careful to avoid simplifying situations that are necessarily complex. And we must be quite sure that those complex situations yield moral conclusions that justify what we feel and what we do.

2. Did Luke Standifer commit a perfect homicide? Even if a prosecutor knew the circumstances leading up to the fatal gunfight, could a legal case be brought against Standifer? Legal opinions are likely to differ. On one hand, he provoked Sharp's response and planned to have the opportunity to kill him. It is entrapment only if Standifer put into Sharp's mind an intention that he did not already have. But Sharp's own inclination was to kill anyone who interfered with him even by accident.

On the other hand, Standifer can argue that he was acting in self-defense. Once Sharp threatened him, he knew that he was in danger and that his only option was to shoot first. But self-defense is not available to someone who provokes the encounter in the first place. Does that erase Standifer's defense? Arguably not. Even if he is the instigator, his right of self-defense is said to revive if the nature of the fight changes, if for example it changes from a non-deadly encounter to a deadly one. It could be said that Standifer's initial act was a non-deadly minor assault. By that standard, Standifer would have no defense against charges based on a fistfight. But when Sharp pulled his gun, the encounter became deadly (and Standifer's right revived). Thus, by standard reasoning in criminal law, the argument based on self-defense would succeed. The flaw in the argument is that Standifer knew from the beginning that the encounter would be deadly. The initial encounter was non-deadly only if one looks at what he did, not at what he intended and foresaw.

Of course, no prosecutor would have access to evidence for making a case against Standifer beyond a reasonable doubt. The defense would argue successfully that his first act was accidental and that the only culpable homicidal intention was Sharp's.

3. To the extent that we see vigilantes as heroic and admirable, that response seems limited to those who act alone. Groups that take law into their own hands, like the Ku Klux Klan, are almost always condemned. And that seems true in fiction as well as fact. The vigilante-hero who acts alone puts himself or herself at risk and relies on wit and strength. Those who act in groups are thought to act as mobs, to need the support of the group to do what they are too cowardly or bigoted to do alone.

This is true, but not universally so. One's judgment depends on the degree of corruption and harm that is object of the struggle. Compare the situation of subversive groups in rural America, such as the Minutemen, which evoke little admiration from ordinary citizens and are rarely roman-ticized, with the Free French underground during the Nazi occupation of France. The latter have been portrayed as heroes. In their own thinking, of course, the Minutemen see themselves as pursuing a similar crusade against evil.

4. Does Standifer present a dangerous precedent? Might others be able to provoke their intended victims in a similar way—and have a good defense against homicide? Note that the strategy can work only against someone with a hair-trigger inclination toward violence. Does such a person present such a danger that he or she "deserves" what he gets?

Defense of Honor

Guy de Maupassant: The Assassin

Honor has gone out of style. We associate the defense of honor with distant times. Knights defended the honor of maidens and feudal courts. Duels were fought in the eighteenth and nineteenth centuries in the name of honor. In the early twentieth century, as in earlier times, husbands who caught their wives *in flagrante* with lovers and responded with homicidal violence, were sometimes given mitigated sentences, if not excused altogether, because their honor was at stake.

Few of us fight duels today and few of us talk of honor. But we do talk about self-respect and pride. In fact, the subculture of gangs puts great emphasis on the defense of respect and pride as a justification for violence. Criminal law admits no defense in terms of honor or respect, but it does allow the defense of duress when "a person of reasonable firmness" is driven to act by threats that such a person could not withstand, and it mitigates crime on the basis of understandable "extreme emotional distress." What was once seen as a matter of honor can now often be seen as disturbing to a person of reasonable firmness or as causing significant distress. It is possible also to find normative bias in what counts as emotional distress for purposes of mitigation. Distress at marital fidelity has long been a textbook example, but distress at insults to the honor of one's gang has never qualified as a basis for mitigation.

Sometimes, but hardly always, honor can lead to self-delusion. What is obvious to everyone else may be invisible to the person whose honor is at stake. This is the situation in de Maupassant's story, "The Assassin." The author (1850-1893) was well-known during his lifetime for his short stories. In the early twentieth century, he was widely read and highly regarded throughout Europe. But his reputation in the U.S. has always lagged behind his fame in the rest of the world.

❧ The Assassin ❧

Guy de Maupassant

The guilty man was defended by a very young lawyer, a beginner, who spoke thus:

"The facts are undeniable, gentlemen of the jury. My client, an honest man, an irreproachable employee, gentle and timid, assassinated his employer in a moment of anger which seems to me incomprehensible. If you will allow me, I would like to look into the psychology of the crime, so to speak, without wasting any time or attempting to excuse anything. We shall then be able to judge better.

"John Nicholas Lougère is the son of very honorable people, who made of him a simple, respectful man.

"That is his crime: respect! It is a sentiment, gentlemen, which we of today no longer know, of which the name alone seems to exist while its power has disappeared. It is necessary to enter certain old, modest families to find this severe tradition, this religion of a thing or of a man, this sentiment where belief takes on a sacred character, this faith which doubts not, nor smiles, nor entertains a suspicion.

"One cannot be an honest man, a truly honest man in the full force of the term, and be respectful. The man who respects has his eyes closed. He believes. We others, whose eyes are wide open upon the world, who live here in this hall of justice, this purger of society, where all infamy runs aground, we others who are the confidants of shame, the devoted defenders of all human meanness, the support, not to say the supporters, of male and female sharpers, from a prince to a tramp, we who welcome with indulgence, with complacence, with a smiling benevolence all the guilty and defend them before you, we who, if we truly love our profession, measure our legal sympathy by the size of the crime, we could never have a respectful soul. We see too much of this river of corruption, which catches the chiefs of power as well as the lowest scamp; we know too much of how it gives and takes and sells itself. Places, offices, honors brutally exchanged for a little money, or skillfully exchanged for titles and interests in industrial enterprises, or sometimes, simply for the kiss of a woman.

"Our duty and our profession force us to be ignorant of nothing, to suspect everybody, because everybody is doubtful; and we are taken by surprise when we find ourselves face to face with a man, like the assassin seated before you, who possesses the religion of respect to such a degree that he will become a martyr for it.

"We others, gentlemen, have a sense of honor, a certain need of propriety, from a disgust of baseness, from a sentiment of personal dignity and pride; but we do not carry at the bottom of our hearts the blind, inborn, brutal faith of this man.

"Let me tell you the story of his life:

"He was brought up, like many another child, to separate all human acts into two parts: the good and the bad. He was shown the good with an irresistible authority which made him only distinguish the bad, as we distinguish day and night. His father did not belong to the superior race of minds who, looking from a height, see the sources of belief and recognize the social necessities born of these distinctions.

"He grew up, religious and confident, enthusiastic and limited. At twenty-two he married. His wife was a cousin, brought up as he was, simple and pure as he was. His was the inestimable privilege of having for a companion an honest woman with a true heart, the rarest and most respectable thing in the world. He had for his mother that veneration which surrounds mothers in patriarchal families, that profound respect which is reserved for divinities. This religion he reflected somewhat upon his wife, and it became scarcely less as conjugal familiarity increased. He lived in absolute ignorance of double dealing, in a state of constant uprightness and tranquil happiness which made him a being apart from the world. Deceiving no one he had never a suspicion that any one would deceive him.

"Some time before his marriage, he had become cashier in the office of Mr. Langlais, the man who was lately assassinated by him.

"We know, gentlemen of the jury, by the testimony of Mrs. Langlais and of her brother, Mr. Perthuis, a partner of her husband, of all the family and of all the higher employees of the bank, that Lougère was a model employee, upright, submissive, gentle, prompt, and deferential toward his superiors. They treated him with the consideration due to his exemplary conduct. He was accustomed to this homage and to a kind of respect shown to Mrs. Lougère, whose worthiness was upon all lips.

"But she died of typhoid fever in a few days' time. He assuredly felt a profound grief, but the cold, calm grief of a methodical heart. Only from his pallor and from a change in his looks was one able to judge how deeply he had been wounded.

"Then, gentlemen, the most natural thing in the world happened.

"This man had been married ten years. For ten years he had been accustomed to feel the presence of a woman near him always. He was habituated to her care, her familiar voice upon his return, the good night at evening, the cheerful greeting of the morning, the gentle rustle of the dress so dear to the feminine heart, to that caress, at once lover-like and maternal, which renders life pleasant, to that loved presence that made the hours move less slowly. He was also accustomed to being spoiled at table, perhaps, and to all those attentions which become, little by little, so indispensable.

"He could no longer live alone. Then, to pass the interminable evenings, he got into the habit of spending an hour or two in a neighboring wine shop. He would drink a glass and sit there motionless, following, with heedless eye, the billiard balls running after one another under the smoke of the pipes, listening to, without hearing, the discussion of the players, the disputes of his neighbors over politics, and the sound of laughter that sometimes went up from the other end of the room, from some unusual joke. He often ended by going to sleep, from sheer lassitude and weariness. But, at the bottom of his heart and of his flesh, there was the irresistible need of a woman's heart and flesh; and, without thinking, he approached each evening a little nearer to the desk where the cashier, a pretty blonde, sat, attracted to her unconquerably, because she was a woman.

"At first they chatted, and he got into the habit, so pleasant for him, of passing the evening by her side. She was gracious and kind, as one learns in this occupation to smile, and she amused herself by making him renew his order as often as possible, which makes business good.

"But each day Lougere was becoming more and more attached to this woman whom he did not know, whose whole existence he was ignorant of, and whom he loved only because he was in the way of seeing nobody else.

"The little creature was crafty, and soon perceived that she could reap some benefit from this guileless man; she then sought out the best means of exploiting him. The most effective, surely, was to marry him.

"This she accomplished without difficulty.

"Need I tell you, gentlemen of the jury, that the conduct of this girl had been most irregular and that marriage, far from putting a check to her flight, seemed on the contrary to render it more shameless?

"From the natural sport of feminine astuteness, she seemed to take pleasure in deceiving this honest man with all the employees of his office. I said with all. We have letters, gentlemen. There was soon a public scandal, of which the husband alone, as usual, was the only one ignorant.

"Finally, this wretch, with an interest easy to understand, seduced the son of the proprietor, a young man nineteen years old, upon whose mind and judgment she had a deplorable influence. Mr. Langlais, whose eyes had been closed up to that time, through friendship for his employee, resented having his son in the hands, I should say in the arms of this dangerous woman, and was legitimately angry.

"He made the mistake of calling Lougère to him on the spot and of speaking to him of his paternal indignation.

"There remains nothing more for me to say, gentlemen, except to read to you the recital of the crime, made by the lips of the dying man, and submitted as evidence. It says:

"'I learned that my son had given to this woman, that same night, ten thousand francs, and my anger was stronger on that account. Certainly, I never suspected the honorableness of Lougère, but a certain kind of blindness is more dangerous than positive faults. And so I had him come to me and told him that I should be obliged to deprive myself of his services.

" 'He remained standing before me, terrified, and not comprehending. He ended by demanding, rather excitedly, some explanation. I refused to give him any, affirming that my reasons were wholly personal. He believed then that I suspected him of indelicacy and, very pale, besought, implored me to explain. Held by this idea, he was strong and began to talk loud. As I kept silent, he abused and insulted me, until he arrived at such a degree of exasperation that I was fearful of results.

" 'Then, suddenly, upon a wounding word that struck upon a full heart, I threw the whole truth in his face.

" 'He stood still some seconds, looking at me with haggard eyes. Then I saw him take from my desk the long shears, which I use for making margins to certain registers, I saw him fall upon me with uplifted arm, and I felt something enter my throat just above the breast, without noticing any pain.'

"This, gentleman of the jury, is the simple recital of this murder. What more can be said for his defense? He respected his second wife with blindness because he respected his first with reason."

After a short deliberation, the prisoner was acquitted.

Discussion Topics

1. What difference does it make that M. Langlais' account of the indiscretions of the second Mme. Lougere was true? Suppose Langlais had been misled and was mistaken about the affair involving his son. In either case, Lougere's beliefs and attitudes would be the same. He would believe his wife to be without fault and would defend her honor. His emotions would be the same. And the legal result would be the same. His belief in her honor would not excuse his crime but it might mitigate his culpability on the basis of emotional distress.

Should the truth or falsity of Langlais' charges against the new wife make a difference in the legal disposition of the case? Does the truth or falsity affect the morality of Lougere's actions?

2. Consider the extent of Lougere's self-deception. Should he be able to benefit from his blindness and faith by getting a mitigated punishment? Or should he be blamed (morally, if not legally) for willful ignorance?

It can be argued that we all have an obligation to see our circumstances as they are. If we know that our neighbor is abusing his spouse or children, we are at fault if we turn a blind eye and ignore the situation or deny to ourselves that it is happening. As citizens, we can be blamed (as Germans citizens in Nazi Germany are often blamed) if we tolerate without protest policies that are morally indefensible and tell ourselves that all is well.

Is Lougere to be blamed in similar fashion — or is his loyalty to his wife something to admire?

Mental Illness and Abnormality

Robert Louis Stevenson: *Dr. Jekyll and Mr. Hyde*

The fact that criminal law rests on a simplified picture of the mind is most acutely evident when mental illness is an issue. Even when it deals with so-called "normal" persons, law presumes an implausibly high degree of awareness and intentionality. It pays little concern, as we have seen, to the unconscious, and it takes for granted that means-ends rationality is the norm. When the law concerns itself with mitigation and excuses, the criterion is whether a rational person with normal resources of control would have succumbed to pressure or been seriously disturbed.

We all know that countless persons are troubled by "mental" illnesses that range from those which frequently affect function (obsessive-compulsive syndrome, bipolar disease, depression) to those which can be altogether disabling (schizophrenia, paranoid fantasies). It is now taken for granted that the term "mental illness" is something of a misnomer and that these conditions often have physical bases and can be treated chemically (as well as cognitively). For the most part, criminal law ignores the infinite shadings of competence and disability that characterize the vast majority of us. One is fully responsible unless one is insane, and the legal test for insanity that is still used most widely requires that, because of mental defect at the time of acting, one did not know the *nature* of the act one was carrying out or was *unable* to tell right from wrong.

An entire chapter is needed to discuss whether and why criminal law needs to draw a clear line between sanity and full responsibility on one hand and insanity on the other. And another chapter would be needed to discuss the merits of the test for sanity (the *McNaghten* test) described above. The most fruitful discussion would be in terms of the ways each condition compromises one's ability to comply with the law and how law might accommodate those situations.

Robert Louis Stevenson's famous novella *Dr. Jekyll and Mr. Hyde* gives us the chance to discuss one small corner of the intersection of criminal law and mental illness. Multiple personality disorder (MPD) is a condition in which several personalities, each organized and seemingly coherent, coexist in the same person. The condition is rare but well-documented, even though it long seemed to be more the fevered dream of fiction writers than the actual experience of anyone. MPD raises special questions of responsibility. Each personality seems to make choices and have some control, but how are we to assess the responsibility of the person who is typically unaware of some of his subpersonalities and their actions?

In Stevenson's story, the main character has multiple lives—but he arrives at that condition in a special way. We will look at the similarities and differences between his plight and that of the typical MPD sufferer. The story itself was an unusual one for Stevenson (1850-1894), who was best known for his adventure narratives (*Treasure Island, Kidnapped*). He himself was an adventurer. Raised in Scotland, he sailed as a crew member to America and made his way to California; in pursuit of a good climate for tuberculosis, which plagued him throughout his short life, he went to Colorado, New York state, and finally the Pacific Islands.

❖ Dr. Jekyll and Mr. Hyde ❖

Robert Louis Stevenson

Mr. Utterson the lawyer was a man of a rugged countenance that was never lighted by a smile; cold, scanty and embarrassed in discourse; backward in sentiment; lean, long, dusty, dreary and yet somehow lovable. At friendly meetings, and when the wine was to his taste, something eminently human beaconed from his eye; something indeed which never found its way into his talk, but which spoke not only in these silent symbols of the after-dinner face, but more often and loudly in the acts of his life. He was austere with himself; drank gin when he was alone, to mortify a taste for vintages; and though he enjoyed the theater, had not crossed the doors of one for twenty years. But he had an approved tolerance for others; sometimes wondering, almost with envy, at the high pressure of spirits involved in their misdeeds; and in any extremity inclined to help rather than to reprove. "I incline to Cain's heresy," he used to say quaintly: "I let my brother go to the devil in his own way." In this character, it was frequently his fortune to be the last reputable acquaintance and the last good influence in the lives of downgoing men. And to such as these, so long as they came about his chambers, he never marked a shade of change in his demeanour.

No doubt the feat was easy to Mr. Utterson; for he was undemonstrative at the best, and even his friendship seemed to be founded in a similar catholicity of good-nature. It is the mark of a modest man to accept his friendly circle ready-made from the hands of opportunity; and that was the lawyer's way. His friends were those of his own blood or those whom he had known the longest; his affections, like ivy, were the growth of time, they implied no aptness in the object. Hence, no doubt the bond that united him to Mr. Richard Enfield, his distant kinsman, the well-known man about town. It was a nut to crack for many, what these two could see in each other, or what subject they could find in common. It was reported by those who encountered them in their Sunday walks, that they said nothing, looked singularly dull and would hail with obvious relief the appearance of a friend. For all that, the two men put the greatest store by these excursions, counted them the chief jewel of each week, and not only set aside occasions of pleasure, but even resisted the calls of business, that they might enjoy them uninterrupted.

It chanced on one of these rambles that their way led them down a by-street in a busy quarter of London. The street was small and what is called quiet, but it drove a thriving trade on the weekdays. The inhabitants were all doing well, it seemed, and all emulously hoping to do better still, and laying out the surplus of their grains in coquetry; so that the shop fronts stood along that thoroughfare with an air of invitation, like rows of smiling saleswomen. Even on Sunday, when it veiled its more florid charms and lay comparatively empty of passage, the street shone out in contrast to its dingy neighbourhood, like a fire in a forest; and with its freshly painted shutters, well-polished brasses, and general cleanliness and gaiety of note, instantly caught and pleased the eye of the passenger.

Two doors from one corner, on the left hand going east the line was broken by the entry of a court; and just at that point a certain sinister block of building thrust forward its gable on the street. It was two storeys high; showed no window, nothing but a door on the lower storey and a blind forehead of discoloured wall on the upper; and bore in every feature, the marks of prolonged and sordid negligence. The door, which was equipped with neither bell nor knocker, was blistered and distained. Tramps slouched into the recess and struck matches on the panels; children kept shop upon the steps; the schoolboy had tried his knife on the mouldings; and for close on a generation, no one had appeared to drive away these random visitors or to repair their ravages. Mr. Enfield and the lawyer were on the other side of the by-street; but when they came abreast of the entry, the former lifted up his cane and pointed.

"Did you ever remark that door?" he asked; and when his companion had replied in the affirmative. "It is connected in my mind," added he, "with a very odd story."

"Indeed?" said Mr. Utterson, with a slight change of voice, "and what was that?"

"Well, it was this way," returned Mr. Enfield: "I was coming home from some place at the end of the world, about three o'clock of a black winter morning, and my way lay through a part of town where there was literally nothing to be seen but lamps. Street after street and all the folks asleep — street after street, all lighted up as if for a procession and all as empty as a church — till at last I got into that state of mind when a man listens and listens and begins to long for the sight of a policeman. All at once, I saw two figures: one a little man who was stumping along eastward at a good walk, and the other a girl of maybe eight or ten who was running as hard as she was able down a cross street. Well, sir, the two ran into one another naturally enough at the corner; and then came the horrible part of the thing; for the man trampled calmly over the child's body and left her screaming on the ground. It sounds nothing to hear, but it was hellish to see. It wasn't like a man; it was like some damned Juggernaut. I gave a few halloa, took to my heels, collared my gentleman, and brought him back to where there was already quite a group about the screaming child. He was perfectly cool and made no resistance, but gave me one look, so ugly that it brought out the sweat on me like running. The people who had turned out were the girl's own family; and pretty soon, the doctor, for whom she had been sent put in his appearance. Well, the child was not much the worse, more frightened, according to the Sawbones; and there you might have supposed would be an end to it. But there was one curious circumstance. I had taken a loathing to my gentleman at first sight. So had the child's family, which was only natural. But the doctor's case was what struck me. He was the usual cut and dry apothecary, of no particular age and colour, with a strong Edinburgh accent and about as emotional as a bagpipe. Well, sir, he was like the rest of us; every time he looked at my prisoner, I saw that Sawbones turn sick and white with desire to kill him. I knew what was in his mind, just as he knew what was in mine; and killing being out of the question, we did the next best. We told the man we could and would make such a scandal out of this as should make his name stink from one end of London to the other. If he had any friends or any credit, we undertook that he should lose them. And all the time, as we were pitching it in red hot, we were keeping the women off him as best we could for they were as wild as harpies. I never saw a circle of such hateful faces; and there was the man in the middle, with a kind of black sneering coolness — frightened to, I could see that — but carrying it off, sir, really like Satan. 'If you choose to make capital out of this accident,' said he, 'I am naturally helpless. No gentleman but wishes to avoid a scene,' says he. 'Name your figure.' Well, we screwed him up to a hundred pounds for the child's family; he would have clearly liked to stick out; but there was something about the lot of us that meant mischief, and at last he struck. The next thing was to get the money; and where do you think he carried us but to that place with the door? — whipped out a key, went in, and presently came back with the matter of ten pounds in gold and a cheque for the balance on

Coutts's, drawn payable to bearer and signed with a name that I can't mention, though it's one of the points of my story, but it was a name at least very well known and often printed. The figure was stiff; but the signature was good for more than that if it was only genuine. I took the liberty of pointing out to my gentleman that the whole business looked apocryphal, and that a man does not, in real life, walk into a cellar door at four in the morning and come out with another man's cheque for close upon a hundred pounds. But he was quite easy and sneering. 'Set your mind at rest,' says he, 'I will stay with you till the banks open and cash the cheque myself.' So we all set off, the doctor, and the child's father, and our friend and myself, and passed the rest of the night in my chambers; and next day, when we had breakfasted, went in a body to the bank. I gave in the cheque myself, and said I had every reason to believe it was a forgery. Not a bit of it. The cheque was genuine."

"Tut-tut," said Mr. Utterson.

"I see you feel as I do," said Mr. Enfield. "Yes, it's a bad story. For my man was a fellow that nobody could have to do with, a really damnable man; and the person that drew the cheque is the very pink of the proprieties, celebrated too, and (what makes it worse) one of your fellows who do what they call good. Blackmail I suppose; an honest man paying through the nose for some of the capers of his youth. Black Mail House is what I call the place with the door, in consequence. Though even that, you know, is far from explaining all," he added, and with the words fell into a vein of musing.

From this he was recalled by Mr. Utterson asking rather suddenly: "And you don't know if the drawer of the cheque lives there?"

"A likely place, isn't it?" returned Mr. Enfield. "But I happen to have noticed his address; he lives in some square or other."

"And you never asked about the — place with the door?" said Mr. Utterson.

"No, sir: I had a delicacy," was the reply. "I feel very strongly about putting questions; it partakes too much of the style of the day of judgment. You start a question, and it's like starting a stone. You sit quietly on the top of a hill; and away the stone goes, starting others; and presently some bland old bird (the last you would have thought of) is knocked on the head in his own back garden and the family have to change their name. No sir, I make it a rule of mine: the more it looks like Queer Street, the less I ask."

"A very good rule, too," said the lawyer.

"But I have studied the place for myself," continued Mr. Enfield. "It seems scarcely a house. There is no other door, and nobody goes in or out of that one but, once in a great while, the gentleman of my adventure. There are three windows looking on the court on the first floor; none below; the windows are always shut but they're clean. And then there is a chimney which is generally smoking; so somebody must live there. And yet it's not so sure; for the buildings are so packed together about the court, that it's hard to say where one ends and another begins."

The pair walked on again for a while in silence; and then "Enfield," said Mr. Utterson, "that's a good rule of yours."

"Yes, I think it is," returned Enfield.

"But for all that," continued the lawyer, "there's one point I want to ask: I want to ask the name of that man who walked over the child."

"Well," said Mr. Enfield, "I can't see what harm it would do. It was a man of the name of Hyde."

"Hm," said Mr. Utterson. "What sort of a man is he to see?"

"He is not easy to describe. There is something wrong with his appearance; something displeasing, something down-right detestable. I never saw a man I so disliked, and yet I scarce know why. He must be deformed somewhere; he gives a strong feeling of deformity, although I couldn't specify the point. He's an extraordinary looking man, and yet I really can name nothing out of the way. No, sir; I can make no hand of it; I can't describe him. And it's not want of memory; for I declare I can see him this moment."

Mr. Utterson again walked some way in silence and obviously under a weight of consideration. "You are sure he used a key?" he inquired at last.

"My dear sir . . ." began Enfield, surprised out of himself.

"Yes, I know," said Utterson; "I know it must seem strange. The fact is, if I do not ask you the name of the other party, it is because I know it already. You see, Richard, your tale has gone home. If you have been inexact in any point you had better correct it."

"I think you might have warned me," returned the other with a touch of sullenness. "But I have been pedantically exact, as you call it. The fellow had a key; and what's more, he has it still. I saw him use it not a week ago."

Mr. Utterson sighed deeply but said never a word; and the young man presently resumed. "Here is another lesson to say nothing," said he. "I am ashamed of my long tongue. Let us make a bargain never to refer to this again."

"With all my heart," said the lawyer. "I shake hands on that, Richard."

That evening Mr. Utterson came home to his bachelor house in sombre spirits and sat down to dinner without relish. It was his custom of a Sunday, when this meal was over, to sit close by the fire, a volume of some dry divinity on his reading desk, until the clock of the neighbouring church rang out the hour of twelve, when he would go soberly and gratefully to bed. On this night however, as soon as the cloth was taken away, he took up a candle and went into his business room. There he opened his safe, took from the most private part of it a document endorsed on the envelope as Dr. Jekyll's Will and sat down with a clouded brow to study its contents. The will was holograph, for Mr. Utterson though he took charge of it now that it was made, had refused to lend the least assistance in the making of it; it provided not only that, in case of the decease of Henry Jekyll, M.D., D.C.L., L.L.D., F.R.S., etc., all his possessions were to pass into the hands of his "friend and benefactor Edward Hyde," but that in case of Dr. Jekyll's "disappearance or unexplained absence for any period exceeding three calendar months," the said Edward Hyde should step into the said Henry Jekyll's shoes without further delay and free from any burthen or obligation beyond the payment of a few small sums to the members of the doctor's household. This document had long been the lawyer's eyesore. It offended him both as a lawyer and as a lover of the sane and customary sides of life, to whom the fanciful was the immodest. And hitherto it was his ignorance of Mr. Hyde that had swelled his indignation; now, by a sudden turn, it was his knowledge. It was already bad enough when the name was but a name of which he could learn no more. It was worse when it began to be clothed upon with detestable attributes; and out of the shifting, insubstantial mists that had so long baffled his eye, there leaped up the sudden, definite presentment of a fiend.

"I thought it was madness," he said, as he replaced the obnoxious paper in the safe, "and now I begin to fear it is disgrace."

With that he blew out his candle, put on a greatcoat, and set forth in the direction of Cavendish Square, that citadel of medicine, where his friend, the great Dr. Lanyon, had his house and received his crowding patients. "If anyone knows, it will be Lanyon," he had thought.

The solemn butler knew and welcomed him; he was subjected to no stage of delay, but ushered direct from the door to the dining-room where Dr. Lanyon sat alone over his wine. This was a hearty, healthy, dapper, red-faced gentleman, with a shock of hair prematurely white, and a boisterous and decided manner. At sight of Mr. Utterson, he sprang up from his chair and welcomed him with both hands. The geniality, as was the way of the man, was somewhat theatrical to the eye; but it reposed on genuine feeling. For these two were old friends, old mates both at school and college, both thorough respectors of themselves and of each other, and what does not always follow, men who thoroughly enjoyed each other's company.

After a little rambling talk, the lawyer led up to the subject which so disagreeably preoccupied his mind.

"I suppose, Lanyon," said he, "you and I must be the two oldest friends that Henry Jekyll has?"

"I wish the friends were younger," chuckled Dr. Lanyon. "But I suppose we are. And what of that? I see little of him now."

"Indeed?" said Utterson. "I thought you had a bond of common interest."

"We had," was the reply. "But it is more than ten years since Henry Jekyll became too fanciful for me. He began to go wrong, wrong in mind; and though of course I continue to take an interest in him for old sake's sake, as they say, I see and I have seen devilish little of the man. Such unscientific balderdash," added the doctor, flushing suddenly purple, "would have estranged Damon and Pythias."

This little spirit of temper was somewhat of a relief to Mr. Utterson. "They have only differed on some point of science," he thought; and being a man of no scientific passions (except in the matter of conveyancing), he even added: "It is nothing worse than that!" He gave his friend a few seconds to recover his composure, and then approached the question he had come to put. Did you ever come across a protege of his—one Hyde?" he asked.

"Hyde?" repeated Lanyon. "No. Never heard of him. Since my time."

That was the amount of information that the lawyer carried back with him to the great, dark bed on which he tossed to and fro, until the small hours of the morning began to grow large. It was a night of little ease to his toiling mind, toiling in mere darkness and besieged by questions.

Six o'clock struck on the bells of the church that was so conveniently near to Mr. Utterson's dwelling, and still he was digging at the problem. Hitherto it had touched him on the intellectual side alone; but now his imagination also was engaged, or rather enslaved; and as he lay and tossed in the gross darkness of the night and the curtained room, Mr. Enfield's tale went by before his mind in a scroll of lighted pictures. He would be aware of the great field of lamps of a nocturnal city; then of the figure of a man walking swiftly; then of a child running from the doctor's; and then these met, and that human Juggernaut trod the child down and passed on regardless of her screams. Or else he would see a room in a rich house, where his friend lay asleep, dreaming and smiling at his dreams; and then the door of that room would be opened, the curtains of the bed plucked apart, the sleeper recalled, and lo! there would stand by his side a figure to whom power was given, and even at that dead hour, he must rise and do its bidding. The figure in these two phases haunted the lawyer all night; and if at any time he dozed over, it was but to see it glide more stealthily through sleeping houses, or move the more swiftly and still the more swiftly, even to dizziness, through wider labyrinths of lamp-lighted city, and at every street corner crush a child and leave her screaming. And still the figure had no face by which he might know it; even in his dreams, it had no face, or one that baffled him and melted before his eyes; and thus it was that there sprang up and grew apace in the lawyer's mind a singularly strong, almost an inordinate, curiosity to behold the features of the real Mr. Hyde. If he could but once set eyes on him, he thought the mystery would lighten and perhaps roll altogether away, as was the habit of mysterious things when well examined. He might see a reason for his friend's strange preference or bondage (call it which you please) and even for the startling clause of the will. At least it would be a face worth seeing: the face of a man who was without bowels of mercy: a face which had but to show itself to raise up, in the mind of the unimpressionable Enfield, a spirit of enduring hatred.

From that time forward, Mr. Utterson began to haunt the door in the by-street of shops. In the morning before office hours, at noon when business was plenty, and time scarce, at night under the face of the fogged city moon, by all lights and at all hours of solitude or concourse, the lawyer was to be found on his chosen post.

"If he be Mr. Hyde," he had thought, "I shall be Mr. Seek."

And at last his patience was rewarded. It was a fine dry night; frost in the air; the streets as clean as a ballroom floor; the lamps, unshaken by any wind, drawing a regular pattern of light and shadow. By ten o'clock, when the shops were closed the by-street was very solitary and, in spite of the low growl of London from all round, very silent. Small sounds carried far; domestic sounds out of the houses were clearly audible on either side of the roadway; and the rumour of the approach of any passenger preceded him by a long time. Mr. Utterson had been some minutes at his post, when he was aware of an odd light footstep drawing near. In the course of his nightly patrols, he had long grown accustomed to the quaint effect with which the footfalls of a single person, while he is still a great way off, suddenly spring out distinct from the vast hum and clatter of the city. Yet his attention had never before been so sharply and decisively arrested; and it was with a strong, superstitious prevision of success that he withdrew into the entry of the court.

The steps drew swiftly nearer, and swelled out suddenly louder as they turned the end of the street. The lawyer, looking forth from the entry, could soon see what manner of man he had to deal with. He was small and very plainly dressed and the look of him, even at that distance, went somehow strongly against the watcher's inclination. But he made straight for the door, crossing the roadway to save time; and as he came, he drew a key from his pocket like one approaching home.

Mr. Utterson stepped out and touched him on the shoulder as he passed. "Mr. Hyde, I think?"

Mr. Hyde shrank back with a hissing intake of the breath. But his fear was only momentary; and though he did not look the lawyer in the face, he answered coolly enough: "That is my name. What do you want?"

"I see you are going in," returned the lawyer. "I am an old friend of Dr. Jekyll's — Mr. Utterson of Gaunt Street — you must have heard of my name; and meeting you so conveniently, I thought you might admit me."

"You will not find Dr. Jekyll; he is from home," replied Mr. Hyde, blowing in the key. And then suddenly, but still without looking up, "How did you know me?" he asked.

"On your side," said Mr. Utterson "will you do me a favour?"

"With pleasure," replied the other. "What shall it be?"

"Will you let me see your face?" asked the lawyer.

Mr. Hyde appeared to hesitate, and then, as if upon some sudden reflection, fronted about with an air of defiance; and the pair stared at each other pretty fixedly for a few seconds. "Now I shall know you again," said Mr. Utterson. "It may be useful."

"Yes," returned Mr. Hyde, "It is as well we have met; and *à propos*, you should have my address." And he gave a number of a street in Soho.

"Good God!" thought Mr. Utterson, "can he, too, have been thinking of the will?" But he kept his feelings to himself and only grunted in acknowledgment of the address.

"And now," said the other, "how did you know me?"

"By description," was the reply.

"Whose description?"

"We have common friends," said Mr. Utterson.

"Common friends," echoed Mr. Hyde, a little hoarsely. "Who are they?"

"Jekyll, for instance," said the lawyer.

"He never told you," cried Mr. Hyde, with a flush of anger. "I did not think you would have lied."

"Come," said Mr. Utterson, "that is not fitting language."

The other snarled aloud into a savage laugh; and the next moment, with extraordinary quickness, he had unlocked the door and disappeared into the house.

The lawyer stood awhile when Mr. Hyde had left him, the picture of disquietude. Then he began slowly to mount the street, pausing every step or two and putting his hand to his brow like a man in mental perplexity. The problem he was thus debating as he walked, was one of a class that is rarely solved. Mr. Hyde was pale and dwarfish, he gave an impression of deformity without any nameable malformation, he had a displeasing smile, he had borne himself to the lawyer with a sort of murderous mixture of timidity and boldness, and he spoke with a husky, whispering and somewhat broken voice; all these were points against him, but not all of these together could explain the hitherto unknown disgust, loathing and fear with which Mr. Utterson regarded him. "There must be something else," said the perplexed gentleman. "There *is* something more, if I could find a name for it. God bless me, the man seems hardly human! Something troglodytic, shall we say? or can it be the old story of Dr. Fell? or is it the mere radience of a foul soul that thus transpires through, and transfigures, its clay continent? The last, I think; for, O my poor old Harry Jekyll, if ever I read Satan's signature upon a face, it is on that of your new friend."

Round the corner from the by-street, there was a square of ancient, handsome houses, now for the most part decayed from their high estate and let in flats and chambers to all sorts and conditions of men; map-engravers, architects, shady lawyers and the agents of obscure enterprises. One house, however, second from the corner, was still occupied entire; and at the door of this, which wore a great air of wealth and comfort, though it was now plunged in darkness except for the fanlight, Mr. Utterson stopped and knocked. A well-dressed, elderly servant opened the door.

"Is Dr. Jekyll at home, Poole?" asked the lawyer.

"I will see, Mr. Utterson," said Poole, admitting the visitor, as he spoke, into a large, low-roofed, comfortable hall paved with flags, warmed (after the fashion of a country house) by a bright, open fire, and furnished with costly cabinets of oak. "Will you wait here by the fire, sir? or shall I give you a light in the dining-room?"

"Here, thank you," said the lawyer, and he drew near and leaned on the tall fender. This hall, in which he was now left alone, was a pet fancy of his friend the doctor's; and Utterson himself was wont to speak of it as the pleasantest room in London. But tonight there was a shudder in his blood; the face of Hyde sat heavy on his memory; he felt (what was rare with him) a nausea and distaste of life; and in the gloom of his spirits, he seemed to read a menace in the flickering of the firelight on the polished cabinets and the uneasy starting of the shadow on the roof. He was ashamed of his relief, when Poole presently returned to announce that Dr. Jekyll was gone out.

"I saw Mr. Hyde go in by the old dissecting room, Poole," he said. "Is that right, when Dr. Jekyll is from home?"

"Quite right, Mr. Utterson, sir," replied the servant. "Mr. Hyde has a key."

"Your master seems to repose a great deal of trust in that young man, Poole," resumed the other musingly.

"Yes, sir, he does indeed," said Poole. "We have all orders to obey him."

"I do not think I ever met Mr. Hyde?" asked Utterson.

"O, dear no, sir. He never *dines* here," replied the butler. Indeed we see very little of him on this side of the house; he mostly comes and goes by the laboratory."

"Well, good-night, Poole."

"Good-night, Mr. Utterson."

And the lawyer set out homeward with a very heavy heart. "Poor Harry Jekyll," he thought, "my mind misgives me he is in deep waters! He was wild when he was young; a long while ago to be sure; but in the law of God, there is no statute of limitations. Ay, it must be that; the ghost of some old sin, the cancer of some concealed disgrace: punishment coming, *pede claudo*, years after memory has forgotten and self-love condoned the fault." And the lawyer, scared by the thought, brooded awhile on his own past, groping in all the corners of memory, least by chance some Jack-in-the-Box of an old iniquity should leap to light there. His past was fairly blameless; few men could read the rolls of their life with less apprehension; yet he was humbled to the dust by the many ill things he had done, and raised up again into a sober and fearful gratitude by the many he had come so near to doing yet avoided. And then by a return on his former subject, he conceived a spark of hope. "This Master Hyde, if he were studied," thought he, "must have secrets of his own, black secrets, by the look of him, secrets compared to which poor Jekyll's worst would be like sunshine. Things cannot continue as they are. It turns me cold to think of this creature stealing like a thief to Harry's bedside; poor Harry, what a wakening! And the danger of it; for if this Hyde suspects the existence of the will, he may grow impatient to inherit. Ay, I must put my shoulders to the wheel — if Jekyll will but let me," he added, "if Jekyll will only let me." For once more he saw before his mind's eye, as clear as transparency, the strange clauses of the will.

A fortnight later, by excellent good fortune, the doctor gave one of his pleasant dinners to some five or six old cronies, all intelligent, reputable men and all judges of good wine; and Mr. Utterson so contrived that he remained behind after the others had departed. This was no new arrangement, but a thing that had befallen many scores of times. Where Utterson was liked, he was liked well. Hosts loved to detain the dry lawyer, when the light-hearted and loose-tongued had already their foot on the threshold; they liked to sit a while in his unobtrusive company, practising for solitude, sobering their minds in the man's rich silence after the expense and strain of gaiety. To this rule, Dr. Jekyll was no exception; and as he now sat on the opposite side of the fire — a large, well-made, smooth-faced man of fifty, with something of a stylish cast perhaps, but every mark of capacity and kindness — you could see by his looks that he cherished for Mr. Utterson a sincere and warm affection.

"I have been wanting to speak to you, Jekyll," began the latter. "You know that will of yours?"

A close observer might have gathered that the topic was distasteful; but the doctor carried it off gaily. "My poor Utterson," said he, "you are unfortunate in such a client. I never saw a man so distressed as you were by my will; unless it were that hidebound pedant, Lanyon, at what he called my scientific heresies. O, I know he's a good fellow — you needn't frown — an excellent fellow, and I always mean to see more of him; but a hide-bound pedant for all that; an ignorant, blatant pedant. I was never more disappointed in any man than Lanyon."

"You know I never approved of it," pursued Utterson, ruthlessly disregarding the fresh topic.

"My will? Yes, certainly, I know that," said the doctor, a trifle sharply. "You have told me so."

"Well, I tell you so again," continued the lawyer. "I have been learning something of young Hyde."

The large handsome face of Dr. Jekyll grew pale to the very lips, and there came a blackness about his eyes. "I do not care to hear more," said he. "This is a matter I thought we had agreed to drop."

"What I heard was abominable," said Utterson.

"It can make no change. You do not understand my position," returned the doctor, with a certain incoherency of manner. "I am painfully situated, Utterson; my position is a very strange — a very strange one. It is one of those affairs that cannot be mended by talking."

"Jekyll," said Utterson, "you know me: I am a man to be trusted. Make a clean breast of this in confidence; and I make no doubt I can get you out of it."

"My good Utterson," said the doctor, "this is very good of you, this is downright good of you, and I cannot find words to thank you in. I believe you fully; I would trust you before any man alive, ay, before myself, if I could make the choice; but indeed it isn't what you fancy; it is not as bad as that; and just to put your good heart at rest, I will tell you one thing: the moment I choose, I can be rid of Mr. Hyde. I give you my hand upon that; and I thank you again and again; and I will just add one little word, Utterson, that I'm sure you'll take in good part: this is a private matter, and I beg of you to let it sleep."

Utterson reflected a little, looking in the fire.

"I have no doubt you are perfectly right," he said at last, getting to his feet.

"Well, but since we have touched upon this business, and for the last time I hope," continued the doctor, "there is one point I should like you to understand. I have really a very great interest in poor Hyde. I know you have seen him; he told me so; and I fear he was rude. But I do sincerely take a great, a very great interest in that young man; and if I am taken away, Utterson, I wish you to promise me that you will bear with him and get his rights for him. I think you would, if you knew all; and it would be a weight off my mind if you would promise."

"I can't pretend that I shall ever like him," said the lawyer.

"I don't ask that," pleaded Jekyll, laying his hand upon the other's arm; "I only ask for justice; I only ask you to help him for my sake, when I am no longer here."

Utterson heaved an irrepressible sigh. "Well," said he, "I promise."

Nearly a year later, in the month of October, 18 — , London was startled by a crime of singular ferocity and rendered all the more notable by the high position of the victim. The details were few and startling. A maid servant living alone in a house not far from the river, had gone upstairs to bed about eleven. Although a fog rolled over the city in the small hours, the early part of the night was cloudless, and the lane, which the maid's window overlooked, was brilliantly lit by the full moon. It seems she was romantically given, for she sat down upon her box, which stood immediately under the window, and fell into a dream of musing. Never (she used to say, with streaming tears, when she narrated that experience), never had she felt more at peace with all men or thought more kindly of the world. And as she so sat she became aware of an aged beautiful gentleman with white hair, drawing near along the lane; and advancing to meet him, another and very small gentleman, to whom at first she paid less attention. When they had come within speech (which was just under the maid's eyes) the older man bowed and accosted the other with a very pretty manner of politeness. It did not seem as if the subject of his address were of great importance; indeed, from his pointing, it some times appeared as if he were only inquiring his way; but the moon shone on his face as he spoke, and the girl was pleased to watch it, it seemed to breathe such an innocent and old-world kindness of disposition, yet with something high too, as of a well-founded self-content. Presently her eye wandered to the other, and she was surprised to recognise in him a certain Mr. Hyde, who had once visited her master and for whom she had conceived a dislike. He had in his hand a heavy cane, with which he was trifling; but he answered never a word, and seemed to listen with an ill-contained impatience. And then all of a sudden he broke out in a great flame of anger, stamping with his foot, brandishing the cane, and carrying on (as the maid described it) like a madman. The old gentleman took a step back, with the air of one very much surprised and a trifle hurt; and at that Mr. Hyde broke out of all bounds and clubbed him to the earth. And next moment, with ape-like fury, he was trampling his victim under foot and hailing down a storm of blows, under which the bones were audibly shattered and the body jumped upon the roadway. At the horror of these sights and sounds, the maid fainted.

It was two o'clock when she came to herself and called for the police. The murderer was gone long ago; but there lay his victim in the middle of the lane, incredibly mangled. The stick with which the deed had been done, although it was of some rare and very tough and heavy wood, had broken in the middle under the stress of this insensate cruelty; and one splintered half had rolled in the neighbouring gutter—the other, without doubt, had been carried away by the murderer. A purse and gold watch were found upon the victim: but no cards or papers, except a sealed and stamped envelope, which he had been probably carrying to the post, and which bore the name and address of Mr. Utterson.

This was brought to the lawyer the next morning, before he was out of bed; and he had no sooner seen it and been told the circumstances, than he shot out a solemn lip. "I shall say nothing till I have seen the body," said he; "this may be very serious. Have the kindness to wait while I dress." And with the same grave countenance he hurried through his breakfast and drove to the police station, whither the body had been carried. As soon as he came into the cell, he nodded.

"Yes," said he, "I recognise him. I am sorry to say that this is Sir Danvers Carew."

"Good God, sir," exclaimed the officer, "is it possible?" And the next moment his eye lighted up with professional ambition. "This will make a deal of noise," he said. "And perhaps you can help us to the man." And he briefly narrated what the maid had seen, and showed the broken stick.

Mr. Utterson had already quailed at the name of Hyde; but when the stick was laid before him, he could doubt no longer; broken and battered as it was, he recognized it for one that he had himself presented many years before to Henry Jekyll.

"Is this Mr. Hyde a person of small stature?" he inquired.

"Particularly small and particularly wicked-looking, is what the maid calls him," said the officer.

Mr. Utterson reflected; and then, raising his head, "If you will come with me in my cab," he said, "I think I can take you to his house."

It was by this time about nine in the morning, and the first fog of the season. A great chocolate-coloured pall lowered over heaven, but the wind was continually charging and routing these embattled vapours; so that as the cab crawled from street to street, Mr. Utterson beheld a marvelous number of degrees and hues of twilight; for here it would be dark like the back-end of evening; and there would be a glow of a rich, lurid brown, like the light of some strange conflagration; and here, for a moment, the fog would be quite broken up, and a haggard shaft of daylight would glance in between the swirling wreaths. The dismal quarter of Soho seen under these changing glimpses, with its muddy ways, and slatternly passengers, and its lamps, which had never been extinguished or had been kindled afresh to combat this mournful reinvasion of darkness, seemed, in the lawyer's eyes, like a district of some city in a nightmare. The thoughts of his mind, besides, were of the gloomiest dye; and when he glanced at the companion of his drive, he was conscious of some touch of that terror of the law and the law's officers, which may at times assail the most honest.

As the cab drew up before the address indicated, the fog lifted a little and showed him a dingy street, a gin palace, a low French eating house, a shop for the retail of penny numbers and two-penny salads, many ragged children huddled in the doorways, and many women of many different nationalities passing out, key in hand, to have a morning glass; and the next moment the fog settled down again upon that part, as brown as umber, and cut him off from his blackguardly surroundings. This was the home of Henry Jekyll's favourite; of a man who was heir to a quarter of a million sterling.

An ivory-faced and silvery-haired old woman opened the door. She had an evil face, smoothed by hypocrisy, but her manners were excellent. Yes, she said, this was Mr. Hyde's, but he was not at home; he had been in that night very late, but he had gone away again in less than an hour; there was nothing strange in that; his habits were very irregular, and he was often absent; for instance, it was nearly two months since she had seen him till yesterday.

"Very well, then, we wish to see his rooms," said the lawyer; and when the woman began to declare it was impossible, "I had better tell you who this person is," he added. "This is Inspector Newcomen of Scotland Yard."

A flash of odious joy appeared upon the woman's face. "Ah!" said she, "he is in trouble! What has he done?"

Mr. Utterson and the inspector exchanged glances. "He don't seem a very popular character," observed the latter. "And now, my good woman, just let me and this gentleman have a look about us."

In the whole extent of the house, which but for the old woman remained otherwise empty, Mr. Hyde had only used a couple of rooms; but these were furnished with luxury and good taste. A closet was filled with wine; the plate was of silver, the napery elegant; a good picture hung upon the walls, a gift (as Utterson supposed) from Henry Jekyll, who was much of a connoisseur; and the carpets were of many plies and agreeable in colour. At this moment, however, the rooms bore every mark of having been recently and hurriedly ransacked; clothes lay about the floor, with their pockets inside out; lock-fast drawers stood open; and on the hearth there lay a pile of grey ashes, as though many papers had been burned. From these embers the inspector disinterred the butt end of a green cheque book, which had resisted the action of the fire; the other half of the stick was found behind the door; and as this clinched his suspicions, the officer declared himself delighted. A visit to the bank, where several thousand pounds were found to be lying to the murderer's credit, completed his gratification.

"You may depend upon it, sir," he told Mr. Utterson: "I have him in my hand. He must have lost his head, or he never would have left the stick or, above all, burned the cheque book. Why, money's life to the man. We have nothing to do but wait for him at the bank, and get out the handbills."

This last, however, was not so easy of accomplishment; for Mr. Hyde had numbered few familiars — even the master of the servant maid had only seen him twice; his family could nowhere be traced; he had never been photographed; and the few who could describe him differed widely, as common observers will. Only on one point were they agreed; and that was the haunting sense of unexpressed deformity with which the fugitive impressed his beholders.

It was late in the afternoon, when Mr. Utterson found his way to Dr. Jekyll's door, where he was at once admitted by Poole, and carried down by the kitchen offices and across a yard which had once been a garden, to the building which was indifferently known as the laboratory or dissecting rooms. The doctor had bought the house from the heirs of a celebrated surgeon; and his own tastes being rather chemical than anatomical, had changed the destination of the block at the bottom of the garden. It was the first time that the lawyer had been received in that part of his friend's quarters; and he eyed the dingy, windowless structure with curiosity, and gazed round with a distasteful sense of strangeness as he crossed the theatre, once crowded with eager students and now lying gaunt and silent, the tables laden with chemical apparatus, the floor strewn with crates and littered with packing straw, and the light falling dimly through the foggy cupola. At the further end, a flight of stairs mounted to a door covered with red baize; and through this, Mr. Utterson was at last received into the doctor's cabinet. It was a large room fitted round with glass presses, furnished, among other things, with a cheval-glass and a business table, and looking out upon the court by three dusty windows barred with iron. The fire burned in the grate; a lamp was set lighted on the chimney shelf, for even in the houses the fog began to lie thickly; and there, close up to the warmth, sat Dr. Jekyll, looking deathly sick. He did not rise to meet his visitor, but held out a cold hand and bade him welcome in a changed voice.

"And now," said Mr. Utterson, as soon as Poole had left them, "you have heard the news?"

The doctor shuddered. "They were crying it in the square," he said. "I heard them in my dining-room."

"One word," said the lawyer. "Carew was my client, but so are you, and I want to know what I am doing. You have not been mad enough to hide this fellow?"

"Utterson, I swear to God," cried the doctor, "I swear to God I will never set eyes on him again. I bind my honour to you that I am done with him in this world. It is all at an end. And indeed he does not want my help; you do not know him as I do; he is safe, he is quite safe; mark my words, he will never more be heard of."

The lawyer listened gloomily; he did not like his friend's feverish manner. "You seem pretty sure of him," said he; "and for your sake, I hope you may be right. If it came to a trial, your name might appear."

"I am quite sure of him," replied Jekyll; "I have grounds for certainty that I cannot share with any one. But there is one thing on which you may advise me. I have — I have received a letter; and I am at a loss whether I should show it to the police. I should like to leave it in your hands, Utterson; you would judge wisely, I am sure; I have so great a trust in you."

"You fear, I suppose, that it might lead to his detection?" asked the lawyer.

"No," said the other. "I cannot say that I care what becomes of Hyde; I am quite done with him. I was thinking of my own character, which this hateful business has rather exposed."

Utterson ruminated awhile; he was surprised at his friend's selfishness, and yet relieved by it. "Well," said he, at last, "let me see the letter."

The letter was written in an odd, upright hand and signed "Edward Hyde": and it signified, briefly enough, that the writer's benefactor, Dr. Jekyll, whom he had long so unworthily repaid for a thousand generosities, need labour under no alarm for his safety, as he had means of escape on which he placed a sure dependence. The lawyer liked this letter well enough; it put a better colour on the intimacy than he had looked for; and he blamed himself for some of his past suspicions.

"Have you the envelope?" he asked. "I burned it," replied Jekyll, "before I thought what I was about. But it bore no postmark. The note was handed in."

"Shall I keep this and sleep upon it?" asked Utterson.

"I wish you to judge for me entirely," was the reply. "I have lost confidence in myself."

"Well, I shall consider," returned the lawyer. "And now one word more: it was Hyde who dictated the terms in your will about that disappearance?"

The doctor seemed seized with a qualm of faintness; he shut his mouth tight and nodded.

"I knew it," said Utterson. "He meant to murder you. You had a fine escape."

"I have had what is far more to the purpose," returned the doctor solemnly: "I have had a lesson—O God, Utterson, what a lesson I have had!" And he covered his face for a moment with his hands.

On his way out, the lawyer stopped and had a word or two with Poole. "By the by," said he, "there was a letter handed in today: what was the messenger like?" But Poole was positive nothing had come except by post; "and only circulars by that," he added.

This news sent off the visitor with his fears renewed. Plainly the letter had come by the laboratory door; possibly, indeed, it had been written in the cabinet; and if that were so, it must be differently judged, and handled with the more caution. The newsboys, as he went, were crying themselves hoarse along the footways: "Special edition. Shocking murder of an M.P." That was the funeral oration of one friend and client; and he could not help a certain apprehension lest the good name of another should be sucked down in the eddy of the scandal. It was, at least, a ticklish decision that he had to make; and self-reliant as he was by habit, he began to cherish a longing for advice. It was not to be had directly; but perhaps, he thought, it might be fished for.

Presently after, he sat on one side of his own hearth, with Mr. Guest, his head clerk, upon the other, and midway between, at a nicely calculated distance from the fire, a bottle of a particular old wine that had long dwelt unsunned in the foundations of his house. The fog still slept on the wing above the drowned city, where the lamps glimmered like carbuncles; and through the muffle and smother of these fallen clouds, the procession of the town's life was still rolling in through the great arteries with a sound as of a mighty wind. But the room was gay with firelight. In the bottle the acids were long ago resolved; the imperial dye had softened with time, as the colour grows richer in stained windows; and the glow of hot autumn afternoons on hillside vineyards, was ready to be set free and to disperse the fogs of London. Insensibly the lawyer melted. There was no man from whom he kept fewer secrets than Mr. Guest; and he was not always sure that he kept as many as he meant. Guest had often been on business to the doctor's; he knew Poole; he could scarce have failed to hear of Mr. Hyde's familiarity about the house; he might draw conclusions: was it not as well, then, that he should see a letter which put that mystery to right? and above all since Guest, being a great student and critic of handwriting, would consider the step natural and obliging? The clerk, besides, was a man of counsel; he could scarce read so strange a document without dropping a remark; and by that remark Mr. Utterson might shape his future course.

"This is a sad business about Sir Danvers," he said.

"Yes, sir, indeed. It has elicited a great deal of public feeling," returned Guest. "The man, of course, was mad."

"I should like to hear your views on that," replied Utterson. "I have a document here in his handwriting; it is between ourselves, for I scarce know what to do about it; it is an ugly business at the best. But there it is; quite in your way: a murderer's autograph."

Guest's eyes brightened, and he sat down at once and studied it with passion. "No sir," he said: "not mad; but it is an odd hand."

"And by all accounts a very odd writer," added the lawyer.

Just then the servant entered with a note.

"Is that from Dr. Jekyll, sir?" inquired the clerk. "I thought I knew the writing. Anything private, Mr. Utterson?"

"Only an invitation to dinner. Why? Do you want to see it?"

"One moment. I thank you, sir;" and the clerk laid the two sheets of paper alongside and sedulously compared their contents. "Thank you, sir," he said at last, returning both; "it's a very interesting autograph."

There was a pause, during which Mr. Utterson struggled with himself. "Why did you compare them, Guest?" he inquired suddenly.

"Well, sir," returned the clerk, "there's a rather singular resemblance; the two hands are in many points identical: only differently sloped."

"Rather quaint," said Utterson.

"It is, as you say, rather quaint," returned Guest.

"I wouldn't speak of this note, you know," said the master.

"No, sir," said the clerk. "I understand."

But no sooner was Mr. Utterson alone that night, than he locked the note into his safe, where it reposed from that time forward. "What!" he thought. "Henry Jekyll forge for a murderer!" And his blood ran cold in his veins.

Time ran on; thousands of pounds were offered in reward, for the death of Sir Danvers was resented as a public injury; but Mr. Hyde had disappeared out of the ken of the police as though he had never existed. Much of his past was unearthed, indeed, and all disreputable: tales came out of the man's cruelty, at once so callous and violent; of his vile life, of his strange associates, of the hatred that seemed to have surrounded his career; but of his present whereabouts, not a whisper. From the time he had left the house in Soho on the morning of the murder, he was simply blotted out; and gradually, as time drew on, Mr. Utterson began to recover from the hotness of his alarm, and to grow more at quiet with himself. The death of Sir Danvers was, to his way of thinking, more than paid for by the disappearance of Mr. Hyde. Now that that evil influence had been withdrawn, a new life began for Dr. Jekyll. He came out of his seclusion, renewed relations with his friends, became once more their familiar guest and entertainer; and whilst he had always been known for charities, he was now no less distinguished for religion. He was busy, he was much in the open air, he did good; his face seemed to open and brighten, as if with an inward con-sciousness of service; and for more than two months, the doctor was at peace.

On the 8th of January Utterson had dined at the doctor's with a small party; Lanyon had been there; and the face of the host had looked from one to the other as in the old days when the trio were inseparable friends. On the 12th, and again on the 14th, the door was shut against the lawyer. "The doctor was confined to the house," Poole said, "and saw no one." On the 15th, he tried again, and was again refused; and having now been used for the last two months to see his friend almost daily, he found this return of solitude to weigh upon his spirits. The fifth night he had in Guest to dine with him; and the sixth he betook himself to Dr. Lanyon's.

There at least he was not denied admittance; but when he came in, he was shocked at the change which had taken place in the doctor's appearance. He had his death-warrant written legibly upon his face. The rosy man had grown pale; his flesh had fallen away; he was visibly balder and older; and yet it was not so much these tokens of a swift physical decay that arrested the lawyer's notice, as a look in the eye and quality of manner that seemed to testify to some deep-seated terror of the mind. It was unlikely that the doctor should fear death; and yet that was what Utterson was tempted to suspect. "Yes," he thought; "he is a doctor, he must know his own state and that his days are counted; and the knowledge is more than he can bear." And yet when Utterson remarked on his ill-looks, it was with an air of great firmness that Lanyon declared himself a doomed man.

"I have had a shock," he said, "and I shall never recover. It is a question of weeks. Well, life has been pleasant; I liked it; yes, sir, I used to like it. I sometimes think if we knew all, we should be more glad to get away."

"Jekyll is ill, too," observed Utterson. "Have you seen him?"

But Lanyon's face changed, and he held up a trembling hand. "I wish to see or hear no more of Dr. Jekyll," he said in a loud, unsteady voice. "I am quite done with that person; and I beg that you will spare me any allusion to one whom I regard as dead."

"Tut-tut," said Mr. Utterson; and then after a considerable pause, "Can't I do anything?" he inquired. "We are three very old friends, Lanyon; we shall not live to make others."

"Nothing can be done," returned Lanyon; "ask himself."

"He will not see me," said the lawyer.

"I am not surprised at that," was the reply. "Some day, Utterson, after I am dead, you may perhaps come to learn the right and wrong of this. I cannot tell you. And in the meantime, if you can sit and talk with me of other things, for God's sake, stay and do so; but if you cannot keep clear of this accursed topic, then in God's name, go, for I cannot bear it."

As soon as he got home, Utterson sat down and wrote to Jekyll, complaining of his exclusion from the house, and asking the cause of this unhappy break with Lanyon; and the next day brought him a long answer, often very pathetically worded, and sometimes darkly mysterious in drift. The quarrel with Lanyon was incurable. "I do not blame our old friend," Jekyll wrote, but I share his view that we must never meet. I mean from henceforth to lead a life of extreme seclusion; you must not be surprised, nor must you doubt my friendship, if my door is often shut even to you. You must suffer me to go my own dark way. I have brought on myself a punishment and a danger that I cannot name. If I am the chief of sinners, I am the chief of sufferers also. I could not think that this earth contained a place for sufferings and terrors so unmanning; and you can do but one thing, Utterson, to lighten this destiny, and that is to respect my silence." Utterson was amazed; the dark influence of Hyde had been withdrawn, the doctor had returned to his old tasks and amities; a week ago, the prospect had smiled with every promise of a cheerful and an honoured age; and now in a moment, friendship, and peace of mind, and the whole tenor of his life were wrecked. So great and unprepared a change pointed to madness; but in view of Lanyon's manner and words, there must lie for it some deeper ground.

A week afterwards Dr. Lanyon took to his bed, and in something less than a fortnight he was dead. The night after the funeral, at which he had been sadly affected, Utterson locked the door of his business room, and sitting there by the light of a melancholy candle, drew out and set before him an envelope addressed by the hand and sealed with the seal of his dead friend. "PRIVATE: for the hands of G. J. Utterson ALONE, and in case of his predecease *to be destroyed unread,*" so it was emphatically superscribed; and the lawyer dreaded to behold the contents. "I have buried one friend to-day," he thought: "what if this should cost me another?" And then he condemned the fear as a disloyalty, and broke the seal. Within there was another enclosure, likewise sealed, and marked upon the cover as "not to be opened till the death or disappearance of Dr. Henry Jekyll." Utterson could not trust his eyes. Yes, it was disappearance; here again, as in the mad will which he had long ago restored to its author, here again were the idea of a disappearance and the name of Henry Jekyll bracketted. But in the will, that idea had sprung from the sinister suggestion of the man Hyde; it was set there with a purpose all too plain and horrible. Written by the hand of Lanyon, what should it mean? A great curiosity came on the trustee, to disregard the prohibition and dive at once to the bottom of these mysteries; but professional honour and faith to his dead friend were stringent obligations; and the packet slept in the inmost corner of his private safe.

It is one thing to mortify curiosity, another to conquer it; and it may be doubted if, from that day forth, Utterson desired the society of his surviving friend with the same eagerness. He thought of him kindly; but his thoughts were disquieted and fearful. He went to call indeed; but he was perhaps relieved to be denied admittance; perhaps, in his heart, he preferred to speak with Poole upon the doorstep and surrounded by the air and sounds of the open city, rather than to be admitted into that house of voluntary bondage, and to sit and speak with its inscrutable recluse. Poole had, indeed, no very pleasant news to communicate. The doctor, it appeared, now more than ever confined himself to the cabinet over the laboratory, where he would sometimes even sleep; he was out of spirits, he had grown very silent, he did not read; it seemed as if he had something on his mind. Utterson became so used to the unvarying character of these reports, that he fell off little by little in the frequency of his visits.

It chanced on Sunday, when Mr. Utterson was on his usual walk with Mr. Enfield, that their way lay once again through the by-street; and that when they came in front of the door, both stopped to gaze on it.

"Well," said Enfield, "that story's at an end at least. We shall never see more of Mr. Hyde."

"I hope not," said Utterson. "Did I ever tell you that I once saw him, and shared your feeling of repulsion?"

"It was impossible to do the one without the other," returned Enfield. "And by the way, what an ass you must have thought me, not to know that this was a back way to Dr. Jekyll's! It was partly your own fault that I found it out, even when I did."

"So you found it out, did you?" said Utterson. "But if that be so, we may step into the court and take a look at the windows. To tell you the truth, I am uneasy about poor Jekyll; and even outside, I feel as if the presence of a friend might do him good."

The court was very cool and a little damp, and full of premature twilight, although the sky, high up overhead, was still bright with sunset. The middle one of the three windows was half-way open; and sitting close beside it, taking the air with an infinite sadness of mien, like some disconsolate prisoner, Utterson saw Dr. Jekyll.

"What! Jekyll!" he cried. "I trust you are better."

"I am very low, Utterson," replied the doctor drearily, "very low. It will not last long, thank God."

"You stay too much indoors," said the lawyer. "You should be out, whipping up the circulation like Mr. Enfield and me. (This is my cousin — Mr. Enfield — Dr. Jekyll.) Come now; get your hat and take a quick turn with us."

"You are very good," sighed the other. "I should like to very much; but no, no, no, it is quite impossible; I dare not. But indeed, Utterson, I am very glad to see you; this is really a great pleasure; I would ask you and Mr. Enfield up, but the place is really not fit."

"Why, then," said the lawyer, good-naturedly, "the best thing we can do is to stay down here and speak with you from where we are."

"That is just what I was about to venture to propose," returned the doctor with a smile. But the words were hardly uttered, before the smile was struck out of his face and succeeded by an expression of such abject terror and despair, as froze the very blood of the two gentlemen below. They saw it but for a glimpse for the window was instantly thrust down; but that glimpse had been sufficient, and they turned and left the court without a word. In silence, too, they traversed the by-street; and it was not until they had come into a neighbouring thoroughfare, where even upon a Sunday there were still some stirrings of life, that Mr. Utterson at last turned and looked at his companion. They were both pale; and there was an answering horror in their eyes.

"God forgive us, God forgive us," said Mr. Utterson.

But Mr. Enfield only nodded his head very seriously, and walked on once more in silence.

Mr. Utterson was sitting by his fireside one evening after dinner, when he was surprised to receive a visit from Poole.

"Bless me, Poole, what brings you here?" he cried; and then taking a second look at him, "What ails you?" he added, "is the doctor ill?"

"Mr. Utterson," said the man, "there is something wrong."

"Take a seat, and here is a glass of wine for you," said the lawyer. "Now, take your time, and tell me plainly what you want."

"You know the doctor's ways, sir," replied Poole, "and how he shuts himself up. Well, he's shut up again in the cabinet; and I don't like it, sir — I wish I may die if I like it. Mr. Utterson, sir, I'm afraid."

"Now, my good man," said the lawyer, "be explicit. What are you afraid of?"

"I've been afraid for about a week," returned Poole, doggedly disregarding the question, "and I can bear it no more."

The man's appearance amply bore out his words; his manner was altered for the worse; and except for the moment when he had first announced his terror, he had not once looked the lawyer in the face. Even now, he sat with the glass of wine untasted on his knee, and his eyes directed to a corner of the floor. "I can bear it no more," he repeated.

"Come," said the lawyer, "I see you have some good reason, Poole; I see there is something seriously amiss. Try to tell me what it is."

"I think there's been foul play," said Poole, hoarsely.

"Foul play!" cried the lawyer, a good deal frightened and rather inclined to be irritated in consequence. "What foul play! What does the man mean?"

"I daren't say, sir," was the answer; "but will you come along with me and see for yourself?"

Mr. Utterson's only answer was to rise and get his hat and greatcoat; but he observed with wonder the greatness of the relief that appeared upon the butler's face, and perhaps with no less, that the wine was still untasted when he set it down to follow.

It was a wild, cold, seasonable night of March, with a pale moon, lying on her back as though the wind had tilted her, and flying wrack of the most diaphanous and lawny texture. The wind made talking difficult, and flecked the blood into the face. It seemed to have swept the streets unusually bare of passengers, besides; for Mr. Utterson thought he had never seen that part of London so deserted. He could have wished it otherwise; never in his life had he been conscious of so sharp a wish to see and touch his fellow-creatures; for struggle as he might, there was borne in upon his mind a crushing anticipation of calamity. The square, when they got there, was full of wind and dust, and the thin trees in the garden were lashing themselves along the railing. Poole, who had kept all the way a pace or two ahead, now pulled up in the middle of the pavement, and in spite of the biting weather, took off his hat and mopped his brow with a red pocket-handkerchief. But for all the hurry of his coming, these were not the dews of exertion that he wiped away, but the moisture of some strangling anguish; for his face was white and his voice, when he spoke, harsh and broken.

"Well, sir," he said, "here we are, and God grant there be nothing wrong."

"Amen, Poole," said the lawyer.

Thereupon the servant knocked in a very guarded manner; the door was opened on the chain; and a voice asked from within, "Is that you, Poole?"

"It's all right," said Poole. "Open the door."

The hall, when they entered it, was brightly lighted up; the fire was built high; and about the hearth the whole of the servants, men and women, stood huddled together like a flock of sheep. At the sight of Mr. Utterson, the housemaid broke into hysterical whim-pering; and the cook, crying out "Bless God! it's Mr. Utterson," ran forward as if to take him in her arms.

"What, what? Are you all here?" said the lawyer peevishly. "Very irregular, very unseemly; your master would be far from pleased."

"They're all afraid," said Poole.

Blank silence followed, no one protesting; only the maid lifted her voice and now wept loudly.

"Hold your tongue!" Poole said to her, with a ferocity of accent that testified to his own jangled nerves; and indeed, when the girl had so suddenly raised the note of her lamentation, they had all started and turned towards the inner door with faces of dreadful expectation. "And now," continued the butler, addressing the knife-boy, "reach me a candle, and we'll get this through hands at once." And then he begged Mr. Utterson to follow him, and led the way to the back garden.

"Now, sir," said he, "you come as gently as you can. I want you to hear, and I don't want you to be heard. And see here, sir, if by any chance he was to ask you in, don't go."

Mr. Utterson's nerves, at this unlooked-for termination, gave a jerk that nearly threw him from his balance; but he recollected his courage and followed the butler into the laboratory building through the surgical theatre, with its lumber of crates and bottles, to the foot of the stair. Here Poole motioned him to stand on one side and listen; while he himself, setting down the candle and making a great and obvious call on his resolution, mounted the steps and knocked with a somewhat uncertain hand on the red baize of the cabinet door.

"Mr. Utterson, sir, asking to see you," he called; and even as he did so, once more violently signed to the lawyer to give ear.

A voice answered from within: "Tell him I cannot see anyone," it said complainingly.

"Thank you, sir," said Poole, with a note of something like triumph in his voice; and taking up his candle, he led Mr. Utterson back across the yard and into the great kitchen, where the fire was out and the beetles were leaping on the floor.

"Sir," he said, looking Mr. Utterson in the eyes, "Was that my master's voice?"

"It seems much changed," replied the lawyer, very pale, but giving look for look.

"Changed? Well, yes, I think so," said the butler. "Have I been twenty years in this man's house, to be deceived about his voice? No, sir; master's made away with; he was made away with eight days ago, when we heard him cry out upon the name of God; and who's in there instead of him, and why it stays there, is a thing that cries to Heaven, Mr. Utterson!"

"This is a very strange tale, Poole; this is rather a wild tale, my man," said Mr. Utterson, biting his finger. "Suppose it were as you suppose, supposing Dr. Jekyll to have been — well, murdered; what could induce the murderer to stay? That won't hold water; it doesn't commend itself to reason."

"Well, Mr. Utterson, you are a hard man to satisfy, but I'll do it yet," said Poole. "All this last week (you must know) him, or it, whatever it is that lives in that cabinet, has been crying night and day for some sort of medicine and cannot get it to his mind. It was sometimes his way — the master's, that is — to write his orders on a sheet of paper and throw it on the stair. We've had nothing else this week back; nothing but papers, and a closed door, and the very meals left there to be smuggled in when nobody was looking. Well, sir, every day, ay, and twice and thrice in the same day, there have been orders and complaints, and I have been sent flying to all the wholesale chemists in town. Every time I brought the stuff back, there would be another paper telling me to return it, because it was not pure, and another order to a different firm. This drug is wanted bitter bad, sir, whatever for."

"Have you any of these papers?" asked Mr. Utterson.

Poole felt in his pocket and handed out a crumpled note, which the lawyer, bending nearer to the candle, carefully examined. Its contents ran thus: "Dr. Jekyll presents his compliments to Messrs. Maw. He assures them that their last sample is impure and quite useless for his present purpose. In the year 18—, Dr. J. purchased a somewhat large quantity from Messrs. M. He now begs them to search with most sedulous care, and should any of the same quality be left, forward it to him at once. Expense is no consideration. The importance of this to Dr. J. can hardly be exaggerated." So far the letter had run composedly enough, but here with a sudden splutter of the pen, the writer's emotion had broken loose. "For God's sake," he added, "find me some of the old."

"This is a strange note," said Mr. Utterson; and then sharply, "How do you come to have it open?"

"The man at Maw's was main angry, sir, and he threw it back to me like so much dirt," returned Poole.

"This is unquestionably the doctor's hand, do you know?" resumed the lawyer.

"I thought it looked like it," said the servant rather sulkily; and then, with another voice, "But what matters hand of write?" he said. "I've seen him!"

"Seen him?" repeated Mr. Utterson. "Well?"

"That's it!" said Poole. "It was this way. I came suddenly into the theater from the garden. It seems he had slipped out to look for this drug or whatever it is; for the cabinet door was open, and there he was at the far end of the room digging among the crates. He looked up when I came in, gave a kind of cry, and whipped upstairs into the cabinet. It was but for one minute that I saw him, but the hair stood upon my head like quills. Sir, if that was my master, why had he a mask upon his face? If it was my master, why did he cry out like a rat, and run from me? I have served him long enough. And then . . ." The man paused and passed his hand over his face.

"These are all very strange circumstances," said Mr. Utterson, "but I think I begin to see daylight. Your master, Poole, is plainly seized with one of those maladies that both torture and deform the sufferer; hence, for aught I know, the alteration of his voice; hence the mask and the avoidance of his friends; hence his eagerness to find this drug, by means of which the poor soul retains some hope of ultimate recovery—God grant that he be not deceived! There is my explanation; it is sad enough, Poole, ay, and appalling to consider; but it is plain and natural, hangs well together, and delivers us from all exorbitant alarms."

"Sir," said the butler, turning to a sort of mottled pallor, "that thing was not my master, and there's the truth. My master"—here he looked round him and began to whisper—"is a tall, fine build of a man, and this was more of a dwarf." Utterson attempted to protest. "O, sir," cried Poole, "do you think I do not know my master after twenty years? Do you think I do not know where his head comes to in the cabinet door, where I saw him every morning of my life? No, sir, that thing in the mask was never Dr. Jekyll — God knows what it was, but it was never Dr. Jekyll; and it is the belief of my heart that there was murder done."

"Poole," replied the lawyer, "if you say that, it will become my duty to make certain. Much as I desire to spare your master's feelings, much as I am puzzled by this note which seems to prove him to be still alive, I shall consider it my duty to break in that door."

"Ah, Mr. Utterson, that's talking!" cried the butler.

"And now comes the second question," resumed Utterson: "Who is going to do it?"

"Why, you and me, sir," was the undaunted reply.

"That's very well said," returned the lawyer; "and whatever comes of it, I shall make it my business to see you are no loser."

"There is an axe in the theatre," continued Poole; "and you might take the kitchen poker for yourself."

The lawyer took that rude but weighty instrument into his hand, and balanced it. "Do you know, Poole," he said, looking up, "that you and I are about to place ourselves in a position of some peril?"

"You may say so, sir, indeed," returned the butler.

"It is well, then that we should be frank," said the other. "We both think more than we have said; let us make a clean breast. This masked figure that you saw, did you recognise it?"

"Well, sir, it went so quick, and the creature was so doubled up, that I could hardly swear to that," was the answer. "But if you mean, was it Mr. Hyde? — why, yes, I think it was! You see, it was much of the same bigness; and it had the same quick, light way with it; and then who else could have got in by the laboratory door? You have not forgot, sir, that at the time of the murder he had still the key with him? But that's not all. I don't know, Mr. Utterson, if you ever met this Mr. Hyde?"

"Yes," said the lawyer, "I once spoke with him."

"Then you must know as well as the rest of us that there was something queer about that gentleman — something that gave a man a turn — I don't know rightly how to say it, sir, beyond this: that you felt in your marrow kind of cold and thin."

"I own I felt something of what you describe," said Mr. Utterson.

"Quite so, sir," returned Poole. "Well, when that masked thing like a monkey jumped from among the chemicals and whipped into the cabinet, it went down my spine like ice. O, I know it's not evidence, Mr. Utterson; I'm book-learned enough for that; but a man has his feelings, and I give you my bible-word it was Mr. Hyde!"

"Ay, ay," said the lawyer. "My fears incline to the same point. Evil, I fear, founded — evil was sure to come — of that connection. Ay truly, I believe you; I believe poor Harry is killed; and I believe his murderer (for what purpose, God alone can tell) is still lurking in his victim's room. Well, let our name be vengeance. Call Bradshaw."

The footman came at the summons, very white and nervous.

"Put yourself together, Bradshaw," said the lawyer. "This suspense, I know, is telling upon all of you; but it is now our intention to make an end of it. Poole, here, and I are going to force our way into the cabinet. If all is well, my shoulders are broad enough to bear the blame. Meanwhile, lest anything should really be amiss, or any malefactor seek to escape by the back, you and the boy must go round the corner with a pair of good sticks and take your post at the laboratory door. We give you ten minutes, to get to your stations."

As Bradshaw left, the lawyer looked at his watch. "And now, Poole, let us get to ours," he said; and taking the poker under his arm, led the way into the yard. The scud had banked over the moon, and it was now quite dark. The wind, which only broke in puffs and draughts into that deep well of building, tossed the light of the candle to and fro about their steps, until they came into the shelter of the theatre, where they sat down silently to wait. London hummed solemnly all around; but nearer at hand, the stillness was only broken by the sounds of a footfall moving to and fro along the cabinet floor.

"So it will walk all day, sir," whispered Poole, "ay, and the better part of the night. Only when a new sample comes from the chemist, there's a bit of a break. Ah, it's an ill conscience that's such an enemy to rest! Ah, sir, there's blood foully shed in every step of it! But hark again, a little closer — put your heart in your ears, Mr. Utterson, and tell me, is that the doctor's foot?"

The steps fell lightly and oddly, with a certain swing, for all they went so slowly; it was different indeed from the heavy creaking tread of Henry Jekyll. Utterson sighed. "Is there never anything else?" he asked.

Poole nodded. "Once," he said. "Once I heard it weeping!"

"Weeping? how that?" said the lawyer, conscious of a sudden chill of horror.

"Weeping like a woman or a lost soul," said the butler. "I came away with that upon my heart, that I could have wept too."

But now the ten minutes drew to an end. Poole disinterred the axe from under a stack of packing straw; the candle was set upon the nearest table to light them to the attack; and they drew near with bated breath to where that patient foot was still going up and down, up and down, in the quiet of the night. "Jekyll," cried Utterson, with a loud voice, "I demand to see you." He paused a moment, but there came no reply. "I give you fair warning, our suspicions are aroused, and I must and shall see you," he resumed; "if not by fair means, then by foul—if not of your consent, then by brute force!"

"Utterson," said the voice, "for God's sake, have mercy!"

"Ah, that's not Jekyll's voice—it's Hyde's!" cried Utterson. "Down with the door, Poole!"

Poole swung the axe over his shoulder; the blow shook the building, and the red baize door leaped against the lock and hinges. A dismal screech, as of mere animal terror, rang from the cabinet. Up went the axe again, and again the panels crashed and the frame bounded; four times the blow fell; but the wood was tough and the fittings were of excellent workmanship; and it was not until the fifth, that the lock burst and the wreck of the door fell inwards on the carpet.

The besiegers, appalled by their own riot and the stillness that had succeeded, stood back a little and peered in. There lay the cabinet before their eyes in the quiet lamplight, a good fire glowing and chattering on the hearth, the kettle singing its thin strain, a drawer or two open, papers neatly set forth on the business table, and nearer the fire, the things laid out for tea; the quietest room, you would have said, and, but for the glazed presses full of chemicals, the most commonplace that night in London.

Right in the middle there lay the body of a man sorely contorted and still twitching. They drew near on tiptoe, turned it on its back and beheld the face of Edward Hyde. He was dressed in clothes far too large for him, clothes of the doctor's bigness; the cords of his face still moved with a semblance of life, but life was quite gone: and by the crushed phial in the hand and the strong smell of kernels that hung upon the air, Utterson knew that he was looking on the body of a self-destroyer.

"We have come too late," he said sternly, "whether to save or punish. Hyde is gone to his account; and it only remains for us to find the body of your master."

The far greater proportion of the building was occupied by the theatre, which filled almost the whole ground storey and was lighted from above, and by the cabinet, which formed an upper story at one end and looked upon the court. A corridor joined the theatre to the door on the by-street; and with this the cabinet communicated separately by a second flight of stairs. There were besides a few dark closets and a spacious cellar. All these they now thoroughly examined. Each closet needed but a glance, for all were empty, and all, by the dust that fell from their doors, had stood long unopened. The cellar, indeed, was filled with crazy lumber, mostly dating from the times of the surgeon who was Jekyll's predecessor; but even as they opened the door they were advertised of the uselessness of further search, by the fall of a perfect mat of cobweb which had for years sealed up the entrance. Nowhere was there any trace of Henry Jekyll dead or alive.

Poole stamped on the flags of the corridor. "He must be buried here," he said, hearkening to the sound.

"Or he may have fled," said Utterson, and he turned to examine the door in the by-street. It was locked; and lying near by on the flags, they found the key, already stained with rust.

"This does not look like use," observed the lawyer.

"Use!" echoed Poole. "Do you not see, sir, it is broken? much as if a man had stamped on it."

"Ay," continued Utterson, "and the fractures, too, are rusty." The two men looked at each other with a scare. "This is beyond me, Poole," said the lawyer. "Let us go back to the cabinet."

They mounted the stair in silence, and still with an occasional awestruck glance at the dead body, proceeded more thoroughly to examine the contents of the cabinet. At one table, there were traces of chemical work, various measured heaps of some white salt being laid on glass saucers, as though for an experiment in which the unhappy man had been prevented.

"That is the same drug that I was always bringing him," said Poole; and even as he spoke, the kettle with a startling noise boiled over.

This brought them to the fireside, where the easy-chair was drawn cosily up, and the tea things stood ready to the sitter's elbow, the very sugar in the cup. There were several books on a shelf; one lay beside the tea things open, and Utterson was amazed to find it a copy of a pious work, for which Jekyll had several times expressed a great esteem, annotated, in his own hand with startling blasphemies.

Next, in the course of their review of the chamber, the searchers came to the cheval-glass, into whose depths they looked with an involuntary horror. But it was so turned as to show them nothing but the rosy glow playing on the roof, the fire sparkling in a hundred repetitions along the glazed front of the presses, and their own pale and fearful countenances stooping to look in.

"This glass has seen some strange things, sir," whispered Poole.

"And surely none stranger than itself," echoed the lawyer in the same tones. "For what did Jekyll" — he caught himself up at the word with a start, and then conquering the weakness — "what could Jekyll want with it?" he said. "You may say that!" said Poole.

Next they turned to the business table. On the desk, among the neat array of papers, a large envelope was uppermost, and bore, in the doctor's hand, the name of Mr. Utterson. The lawyer unsealed it, and several enclosures fell to the floor. The first was a will, drawn in the same eccentric terms as the one which he had returned six months before, to serve as a testament in case of death and as a deed of gift in case of disappearance; but in place of the name of Edward Hyde, the lawyer, with indescribable amazement read the name of Gabriel John Utterson. He looked at Poole, and then back at the paper, and last of all at the dead malefactor stretched upon the carpet.

"My head goes round," he said. "He has been all these days in possession; he had no cause to like me; he must have raged to see himself displaced; and he has not destroyed this document."

He caught up the next paper; it was a brief note in the doctor's hand and dated at the top. "O Poole!" the lawyer cried, "he was alive and here this day. He cannot have been disposed of in so short a space; he must be still alive, he must have fled! And then, why fled? and how? and in that case, can we venture to declare this suicide? O, we must be careful. I foresee that we may yet involve your master in some dire catastrophe."

"Why don't you read it, sir?" asked Poole.

"Because I fear," replied the lawyer solemnly. "God grant I have no cause for it!" And with that he brought the paper to his eyes and read as follows:

"My dear Utterson, — When this shall fall into your hands, I shall have disappeared, under what circumstances I have not the penetration to foresee, but my instinct and all the circumstances of my nameless situation tell me that the end is sure and must be early. Go then, and first read the narrative which Lanyon warned me he was to place in your hands; and if you care to hear more, turn to the confession of

"Your unworthy and unhappy friend,

"Henry Jekyll."

"There was a third enclosure?" asked Utterson.

"Here, sir," said Poole, and gave into his hands a considerable packet sealed in several places.

The lawyer put it in his pocket. "I would say nothing of this paper. If your master has fled or is dead, we may at least save his credit. It is now ten; I must go home and read these documents in quiet; but I shall be back before midnight, when we shall send for the police."

They went out, locking the door of the theatre behind them; and Utterson, once more leaving the servants gathered about the fire in the hall, trudged back to his office to read the two narratives in which this mystery was now to be explained.

Lanyon's Narrative

On the ninth of January, now four days ago, I received by the evening delivery a registered envelope, addressed in the hand of my colleague and old school companion, Henry Jekyll. I was a good deal surprised by this; for we were by no means in the habit of correspondence; I had seen the man, dined with him, indeed, the night before; and I could imagine nothing in our intercourse that should justify formality of registration. The contents increased my wonder; for this is how the letter ran:

"10th December, 18 — .

"Dear Lanyon, — You are one of my oldest friends; and although we may have differed at times on scientific questions, I cannot remember, at least on my side, any break in our affection. There was never a day when, if you had said to me, 'Jekyll, my life, my honour, my reason, depend upon you,' I would not have sacrificed my left hand to help you. Lanyon, my life, my honour, my reason, are all at your mercy; if you fail me to-night, I am lost. You might suppose, after this preface, that I am going to ask you for something dishonourable to grant. Judge for yourself.

"I want you to postpone all other engagements for to-night — ay, even if you were summoned to the bedside of an emperor; to take a cab, unless your carriage should be actually at the door; and with this letter in your hand for consultation, to drive straight to my house. Poole, my butler, has his orders; you will find him waiting your arrival with a locksmith. The door of my cabinet is then to be forced: and you are to go in alone; to open the glazed press (letter E) on the left hand, breaking the lock if it be shut; and to draw out, with all its contents as they stand, the fourth drawer from the top or (which is the same thing) the third from the bottom. In my extreme distress of mind, I have a morbid fear of misdirecting you; but even if I am in error, you may know the right drawer by its contents: some powders, a phial and a paper book. This drawer I beg of you to carry back with you to Cavendish Square exactly as it stands.

"That is the first part of the service: now for the second. You should be back, if you set out at once on the receipt of this, long before midnight; but I will leave you that amount of margin, not only in the fear of one of those obstacles that can neither be prevented nor foreseen, but because an hour when your servants are in bed is to be preferred for what will then remain to do. At midnight, then, I have to ask you to be alone in your consulting room, to admit with your own hand into the house a man who will present himself in my name, and to place in his hands the drawer that you will have brought with you from my cabinet. Then you will have played your part and earned my gratitude completely. Five minutes afterwards, if you insist upon an explanation, you will have understood that these arrangements are of capital importance; and that by the neglect of one of them, fantastic as they must appear, you might have charged your conscience with my death or the shipwreck of my reason.

"Confident as I am that you will not trifle with this appeal, my heart sinks and my hand trembles at the bare thought of such a possibility. Think of me at this hour, in a strange place, labouring under a blackness of distress that no fancy can exaggerate, and yet well aware that, if you will but punctually serve me, my troubles will roll away like a story that is told. Serve me, my dear Lanyon and save

"Your friend,
"H.J.

"P.S. — I had already sealed this up when a fresh terror struck upon my soul. It is possible that the post-office may fail me, and this letter not come into your hands until to-morrow morning. In that case, dear Lanyon, do my errand when it shall be most convenient for you in the course of the day; and once more expect my messenger at midnight. It may then already be too late; and if that night passes without event, you will know that you have seen the last of Henry Jekyll."

Upon the reading of this letter, I made sure my colleague was insane; but till that was proved beyond the possibility of doubt, I felt bound to do as he requested. The less I understood of this farrago, the less I was in a position to judge of its importance; and an appeal so worded could not be set aside without a grave responsibility. I rose accordingly from table, got into a hansom, and drove straight to Jekyll's house. The butler was awaiting my arrival; he had received by the same post as mine a registered letter of instruction, and had sent at once for a locksmith and a carpenter. The tradesmen came while we were yet speaking; and we moved in a body to old Dr. Denman's surgical theatre, from which (as you are doubtless aware) Jekyll's private cabinet is most conveniently entered. The door was very strong, the lock excellent; the carpenter avowed he would have great trouble and have to do much damage, if force were to be used; and the locksmith was near despair. But this last was a handy fellow, and after two hour's work, the door stood open. The press marked E was unlocked; and I took out the drawer, had it filled up with straw and tied in a sheet, and returned with it to Cavendish Square.

Here I proceeded to examine its contents. The powders were neatly enough made up, but not with the nicety of the dispensing chemist; so that it was plain they were of Jekyll's private manufacture: and when I opened one of the wrappers I found what seemed to me a simple crystalline salt of a white colour. The phial, to which I next turned my attention, might have been about half full of a blood-red liquor, which was highly pungent to the sense of smell and seemed to me to contain phosphorus and some volatile ether. At the other ingredients I could make no guess. The book was an ordinary version book and contained little but a series of dates. These covered a period of many years, but I observed that the entries ceased nearly a year ago and quite abruptly. Here and there a brief remark was appended to a date, usually no more than a single word: "double" occurring perhaps six times in a total of several hundred entries; and once very early in the list and followed by several marks of exclamation, "total failure!!!" All this, though it whetted my curiosity, told me little that was definite. Here were a phial of some salt, and the record of a series of experiments that had led (like too many of Jekyll's investigations) to no end of practical usefulness. How could the presence of these articles in my house affect either the honour, the sanity, or the life of my flighty colleague? If his messenger could go to one place, why could he not go to another? And even granting some impediment, why was this gentleman to be received by me in secret? The more I reflected the more convinced I grew that I was dealing with a case of cerebral disease; and though I dismissed my servants to bed, I loaded an old revolver, that I might be found in some posture of self-defence.

Twelve o'clock had scarce rung out over London, ere the knocker sounded very gently on the door. I went myself at the summons, and found a small man crouching against the pillars of the portico.

"Are you come from Dr. Jekyll?" I asked.

He told me "yes" by a constrained gesture; and when I had bidden him enter, he did not obey me without a searching backward glance into the darkness of the square. There was a policeman not far off, advancing with his bull's eye open; and at the sight, I thought my visitor started and made greater haste.

These particulars struck me, I confess, disagreeably; and as I followed him into the bright light of the consulting room, I kept my hand ready on my weapon. Here, at last, I had a chance of clearly seeing him. I had never set eyes on him before, so much was certain. He was small, as I have said; I was struck besides with the shocking expression of his face, with his remarkable combination of great muscular activity and great apparent debility of constitution, and — last but not least — with the odd, subjective disturbance caused by his neighbourhood. This bore some resemblance to incipient rigour, and was accompanied by a marked sinking of the pulse. At the time, I set it down to some idiosyncratic, personal distaste, and merely wondered at the acuteness of the symptoms; but I have since had reason to believe the cause to lie much deeper in the nature of man, and to turn on some nobler hinge than the principle of hatred.

This person (who had thus, from the first moment of his entrance, struck in me what I can only, describe as a disgustful curiosity) was dressed in a fashion that would have made an ordinary person laughable; his clothes, that is to say, although they were of rich and sober fabric, were enormously too large for him in every measurement — the trousers hanging on his legs and rolled up to keep them from the ground, the waist of the coat below his haunches, and the collar sprawling wide upon his shoulders. Strange to relate, this ludicrous accoutrement was far from moving me to laughter. Rather, as there was something abnormal and misbegotten in the very essence of the creature that now faced me — something seizing, surprising and revolting — this fresh disparity seemed but to fit in with and to reinforce it; so that to my interest in the man's nature and character, there was added a curiosity as to his origin, his life, his fortune and status in the world.

These observations, though they have taken so great a space to be set down in, were yet the work of a few seconds. My visitor was, indeed, on fire with sombre excitement.

"Have you got it?" he cried. "Have you got it?" And so lively was his impatience that he even laid his hand upon my arm and sought to shake me.

I put him back, conscious at his touch of a certain icy pang along my blood. "Come, sir," said I. "You forget that I have not yet the pleasure of your acquaintance. Be seated, if you please." And I showed him an example, and sat down myself in my customary seat and with as fair an imitation of my ordinary manner to a patient, as the lateness of the hour, the nature of my preoccupations, and the horror I had of my visitor, would suffer me to muster.

"I beg your pardon, Dr. Lanyon," he replied civilly enough. "What you say is very well founded; and my impatience has shown its heels to my politeness. I come here at the instance of your colleague, Dr. Henry Jekyll, on a piece of business of some moment; and I understood . . ." He paused and put his hand to his throat, and I could see, in spite of his collected manner, that he was wrestling against the approaches of the hysteria — "I understood, a drawer . . ."

But here I took pity on my visitor's suspense, and some perhaps on my own growing curiosity.

"There it is, sir," said I, pointing to the drawer, where it lay on the floor behind a table and still covered with the sheet.

He sprang to it, and then paused, and laid his hand upon his heart: I could hear his teeth grate with the convulsive action of his jaws; and his face was so ghastly to see that I grew alarmed both for his life and reason.

"Compose yourself," said I.

He turned a dreadful smile to me, and as if with the decision of despair, plucked away the sheet. At sight of the contents, he uttered one loud sob of such immense relief that I sat petrified. And the next moment, in a voice that was already fairly well under control, "Have you a graduated glass?" he asked.

I rose from my place with something of an effort and gave him what he asked.

He thanked me with a smiling nod, measured out a few minims of the red tincture and added one of the powders. The mixture, which was at first of a reddish hue, began, in proportion as the crystals melted, to brighten in colour, to effervesce audibly, and to throw off small fumes of vapour. Suddenly and at the same moment, the ebullition ceased and the compound changed to a dark purple, which faded again more slowly to a watery green. My visitor, who had watched these metamorphoses with a keen eye, smiled, set down the glass upon the table, and then turned and looked upon me with an air of scrutiny.

"And now," said he, "to settle what remains. Will you be wise? will you be guided? will you suffer me to take this glass in my hand and to go forth from your house without further parley? or has the greed of curiosity too much command of you? Think before you answer, for it shall be done as you decide. As you decide, you shall be left as you were before, and neither richer nor wiser, unless the sense of service rendered to a man in mortal distress may be counted as a kind of riches of the soul. Or, if you shall so prefer to choose, a new province of knowledge and new avenues to fame and power shall be laid open to you, here, in this room, upon the instant; and your sight shall be blasted by a prodigy to stagger the unbelief of Satan."

"Sir," said I, affecting a coolness that I was far from truly possessing, "you speak enigmas, and you will perhaps not wonder that I hear you with no very strong impression of belief. But I have gone too far in the way of inexplicable services to pause before I see the end."

"It is well," replied my visitor. "Lanyon, you remember your vows: what follows is under the seal of our profession. And now, you who have so long been bound to the most narrow and material views, you who have denied the virtue of transcendental medicine, you who have derided your superiors—behold!"

He put the glass to his lips and drank at one gulp. A cry followed; he reeled, staggered, clutched at the table and held on, staring with injected eyes, gasping with open mouth; and as I looked there came, I thought, a change — he seemed to swell — his face became suddenly black and the features seemed to melt and alter — and the next moment, I had sprung to my feet and leaped back against the wall, my arms raised to shield me from that prodigy, my mind submerged in terror.

"O God!" I screamed, and "O God!" again and again; for there before my eyes — pale and shaken, and half fainting, and groping before him with his hands, like a man restored from death — there stood Henry Jekyll!

What he told me in the next hour, I cannot bring my mind to set on paper. I saw what I saw, I heard what I heard, and my soul sickened at it; and yet now when that sight has faded from my eyes, I ask myself if I believe it, and I cannot answer. My life is shaken to its roots; sleep has left me; the deadliest terror sits by me at all hours of the day and night; and I feel that my days are numbered, and that I must die; and yet I shall die incredulous. As for the moral turpitude that man unveiled to me, even with tears of penitence, I can not, even in memory, dwell on it without a start of horror. I will say but one thing, Utterson, and that (if you can bring your mind to credit it) will be more than enough. The creature who crept into my house that night was, on Jekyll's own confession, known by the name of Hyde and hunted for in every corner of the land as the murderer of Carew.

Hastie Lanyon

Henry Jekyll's Full Statement of the Case

I was born in the year 18 — to a large fortune, endowed besides with excellent parts, inclined by nature to industry, fond of the respect of the wise and good among my fellowmen, and thus, as might have been supposed, with every guarantee of an honourable and distinguished future. And indeed the worst of my faults was a certain impatient gaiety of disposition, such as has made the happiness of many, but such as I found it hard to reconcile with my imperious desire to carry my head high, and wear a more than commonly grave countenance before the public. Hence it came about that I concealed my pleasures; and that when I reached years of reflection, and began to look round me and take stock of my progress and position in the world, I stood already committed to a profound duplicity of me. Many a man would have even blazoned such irregularities as I was guilty of; but from the high views that I had set before me, I regarded and hid them with an almost morbid sense of shame. It was thus rather the exacting nature of my aspirations than any particular degradation in my faults, that made me what I was, and, with even a deeper trench than in the majority of men, severed in me those provinces of good and ill which divide and compound man's dual nature. In this case, I was driven to reflect deeply and inveterately on that hard law of life, which lies at the root of religion and is one of the most plentiful springs of distress. Though so profound a double-dealer, I was in no sense a hypocrite; both sides of me were in dead earnest; I was no more myself when I laid aside restraint and plunged in shame, than when I laboured, in the eye of day, at the futherance of knowledge or the relief of sorrow and suffering. And it chanced that the direction of my scientific studies, which led wholly towards the mystic and the transcendental, reacted and shed a strong light on this conscious- ness of the perennial war among my members. With every day, and from both sides of my intelligence, the moral and the intellectual, I thus drew steadily nearer to that truth, by whose partial discovery I have been doomed to such a dreadful shipwreck: that man is not truly one, but truly two. I say two, because the state of my own knowledge does not pass beyond that point. Others will follow, others will outstrip me on the same lines; and I hazard the guess that man will be ultimately known for a mere polity of multifarious, incongruous and independent denizens. I, for my part, from the nature of my life, advanced infallibly in one direction and in one direction only. It was on the moral side, and in my own person, that I learned to recognise the thorough and primitive duality of man; I saw that, of the two natures that contended in the field of my consciousness, even if I could rightly be said to be either, it was only because I was radically both; and from an early date, even before the course of my scientific discoveries had begun to suggest the most naked possibility of such a miracle, I had learned to dwell with pleasure, as a beloved daydream, on the thought of the sep- aration of these elements. If each, I told myself, could be housed in separate identities, life would be relieved of all that was unbearable; the unjust might go his way, delivered from the aspirations and remorse of his more upright twin; and the just could walk stead- fastly and securely on his upward path, doing the good things in which he found his pleasure, and no longer exposed to disgrace and penitence by the hands of this extraneous evil. It was the curse of mankind that these incongruous faggots were thus bound together — that in the agonised womb of consciousness, these polar twins should be continuously struggling. How, then were they dissociated?

I was so far in my reflections when, as I have said, a side light began to shine upon the subject from the laboratory table. I began to perceive more deeply than it has ever yet been stated, the trembling immateriality, the mistlike transience, of this seemingly so solid body in which we walk attired. Certain agents I found to have the power to shake and pluck back that fleshly vestment, even as a wind might toss the curtains of a pavilion. For two good reasons, I will not enter deeply into this scientific branch of my confession. First, because I have been made to learn that the doom and burthen of our life is bound for ever on man's shoulders, and when the attempt is made to cast it off, it but returns upon us with more unfamiliar and more awful pressure. Second, because, as my narrative will make, alas! too evident, my discoveries were incomplete. Enough then, that I not only recognised my natural body from the mere aura and effulgence of certain of the powers that made up my spirit, but managed to compound a drug by which these powers should be dethroned from their supremacy, and a second form and countenance substituted, none the less natural to me because they were the expression, and bore the stamp of lower elements in my soul.

I hesitated long before I put this theory to the test of practice. I knew well that I risked death; for any drug that so potently controlled and shook the very fortress of identity, might, by the least scruple of an overdose or at the least inopportunity in the moment of exhibition, utterly blot out that immaterial tabernacle which I looked to it to change. But the temptation of a discovery so singular and profound at last overcame the suggestions of alarm. I had long since prepared my tincture; I purchased at once, from a firm of wholesale chemists, a large quantity of a particular salt which I knew, from my experiments, to be the last ingredient required; and late one accursed night, I compounded the elements, watched them boil and smoke together in the glass, and when the ebullition had subsided, with a strong glow of courage, drank off the potion.

The most racking pangs succeeded: a grinding in the bones, deadly nausea, and a horror of the spirit that cannot be exceeded at the hour of birth or death. Then these agonies began swiftly to subside, and I came to myself as if out of a great sickness. There was something strange in my sensations, something indescribably new and, from its very novelty, incredibly sweet. I felt younger, lighter, happier in body; within I was conscious of a heady recklessness, a current of disordered sensual images running like a millrace in my fancy, a solution of the bonds of obligation, an unknown but not an innocent freedom of the soul. I knew myself, at the first breath of this new life, to be more wicked, tenfold more wicked, sold a slave to my original evil; and the thought, in that moment, braced and delighted me like wine. I stretched out my hands, exulting in the freshness of these sensations; and in the act, I was suddenly aware that I had lost in stature.

There was no mirror, at that date, in my room; that which stands beside me as I write, was brought there later on and for the very purpose of these transformations. The night however, was far gone into the morning — the morning, black as it was, was nearly ripe for the conception of the day — the inmates of my house were locked in the most rigorous hours of slumber; and I determined, flushed as I was with hope and triumph, to venture in my new shape as far as to my bedroom. I crossed the yard, wherein the constellations looked down upon me, I could have thought, with wonder, the first creature of that sort that their unsleeping vigilance had yet disclosed to them; I stole through the corridors, a stranger in my own house; and coming to my room, I saw for the first time the appearance of Edward Hyde.

I must here speak by theory alone, saying not that which I know, but that which I suppose to be most probable. The evil side of my nature, to which I had now transferred the stamping efficacy, was less robust and less developed than the good which I had just deposed. Again, in the course of my life, which had been, after all, nine tenths a life of effort, virtue and control, it had been much less exercised and much less exhausted. And hence, as I think, it came about that Edward Hyde was so much smaller, slighter and younger than Henry Jekyll. Even as good shone upon the countenance of the one, evil was written broadly and plainly on the face of the other. Evil besides (which I must still believe to be the lethal side of man) had left on that body an imprint of deformity and decay. And yet when I looked upon that ugly idol in the glass, I was conscious of no repugnance, rather of a leap of welcome. This, too, was myself. It seemed natural and human. In my eyes it bore a livelier image of the spirit, it seemed more express and single, than the imperfect and divided countenance I had been hitherto accustomed to call mine. And in so far I was doubtless right. I have observed that when I wore the semblance of Edward Hyde, none could come near to me at first without a visible misgiving of the flesh. This, as I take it, was because all human beings, as we meet them, are commingled out of good and evil: and Edward Hyde, alone in the ranks of mankind, was pure evil.

I lingered but a moment at the mirror: the second and conclusive experiment had yet to be attempted; it yet remained to be seen if I had lost my identity beyond redemption and must flee before daylight from a house that was no longer mine; and hurrying back to my cabinet, I once more prepared and drank the cup, once more suffered the pangs of dissolution, and came to myself once more with the character, the stature and the face of Henry Jekyll.

That night I had come to the fatal cross-roads. Had I approached my discovery in a more noble spirit, had I risked the experiment while under the empire of generous or pious aspirations, all must have been otherwise, and from these agonies of death and birth,

I had come forth an angel instead of a fiend. The drug had no discriminating action; it was neither diabolical nor divine; it but shook the doors of the prisonhouse of my disposition; and like the captives of Philippi, that which stood within ran forth. At that time my virtue slumbered; my evil, kept awake by ambition, was alert and swift to seize the occasion; and the thing that was projected was Edward Hyde. Hence, although I had now two characters as well as two appearances, one was wholly evil, and the other was still the old Henry Jekyll, that incongruous compound of whose reformation and improvement I had already learned to despair. The movement was thus wholly toward the worse.

Even at that time, I had not conquered my aversions to the dryness of a life of study. I would still be merrily disposed at times; and as my pleasures were (to say the least) undignified, and I was not only well known and highly considered, but growing towards the elderly man, this incoherency of my life was daily growing more unwelcome. It was on this side that my new power tempted me until I fell in slavery. I had but to drink the cup, to doff at once the body of the noted professor, and to assume, like a thick cloak, that of Edward Hyde. I smiled at the notion; it seemed to me at the time to be humourous; and I made my preparations with the most studious care. I took and furnished that house in Soho, to which Hyde was tracked by the police; and engaged as a housekeeper a creature whom I knew well to be silent and unscrupulous. On the other side, I announced to my servants that a Mr. Hyde (whom I described) was to have full liberty and power about my house in the square; and to parry mishaps, I even called and made myself a familiar object, in my second character. I next drew up that will to which you so much objected; so that if anything befell me in the person of Dr. Jekyll, I could enter on that of Edward Hyde without pecuniary loss. And thus fortified, as I supposed, on every side, I began to profit by the strange immunities of my position.

Men have before hired bravos to transact their crimes, while their own person and reputation sat under shelter. I was the first that ever did so for his pleasures. I was the first that could plod in the public eye with a load of genial respectability, and in a moment, like a schoolboy, strip off these lendings and spring headlong into the sea of liberty. But for me, in my impenetrable mantle, the safety was complete. Think of it — I did not even exist! Let me but escape into my laboratory door, give me but a second or two to mix and swallow the draught that I had always standing ready; and whatever he had done, Edward Hyde would pass away like the stain of breath upon a mirror; and there in his stead, quietly at home, trimming the midnight lamp in his study, a man who could afford to laugh at suspicion, would be Henry Jekyll.

The pleasures which I made haste to seek in my disguise were, as I have said, undignified; I would scarce use a harder term. But in the hands of Edward Hyde, they soon began to turn toward the monstrous. When I would come back from these excursions, I was often plunged into a kind of wonder at my vicarious depravity. This familiar that I called out of my own soul, and sent forth alone to do his good pleasure, was a being inherently malign and villainous; his every act and thought centered on self; drinking pleasure with bestial avidity from any degree of torture to another; relentless like a man of stone. Henry Jekyll stood at times aghast before the acts of Edward Hyde; but the situation was apart from ordinary laws, and insidiously relaxed the grasp of conscience. It was Hyde, after all, and Hyde alone, that was guilty. Jekyll was no worse; he woke again to his good qualities seemingly unimpaired; he would even make haste, where it was possible, to undo the evil done by Hyde. And thus his conscience slumbered.

Into the details of the infamy at which I thus connived (for even now I can scarce grant that I committed it) I have no design of entering; I mean but to point out the warnings and the successive steps with which my chastisement approached. I met with one accident which, as it brought on no consequence, I shall no more than mention. An act of cruelty to a child aroused against me the anger of a passer-by, whom I recognised the other day in the person of your kinsman; the doctor and the child's family joined him; there were moments when I feared for my life; and at last, in order to pacify their too just resentment, Edward Hyde had to bring them to the door, and pay them in a cheque drawn in the name of Henry Jekyll. But this danger was easily eliminated from the future, by opening an account at another bank in the name of Edward Hyde himself; and when, by sloping my own hand backward, I had supplied my double with a signature, I thought I sat beyond the reach of fate.

Some two months before the murder of Sir Danvers, I had been out for one of my adventures, had returned at a late hour, and woke the next day in bed with somewhat odd sensations. It was in vain I looked about me; in vain I saw the decent furniture and tall proportions of my room in the square; in vain that I recognised the pattern of the bed curtains and the design of the mahogany frame; something still kept insisting that I was not where I was, that I had not wakened where I seemed to be, but in the little room in Soho where I was accustomed to sleep in the body of Edward Hyde. I smiled to myself, and in my psychological way, began lazily to inquire into the elements of this illusion, occasionally, even as I did so, dropping back into a comfortable morning doze. I was still so engaged when, in one of my more wakeful moments, my eyes fell upon my hand. Now the hand of Henry Jekyll (as you have often remarked) was professional in shape and size: it was large, firm, white and comely. But the hand which I now saw, clearly enough, in the yellow light of a mid-London morning, lying half shut on the bedclothes, was lean, corded, knuckly, of a dusky pallor and thickly shaded with a swart growth of hair. It was the hand of Edward Hyde.

I must have stared upon it for near half a minute, sunk as I was in the mere stupidity of wonder, before terror woke up in my breast as sudden and startling as the crash of cymbals; and bounding from my bed I rushed to the mirror. At the sight that met my eyes, my blood was changed into something exquisitely thin and icy. Yes, I had gone to bed Henry Jekyll, I had awakened Edward Hyde. How was this to be explained? I asked myself; and then, with another bound of terror—how was it to be remedied? It was well on in the morning; the servants were up; all my drugs were in the cabinet—a long journey down two pairs of stairs, through the back passage, across the open court and through the anatomical theatre, from where I was then standing horror-struck. It might indeed be possible to cover my face; but of what use was that, when I was unable to conceal the alteration in my stature? And then with an overpowering sweetness of relief, it came back upon my mind that the servants were already used to the coming and going of my second self. I had soon dressed, as well as I was able, in clothes of my own size: had soon passed through the house, where Bradshaw stared and drew back at seeing Mr. Hyde at such an hour and in such a strange array; and ten minutes later, Dr. Jekyll had returned to his own shape and was sitting down, with a darkened brow, to make a feint of breakfasting.

Small indeed was my appetite. This inexplicable incident, this reversal of my previous experience, seemed, like the Babylonian finger on the wall, to be spelling out the letters of my judgment; and I began to reflect more seriously than ever before on the issues and possibilities of my double existence. That part of me which I had the power of projecting, had lately been much exercised and nourished; it had seemed to me of late as though the body of Edward Hyde had grown in stature, as though (when I wore that form) I were conscious of a more generous tide of blood; and I began to spy a danger that, if this were much prolonged, the balance of my nature might be permanently overthrown, the power of voluntary change be forfeited, and the character of Edward Hyde become irrevocably mine. The power of the drug had not been always equally displayed. Once, very early in my career, it had totally failed me; since then I had been obliged on more than one occasion to double, and once, with infinite risk of death, to treble the amount; and these rare uncertainties had cast hitherto the sole shadow on my contentment. Now, however, and in the light of that morning's accident, I was led to remark that whereas, in the beginning, the difficulty had been to throw off the body of Jekyll, it had of late gradually but decidedly transferred itself to the other side. All things therefore seemed to point to this; that I was slowly losing hold of my original and better self, and becoming slowly incorporated with my second and worse.

Between these two, I now felt I had to choose. My two natures had memory in common, but all other faculties were most unequally shared between them. Jekyll (who was composite) now with the most sensitive apprehensions, now with a greedy gusto, projected and shared in the pleasures and adventures of Hyde; but Hyde was indifferent to Jekyll, or but remembered him as the mountain bandit remembers the cavern in which he conceals himself from pursuit. Jekyll had more than a father's interest; Hyde had more than a son's indifference. To cast in my lot with Jekyll, was to die to those appetites which I had long secretly indulged and had of late begun to pamper. To cast it in with Hyde, was to die to a thousand interests and aspirations, and to become, at a blow and forever, despised and friendless. The bargain might appear unequal; but there was still another consideration in the scales; for while Jekyll would suffer smartingly in the fires of abstinence, Hyde would be not even conscious of all that he had lost. Strange as my circumstances were, the terms of this debate are as old and commonplace as man; much the same inducements and alarms cast the die for any tempted and trembling sinner; and it fell out with me, as it falls with so vast a majority of my fellows, that I chose the better part and was found wanting in the strength to keep to it.

Yes, I preferred the elderly and discontented doctor, surrounded by friends and cherishing honest hopes; and bade a resolute farewell to the liberty, the comparative youth, the light step, leaping impulses and secret pleasures, that I had enjoyed in the disguise of Hyde. I made this choice perhaps with some unconscious reservation, for I neither gave up the house in Soho, nor destroyed the clothes of Edward Hyde, which still lay ready in my cabinet. For two months, however, I was true to my determination; for two months, I led a life of such severity as I had never before attained to, and enjoyed the compensations of an approving conscience. But time began at last to obliterate the freshness of my alarm; the praises of conscience began to grow into a thing of course; I began to be tortured with throes and longings, as of Hyde struggling after freedom; and at last, in an hour of moral weakness, I once again compounded and swallowed the transforming draught.

I do not suppose that, when a drunkard reasons with himself upon his vice, he is once out of five hundred times affected by the dangers that he runs through his brutish, physical insensibility; neither had I, long as I had considered my position, made enough allowance for the complete moral insensibility and insensate readiness to evil, which were the leading characters of Edward Hyde. Yet it was by these that I was punished. My devil had been long caged, he came out roaring. I was conscious, even when I took the draught, of a more unbridled, a more furious propensity to ill. It must have been this, I suppose, that stirred in my soul that tempest of impatience with which I listened to the civilities of my unhappy victim; I declare, at least, before God, no man morally sane could have been guilty of that crime upon so pitiful a provocation; and that I struck in no more reasonable spirit than that in which a sick child may break a plaything. But I had voluntarily stripped myself of all those balancing instincts by which even the worst of us continues to walk with some degree of steadiness among temptations; and in my case, to be tempted, however slightly, was to fall.

Instantly the spirit of hell awoke in me and raged. With a transport of glee, I mauled the unresisting body, tasting delight from every blow; and it was not till weariness had begun to succeed, that I was suddenly, in the top fit of my delirium, struck through the heart by a cold thrill of terror. A mist dispersed; I saw my life to be forfeit; and fled from the scene of these excesses, at once glorying and trembling, my lust of evil gratified and stimulated, my love of life screwed to the topmost peg. I ran to the house in Soho, and (to make assurance doubly sure) destroyed my papers; thence I set out through the lamplit streets, in the same divided ecstasy of mind, gloating on my crime, light-headedly devising others in the future, and yet still hastening and still hearkening in my wake for the steps of the avenger. Hyde had a song upon his lips as he compounded the draught, and as he drank it, pledged the dead man. The pangs of transformation had not done tearing him, before Henry Jekyll, with streaming tears of gratitude and remorse, had fallen upon his knees and lifted his clasped hands to God. The veil of self-indulgence was rent from head to foot. I saw my life as a whole: I followed it up from the days of childhood, when I had walked with my father's hand, and through the self-denying toils of my professional life, to arrive again and again, with the same sense of unreality, at the damned horrors of the evening. I could have screamed aloud; I sought with tears and prayers to smother down the crowd of hideous images and sounds with which my memory swarmed against me; and still, between the petitions, the ugly face of my iniquity stared into my soul. As the acuteness of this remorse began to die away, it was succeeded by a sense of joy. The problem of my conduct was solved.

Hyde was thenceforth impossible; whether I would or not, I was now confined to the better part of my existence; and O, how I rejoiced to think of it! with what willing humility I embraced anew the restrictions of natural life! with what sincere renunciation I locked the door by which I had so often gone and come, and ground the key under my heel!

The next day, came the news that the murder had been overlooked, that the guilt of Hyde was patent to the world, and that the victim was a man high in public estimation. It was not only a crime, it had been a tragic folly. I think I was glad to know it; I think I was glad to have my better impulses thus buttressed and guarded by the terrors of the scaffold. Jekyll was now my city of refuge; let but Hyde peep out an instant, and the hands of all men would be raised to take and slay him. I resolved in my future conduct to redeem the past; and I can say with honesty that my resolve was fruitful of some good. You know yourself how earnestly, in the last months of the last year, I laboured to relieve suffering; you know that much was done for others, and that the days passed quietly, almost happily for myself. Nor can I truly say that I wearied of this beneficent and innocent life; I think instead that I daily enjoyed it more completely; but I was still cursed with my duality of purpose; and as the first edge of my penitence wore off, the lower side of me, so long indulged, so recently chained down, began to growl for licence. Not that I dreamed of resuscitating Hyde; the bare idea of that would startle me to frenzy: no, it was in my own person that I was once more tempted to trifle with my conscience; and it was as an ordinary secret sinner that I at last fell before the assaults of temptation.

There comes an end to all things; the most capacious measure is filled at last; and this brief condescension to my evil finally destroyed the balance of my soul. And yet I was not alarmed; the fall seemed natural, like a return to the old days before I had made my discovery. It was a fine, clear, January day, wet under foot where the frost had melted, but cloudless overhead; and the Regent's Park was full of winter chirrupings and sweet with spring odours. I sat in the sun on a bench; the animal within me licking the chops of memory; the spiritual side a little drowsed, promising subsequent penitence, but not yet moved to begin. After all, I reflected, I was like my neighbours; and then I smiled, comparing myself with other men, comparing my active good-will with the lazy cruelty of their neglect. And at the very moment of that vainglorious thought, a qualm came over me, a horrid nausea and the most deadly shuddering. These passed away, and left me faint; and then as in its turn faintness subsided, I began to be aware of a change in the temper of my thoughts, a greater boldness, a contempt of danger, a solution of the bonds of obligation. I looked down; my clothes hung formlessly on my shrunken limbs; the hand that lay on my knee was corded and hairy. I was once more Edward Hyde. A moment before I had been safe of all men's respect, wealthy, beloved — the cloth laying for me in the dining-room at home; and now I was the common quarry of mankind, hunted, houseless, a known murderer, thrall to the gallows.

My reason wavered, but it did not fail me utterly. I have more than once observed that in my second character, my faculties seemed sharpened to a point and my spirits more tensely elastic; thus it came about that, where Jekyll perhaps might have succumbed, Hyde rose to the importance of the moment. My drugs were in one of the presses of my cabinet; how was I to reach them? That was the problem that (crushing my temples in my hands) I set myself to solve. The laboratory door I had closed. If I sought to enter by the house, my own servants would consign me to the gallows. I saw I must employ another hand, and thought of Lanyon. How was he to be reached? how persuaded? Supposing that I escaped capture in the streets, how was I to make my way into his presence? and how should I, an unknown and displeasing visitor, prevail on the famous physician to rifle the study of his colleague, Dr. Jekyll? Then I remembered that of my original character, one part remained to me: I could write my own hand; and once I had conceived that kindling spark, the way that I must follow became lighted up from end to end.

Thereupon, I arranged my clothes as best I could, and summoning a passing hansom, drove to an hotel in Portland Street, the name of which I chanced to remember. At my appearance (which was indeed comical enough, however tragic a fate these garments covered) the driver could not conceal his mirth. I gnashed my teeth upon him with a gust of devilish fury; and the smile withered from his face — happily for him — yet more happily for myself, for in another instant I had certainly dragged him from his perch. At the inn, as I entered, I looked about me with so black a countenance as made the attendants tremble; not a look did they exchange in my presence; but obsequiously took my orders, led me to a private room, and brought me wherewithal to write. Hyde in danger of his life was a creature new to me; shaken with inordinate anger, strung to the pitch of murder, lusting to inflict pain. Yet the creature was astute; mastered his fury with a great effort of the will; composed his two important letters, one to Lanyon and one to Poole; and that he might receive actual evidence of their being posted, sent them out with directions that they should be registered. Thenceforward, he sat all day over the fire in the private room, gnawing his nails; there he dined, sitting alone with his fears, the waiter visibly quailing before his eye; and thence, when the night was fully come, he set forth in the corner of a closed cab, and was driven to and fro about the streets of the city. He, I say — I cannot say, I. That child of Hell had nothing human; nothing lived in him but fear and hatred. And when at last, thinking the driver had begun to grow suspicious, he discharged the cab and ventured on foot, attired in his misfitting clothes, an object marked out for observation, into the midst of the nocturnal passengers, these two base passions raged within him like a tempest. He walked fast, hunted by his fears, chattering to himself, skulking through the less frequented thoroughfares, counting the minutes that still divided him from midnight. Once a woman spoke to him, offering, I think, a box of lights. He smote her in the face, and she fled.

When I came to myself at Lanyon's, the horror of my old friend perhaps affected me somewhat: I do not know; it was at least but a drop in the sea to the abhorrence with which I looked back upon these hours. A change had come over me. It was no longer the fear of the gallows, it was the horror of being Hyde that racked me. I received Lanyon's condemnation partly in a dream; it was partly in a dream that I came home to my own house and got into bed. I slept after the prostration of the day, with a stringent and profound slumber which not even the nightmares that wrung me could avail to break. I awoke in the morning shaken, weakened, but refreshed. I still hated and feared the thought of the brute that slept within me, and I had not of course forgotten the appalling dangers of the day before; but I was once more at home, in my own house and close to my drugs; and gratitude for my escape shone so strong in my soul that it almost rivalled the brightness of hope.

I was stepping leisurely across the court after breakfast, drinking the chill of the air with pleasure, when I was seized again with those indescribable sensations that heralded the change; and I had but the time to gain the shelter of my cabinet, before I was once again raging and freezing with the passions of Hyde. It took on this occasion a double dose to recall me to myself; and alas! six hours after, as I sat looking sadly in the fire, the pangs returned, and the drug had to be re-administered. In short, from that day forth it seemed only by a great effort as of gymnastics, and only under the immediate stimulation of the drug, that I was able to wear the countenance of Jekyll. At all hours of the day and night, I would be taken with the premonitory shudder; above all, if I slept, or even dozed for a moment in my chair, it was always as Hyde that I awakened. Under the strain of this continually impending doom and by the sleeplessness to which I now condemned myself, ay, even beyond what I had thought possible to man, I became, in my own person, a creature eaten up and emptied by fever, languidly weak both in body and mind, and solely occupied by one thought: the horror of my other self. But when I slept, or when the virtue of the medicine wore off, I would leap almost without transition (for the pangs of transformation grew daily less marked) into the possession of a fancy brimming with images of terror, a soul boiling with causeless hatreds, and a body that seemed not strong enough to contain the raging energies of life. The powers of Hyde seemed to have grown with the sickliness of Jekyll. And certainly the hate that now divided them was equal on each side. With Jekyll, it was a thing of vital instinct. He had now seen the full deformity of that creature that shared with him some of the phenomena of consciousness, and was co-heir with him to death: and beyond these links of community, which in themselves made the most poignant part of his distress, he thought of Hyde, for all his energy of life, as of something not only hellish but inorganic. This was the shocking thing; that the slime of the pit seemed to utter cries and voices; that the amorphous dust gesticulated and sinned; that what was dead, and had no shape, should usurp the offices of life. And this again, that that insurgent horror was knit to him closer than a wife, closer than an eye; lay caged in his flesh, where he heard it mutter and felt it struggle to be born; and at every hour of weakness, and in the confidence of slumber, prevailed against him, and deposed him out of life. The hatred of Hyde for Jekyll was of a different order. His terror of the gallows drove him continually to commit temporary suicide, and return to his subordinate station of a part instead of a person; but he loathed the necessity, he loathed the despondency into which Jekyll was now fallen, and he resented the dislike with which he was himself regarded. Hence the ape-like tricks that he would play me, scrawling in my own hand blasphemies on the pages of my books, burning the letters and destroying the portrait of my father; and indeed, had it not been for his fear of death, he would long ago have ruined himself in order to involve me in the ruin. But his love of me is wonderful; I go further: I, who sicken and freeze at the mere thought of him, when I recall the abjection and passion of this attachment, and when I know how he fears my power to cut him off by suicide, I find it in my heart to pity him.

It is useless, and the time awfully fails me, to prolong this description; no one has ever suffered such torments, let that suffice; and yet even to these, habit brought — no, not alleviation — but a certain callousness of soul, a certain acquiescence of despair; and my punishment might have gone on for years, but for the last calamity which has now fallen, and which has finally severed me from my own face and nature. My provision of the salt, which had never been renewed since the date of the first experiment, began to run low. I sent out for a fresh supply and mixed the draught; the ebullition followed, and the first change of colour, not the second; I drank it and it was without efficiency. You will learn from Poole how I have had London ransacked; it was in vain; and I am now persuaded that my first supply was impure, and that it was that unknown impurity which lent efficacy to the draught.

About a week has passed, and I am now finishing this statement under the influence of the last of the old powders. This, then, is the last time, short of a miracle, that Henry Jekyll can think his own thoughts or see his own face (now how sadly altered!) in the glass. Nor must I delay too long to bring my writing to an end; for if my narrative has hitherto escaped destruction, it has been by a combination of great prudence and great good luck. Should the throes of change take me in the act of writing it, Hyde will tear it in pieces; but if some time shall have elapsed after I have laid it by, his wonderful selfishness and circumscription to the moment will probably save it once again from the action of his ape-like spite. And indeed the doom that is closing on us both has already changed and crushed him. Half an hour from now, when I shall again and forever reindue that hated personality, I know how I shall sit shuddering and weeping in my chair, or continue, with the most strained and fearstruck ecstasy of listening, to pace up and down this room (my last earthly refuge) and give ear to every sound of menace. Will Hyde die upon the scaffold? or will he find courage to release himself at the last moment? God knows; I am careless; this is my true hour of death, and what is to follow concerns another than myself. Here then, as I lay down the pen and proceed to seal up my confession, I bring the life of that unhappy Henry Jekyll to an end.

Discussion Topics

1. What common modern disability best approximates that of Dr. Jekyll? While there are similarities to MPD, as we will see below, a crucial fact is that he chose to take the potion that transformed him. Over time, the transformation slipped out of his control. An obvious analogy is to addiction. Whether the object is alcohol, drugs, or gambling, an addict initially chooses to indulge and finds it ever harder to resist.

The approach of law to addictions is generally to assume that they remain within control of the addict. The person who commits petty thefts and assaults for drug money is held responsible, just as she is responsible for any crimes involving the possession, purchase, and sale of drugs. Similarly, the alcoholic who drives drunk is held to be no less responsible than the person who drinks socially and can readily stop drinking. The addicted gambler who, because of his habit, has no funds for child support is liable in the same way as the non-addict.

One explanation is tough love or just plain toughness. Addiction, in other words, is not seen as a disability or medical/psychological condition but as an optional, freely chosen series of acts. How is this justified? Consider two arguments. The first is that treating the addict as one would treat others will bring about deterrence and compliance with law. In fact, the evidence for this assumption is not strong. If one moves away from deterrence and other such consequentialist arguments, a second argument is retributive, namely that the addict is as blameworthy as anyone else. *If this is true, law should not differentiate between wrongdoers even if punishment turns out to be less effective.*

Medical and legal models of addiction clash. The clash can be seen as a matter of fact or a matter of value. Seen as fact, it comes down to the question of control, whether the addict has control over her relevant acts, whether they are really choices. Seen as value, it comes down to whether the addict can be blamed and held responsible for the results of her actions.

Consider your own position on these questions. And consider as well the extent to which you would hold Dr. Jekyll morally and legally responsible for the acts committed by Mr. Hyde. In what ways does this situation differ from addiction?

2. Stevenson's story continues to strike a chord in popular culture because it is a potent example of the idea that each of us is split between two selves, a hedonistic and self-indulgent person that lives for the moment and another self that does long-term planning, follows moral and legal rules, and obeys the constraints of civilized social life. The first is held in check by the second, and life is a struggle between the two.

This was Jekyll's great "discovery" along with a method for freeing the first self from the second. Is this a deep insight into human nature or a simplistic and misleading myth? If it is a myth, it has played an enormous role in shaping Western culture. A theory of the parts of the soul, whereby the rational part holds the other parts in check, is put forth in Plato's *Republic*. In the Bible, both old and new testaments, the efforts of man to keep his bad instincts in check, to resist temptation, is a constant theme from the story of the garden of Eden to that of Cain and Abel—and so on. The eschatology of a war between angels and devils, between God and Satan, is inseparable from the history of Christianity. To this day, fundamentalists stress that life is a battle to keep Satanic urges in check.

A similar model is offered by Freudian psychology. The *id* is the instinctive, non-rational, pleasure-seeking, primitive part of human nature. The *superego* is the seat of conscience, the cultural voice of order and discipline. And the *ego*, the self-aware rational part, mediates between the id and superego. It is hard not to see Mr. Hyde as the embodiment of the id and Dr. Jekyll as consumed by the ego's involvement in the battle between id and superego, the demands of society.

This kind of account of human nature comes in two flavors. In one version, the two basic parts are equal: one part connects with the rest of society and shares its interests and needs, and the other part is out for itself and seeks pleasure and gratification in the short run. (The Harvard legal theorist Duncan Kennedy has a version of this account by which we are all drawn by conflicting agendas that can be called altruistic and individualistic.) Thus, our lives involve tacking between these two agendas and sets of goals even though they cannot ultimately be made harmonious.

The second version does not treat the two poles as equal. It claims that the fundamental, truest nature of persons is willful and selfish, even mean and cruel, and that these "demonic" aspects need to be curbed in the interest of society. Education and socialization work to alienate us from this basic nature. The second version is, of course, the one that is familiar in Christianity and in Freud's thinking. For Freud, the id energizes us; for Christians, we are all born in sin.

How rash is it to question this pervasive aspect of Western culture? The fact that we have moral choices and that we do some admirable and some not-so-admirable things hardly means that we are fundamentally divided. Most psychologists suggest it is simplistic and dangerous to think that we are fundamentally corrupt or that life is basically a struggle with evil. More importantly, they do not see two selves at war — but rather describe a complex mix of experiences and responses that owes much both to genetics (or nature) and nurture.

How useful and how misleading is the Jekyll-Hyde dichotomy in understanding human nature?

3. In spite of significant dissimilarities, the legal dilemma of holding a person with multiple personalities responsible for the actions of one of her multiples is a lot like the question of holding Jekyll responsible for the crimes of Mr. Hyde. Consider some of the similarities and differences. Jekyll had no foreknowledge of Hyde's acts. Moreover, he had virtually no control over Hyde. Beyond a certain point, he also had no control over the emergence of the Hyde persona, which began to occur spontaneously. All of these aspects are true of so-called multiples. A major difference is that Jekyll remained conscious of Hyde's actions while they happened and remembered them afterwards.

Perhaps the most sustained and thoughtful examination of the legal status of MPD is "Multiple Personality Disorder and Criminal Responsibility," by Professor Elyn Saks (25 *University of California, Davis, Law Review* 383 (1992)). Saks looks at how we individuate characters and how we assign responsibility. She argues that we should not hold multiples responsible in large part because the dominant personality is unaware of the acts of the other personalities both when they happen and afterwards. She concludes that "responsibility requires at least a minimal degree of unity and continuity in a person's mental life. . . . [R]esponsibility cannot coexist with a true cleavage in the mind — dissociation so complete that ever the appearance of conflict is obliterated." This does not mean, of course, that the law would be incapable of intervening if the person were found dangerous to herself or others.

Dr. Jekyll, however, did not suffer the amnesia typical of those with MPD. Is that a sufficient basis for trying him criminally for Mr. Hyde's crimes? In what sense did he have the intentions relevant for criminal liability? Is his dissociation from Mr. Hyde greater in some sense than that of the drug addict who commits a crime in desperation for a fix or who commits an aggressive assault because methamphetamine has altered his personality?

✎ Further Reading

This chapter is about entering the criminal mind, understanding what aspects of it play a significant role in criminal law, and determining what factors are legally irrelevant. The following works help us identify situations, motives, and attitudes that give rise to criminality and sort them into various categories.

(1) Power, ambition, and the sense that one has a special right to transcend the rules that govern others are common themes in literature. Shakespeare's *Macbeth* gives pure expression to the seductiveness of power; his *Richard III* is even more uncompromising in its examination of ruthlessness. In both plays, war and politics, rather than law, bring about some form of cosmic justice.

Wealth and privilege and the ways they provide both motive and opportunity for evading the law are examined by F. Scott Fitzgerald in his classic novel, *The Great Gatsby*.

Colonial administrators often enjoyed exemptions from the laws they enforced. Joseph Conrad's novella, *Heart of Darkness*, compellingly translated to film by Francis Ford Coppola in *Apocalypse Now*, is a clear statement of how an administrator's "journey into the interior" in colonial Africa turns him, in his own imaginings, into a god unbounded by moral or legal rules.

Psychopaths, lacking emotional identification and moral constraints, also see themselves as more powerful than other persons. Bret Easton Ellis' highly controversial novel, *American Psycho*, is an effective look at psychopathy.

(2) Some of the greatest criminals in fiction believe they see the world from a unique perspective, one that entitles them to act in ways that the

benighted world condemns. Fyodor Dostoyevsky's *Crime and Punishment* is the story of student who murders a shopkeeper in accord with his utilitarian theory that her death will bring greater good to the world than her continued existence. Raskolnikov, the student, is often interpreted as acting on the philosophical conviction that he lives (in Nietzsche's phrase) "beyond good and evil."

A special kind of sexual and esthetic passion supposedly gives Humbert Humbert, the protagonist of Vladimir Nabokov's *Lolita*, his special license to pursue what the law condemns. The novel is elegant and touching in its exploration of self-justification and self-delusion.

(3) The African-American underclass has historically had special reasons to question the even-handedness of law and special motivation to make a political statement in breaking the law. William Styron's *The Confessions of Nat Turner* offers a first-person narrative, significantly fictionalized, of a pivotal slave rebellion. Richard Wright's *Native Son* offers a largely realistic portrait of a young black man in 1940s Chicago, limited by racism and poverty, who accidentally kills a young white woman and is snared by the processes of law and his own misguided responses.

(4) Three books illustrate the ease with which human nature and marginal situations can work together to produce horrific and often tragically inhuman results. Truman Capote's *In Cold Blood,* an exploration of true events, is an intimate description of the slaughter of the Clutter family in rural Kansas by two itinerants. Capote conveys particularly well the flux of motives and intentions, the psychological interplay between the killers, the mix of bravado and bewilderment in their self-understanding.

The Lord of the Flies by William Golding shows the emergence and triumph of sadism and cruelty in the interaction of young boys. The novel takes a Hobbesian stance on the need for rules and discipline. It implies that one's natural disposition is to take advantage of others and take pleasure in their misery.

Finally, John Steinbeck's *Of Mice and Men* describes the casualness with which a motiveless killing can occur. Even in the absence of malice, innocuous acts can have fatal and tragic results.

FIVE

Trial and Punishment

For the most part, fiction looks at law by looking at trials. Legal drama on television or in the movies generally means stories about preparing for trials, usually criminal trials, or participating in them. The success of *CSI* and *Law and Order* is nothing new. We can go back fifty years to *Perry Mason* or four hundred years to *The Merchant of Venice*. The situation is no different with novels. John Grisham is only the current beneficiary of a fascination with the vagaries of individual fortune in court that goes back to ancient Greek tragedy.

Why are we fascinated? When violence occurs, we want to know what happened and why it happened. Ideally, the courtroom is the place where guilt and innocence are declared on the basis of a process designed to uncover the truth. We all know that this ideal is rarely realized.

Thus, we attend to stories of investigation and trial for several reasons. First, we want to know the truth about events. Second, we want to know whether the truth will see the light of day within the story. Third, we want to know whether the wrongdoers will be punished justly. The storytelling itself becomes ever more sophisticated and seemingly realistic. Because of the various new forensic series on television, not merely the *CSI* triad, we know a lot about the technology of evidence. In light of programs such as *Law and Order*, we know about plea negotiations, the moral dilemmas of prosecutors, the constraints on arguments and evidence, and the vagaries of jury decision-making. We know not only that the truth often fails to emerge in the courtroom; we also know why. Truth and justice are only two of many goals that lawyers, not just those who play them on TV, pursue and sometimes achieve.

The television series and novels based on the investigation of crime and trials flourish because the subject is inexhaustible. In this chapter we will touch on two aspects, the control an attorney has over her case in court and the moral questions that may arise as she constructs her strategy. Every attorney wants as much control as possible, wants to avoid being surprised by evidence and witness testimony. And every attorney wants to win. But surprise is inevitable, and winning is possible only if the rules of the game are followed. We will look at both the legal rules of the game, which are often but not always explicit, and the moral rules, which are implicit and often in the eye of the beholder.

The chapter looks at punishment as well as trials. Again, the topic is inexhaustible. We can raise sound and difficult questions about *why* we punish, *how* we punish, and *how severely* we punish. Answers to the first question are of two kinds. Many answers are called "consequentialist" because they justify punishment in terms of the consequences of punishing. Theories of this kind involve specific deterrence (keeping the offender from being in a position to cause further harm), general deterrence (making it clear that harm-causing of a similar kind will be punished, and thus giving a general incentive to refrain), and rehabilitation (making the offender a law-obeying and productive citizen). But other answers to the question of why we punish appeal to a sense of justice and fairness. They argue that the offender has put herself in such a position that a general sense of fairness requires not only blaming her but making her suffer harm that is in some way comparable to the harm she herself has caused. These accounts of punishment's justification are often called retributive.

The two kinds of explanations or justifications of punishment begin with different premises. The first kind assumes that to justify something involves showing how it will make society a better place in the future. The second kind assumes that doing justice—blaming and punishing when they are justly deserved—is a self-evident mandate of morality. But some observers have argued that we accomplish consequentialist and retributive goals at the same time. By punishing those who have willfully done wrong, and doing so *because* they have done wrong, we are also sending the message that we will punish future wrongs and take the underlying rules seriously as norms to live by. Thus, our practice achieves consequentialist goals as well.

The question of *how* to punish is the one that we will examine most seriously from a literary and theoretical perspective. Three hundred years ago, punishment was often physical and public. Public hangings, drawing-and-quarterings, and whippings were events that brought communities together. Incarceration, the most common punishment of the last century and a half, is neither physical nor public. The motive behind it, according to the French theorist Michel Foucault in his extraordinary book *Discipline and Punish,* was to reform and rehabilitate (hence the terms, reformatory and penitentiary). But the more insidious effects seem to be that we have made punishment invisible so that ordinary persons feel no responsibility for it and that we have become oblivious to the psychological harms it causes.

There is much evidence that our system of imprisonment does not deter or rehabilitate very well. Many writers have looked for better results from alternative punishments. As we will see, some of them have focused on renewing the public role in punishment. Dan Kahan at Yale has recommended shaming punishments that bring home to the offender society's condemnation. Others have suggested that the crucial element in effective shaming is that it also educates the offender with regard to the significance of his crime. We will look at this debate at the end of the chapter and will consider other kinds of alternative sanctions as well.

The third question, *how much* to punish, draws attention to societal comparisons. In the U.S., we punish more severely than do most other Western societies. We are unique among them in using the death penalty. And our sentences tend to be much longer for the same crimes. Are there cultural, social, and political differences that explain these variations? If not, how can the differences be justified? And, if they cannot be justified, how can they be explained?

Aside from such comparisons, the problem of how much to punish also implicates comparative seriousness. Should so-called white collar crimes be punished less seriously than crimes of violence? It is hardly clear that they cause less harm. The crimes of the Enron executives cause havoc and economic ruin in the lives of thousands of people. How do we compare that with a single rape or assault? We are translating qualitative results that are in no way commensurate into a quantitative scale. It is hardly clear that we can ever do this with absolute success.

Trial Practice: Controlling the Process

Witness Testimony
Peter Ustinov: There Are 43,200 Seconds in a Day

Witnesses are inherently unreliable—because human nature is inherently unpredictable. What we see often depends on our expectations and emotions; witnesses testifying to the same event may "see" different things. In giving testimony, witnesses are affected by many circumstances—fear about involvement, apprehension about how they will be seen, the uncomfortable sense of their power to affect verdicts, and the attitudes and demeanor of their questioners. And all these variations occur even when the witness is sincere and conscientious about telling the truth. Many witnesses in fact lie, and the possibility of being prosecuted for the crime of perjury deters them no more than other laws deter crime.

The difficulty of controlling witness testimony is one reason many defense attorneys prefer to settle cases through plea bargaining or other means before trial. The Model Rules of Professional Responsibility

(Rule 3.3(3)) prohibit a lawyer from offering testimony or other evidence that she knows is false and requires remedial measures if she discovers the falsity after the evidence is entered. Ironically and perversely, some lawyers *avoid* investigating the true facts of the case so that they maintain deniability if accused of *knowingly* presenting false accounts.

The following story, by the British actor, playwright, and author, Peter Ustinov, presents us with a witness who is as honest as possible. He is punctilious about presenting the truth precisely. But that hardly makes him the ideal witness. Ustinov (1921-2004) used humor and gentle ridicule in most of his plays and stories, and he was a renowned comic actor. One of the most talented comedians of his generation, he won the Academy Award for best supporting actor twice. His Russian ancestors were influential in the arts for generations. As an internationalist, he spent his last thirty years working for Unicef, the United Nations international health organization.

❧ There Are 43,200 Seconds in a Day ❧

Peter Ustinov

Edwin Applecote used to go to the zoo, not to see the lions, but to see the rabbits. Nature he considered marvelous, because every facet of man, every temperament, was reflected in it. The comptroller of his department at the British Broadcasting Corporation was a lion by nature, a red-bearded Scot with a slow but diabolical temper, forever wrapped in hairy tweeds. Miss Butler, the producer of his program, was a bit of a horse, even more of a gnu, that South African animal with a vast, horny nose and tiny hangover eyes. Mustn't be cruel to Miss Butler, though. She might not be a thing of beauty, but she had a beautiful spirit. Miss Mowberry, who ran the section devoted to music and movement for the under fours, was a hen. When she performed her callisthenics on a toe she imagined to be both light and fantastic, she bore a terrible resemblance to a hen rushing in panic from under the wheels of an approaching car. Miss Alsop, the lyric soprano, was a giraffe. Her neck was so long that you could practically follow the notes on the way from the diaphragm into the open air. And he, Edwin Applecote, the high tenor, was a rabbit.

His mother had been an old maid by inclination, and his father a confirmed bachelor. They had married late in life, and it had been a union of two habitual wallflowers. Edwin always blushed at the thought of the process which had given him life, since his parents had always seemed to him far too nice to forget themselves in such an intensely personal way. It only happened once, however. He was an only child.

He had been very close to his mother, but then he had been very close to his father also, since his parents had resembled each other in the most remarkable way, and there was nothing left for him but to resemble them both. Family life had been harmonious, with never an angry word exchanged. Breakfast had been taken at 8:00, lunch at 1:00 sharp, tea at 4:30, supper at 7:45. Mr. Applecote had worked as an assistant in a draper's shop all his life with no thought of promotion. Although a devout man, neither God nor even the King were the figures who crowned his imagination, but Mr. Perry, the owner of the shop he worked in. Mr. Perry this, and Mr. Perry that, dominated every conversation, and Mrs. Applecote was tactful enough to ask "What did Mr. Perry say today?" when she caught her husband daydreaming for a moment.

Even in death his parents had been decent and undramatic, each dying during sleep, the expressions on their faces untroubled by pain, doubt, or even experience.

Edwin had had an average education, and had culled average marks. He hated games, but was too timid to admit it, and so threw himself into them with touching abandon, his games master describing him as a "tryer." The Army discharged him after six months for anemia, and he had found a job near the end of the war, while the competition was negligible, which both suited his temperament and enabled him to eat.

For sixteen years now he had worked on the children's radio program, singing nursery rhymes with Miss Alsop, and lending his voice to an animated puppet called Siegfried, who was a top-hatted rabbit, and a great favorite with the kids.

This work gave him considerable free time, and there was nothing he liked better than to spend his hours of leisure at the zoo, watching the small defenseless creatures of nature engaged in their harmless pursuits. He knew a way of reaching the houses in which they were kept without going too near the large and dangerous mammals. Whenever he was compelled to pass the lions and the tigers, he would imagine ways in which he could save himself if by some chance one of them escaped while he was in the vicinity. He eyed every railing, judging its height, and would walk a little quicker when he was nowhere near a door.

In traffic, too, he would sometimes remain alone on the pavement while a herd of people crossed against the light, trusting in safety in numbers. He could not mount or dismount from a moving bus, nor could he face the escalator in the subway. He was haunted by visions of catching his foot in the machine, and often dreamed about it. The electric rail both fascinated and terrified him, and he couldn't bring himself to travel that way during the rush hour, for fear of being pushed onto it by the crowd. Elevators were another conveyance of which he had a mortal fear. If the car suddenly should drop, he often wondered if it wouldn't be possible to jump in the air at the moment of impact with the bottom, and made elaborate plans for just such a contingency.

Once he had tried to ride a bicycle, and had found it fairly easy to retain his balance, but the sound of any internal combustion engine behind him made him wobble and eventually fall. Being a very phlegmatic person basically, he needed no psychiatric assistance, since no wise man would ever make him braver, and it was merely association with other people, with crowds and machines and open spaces which confused him. Alone, at home, with his few bits of Victorian furniture, his brown velvet curtains, and his odds and ends, all inherited and remembered with affection from the days of a poor but untroubled youth, he felt entirely confident and controlled. When he made himself some tea, and it was often, he laid all the dainty implements out as though he were expecting company. He sipped the tea out of a cup decorated with fading roses, and passed a few polite remarks about it in a small, high voice, taking nine or ten minute mouthfuls to dispose of a scone, and wiping his hands on a monogrammed napkin as though trying to remove bloodstains afterwards. He always washed up after every meal, wearing a mauve apron which had been his mother's. The place was invariably spotless, even if it smelled of age, dampness, and the acrid odor of methylated spirit used to clean the pewter mugs and horse brasses which hung, cottage-like, around the mantelpiece.

This peaceful haven was a two-room apartment on the second floor of a low house in Bayswater, London, north of the park. It is an area of decaying opulence, which finally received its coup de grace during the war, when the bombs felled buildings which would have fallen down anyway. The only other occupant of the house was a Mrs. Sidney, whom Edwin often greeted in the entrance hall, since she appeared to go in and out of her flat with extraordinary frequency. She was a polite lady with a careworn expression and a common voice, and her perfume was disagreeably intense. A Sealyham terrier.

One summer's day Edwin finished his radio program a little earlier than usual, and after returning home briefly for tea, he sped to the zoo in a bus. He pursued his usual complicated path to his friends, the rabbits. He stayed there a full two hours, reflecting that there is no greater consolation in life than to find a creature who shares your fears. So long as rabbits were part of nature, with their innocent eyes and contented chewing, he was just a timid man, not a freak.

When he emerged into the open, it was already beginning to get dark. The zoo was on the point of closing for the night, and he hurried back the way he had come, only to find about halfway to the turnstile that his path was blocked by a barrier. They had begun to work on some underground cables. There was nothing for it, he had to retrace his steps and take the shorter road by the lion house. He began to run, not only because of his fear of being locked in the zoo for the night, but also because the lions were in a fretful mood, and roaring.

The twilight played all manner of cruel tricks on him. As he ran, he believed he saw shapes moving before him, crouching in the shadows, encircling him silently. He staggered through the turnstile and stood for five minutes in the street, leaning on a lamp post, recovering his breath. His thin white brow was beaded with perspiration. It was a bad way to start an evening.

The bus stopped near his home, and he was about to step off, when, with a lurch, it left again. He remonstrated with the conductor, who was not very helpful, but at least made sure that he got off at the next stop before it left again. As he alighted, he apologized to the conductor out of force of habit, although he had absolutely nothing to apologize about.

He walked back towards his home absently, his imagination crowding with leaping lions and crouching pumas. Oh, dear, if it was like this when he was awake, what would it be like when he was asleep? He would have to take a pill and set the alarm. Near his front door, he looked up and saw the police. Not one bobby, but four of them, a squad car, an ambulance, and a couple of plainclothes men.

He stopped dead. This was worse than lions. He couldn't see their eyes, which were hidden in the shadow of their hats and helmets, but there was no mistaking the fact that they were looking at him. What had he done? His radio license had been posted on time, unless it had been mislaid in the mail. The rent had been paid, and the rates. His income tax was deducted at source. During the war, his record had been impeccable as far as his rations were concerned. Admittedly, he had accepted a little extra sugar, but only from a diabetic friend. He had a sweet tooth. Was that a crime? And if it was, did it warrant an entire platoon of policemen and detectives?

The longer he stood there, the more guilt he felt. Suddenly, he could stand the tension no longer. He turned and walked away. Behind him he could hear one, two, three footfalls. This was like riding a bicycle. The feet seemed to be gaining on him. He walked faster. As he passed a lamp post, he saw his shadow lengthen grotesquely, and just before he walked out of range of the light, the shadows of three helmets shot past his feet like arrows and disappeared into the gloom. At the next lamp post, the three helmets were closer behind him. He started to run and reached the road. Here he paused in order to be certain that no traffic was approaching. He looked right, left, right again, as he had been taught in the propaganda against jaywalking, and they caught him.

"Are you Edwin Applecote?" asked a stout policeman.

"No."

"You aren't Edwin Applecote?"

"Yes," said Edwin, crestfallen.

"Then why did you say you wasn't?"

"I don't know, sir. I lost my head."

"What made you run away?"

"Same reason, I suppose. What have I done?"

"I don't know. We want you to answer a few questions."

"What about?"

"There's been a murder."

"Murder?"

Edwin fainted in the arms of the policeman who was standing behind him, and they carried him back to his house.

Detective-Inspector McGlashan saw the strange cortege approaching and called out, "Did you get him?"

He was a no-nonsense man with a glorious record in the Western Desert, where Montgomery had helped him to win the campaign.

His eyes narrowed as he said, "Resisted, did he? The blighter."

"No, fainted," answered Constable Matley. "Fainted clear away when he heard there'd been a murder."

They put Edwin gently in the gutter to rest.

"So that's Applecote, is it?" snarled McGlashan. "Pretty poor specimen."

"I'd say he weighed about ninety pounds," laughed Matley. "Some people have all the luck."

Constable Norton was very young. Seeing the intense expression on McGlashan's face, he said, excitedly, "You don't think he did it, do you, sir?"

McGlashan shot a withering look at the boy.

"I know, Norton, that in the detective stories, criminals always return to the scene of their crime, but they usually allow a decent interval of time to elapse. If you committed a murder, would you come back an hour later?"

"No, sir."

"Why not?"

"Well . . . well . . ."

"You'd be frightened that you'd run headlong into the police, wouldn't you?"

"Yes, sir."

"Very well, then, stop talking through the back of your head."

"Yes, sir." Norton wasn't defeated. His keen young face lit up again.

"Of course, he may be a loony, sir."

McGlashan looked sourly at Edwin.

"I wouldn't put it past him at that," he growled.

"Where am I?" asked Edwin, who was in time to see a body being carried from his house on a stretcher.

"Hold it," said McGlashan to the stretcher bearers, and then turning to Edwin, asked, "Did you know Mrs. Sidney?"

"Yes — that is, I didn't know her exactly."

"You'd recognize her if you saw her again?"

"Oh, yes. She's been living here for over three years."

McGlashan helped Edwin to his feet and walked him to the stretcher.

With a brisk, unemotional gesture, he pulled the blanket away to reveal the face of Mrs. Sidney, hideously mangled and spattered with blood.

Edwin screamed and fainted again. McGlashan caught him and called in a disgusted voice, "It's her all right. Norton, Mayhew, get him off me."

The pathologist, Dr. Golly, came slowly out of the house.

"She's been dead less than an hour," he said. "Evidently she didn't die at once."

"Of course not. She called the police," said McGlashan. "Death was caused by the cumulative effects of a beating, both with fists and with a stick, as far as I can see at the moment. She had been drinking. Very sordid."

Edwin was white. He had a splitting headache, and wished to be sick.

"Let's go up to your flat," said McGlashan.

"All right."

Edwin led the way, but stopped when he saw some dark patches on the wooden floor of the entrance hall.

"What's that?" he asked.

"Blood."

Edwin vomited, and then declared that he couldn't stay there a moment longer.

They took him to the station and gave him a cup of tea. As he drank it, he was composed enough to reflect that their tea wasn't a patch on his.

"Now," said McGlashan, "where were you an hour ago, that is at about seven-fifteen to seven-thirty?"

"I was at the zoo."

"The zoo closes at six."

"Not in summer."

McGlashan nodded. Edwin had escaped from that trap.

"What were you doing at the zoo?"

"I often go."

"That's no answer."

"I like the zoo. I go to look at the animals."

"Which animals?"

"Lions, tigers, all animals," he lied, and blushed. He was seized with a feeling that he had deserted his little friends. "Rabbits," he added lamely.

"Rabbits," said McGlashan, with more intensity than the word could carry. He lit a cigarette in order to appear casual.

"Cigarette?"

"I neither smoke nor drink. May I have a butterscotch pastille? They steady me."

McGlashan was beginning to wonder whether Edwin wasn't slightly mad, or perhaps just acting stupid.

"You say you go to the zoo often. You must have a very special kind of work to get so much free time."

"I work for the BBC."

"What are you, a sports commentator?"

"Oh, lordie, no. I work on the children's program *Come Out to Play*, at three-fifteen daily."

"My daughters watch that."

"Do they?" cried Edwin with delight. "How old are they?"

"One's five, one's two."

"Ah, the two-year-old would be a little young to understand."

"She's old for her age."

"Has she any favorites?"

"Wumbly the Mule."

"Ah, yes, that's Miss Alsop."

"I beg your pardon?"

"Miss Alsop lends her voice to Wumbly. I do Siegfried the Rabbit."

"Rabbit," said McGlashan, putting two and two together and finding no satisfaction in the result. "Give me your autograph, will you, for Jennifer?"

"Really? D'you mean it?" Edwin hesitated. "But this is an official document."

"Doesn't matter." McGlashan smiled wanly. "It's O.K. I'm not tricking you into confessing to a crime you didn't commit. Just sign Siegfried the Rabbit if you wish."

Edwin did so, feeling that there was warmth in the coldest heart if you probed long enough.

"Now," said McGlashan, pocketing the autograph, "let's get down to cases. You often saw Mrs. Sidney?"

"Oh, poor lady, yes, indeed I did. She always seemed to be going in or out."

McGlashan smiled grimly. "I'm not surprised, seeing the nature of her work, are you?"

"What exactly was the nature of her work, sir? I often wondered, but I didn't wish to appear inquisitive. I always imagined she must have had private means."

McGlashan stared at him, incredulous.

"How long have you been living there?" he asked.

"Three years."

"And how long has Mrs. Sidney been living there?"

"She was there when I moved in."

"You noticed nothing?"

"I noticed that she seemed very popular. She was always receiving visitors. In fact, truth to tell, I was a little puzzled that she never asked me in. After all, I was her neighbor." He smiled sadly. "She used to play her radio at all hours, but I didn't really mind. I never liked to bother her. Every time I went down to ask her up for a cup of tea, I could hear through the door that she had company."

There was a pause.

"Don't sit on the edge of the chair," said McGlashan. "Lean back. We don't want you to faint again." He cleared his throat. "Mrs. Sidney was a common harlot."

"A what?" asked Edwin politely.

"A strumpet, a tart."

"I'm sorry, I don't understand."

McGlashan rolled his eyes with exasperation and brought his fist down on his desk. Steadied, he put on a sweet expression and said, "A lady of easy virtue."

"Oh, no," whispered Edwin, turning purple. "Mrs. Sidney? Surely not."

"She picked up customers in the park and brought them back to the flat below yours."

For the first time in his life, Edwin lost his temper. "How disgusting!" he cried in his small voice.

His display of spirit had taken a lot out of him, and he was obviously in no condition to continue answering questions. As he only had very little money on him and clearly couldn't face his own apartment, McGlashan lent him a pound, and the police found him a room in a small hotel in the area. After he had gone,

Constable Matley asked McGlashan whether any information had been gleaned from Edwin.

"No," McGlashan grunted. "He's a dear little fellow, but he's going to be a bloody awful witness when the time comes," and then added, "I don't know how a man like that can survive in this day and age."

Edwin didn't sleep a wink all night, and he worried his colleagues at work. He forgot the words of Oranges and Lemons right in the middle of the program, and seemed quite unable to take a prompt from Miss Alsop. Siegfried the Rabbit was particularly morose that day, and even incoherent. Mothers all over England telephoned to complain that their children had been unable to understand all that Siegfried had said.

He cashed a check and bought a shirt, but couldn't bring himself to go anywhere near the zoo. He returned to the hotel, and just sat down, staring at nothing. At halfpast six, Mr. McGlashan dropped around. "Cheer up," he said.

Edwin hardly reacted.

McGlashan sat down on the bed.

"The main thing is to take an interest in what's going on," he said. "Don't let your mind go blank. You'll have a breakdown."

"Take an interest in what?"

"In our work. You're part of the case, you know. Seen the evening paper?"

"No."

McGlashan put it on Edwin's lap.

The headlines announced that a man had been arrested for the murder of Gertrude O'Toole, otherwise Mrs. Sidney.

"Yes," said McGlashan, "we got him this morning. An easy case. I'm glad we got him that quick. The public was beginning to get restless. So many unsolved murders. We found some letters from him in her handbag, and we picked him up early this morning, asleep on a bench on the Embankment."

"Who is he?" asked Edwin involuntarily.

"A pimp."

"A what?"

The devil wouldn't know where to begin tempting this one. McGlashan felt he was dealing with a clergyman's daughter.

"A man who lives on the immoral earnings of a woman or women," said McGlashan, making it sound as natural as he could.

"How is that possible?" asked Edwin, his voice trembling.

"The woman earns the money, by soliciting, then she gives most of it to her male friend. Women who live that way are curious emotionally. They only live half a life, and this crazy kind of generosity may be their gesture towards the normal life they're forced to do without. I don't know. I'm not a psychologist. I just see the seamy side of life, recognize its patterns, but beyond that I'm not qualified to go. Can't change anything."

"But what about the men . . . the men who accept such money?"

Edwin's face was a mask of real suffering, of horror.

McGlashan kept the tone of his voice as relaxed as he was able, almost weary.

"There'll always be men who think it's smart to get something for nothing, just as there'll always be men who think the male sex is superior to the female. Their instincts invariably seem to lead them to women who agree with them, and who get a vicious kick out of being victimized and pushed around." McGlashan was an intelligent, even an interesting man. His undoubted physical courage was matched by an inquiring and often paradoxical mind which hardly seemed to suit his very active face. He recognized that it took all sorts to make a world, and he was not content with just saying so as a platitude when the occasion arose.

Now he sat facing Edwin, dealing with the situation with the tenderness of a regular sergeant who realizes that some wretched conscript is totally unsuited to his life, and that he is doing his unit more harm than good by his presence there. He leaned forward confidentially.

"I know all these facts are pretty shocking to you, Applecote, but these things exist, and we're not being quite realistic if we try to pretend they don't. Mind you, I'm not telling you all this just in order to get a rise out of you, or to see you flinch. I realize you must have lived a pretty sheltered life, or you'd hardly be surprised by all this. You'd have known Mrs. Sidney for what she was. You might even have moved house. But look here, you're bound to be called on to give evidence—"

"Me?" cried Edwin.

"Yes."

"I'd die!"

"No, you won't die. I just don't want you to make a fool of yourself when the time comes. I don't want you to stand up there and pretend you didn't know what Mrs. Sidney was up to. Nobody'd ever believe you."

"You believe me, don't you?" asked Edwin, averting his eyes.

"I believe you, but it took me nearly twenty-four hours, and you won't be that long in the witness box. Some of these legal guys are tough customers. Too tough, I think. None of them care much for the police, that's how I know. If it should be Sir Cleverdon Bowyer or Sir Giles Parrish prosecuting, well, they're pretty impatient and sarcastic. They're out to rattle you. They want a conviction more than they want the truth."

"Oh, I don't believe that, not in England."

"Anywhere, Applecote. They're like boxers. They've got their reputations to think of, same as you and I. And the way they lose their reputations is by losing cases."

Edwin became sullen and uncommunicative, so McGlashan rose and went to the door.

"I'm going to be proud of you," he said.

"I owe you a pound," said Edwin.

"Never mind about that now —" For the first time McGlashan was embarrassed, and he left.

Back at the station, he confided in Constable Matley.

"I don't give a damn for the killer, he's got it coming to him. I'm worried about Applecote, though. If he falls foul of Bowyer or Parrish, they'll eat him up. Silly to call him really, but I bet they do."

After a few days the producer of Edwin's show, Miss Butler, took him aside and asked him if he was ill. He obviously couldn't concentrate properly, his complexion was appalling, there were pendulous bags under his eyes, and everyone in the department was very concerned about him. He blurted out the truth to her and burst into tears. They were all very kind and understanding, and he was given a week's leave with pay to recuperate.

This enforced absence did him no good whatsoever, since he just sat in his hotel and brooded for four days, eating nothing and sleeping not at all. On the fifth day, he was summoned as a witness for the prosecution. He was expecting this, since he had been interviewed by the clerk of the redoubtable Sir Cleverdon Bowyer, who was prosecuting in the trial of Arnold Ahoe, the alleged murderer. The meeting had passed in a dream, and Edwin could remember nothing of it. He was invaded by a great feeling of emptiness. He could no longer see clearly. Black spots exploded in his eyes, and strange embryonic shapes kept passing sideways across his vision. There was a high, distant song in his ears.

He sat waiting to be called without emotion. Then at last he heard his name chanted by what sounded like an army of toast-masters, and he emerged into the courtroom. The glands at the back of his neck were swollen, and the nerves contorted. Every time he moved his head, it was as though a cargo of packing cases were shifting from one temple to the other in a rough sea.

The judge, Lord Stobury, had the characteristic traits of his profession. A vulture's head was set below the hunched line of the shoulders, the white wig seeming to be powdered with the dust of death. It was hard to tell whether the eyes were open or shut, since the shadows which the brow cast on the eyelids looked strangely like dull, dark pupils. Behind Lord Stobury, a vast lion and unicorn propped up the arms of the realm on the wall, their expressions vindictive and intolerant. Sir Cleverdon Bowyer stood with his thumbs in his waistcoat pocket, a picture of assured arrogance, his single uninterrupted black eyebrow hanging like a canopy over his steel-gray eyes. Mr. Herbert Ammons, the council for the defense, sat with the florid benignity of a fresh Dutch cheese on a welcoming buffet, expressing nothing as yet, his lips curved maliciously in repose. Ahoe, the prisoner, stood listlessly in the dock, an insignificant enough man who seemed quite unworthy of being the pretext for this heraldic assemblage.

This, then, was the place where British justice was dispensed, the place where men were told that they were innocent until proved guilty, but where the atmosphere told them that they were pretty guilty even if proved innocent. Edwin took the oath, and Sir Cleverdon wheeled himself into the position of assault like a wicked piece of artillery. He was a man who had done everything in his life with skill and application. In the 1930's he had run a mile in only very little over four minutes, he had represented his country in a bobsleigh on the Cresta Run, he had won races as a yachtsman and a rally driver, and he had once taken ten games off Tilden. Now he looked as though he were embarking on a sporting contest which he intended to win.

"You are Edwin Applecote?"

"Yes," said Edwin inaudibly.

"Do I pronounce your name right? Is it Cote or Cott?"

"Whichever you prefer."

"You are really most accommodating. You live, as I understand it, in the flat above that of Mrs. Sidney, the murdered woman?"

"Yes."

"How long have you lived there?"

"Three years."

The judge interrupted.

"You must speak up," he said. "I can't hear the answers, and I must hear the answers. That is the cardinal rule of giving evidence. Whatever you say, be audible at all times."

Edwin bowed elaborately.

"Proceed."

The questions at the beginning were fairly pedestrian, since Sir Cleverdon was sure of victory.

"You were, of course, aware of the fact that she was a common harlot," he said suddenly, after several minutes.

"No," said Edwin, his eyes shut. This was terrible, terrible, all these questions in public.

Sir Cleverdon looked up, quick as lightning.

"You were not aware of the fact that the woman was a harlot? Come, come, do you expect me to believe that?"

He shot a look at his clerk, who was completely dumfounded. In the preliminary meeting, Edwin had said everything McGlashan had told him to say, but now, for some reason, he was being utterly honest.

"Is it not a fact," Sir Cleverdon proceeded, "that the deceased was in the habit of entertaining frequently?"

"Yes."

"She arranged her entertainments so that there was only one guest at a time, did she not?"

"I don't know."

"Well, you never saw any women entering her apartment did you?"

"Not that I can recall, sir."

"Did you see men enter her apartment?"

"On one or two occasions, yes."

"Did you ever see the prisoner enter Mrs. Sidney's apartment?"

Edwin looked at Arnold Ahoe.

"I can't tell without my glasses, sir."

"Have you got them with you?"

"Yes."

"Then put them on by all means," Sir Cleverdon thundered, his face suffused with irritation. "Well?"

"I may have done. I can't be sure."

"'You can't be sure'?" Sir Cleverdon repeated incredulously.

"Yes, I think I have seen the gentleman before, but I wouldn't know where I'd seen him."

"The gentleman?"

There was a ripple of laughter in court. Even the prisoner grinned bleakly. The judge rapped his gavel.

Sir Cleverdon had never come across anything like it. What Edwin had said before was entirely different, and Sir Cleverdon was relying upon him to establish an odious and salacious character for the deceased, and therefore, by implication, for the company she kept.

"Do you feel quite well?" asked Sir Cleverdon.

"I haven't been feeling very well recently."

"Perhaps in that case it would be better if we were to excuse you from testifying until such a time as you feel better."

Mr. Ammons was on his feet at once, his cheeks flushed with the pressure of blood and ambition.

"If my honorable and learned friend has finished, I would like to ask the witness a few questions."

"The witness is ill, m'lud," Sir Cleverdon remonstrated.

"He seems able to stand," said the judge in chilly tones, "he is vertical and breathing. The idea that he is ill emanated from you." The judge looked over his glasses at Edwin. "Would you describe yourself as ill?"

Edwin felt a great temptation to give up, but he was too truthful.

"No, my lord."

"Very well. Have you finished, Sir Cleverdon?"

"For the time being, m'lud," said Sir Cleverdon bitterly.

"Proceed, Mr. Ammons."

Sir Cleverdon leaned back and whispered furiously to his clerk, who shrugged his shoulders and wrung his hands.

A pinched smile spread over Ammons's face, a smile of conditional friendship.

"Mr. Applecote, what is the nature of your employment?"

"I'm employed by the BBC, sir."

"The British Broadcasting Corporation," said Ammons, turning towards the jury, and making it sound like a piece of the national heritage. "What function do you serve in that august body?"

"I work on the program for children *Come Out to Play*."

"As an artist?"

"As a singer, sir."

"And how long have you been employed in such a manner?"

"About sixteen years, sir."

"Sixteen years!" cried Ammons, as though it were a century. He grasped his lapels and lowered his head for the charge. "In other words, the British Broadcasting Corporation has seen fit to employ you for sixteen years on a program designed for the pleasure and edification of the young, the men and women of tomorrow, my friends, in their most formative years, the years in which the seeds of hatred, of corruption are, alas, most easily sown. It follows from this that the British Broadcasting Corporation considers you a responsible man. Do you agree with the corporation? Do you consider yourself responsible?"

"Yes, sir, I like to think I am."

"There is no need to be modest here, you know. Would you consider yourself a moral man?"

"I hope so."

"Kindly confine your answers to yes and no," snapped Ammons, losing his smile for a moment. He hated this English incapacity to think highly of oneself in public when it was most urgently needed.

"I would like to be a moral man, sir."

"You don't consider yourself immoral, do you?"

"Oh, no, sir," said Edwin, horrified.

"Very well then. Would you, a moral, responsible man, knowingly take a flat above that of a known woman of the night?"

"Woman of the night, sir?"

"Prostitute," barked Ammons.

"Oh, no."

"How long have you been in residence at your present address?"

"Three years, sir."

"And Mrs. Sidney was living there when you moved in?"

"Yes, sir."

"It stands to reason, therefore, that she gave no appearance of being a woman who lived by commercializing her body, or you would not have stayed?"

"No, sir, I don't think I would."

"And in the three years, the suspicion never entered your mind that she might have belonged to the world's oldest profession?"

"The world's oldest what, sir? I didn't catch that."

"That she was a . . . a prostitute," Ammons practically shouted. He detested having the elegance of his delivery frustrated by stupidity. He glanced at Sir Cleverdon, who smiled grimly.

"No, sir, I didn't know."

"But you do know now, is that it?"

"I've been told."

"Told? By whom?"

"The police."

There was a stir. Ammons looked at the jury. "An allegation, a slur on the character of a woman who is not here to defend herself has been cooked up callously by the police, eager for a quick conviction, whereas a responsible, a moral man, living in the closest possible proximity to the deceased noticed no sign of his neighbor's immoral practices over a span of three years, of thirty-six months, of well over a thousand days!"

Sir Cleverdon objected. Mr. Ammons's job was to cross-examine the witness, not to make speeches to the jury.

The judge upheld the objection, and Mr. Ammons apologized without contrition.

"Take a good look at the accused. I suggest to you that you have never seen him before."

"I couldn't swear it."

"Would you call the face of the accused a distinctive one?"

"I wouldn't know how to answer that, sir."

"Wouldn't you? Then I will tell you. You would answer it by a yes or a no."

"I don't like passing personal remarks about people's faces, sir. After all they can't help the faces they are born with."

The judge answered Ammons's mute appeal with a rap of the gavel.

"That does not seem to me a very fruitful line of country to explore, Mr. Ammons," said the judge.

"I only want to establish the fact that the accused had never been seen before by Mr. Applecote, M'lud."

"The witness has already said that he could not swear to it. Since he is under oath, we must accept his answer at its face value. He may have seen the accused, for all he knows."

"And I may not," said Edwin recklessly.

"I beg your pardon?"

Now even the judge was beginning to become a little rattled.

"You see, my lord," said Edwin, "I may have seen Mr. Ahoe's face on a bus, or in the street. It certainly looks familiar, and yet it may be just that I have seen a face very much like it somewhere or other."

"We are not here to test your memory for human physiognomy," said the judge acidly. "Perhaps, with Mr. Ammons's permission, I may be allowed to ask you whether you actually saw the accused entering the deceased's place of residence at any time."

"I may have done, for all I know."

"And you may not. Very well, proceed," muttered the judge with a huge sigh. "The answer is no."

"Well—"

"That's enough of that," said the judge. "We are wasting time."

"Did you ever speak to Mrs. Sidney?" Mr. Ammons resumed.

"Yes, sir. Never much more than a good morning or a good day."

"Would you describe her as a pleasant, well-spoken person?"

"Yes, sir. Very pleasant. And very well spoken. Her use of language was a little common perhaps, but that's not for me to say."

"How can a person be well spoken and common at the same time?" rasped the judge.

"It is difficult, I admit, sir. I don't like speaking ill of people. It's not my place."

"It is your place to tell us what you know, and not to indulge in niceties here. Now, was she, in your opinion, well spoken or vulgar?" The judge hated gray as much as he loved black and white.

"She was well spoken, I would say."

"Very well. Proceed."

"With a tendency towards vulgarity."

The judge threw up his hands.

Edwin added quickly, "I don't think she could help it, you see."

"She had none of the traits you would associate with her alleged profession, had she?" asked Mr. Ammons. "No excessive paint, no perfume, no high heels or black stockings or the like?"

"Well, she used a very strong perfume, sir, which I could smell upstairs."

"Are you suggesting that her perfume penetrated through the floorboards and the carpeting?"

"Oh, yes, sir, it gave me headaches. I complained once or twice, in a polite way."

"Did you complain orally?"

"No. Every time I went down, I could hear through the door that she had company. When she hadn't got company, she was out."

"You mean you listened at her door?"

"Oh, no, sir, you could hear their voices halfway up the stairs."

"Did you listen to the conversations halfway up the stairs?"

"No, sir, I only heard the conversations, I never listened. It wouldn't have been right. And it wasn't always conversation. Sometimes it was just the radio and some furniture moving sounds."

Ammons cleared his throat. "I see. How did you transmit your messages of complaint since you didn't do it orally?"

"I wrote notes, which I pushed under her door."

"Were they ever answered?"

"Never. Except—" Edwin stopped.

"Yes?"

"Once the door opened when I had just pushed my message under it."

"Who appeared?"

"A gentleman."

"A gentleman? How was he dressed?"

"In an undervest."

"And?"

"That's all."

Mr. Ammons faltered. "Do you mean to tell this Court that Mrs. Sidney's door was opened by a man dressed in nothing but an undervest?"

"He may have had socks on, I can't remember."

"No further questions."

Sir Cleverdon rose, his eyebrow arched in triumph.

"With your lordship's permission, I would like to ask the witness a few more questions."

"Not too many, I hope. Proceed."

"Do you remember the face of this man or gentleman, if you prefer it. Would you recognize it again?"

"Well, he was of medium height, dark, fair skin."

"Did he look at all like the accused?"

"Yes, now that you mention it, very much, but I could never swear it was him."

There was some excitement in court, and Ahoe looked at Edwin with sheer hatred.

"And what did this man say to you?"

"I didn't understand what he said to me, but it sounded like — " And here Edwin spoke two words which are never used in any society. There was a gasp in court, a girl giggled, an elderly man shouted something incomprehensible, and the judge demanded order.

"We may see from this the degree of refinement which the friends of your well-spoken neighbor were wont to reach," said Sir Cleverdon.

"What does it mean?" asked Edwin, sick at heart.

"Never mind," said Sir Cleverdon, "but I would advise you not to use it as an expletive in civilian life, however popular it may be in the Armed Forces." And then he added, to put Edwin out of his misery, "It is a way of saying please go away." (Laughter.)

When silence had been re-established, Sir Cleverdon went on, "When did this occur?"

"About eleven o'clock in the morning."

"But when?"

"Oh." Edwin had not recovered from his shock. "On the morning of the murder."

There was consternation. In the previous testimony, Ahoe, who was a truck driver, had freely admitted knowing Mrs. Sidney as a casual acquaintance, but had said that he was with his sister in Islington from nine in the morning of the day of the murder until after the murder. His sister had confirmed his alibi.

"Are you sure of this? On the seventh of July?"

"I don't remember the date, but it was that day. I was on my way to work."

"What time did you leave for work?"

"About eleven."

"Don't you know the precise time of your departure?"

"About eleven."

"Do you mean to tell this Court that you don't know what time you leave for work?"

Edwin began to falter. This was the last straw.

"Do people usually know exactly the time they leave for work?"

"Yes," snapped Sir Cleverdon.

Was he alone in the world, a freak after all? The rabbits could never share this terrible experience with him. How long could he stand this nightmarish room, which seemed to be full of people who knew exactly what they were doing at all hours of the day, and even knew what others should be doing.

"About eleven," he heard his voice saying.

"What time are you due at the BBC?"

"Eleven o'clock."

"Do you mean you leave at about eleven to reach a destination halfway across town at the same hour?"

"I was late that day."

"What time did you arrive?"

"Some time after eleven."

"How long after eleven?"

"About ten past . . . a quarter past."

"How long does it take you to get from home to the BBC?"

"About twenty minutes."

"So it is logical to suppose that you left home between five and ten to eleven?"

"I suppose so."

"Why couldn't you have told me that at the outset?"

"Why?" Edwin blurted. "Because I have sworn to tell the truth and nothing but the truth, and I was wrong to swear it."

"What was that?" asked the judge.

"I don't know the truth," he cried, wide-eyed. "I know I should know exactly about everything, but I don't. I don't know what time I left home, and even if I knew it to the minute, I probably wouldn't know it to the second, and if I couldn't tell you everything, in the minutest detail, I wouldn't be telling you the truth."

"You must speak up," said the judge.

Funny, Edwin thought he had been shouting. Now it appeared he had been muttering all this to himself. He shook his head violently from side to side, closing his eyes, and saw no clearer when he opened them again.

Sir Cleverdon was looking at him intensely, an eagle. So was the judge, a vulture, and Mr. Ammons, a mole.

"In any case, you left home after half-past ten in the morning?"

"I must have done."

"Did you return home again before seven o'clock?"

"Yes, I think so."

"You think so."

"Please don't speak so quickly."

"You must speak up," said the judge.

With a superhuman effort, Edwin pulled himself together.

"The program goes on the air at three-fifteen," he said. "Three-fifteen sharp. It lasts till three-forty-five."

"What did you do after it was over?"

"I returned home to make myself a cup of tea."

"Straight away?"

"Yes."

"So we can assume that you arrived home between four and four-fifteen?"

"I suppose so."

"What do you mean, you suppose so. It stands to reason, doesn't it?"

"If you say so, sir."

"I do. How long did you stay at home?"

"Long enough to make a cup of tea and eat a scone. I had one scone, with margarine and raspberry jam. Then I washed up, dried the dishes, put them in the cupboard, and left for the zoo."

"So, that might have taken another quarter of an hour?"

"I don't know."

"Are you an exceptionally slow eater?"

"I don't know."

"It really is extraordinary that there are people who go through life with no knowledge of when they do what they do or indeed how they do it. Now, concentrate if you will. During your visit to your flat in order to have your cup of tea, was there any evidence of the man's continued presence in Mrs. Sidney's flat?"

"I heard voices."

"Voices?"

"A man was shouting. The radio was on, playing dance music. There was a noise like glass breaking."

"Did you recognize the voice as being the same as the one which had uttered that filthy expletive to your face?"

"I can't tell. It may have been, it may not."

"Did you hear any of the words this voice uttered?"

"Yes. No, I daren't say them, for fear they may be immodest."

"I instruct you to tell us what you heard," said the judge, leaning forward, "and speak up."

"I heard something like — one more crack, or clack out of you, and I will mash you — something like that."

"That was the man talking?"

"Yes, is it very terrible? I remember that because I didn't understand it."

"Did you hear her voice?"

"No, just her laugh. I kept hearing her laugh, right up to the time I left."

"And what did you think when you heard the glass break?"

"I thought someone had dropped a glass."

"Was it not a more violent sound than that? Was it not the sound of a glass which had been thrown rather than dropped?"

"What would be the point of that?"

"A glass can injure if it is thrown hard enough and hits its target."

"I've never heard of anyone doing that."

"Speak up," said the judge.

"Now, when you left to go to the zoo," asked Sir Cleverdon intensely, "did you see a vehicle parked outside the house?"

"I don't remember."

"A six-wheeled truck?"

"I don't know."

"You noticed no vehicle at all?"

"Oh, I do remember some boys playing cricket in the street. The ball rolled under a car, and one of the boys went underneath to get it. I told him to be careful, as it was dangerous, and I looked into the driving compartment to make sure that the driver wasn't there."

"How old was the boy?"

"About ten, twelve, fourteen perhaps. I'm not very good at the ages of children."

"If he was playing cricket, he was presumably over six."

"Oh, I think so, he was smoking."

"Smoking? You said it was a car. Would a boy of an age to smoke find it easy to clamber under a modern car?"

"No, it must have been bigger than a car."

"Did you have to stoop in order to look into the driving compartment?"

"No, I had to stand on tiptoe."

"Stand on tiptoe? Unless the car was built before 1910, I suggest it was a truck—a gay Leyland truck, perhaps, with the name of the Hiscox Brothers, of Hemel Hempstead in white letters on the door?"

Ammons objected to the form of the question. Sir Cleverdon withdrew the question, but no one could deny that he had asked it.

"I do remember something about it," Edwin volunteered, his hand over his forehead.

Ahoe tensed visibly.

"Speak louder," commanded the judge.

"I remember there was a picture . . . a transfer I suppose it was . . . of a young lady rather immodestly dressed in a bathing costume . . . holding a colored ball . . . it was stuck on the window the drivers have to look through to see the road . . . the windscreen, is it? I remember wondering how the police could tolerate such a thing, placed as it was, in the line of vision, and rather disgustingly suggestive."

Although this was quite inconclusive as evidence, Ahoe evidently thought he had fallen into a trap, and being a man of short and vitriolic temper, he rose to his feet and yelled a repulsive phrase at Edwin, which Edwin mercifully didn't understand.

Sir Cleverdon threw down his papers dramatically. Ammons muttered, "No further questions."

The judge looked straight at Edwin and said, in the crackling tones of a boot on autumn leaves, "If it should ever fall to your lot to give evidence again, I strongly advise you to be more observant and also more coherent. Today you initially gave the deceased a rosy and innocuous character, and then, under cross-examination, you proceeded to attribute to her a character so different that it is hard not to suspect you of mendacious intentions at the outset. I do not believe this is so, since you are clearly a man who is not used to giving evidence, and who sincerely believes that a person should be accorded the benefit of the doubt. But a benefit of the doubt is one thing, and a total blindness to the facts is another. It leads to dangerous evidence, which might, if not subjected to the most stringent methods of our legal system, even entail grave miscarriages of justice. I urge you to reflect on what I have said, since your evidence here today has been, in all my experience, the most misleading and the most illogical. Next witness, please."

Edwin was not the key witness by any means. Ahoe's sister, on re-examination, broke down and confessed that her alibi had been a lie. The truck had been over twenty-four hours overdue, and the police found letters and fingerprints which eventually sent Ahoe to prison for life.

But Ahoe was not the only one whose mode of living was affected by this case. Edwin could no longer go home. He stayed on in the hotel, taking care to lock the door on every occasion. He bought a little book, and carefully inscribed the exact minute he left for work and the exact moment he arrived for work. As he sat in the bus, his eye scanned the road for anything suspicious or noteworthy. His perception was unnecessarily acute, and his manner had become curiously abrupt.

At work, he would greet his old friend Miss Alsop by saying things he had never said before. "Good morning, Miss Alsop, you are wearing green, I see. Green tweed, is it? And a cameo depicting the head of a Georgian lady in profile. Shoes? Brown brogues, lisle stockings. Thank you. That will be all for the moment." And he would note all these details in his book. Miss Butler was subjected to the same strange treatment, and he would even stop singing the middle of his nursery rhymes, not because he had forgotten the lines, but because he suddenly noticed as he sang that the studio clock did not tally to the minute with the watch on his wrist. Only when playing Siegfried the Rabbit was he entirely his old self, tender, whimsical and slightly tragic.

Miss Butler tried valiantly to understand his problem. "Do you never go to the zoo as you used to?" she asked kindly.

A sly look came into his eye. "Oh, no," he answered, "animals can't talk. If anything were to happen to me there, they could never give evidence."

"What could happen to you?"

"Murder." said Edwin, unmoved.

"Murder? Who would want to murder you?"

"There are millions of people in London," Edwin said evasively, "but they'd never get away with it, not now. Do you know, when I go home at night, I lock the door and write out on a piece of paper who I am and what I do, addressed to whom it may concern, and I hide it under the mattress. I outline all my movements for that day, whom I have talked to and what we talked about. You, Miss Butler, will be on it tonight, and so will our conversation." He glanced at his watch. "It's four-oh-eight."

"But why do you do this, Mr. Applecote?" asked Miss Butler, beginning to feel distinctly uncomfortable.

"To classify the evidence, Miss Butler. I don't know whether you've ever given evidence, but it must be clear and audible. I don't know whether you've noticed it, but I've been training myself to speak in a rather louder voice."

"The engineers have noticed it. You're giving them a very bad time."

Edwin laughed. "You see, by putting the paper under the mattress, the police would discover it, but no murderer would have the presence of mind to look there." He frowned uncertainly. "Or perhaps he would, perhaps I'd better put it somewhere else?"

It was with genuine regret that the Children's Broadcast Department were forced to say good-bye to Edwin Applecote, but his nursery rhymes were becoming really too erratic, and his behavior more and more disconcerting. With unconscious cruelty, they gave him a beautifully inscribed clock as a farewell present. No two clocks ever tell precisely the same time for long, and Edwin was to spend many harassed hours checking watch and clock, and trying to find which one of them was correct.

Inspector McGlashan waited in the anteroom to see Dr. Feindienst, a large cardboard box under his arm. Eventually the doctor entered the room, and the two men shook hands.

"How is he?" asked McGlashan.

"He's a dear little fellow," said Dr. Fiendienst, with a light Austrian accent. "Quite harmless, and no trouble, not like some of them, violent paranoiacs and so on. You wish to see him?"

"May I?"

"Of course, follow me."

"May I leave this packet here?"

"Surely."

As they walked down the corridor, Dr. Feindienst said, "Our main problem is to keep him quiet. He is so intensely observant that he exhausts himself by noticing everything and by noting it down."

McGlashan entered Edwin's room. The blinds were drawn.

"Remember me, McGlashan?"

"Certainly I do, the German shepherd."

"Eh?"

Edwin was more than cordial. "Please sit down, Inspector. Well, you'll never catch me napping again. They draw the blinds to keep me quiet, but when they're gone, I peep out. I was peeping out when I heard you coming down the corridor. You nearly caught me at it, but not quite."

"What have you been doing?" asked the inspector.

He hardly expected the answer he got.

"Me? I'll tell you. I woke up at six-thirty-seven, washed from six-thirty-nine to six-fifty-one, brushed my teeth at six-fifty-two, had breakfast consisting of a boiled egg, from New Zealand it was, said so on the shell, tea, two rolls and butter, with one lump of sugar in the tea. This took from precisely seven-oh-nine to seven-twenty-one. I read the paper, the News Chronicle, second edition, from seven-thirteen, when I picked it up, to seven-twenty-nine, when I put it down. Since then, I have been here in my room, except for a short walk. I left at ten-nineteen and returned at ten-forty-six. It was ten-fifty-seven when you stepped into the room. Incidentally, Inspector, what is the time on your watch?"

"Eleven sharp."

"You're almost a minute fast."

"Oh, thanks." McGlashan pretended to adjust his watch.

"I say, if there should be a crime committed across the way," Edwin whispered, indicating the window with his finger, "at No. 18, a blue Austin station wagon pulled up there at nine-forty-one, and it's been there ever since. The number is BXC715."

"Thank you very much," said McGlashan sadly, pretending to write the number down. "When we catch him, it'll be thanks to you."

There was a shy pause, during which McGlashan tried to hypnotize him back to sanity.

"Don't you miss your rabbits?" he said at length.

"No," answered Edwin, "they're happy where they are. They don't have the problems we have."

"Perhaps they do, but we just don't understand their language."

"Yes, perhaps they do," said Edwin, with a noncommittal sigh.

"And don't you miss the BBC?"

"Not now that I'm doing really important work, collecting evidence."

"They miss you."

"Who?"

"The children."

"I've no time for children now. This is a man's world. You mustn't be too gentle, mustn't be blind to the facts." He gave this quote from the judge a fearful emphasis.

Back in the office, Dr. Feindienst asked, "How did you find him?"

"Damn the legal profession," said McGlashan with venom. "What do they do? For the purposes of argument they take a completely extraordinary event, full of extraordinary and perverted aspects, and make it sound ordinary and natural. Why should a little fellow like that know all the horrible uses to which life is put by those who take it for granted? Why shouldn't he have the right to be naive and simple. They convicted a murderer and they sent a witness off his head. That's called justice. And where are they now? In their clubs thinking of ways to make our job impossible, while that poor little bastard is in here, thinking up a lot of evidence he'll never be called on to give. It makes me sick."

Dr. Feindienst smiled. "You sound as if you're ready to occupy one of our padded cells."

McGlashan leaned forward conspiratorially. "I'll tell you something, Doctor, that little fellow had something, and I'm not making this up, and I didn't get it out of my own head. I got it from my girl, aged five. I went up to say good night to her at bedtime yesterday, and she looked up at me and asked, 'Daddy, why's Siegfried the Rabbit got a different voice now?' By god, Doctor, I could have told her. I could have told her, and I will one day."

"Well, who knows, he may be back in a year or two."

McGlashan shook his head. "You know as well as I do that isn't true, Doctor. They hurt him too much out there. He can't take it. And all I say is, things should be arranged so he can take it."

The doctor sighed. "It's a cruel world, Inspector. Both our professions should tell us that."

"Cruel?" said McGlashan. "It's filthy. Filthy. And often its those who look the cleanest who are the filthiest. Those with responsibilities."

McGlashan picked up his package carefully and went to the door. Before going out, he turned and said, "We don't have to complain. We can look after ourselves." With a strange delicacy he looked at the box he was carrying. "I had brought him a present, but I'd better not give it him, though, after our conversation. I'll give it to my girl."

"What is it?" asked Dr. Feindienst.

McGlashan poked a piece of protruding lettuce back into the box and said softly, "A rabbit."

Discussion Topics

1. Does this story make you question the usefulness and efficacy of a trial as a way of determining facts? As a witness, does Edwin help or hurt the prosecution's case? If you were the prosecutor, how would you reach the decision whether to call him to testify? Note that he is perhaps uniquely situated to have seen events that no one else saw. The decision to do without his story may make the prosecutor's job harder.

2. Can we fault the prosecutor for doing his job badly? We generally distinguish between advising or coaching witnesses to give false testimony, which is prohibited, and preparing witnesses to give a coherent and intelligible version of the true facts as they see them. On one hand, the story gives us no sense that Edwin has been given the chance to anticipate the questions and consider his answers. On the other hand, perhaps he is inherently unteachable. His naïveté and limited powers of inference are striking. Some readers conclude that he is mentally disabled. Is that a plausible inference about Ustinov's intentions?

(The prosecutor's surprise, frustration, and inability to control Edwin's story may be explained by the English practice of separating the job of solicitor and barrister. The solicitor prepares the case; the barrister argues in court. Since the barrister's contact with the parties is through the solicitor, it is likely that he had no prior acquaintance with Edwin.)

3. Edwin is a sympathetic figure — for most readers. He illustrates the English tolerance and even encouragement of eccentricity. But is he ethically beyond reproach? The consequences of naïveté can be great. Suppose violent child abuse or spousal abuse were occurring in the downstairs apartment, and suppose Edwin chose to interpret the distinctive screams as evidence of game-playing or loud television shows. It can be argued that we are all responsible, at least minimally, for the well-being of our neighbors and fellow citizens and that we must not ignore obvious predicaments when we can, with little dislocation of our own lives, intervene. If we see danger by the side of the road, may we drive on knowing that the drivers behind us will be imperiled?

Doctored Evidence
Agatha Christie: Witness for the Prosecution

Physical evidence rarely betrays the litigator if it is appropriately examined before trial. The attorney vouches for the evidence he introduces. If he makes false claims for it, he is bound by Model Rule 3.3(3) of the Model Rules of Professional Responsibility to correct the claims. He can, of course, neither destroy evidence with impunity nor manufacture evidence.

The lawyer's interest in winning a case can seduce him into taking evidence at face value when its origins and existence may warrant further investigation. Agatha Christie's "Witness for the Prosecution" shows how readily a lawyer may embrace evidence that he receives in suspicious circumstances. It shows us, as well, that the various players in a trial may have complex strategies that play on each other's strengths and weaknesses. The story, one of Ms. Christie's best-known in her vast corpus of mysteries, was made into an extraordinary 1957 film with three of most charismatic stars of that period, Marlene Dietrich, Charles Laughton, and Tyrone Power.

❧ Witness for the Prosecution ❧

Agatha Christie

Mr. Mayherne adjusted his pince-nez and cleared his throat with a little dry-as-dust cough that was wholly typical of him. Then he looked again at the man opposite him, the man charged with willful murder.

Mr. Mayherne was a small man, precise in manner, neatly, not to say foppishly dressed, with a pair of very shrewd and piercing gray eyes. By no means a fool. Indeed, as a solicitor, Mr. Mayherne's reputation stood very high. His voice, when he spoke to his client, was dry but not unsympathetic.

"I must impress upon you again that you are in very grave danger, and that the utmost frankness is necessary."

Leonard Vole, who had been staring in a dazed fashion at the blank wall in front of him, transferred his glance to the solicitor.

"I know," he said hopelessly. "You keep telling me so. But I can't seem to realize yet that I'm charged with murder—*murder*. And such a dastardly crime, too."

Mr. Mayherne was practical, not emotional. He coughed again, took off his pince-nez, polished them carefully, and replaced them on his nose. Then he said, "Yes, yes, yes. Now, my dear Mr. Vole, we're going to make a determined effort to get you off — and we shall succeed — we shall succeed. But I must have all the facts. I must know just how damaging the case against you is likely to be. Then we can fix upon the best line of defense."

Still the young man looked at him in the same dazed, hopeless fashion. To Mr. Mayherne the case had seemed black enough, and the guilt of the prisoner assured. Now, for the first time, he felt a doubt.

"You think I'm guilty," said Leonard Vole, in a low voice. "But I swear I'm not! It looks pretty black against me, I know that. I'm like a man caught in a net — the meshes of it all round me, entangling me whichever way I turn. But I didn't do it, Mr. Mayherne, I didn't do it!"

In such a position a man was bound to protest his innocence. Mr. Mayherne knew that. Yet, in spite of himself, he was impressed. It might be, after all, that Leonard Vole was innocent.

"You are right, Mr. Vole," he said gravely. "The case does look very black against you. Nevertheless, I accept your assurance. Now, let us get to facts. I want you to tell me in your own words exactly how you came to make the acquaintance of Miss Emily French."

"It was one day in Oxford Street. I saw an elderly lady crossing the road. She was carrying a lot of parcels. In the middle of the street she dropped them, tried to recover them, found a bus was almost on top of her, and just managed to reach the curb safely, dazed and bewildered by people having shouted at her. I recovered her parcels, wiped the mud off them as best I could, retied the string of one, and returned them to her."

"There was no question of your having saved her life?"

"Oh, dear me, no! All I did was to perform a common act of courtesy. She was extremely grateful, thanked me warmly, and said something about my manners not being those of most of the younger generation — I can't remember the exact words. Then I lifted my hat and went on. I never expected to see her again. But life is full of coincidences. That very evening I came across her at a party at a friend's house. She recognized me at once and asked that I should be introduced to her. I then found out that she was a Miss Emily French and that she lived at Cricklewood. I talked to her for some time. She was, I imagine, an old lady who took sudden and violent fancies to people. She took one to me on the strength of a perfectly simple action which anyone might have performed. On leaving, she shook me warmly by the hand and asked me to come and see her. I replied, of course, that I should be very pleased to do so, and she then urged me to name a day. I did not want particularly to go, but it would have seemed churlish to refuse, so I fixed on the following Saturday. After she had gone, I learned something about her from my friends. That she was rich, eccentric, lived alone with one maid, and owned no less than eight cats."

"I see," said Mr. Mayherne. "The question of her being well off came up as early as that?"

"If you mean that I inquired — " began Leonard Vole hotly, but Mr. Mayherne stilled him with a gesture.

"I have to look at the case as it will be presented by the other side. An ordinary observer would not have supposed Miss French to be a lady of means. She lived poorly, almost humbly. Unless you had been told the contrary, you would in all probability have considered her to be in poor circumstances — at any rate to begin with. Who was it exactly who told you that she was well off?"

"My friend, George Harvey, at whose house the party took place."

"Is he likely to remember having done so?"

"I really don't know. Of course it is some time ago now."

"Quite so, Mr. Vole. You see, the first aim of the prosecution will be to establish that you were in low water financially — that is true, is it not?"

Leonard Vole flushed.

"Yes," he said, in a low voice. "I'd been having a run of infernal bad luck just then."

"Quite so," said Mr. Mayherne again. "That being, as I say, in low water financially, you met this rich old lady and cultivated her acquaintance assiduously. Now if we are in a position to say that you had no idea she was well off, and that you visited her out of pure kindness of heart — "

"Which is the case."

"I dare say. I am not disputing the point. I am looking at it from the outside point of view. A great deal depends on the memory of Mr. Harvey. Is he likely to remember that conversation or is he not? Could he be confused by counsel into believing that it took place later?"

Leonard Vole reflected for some minutes. Then he said steadily enough, but with a rather pale face, "I do not think that that line would be successful, Mr. Mayherne. Several of those present heard his remark, and one or two of them chaffed me about my conquest of a rich old lady."

The solicitor endeavored to hide his disappointment with a wave of the hand.

"Unfortunate," he said. "But I congratulate you upon your plain speaking, Mr. Vole. It is to you I look to guide me. Your judgment is quite right. To persist in the line I spoke of would have been disastrous. We must leave that point. You made the acquaintance of Miss French, you called upon her, the acquaintanceship progressed.

We want a clear reason for all this. Why did you, a young man of thirty-three, good-looking, fond of sport, popular with your friends, devote so much of your time to an elderly woman with whom you could hardly have anything in common?"

Leonard Vole flung out his hands in a nervous gesture.

"I can't tell you—I really can't tell you. After the first visit, she pressed me to come again, spoke of being lonely and unhappy. She made it difficult for me to refuse. She showed so plainly her fondness and affection for me that I was placed in an awkward position. You see, Mr. Mayherne, I've got a weak nature—I drift— I'm one of those people who can't say no. And believe me or not, as you like, after the third or fourth visit I paid her I found myself getting genuinely fond of the old thing. My mother died when I was young, an aunt brought me up, and she, too, died before I was fifteen. If I told you that I genuinely enjoyed being mothered and pampered, I dare say you'd only laugh."

Mr. Mayherne did not laugh. Instead he took off his pince-nez again and polished them, a sign with him that he was thinking deeply.

"I accept your explanation, Mr. Vole," he said at last. "I believe it to be psychologically probable. Whether a jury would take that view of it is another matter. Please continue your narrative. When was it that Miss French first asked you to look into her business affairs?"

"After my third or fourth visit to her. She understood very little of money matters, and was worried about some investments."

Mr. Mayherne looked up sharply.

"Be careful, Mr. Vole. The maid, Janet Mackenzie, declares that her mistress was a good woman of business and transacted all her own affairs, and this is borne out by the testimony of her bankers."

"I can't help that," said Vole earnestly. "That's what she said to me."

Mr. Mayherne looked at him for a moment or two in silence. Though he had no intention of saying so, his belief in Leonard Vole's innocence was at that moment strengthened. He knew something of the mentality of elderly ladies. He saw Miss French, infatuated with the good-looking young man, hunting about for pretexts that would bring him to the house. What more likely than that she would plead ignorance of business, and beg him to help her with her money affairs? She was enough of a woman of the world to realize that any man is slightly flattered by such an admission of his superiority. Leonard Vole had been flattered. Perhaps, too, she had not been averse to letting this young man know that she was wealthy. Emily French had been a strong-willed old woman, willing to pay her price for what she wanted. All this passed rapidly through Mr. Mayherne's mind, but he gave no indication of it, and asked instead a further question.

"And did you handle her affairs for her at her request?"

"I did."

"Mr. Vole," said the solicitor, "I am going to ask you a very serious question, and one to which it is vital I should have a truthful answer. You were in low water financially. You had the handling of an old lady's affairs — an old lady who, according to her own statement, knew little or nothing of business. Did you at any time, or in any manner, convert to your own use the securities which you handled? Did you engage in any transaction for your own pecuniary advantage which will not bear the light of day?" He quelled the other's response. "Wait a minute before you answer. There are two courses open to us. Either we can make a feature of your probity and honesty in conducting her affairs while pointing out how unlikely it is that you would commit murder to obtain money which you might have obtained by such infinitely easier means. If, on the other hand, there is anything in your dealings which the prosecution will get hold of — if, to put it badly, it can be proved that you swindled the old lady in any way, we must take the line that you had no motive for the murder, since she was already a profitable source of income to you. You perceive the distinction. Now, I beg of you, take your time before you reply."

But Leonard Vole took no time at all.

"My dealings with Miss French's affairs were all perfectly fair and above board. I acted for her interests to the very best of my ability, as anyone will find who looks into the matter."

"Thank you," said Mr. Mayherne. "You relieve my mind very much. I pay you the compliment of believing that you are far too clever to lie to me over such an important matter."

"Surely," said Vole eagerly, "the strongest point in my favor is the lack of motive. Granted that I cultivated the acquaintanceship of a rich old lady in the hopes of getting money out of her — that, I gather, is the substance of what you have been saying — surely her death frustrates all my hopes?"

The solicitor looked at him steadily. Then, very deliberately, he repeated his unconscious trick with his pince-nez. It was not until they were firmly replaced on his nose that he spoke.

"Are you not aware, Mr. Vole, that Miss French left a will under which you are the principal beneficiary?"

"What?" The prisoner sprang to his feet. His dismay was obvious and unforced. "What are you saying? She left her money to me?"

Mr. Mayherne nodded slowly. Vole sank down again, his head in his hands.

"You pretend you know nothing of this will?"

"Pretend? There's no pretense about it. I knew nothing about it."

"What would you say if I told you that the maid, Janet Mackenzie, swears that you did know? That her mistress told her distinctly that she had consulted you in the matter, and told you of her intentions?"

"Say? That she's lying! No, I go too fast. Janet is an elderly woman. She was a faithful watchdog to her mistress, and she didn't like me. She was jealous and suspicious. I should say that Miss French confided her intentions to Janet, and that Janet either mistook something she said, or else was convinced in her own mind that I had persuaded the old lady into doing it. I dare say that she herself believes now that Miss French actually told her so."

"You don't think she dislikes you enough to lie deliberately about the matter?"

Leonard Vole looked shocked and startled.

"No, indeed! Why should she?"

"I don't know," said Mr. Mayherne thoughtfully. "But she's very bitter against you."

The wretched young man groaned again.

"I'm beginning to see," he muttered. "It's frightful. I made up to her, that's what they'll say, I got her to make a will leaving her money to me, and then I go there that night, and there's nobody in the house — they find her the next day — oh, it's awful!"

"You are wrong about there being nobody in the house," said Mr. Mayherne. "Janet, as you remember, was to go out for the evening. She went, but about half past nine she returned to fetch the pattern of a blouse sleeve which she had promised to a friend. She let herself in by the back door, went upstairs and fetched it, and went out again. She heard voices in the sitting-room, though she could not distinguish what they said, but she will swear that one of them was Miss French's and one was a man's."

"At half past nine," said Leonard Vole. "At half past nine —" He sprang to his feet. "But then I'm saved — saved —"

"What do you mean, saved?" cried Mr. Mayherne, astonished.

"By half past nine I was at home again! My wife can prove that. I left Miss French about five minutes to nine. I arrived home about twenty past nine. My wife was there waiting for me. Oh, thank God — thank God! And bless Janet Mackenzie's sleeve pattern."

In his exuberance, he hardly noticed that the grave expression on the solicitor's face had not altered. But the latter's words brought him down to earth with a bump.

"Who, then, in your opinion, murdered Miss French?"

"Why, a burglar, of course, as was thought at first. The window was forced, you remember. She was killed with a heavy blow from a crowbar, and the crowbar was found lying on the floor beside the body. And several articles were missing. But for Janet's absurd suspicions and dislike of me, the police would never have swerved from the right track."

"That will hardly do, Mr. Vole," said the solicitor. "The things that were missing were mere trifles of no value, taken as a blind. And the marks on the window were not at all conclusive. Besides, think for yourself. You say you were no longer in the house by half past nine. Who, then, was the man Janet heard talking to Miss French in the sitting-room? She would hardly be having an amicable conversation with a burglar."

"No," said Vole. "No—" He looked puzzled and discouraged. "But, anyway," he added with reviving spirit, "it lets me out. I've got an alibi. You must see Romaine—my wife—at once."

"Certainly," acquiesced the lawyer. "I should already have seen Mrs. Vole but for her being absent when you were arrested. I wired to Scotland at once, and I understand that she arrives back tonight. I am going to call upon her immediately I leave here."

Vole nodded, a great expression of satisfaction settling down over his face.

"Yes, Romaine will tell you. It's a lucky chance that."

"Excuse me, Mr. Vole, but you are very fond of your wife?"

"Of course."

"And she of you?"

"Romaine is devoted to me. She'd do anything in the world for me."

He spoke enthusiastically, but the solicitor's heart sank a little lower. The testimony of a devoted wife—would it gain credence?

"Was there anyone else who saw you return at nine-twenty. A maid, for instance?"

"We have no maid."

"Did you meet anyone in the street on the way back?"

"Nobody I knew. I rode part of the way in a bus. The conductor might remember."

Mr. Mayherne shook his head doubtfully.

"There is no one, then, who can confirm your wife's testimony?"

"No. But it isn't necessary, surely?"

"I dare say not. I dare say not," said Mr. Mayherne hastily. "Now there's just one thing more. Did Miss French know that you were a married man?"

"Oh, yes."

"Yet you never took your wife to see her. Why was that?"

For the first time, Leonard Vole's answer came halting and uncertain.

"Well—I don't know."

"Are you aware that Janet Mackenzie says her mistress believed you to be single, and contemplated marrying you in the future?"

Vole laughed. "Absurd! There was forty years' difference in age between us."

"It has been done," said the solicitor dryly. "The fact remains. Your wife never met Miss French?"

"No—" Again the constraint.

"You will permit me to say," said the lawyer, "that I hardly understand your attitude in the matter."

Vole flushed, hesitated, and then spoke.

"I'll make a clean breast of it. I was hard up, as you know. I hoped that Miss French might lend me some money. She was fond of me, but she wasn't at all interested in the struggles of a young couple. Early on, I found that she had taken it for granted that my wife and I didn't get on—were living apart. Mr. Mayherne—I wanted the money—for Romaine's sake. I said nothing, and allowed the old lady to think what she chose. She spoke of my being an adopted son to her. There was never any question of marriage—that must be just Janet's imagination."

"And that is all?"

"Yes—that is all."

Was there just a shade of hesitation in the words? The lawyer fancied so. He rose and held out his hand.

"Good-by, Mr. Vole." He looked into the haggard young face and spoke with an unusual impulse. "I believe in your innocence in spite of the multitude of facts arrayed against you. I hope to prove it and vindicate you completely."

Vole smiled back at him.

"You'll find the alibi is all right," he said cheerfully.

Again he hardly noticed that the other did not respond.

"The whole thing hinges a good deal on the testimony of Janet Mackenzie," said Mr. Mayherne. "She hates you. That much is clear."

"She can hardly hate me," protested the young man.

The solicitor shook his head as he went out. *Now* for Mrs. Vole, he said to himself. He was seriously disturbed by the way the thing was shaping.

The Voles lived in a small shabby house near Paddington Green. It was to this house that Mr. Mayherne went.

In answer to his ring, a big slatternly woman, obviously a charwoman, answered the door.

"Mrs. Vole? Has she returned yet?"

"Got back an hour ago. But I dunno if you can see her."

"If you will take my card to her," said Mr. Mayherne quietly. "I am quite sure that she will do so."

The woman looked at him doubtfully, wiped her hand on her apron, and took the card. Then she closed the door in his face and left him on the step outside.

In a few minutes, however, she returned with a slightly altered manner.

"Come inside, please."

She ushered him into a tiny drawing-room. Mr. Mayherne, examining a drawing on the wall, started up suddenly to face a tall, pale woman who had entered so quietly that he had not heard her.

"Mr. Mayherne? You are my husband's solicitor, are you not? You have come from him? Will you please sit down?"

Until she spoke he had not realized that she was not English. Now, observing her more closely, he noticed the high cheekbones, the dense blue-black of the hair, and an occasional very slight movement of the hands that was distinctly foreign. A strange woman, very quiet. So quiet as to make one uneasy. From the very first Mr. Mayherne was conscious that he was up against something that he did not understand.

"Now, my dear Mrs. Vole," he began, "you must not give way—"

He stopped. It was so very obvious that Romaine Vole had not the slightest intention of giving way. She was perfectly calm and composed.

"Will you please tell me about it?" she said. "I must know everything. Do not think to spare me. I want to know the worst." She hesitated, then repeated in a lower tone, with a curious emphasis which the lawyer did not understand, "I want to know the worst."

Mr. Mayherne went over his interview with Leonard Vole. She listened attentively, nodding her head now and then.

"I see," she said, when he had finished. "He wants me to say that he came in at twenty minutes past nine that night?"

"He did come in at that time?" said Mr. Mayherne sharply.

"That is not the point," she said coldly. "Will my saying so acquit him? Will they believe me?"

Mr. Mayherne was taken aback. She had gone so quickly to the core of the matter.

"That is what I want to know," she said. "Will it be enough? Is there anyone else who can support my evidence?"

There was a suppressed eagerness in her manner that made him vaguely uneasy.

"So far there is no one else," he said reluctantly.

"I see," said Romaine Vole.

She sat for a minute or two perfectly still. A little smile played over her lips.

The lawyer's feeling of alarm grew stronger and stronger.

"Mrs. Vole —" he began. "I know what you must feel —"

"Do you?" she asked. "I wonder."

"In the circumstances —"

"In the circumstances — I intend to play a lone hand."

He looked at her in dismay.

"But, my dear Mrs. Vole — you are overwrought. Being so devoted to your husband —"

"I beg your pardon?"

The sharpness of her voice made him start. He repeated in a hesitating manner, "Being so devoted to your husband —"

Romaine Vole nodded slowly, the same strange smile on her lips.

"Did he tell you that I was devoted to him?" she asked softly. "Ah! yes, I can see he did. How stupid men are! Stupid — stupid — stupid —"

She rose suddenly to her feet. All the intense emotion that the lawyer had been conscious of in the atmosphere was now concentrated in her tone.

"I hate him, I tell you! I hate him. I hate him. I hate him! I would like to see him hanged by the neck till he is dead."

The lawyer recoiled before her and the smoldering passion in her eyes.

She advanced a step nearer and continued vehemently.

"Perhaps I shall see it. Supposing I tell you that he did not come in that night at twenty past nine, but at twenty past ten? You say that he tells you he knew nothing about the money coming to him. Supposing I tell you he knew all about it, and counted on it, and committed murder to get it? Supposing I tell you that he admitted to me that night when he came in what he had done? That there was blood on his coat? What then? Supposing that I stand up in court and say all these things?"

Her eyes seemed to challenge him. With an effort he concealed his growing dismay, and endeavored to speak in a rational tone.

"You cannot be asked to give evidence against your husband —"

"I should like you to tell me one thing," said Mr. Mayherne. He contrived to appear as cool and unemotional as ever. "Why are you so bitter against Leonard Vole?"

She shook her head, smiling a little.

"Yes, you would like to know. But I shall not tell you. I will keep my secret."

Mr. Mayherne gave his dry little cough and rose.

"There seems no point in prolonging this interview," he remarked. "You will hear from me again after I have communicated with my client."

She came closer to him, looking into his eyes with her own wonderful dark ones.

"Tell me," she said, "did you believe — honestly — that he was innocent when you came here today?"

"I did," said Mr. Mayherne.

"You poor little man." She laughed.

"And I believe so still," finished the lawyer. "Good evening, madam."

He went out of the room, taking with him the memory of her startled face. *This is going to be the devil of a business*, said Mr. Mayherne to himself as he strode along the street.

Extraordinary, the whole thing. An extraordinary woman. A very dangerous woman. Women were the devil when they got their knife into you.

What was to be done? That wretched young man hadn't a leg to stand upon. Of course, possibly he did commit the crime.

No, said Mr. Mayherne to himself. *No — there's almost too much evidence against him. I don't believe this woman. She was trumping up the whole story. But she'll never bring it into court.*

He wished he felt more conviction on the point.

The police court proceedings were brief and dramatic. The principal witnesses for the prosecution were Janet Mackenzie, maid to the dead woman, and Romaine Heilger.

Mr. Mayherne sat in court and listened to the damning story that the latter told. It was on the lines she had indicated to him in their interview.

The prisoner reserved his defense and was committed for trial.

Mr. Mayherne was at his wits' end. The case against Leonard Vole was black beyond words. Even the famous K.C. who was engaged for the defense held out little hope.

"If we can shake that woman's testimony, we might do something," he said dubiously. "But it's a bad business."

Mr. Mayherne had concentrated his energies on one single point. Assuming Leonard Vole to be speaking the truth, and to have left the murdered woman's house at nine o'clock, who was the man Janet heard talking to Miss French at half past nine?

The only ray of light was in the shape of a scapegrace nephew who had in bygone days cajoled and threatened his aunt out of various sums of money. Janet Mackenzie, the solicitor learned, had always been attached to this young man, and had never ceased urging his claims upon her mistress. It certainly seemed possible that it was this nephew who had been with Miss French after

Leonard Vole left, especially as he was not to be found in any of his old haunts.

In all other directions, the lawyer's researches had been negative in their result. No one had seen Leonard Vole entering his own house, or leaving that of Miss French. No one had seen any other man enter or leave the house in Cricklewood. All inquiries drew blank.

It was the eve of the trial when Mr. Mayherne received the letter which was to lead his thoughts in an entirely new direction.

It came by the six-o'clock post. An illiterate scrawl, written on common paper and enclosed in a dirty envelope with the stamp stuck on crooked.

Mr. Mayherne read it through once or twice before he grasped its meaning.

Dear Mister:
Youre the lawyer chap wot acts for the young feller. If you want that painted foreign hussy showd up for wot she is an her pack of lies you come to 16 Shaw's Rents Stepney tonight It ull cawst you 2 hundred quid Arsk for Missis Mogson.

The solicitor read and reread this strange epistle. It might of course, be a hoax, but when he thought it over, he became increasingly convinced that it was genuine, and also convinced that it was the one hope for the prisoner. The evidence of Romaine Heilger damned him completely, and the line the defense meant to pursue, the line that the evidence of a woman who had admittedly lived an immoral life was not to be trusted, was at best a weak one.

Mr. Mayherne's mind was made up. It was his duty to save his client at all costs. He must go to Shaw's Rents.

He had some difficulty in finding the place, a ramshackle building in an evil-smelling slum, but at last he did so, and on inquiry for Mrs. Mogson was sent up to a room on the third floor. On this door he knocked, and getting no answer, knocked again.

At this second knock, he heard a shuffling sound inside, and presently the door was opened cautiously half an inch and a bent figure peered out.

Suddenly the woman, for it was a woman, gave a chuckle and opened the door wider.

"So it's you, dearie," she said, in a wheezy voice. "Nobody with you, is there? No playing tricks? That's right. You can come in — you can come in."

With some reluctance the lawyer stepped across the threshold into the small, dirty room, with its flickering gas jet. There was an untidy unmade bed in a corner, a plain deal table, and two rickety chairs. For the first time Mr. Mayherne had a full view of the tenant of this unsavory apartment. She was a woman of middle age, bent in figure, with a mass of untidy gray hair and a scarf wound tightly round her face. She saw him looking at this and laughed again, the same curious, toneless chuckle.

"Wondering why I hide my beauty, dear? He, he, he. Afraid it may tempt you, eh? But you shall see — you shall see."

She drew aside the scarf, and the lawyer recoiled involuntarily before the almost formless blur of scarlet. She replaced the scarf again.

"So you're not wanting to kiss me, dearie? He, he, I don't wonder. And yet I was a pretty girl once — not so long ago as you'd think, either. Vitriol, dearie, vitriol — that's what did that. Ah! but I'll be even with 'em — "

She burst into a hideous torrent of abuse which Mr. Mayherne tried vainly to quell. She fell silent at last, her hands clenching and unclenching themselves nervously.

"Enough of that," said the lawyer sternly. "I've come here because I have reason to believe you can give me information which will clear my client, Leonard Vole. Is that the case?"

Her eyes leered at him cunningly.

"What about the money, dearie?" she wheezed. "Two hundred quid, you remember."

"It is your duty to give evidence, and you can be called upon to do so."

"That won't do, dearie. I'm an old woman, and I know nothing. But you give me two hundred quid, and perhaps I can give you a hint or two. See?"

"What kind of hint?"

"What should you say to a letter? A letter from *her*. Never mind how I got hold of it. That's my business. It'll do the trick. But I want my two hundred quid."

Mr. Mayherne looked at her coldly, and made up his mind.

"I'll give you ten pounds, nothing more. And only that if this letter is what you say it is."

"Ten pounds?" She screamed and raved at him.

"Twenty," said Mr. Mayherne, "and that's my last word."

He rose as if to go. Then, watching her closely, he drew out a pocketbook, and counted out twenty one-pound notes.

"You see," he said. "That is all I have with me. You can take it or leave it."

But already he knew that the sight of the money was too much for her. She cursed and raved impotently, but at last she gave in. Going over to the bed, she drew something from beneath the tattered mattress.

"Here you are," she snarled. "It's the top one you want."

It was a bundle of letters that she threw to him, and Mr. Mayherne untied them and scanned them in his usual cool, methodical manner. The woman, watching him eagerly, could gain no clue from his impassive face.

He read each letter through, then returned again to the top one and read it a second time. Then he tied the whole bundle up again carefully.

They were love letters, written by Romaine Heilger, and the man they were written to was not Leonard Vole. The top letter was dated the day of the latter's arrest.

"I spoke true, dearie, didn't I?" whined the woman. "It'll do for her, that letter?"

Mr. Mayherne put the letters in his pocket, then he asked a question.

"How did you get hold of this correspondence?"

"That's telling," she said with a leer. "But I know something more. I heard in court what that hussy said. Find out where she was at twenty past ten, the time she says she was at home. Ask at the Lion Road Cinema. They'll remember—a fine upstanding girl like that—curse her!"

"Who is the man?" asked Mr. Mayherne. "There's only a Christian name here."

The other's voice grew thick and hoarse, her hands clenched and unclenched. Finally she lifted one to her face.

"He's the man that did this to me. Many years ago now. She took him away from me—a chit of a girl she was then. And when I went after him—and went for him, too—he threw the cursed stuff at me! And she laughed! I've had it in for her for years. Followed her, I have, spied upon her. And now I've got her! She'll suffer for this, won't she, Mr. Lawyer? She'll suffer?"

"She will probably be sentenced to a term of imprisonment for perjury," said Mr. Mayherne quietly.

"Shut away—that's what I want. You're going, are you? Where's my money? Where's that good money?"

Without a word, Mr. Mayherne put down the notes on the table. Then, drawing a deep breath, he turned and left the squalid room. Looking back, he saw the old woman crooning over the money.

He wasted no time. He found the cinema in Lion Road easily enough, and, shown a photograph of Romaine Heilger, the commissionaire recognized her at once. She had arrived at the cinema with a man some time after ten o'clock on the evening in question. He had not noticed her escort particularly, but he remembered the lady who had spoken to him about the picture that was showing. They stayed until the end, about an hour later.

Mr. Mayherne was satisfied. Romaine Heilger's evidence was a tissue of lies from beginning to end. She had evolved it out of her passionate hatred. The lawyer wondered whether he would ever know what lay behind that hatred. What had Leonard Vole done to her? He had seemed dumfounded when the solicitor had reported her attitude to him. He had declared earnestly that such a thing was incredible — yet it had seemed to Mr. Mayherne that after the first astonishment his protests had lacked sincerity.

He did know. Mr. Mayherne was convinced of it. He knew, but he had no intention of revealing the fact. The secret between those two remained a secret. Mr. Mayherne wondered if some day he should come to learn what it was.

The solicitor glanced at his watch. It was late, but time was everything. He hailed a taxi and gave an address.

"Sir Charles must know of this at once," he murmured to himself as he got in.

The trial of Leonard Vole for the murder of Emily French aroused widespread interest. In the first place the prisoner was young and good-looking, then he was accused of a particularly dastardly crime, and there was the further interest of Romaine Heilger, the principal witness for the prosecution. There had been pictures of her in many papers, and several fictitious stories as to her origin and history.

The proceedings opened quietly enough. Various technical evidence came first. Then Janet Mackenzie was called. She told substantially the same story as before. In cross-examination counsel for the defense succeeded in getting her to contradict herself once or twice over her account of Vole's association with Miss French; he emphasized the fact that though she had heard a man's voice in the sitting-room that night, there was nothing to show that it was Vole who was there, and he managed to drive home a feeling that jealousy and dislike of the prisoner were at the bottom of a good deal of her evidence.

Then the next witness was called.

"Your name is Romaine Heilger?"

"Yes."

"You are an Austrian subject?"

"Yes."

"For the last three years you have lived with the prisoner and passed yourself off as his wife?"

Just for a moment Romaine Heilger's eyes met those of the man in the dock. Her expression held something curious and unfathomable.

"Yes."

The questions went on. Word by word the damning facts came out. On the night in question the prisoner had taken out a crowbar with him. He had returned at twenty minutes past ten, and had confessed to having killed the old lady. His cuffs had been stained with blood, and he had burned them in the kitchen stove. He had terrorized her into silence by means of threats.

As the story proceeded, the feeling of the court which had, to begin with, been slightly favorable to the prisoner, now set dead against him. He himself sat with downcast head and moody air, as though he knew he were doomed.

Yet it might have been noted that her own counsel sought to restrain Romaine's animosity. He would have preferred her to be more unbiased. Formidable and ponderous, counsel for the defense arose.

He put it to her that her story was a malicious fabrication from start to finish, that she had not even been in her own house at the time in question, that she was in love with another man and was deliberately seeking to send Vole to his death for a crime he did not commit.

Romaine denied these allegations with superb insolence.

Then came the surprising denouement, the production of the letter. It was read aloud in court in the midst of a breathless stillness.

"Max, beloved, the Fates have delivered him into our hands! He has been arrested for murder—but, yes, the murder of an old lady! Leonard, who would not hurt a fly! At last I shall have my revenge. The poor chicken! I shall say that he came in that night with blood upon him—that he confessed to me. I shall hang him, Max—and when he hangs he will know and realize that it was Romaine who sent him to his death. And then—happiness, Beloved! Happiness at last!"

There were experts present ready to swear that the handwriting was that of Romaine Heilger, but they were not needed. Confronted with the letter, Romaine broke down utterly and confessed everything. Leonard Vole had returned to the house at the time he said, twenty past nine. She had invented the whole story to ruin him.

With the collapse of Romaine Heilger, the case for the Crown collapsed also. Sir Charles called his few witnesses, the prisoner himself went into the box and told his story in a manly straightforward manner, unshaken by cross-examination.

The prosecution endeavored to rally, but without great success. The judge's summing up was not wholly favorable to the prisoner, but a reaction had set in and the jury needed little time to consider their verdict.

"We find the prisoner not guilty."

Leonard Vole was free!

Little Mr. Mayherne hurried from his seat. He must congratulate his client.

He found himself polishing his pince-nez vigorously, and checked himself. His wife had told him only the night before that he was getting a habit of it. Curious things, habits. People themselves never knew they had them.

An interesting case—a very interesting case. That woman, now, Romaine Heilger.

The case was dominated for him still by the exotic figure of Romaine Heilger. She had seemed a pale, quiet woman in the house at Paddington, but in court she had flamed out against the sober background, flaunting herself like a tropical flower.

If he closed his eyes he could see her now, tall and vehement, her exquisite body bent forward a little, her right hand clenching and unclenching itself unconsciously all the time.

Curious things, habits. That gesture of hers with the hand was her habit, he supposed. Yet he had seen someone else do it quite lately. Who was it now?

He drew in his breath with a gasp as it came back to him. The woman in Shaw's Rents.

He stood still, his head whirling. It was impossible—impossible—Yet, Romaine Heilger was an actress.

The K.C. came up behind him and clapped him on the shoulder.

"Congratulated our man yet? He's had a narrow shave, you know. Come along and see him."

But the little lawyer shook off the other's hand.

He wanted one thing only—to see Romaine Heilger face to face.

He did not see her until some time later, and the place of their meeting is not relevant.

"So you guessed," she said, when he had told her all that was in his mind. "The face? Oh that was easy enough, and the light of that gas jet was too bad for you to see the makeup."

"But why—why—"

"'Why did I play a lone hand?'" She smiled a little, remembering the last time she had used the words.

"Such an elaborate comedy!"

"My friend—I had to save him. The evidence of a woman devoted to him would not have been enough—you hinted as much yourself. But I know something of the psychology of crowds. Let my evidence be wrung from me, as an admission, damning me in the eyes of the law, and a reaction in favor of the prisoner would immediately set in."

"And the bundle of letters?"

"One alone, the vital one, might have seemed like a—what do you call it?—put-up job."

"Then the man called Max?"

"Never existed, my friend."

"I still think," said little Mr. Mayherne, in an aggrieved manner, "that we could have got him off by the—er—normal procedure."

"I dared not risk it. You see you thought he was innocent—"

"And you knew it? I see," said little Mr. Mayherne.

"My dear Mr. Mayherne," said Romaine, "you do not see at all. I knew—he was guilty!"

Discussion Topics

1. One of the most controversial aspects of litigation is the strategy of discrediting or impeaching a witness. Impeaching a witness is generally a formal procedure of introducing evidence to demonstrate the unreliability of the witness or her testimony. Discrediting is more informal; it involves showing that the witness had motives, character flaws, or experiences that suggest she is not to be trusted. Of course there are many circumstances in which these strategies are useful, necessary, and handled in an honest way. But they are important tools that can easily be mishandled. Lawyers are reined in to some extent by the prohibitions on introducing irrelevant evidence, but the criteria for relevance are elastic.

In Christie's story, Romaine arranges to impeach her own testimony, reasoning that, since she is a crucial witness for the prosecution, the discrediting of her testimony will decisively help the defense. Consider how likely it is as a general matter that the strategy will be abused. Would it be possible to set rules to constrain it? If not, can you come up with a moral standard that a conscientious lawyer could use as a guideline for such opportunities?

2. Good lawyers never introduce evidence without assuring themselves that it is reliable and from a dependable source. Was Mayherne at fault for taking Romaine's letters at face value? Could he have investigated the matter further? Did he have convincing reasons to believe the story told him by Romaine-in-disguise? Consider how you or some other skilled lawyer would have handled this. And keep in mind that the case for the prosecution was, in all respects, strong.

Jurors and Their Qualifications
William Faulkner: Tomorrow

The process of juror examination and selection has become immensely sophisticated. Jury behavior is a subspecialty within social psychology;

the field has given rise to countless studies and theories. Its conclusions range from the obvious (that rape victims tend to be unforgiving to defendants accused of rape) to the counterintuitive (that jurors involved in law enforcement can often favor defendants). Experts, both real and self-anointed, hire themselves out as consultants to attorneys and charge generous fees.

Jury selection is constrained by legal rules. Jurors cannot be selected in a way that shows evident gender or race bias. A jury "of one's peers" does not mean that a female defendant gets to be tried by a jury of women any more than it means that a racial bigot can be tried by a jury of racists. Selection usually occurs through a process in which both sides examine the jurors; the questioning is called *voir dire* (literally, to see to say). Usually each side can exclude a certain number of potential jurors for evident reasons (i.e., for cause) and an additional number for unspecified, discretionary reasons.

Attorneys must, therefore, anticipate all relevant situations that may affect jurors' decisions. But he cannot consider every possibility, however remote. In William Faulkner's story, "Tomorrow," one juror's personal history becomes crucial to the resolution of a murder trial—and it is a history that an outsider could hardly guess. Faulkner (1897-1962), a winner of the Nobel prize, is the most acclaimed writer of the Old South. His twenty novels and numerous stories reflect the flow of consciousness— with its dislocations of time and rapid shifts in point of view.

❧ Tomorrow ❧

William Faulkner

Uncle Gavin had not always been county attorney. But the time when he had not been was more than twenty years ago and it had lasted for such a short period that only the old men remembered it, and even some of them did not. Because in that time he had had but one case.

He was a young man then, twenty-eight, only a year out of the state University law school where, at grandfather's instigation, he had gone after his return from Harvard and Heidelberg; and he had taken the case voluntarily, persuaded grandfather to let him handle it alone, which grandfather did, because everyone believed the trial would be a mere formality.

So he tried the case. Years afterward he still said it was the only case, either as a private defender or a public prosecutor, in which he was convinced that right and justice were on his side, that he ever lost. Actually he did not lose it—a mistrial in the fall court term, an acquittal in the following spring term—the defendant a solid, well-to-do farmer, husband and father, too, named Bookwright, from a section called Frenchman's Bend in the remote southeastern corner of the county; the victim a swaggering bravo calling himself Buck Thorpe and called Bucksnort by the other young men whom he had subjugated with his fists during the three years he had been in Frenchman's Bend; kinless, who had appeared overnight from nowhere, a brawler, a gambler, known to be a distiller of illicit whiskey and caught once on the road to Memphis with a small drove of stolen cattle, which the owner promptly identified. He had a bill of sale for them, but none in the country knew the name signed to it.

And the story itself was old and unoriginal enough: The country girl of seventeen, her imagination fired by the swagger and the prowess and the daring and the glib tongue; the father who tried to reason with her and got exactly as far as parents usually do in such cases; then the interdiction, the forbidden door, the inevitable elopement at midnight; and at four o'clock the next morning Bookwright waked Will Varner, the justice of the peace and the chief officer of the district, and handed Varner his pistol and said. 'I have come to surrender. I killed Thorpe two hours ago.' And a neighbor named Quick, who was first on the scene, found the half-drawn pistol in Thorpe's hand; and a week after the brief account was printed in the Memphis papers, a woman appeared in Frenchman's Bend who claimed to be Thorpe's wife, and with a wedding license to prove it, trying to claim what money or property he might have left.

I can remember the surprise that the grand jury even found a true bill; when the clerk read the indictment, the betting was twenty to one that the jury would not be out ten minutes. The district attorney even conducted the case through an assistant, and it did not take an hour to submit all the evidence. Then Uncle Gavin rose, and I remember how he looked at the jury — the eleven farmers and storekeepers and the twelfth man, who was to ruin his case — a farmer, too, a thin man, small, with thin gray hair and that appearance of hill farmers — at once frail and work-worn, yet curiously imperishable — who seem to become old men at fifty and then become invincible to time. Uncle Gavin's voice was quiet, almost monotonous, not ranting as criminal-court trials had taught us to expect; only the words were a little different from the ones he would use in later years. But even then, although he had been talking to them for only a year, he could already talk so that all the people in our country — the Negroes, the hill people, the rich flatland plantation owners — understood what he said.

"All of us in this country, the South, have been taught from birth a few things which we hold to above all else. One of the first of these — not the best; just one of the first — is that only a life can pay for the life it takes; that the one death is only half complete. If that is so, then we could have saved both these lives by stopping this defendant before he left his house that night; we could have saved at least one of them, even if we had had to take this defendant's life from him in order to stop him. Only we didn't know in time. And that's what I am talking about — not about the dead man and his character and the morality of the act he was engaged in; not about self-defense, whether or not this defendant was justified in forcing the issue to the point of taking life, but about us who are not dead and what we don't know — about all of us, human beings who at bottom want to do right, want not to harm others; human beings with all the complexity of human passions and feelings and beliefs, in the accepting or rejecting of which we had no choice, trying to do the best we can with them or despite them — this defendant, another human being with that same complexity of passions and instincts and beliefs, faced by a problem — the inevitable misery of his child who, with the headstrong folly of youth — again that same old complexity which she, too, did not ask to inherit — was incapable of her own preservation — and solved that problem to the best of his ability and beliefs, asking help of no one, and then abode by his decision and his act."

He sat down. The district attorney's assistant merely rose and bowed to the court and sat down again. The jury went out and we didn't even leave the room. Even the judge didn't retire. And I remember the long breath, something, which went through the room when the clock hand above the bench passed the ten-minute mark and then passed the half-hour mark, and the judge beckoned a bailiff and whispered to him, and the bailiff went out and returned and whispered to the judge, and the judge rose and banged his gavel and recessed the court.

I hurried home and ate my dinner and hurried back to town. The office was empty. Even grandfather, who took his nap after dinner, regardless of who hung and who didn't, returned first; after three o'clock then, and the whole town knew now that Uncle Gavin's jury was hung by one man, eleven to one for acquittal; then Uncle Gavin came in fast, and grandfather said, "Well, Gavin, at least you stopped talking in time to hang just your jury and not your client."

"That's right, sir," Uncle Gavin said. Because he was looking at me with his bright eyes, his thin, quick face, his wild hair already beginning to turn white. "Come here, Chick," he said. "I need you for a minute."

"Ask Judge Frazier to allow you to retract your oration, then let Charley sum up for you," grandfather said. But we were outside then, on the stairs, Uncle Gavin stopping halfway down, so that we stood exactly halfway from anywhere, his hand on my shoulder, his eyes brighter and intenter than ever.

"This is not cricket," he said. "But justice is accomplished lots of times by methods that won't bear looking at. They have moved the jury to the back room in Mrs. Rouncewell's boardinghouse. The room right opposite that mulberry tree. If you could get into the back yard without anybody seeing you, and be careful when you climb the tree—"

Nobody saw me. But I could look through the windy mulberry leaves into the room, and see and hear, both—the nine angry and disgusted men sprawled in chairs at the far end of the room; Mr. Holland, the foreman, and another man standing in front of the chair in which the little, worn, dried-out hill man sat. His name was Fentry. I remembered all their names, because Uncle Gavin said that to be a successful lawyer and politician in our country you did not need a silver tongue nor even an intelligence; you needed only an infallible memory for names. But I would have remembered his name anyway, because it was Stonewall Jackson—Stonewall Jackson Fentry.

"Don't you admit that he was running off with Bookwright's seventeen-year-old daughter?" Mr. Holland said. "Don't you admit that he had a pistol in his hand when they found him? Don't you admit that he wasn't hardly buried before that woman turned up and proved she was already his wife? Don't you admit that he was not only no-good but dangerous, and that if it hadn't been Bookwright, sooner or later somebody else would have had to, and that Bookwright was just unlucky?"

"Yes," Fentry said.

"Then what do you want?' Mr. Holland said. "What do you want?"

"I can't help it," Fentry said. "I ain't going to vote Mr. Bookwright free."

And he didn't. And that afternoon Judge Frazier discharged the jury and set the case for retrial in the next term of court; and the next morning Uncle Gavin came for me before I had finished breakfast.

"Tell your mother we might be gone overnight," he said. "Tell her I promise not to let you get either shot, snake-bit or surfeited with soda pop. . . . Because I've got to know," he said. We were driving fast now, out the northeast road, and his eyes were bright, not baffled, just intent and eager. "He was born and raised and lived all his life out here at the very other end of the county, thirty miles from Frenchman's Bend. He said under oath that he had never even seen Bookwright before, and you can look at him and see that he never had enough time off from hard work to learn how to lie in. I doubt if he ever even heard Bookwright's name before."

We drove until almost noon. We were in the hills now, out of the rich flat land, among the pine and bracken, the poor soil, the little tilted and barren patches of gaunt corn and cotton which somehow endured, as the people they clothed and fed somehow endured; the roads we followed less than lanes, winding and narrow, rutted and dust choked, the car in second gear half the time. Then we saw the mailbox, the crude lettering: G. A. FENTRY; beyond it, the two-room log house with an open hall, and even I, a boy of twelve, could see that no woman's hand had touched it in a lot of years. We entered the gate.

Then a voice said, "Stop! Stop where you are!" And we hadn't even seen him—an old man, barefoot, with a fierce white bristle of mustache, in patched denim faded almost to the color of skim milk, smaller, thinner even than the son, standing at the edge of the worn gallery, holding a shotgun across his middle and shaking with fury or perhaps with the palsy of age.

"Mr. Fentry—" Uncle Gavin said.

"You've badgered and harried him enough!" the old man said. It was fury; the voice seemed to rise suddenly with a fiercer, an uncontrollable blaze of it: "Get out of here! Get off my land! Go!"

"Come," Uncle Gavin said quietly. And still his eyes were only bright, eager, intent and grave. We did not drive fast now. The next mailbox was within the mile, and this time the house was even painted, with beds of petunias beside the steps, and the land about it was better, and this time the man rose from the gallery and came down to the gate.

"Howdy, Mr. Stevens," he said. "So Jackson Fentry hung your jury for you."

"Howdy, Mr. Pruitt," Uncle Gavin said. "It looks like he did. Tell me."

And Pruitt told him, even though at that time Uncle Gavin would forget now and then and his language would slip back to Harvard and even to Heidelberg. It was as if people looked at his face and knew that what he asked was not just for his own curiosity or his own selfish using.

"Only ma knows more about it than I do," Pruitt said. "Come up to the gallery."

We followed him to the gallery, where a plump, whitehaired old lady in a clean gingham sunbonnet and dress and a clean white apron sat in a low rocking chair, shelling field peas into a wooden bowl. "This is Lawyer Stevens," Pruitt said. "Captain Stevens' son, from town. He wants to know about Jackson Fentry."

So we sat, too, while they told it, the son and the mother talking in rotation.

"That place of theirs," Pruitt said. "You seen some of it from the road. And what you didn't see don't look no better. But his pa and his grandpa worked it, made a living for themselves and raised families and paid their taxes and owed no man. I don't know how they done it, but they did. And Jackson was helping from the time he got big enough to reach up to the plow handles. He never got much bigger than that neither. None of them ever did. I reckon that was why. And Jackson worked it, too, in his time, until he was about twenty-five and already looking forty, asking no odds of nobody, not married and not nothing, him and his pa living alone and doing their own washing and cooking, because how can a man afford to marry when him and his pa have just one pair of shoes between them. If it had been worth while getting a wife at all, since that place had already killed his ma and his grandma both before they were forty years old. Until one night —"

"Nonsense," Mrs. Pruitt said. "When your pa and me married, we didn't even own a roof over our heads. We moved into a rented house, or rented land —"

"All right," Pruitt said. "Until one night he come to me and said how he had got him a sawmilling job down at Frenchman's Bend."

"Frenchman's Bend?" Uncle Gavin said, and now his eyes were much brighter and quicker than just intent. "Yes," he said.

"A day-wage job," Pruitt said. "Not to get rich; just to earn a little extra money maybe, risking a year or two to earn a little extra money, against the life his grandpa led until he died between the plow handles one day, and that his pa would lead until he died in a corn furrow, and then it would be his turn, and not even no son to come and pick him up out of the dirt. And that he had traded with a nigger to help his pa work their place while he was gone, and would I kind of go up there now and then and see that his pa was all right."

"Which you did," Mrs. Pruitt said.

"I went close enough," Pruitt said. "I would get close enough to the field to hear him cussing at the nigger for not moving fast enough and to watch the nigger trying to keep up with him, and to think what a good thing it was Jackson hadn't got two niggers to work the place while he was gone, because if that old man — and he was close to sixty then — had had to spend one full day sitting in a chair in the shade with nothing in his hands to chop or hoe with, he would have died before sundown. So Jackson left. He walked. They didn't have but one mule. They ain't never had but one mule. But it ain't but about thirty miles. He was gone about two and a half years. Then one day —"

"He come home that first Christmas," Mrs. Pruitt said.

"That's right," Pruitt said. "He walked them thirty miles home and spent Christmas Day, and walked them other thirty miles back to the sawmill."

"Whose sawmill?" Uncle Gavin said.

"Quick's," Pruitt said. "Old Man Ben Quick's. It was the second Christmas he never come home. Then, about the beginning of March, about when the river bottom at Frenchman's Bend would be starting to dry out to where you could skid logs through it and you would have thought he would be settled down good to his third year of sawmilling, he come home to stay. He didn't walk this time. He come in a hired buggy. Because he had the goat and the baby."

"Wait," Uncle Gavin said.

"We never knew how he got home," Mrs. Pruitt said. "Because he had been home over a week before we even found out he had the baby."

"Wait," Uncle Gavin said.

They waited, looking at him, Pruitt sitting on the gallery railing and Mrs. Pruitt's fingers still shelling the peas out of the long brittle hulls, looking at Uncle Gavin. His eyes were not exultant now any more than they had been baffled or even very speculative before; they had just got brighter, as if whatever it was behind them had flared up, steady and fiercer, yet still quiet, as if it were going faster than the telling was going.

"Yes," he said. "Tell me."

"And when I finally heard about it and went up there," Mrs. Pruitt said, "that baby wasn't two weeks old. And how he had kept it alive, and just on goat's milk—"

"I don't know if you know it," Pruitt said. "A goat ain't like a cow. You milk a goat every two hours or so. That means all night too."

"Yes," Mrs. Pruitt said. "He didn't even have diaper cloths, He had some split floursacks the midwife had showed him how to put on. So I made some cloths and I would go up there; he had kept the nigger on to help his pa in the field and he was doing the cooking and washing and nursing that baby, milking the goat to feed it; and I would say, 'Let me take it. At least until he can be weaned. You come stay at my house, too, if you want,' and him just looking at me—little, thin, already wore-out something that never in his whole life had ever set down to a table and et all he could hold—saying, 'I thank you, ma'am. I can make out.'"

"Which was correct," Pruitt said. "I don't know how he was at sawmilling, and he never had no farm to find out what kind of a farmer he was. But he raised that boy."

"Yes," Mrs. Pruitt said. "And I kept on after him: 'We hadn't even heard you was married,' I said. 'Yessum,' he said. 'We was married last year. When the baby come, she died.' 'Who was she?' I said. 'Was she a Frenchman Bend girl?' 'No'm,' he said, 'She come from downstate.' 'What was her name?' I said, 'Miss Smith,' he said."

"He hadn't even had enough time off from hard work to learn how to lie either," Pruitt said. "But he raised that boy. After their crops were in in the fall, he let the nigger go, and next spring him and the old man done the work like they use to. He had made a kind of satchel, like they say Indians does, to carry the boy in. I would go up there now and then while the ground was still cold and see Jackson and his pa plowing and chopping brush, and that satchel hanging on a fence post and that boy asleep bolt upright in it like it was a feather bed. He learned to walk that spring, and I would stand there at the fence and watch that durn little critter out there in the middle of the furrow, trying his best to keep up with Jackson, until Jackson would stop the plow at the turn row and go back and get him and set him straddle of his neck and take up the plow and go on. In the late summer he could walk pretty good. Jackson made him a little hoe out of a stick and a scrap of shingle, and you could see Jackson chopping in the middle-thigh cotton, but you couldn't see the boy at all; you could just see the cotton shaking where he was."

"Jackson made his clothes," Mrs. Pruitt said. "Stitched them himself, by hand. I made a few garments and took them up there. I never done it but once though. He took them and he thanked me. But you could see it. It was like he even begrudged the earth itself for what the child had to eat to keep alive. And I tried to persuade Jackson to take him to church, have him baptized. 'He's already named,' he said. 'His name is Jackson and Longstreet Fentry. Pa fit under both of them.'

"He never went nowhere," Pruitt said. "Because where you saw Jackson, you saw that boy. If he had had to steal that boy down there at Frenchman's Bend, he couldn't 'a' hid no closer. It was even the old man that would ride over to Haven Hill store to buy their supplies, and the only time Jackson and that boy was separated as much as one full breath was once a year when Jackson would ride in to Jefferson to pay their taxes, and when I first seen the boy I thought of a setter puppy, until one day I knowed Jackson had gone to pay their taxes and I went up there and the boy was under the bed, not making any fuss, just backed up into the corner, looking out at me. He didn't blink once. He was exactly like a fox or a wolf cub somebody had caught just last night."

We watched him take from his pocket a tin of snuff and tilt a measure of it into the lid and then into his lower lip, tapping the final grain from the lid with delicate deliberation.

"All right," Uncle Gavin said, "Then what?"

"That's all," Pruitt said. "In the next summer him and the boy disappeared."

"Disappeared?" Uncle Gavin said.

"That's right. They were just gone one morning. I didn't know when. And one day I couldn't stand it no longer, I went up there and the house was empty, and I went on to the field where the old man was plowing, and at first I thought the spreader between his plow handles had broke and he had tied a sapling off, and it was that shotgun, and I reckon what he said to me was about what he said to you this morning when you stopped there. Next year he had the nigger helping him again. Then, about five years later, Jackson come back. I don't know when. He was just there one morning. And the nigger was gone again, and him and his pa worked the place like they use to. And one day I couldn't stand it no longer, I went up there and I stood at the fence where he was plowing, until after a while the land he was breaking brought him up to the fence, and still he hadn't never looked at me; he plowed right by me, not ten feet away, still without looking at me, and he turned and come back, and I said, 'Did he die, Jackson?' and then he looked at me. 'The boy,' I said. And he said, 'What boy?'"

They invited us to stay for dinner.

Uncle Gavin thanked them. "We brought a snack with us," he said. "And it's thirty miles to Varner's store, and twenty-two from there to Jefferson. And our roads ain't quite used to automobiles yet."

So it was just sundown when we drove up to Varner's store in Frenchman's Bend Village; again a man rose from the deserted gallery and came down the steps to the car.

It was Isham Quick, the witness who had first reached Thorpe's body—a tall, gangling man in the middle forties, with a dreamy kind of face and near-sighted eyes, until you saw there was something shrewd behind them, even a little quizzical.

"I been waiting for you," he said "Looks like you made a water haul." He blinked at Uncle Gavin. "That Fentry."

"Yes," Uncle Gavin said. "Why didn't you tell me?"

"I didn't recognize it myself," Quick said. "It wasn't until I heard your jury was hung, and by one man, that I associated them names."

"Names?" Uncle Gavin said. "What na—Never mind. Just tell it."

So we sat on the gallery of the locked and deserted store while the cicadas shrilled and rattled in the trees and the lightning bugs blinked and drifted above the dusty road, and Quick told it, sprawled on the bench beyond Uncle Gavin, loose-jointed, like he would come all to pieces the first time he moved, talking in a lazy sardonic voice, like he had all night to tell it in and it would take all night to tell it. But it wasn't that long. It wasn't long enough for what was in it. But Uncle Gavin says it don't take many words to tell the sum of any human experience; that somebody has already done it in eight: He was born, he suffered and he died.

"It was pap that hired him. But when I found out where he had come from, I knowed he would work, because folks in that country hadn't never had time to learn nothing but hard work. And I knowed he would be honest for the same reason: that there wasn't nothing in his country a man could want bad enough to learn how to steal it. What I seem to have underestimated was his capacity for love. I reckon I figured that, coming from where he come from, he never had none a-tall, and for that same previous reason — that even the comprehension of love had done been lost out of him back down the generations where the first one of them had had to take his final choice between the pursuit of love and the pursuit of keeping on breathing.

"So he come to work, doing the same work and drawing the same pay as the niggers done. Until in the late fall, when the bottom got wet and we got ready to shut down for the winter, I found out he had made a trade with pap to stay on until spring as watchman and caretaker, with three days out to go home Christmas. And he did, and the next year when we started up, he had done learned so much about it and he stuck to it so, that by the middle of summer he was running the whole mill hisself, and by the end of summer pap never went out there no more a-tall and I just went when I felt like it, maybe once a week or so; and by fall pap was even talking about building him a shack to live in in place of that shuck mattress and a old broke-down cookstove in the boiler shed. And he stayed through that winter too. When he went home that Christmas we never even knowed it, when he went or when he come back, because even I hadn't been out there since fall.

"Then one afternoon in February — there had been a mild spell and I reckon I was restless — I rode out there. The first thing I seen was her, and it was the first time I had ever done that — a woman, young, and maybe when she was in her normal health she might have been pretty, too; I don't know. Because she wasn't just thin, she was gaunted. She was sick, more than just starved-looking, even if she was still on her feet, and it wasn't just because she was going to have that baby in a considerable less than another month. And I says, 'Who is that?' and he looked at me and says, 'That's my wife,' and I says, 'Since when? You never had no wife last fall. And that child ain't a month off.' And he says, 'Do you want us to leave?' and I says, 'What do I want you to leave for?' I'm going to tell this from what I know now, what I found out after them two brothers showed up here three years later with their court paper, not from what he ever told me, because he never told nobody nothing."

"All right," Uncle Gavin said. "Tell."

"I don't know where he found her. I don't know if he found her somewhere, or if she just walked into the mill one day or one night and he looked up and seen her, and it was like the fellow says — nobody knows where or when love or lightning either is going to strike, except that it ain't going to strike there twice, because it don't have to. And I don't believe she was hunting for the husband that had deserted her — likely he cut and run soon as she told him about the baby — and I don't believe she was scared or ashamed to go back home just because her brothers and father had tried to keep her from marrying the husband, in the first place. I believe it was just some more of that same kind of black-complected and not extra-intelligent and pretty durn ruthless blood pride that them brothers themselves was waving around here for about a hour that day.

"Anyway, there she was, and I reckon she knowed her time was going to be short, and him saying to her, 'Let's get married,' and her saying, 'I can't marry you. I've already got a husband.' And her time come and she was down then, on that shuck mattress, and him feeding her with a spoon, likely, and I reckon she knowed she wouldn't get up from it, and he got the midwife, and the baby was born, and likely her and the midwife both knowed by then she would never get up from that mattress and maybe they even convinced him at last, or maybe she knowed it wouldn't make no difference nohow and said yes, and he taken the mule pap let him keep at the mill and rid seven miles to Preacher Whitfield's and brung Whitfield back about daylight, and Whitfield married them and she died, and him and Whitfield buried her. And that night he come to the house and told pap he was quitting, and left the mule, and I went out to the mill a few days later and he was gone — just the shuck mattress and the stove, and the dishes and skillet mammy let him have, all washed and clean and set on the shelf. And in the third summer from then, them two brothers, them Thorpes — "

"Thorpes," Uncle Gavin said. It wasn't loud. It was getting dark fast now, as it does in our country, and I couldn't see his face at all any more. "Tell," he said.

"Black-complected like she was—the youngest one looked a heap like her—coming up in the surrey, with the deputy or bailiff or whatever he was, and the paper all wrote out and stamped and sealed all regular, and I says, 'You can't do this. She come here of her own accord, sick and with nothing, and he taken her in and fed her and nursed her and got help to born that child and a preacher to bury her; they was even married before she died. The preacher and the midwife both will prove it.' And the oldest brother says, 'He couldn't marry her. She already had a husband. We done already attended to him.' And I says, 'All right. He taken that boy when nobody come to claim him. He has raised that boy and clothed and fed him for two years and better.' And the oldest one drawed a money purse half outen his pocket and let it drop back again. 'We aim to do right about that, too—when we have seen the boy,' he says. 'He is our kin. We want him and we aim to have him.' And that wasn't the first time it ever occurred to me that this world ain't run like it ought to be run a heap of more times than what it is, and I says, 'It's thirty miles up there. I reckon you all will want to lay over here tonight and rest your horses.' And the oldest one looked at me and says, 'The team ain't tired. We won't stop.' 'Then I'm going with you,' I says. 'You are welcome to come,' he says.

"We drove until midnight. So I thought I would have a chance then, even if I never had nothing to ride. But when we unhitched and laid down on the ground, the oldest brother never laid down. 'I ain't sleepy,' he says. 'I'll set up a while.' So it wasn't no use, and I went to sleep and then the sun was up and it was too late then, and about middle morning we come to that mailbox with the name on it you couldn't miss, and the empty house with nobody in sight or hearing neither, until we heard the ax and went around to the back, and he looked up from the woodpile and seen what I reckon he had been expecting to see every time the sun rose for going on three years now. Because he never even stopped. He said to the little boy, 'Run. Run to the field to grandpap. Run,' and come straight at the oldest brother with the ax already raised and the down-stroke already started, until I managed to catch it by the haft just as the oldest brother grabbed him and we lifted him clean off the ground, holding him, or trying to. 'Stop it, Jackson!' I says. 'Stop it! They got the law!'

"Then a puny something was kicking and clawing me about the legs; it was the little boy, not making a sound, just swarming around me and the brother both, hitting at us as high as he could reach with a piece of wood Fentry had been chopping. 'Catch him and take him on to the surrey,' the oldest one says. So the youngest one caught him; he was almost as hard to hold as Fentry, kicking and plunging even after the youngest one had picked him up, and still not making a sound, and Fentry jerking and lunging like two men until the youngest one and the boy was out of sight. Then he collapsed. It was like all his bones had turned to water, so that me and the oldest brother lowered him down to the chopping block like he never had no bones a-tall, laying back against the wood he had cut, panting, with a little froth of spit at each corner of his mouth. 'It's the law, Jackson,' I says. 'Her husband is still alive.'

" 'I know it,' he says. It wasn't much more than whispering. 'I been expecting it. I reckon that's why it taken me so by surprise. I'm all right now.'

" 'I'm sorry for it,' the brother says. 'We never found out about none of it until last week. But he is our kin. We want him home. You done well by him. We thank you. His mother thanks you. Here,' he says. He taken the money purse outen his pocket and puts it into Fentry's hand. Then he turned and went away. After a while I heard the carriage turn and go back down the hill. Then I couldn't hear it any more. I don't know whether Fentry ever heard it or not.

" 'It's the law, Jackson,' I says. 'But there's two sides to the law. We'll go to town and talk to Captain Stevens. I'll go with you.'

"Then he set up on the chopping block, setting up slow and stiff. He wasn't panting so hard now and he looked better now, except for his eyes, and they was mostly just dazed looking. Then he raised the hand that had the money purse in it and started to mop his face with the money purse, like it was a handkerchief; I don't believe he even knowed there was anything in his hand until then, because he taken his hand down and looked at the money purse for maybe five seconds, and then he tossed it — he didn't fling it; he just tossed it like you would a handful of dirt you had been examining to see what it would make — over behind the chopping block and got up and walked across the yard toward the woods, walking straight and not fast, and not looking much bigger than that little boy, and into the woods. 'Jackson,' I says. But he never looked back.

"And I stayed that night at Rufus Pruitt's and borrowed a mule from him; I said I was just looking around, because I didn't feel much like talking to nobody, and the next morning I hitched the mule at that gate and started up the path, and I didn't see old man Fentry on the gallery at all at first.

"When I did see him he was moving so fast I didn't even know what he had in his hands until it went "boom!" and I heard the shot rattling in the leaves overhead and Rufus Pruitt's mule trying his durn best either to break the hitch rein or hang hisself from the gatepost.

"And one day about six months after he had located here to do the balance of his drinking and fighting and sleight-of-hand with other folks' cattle, Bucksnort was on the gallery here, drunk still and running his mouth, and about a half dozen of the ones he had beat unconscious from time to time by foul means and even by fair on occasion, as such emergencies arose, laughing every time he stopped to draw a fresh breath. And I happened to look up, and Fentry was setting on his mule out there in the road.

"He was just setting there, with the dust of them thirty miles caking into the mule's sweat, looking at Thorpe. I don't know how long he had been there, not saying nothing, just setting there and looking at Thorpe; then he turned the mule and rid back up the road toward them hills he hadn't ought to never have left. Except maybe it's like the fellow says, and there ain't nowhere you can hide from either lightning or love. And I didn't know why then. I hadn't associated them names. I knowed that Thorpe was familiar to me, but that other business had been twenty years ago and I had forgotten it until I heard about that hung jury of yourn. Of course he wasn't going to vote Bookwright free. . . . It's dark. Let's go to supper."

But it was only twenty-two miles to town now, and we were on the highway now, the gravel; we would be home in an hour and a half, because sometimes we could make thirty and thirty-five miles an hour, and Uncle Gavin said that someday all the main roads in Mississippi would be paved like the streets in Memphis and every family in America would own a car. We were going fast now.

"Of course he wasn't," Uncle Gavin said. "The lowly and invincible of the earth—to endure and endure and then endure, tomorrow and tomorrow and tomorrow. Of course he wasn't going to vote Bookwright free."

"I would have," I said. "I would have freed him. Because Buck Thorpe was bad. He—"

"No, you wouldn't," Uncle Gavin said. He gripped my knee with one hand even though we were going fast, the yellow light beam level on the yellow road, the bugs swirling down into the light beam and ballooning away. "It wasn't Buck Thorpe, the adult, the man. He would have shot that man as quick as Bookwright did, if he had been in Bookwright's place. It was because somewhere in that debased and brutalized flesh which Bookwright slew there still remained, not the spirit maybe, but at least the memory, of that little boy, that Jackson and Longstreet Fentry, even though the man the boy had become didn't show it, and only Fentry did. And you wouldn't have freed him either. Don't ever forget that. Never."

Discussion Topics

1. Should Uncle Gavin have uncovered the history of Jackson Fentry and Buck Thorpe? Would *voir dire,* as it is now generally conducted, uncover a connection of that kind? Consider the questions that a lawyer with common sense and caution would ask while selecting a jury and probing for sources of bias.

2. It is likely that Jackson Fentry was required to pledge that he would be able to perform the function of a juror without bias and preconceptions. Do you think it was psychologically possible for him to do so in good conscience? Does his history with Buck Thorpe necessarily prevent him from doing the proper job of a juror in this case? Is it possible that in some sense he would be a *better* juror, would be better able to do justice, than a stranger?

3. Contrast the treatment of character in "Tomorrow" with O. Henry's presentation of Benton Sharp in "A Departmental Case." Both are unmitigated villains. Their killers are generally seen to have served justice. But Faulkner's story has the added dimension of showing that Buck Thorpe, like every outlaw and villain, was once a child and remains cherished by his surrogate father. He hints at Thorpe's difficult childhood and allows us to guess why Thorpe became the man he did.

Our legal system, in particular our jury system, works hard to exclude the point of view toward defendants that Fentry has toward Thorpe. We assume that parental indulgence and forgiveness is at war with the interests of justice, that the two points of view cannot be reconciled. Consider whether you agree and whether society would be better off if the parental attitude could be seen as relevant to a just resolution.

Trial Practice: Going for Broke and Respecting Morality

Ernest Gaines: *A Lesson Before Dying* and
Harper Lee: *To Kill a Mockingbird*

The Model Rules of Professional Responsibility (Rule 1.3, note 1) require that a lawyer "shall take whatever lawful and ethical measures are required to vindicate a client's cause or endeavor. A lawyer must also act . . . with zeal in advocacy upon the client's behalf." Lawyers interpret the mandate in different ways. Some believe that they are required to put the client's interest above all other interests. If a tactic will benefit the client and is lawful, the fact that other parties or society in general will be harmed is at best secondary and more likely irrelevant. Others emphasize that the rule mandates "lawful and *ethical* measures."

They stress that lawyers are required by the Model Rules to serve the cause of justice as well as the causes represented by clients. Accordingly, they conclude that a practice that serves a client but also damages others in a significant way may not pass the ethical test. Thus, one lawyer may do for his client what another will shun.

One kind of example recurs in law and literature and brings the questions into focus. A lawyer may find it opportune to use damaging and false stereotypes in defending her client. A client who is being tried for organizing a criminal enterprise may be defended with an argument that because of his race or gender, he was incapable of taking initiative or carrying out a serious crime. A lawyer for a homosexual defendant may say that her client has diminished capacity because gay persons are emotionally unstable. A lawyer for an elderly defendant may argue that all old people are close to senility and easily influenced by others.

In practice arguments of this kind may be effective with juries. A similar, and equally questionable, strategy would be to suggest by innuendo that an adverse witness or the victim is untrustworthy because of her ethnic background, race, etc. In all these cases, opinion is divided. Some lawyers argue that zealous advocacy requires their use once it is evident that they can be effective. Others reject them, arguing that serving justice and ethics means that they must refrain from inflaming prejudice.

Two literary examples illustrate these options. Both involve African-American defendants in the segregated South facing the death penalty. Ernest Gaines' *A Lesson Before Dying* is set in a small Louisiana town in the late 1940s. The first chapter, reprinted below, gives us the defense summation and the sentence. Gaines himself is a prolific writer who divides his time and his teaching between Louisiana, where he was raised, and San Francisco. Our other example is Atticus Finch's summation in his defense of Tom Robinson in Harper Lee's 1960 novel, *To Kill a Mockingbird*. The well-known and influential book remains her only novel.

❧ A Lesson Before Dying (chapter 1) ❧

Ernest Gaines

I was not there, yet I was there. No, I did not go to the trial, I did not hear the verdict, because I knew all the time what it would be. Still, I was there. I was there as much as anyone else was there. Either I sat behind my aunt and his godmother or I sat beside them. Both are large women, but his godmother is larger. She is of average height, five four, five five, but weighs nearly two hundred pounds. Once she and my aunt had found their places — two rows behind the table where he sat with his court-appointed attorney — his godmother became as immobile as a great stone or as one of our oak or cypress stumps. She never got up once to get water or go to the bathroom down in the basement. She just sat there staring at the boy's clean-cropped head where he sat at the front table with his lawyer. Even after he had gone to await the jurors' verdict, her eyes remained in that one direction. She heard nothing said in the courtroom. Not by the prosecutor, not by the defense attorney, not by my aunt. (Oh, yes, she did hear one word — one word, for sure: "hog.") It was my aunt whose eyes followed the prosecutor as he moved from one side of the courtroom to the other, pounding his fist into the palm of his hand, pounding the table where his papers lay, pounding the rail that separated the jurors from the rest of the courtroom. It was my aunt who followed his every move, not his godmother. She was not even listening. She had gotten tired of listening. She knew, as we all knew, what the outcome would be. A white man had been killed during a robbery, and though two of the robbers had been killed on the spot, one had been captured, and he, too, would have to die. Though he told them no, he had nothing to do with it, that he was on his way to the White Rabbit Bar and Lounge when Brother and Bear drove up beside him and offered him a ride. After he got into the car, they asked him if he had any money. When he told them he didn't have a solitary dime, it was then that Brother and Bear started talking credit, saying that old Grope should not mind crediting them a pint since he knew them well, and he knew that the grinding season was coming soon, and they would be able to pay him back then.

The store was empty, except for the old storekeeper, Alcee Grope, who sat on a stool behind the counter. He spoke first. He asked Jefferson about his godmother. Jefferson told him his nannan was all right. Old Grope nodded his head. "You tell her for me I say hello," he told Jefferson. He looked at Brother and Bear. But he didn't like them. He didn't trust them. Jefferson could see that in his face. "Do for you boys?" he asked. "A bottle of that Apple White, there, Mr. Grope," Bear said. Old Grope got the bottle off the shelf, but he did not set it on the counter. He could see that the boys had already been drinking, and he became suspicious. "You boys got money?" he asked. Brother and Bear spread out all the money they had in their pockets on top of the counter. Old Grope counted it with his eyes. "That's not enough," he said. "Come on, now, Mr. Grope," they pleaded with him. "You know you go'n get your money soon as grinding start." "No," he said. "Money is slack everywhere. You bring the money, you get your wine." He turned to put the bottle back on the shelf. One of the boys, the one called Bear, started around the counter. "You, stop there," Grope told him. "Go back." Bear had been drinking, and his eyes were glossy, he walked unsteadily, grinning all the time as he continued around the counter. "Go back," Grope told him. "I mean, the last time now — go back." Bear continued. Grope moved quickly toward the cash register, where he withdrew a revolver and started shooting. Soon there was shooting from another direction. When it was quiet again, Bear, Grope, and Brother were all down on the floor, and only Jefferson was standing.

He wanted to run, but he couldn't run. He couldn't even think. He didn't know where he was. He didn't know how he had gotten there. He couldn't remember ever getting into the car. He couldn't remember a thing he had done all day.

He heard a voice calling. He thought the voice was coming from the liquor shelves. Then he realized that old Grope was not dead, and that it was he who was calling. He made himself go to the end of the counter. He had to look across Bear to see the storekeeper. Both lay between the counter and the shelves of alcohol. Several bottles had been broken, and alcohol and blood covered their bodies as well as the floor. He stood there gaping at the old man slumped against the bottom shelf of gallons and half gallons of wine. He didn't know whether he should go to him or whether he should run out of there. The old man continued to call: "Boy? Boy? Boy?" Jefferson became frightened. The old man was still alive. He had seen him. He would tell on him. Now he started babbling. "It wasn't me. It wasn't me, Mr. Grope. It was Brother and Bear. Brother shot you. It wasn't me. They made me come with them. You got to tell the law that, Mr. Grope. You hear me, Mr. Grope?"

But he was talking to a dead man.

Still he did not run. He didn't know what to do. He didn't believe that this had happened. Again he couldn't remember how he had gotten there. He didn't know whether he had come there with Brother and Bear, or whether he had walked in and seen all this after it happened.

He looked from one dead body to the other. He didn't know whether he should call someone on the telephone or run. He had never dialed a telephone in his life, but he had seen other people use them. He didn't know what to do. He was standing by the liquor shelf, and suddenly he realized he needed a drink and needed it badly. He snatched a bottle off the shelf, wrung off the cap, and turned up the bottle, all in one continuous motion. The whiskey burned him like fire — his chest, his belly, even his nostrils. His eyes watered; he shook his head to clear his mind. Now he began to realize where he was. Now he began to realize fully what had happened. Now he knew he had to get out of there. He turned. He saw the money in the cash register, under the little wire clamps.

He knew taking money was wrong. His nannan had told him never to steal. He didn't want to steal. But he didn't have a solitary dime in his pocket. And nobody was around, so who could say he stole it? Surely not one of the dead men.

He was halfway across the room, the money stuffed inside his jacket pocket, the half bottle of whiskey clutched in his hand, when two white men walked into the store.

That was his story.

The prosecutor's story was different. The prosecutor argued that Jefferson and the other two had gone there with the full intention of robbing the old man and then killing him so that he could not identify them. When the old roan and the other two robbers were all dead, this one—it proved the kind of animal he really was—stuffed the money into his pockets and celebrated the event by drinking over their still-bleeding bodies.

The defense argued that Jefferson was innocent of all charges except being at the wrong place at the wrong time. There was absolutely no proof that there had been a conspiracy between himself and the other two. The fact that Mr. Grope shot only Brother and Bear was proof of Jefferson's innocence. Why did Mr. Grope shoot one boy twice and never shoot at Jefferson once? Because Jefferson was merely an innocent bystander. He took the whiskey to calm his nerves, not to celebrate. He took the money out of hunger and plain stupidity.

"Gentlemen of the jury, look at this—this—this boy. I almost said man, but I can't say man. Oh, sure, he has reached the age of twenty-one, when we, civilized men, consider the male species has reached manhood, but would you call this—this—this a man? No, not I. I would call it a boy and a fool. A fool is not aware of right and wrong. A fool does what others tell him to do. A fool got into that automobile. A man with a modicum of intelligence would have seen that those racketeers meant no good. But not a fool. A fool got into that automobile. A fool rode to the grocery store. A fool stood by and watched this happen, not having the sense to run.

"Gentlemen of the jury, look at him—look at him—look at this. Do you see a man sitting here? Do you see a man sitting here? I ask you, I implore, look carefully—do you see a man sitting here? Look at the shape of this skull, this face as flat as the palm of my hand—look deeply into those eyes. Do you see a modicum of intelligence? Do you see anyone here who could plan a murder, a robbery, can plan—can plan—can plan anything? A cornered animal to strike quickly out of fear, a trait inherited from his ancestors in the deepest jungle of blackest Africa—yes, yes, that he can do—but to plan? To plan, gentlemen of the jury? No, gentlemen, this skull here holds no plans. What you see here is a thing that acts on command. A thing to hold the handle of a plow, a thing to load your bales of cotton, a thing to dig your ditches, to chop your wood, to pull your corn. That is what you see here, but you do not see anything capable of planning a robbery or a murder. He does not even know the size of his clothes or his shoes. Ask him to name the months of the year. Ask him does Christmas come before or after the Fourth of July? Mention the names of Keats, Byron, Scott, and see whether the eyes will show one moment of recognition. Ask him to describe a rose, to quote one passage from the Constitution or the Bill of Rights. Gentlemen of the jury, this man planned a robbery? Oh, pardon me, pardon me, I surely did not mean to insult your intelligence by saying 'man'—would you please forgive me for committing such an error?

"Gentlemen of the jury, who would be hurt if you took this life? Look back to that second row. Please look. I want all twelve of you honorable men to turn your heads and look back to that second row. What you see there has been everything to him—mama, grandmother, godmother—everything. Look at her, gentlemen of the jury, look at her well. Take this away from her, and she has no reason to go on living. We may see him as not much, but he's her reason for existence. Think on that, gentlemen, think on it.

"Gentlemen of the jury, be merciful. For God's sake, be merciful. He is innocent of all charges brought against him.

"But let us say he was not. Let us for a moment say he was not. What justice would there be to take this life? Justice, gentlemen? Why, I would just as soon put a hog in the electric chair as this.

"I thank you, gentlemen, from the bottom of my heart, for your kind patience. I have no more to say, except this: We must live with our own conscience. Each and every one of us must live with his own conscience."

The jury retired, and it returned a verdict after lunch: guilty of robbery and murder in the first degree. The judge commended the twelve white men for reaching a quick and just verdict. This was Friday. He would pass sentence on Monday.

Ten o'clock on Monday, Miss Emma and my aunt sat in the same seats they had occupied on Friday. Reverend Mose Ambrose, the pastor of their church, was with them. He and my aunt sat on either side of Miss Emma. The judge, a short, red-faced man with snow-white hair and thick black eyebrows, asked Jefferson if he had anything to say before the sentencing. My aunt said that Jefferson was looking down at the floor and shook his head. The judge told Jefferson that he had been found guilty of the charges brought against him, and that the judge saw no reason that he should not pay for the part he played in this horrible crime.

Death by electrocution. The governor would set the date.

❦ *from* To Kill a Mockingbird ❦

Harper Lee

We raced back to the courthouse, up the steps, up two flights of stairs, and edged our way along the balcony rail. Reverend Sykes had saved our seats.

The courtroom was still, and again I wondered where the babies were. Judge Taylor's cigar was a brown speck in the center of his mouth; Mr. Gilmer was writing on one of the yellow pads on his table, trying to outdo the court reporter, whose hand was jerking rapidly. "Shoot," I muttered, "we missed it."

Atticus was halfway through his speech to the jury. He had evidently pulled some papers from his briefcase that rested beside his chair, because they were on his table. Tom Robinson was toying with them.

"... absence of any corroborative evidence, this man was indicted on a capital charge and is now on trial for his life . . .

I punched Jem. "How long's he been at it?"

"He's just gone over the evidence," Jem whispered, "and we're gonna win, Scout. I don't see how we can't. He's been at it 'bout five minutes. He made it as plain and easy as — well, as I'da explained it to you. You could've understood it, even."

"Did Mr. Gilmer — ?"

"Sh-h. Nothing new, just the usual. Hush now."

We looked down again. Atticus was speaking easily, with the kind of detachment he used when he dictated a letter. He walked slowly up and down in front of the jury, and the jury seemed to be attentive: their heads were up, and they followed Atticus's route with what seemed to be appreciation. I guess it was because Atticus wasn't a thunderer.

Atticus paused, then he did something he didn't ordinarily do. He unhitched his watch and chain and placed them on the table, saying, "With the court's permission — "

Judge Taylor nodded, and then Atticus did something I never saw him do before or since, in public or in private: he unbuttoned his vest, unbuttoned his collar, loosened his tie, and took off his coat. He never loosened a scrap of his clothing until he undressed at bedtime, and to Jem and me, this was the equivalent of him standing before us stark naked. We exchanged horrified glances.

Atticus put his hands in his pockets, and as he returned to the jury, I saw his gold collar button and the tips of his pen and pencil winking in the light.

"Gentlemen," he said. Jem and I again looked at each other. Atticus might have said, "Scout." His voice had lost its aridity, its detachment, and he was talking to the jury as if they were folks on the post office corner.

"Gentlemen," he was saying, "I shall be brief, but I would like to use my remaining time with you to remind you that this case is not a difficult one, it requires no minute sifting of complicated facts, but it does require you to be sure beyond all reasonable doubt as to the guilt of the defendant. To begin with, this case should never have come to trial. This case is as simple as black and white.

"The state has not produced one iota of medical evidence to the effect that the crime Tom Robinson is charged with ever took place. It has relied instead upon the testimony of two witnesses whose evidence has not only been called into serious question on cross-examination, but has been flatly contradicted by the defendant. The defendant is not guilty, but somebody in this courtroom is.

"I have nothing but pity in my heart for the chief witness for the state but my pity does not extend so far as to her putting a man's life at stake which she has done in an effort to get rid of her own guilt.

"I say guilt, gentlemen, because it was guilt that motivated her. She has committed no crime, she has merely broken a rigid and time-honored code of our society, a code so severe that whoever breaks it is hounded from our midst as unfit to live with. She is the victim of cruel poverty and ignorance, but I cannot pity her: she is white. She knew full well the enormity of her offense, but because her desires were stronger than the code she was breaking, she persisted in breaking it. She persisted, and the subsequent reaction is something that all of us have known at one time or another. She did something every child has done—she tried to put the evidence of her offense away from her. But in this case she was no child hiding stolen contraband: she struck out at her victim—of necessity she must put him away from her—he must be removed from her presence from this world. She must destroy the evidence of her offense.

"What was the evidence of her offense? Tom Robinson, a human being. She must put Tom Robinson away from her. Tom Robinson was her daily reminder of what she did. What did she do? She tempted a Negro.

"She was white, and she tempted a Negro. She did something that in our society is unspeakable: she kissed a black man. Not an old Uncle, but a strong young Negro man. No code mattered to her before she broke it but it came crashing down on her afterwards.

"Her father saw it, and the defendant has testified as to his remarks. What did her father do? We don't know, but there is circumstantial evidence to indicate that Mayella Ewell was beaten savagely by someone who led almost exclusively with his left. We do know in part what Mr. Ewell did: he did what any God-fearing, persevering, respectable white man would do under the circumstances—he swore out a warrant, no doubt signing it with his left hand, and Tom Robinson now sits before you, having taken the oath with the only good hand he possesses—his right hand.

"And so a quiet, respectable, humble Negro who had the unmitigated temerity to 'feel sorry' for a white woman has had to put his word against two white people's. I need not remind you of their appearance and conduct on the stand—you saw them for yourselves. The witnesses for the state, with the exception of the sheriff of Maycomb County, have presented themselves to you gentlemen, to this court, in the cynical confidence that their testimony would not be doubted, confident that you gentlemen would go along with them on the assumption—the evil assumption—that all Negroes lie, that all Negroes are basically immoral beings, that all Negro men are not to be trusted around our women, an assumption one associates with minds of their caliber.

"Which, gentlemen, we know is in itself a lie as black as Tom Robinson's skin, a lie I do not have to point out to you. You know the truth, and the truth is this: some Negroes lie, some Negroes are immoral, some Negro men are not to be trusted around women—black or white. But this is a truth that applies to the human race and to no particular race of men. There is not a person in this courtroom who has never told a lie, who has never done an immoral thing, and there is no man living who has never looked upon a woman without desire."

Atticus paused and took out his handkerchief. Then he took off his glasses and wiped them, and we saw another "first": we had never seen him sweat—he was one of those men whose faces never perspired, but now it was shining tan.

"One more thing, gentlemen, before I quit. Thomas Jefferson once said that all men are created equal, a phrase that the Yankees and the distaff side of the Executive branch in Washington are fond of hurling at us. There is a tendency in this year of grace, 1935, for certain people to use this phrase out of context, to satisfy all conditions. The most ridiculous example I can think of is that the people who run public education promote the stupid and idle along with the industrious—because all men are created equal, educators will gravely tell you, the children left behind suffer terrible feelings of inferiority. We know all men are not created equal in the sense some people would have us believe—some people are smarter than others, some people have more opportunity because they're born with it, some men make more money than others, some ladies make better cakes than others — some people are born gifted beyond the normal scope of most men.

"But there is one way in this country in which all men are created equal — there is one human institution that makes a pauper the equal of a Rockefeller, the stupid man the equal of an Einstein, and the ignorant man the equal of any college president. That institution, gentlemen, is a court. It can be the Supreme Court of the United States or the humblest J. P. court in the land, or this honorable court which you serve. Our courts have their faults, as does any human institution, but in this country our courts are the great levelers, and in our courts all men are created equal. "I'm no idealist to believe firmly in the integrity of our courts and in the jury system — that is no ideal to me, it is a living, working reality. Gentlemen, a court is no better than each man of you sitting before me on this jury. A court is only as sound as its jury, and a jury is only as sound as the men who make it up. I am confident that you gentlemen will review without passion the evidence you have heard, come to a decision, and restore this defendant to his family. In the name of God, do your duty."

Atticus's voice had dropped, and as he turned away from the jury he said something I did not catch. He said it more to himself than to the court. I punched Jem. "What'd he say?"

" 'In the name of God, believe him,' I think that's what he said."

Dill suddenly reached over me and tugged at Jem. "Looka yonder!"

We followed his finger with sinking hearts. Calpurnia was making her way up the middle aisle, walking straight toward Atticus.

She stopped shyly at the railing and waited to get Judge Taylor's attention. She was in a fresh apron and she carried an envelope in her hand.

Judge Taylor saw her and said, "It's Calpurnia, isn't it?"

"Yes sir," she said. "Could I just pass this note to Mr. Finch, please sir? It hasn't got anything to do with — with the trial."

Judge Taylor nodded and Atticus took the envelope from Calpurnia. He opened it, read its contents and said, "Judge, I — this note is from my sister. She says my children are missing, haven't turned up since noon . . . I . . . could you — "

"I know where they are, Atticus." Mr. Underwood spoke up. "They're right up yonder in the colored balcony — been there since precisely one-eighteen P.M."

Our father turned around and looked up. "Jem, come down from there," he called. Then he said something to the Judge we didn't hear. We climbed across Reverend Sykes and made our way to the staircase.

Atticus and Calpurnia met us downstairs. Calpurnia looked peeved, but Atticus looked exhausted.

Jem was jumping in excitement. "We've won, haven't we?"

"I've no idea," said Atticus shortly. "You've been here all afternoon? Go home with Calpurnia and get your supper — and stay home."

"Aw, Atticus, let us come back," pleaded Jem. "Please let us hear the verdict, *please* sir."

"The jury might be out and back in a minute, we don't know — " but we could tell Atticus was relenting. "Well, you've heard it all, so you might as well hear the rest. Tell you what, you all can come back when you've eaten your supper — eat slowly, now, you won't miss anything important — and if the jury's still out, you can wait with us. But I expect it'll be over before you get back."

"You think they'll acquit him that fast?" asked Jem.

Atticus opened his mouth to answer, but shut it and left us.

I prayed that Reverend Sykes would save our seats for us, but stopped praying when I remembered that people got up and left in droves when the jury was out — tonight, they'd overrun the drugstore, the O.K. Café and the hotel, that is, unless they had brought their suppers too.

Calpurnia marched us home: " — skin every one of you alive, the very idea, you children listenin' to all that! Mister Jem, don't you know better'n to take your little sister to that trial? Miss Alexandra'll absolutely have a stroke of paralysis when she finds out! Ain't fittin' for children to hear . . ."

The streetlights were on, and we glimpsed Calpurnia's indignant profile as we passed beneath them. "Mister Jem, I thought you was gettin' some kinda head on your shoulders — the very idea, she's your little sister! The very idea, sir! You oughta be perfectly ashamed of yourself — ain't you got any sense at all?"

I was exhilarated. So many things had happened so fast I felt it would take years to sort them out, and now here was Calpurnia giving her precious Jem down the country — what new marvels would the evening bring?

Jem was chuckling. "Don't you want to hear about it, Cal?"

"Hush your mouth, sir! When you oughta be hangin' your head in shame you go along laughin' — " Calpurnia revived a series of rusty threats that moved Jem to little remorse, and she sailed up the front steps with her classic, "If Mr. Finch don't wear you out, I will — get in that house, sir!"

Jem went in grinning, and Calpurnia nodded tacit consent to having Dill in to supper. "You all call Miss Rachel right now and tell her where you are," she told him. "She's run distracted lookin' for you — you watch out she don't ship you back to Mer-idian first thing in the mornin'."

Aunt Alexandra met us and nearly fainted when Calpurnia told her where we were. I guess it hurt her when we told her Atticus said we could go back, because she didn't say a word during supper. She just rearranged food on her plate, looking at it sadly while Calpurnia served Jem, Dill and me with a vengeance. Calpurnia poured milk, dished out potato salad and ham, mutter-ing, "'shamed of yourselves," in varying degrees of intensity. "Now you all eat slow," was her final command.

Reverend Sykes had saved our places. We were surprised to find that we had been gone nearly an hour, and were equally surprised to find the courtroom exactly as we had left it, with minor changes: the jury box was empty, the defendant was gone. Judge Taylor had been gone, but he reappeared as we were seating ourselves.

"Nobody's moved, hardly," said Jem.

"They moved around some when the jury went out," said Reverend Sykes. "The menfolk down there got the womenfolk their suppers, and they fed their babies."

"How long have they been out?" asked Jem.

" 'bout thirty minutes. Mr. Finch and Mr. Gilmer did some more talkin', and Judge Taylor charged the jury."

"How was he?" asked Jem.

"What say? Oh, he did right well. I ain't complainin' one bit — he was mighty fair-minded. He sorta said if you believe this, then you'll have to return one verdict, but if you believe this, you'll have to return another one. I thought he was leanin' a little to our side — " Reverend Sykes scratched his head.

Jem smiled. "He's not supposed to lean, Reverend, but don't fret, we've won it," he said wisely. "Don't see how any jury could convict on what we heard — "

"Now don't you be so confident, Mr. Jem, I ain't ever seen any jury decide in favor of a colored man over a white man. . . ." But Jem took exception to Reverend Sykes, and we were subjected to a lengthy review of the evidence with Jem's ideas on the law regard-ing rape: it wasn't rape if she let you, but she had to be eighteen — in Alabama, that is — and Mavella was nineteen. Apparently you had to kick and holler, you had to be overpowered and stomped on, preferably knocked stone cold. If you were under eighteen, you didn't have to go through all this.

"Mr. Jem," Reverend Sykes demurred, "this ain't a polite thing for little ladies to hear . . ."

"Aw, she doesn't know what we're talkin' about," said Jem. "Scout, this is too old for you, ain't it?"

"It most certainly is not, I know every word you're saying." Perhaps I was too convincing, because Jem hushed and never discussed the subject again.

"What time is it, Reverend?" he asked.

"Gettin' on toward eight."

I looked down and saw Atticus strolling around with his hands in his pockets: he made a tour of the windows, then walked by the railing over to the jury box. He looked in it, inspected Judge Taylor on his throne, then went back to where he started. I caught his eye and waved to him. He acknowledged my salute with a nod, and resumed his tour.

Mr. Gilmer was standing at the windows talking to Mr. Underwood. Bert, the court reporter, was chain-smoking: he sat back with his feet on the table.

But the officers of the court, the ones present—Atticus, Mr. Gilmer, Judge Taylor sound asleep, and Bert, were the only ones whose behavior seemed normal. I had never seen a packed courtroom so still. Sometimes a baby would cry out fretfully, and a child would scurry out, but the grown people sat as if they were in church. In the balcony, the Negroes sat and stood around us with biblical patience.

The old courthouse clock suffered its preliminary strain and struck the hour, eight deafening bongs that shook our bones.

When it bonged eleven times I was past feeling: tired from fighting sleep, I allowed myself a short nap against Reverend Sykes's comfortable arm and shoulder. I jerked awake and made an honest effort to remain so, by looking down and concentrating on the heads below: there were sixteen bald ones, fourteen men that could pass for redheads, forty heads varying between brown and black, and—I remembered something Jem had once explained to me when he went through a brief period of psychical research: he said if enough people—a stadium full, maybe—were to concentrate on one thing, such as setting a tree afire in the woods, that the tree would ignite of its own accord. I toyed with the idea of asking everyone below to concentrate on setting Tom Robinson free, but thought if they were as tired as I, it wouldn't work.

Dill was sound asleep, his head on Jem's shoulder, and Jem was quiet.

"Ain't it a long time?" I asked him.

"Sure is, Scout," he said happily.

"Well, from the way you put it, it'd just take five minutes."

Jem raised his eyebrows. "There are things you don't understand," he said, and I was too weary to argue.

But I must have been reasonably awake, or I would not have received the impression that was creeping into me. It was not unlike one I had last winter, and I shivered, though the night was hot. The feeling grew until the atmosphere in the courtroom was exactly the same as a cold February morning, when the mockingbirds were still, and the carpenters had stopped hammering on Miss Maudie's new house, and every wood door in the neighborhood was shut as tight as the doors of the Radley place. A deserted, waiting, empty street, and the courtroom was packed with people. A steaming summer night was no different from a winter morning. Mr. Heck Tate, who had entered the courtroom and was talking to Atticus, might have been wearing his high boots and lumber jacket. Atticus had stopped his tranquil journey and had put his foot onto the bottom rung of a chair; as he listened to what Mr. Tate was saying, he ran his hand slowly up and down his thigh. I expected Mr. Tate to say any minute, "Take him, Mr. Finch. . . ."

But Mr. Tate said, "This court will come to order," in a voice that rang with authority, and the heads below us jerked up. Mr. Tate left the room and returned with Tom Robinson. He steered Tom to his place beside Atticus, and stood there. Judge Taylor had roused himself to sudden alertness and was sitting up straight, looking at the empty jury box.

What happened after that had a dreamlike quality; in a dream I saw the jury return, moving like underwater swimmers, and Judge Taylor's voice came from far away, and was tiny. I saw something only a lawyer's child could be expected to see, could be expected to watch for, and it was like watching Atticus walk into the street, raise a rifle to his shoulder and pull the trigger, but watching all the time knowing that the gun was empty.

A jury never looks at a defendant it has convicted, and when this jury came in, not one of them looked at Tom Robinson. The foreman handed a piece of paper to Mr. Tate who handed it to the clerk who handed it to the judge. . . .

I shut my eyes. Judge Taylor was polling the jury: "Guilty . . . guilty . . . guilty . . . guilty . . ." I peeked at Jem: his hands were white from gripping the balcony rail, and his shoulders jerked as if each "guilty" was a separate stab between them.

Judge Taylor was saying something. His gavel was in his fist, but he wasn't using it. Dimly, I saw Atticus pushing papers from the table into his briefcase. He snapped it shut, went to the court reporter and said something, nodded to Mr. Gilmer, and then went to Tom Robinson and whispered something to him. Atticus put his hand on Tom's shoulder as he whispered. Atticus took his coat off the back of his chair and pulled it over his shoulder. Then he left the courtroom, but not by his usual exit.

He must have wanted to go home the short way, because he walked quickly down the middle aisle toward the south exit. I followed the top of his head as he made his way to the door. He did not look up.

Someone was punching me, but I was reluctant to take my eyes from the people below us, and from the image of Atticus's lonely walk down the aisle.

"Miss Jean Louise?"

I looked around. They were standing. All around us and in the balcony on the opposite wall, the Negroes were getting to their feet. Reverend Sykes's voice was as distant as Judge Taylor's:

"Miss Jean Louise, stand up. Your father's passin'."

It was Jem's turn to cry. His face was streaked with angry tears as we made our way through the cheerful crowd. "It ain't right," he muttered, all the way to the corner of the square where we found Atticus waiting. Atticus was standing under the street light looking as though nothing had happened: his vest was buttoned, his collar and tie were neatly in place, his watch-chain glistened, he was his impassive self again.

"It ain't right, Atticus." said Jem.

"No son, it's not right."

We walked home.

Aunt Alexandra was waiting up. She was in her dressing gown, and I could have sworn she had on her corset underneath it. "I'm sorry, brother," she murmured. Having never heard her call Atticus "brother" before, I stole a glance at Jem, but he was not listening. He would look up at Atticus, then down at the floor, and I wondered if he thought Atticus somehow responsible for Tom Robinson's conviction.

"Is he all right?" Aunty asked, indicating Jem.

"He'll be so presently," said Atticus. "It was a little too strong for him." Our father sighed. "I'm going to bed," he said. "If I don't wake up in the morning, don't call me."

"I didn't think it wise in the first place to let them — "

"This is their home, sister," said Atticus. "We've made it this way for them, they might as well learn to cope with it."

"But they don't have to go to the courthouse and wallow in it — "

"It's just as much Maycomb County as missionary teas."

"Atticus — " Aunt Alexandra's eyes were anxious. "You are the last person I thought would turn bitter over this."

"I'm not bitter, just tired. I'm going to bed."

"Atticus — " said Jem bleakly.

He turned in the doorway. "What, son?"

"How could they do it, how could they?"

"I don't know, but they did it. They've done it before and they did it tonight and they'll do it again and when they do it — seems that only children weep. Good night."

But things are always better in the morning. Atticus rose at his usual ungodly hour and was in the living room behind the Mobile Register when we stumbled in. Jem's morning face posed the question his sleepy lips struggled to ask.

"It's not time to worry yet," Atticus reassured him, as we went to the dining room. "We're not through yet. There'll be an appeal, you can count on that. Gracious alive, Cal, what's all this?" He was staring at his breakfast plate.

Calpurnia said, "Tom Robinson's daddy sent you along this chicken this morning. I fixed it."

"You tell him I'm proud to get it — bet they don't have chicken for breakfast at the White House. What are these?"

"Rolls," said Calpurnia. "Estelle down at the hotel sent 'em."

Atticus looked up at her, puzzled, and she said, "You better step out here and see what's in the kitchen, Mr. Finch."

We followed him. The kitchen table was loaded with enough food to bury the family: hunks of salt pork, tomatoes, beans, even scuppernongs. Atticus grinned when he found a jar of pickled pigs' knuckles. "Reckon Aunty'll let me eat these in the dining room?"

Calpurnia said, "This was all 'round the back steps when I got here this morning. They — they 'preciate what you did, Mr. Finch. They — they aren't oversteppin' themselves, are they?"

Atticus's eyes filled with tears. He did not speak for a moment. "Tell them I'm very grateful," he said. "Tell them — tell them they must never do this again. Times are too hard. . . ."

He left the kitchen, went in the dining room and excused himself to Aunt Alexandra, put on his hat and went to town.

We heard Dill's step in the hall, so Calpurnia left Atticus's uneaten breakfast on the table. Between rabbit-bites Dill told us of Miss Rachel's reaction to last night, which was: if a man like Atticus Finch wants to butt his head against a stone wall it's his head.

"I'da got her told," growled Dill, gnawing a chicken leg, "but she didn't look much like tellin' this morning. Said she was up half the night wonderin' where I was, said she'da had the sheriff after me but he was at the hearing."

"Dill, you've got to stop goin' off without tellin' her," said Jem. "It just aggravates her."

Dill sighed patiently. "I told her till I was blue in the face where I was goin' — she's just seein' too many snakes in the closet. Bet that woman drinks a pint for breakfast every morning — know she drinks two glasses full. Seen her."

"Don't talk like that, Dill," said Aunt Alexandra. "It's not becoming to a child. It's — cynical."

"I ain't cynical, Miss Alexandra. Tellin' the truth's not cynical, is it?"

"The way you tell it, it is."

Jem's eyes flashed at her, but he said to Dill, "Let's go. You can take that runner with you."

When we went to the front porch, Miss Stephanie Crawford was busy telling it to Miss Maudie Atkinson and Mr. Avery. They looked around at us and went on talking. Jem made a feral noise in his throat. I wished for a weapon.

"I hate grown folks lookin' at you," said Dill. "Makes you feel like you've done something."

Miss Maudie yelled for Jem Finch to come there.

Jem groaned and heaved himself up from the swing. "We'll go with you," Dill said.

Miss Stephanie's nose quivered with curiosity. She wanted to know who all gave us permission to go to court — she didn't see us but it was all over town this morning that we were in the Colored balcony. Did Atticus put us up there as a sort of — ? Wasn't it right close up there with all those — ? Did Scout understand all the — ? Didn't it make us mad to see our daddy beat?

"Hush, Stephanie." Miss Maudie's diction was deadly. "I've not got all the morning to pass on the porch — Jem Finch, I called to find out if you and your colleagues can eat some cake. Got up at five to make it, so you better say yes. Excuse us, Stephanie. Good morning, Mr. Avery."

There was a big cake and two little ones on Miss Maudie's kitchen table. There should have been three little ones. It was not like Miss Maudie to forget Dill, and we must have shown it. But we understood when she cut from the big cake and gave the slice to Jem.

As we ate, we sensed that this was Miss Maudie's way of saying that as far as she was concerned, nothing had changed. She sat quietly in a kitchen chair, watching us.

Suddenly she spoke: "Don't fret, Jem. Things are never as bad as they seem."

Indoors, when Miss Maudie wanted to say something lengthy she spread her fingers on her knees and settled her bridgework. This she did, and we waited.

"I simply want to tell you that there are some men in this world who were born to do our unpleasant jobs for us. Your father's one of them."

"Oh," said Jem. "Well."

"Don't you oh well me, sir," Miss Maudie replied, recognizing Jem's fatalistic noises, "you are not old enough to appreciate what I said."

Jem was staring at his half-eaten cake. "It's like bein' a caterpillar in a cocoon, that's what it is," he said. "Like somethin' asleep wrapped up in a warm place. I always thought Maycomb folks were the best folks in the world, least that's what they seemed like."

"We're the safest folks in the world," said Miss Maudie. "We're so rarely called on to be Christians, but when we are, we've got men like Atticus to go for us."

Jem grinned ruefully. "Wish the rest of the county thought that."

"You'd be surprised how many of us do."

"Who?" Jem's voice rose. "Who in this town did one thing to help Tom Robinson, just who?"

"His colored friends for one thing, and people like us. People like Judge Taylor. People like Mr. Heck Tate. Stop eating and start thinking, Jem. Did it ever strike you that Judge Taylor naming Atticus to defend that boy was no accident? That Judge Taylor might have had his reasons for naming him?"

This was a thought. Court-appointed defenses were usually given to Maxwell Green, Maycomb's latest addition to the bar, who needed the experience. Maxwell Green should have had Tom Robinson's case.

"You think about that," Miss Maudie was saying. "It was no accident. I was sittin' there on the porch last night, waiting. I waited and waited to see you all come down the sidewalk, and as I waited I thought, Atticus Finch won't win, he can't win, but he's the only man in these parts who can keep a jury out so long in a case like that. And I thought to myself, well, we're making a step—it's just a baby-step, but it's a step."

" 't's all right to talk like that—can't any Christian judges an' lawyers make up for heathen juries," Jem muttered. "Soon's I get grown—"

"That's something you'll have to take up with your father," Miss Maudie said.

We went down Miss Maudie's cool new steps into the sunshine and found Mr. Avery and Miss Stephanie Crawford still at it. They had moved down the sidewalk and were standing in front of Miss Stephanie's house. Miss Rachel was walking toward them.

"I think I'll be a clown when I get grown," said Dill.

Jem and I stopped in our tracks.

"Yes sir, a clown," he said. "There ain't one thing in this world I can do about folks except laugh, so I'm gonna join the circus and laugh my head off."

"You got it backwards, Dill," said Jem. "Clowns are sad, it's folks that laugh at them."

"Well I'm gonna be a new kind of clown. I'm gonna stand in the middle of the ring and laugh at the folks. Just looka yonder," he pointed. "Every one of 'em oughta be ridin' broomsticks. Aunt Rachel already does."

Miss Stephanie and Miss Rachel were waving wildly at us, in a way that did not give the lie to Dill's observation.

"Oh gosh," breathed Jem. "I reckon it'd be ugly not to see 'em."

Something was wrong. Mr. Avery was red in the face from a sneezing spell and nearly blew us off the sidewalk when we came up. Miss Stephanie was trembling with excitement, and Miss Rachel caught Dill's shoulder. "You get on in the back yard and stay there," she said. "There's danger a'comin'."

" 's matter?" I asked.

"Ain't you heard yet? It's all over town—"

At that moment Aunt Alexandra came to the door and called us, but she was too late. It was Miss Stephanie's pleasure to tell us: this morning Mr. Bob Ewell stopped Atticus on the post office corner, spat in his face, and told him he'd get him if it took the rest of his life.

"I wish Bob Ewell wouldn't chew tobacco," was all Atticus said about it.

According to Miss Stephanie Crawford, however, Atticus was leaving the post office when Mr. Ewell approached him, cursed him, spat on him, and threatened to kill him. Miss Stephanie (who, by the time she had told it twice was there and had seen it all—passing by from the Jitney Jungle, she was)—Miss Stephanie said Atticus didn't bat an eye, just took out his handkerchief and wiped his face and stood there and let Mr. Ewell call him names wild horses could not bring her to repeat. Mr. Ewell was a veteran of an obscure war; that plus Atticus's peaceful reaction probably prompted him to inquire, "Too proud to fight, you nigger-lovin' bastard?" Miss Stephanie said Atticus said, "No, too old," put his hands in his pockets and strolled on. Miss Stephanie said you had to hand it to Atticus Finch, he could be right dry sometimes.

Jem and I didn't think it entertaining.

"After all, though," I said, "he was the deadest shot in the county one time. He could—"

"You know he wouldn't carry a gun, Scout. He ain't even got one—"said Jem. "You know he didn't even have one down at the jail that night. He told me havin' a gun around's an invitation to somebody to shoot you."

"This is different," I said. "We can ask him to borrow one."

We did, and he said, "Nonsense."

Dill was of the opinion that an appeal to Atticus's better nature might work: after all, we would starve if Mr. Ewell killed him, besides be raised exclusively by Aunt Alexandra, and we all knew the first thing she'd do before Atticus was under the ground good would be to fire Calpurnia. Jem said it might work if I cried and flung a fit, being young and a girl. That didn't work either.

But when he noticed us dragging around the neighborhood, not eating, taking little interest in our normal pursuits, Atticus discovered how deeply frightened we were. He tempted Jem with a new football magazine one night; when he saw Jem flip the pages and toss it aside, he said, "What's bothering you, son?"

Jem came to the point: "Mr. Ewell."

"What has happened?"

"Nothing's happened. We're scared for you, and we think you oughta do something about him."

Atticus smiled wryly. "Do what? Put him under a peace bond?"

"When a man says he's gonna get you, looks like he means it."

"He meant it when he said it," said Atticus. "Jem, see if you can stand in Bob Ewell's shoes a minute. I destroyed his last shred of credibility at that trial, if he had any to begin with. The man had to have some kind of comeback, his kind always does. So if spitting in my face and threatening me saved Mayella Ewell one extra beating, that's something I'll gladly take. He had to take it out on somebody and I'd rather it be me than that houseful of children out there. You understand?"

Jem nodded.

Aunt Alexandra entered the room as Atticus was saying, "We don't have anything to fear from Bob Ewell, he got it all out of his system that morning."

"I wouldn't be so sure of that, Atticus," she said. "His kind'd do anything to pay off a grudge. You know how those people are."

"What on earth could Ewell do to me, sister?"

"Something furtive," Aunt Alexandra said. "You may count on that."

"Nobody has much chance to be furtive in Maycomb," Atticus answered.

After that, we were not afraid. Summer was melting away, and we made the most of it. Atticus assured us that nothing would happen to Tom Robinson until the higher court reviewed his case, and that Tom had a good chance of going free, or at least of having a new trial. He was at Enfield Prison Farm, seventy miles away in Chester County. I asked Atticus if Tom's wife and children were allowed to visit him, but Atticus said no.

"If he loses his appeal," I asked one evening, "what'll happen to him?"

"He'll go to the chair," said Atticus, "unless the Governor commutes his sentence. Not time to worry yet, Scout. We've got a good chance."

Jem was sprawled on the sofa reading *Popular Mechanics*. He looked up. "It ain't right. He didn't kill anybody even if he was guilty. He didn't take anybody's life."

"You know rape's a capital offense in Alabama." said Atticus.

"Yessir, but the jury didn't have to give him death—if they wanted to they could've gave him twenty years."

"Given," said Atticus. "Tom Robinson's a colored man, Jem. No jury in this part of the world's going to say, 'We think you're guilty, but not very,' on a charge like that. It was either a straight acquittal or nothing."

Jem was shaking his head. "I know it's not right, but I can't figure out what's wrong—maybe rape shouldn't be a capital offense. . . ."

Atticus dropped his newspaper beside his chair. He said he didn't have any quarrel with the rape statute, none whatever, but he did have deep misgivings when the state asked for and the jury gave a death penalty on purely circumstantial evidence. He glanced at me, saw I was listening, and made it easier. "—I mean, before a man is sentenced to death for murder, say, there should be one or two eyewitnesses. Someone should be able to say, 'Yes, I was there and saw him pull the trigger.'"

"But lots of folks have been hung—hanged—on circumstantial evidence," said Jem.

"I know, and lots of 'em probably deserved it, too—but in the absence of eye-witnesses there's always a doubt, sometimes only the shadow of a doubt. The law says 'reasonable doubt,' but I think a defendant's entitled to the shadow of a doubt. There's always the possibility, no matter how improbable, that he's innocent."

"Then it all goes back to the jury, then. We oughta do away with juries." Jem was adamant.

Atticus tried hard not to smile but couldn't help it. "You're rather hard on us, son. I think maybe there might be a better way. Change the law. Change it so that only judges have the power of fixing the penalty in capital cases."

"Then go up to Montgomery and change the law."

"You'd be surprised how hard that'd be. I won't live to see the law changed, and if you live to see it you'll be an old man."

This was not good enough for Jem. "No sir, they oughta do away with juries. He wasn't guilty in the first place and they said he was."

"If you had been on that jury, son, and eleven other boys like you, Tom would be a free man," said Atticus. "So far nothing in your life has interfered with your reasoning process. Those are twelve reasonable men in everyday life, Tom's jury, but you saw something come between them and reason. You saw the same thing that night in front of the jail. When that crew went away, they didn't go as reasonable men, they went because we were there. There's something in our world that makes men lose their heads — they couldn't be fair if they tried. In our courts, when it's a white man's word against a black man's, the white man always wins. They're ugly, but those are the facts of life."

"Doesn't make it right," said Jem stolidly. He beat his fist softly on his knee. "You just can't convict a man on evidence like that — you can't."

"You couldn't, but they could and did. The older you grow the more of it you'll see. The one place where a man ought to get a square deal is in a courtroom, be he any color of the rainbow, but people have a way of carrying their resentments right into a jury box. As you grow older, you'll see white men cheat black men every day of your life, but let me tell you something and don't you forget it — whenever a white man does that to a black man, no matter who he is, how rich he is, or how fine a family he comes from, that white man is trash."

Atticus was speaking so quietly his last word crashed on our ears. I looked up, and his face was vehement. "There's nothing more sickening to me than a low-grade white man who'll take advantage of a Negro's ignorance. Don't fool yourselves — it's all adding up and one of these days we're going to pay the bill for it. I hope it's not in you children's time."

Discussion Topics

1. Consider the defense argument in Gaines' *A Lesson Before Dying*. Thinking solely of the goal of forestalling a death sentence, did this argument give the defense its best shot? Two distinct points are made. The first is that Jefferson was an accidental bystander and not an intending participant; this point hardly depends on his intelligence and skills. The second is that he was incapable of being a co-conspirator and accomplice. The defense attorney emphasizes the second presumably because he lacks evidence for the first (circumstances suggest the opposite might be true) and because he knows the jury's prejudices. But the argument is weak if the jury hardly regards intelligence as necessary for committing armed robbery and murder.

Think also about the extent to which the defense argument reinforces and spreads prejudice. Is the attorney preaching to the choir so that his words have no risk of changing minds? Or is the effect likely to be more insidious?

2. Almost every high school student has learned to admire Atticus Finch. His defense speech is noble, high-minded, and candid. He describes matters as they are as he asks the jury to reflect on its biases and beliefs. But is it a model of good lawyering? Does he have a chance of convincing *this audience* that his client, Tom Robinson, should be spared? We admire him because he is talking to the ages and tearing the veil off class bias. But can he be criticized for using his client's predicament as a pretext for giving political and moral instruction?

(Atticus Finch gets mixed reviews from academic commentators. Monroe Freedman, in "Atticus Finch — Right and Wrong," at 45 *Alabama Law Review* 404 (1994), calls him "fatuous." In "Atticus Finch — The End of Honor: A Discussion of *To Kill a Mockingbird*," at 30 *University of San Francisco Law Review* 1139 (1996), John Jay Osborn, who wrote *The Paper Chase*, argues that the novel's posture is hypocritical and childish.)

Note that in the period of civil rights litigation in the 1960s and '70s lawyers were often accused of using clients to create legal opportunities that would benefit society at large more than they would help the particular clients.

3. One of the most controversial and eloquent responses to the underlying moral dilemma is Abbe Smith's in her article, "Defending Defending: The Case for Unmitigated Zeal on Behalf of People Who Do Terrible Things," 28 *Hofstra Law Review* 925. Consider the argument in her own words.

❧ *from* Defending Defending ❧

Abbe Smith

When Haitian immigrant Abner Louima accused Officer John Volpe of committing an act of unspeakable brutality on him in a Brooklyn police station in 1997 — shoving a broom handle into Louima's rectum so hard he caused massive internal injuries — one has to imagine that Volpe vehemently disavowed the charge and asserted his innocence. One has to imagine that Volpe called Louima a liar, a charlatan, or worse — and insisted that he was incapable of even contemplating such conduct.

How could Volpe not have denied it? He has family, friends, a good job, and standing in the community. He has an African American girlfriend. If, as he later admitted, he had actually brutalized Louima, he was no doubt in a state of shock and denial about his own shameful conduct, for he certainly knows he had crossed a line. Even those who think police officers have a right to engage in a little "street justice" were offended by the allegation; this was not simply a case of big-city cops getting carried away in the heat of battle, but outright torture.

In any event, the likelihood is that Volpe's lawyer, Marvyn Kornberg, had before him a client who insisted he was not guilty, insisted the allegations against him were untrue or overblown, and insisted on going to trial. Kornberg, an experienced criminal lawyer, likely probed Volpe's story in order to learn as much as he could from his client about both the government's case and any possible defenses. Undoubtedly, as the evidence began to mount, the probing became more confrontational. However, some clients can be unbudging, and at some point the lawyer may cause too much damage by challenging the client's story, conduct, or character.

What was Kornberg to do? Let us imagine he did not believe this client and thought he had before him a sadistic, racist cop who, in some sort of monstrous rage, had brutalized an innocent, hard-working immigrant who had the misfortune to cross Volpe's path. Reportedly, Marvyn Kornberg has a sign in his office that reads, "Kornberg's Rule of Law: Presumption of Innocence Commences with Payment of Retainer." Holding aside the crudeness of such a placard, it does make explicit the way in which the right to counsel is the life blood of the fundamental principles afforded the accused in this country: the presumption of innocence, the government's burden to prove guilt, and the high evidentiary standard of proof beyond a reasonable doubt. It also makes plain one of the most important things a defense lawyer can offer a client accused of a terrible crime: suspension of judgment.

So Kornberg attempted to fashion a defense. He did what defense lawyers have always done, what defense lawyers always must do: he challenged the government's case. He did so in the time-honored way: by attacking the credibility of the government's chief witness, by attempting to discredit the other government witnesses; by offering alternative explanations for the government's physical, medical, and scientific evidence.

As he is ethically required to do, Kornberg advocated on behalf of his client with zeal. Kornberg also took to the press, as the case was high profile from the start. The defense theory he began to build and later articulate in his opening statement used what he had: a chief government witness who could not seem to keep his story straight, who could thus be portrayed as a liar, a trouble-maker, and a mercenary; police officer informants who were not present during the incident, have no direct knowledge of what happened, and were motivated by their own self-interest; and evidence of physical injuries that could have occurred in a manner other than what was alleged. With rare exception, Kornberg's cross-examinations of witnesses were intense and aggressive.

Of course, it is the aspect of the defense theory having to do with Louima's injuries that is the source of the controversy. Kornberg's suggestion that Louima's injuries were the result not of police brutality, but of consensual anal sex with another man. Although Kornberg laid out this theory rather clumsily, if emphatically — "the injuries sustained by Mr. Louima are not, I repeat, not consistent with a nonconsensual insertion of an object into his rectum" — he set the groundwork for arguing consensual homosexual sex. Kornberg noted "that a trace of Mr. Louima's feces found in the police station bathroom 'contains the DNA of another male,'" and told the jury, "[y]ou are going to be shown how somebody else's DNA can get into another individual's feces."

Although some dismissed this theory as "absurd" or "crazy," others self-righteously denounced it as a "vile insinuation," a "vile fantasy," and even as "a second rape." One commentator astutely suggested that the "outrage over the supposed slight shows that Kornberg was onto something" larger than the refutation of medical evidence at trial. This commentator argued that, holding aside the implausibility of the defense, "it cleverly played on the expectation that the jury of ordinary Americans would still see homosexuality as vile, and see violence as normal in a homosexual act — at least in preference to seeing sadism as normal in a heterosexual arrest. How else explain a torn rectum and bladder?

Still, *how else explain a torn rectum and bladder?* Kornberg certainly did not invent the "rough sex" defense — many a defender has raised the defense, which gained notoriety in the "Preppy Murder" case in the 1980s. In rape cases in which there are physical injuries and no viable mistaken identification defense, the only possible defense is rough sex or accidental injury in the course of some sort of sex play. What else is there if a client insists on going to trial?

Yet, Kornberg has been roundly reviled for his defense of Volpe. He has been called a "racist," a "villain," a liar, an "opportunist," and a publicity seeker. He has even been attacked by fellow criminal defense lawyers. One can only imagine what the usual critics of criminal defense advocacy are saying.

Although defending defending may be an endless pursuit, I cannot help taking it on. I am, after all, a defender myself, and defending fellow defenders seems to go with the territory. Of course, attacks on criminal defenders do not come out of nowhere — difficult and complex questions often arise in criminal defense work. Unfortunately, the questions raised in the aftermath of a high profile case such as the Abner Louima case are usually the easy ones — questions that have more to do with the nature of the adversarial system than with the values or ethics of individual defense lawyers or the power structure of our legal and political systems.

[In the middle sections of her article, Smith makes clear the importance of providing representation even for the "most unpopular and the most vilified" in our society. At the same time, she makes clear that lawyers have wide discretion to choose clients, even though they have no discretion whether to defend them "zealously" once the choice has been made. She indicates that she herself would have declined to take Volpe as a client.

[At the end of her article, she makes clearer her position on the underlying debate along with the reasons for her position.]

The burning question raised by Kornberg's advocacy is whether he crossed an "ethical line" when he suggested in his opening statement that Louima's injuries were the result of consensual homosexual sex and not police brutality. As discussed above, Kornberg was well within ethical bounds to offer a *flimsy* theory of defense, even if the evidence to support it was largely illusory. The more interesting question relates to the propriety of putting forward a theory of defense built on the exploitation of potential juror prejudice.

There is a growing body of legal scholarship criticizing the exploitation of bias in lawyering strategies, most of which focuses on social bias. Some scholars have singled out criminal defense lawyers for criticism. . . .

Anthony Alfieri, the most prominent progressive scholar on this subject, wants to have it both ways. He would like criminal defense lawyers to be more "community-centered," and to embrace a "color-conscious, pluralist approach to advocacy that honors the integrity of diverse individual and collective . . . identities *without sacrificing effective representation.*" This is both untenable and disingenuous. In truth, he wants to transform criminal defense lawyers from defenders of individuals accused of crime to defenders of the community and of certain values he holds dear.

It is difficult, if not impossible, to zealously represent the criminally accused and simultaneously tend to the feelings of others. This is so in any political climate, but even more so in a time when criminal punishment is regarded as the answer to almost all of our social problems. We cannot seem to build prisons fast enough, and we are on the road to the virtual banishment of young African American men from society. It is simply wrong to place an additional burden on criminal defense lawyers to make the world a better place as they labor to represent individuals facing loss of liberty or life. . . .

There is nothing unethical about using racial, gender, ethnic, or sexual stereotypes in criminal defense. It is simply an aspect of zealous advocacy. Prejudice exists in the community and in the courthouse, and criminal defense lawyers would be foolhardy not to recognize this as a fact of life. Of course, most bias and prejudice works against the accused, disproportionate numbers of whom are poor and nonwhite. Defense lawyers must incorporate this knowledge, as well as knowledge about the stereotypes that might apply, to the prosecution and defense witnesses in all their trial decisions.

A trial is theater. Defense lawyers cannot afford to be color-blind, gender-blind, or even slightly near-sighted when it comes to race, gender, sexual orientation, and ethnicity, because jurors will be paying close attention and they have come to the trial with their own feelings about these issues. Many stereotypes arise in a criminal trial, whether or not they are actively exploited by either party. Sometimes the exploitation of stereotypes is unavoidable. . . .

a. Smith is an eloquent defender of one side of a continuing debate. She seems to suggest that a lawyer should pull out all stops, especially in defending the "unpopular and the vilified," and that this is what the adversary system is all about. But it is important to keep in mind that lawyers have always had to observe all kinds of constraints in devising their strategies and making their arguments. They cannot destroy or with-hold evidence. They cannot create false evidence. And they cannot present matters as "fact" if they are not supported by evidence. The prosecution cannot withhold exculpatory evidence from the defense. Nor can lawyers solicit perjured testimony. We have seen that they must correct testimony if they discover after the fact that it is false.

Given all of these constraints, is it much of an intellectual stretch to think that they are ethically constrained not to harm other individuals by their actions? To put it another way, the rights of the defendant to zealousness on the part of her counsel is hemmed in in all kinds of ways that are not evident to the layperson. Might ethical strictures not be part of that framework?

b. If we look closely at Smith's defense of Kornberg, we note that she says that he offered a "flimsy" argument about the source of Louima's injuries; she does not say that it is an argument wholly unsupported by evidence. Is it were the latter, it would be outside permissible bounds. Is the line between a flimsy argument and an unsupported argument clear? And is it clear on which side Kornberg lands?

c. Smith makes the sensible point that stereotypes inevitably play a role when cases are litigated. Not only jurors, but also lawyers and judges, cannot leave their prejudices at the door. But there may be a significant distinction between being aware of prejudice and taking it into account, on the one hand, and inflaming prejudice, on the other. Is Kornberg's argument more offensive than, say, the defense argument in Gaines' chapter? Arguably, the prejudice, however offensive, that existed in Louisiana in the 1940s is merely echoed in the argument. By contrast, Kornberg is inventing a connection between Louima and a disparaged group for the sake of using biases that have no connection to the case at all.

Punishment, Prisons, and Alternatives

Franz Kafka: In the Penal Colony

The ever-expanding prison population is, it is said, evidence of a failure of imagination. We no longer have confidence in alternative methods of punishment. Rather, we want to make the very fact of punishment invisible by hiding offenders in places that few of us have ever seen.

Another way of making the same point is that we have given up, for the most part, on most of the goals of punishment except specific deterrence (or restraint) and retribution. We believe that, as far as general deterrence goes, the economic, sociological, and psychological causes of crime are much more determinative than the likely severity or nature of sanctions. Offenders expect to get away with their crimes, not to be punished for them. The consequences of getting caught are not a factor in their plans. As for rehabilitation, we seem to recognize that, while educative efforts may reform many prisoners, even more prisoners use prisons to acquire the skills, connections, and attitudes to become more effective and more committed criminals.

George Bernard Shaw, who was one of the most influential playwrights and essayists in the first half of the twentieth century, argues that "imprisonment is at once the most cruel of punishments and the one that those who inflict it without having ever experienced it cannot believe to be cruel." His point is that most of us cannot begin to understand the effects of long-term deprivation of liberty and of contact with the general public. His guess is that no physical punishment approaches the psychological dislocation caused by imprisonment.

A different consideration is raised by the renowned psychologist, Karl Menninger, who points out that, in making imprisonment the almost universal punishment, we homogenize the needs and deserts of very different kinds of offenders. He discusses the "persistent failure of the law to distinguish between crime as an accidental, incidental, explosive event, crime as a behavior pattern expressive of chronic unutterable rage and frustration, and crime as a business or elected way of life." The suitability of imprisonment as a punishment for members of each category must be considered separately. With its emphasis on intention and choice and with its tacit denial of the role of the unconscious and the emotions, criminal law seems to assimilate all criminals to Menninger's third category.

The materials in the rest of this chapter give us opportunities to think about the pros and cons of alternative punishments as well as to rethink the arguments for imprisonment. Franz Kafka's "In the Penal Colony" imagines a colonial community in which guilt is presumed and capital punishment is the normal remedy. As always, Kafka is not a literalist. He asks us to interpret the elements of his story symbolically. It is useful to look beyond the obvious differences between the system in this penal colony and our own society to see what attitudes and practices we might have in common.

❧ In the Penal Colony ❧

Franz Kafka

"It's a remarkable piece of apparatus," said the officer to the explorer and surveyed with a certain air of admiration the apparatus which was after all quite familiar to him. The explorer seemed to have accepted merely out of politeness the Commandant's invitation to witness the execution of a soldier condemned to death for disobedience and insulting behavior to a superior. Nor did the colony itself betray much interest in this execution. At least, in the small sandy valley, a deep hollow surrounded on all sides by naked crags, there was no one present save the officer, the explorer, the condemned man, who was a stupid-looking, wide-mouthed creature with bewildered hair and face, and the soldier who held the heavy chain controlling the small chains locked on the prisoner's ankles, wrists, and neck, chains that were themselves attached to each other by communicating links. In any case, the condemned man looked so like a submissive dog that one might have thought he could be left to run free on the surrounding hills and would only need to be whistled for when the execution was due to begin.

The explorer did not much care about the apparatus and walked up and down behind the prisoner with almost visible indifference while the officer made the last adjustments, now creeping beneath the structure, which was bedded deep in the earth, now climbing a ladder to inspect its upper parts. These were tasks that might well have been left to a mechanic, but the officer performed them with great zeal, whether because he was a devoted admirer of the apparatus or because of other reasons the work could be entrusted to no one else. "Ready now!" he called at last and climbed down from the ladder. He looked uncommonly limp, breathed with his mouth wide open, and had tucked two fine ladies' handkerchiefs under the collar of his uniform. "These uniforms are too heavy for the tropics, surely," said the explorer, instead of making some inquiry about the apparatus, as the officer had expected. "Of course," said the officer, washing his oily and greasy hands in a bucket of water that stood ready, "but they mean home to us; we don't want to forget about home. Now just have a look at this machine," he added at once, simultaneously drying his hands on a towel and indicating the apparatus. "Up till now a few things still had to be set by hand, but from this moment it works all by itself." The explorer nodded and followed him. The officer, anxious to secure himself against all contingencies, said: "Things sometimes go wrong, of course; I hope that nothing goes wrong today, but we have to allow for the possibility. The machinery should go on working continuously for twelve hours. But if anything does go wrong it will only be some small matter that can be set right at once."

"Won't you take a seat?" he asked finally, drawing a cane chair out from among a heap of them and offering it to the explorer, who could not refuse it. He was now sitting at the edge of a pit, into which he glanced for a fleeting moment. It was not very deep. On one side of the pit the excavated soil had been piled up in a rampart, on the other side of it stood the apparatus. "I don't know," said the officer, "if the Commandant has already explained this apparatus to you." The explorer waved one hand vaguely; the officer asked for nothing better, since now he could explain the apparatus himself. "This apparatus," he said, taking hold of a crank handle and leaning against it, "was invented by our former Commandant. I assisted at the very earliest experiments and had a share in all the work until its completion. But the credit of inventing it belongs to him alone. Have you ever heard of our former Commandant? No? Well, it isn't saying too much if I tell you that the organization of the whole penal colony is his work. We who were his friends knew even before he died that the organization of the colony was so perfect that his successor, even with a thousand new schemes in his head, would find it impossible to alter anything, at least for many years to come. And our prophecy has come true; the new

Commandant has had to acknowledge its truth. A pity you never met the old Commandant! — But," the officer interrupted himself, "I am rambling on, and here stands his apparatus before us. It consists, as you see, of three parts. In the course of time each of these parts has acquired a kind of popular nickname. The lower one is called the 'Bed,' the upper one the 'Designer,' and this one here in the middle that moves up and down is called the 'Harrow.' "

"The Harrow?" asked the explorer. He had not been listening very attentively, the glare of the sun in the shadeless valley was altogether too strong, it was difficult to collect one's thoughts. All the more did he admire the officer, who in spite of his tightfitting full-dress uniform coat, amply befrogged and weighed down by epaulettes, was pursuing his subject with such enthusiasm and, besides talking, was still tightening a screw here and there with a spanner. As for the soldier, he seemed to be in much the same condition as the explorer. He had wound the prisoner's chain around both his wrists, propped himself on his rifle, let his head hang, and was paying no attention to anything. That did not surprise the explorer, for the officer was speaking French, and certainly neither the soldier nor the prisoner understood a word of French. It was all the more remarkable, therefore, that the prisoner was nonetheless making an effort to follow the officer's explanations. With a kind of drowsy persistence he directed his gaze wherever the officer pointed a finger, and at the interruption of the explorer's question he, too, as well as the officer, looked around.

"Yes, the Harrow," said the officer, "a good name for it. The needles are set in like the teeth of a harrow and the whole thing works something like a harrow, although its action is limited to one place and contrived with much more artistic skill. Anyhow, you'll soon understand it. On the Bed here the condemned man is laid — I'm going to describe the apparatus first before I set it in motion. Then you'll be able to follow the proceedings better. Besides, one of the cogwheels in the Designer is badly worn; it creaks a lot when it's working; you can hardly hear yourself speak; spare parts, unfortunately, are difficult to get here. — Well, here is the Bed, as I told you. It is completely covered with a layer of cotton wool; you'll find out why later. On this cotton wool the condemned man is laid, face down, quite naked, of course; here are straps for the hands, here for the feet, and here for the neck, to bind him fast. Here at the head of the Bed, where the man, as I said, first lays down his face, is this little gag of felt, which can be easily regulated to go straight into his mouth. It is meant to keep him from screaming and biting his tongue. Of course the man is forced to take the felt into his mouth, for otherwise his neck would be broken by the strap."

"Is that cotton wool?" asked the explorer, bending forward. "Yes, certainly," said the officer, with a smile, "feel it for yourself." He took the explorer's hand and guided it over the Bed. "It's specially prepared cotton wool, that's why it looks so different; I'll tell you presently what it's for." The explorer already felt a dawning interest in the apparatus; he sheltered his eyes from the sun with one hand and gazed up at the structure. It was a huge affair. The Bed and the Designer were of the same size and looked like two dark wooden chests. The Designer hung about two meters above the Bed; each of them was bound at the corners with four rods of brass that almost flashed out rays in the sunlight. Between the chests shuttled the Harrow on a ribbon of steel.

The officer had scarcely noticed the explorer's previous indifference, but he was now well aware of his dawning interest; so he stopped explaining in order to leave a space of time for quiet observation. The condemned man imitated the explorer; since he could not use a hand to shelter his eyes he gazed upwards without shade.

"Well, the man lies down," said the explorer, leaning back in his chair and crossing his legs.

"Yes," said the officer, pushing his cap back a little and passing one hand over his heated face, "now listen! Both the Bed and the Designer have an electric battery each; the Bed needs one for itself, the Designer for the Harrow. As soon as the man is strapped down, the Bed is set in motion. It quivers in minute, very rapid vibrations, both from side to side and up and down. You will have seen similar apparatus in hospitals; but in our Bed the movements are all precisely calculated; you see, they have to correspond very exactly to the movements of the Harrow. And the Harrow is the instrument for the actual execution of the sentence."

"And how does the sentence run?" asked the explorer.

"You don't know that either?" said the officer in amazement, and bit his lips. "Forgive me if my explanations seem rather incoherent. I do beg your pardon. You see, the Commandant always used to do the explaining; but the new Commandant shirks this duty; yet that such an important visitor"—the explorer tried to deprecate the honor with both hands, the officer, however, insisted—"that such an important visitor should not even be told about the kind of sentence we pass is a new development, which—" He was just on the point of using strong language but checked himself and said only: "I was not informed, it is not my fault. In any case, I am certainly the best person to explain our procedure, since I have here"—he patted his breast pocket—"the relevant drawings made by our former Commandant."

"The Commandant's own drawings?" asked the explorer. "Did he combine everything in himself, then? Was he soldier, judge, mechanic, chemist, and draughtsman?"

"Indeed he was," said the officer, nodding assent, with a remote, glassy look. Then he inspected his hands critically; they did not seem clean enough to him for touching the drawings; so he went over to the bucket and washed them again. Then he drew out a small leather wallet and said: "Our sentence does not sound severe. Whatever commandment the prisoner has disobeyed is written upon his body by the Harrow. This prisoner, for instance" — the officer indicated the man — "will have written on his body: HONOR THY SUPERIORS!"

The explorer glanced at the man; he stood, as the officer pointed him out, with bent head, apparently listening with all his ears in an effort to catch what was being said. Yet the movement of his blubber lips, closely pressed together, showed clearly that he could not understand a word. Many questions were troubling the explorer, but at the sight of the prisoner he asked only: "Does he know his sentence?"

"No," said the officer, eager to go on with his exposition, but the explorer interrupted him: "He doesn't know the sentence that has been passed on him?" "No," said the officer again, pausing a moment as if to let the explorer elaborate his question, and then said: "There would be no point in telling him. He'll learn it on his body."

The explorer intended to make no answer, but he felt the prisoner's gaze turned on him; it seemed to ask if he approved such goings-on. So he bent forward again, having already leaned back in his chair, and put another question: "But surely he knows that he has been sentenced?"

"Nor that either," said the officer, smiling at the explorer as if expecting him to make further surprising remarks.

"No," said the explorer, wiping his forehead, "then he can't know either whether his defense was effective?"

"He has had no chance of putting up a defense," said the officer, turning his eyes away as if speaking to himself and so sparing the explorer the shame of hearing self-evident matters explained.

"But he must have had some chance of defending himself," said the explorer, and rose from his seat.

The officer realized that he was in danger of having his exposition of the apparatus held up for a long time; so he went up to the explorer, took him by the arm, waved a hand toward the condemned man, who was standing very straight now that he had so obviously become the center of attention — the soldier had also given the chain a jerk — and said: "This is how the matter stands. I have been appointed judge in this penal colony. Despite my youth. For I was the former Commandant's assistant in all penal matters and know more about the apparatus than anyone. My guiding principle is this: Guilt is never to be doubted. Other courts cannot follow that principle, for they consist of several opinions and have higher courts to scrutinize them. That is not the case here, or at least, it was not the case in the former Commandant's time. The new man has certainly shown some inclination to interfere with my judgments, but so far I have succeeded in fending him off and will go on succeeding. You wanted to have the case explained; it is quite simple, like all of them. A captain reported to me this morning that this man, who had been assigned to him as a servant and sleeps before his door, had been asleep on duty. It is his duty, you see, to get up every time the hour strikes and salute the captain's door. Not an exacting duty, and very necessary, since he has to be a sentry as well as a servant, and must be alert in both functions. Last night the captain wanted to see if the man was doing his duty. He opened the door as the clock struck two and there was his man curled up asleep. He took his riding whip and lashed him across the face. Instead of getting up and begging pardon, the man caught hold of his master's legs, shook him, and cried: 'Throw that whip away or I'll eat you alive.' — That's the evidence. The captain came to me an hour ago, I wrote down his statement and appended the sentence to it. Then I had the man put in chains. That was all quite simple. If I had first called the man before me and interrogated him, things would have got into a confused tangle. He would have told lies, and had I exposed these lies he would have backed them up with more lies, and so on and so forth. As it is, I've got him and I won't let him go. — Is that quite clear now? But we're wasting time, the execution should be beginning and I haven't finished explaining the apparatus yet."

He pressed the explorer back into his chair, went up again to the apparatus, and began: "As you see, the shape of the Harrow corresponds to the human form; here is the harrow for the torso, here are the harrows for the legs. For the head there is only this one small spike. Is that quite clear?" He bent amiably forward toward the explorer, eager to provide the most comprehensive explanations.

The explorer considered the Harrow with a frown. The explanation of the judicial procedure had not satisfied him. He had to remind himself that this was in any case a penal colony where extraordinary measures were needed and that military discipline must be enforced to the last. He also felt that some hope might be set on the new Commandant, who was apparently of a mind to bring in, although gradually, a new kind of procedure which the officer's narrow mind was incapable of understanding. This train of thought prompted his next question: "Will the Commandant attend the execution?"

"It is not certain," said the officer, wincing at the direct question, and his friendly expression darkened. "That is just why we have to lose no time. Much as I dislike it, I shall have to cut my explanations short. But of course tomorrow, when the apparatus has been cleaned — its one drawback is that it gets so messy — I can recapitulate all the details. For the present, then, only the essentials. — When the man lies down on the Bed and it begins to vibrate, the Harrow is lowered onto his body. It regulates itself automatically so that the needles barely touch his skin; once contact is made the steel ribbon stiffens immediately into a rigid band. And then the performance begins. An ignorant onlooker would see no difference between one punishment and another. The Harrow appears to do its work with uniform regularity. As it quivers, its points pierce the skin of the body which is itself quivering from the vibration of the Bed. So that the actual progress of the sentence can be watched, the Harrow is made of glass. Getting the needles fixed in the glass was a technical problem, but after many experiments we overcame the difficulty. No trouble was too great for us to take, you see. And now anyone can look through the glass and watch the inscription taking form on the body. Wouldn't you care to come a little nearer and have a look at the needles?"

The explorer got up slowly, walked across, and bent over the Harrow.

"You see," said the officer, "there are two kinds of needles arranged in multiple patterns. Each long needle has a short one beside it. The long needle does the writing, and the short needle sprays a jet of water to wash away the blood and keep the inscription clear. Blood and water together are then conducted here through small runnels into this main runnel and down a waste pipe into the pit." With his finger the officer traced the exact course taken by the blood and water. To make the picture as vivid as possible he held both hands below the outlet of the waste pipe as if to catch the outflow, and when he did this the explorer drew back his head and feeling behind him with one hand sought to return to his chair. To his horror he found that the condemned man too had obeyed the officer's invitation to examine the Harrow at close quarters and had followed him. He had pulled forward the sleepy soldier with the chain and was bending over the glass. One could see that his uncertain eyes were trying to perceive what the two gentlemen had been looking at, but since he had not understood the explanation he could not make head or tail of it. He was peering this way and that way. He kept running his eyes along the glass. The explorer wanted to drive him away, since what he was doing was probably culpable. But the officer firmly restrained the explorer with one hand and with the other took a clod of earth from the rampart and threw it at the soldier. He opened his eyes with a jerk, saw what the condemned man had dared to do, let his rifle fall, dug his heels into the ground, dragged his prisoner back so that he stumbled and fell immediately, and then stood looking down at him, watching him struggling and rattling in his chains.

"Set him on his feet!" yelled the officer, for he noticed that the explorer's attention was being too much distracted by the prisoner. In fact he was even leaning right across the Harrow, without taking any notice of it, intent only on finding out what was happening to the prisoner.

"Be careful with him!" cried the officer again. He ran around the apparatus, himself caught the condemned man under the shoulders, and with the soldier's help got him up on his feet, which kept slithering from under him.

"Now I know all about it," said the explorer as the officer came back to him.

"All except the most important thing," he answered, seizing the explorer's arm and pointing upwards: "In the Designer are all the cogwheels that control the movements of the Harrow, and this machinery is regulated according to the inscription demanded by the sentence. I am still using the guiding plans drawn by the former Commandant. Here they are" — he extracted some sheets from the leather wallet — "but I'm sorry I can't let you handle them, they are my most precious possessions. Just take a seat and I'll hold them in front of you like this, then you'll be able to see everything quite well." He spread out the first sheet of paper. The explorer would have liked to say something appreciative, but all he could see was a labyrinth of lines crossing and recrossing each other, which covered the paper so thickly that it was difficult to discern the blank spaces between them.

"Read it," said the officer.

"I can't," said the explorer. "Yet it's clear enough," said the officer.

"It's very ingenious," said the explorer evasively, "but I can't make it out."

"Yes," said the officer with a laugh, putting the paper away again, "it's no calligraphy for school children. It needs to be studied closely. I'm quite sure that in the end you would understand it too. Of course the script can't be a simple one; it's not supposed to kill a man straight off, but only after an interval of, on an average, twelve hours; the turning point is reckoned to come at the sixth hour. So there have to be lots and lots of flourishes around the actual script; the script itself runs around the body only in a narrow girdle; the rest of the body is reserved for the embellishments. Can you appreciate now the work accomplished by the Harrow and the whole apparatus? — Just watch it!" He ran up the ladder, turned a wheel, called down: "Look out, keep to one side!" and everything started working. If the wheel had not creaked, it would have been marvelous. The officer, as if surprised by the noise of the wheel, shook his fist at it, then spread out his arms in excuse to the explorer, and climbed down rapidly to peer at the working of the machine from below. Something perceptible to no one save himself was still not in order; he clambered up again, did something with both hands in the interior of the Designer, then slid down one of the rods, instead of using the ladder, so as to get down quicker, and with the full force of his lungs, to make himself heard at all in the noise, yelled in the explorer's ear: "Can you follow it? The Harrow is beginning to write; when it finishes the first draft of the inscription on the man's back, the layer of cotton wool begins to roll and slowly turns the body over, to give the Harrow fresh space for writing. Meanwhile the raw part that has been written on lies on the cotton wool, which is specially prepared to staunch the bleeding and so makes all ready for a new deepening of the script. Then these teeth at the edge of the Harrow, as the body turns further around, tear the cotton wool away from the wounds, throw it into the pit, and there is more work for the Harrow. So it keeps on writing deeper and deeper for the whole twelve hours. The first six hours the condemned man stays alive almost as before, he suffers only pain. After two hours the felt gag is taken away, for he has no longer strength to scream. Here, into this electrically heated basin at the head of the Bed, some warm rice pap is poured, from which the man, if he feels like it, can take as much as his tongue can lap. Not one of them ever misses the chance. I can remember none, and my experience is extensive. Only about the sixth hour does the man lose all desire to eat. I usually kneel down here at that moment and observe what happens. The man rarely swallows his last mouthful, he only rolls it around his mouth and spits it out into the pit. I have to duck just then or he would spit it in my face. But how quiet he grows at just about the sixth hour! Enlightenment comes to the most dull-witted. It begins around the eyes. From there it radiates. A moment that might tempt one to get under the Harrow oneself. Nothing more happens than that the man begins to understand the inscription, he purses his mouth as if he were listening. You have seen how difficult it is to decipher the script with one's eyes; but our man deciphers it with his wounds. To be sure, that is a hard task; he needs six hours to accomplish it. By that time the Harrow has pierced him quite through and casts him into the pit, where he pitches down upon the blood and water and the cotton wool. Then the judgment has been fulfilled, and we, the soldier and I, bury him."

The explorer had inclined his ear to the officer and with his hands in his jacket pockets watched the machine at work. The condemned man watched it too, but uncomprehendingly. He bent forward a little and was intent on the moving needles when the soldier, at a sign from the officer, slashed through his shirt and trousers from behind with a knife, so that they fell off; he tried to catch at his falling clothes to cover his nakedness, but the soldier lifted him into the air and shook the last remnants from him. The officer stopped the machine, and in the sudden silence the condemned man was laid under the Harrow. The chains were loosened and the straps fastened on instead; in the first moment that seemed almost a relief to the prisoner. And now the Harrow was adjusted a little lower, since he was a thin man. When the needle points touched him a shudder ran over his skin; while the soldier was busy strapping his right hand, he flung out his left hand blindly; but it happened to be in the direction toward where the explorer was standing. The officer kept watching the explorer sideways, as if seeking to read from his face the impression made on him by the execution, which had been at least cursorily explained to him.

The wrist strap broke; probably the soldier had drawn it too tight. The officer had to intervene; the soldier held up the broken piece of strap to show him. So the officer went over to him and said, his face still turned toward the explorer: "This is a very complex machine, it can't be helped that things are breaking or giving way here and there; but one must not thereby allow oneself to be diverted in one's general judgment. In any case, this strap is easily made good; I shall simply use a chain; the delicacy of the vibrations for the right arm will of course be a little impaired." And while he fastened the chains, he added: "The resources for maintaining the machine are now very much reduced. Under the former Commandant I had free access to a sum of money set aside entirely for this purpose. There was a store, too, in which spare parts were kept for repairs of all kinds. I confess I have been almost prodigal with them, I mean in the past, not now as the new Commandant pretends, always looking for an excuse to attack our old way of doing things. Now he has taken charge of the machine money himself, and if I send for a new strap they ask for the broken old strap as evidence, and the new strap takes ten days to appear and then is of shoddy material and not much good. But how I am supposed to work the machine without a strap; that's something nobody bothers about."

The explorer thought to himself: It's always a ticklish matter to intervene decisively in other people's affairs. He was neither a member of the penal colony nor a citizen of the state to which it belonged. Were he to denounce this execution or actually try to stop it, they could say to him: You are a foreigner, mind your own business. He could make no answer to that, unless he were to add that he was amazed at himself in this connection, for he traveled only as an observer, with no intention at all of altering other people's methods of administering justice. Yet here he found himself strongly tempted. The injustice of the procedure and the inhumanity of the execution were undeniable. No one could suppose that he had any selfish interest in the matter, for the condemned man was a complete stranger, not a fellow countryman or even at all sympathetic to him. The explorer himself had recommendations from high quarters, had been received here with great courtesy, and the very fact that he had been invited to attend the execution seemed to suggest that his views would be welcome. And this was all the more likely since the Commandant, as he had heard only too plainly, was no upholder of the procedure and maintained an attitude almost of hostility to the officer.

At that moment the explorer heard the officer cry out in rage. He had just, with considerable difficulty, forced the felt gag into the condemned man's mouth when the man in an irresistible access of nausea shut his eyes and vomited. Hastily the officer snatched him away from the gag and tried to hold his head over the pit; but it was too late, the vomit was running all over the machine. "It's all the fault of that Commandant!" cried the officer, senselessly shaking the brass rods in front, "the machine is befouled like a pigsty." With trembling hands he indicated to the explorer what had happened. "Have I not tried for hours at a time to get the Commandant to understand that the prisoner must fast for a whole day before the execution. But our new, mild doctrine thinks otherwise. The Commandant's ladies stuff the man with sugar candy before he's led off. He has lived on stinking fish his whole life long and now he has to eat sugar candy! But it could still be possible, I should have nothing to say against it, but why won't they get me a new felt gag, which I have been begging for the last three months. How should a man not feel sick when he takes a felt gag into his mouth which more than a hundred men have already slobbered and gnawed in their dying moments?"

The condemned man had laid his head down and looked peaceful, the soldier was busy trying to clean the machine with the prisoner's shirt. The officer advanced toward the explorer; who in some vague presentiment fell back a pace, but the officer seized him by the hand, and drew him to one side. "I should like to exchange a few words with you in confidence," he said, "May I?"

"Of course," said the explorer, and listened with downcast eyes.

"This procedure and method of execution, which you are now having the opportunity to admire, has at the moment no longer any open adherents in our colony. I am its sole advocate, and at the same time the sole advocate of the old Commandant's tradition. I can no longer reckon on any further extension of the method, it takes all my energy to maintain it as it is. During the old Commandant's lifetime the colony was full of his adherents; his strength of conviction I still have in some measure, but not an atom of his power; consequently the adherents have skulked out of sight, there are still many of them but none of them will admit it. If you were to go into the teahouse today, on execution day, and listen to what is being said, you would perhaps hear only ambiguous remarks. These would all be made by adherents, but under the present Commandant and his present doctrines they are of no use to me. And now I ask you: because of this Commandant and the women who influence him, is such a piece of work, the work of a lifetime" — he pointed to the machine — "to perish? Ought one to let that happen? Even if one has only come as a stranger to our island for a few days? But there's no time to lose, an attack of some kind is impending on my function as judge; conferences are already being held in the Commandant's office from which I am excluded; even your coming here today seems to me a significant move; they are cowards and use you as a screen, you, a stranger. — How different an execution was in the old days! A whole day before the ceremony the valley was packed with people; they all came only to look on; early in the morning the Commandant appeared with his ladies; fanfares roused the whole camp; I reported that everything was in readiness; the assembled company — no high official dared to absent himself — arranged itself around the machine; this pile of cane chairs is a miserable survival from that epoch. The machine was freshly cleaned and glittering, I got new spare parts for almost every execution. Before hundreds of spectators — all of them standing on tiptoe as far as the heights there — the condemned man was laid under the Harrow by the Commandant himself. What is left today for a common soldier to do was then my task, the task of the presiding judge, and was an honor for me. And then the execution began! No discordant noise spoiled the working of the machine. Many did not care to watch it but lay with closed eyes in the sand; they all knew: Now Justice is being done. In the silence one heard nothing but the condemned man's sighs, half-muffled by the felt gag. Nowadays the machine can no longer wring from anyone a sigh louder than the felt gag can stifle; but in those days the writing needles let drop an acid fluid, which we're no longer permitted to use. Well, and then came the sixth hour! It was impossible to grant all the requests to be allowed to watch it from nearby. The Commandant in his wisdom ordained that the children should have the preference; I, of course, because of my office had the privilege of always being at hand; often enough I would be squatting there with a small child in either arm. How we all absorbed the look of transfiguration on the face of the sufferer, how we bathed our cheeks in the radiance of that justice, achieved at last and fading so quickly! What times these were, my comrade!" The officer had obviously forgotten whom he was addressing; he had embraced the explorer and laid his head on his shoulder. The explorer was deeply embarrassed, impatiently he stared over the officer's head. The soldier had finished his cleaning job and was now pouring rice pap from a pot into the basin. As soon as the condemned man, who seemed to have recovered entirely, noticed this action he began to reach for the rice with his tongue. The soldier kept pushing him away, since the rice pap was certainly meant for a later hour, yet it was just as unfitting that the soldier himself should thrust his dirty hands into the basin and eat out of it before the other's avid face.

The officer quickly pulled himself together. "I didn't want to upset you," he said, "I know it is impossible to make those days credible now. Anyhow, the machine is still working and it is still effective in itself. It is effective in itself even though it stands alone in this valley. And the corpse still falls at the last into the pit with an incomprehensibly gentle wafting motion, even though there are no hundreds of people swarming around like flies as formerly. In those days we had to put a strong fence around the pit, it has long since been torn down."

The explorer wanted to withdraw his face from the officer and looked around him at random. The officer thought he was surveying the valley's desolation; so he seized him by the hands, turned him around to meet his eyes, and asked: "Do you realize the shame of it?"

But the explorer said nothing. The officer left him alone for a little; with legs apart, hands on hips, he stood very still, gazing at the ground. Then he smiled encouragingly at the explorer and said: "I was quite near you yesterday when the Commandant gave you the invitation. I heard him giving it. I know the Commandant. I divined at once what he was after. Although he is powerful enough to take measures against me, he doesn't dare to do it yet, but he certainly means to use your verdict against me, the verdict of an illustrious foreigner. He has calculated it carefully: this is your second day on the island, you did not know the old Commandant and his ways, you are conditioned by European ways of thought, perhaps you object on principle to capital punishment in general and to such mechanical instruments of death in particular, besides you will see that the execution has no support from the public, a shabby ceremony—carried out with a machine already somewhat old and worn—now, taking all that into consideration, would it not be likely (so thinks the Commandant) that you might disapprove of my methods? And if you disapprove, you wouldn't conceal the fact (I'm still speaking from the Commandant's point of view), for you are a man to feel confidence in your own well-tried conclusions. True, you have seen and learned to appreciate the peculiarities of many peoples, and so you would not be likely to take a strong line against our proceedings, as you might do in your own country. But the Commandant has no need of that. A casual, even an unguarded remark will be enough. It doesn't even need to represent what you really think, so long as it can be used speciously to serve his purpose. He will try to prompt you with sly questions, of that I am certain. And his ladies will sit around you and prick up their ears; you might be saying something like this: 'In our country we have a different criminal procedure,' or 'In our country the prisoner is interrogated before he is sentenced,' or 'We haven't used torture since the Middle Ages.' All these statements are as true as they seem natural to you, harmless remarks that pass no judgment on my methods. But how would the Commandant react to them? I can see him, our good Commandant, pushing his chair away immediately and rushing onto the balcony, I can see his ladies streaming out after him, I can hear his voice — the ladies call it a voice of thunder — well, and this is what he says: 'A famous Western investigator, sent out to study criminal procedure in all the countries of the world, has just said that our old tradition of administering justice is inhumane. Such a verdict from such a personality makes it impossible for me to countenance these methods any longer. Therefore from this very day I ordain . . .' and so on. You may want to interpose that you never said any such thing, that you never called my methods inhumane, on the contrary your profound experience leads you to believe they are most humane and most in consonance with human dignity, and you admire the machine greatly — but it will be too late; you won't even get onto the balcony, crowded as it will be with ladies; you may try to draw attention to yourself; you may want to scream out; but a lady's hand will close your lips — and I and the work of the old Commandant will be done for."

The explorer had to suppress a smile; so easy, then, was the task he had felt to be so difficult. He said evasively: "You overestimate my influence; the Commandant has read my letters of recommendation, he knows that I am no expert in criminal procedure. If I were to give an opinion, it would be as a private individual, an opinion no more influential than that of any ordinary person, and in any case much less influential than that of the Commandant, who, I am given to understand, has very extensive powers in this penal colony. If his attitude to your procedure is as definitely hostile as you believe, then I fear the end of your tradition is at hand, even without any humble assistance from me."

Had it dawned on the officer at last? No, he still did not understand. He shook his head emphatically, glanced briefly around at the condemned man and the soldier, who both flinched away from the rice, came close up to the explorer, and without looking at his face but fixing his eye on some spot on his coat said in a lower voice than before: "You don't know the Commandant; you feel yourself — forgive the expression — a kind of outsider so far as all of us are concerned; yet, believe me, your influence cannot be rated too highly. I was simply delighted when I heard that you were to attend the execution all by yourself. The Commandant arranged it to aim a blow at me, but I shall turn it to my advantage. Without being distracted by lying whispers and contemptuous glances — which could not have been avoided had a crowd of people attended the execution — you have heard my explanations, seen the machine, and are now in course of watching the execution. You have doubtless already formed your own judgment; if you still have some small uncertainties the sight of the execution will resolve them. And now I make this request to you: help me against the Commandant!"

The explorer would not let him go on. "How could I do that," he cried, "it's quite impossible. I can neither help nor hinder you."

"Yes, you can," the officer said. The explorer saw with a certain apprehension that the officer had clenched his fists. "Yes, you can," repeated the officer, still more insistently. "I have a plan that is bound to succeed. You believe your influence is insufficient. I know that it is sufficient. But even granted that you are right, is it not necessary, for the sake of preserving this tradition, to try even what might prove insufficient? Listen to my plan, then. The first thing necessary for you to carry it out is to be as reticent as possible today regarding your verdict on these proceedings. Unless you are asked a direct question you must say nothing at all; but what you do say must be brief and general; let it be remarked that you would prefer not to discuss the matter, that you are out of patience with it, that if you are to let yourself go you would use strong language. I don't ask you to tell any lies; by no means; you should only give curt answers, such as: 'Yes, I saw the execution,' or 'Yes, I had it explained to me.' Just that, nothing more. There are grounds enough for any impatience you betray, although not such as will occur to the Commandant. Of course, he will mistake your meaning and interpret it to please himself. That's what my plan depends on. Tomorrow in the Commandant's office there is to be a large conference of all the high administrative officials, the Commandant presiding. Of course the Commandant is the kind of man to have turned these conferences into public spectacles. He has had a gallery built that is always packed with spectators. I am compelled to take part in the conferences, but they make me sick with disgust. Now, whatever happens, you will certainly be invited to this conference; if you behave today as I suggest, the invitation will become an urgent request. But if for some mysterious reason you're not invited, you'll have to ask for an invitation; there's no doubt of your getting it then. So tomorrow you're sitting in the Commandant's box with the ladies. He keeps looking up to make sure you're there. After various trivial and ridiculous matters, brought in merely to impress the audience — mostly harbor works, nothing but harbor works! — our judicial procedure comes up for discussion too. If the Commandant doesn't introduce it, or not soon enough, I'll see that it's mentioned. I'll stand up and report that today's execution has taken place. Quite briefly, only a statement. Such a statement is not usual, but I shall make it. The Commandant thanks me, as always, with an amiable smile, and then he can't restrain himself, he seizes the excellent opportunity. 'It has just been reported,' he will say, or words to that effect, 'that an execution has taken place: I should like merely to add that this execution was witnessed by the famous explorer who has, as you all know, honored our colony so greatly by his visit to us. His presence at today's session of our conference also contributes to the importance of this occasion. Should we not now ask the famous explorer to give us his verdict on our traditional mode of execution and the procedure that leads up to it?' Of course there is loud applause, general agreement, I am more insistent than anyone. The Commandant bows to you and says: 'Then in the name of the assembled company, I put the question to you.' And now you advance to the front of the box. Lay your hands where everyone can see them, or the ladies will catch them and press your fingers. — And then at last you can speak out. I don't know how I'm going to endure the tension of waiting for that moment. Don't put any restraint on yourself when you make your speech, publish the truth aloud, lean over the front of the box, shout, yes indeed, shout your verdict, your unshakable conviction, at the Commandant. Yet perhaps you wouldn't care to do that, it's not in keeping with your character, in your country perhaps people do these things differently, well, that's all right too, that will be quite as effective, don't even stand up, just say a few words, even in a whisper, so that only the officials beneath you will hear them, that will be quite enough, you don't even need to mention the lack of public support for the execution, the creaking wheel, the broken strap, the filthy gag of felt, no, I'll take all that upon me, and, believe me, if my indictment doesn't drive him out of the conference hall, it will force him to his knees to make the acknowledgment: Old Commandant, I humble myself before you. — That is my plan; will you help me to carry it out? But of course you are willing, what is more, you must." And the officer seized the explorer by both arms and gazed, breathing heavily, into his face. He had shouted the last sentence so loudly that even the soldier and the condemned man were startled into attending; they had not understood a word but they stopped eating and looked over at the explorer, chewing their previous mouthfuls.

From the very beginning the explorer had no doubt about what answer he must give; in his lifetime he had experienced too much to have any uncertainty here; he was fundamentally honorable and unafraid. And yet now, facing the soldier and the condemned man, he did hesitate, for as long as it took to draw one breath. At last, however, he said, as he had to: "No."

The officer blinked several times but did not turn his eyes away.

"Would you like me to explain?" asked the explorer.

The officer nodded wordlessly.

"I do not approve of your procedure," said the explorer then, "even before you took me into your confidence — of course I shall never in any circumstances betray your confidence — I was already wondering whether it would be my duty to intervene and whether my intervention would have the slightest chance of success. I realized to whom I ought to turn: to the Commandant, of course. You have made that fact even clearer, but without having strengthened my resolution, on the contrary, your sincere conviction has touched me, even though it cannot influence my judgment."

The officer remained mute, turned to the machine, caught hold of a brass rod, and then, leaning back a little, gazed at the Designer as if to assure himself that all was in order. The soldier and the condemned man seemed to have come to some understanding; the condemned man was making signs to the soldier, difficult though his movements were because of the tight straps; the soldier was bending down to him; the condemned man whispered something and the soldier nodded.

The explorer followed the officer and said: "You don't know yet what I mean to do. I shall tell the Commandant what I think of the procedure, certainly, but not at a public conference, only in private; nor shall I stay here long enough to attend any conference; I am going away early tomorrow morning, or at least embarking on my ship."

It did not look as if the officer had been listening. "So you did not find the procedure convincing," he said to himself and smiled, as an old man smiles at childish nonsense and yet pursues his own meditations behind the smile.

"Then the time has come," he said at last, and suddenly looked at the explorer with bright eyes that held some challenge, some appeal for cooperation. "The time for what?" asked the explorer uneasily, but got no answer.

"You are free," said the officer to the condemned man in the native tongue. The man did not believe it at first. "Yes, you are set free," said the officer. For the first time the condemned man's face woke to real animation. Was it true? Was it only a caprice of the officer's, that might change again? Had the foreign explorer begged him off? What was it? One could read these questions on his face. But not for long. Whatever it might be, he wanted to be really free if he might, and he began to struggle so far as the Harrow permitted him.

"You'll burst my straps," cried the officer, "lie still! We'll soon loosen them." And signing the soldier to help him, he set about doing so. The condemned man laughed wordlessly to himself, now he turned his face left toward the officer, now right toward the soldier, nor did he forget the explorer.

"Draw him out," ordered the officer. Because of the Harrow this had to be done with some care. The condemned man had already torn himself a little in the back through his impatience.

From now on, however, the officer paid hardly any attention to him. He went up to the explorer, pulled out the small leather wallet again, turned over the papers in it, found the one he wanted, and showed it to the explorer.

"Read it," he said.

"I can't," said the explorer, "I told you before that I can't make out these scripts." "Try taking a close look at it," said the officer and came quite near to the explorer so that they might read it together. But when even that proved useless, he outlined the script with his little finger, holding it high above the paper as if the surface dared not be sullied by touch, in order to help the explorer to follow the script in that way. The explorer did make an effort, meaning to please the officer in this respect at least, but he was quite unable to follow. Now the officer began to spell it, letter by letter, and then read out the words. " 'BE JUST!' is what is written there," he said, "surely you can read it now." The explorer bent so close to the paper that the officer feared he might touch it and drew it farther away; the explorer made no remark, yet it was clear that he still could not decipher it.

" 'BE JUST!' is what is written there," said the officer once more.

"Maybe," said the explorer, "I am prepared to believe you."

"Well, then," said the officer, at least partly satisfied, and climbed up the ladder with the paper; very carefully he laid it inside the Designer and seemed to be changing the disposition of all the cogwheels; it was a troublesome piece of work and must have involved wheels that were extremely small, for sometimes the officer's head vanished altogether from sight inside the Designer, so precisely did he have to regulate the machinery.

The explorer, down below, watched the labor uninterruptedly, his neck grew stiff and his eyes smarted from the glare of sunshine over the sky. The soldier and the condemned man were now busy together. The man's shirt and trousers, which were already lying in the pit, were fished out by the point of the soldier's bayonet. The shirt was abominably dirty and its owner washed it in the bucket of water. When he put on the shirt and trousers both he and the soldier could not help guffawing, for the garments were of course slit up behind. Perhaps the condemned man felt it incumbent on him to amuse the soldier, he turned around and around in his slashed garments before the soldier, who squatted on the ground beating his knees with mirth. All the same, they presently controlled their mirth out of respect for the gentlemen.

When the officer had at length finished his task aloft, he surveyed the machinery in all its details once more, with a smile, but this time shut the lid of the Designer, which had stayed open till now, climbed down, looked into the pit and then at the condemned man, noting with satisfaction that the clothing had been taken out, then went over to wash his hands in the water bucket, perceived too late that it was disgustingly dirty, was unhappy because he could not wash his hands, in the end thrust them into the sand — this alternative did not please him, but he had to put up with it — then stood upright and began to unbutton his uniform jacket. As he did this, the two ladies' handkerchiefs he had tucked under his collar fell into his hands. "Here are your handkerchiefs," he said, and threw them to the condemned man. And to the explorer he said in explanation: "A gift from the ladies."

In spite of the obvious haste with which he was discarding first his uniform jacket and then all his clothing, he handled each garment with loving care, he even ran his fingers caressingly over the silver lace on the jacket and shook a tassel into place. This loving care was certainly out of keeping with the fact that as soon as he had a garment off he flung it at once with a kind of unwilling jerk into the pit. The last thing left to him was his short sword with the sword belt. He drew it out of the scabbard, broke it, then gathered all together, the bits of the sword, the scabbard, and the belt, and flung them so violently down that they clattered into the pit.

Now he stood naked there. The explorer bit his lips and said nothing. He knew very well what was going to happen, but he had no right to obstruct the officer in anything. If the judicial procedure which the officer cherished were really so near its end — possibly as a result of his own intervention, as to which he felt himself pledged — then the officer was doing the right thing; in his place the explorer would not have acted otherwise.

The soldier and the condemned man did not understand at first what was happening, at first they were not even looking on. The condemned man was gleeful at having got the handkerchiefs back, but he was not allowed to enjoy them for long, since the soldier snatched them with a sudden, unexpected grab. Now the condemned man in turn was trying to twitch them from under the belt where the soldier had tucked them, but the soldier was on his guard. So they were wrestling, half in jest. Only when the officer stood quite naked was their attention caught. The condemned man especially seemed struck with the notion that some great change was impending. What had happened to him was now going to happen to the officer. Perhaps even to the very end. Apparently the foreign explorer had given the order for it. So this was revenge. Although he himself had not suffered to the end, he was to be revenged to the end. A broad, silent grin now appeared on his face and stayed there all the rest of the time.

The officer, however, had turned to the machine. It had been clear enough previously that he understood the machine well, but now it was almost staggering to see how he managed it and how it obeyed him. His hand had only to approach the Harrow for it to rise and sink several times till it was adjusted to the right position for receiving him; he touched only the edge of the Bed and already it was vibrating; the felt gag came to meet his mouth, one could see that the officer was really reluctant to take it but he shrank from it only a moment, soon he submitted and received it. Everything was ready, only the straps hung down at the sides, yet they were obviously unnecessary, the officer did not need to be fastened down. Then the condemned man noticed the loose straps, in his opinion the execution was incomplete unless the straps were buckled, he gestured eagerly to the soldier and they ran together to strap the officer down. The latter had already stretched out one foot to push the lever that started the Designer; he saw the two men coming up; so he drew his foot back and let himself be buckled in. But now he could not reach the lever; neither the soldier nor the condemned man would be able to find it, and the explorer was determined not to lift a finger. It was not necessary; as soon as the straps were fastened the machine began to work; the Bed vibrated, the needles flickered above the skin, the Harrow rose and fell. The explorer had been staring at it quite a while before he remembered that a wheel in the Designer should have been creaking; but everything was quiet, not even the slightest hum could be heard.

Because it was working so silently the machine simply escaped one's attention. The explorer observed the soldier and the condemned man. The latter was the more animated of the two, everything in the machine interested him, now he was bending down and now stretching up on tiptoe, his forefinger was extended all the time pointing out details to the soldier. This annoyed the explorer. He was resolved to stay till the end, but he could not bear the sight of these two. "Go back home," he said. The soldier would have been willing enough, but the condemned man took the order as a punishment. With clasped hands he implored to be allowed to stay, and when the explorer shook his head and would not relent, he even went down on his knees. The explorer saw that it was no use merely giving orders, he was on the point of going over and driving them away. At that moment he heard a noise above him in the Designer. He looked up. Was that cogwheel going to make trouble after all? But it was something quite different. Slowly the lid of the Designer rose up and then clicked wide open. The teeth of a cogwheel showed themselves and rose higher, soon the whole wheel was visible, it was as if some enormous force were squeezing the Designer so that there was no longer room for the wheel, the wheel moved up till it came to the very edge of the Designer, fell down, rolled along the sand a little on its rim, and then lay flat. But a second wheel was already rising after it, followed by many others, large and small and indistinguishably minute, the same thing happened to all of them, at every moment one imagined the Designer must now really be empty, but another complex of numerous wheels was already rising into sight, falling down, trundling along the sand, and lying flat. This phenomenon made the condemned man completely forget the explorer's command, the cogwheels fascinated him, he was always trying to catch one and at the same time urging the soldier to help, but always drew back his hand in alarm, for another wheel always came hopping along which, at least on its first advance, scared him off.

The explorer, on the other hand, felt greatly troubled; the machine was obviously going to pieces; its silent working was a delusion; he had a feeling that he must now stand by the officer, since the officer was no longer able to look after himself. But while the tumbling cogwheels absorbed his whole attention he had forgotten to keep an eye on the rest of the machine; now that the last cogwheel had left the Designer, however, he bent over the Harrow and had a new and still more unpleasant surprise. The Harrow was not writing, it was only jabbing, and the Bed was not turning the body over but only bringing it up quivering against the needles. The explorer wanted to do something, if possible, to bring the whole machine to a standstill, for this was no exquisite torture such as the officer desired, this was plain murder. He stretched out his hands. But at that moment the Harrow rose with the body spitted on it and moved to the side, as it usually did only when the twelfth hour had come. Blood was flowing in a hundred streams, not mingled with water, the water jets too had failed to function. And now the last action failed to fulfill itself, the body did not drop off the long needles, streaming with blood it went on hanging over the pit without falling into it. The Harrow tried to move back to its old position, but as if it had itself noticed that it had not yet got rid of its burden it stuck after all where it was, over the pit. "Come and help!" cried the explorer to the other two, and himself seized the officer's feet. He wanted to push against the feet while the others seized the head from the opposite side and so the officer might be slowly eased off the needles. But the other two could not make up their minds to come; the condemned man actually turned away; the explorer had to go over to them and force them into position at the officer's head. And here, almost against his will, he had to look at the face of the corpse. It was as it had been in life; no sign was visible of the promised redemption; what the others had found in the machine the officer had not found; the lips were firmly pressed together, the eyes were open, with the same expression as in life, the look was calm and convinced, through the forehead went the point of the great iron spike.

As the explorer, with the soldier and the condemned man behind him, reached the first houses of the colony, the soldier pointed to one of them and said: "There is the teahouse."

In the ground floor of the house was a deep, low, cavernous space, its walls and ceiling blackened with smoke. It was open to the road all along its length. Although this teahouse was very little different from the other houses of the colony, which were all very dilapidated, even up to the Commandant's palatial headquarters, it made on the explorer the impression of a historic tradition of some kind, and he felt the power of past days. He went near to it, followed by his companions, right up between the empty tables that stood in the street before it, and breathed the cool, heavy air that came from the interior. "The old man's buried here," said the soldier, "the priest wouldn't let him lie in the churchyard. Nobody knew where to bury him for a while, but in the end they buried him here. The officer never told you about that, for sure, because of course that's what he was most ashamed of. He even tried several times to dig the old man up by night, but he was always chased away."

"Where is the grave?" asked the explorer, who found it impossible to believe the soldier. At once both of them, the soldier and the condemned man, ran before him pointing with outstretched hands in the direction where the grave should be. They led the explorer right up to the back wall, where guests were sitting at a few tables. They were apparently dock laborers, strong men with short, glistening, full black beards. None had a jacket, their shirts were torn, they were poor, humble creatures. As the explorer drew near, some of them got up, pressed close to the wall, and stared at him. "It's a foreigner," ran the whisper around him, "he wants to see the grave." They pushed one of the tables aside, and under it there was really a gravestone. It was a simple stone, low enough to be covered by a table. There was an inscription on it in very small letters, the explorer had to kneel down to read it. This was what it said: "Here rests the old Commandant. His adherents, who now must be nameless, have dug this grave and set up this stone. There is a prophecy that after a certain number of years the Commandant will rise again and lead his adherents from this house to recover the colony. Have faith and wait!" When the explorer had read this and risen to his feet he saw all the bystanders around him smiling, as if they too had read the inscription, had found it ridiculous, and were expecting him to agree with them. The explorer ignored this, distributed a few coins among them, waiting till the table was pushed over the grave again, quitted the teahouse, and made for the harbor.

The soldier and the condemned man had found some acquaintances in the teahouse, who detained them. But they must have soon shaken them off, for the explorer was only halfway down the long flight of steps leading to the boats when they came rushing after him. Probably they wanted to force him at the last minute to take them with him. While he was bargaining below with a ferryman to row him to the steamer, the two of them came headlong down the steps, in silence, for they did not dare to shout. But by the time they reached the foot of the steps the explorer was already in the boat, and the ferryman was just casting off from the shore. They could have jumped into the boat, but the explorer lifted a heavy knotted rope from the floor boards, threatened them with it, and so kept them from attempting the leap.

Discussion Topics

1. Do the practices in the colony remind us in any way of our own beliefs, sources of skepticism, and practices? Mysteriously, the machine inscribes the name of the punishment, the rule that the offender broke, into the body of the convict. What is the point of doing this, and in particular of inscribing *a different rule* for each different crime? In our own system, we aspire in some sense (under the rubric of retribution) to make the punishment fit the crime. In Kafka's colony, the punishment fits the crime *to the letter*. We can ask whether this fit is any better than the fit we achieve by punishing a heroin addict's possession and purchase of drugs by putting her in a cell for twenty years.

We are tempted to contrast the determination of guilt in the colony with our own system of trial. We like to think that defendants, in consulting with their attorneys, achieve meaningful participation in their cases. But we can also question how deep and sophisticated their knowledge goes and how much of an effort lawyers put out to understand and act upon their clients' preferences.

Moreover, we might think that in the colony guilt is presumed while we, in our system, have a presumption of innocence. And yet we also believe that the court of public opinion and the figurative courtroom of the media leave very little room for any presumption of innocence. How many of us think that a person would not be charged with a crime unless the evidence was compelling?

2. Note the role of the justice system in the regime of the old commandant and the officer. Executions are ceremonies that tie the community together and reinforce social attitudes. Children have pride of place.

Compare these events with religious celebrations. The story is full of religious metaphors. The prisoner is said, after six hours on the rack, to achieve enlightenment. The prisoner is attached by his limbs in a way that might be said to mimic Christ on the cross. If the story reflects communal religion, does the succession involving the new commandant suggest the coming of secularism and the decline of a religious community?

3. Keep in mind that this is a penal colony and that the system is one of military justice. Military procedures have never operated by the same conventions or constraints as civilian courts. Does this partially explain and even excuse the peremptory nature of justice in this setting?

4. The motivations of the characters are somewhat obscure. The explorer is slow to reach judgment and reluctant to share his decision. Is he genuinely uncertain about the merits of the machine and all it represents? Or is he uncertain whether his verdict will be effective in changing the practice in the colony? In the end, he keeps the condemned man and the soldier from boarding his boat and escaping. Why?

The officer has been committed to the machine and the regime of the old commandant all his life. He is a fervent defender of the system. And yet, after one decisive word from the explorer, he abandons his cause and condemns himself to be punished on the machine with the inscription, "Be just." It seems facile to conclude that he has reversed himself and realized that he has violated the norms of justice. But how do we explain his decision? And why, at this very point, does the machine malfunction and self-destruct so dramatically?

5. Capital punishment has long been controversial. The U. S. is the only western society in which it is currently used and tolerated. Consider whether Kafka is implying that all systems of punishment by death are as cruel and indefensible as the one in the penal colony.

Shaming and Educative Punishments

Nathaniel Hawthorne: *The Scarlet Letter* and
Anthony Burgess: *A Clockwork Orange**

Two extraordinary novels, written in different cultures more than a hundred years apart, offer an opportunity to consider alternative punishments. They raise questions not only about efficacy but also about moral limits. However effective a punishment may be, it must also be seen as morally acceptable. The main objection to the death penalty outside the United States is that it is morally intolerable for a nation to put citizens, *any* citizens, to death deliberately. It is important to keep in mind how fluid moral attitudes toward punishment can be within a culture. Corporal punishment was once accepted as the default, much as imprisonment is taken for granted today.

The Scarlet Letter by Nathaniel Hawthorne is one of the most familiar and influential books in American literature. Published in 1850, it looks back two hundred years to the Puritan colony of Boston. Its central character is a young woman, Hester Prynne, who is punished for giving birth to her daughter, Pearl, out of wedlock. She refuses to name the child's father, and her punishment consists of wearing the scarlet letter "A" (for adultery) embroidered on her clothes. The letter symbolizes that she is to be treated as an outcast in her society, an internal exile. The novel traces the effects of her punishment over several years, a period in which her emotional ties to Pearl's father, Arthur Dimmesdale, the respected minister of the colony, remain complicated. Another complication is the presence in Boston of a man who goes by the name of Roger Chillingsworth, a scholar who had a loveless marriage with Hester, was separated from her, and has followed her to the new world.

The punishment of shaming in *The Scarlet Letter* is intended to serve an educative function, to make Hester aware of the moral rules she has flouted and to educate others about the social consequences of extramarital sex. Punishment as re-education is also the subject of Anthony Burgess' 1962 novel, *A Clockwork Orange*. Set in the indefinite future in a European city, perhaps London, it chronicles the rampages of teenage gangs that terrorize the rest of the population and the Draconian methods used by authorities to limit crime. Alex, the narrator and protagonist, is

---

*Strongly recommended additional reading: This novel does not appear in this volume and must be purchased separtely.

eventually subjected to "re-conditioning" through aversion therapy. He is emotionally re-wired (through the "Ludovico method") to be made violently ill by any acts or artifacts associated with his former antisocial behavior.

We will see in the next section that legal theorists currently debate the merits of shaming and educative punishments as alternatives to prison. But these two novels allow us to anticipate the most interesting questions.

Here are some discussion topics for *The Scarlet Letter*.

(1) The punishment itself and its effects have many dimensions. For one thing, Hester's status among her neighbors has changed significantly, but she is hardly shunned and excluded. In time, she performs a valuable function with her gift for embroidery. The other colonists take various attitudes toward her, and they are not prohibited from social contact. It is arguable that Hester, having given birth to Pearl without a husband, would be made something of an outsider whether or not the punishment had been formalized. It is also arguable that her aloneness turns her into a reflective and noble person, that she has benefitted from her predicament. But, even if this is true, it is quite possibly the idiosyncracy of her character rather than a general effect of shame.

(2) It is sometimes suggested that shaming works only in small, traditional, closely knit communities where persons are interdependent and reliant on others' good opinion. It seems to follow that in a large modern urban society, one can achieve anonymity. But it is possible to argue quite the opposite. In contemporary society, one's reputation can be tracked easily. One can be Googled in a matter of minutes; other Internet resources are available to make anonymity impossible. And, by contrast, in the colonial era of the novel, we note that Chillingsworth left his identity behind and reinvented himself easily. Hester and Dimmesdale also considered this option.

(3) Dimmesdale is the most controversial character in the novel. On one hand, he is arguably a coward in failing to acknowledge his relationship with Hester. She takes the fall for him. On the other hand, he is destroyed by his actions and his conscience. He calls on us for pity. It is clear that he has the most to lose by admitting his role, and he genuinely believes that he is the conscience of the colony.

(4) Chillingsworth is ambiguous in a different way. He wields demonic power over Dimmesdale. But how much does he in fact achieve? The dynamic of Dimmesdale's self-destruction, it seems, would go forward because of his own flaws whether or not Chillingsworth were present to exacerbate the agony. And yet it is clear that Hawthorne sees Chillingsworth as an active malign presence.

The questions raised by *A Clockwork Orange* reflect, in large part, the time and climate in which it was written.

(1) Writing after World War II and after horrifying revelations about Soviet communism, Burgess was thinking about legal practices that violated physical and mental integrity. Neither the body nor the mind of the criminal defendant were beyond intervention and change under fascism and in Stalin's Russia. For the most part, western Europe and the United States observed a strict moral taboo that prohibited corporal punishment as well as punishment that involved changing the body or the psychology of the individual.

(2) There is a deep moral revulsion at punishments that change one's bodily or mental capacities. The Islamic legal system (Sha-ria), which seeks physical incapacitation, for example by cutting off the hands of a thief or sterilizing a rapist, seems barbaric to many Westerners. The notion that one might be surgically altered (lobotomized) to eliminate a disposition to violence is similarly disturbing, as is the suggestion that pedophiles be castrated.

The reasons for this are not transparent. It may be said that we have an obligation to all persons to keep their bodies and minds intact, to return them to society (after serving time) as the same persons they were when they entered the system of trial and punishment. But we hardly can be said to do that. If Shaw is right, the psychological impact of imprisonment can be dramatic and irreversible. If we imagine one serving a long sentence, we can be said to take away thirty or forty years from the individual — with all the irreversible physical change that that implies. Thus, we are responsible for physical and mental change indirectly, even if we are prohibited from bringing them about directly.

Nonetheless, the prohibition remains important. But we need to investigate why changes that are the inevitable by-products of curtailing liberty for a long time are acceptable while changing the body or mind surgically, chemically, or through other radical interventions is unacceptable. (Of course, the death penalty remains the exception. We cannot take a hand as punishment, but we can take a life.)

(3) Notwithstanding these moral taboos, we do in fact experiment with such treatments as chemical castration for inveterate pedophiles or other sexual predators. We circumvent the moral argument by calling them treatments rather than punishments and by giving offenders the choice to remain in prison or take their medicine. It remains morally doubtful whether this is much of a free choice and whether the treatment/punishment distinction bears scrutiny.

(4) Time and maturation turn Alex into a law-abiding citizen even after the Ludovico method fails. Is his renunciation of crime believable? Burgess originally published the novel in the U.S. without the last chapter. Which version of the story is more convincing? Answering this requires us to rethink the motives of Alex's lawlessness. Is it more than youthful exuberance, as the final chapter suggests? Is it, in fact, a deep pathology that is unlikely to be cured by time?

Shaming and Educative Punishment: The Academic Debate

In the last decade, the concerns of Hawthorne and Burgess came alive again. Disillusioned both by the near-universality of imprisonment and the persistence of capital punishment, academic law scholars looked at alternative punishments with new interest.

Dan Kahan at Yale Law School has helped define the parameters of discussion. He has pointed out the alternative punishments that have received the most attention historically, fines and community service, are systematically flawed. The problem is what Kahan calls "the expressive dimension of punishment," its public meaning. To be meaningful, punishment must express moral condemnation and underline the seriousness of the offense. Fines, according to Kahan, lack this dimension, because they imply that crime, like other indulgences, simply has its price on the market. One can buy one's way out of liability. Community service is "expressively irrational . . . not just because it doesn't condemn, but because it threatens the integrity of expressive conventions that the public deeply values," serving needs as a charitable and altruistic contribution to society. See Dan Kahan, "What Do Alternative Sanctions Mean," 63 *University of Chicago Law Review* 591 (1996), at 629.

Kahan goes on to explore shaming as an alternative punishment that expresses the appropriate values. His categories and examples include (1) "literal stigmatization," for example being sentenced to wear a T-shirt that says "DUI convict" or "I write bad checks;" (2) "self-debasement" which is illustrated by standing in a public space with signs describing one's offense or being forced to live in the rat-infested tenement that one has owned and managed; (3) "contrition," exemplified by a regime in which one has to give public speeches describing one's wrongdoing or carry out apology rituals to one's victims; and finally (4) "stigmatizing publicity" whereby, for example, one's name is published in the local newspaper or official local public records website as a solicitor of prostitutes or purchaser of marijuana. Kahan claims for all of these variant forms of shaming punishment that they have a good chance of achieving retribution and deterrence and reinforcing the community's values.

In a response to Kahan, Cornell Law School professor Stephen Garvey concludes that, even if shaming punishments are effective, it is not clear that they are justified. See Stephen Garvey, "Can Shaming Punishments Educate?" 65 *University of Chicago Law Review* 733 (1998). Garvey argues that shaming penalties "may be disproportionately too weak, or disproportionately too strong." What explains the appeal of many of Kahan's examples, according to Garvey, is not simply their connection to shame, but rather their connection to "education of a peculiar sort." Considering the expressive dimension of punishment, which Garvey agrees is crucial, he emphasizes not the message about community disseminated to all citizens but the message conveyed to the offender. Thus, he means something quite different than Kahan does when he invokes the expressive dimension.

Addressing the questions of whether punishment can and should "educate," Garvey considers what he calls the *lex talionis*, the old-fashioned conception of punishment as "an eye for an eye," or more generally as making the offender experience the crime from the standpoint of his victim. Moving significantly away from the notion suggested by "an eye for an eye," Garvey offers as examples the following: having a rapist attend meetings in which rape victims describe their experiences and the consequences of their rapes; having an offender who commits a race crime see the movie "Mississippi Burning" many times in succession; and giving a theft victim the right to "steal" items of equal value from the thief. Garvey contends that these punishments would put the offender appropriately in a situation comparable to those of his victims.

Discussion Topics

1. Kahan and Garvey have an opportunity to present many dimensions of their arguments in the full versions of their articles. Before completely embracing or rejecting their suggestions, you might look up their writings.

Consider the emphasis that both writers put on the expressive role of punishment. Do imprisonment and capital punishment express moral condemnation in the appropriate and proportionate way? Can alternative sanctions do the job of binding the community together more effectively?

2. Consider the specific examples offered by the writers. Do they help make their arguments more persuasive, or do they undermine them? Obviously, these punishments would not be used for offenders who present a significant public danger. If the recommended punishments seem minor, does this imply that they are too weak or that we should consider decriminalization of the underlying conduct? Obviously, this argument is more relevant, perhaps, to prostitution than it is to theft or rape.

⧉ Further Reading

(1) The unreliability of witness identification is a common and tantalizing theme of fiction, psychology, and criminology. Two exceptional literary portrayals of the ways in which events can be seen from multiple points of view and of the ways in which truth can be elusive are the following. A relatively little-known story about a putative rape by the Japanese writer, Ryunosuke Akutagawa, called "Rashomon," was made in a legendary film by Akira Kurosawa. The title has become synonymous with the problem of establishing truth in the reconstruction of events. Gabriel Garcia Marquez's short novel, *A Chronicle of a Death Foretold*, is also a perceptive account of the difficulty of reconciling points of view.

Susan Glaspell's well-known short story, "A Jury of Her Peers," is a persuasive and sly exploration of how a woman's point of view may distinctively facilitate a criminal investigation.

(2) Two novels that present the challenges of trial preparation and conduct in a particularly gripping and sophisticated way are Robert Traver's *Anatomy of a Murder* and Scott Turow's *Presumed Innocent*. The screenplay and film of Reginald Rose's *Twelve Angry Men* are instructive on the subject of jury deliberation. A quite different point of view on the logic (or lack thereof) of trial procedure and content is the trial of the Knave of Hearts as it is presented in Lewis Carroll's *Alice in Wonderland*.

(3) The French philosopher and sociologist, Michel Foucault, examines the history and justifications of incarceration in his exceptionally influential book, *Discipline and Punish: The Birth of the Prison*. He emphasizes the idealism that characterized the invention and creation of "penitentiaries," places of penitence and reform.

The first book of Dante Alighieri's *Divine Comedy*, the *Inferno*, is an account of a tour of the circles of Hell and the punishments inflicted on those confined to these regions. Dante takes every effort to make the punishment fit the crime. A particularly imaginative kind of punishment is the subject of Edgar Allan Poe's short story, "A Cask of Amontillado."

The subculture of inmates and the effects of long-term incarceration are the subjects of Alexander Solzhenitsyn's short novel, *One Day in the Life of Ivan Denisovich*, and his encyclopedic work, *The Gulag Archipelago*. Fyodor Dostoyevsky's *The House of the Dead* looks at prison life in Russia a cetury earlier. In the American context, John Cheever examines imprisonment in the twentieth century in *Falconer*.

Finally, Sister Helen Prejean's nonfiction work *Dead Man Walking* and the film derived from it comment eloquently on the nature and social consequences of capital punishment.

Six

Finding Meaning

Many scholars who write about law and literature do not write about works of fiction. Their interests are a bit more general and abstract. For the most part, they are inspired by a legal phenomenon, judicial decision-making. In the United States, the robust tradition of judicial review by the Supreme Court means that judges are regularly interpreting Constitutional provisions and thus making law that affects us all. Many cases require judges to scrutinize phrases like "due process of law," "equal protection of the law," "interstate commerce," and "cruel and unusual punishment." These phrases do not wear their meaning on their sleeve; judges have often disagreed about their meaning and will no doubt continue to do so.

There are two simplistic ways of looking at the job judges perform in these cases. One is to say that there is a genuine objective method of determining the meaning of, say, "equal protection," and that the scholar's job is to enlighten judges once and for all about what it is. The other is to say that the job is completely indeterminate, that a judge has many options and cannot have a good reason for choosing one of the options over others. Thus, her subjective preferences will be her ultimate trump card.

It takes very little reflection to see that both of these positions are unpersuasive. If there were a method, it would be evident by now. Smart and ingenious thinkers have been trying to find such a method for quite some time. What the smartest of them have produced are good arguments why the method will never be found. The matters at hand — equal protection, due process — are matters about which political analysts have disagreed for as long as they have been writing; they reflect deeply unsettled views about how much government should intrude on individual lives, what the basic entitlements of each person should be, and how we should live collectively. These questions do not yield to easily accessible formulas.

On the other hand, it is equally clear that the range of plausible views about these matters is relatively confined. No one thinks that equal protection is secured if the traffic laws and no others laws are applied impartially. No one thinks due process involves giving each criminal defendant a lawyer with exactly the same skills and talents as every other lawyer. Because we are all part of the same culture, we tend to think in many of the same ways about many issues; we make similar assumptions. This makes it possible for us to debate about known and anticipated alternatives, to have discussions about due process and fairness—and countless other things. Because many of our ways of thinking are similar, discourse of this kind gets off the ground; because we bring different experiences and some different assumptions with us, discourse may in many cases remain unresolved.

This is where literature comes in. Debates about the meanings of works of literature have been going for centuries; critics have come up with sophisticated theories about how and why these debates occur, how and why various interpretations flourish and become influential. It has occurred to contemporary scholars that legal and literary texts may be similar in interesting ways and that legal interpreters, including judges, might have something to learn from literary interpreters.

Like the kinds of legal questions we've glanced at, literary questions such as the meaning of *Macbeth*—the lessons that Shakespeare teaches us about politics, power, and psychology—may have no single objective answer. But in sharing a culture, we share a sense of the shape of the ballpark of debate. Only a small number of theories will sustain interesting debate for very long.

When scholars turn to literature to shed light on legal interpretation, they acknowledge that their enterprise is part of a field called "hermeneutics." This is a Greek term for the art of interpretation. The focus of hermeneutics for many centuries was the interpretation of scripture. In the last fifty years the term has shed its religious connotations and refers generally to the interpretative tools any reader brings to interpreting a text.

The emphasis of hermeneutics is on the specific background and expectations that each individual reader has. Thus, there is a tendency in hermeneutics to relativize and individualize the process, to say that the text is different for each reader because the expectations each reader brings are different. While this is true, it is easily exaggerated—and with sufficient exaggeration it becomes nonsense. Notice that in both law and literature we are interested in texts that because of their history and/or complexity can be seen in different ways. That is hardly true of all texts.

Consider, for example, a STOP sign. It would be absurd to say that the sign's meaning depends on the reader. The very purpose of the sign would be defeated if that were so; it works only because it means the same thing to all of us. Of course, that's not to say that we have the same associations or feelings. One person might find it frustrating to stop; another might merely be indifferent. Another example is a restaurant menu. It works only if we find pretty much the same meaning in "tuna fish sandwich on pumpernickel."

Even in a document like the American Constitution there are levels of complexity and disagreement. The requirement that one is eligible to be president only after one has turned 35 is straightforward. It would be captious to argue that it is vague, that it might mean emotional rather than chronological age. (If it meant the former, we might have had to rule out many promising candidates.) By contrast, some provisions, such as the requirement of due process, are obviously read in different ways by different readers. Whether a provision is or is not transparent or opaque in this way may itself be controversial. A person might think that the ban on cruel and unusual punishment is transparent, comparable to the age requirement for presidents, but that person would be in the minority.

The same, of course, is true of literature, both at the level of work as a whole and at the level of its individual parts. Many aspects are straightforward. But the meaning of a Shakespeare sonnet or of James Joyce's *Ulysses* will always be controversial. The meanings of particular passages in each of these works will also support conflicting readings. But not every passage is equally interesting or controversial. The Dublin streets in Joyce's novel are the actual streets of the city. Plucking a flower petal is an act that everyone understands.

What scholars of hermeneutics tell us, therefore, must be seen in terms of the problems they are trying to address. They are not trying to explain our understanding of STOP signs or age requirements. They *can* explain these experiences, but to do so would be trivial and predictable. They are concerned instead with difficulties, with the intriguing fact, as we have seen, that on the one hand, there will never by a knockdown decision procedure for the meaning of many terms, but on the other hand, there can be genuine discovery and invention in the give-and-take of discourse. The process involves coming up with better answers, whether they are judicial decisions or literary analyses. This is possible because the discussion is constrained. As part of a culture, we share not only an understanding of the problems and why they matter, but also a sense of what counts as a good explanation and a bad one and how much clarity is possible. We are not perfectly congruent in the standards we bring to bear, but we are congruent enough to have the experience of enlightenment and progress.

In the context of both law and literature, this has, I hope, been illustrated by your experience with the first five chapters of this book. The various stories are relatively transparent, some more than others. Perhaps "American Express" is among the clearer ones and the Kafka parables, and possibly "Bartleby the Scrivener," are among the more opaque. For each of the stories, you probably concluded that there was no way of resolving all questions about meaning once and for all. Certainly there was no quasi-mathematical or scientific way of answering, no method that was purely objective and final. At the same time, you probably noticed that the range of plausible and interesting opinions was hardly limitless.

Even a story as complex as "Bartleby" or "An Imperial Message" raises only relatively few tantalizing possibilities. You may well have observed not only that these various possibilities were common ground for discourse with other readers but also that the methods of arguing (what counts as evidence, what counts as decisive) were shared. And finally you may have realized about yourself and others that in finding a position persuasive and being willing to argue for it, you revealed something about yourself—your personal background, values, and commitments.

It is sometimes said about philosophy that it reveals to us what we have in fact always known but known unconsciously and in a way that we could not quite formulate. In that sense, hermeneutics (which some see as a branch of philosophy) does that for the topic of meaning. When we debate about the meaning of a story or when judges consider the meaning of a Constitutional provision, they don't have to stop and reflect on the rules governing what they are doing. They know how to proceed; they know their way about. But this knowledge is implicit — and the devil is in making it explicit and clear.

When we do try to make it clear, it is easy to create false alternatives that reflect false expectations. For example, we sometimes say that meaning must be *objective*, that one person must be able to discover it in the same way as another. We defend this claim by saying if meaning were *subjective*, it would vary so much from person to person that anything or nothing would do. But we have already seen that this is a false opposition and that such terms are mostly unhelpful. Meaning is objective insofar as it is derived through the application of interpersonal standards and measured through interpersonal discourse. But it is subjective insofar as those standards will be deployed somewhat differently and answers will be more or less satisfactory depending on who one is and how one thinks.

These are difficult and subtle distinctions. They are worth exploring as long as one believes in the fundamental premise of Western culture that life is to be examined. (Socrates made the stronger claim that the unexamined life is not worth living.) The materials in the rest of this chapter explore the conditions for finding meaning in law and in literature. They give clues about why we agree and disagree and about how much closure we can expect in our discussions. And, finally, they show how the gift of literature helps resolve some of the questions we have about law.

Cultural Frameworks

Richard Hyland: Babel: a she'ur

Each of us is the product of a particular culture. Indeed some of us have been influenced by several cultures. The culture of our family may not be the culture in which we live our daily lives. And one's family may be a mix of several cultures. As we grow older, we may choose to immerse ourselves in cultures that are neither those of our heritage nor our original home.

Notwithstanding the fact that we are in some ways cultural hybrids, the place where we live and are educated and employed plays a powerful role. Daily exposure to American culture — political, moral, and esthetic — gives us common tools. In ways that are hard to define, there is a distinctive way of thinking that can be called American, just as there are French, German, and Chinese ways of thinking. It is easy to oversimplify this point. One can be distinctively American and have a variety of political agendas from pacifism to world domination, a variety of character dispositions from saintliness to narcissistic selfishness, and a variety of attitudes toward other cultures that range from admiration and respect to chauvinism (in the old sense of the term). But beneath these differences, there may be fundamental ways of proceeding. Perhaps pragmatism is distinctively American. Perhaps individualism and a sense of a personal destiny, aside from the destiny of one's family or government, is distinctive. But for every suggestion about the special features of our culture, one can expect a chorus of deniers who will offer a different list and another chorus of deniers who will disparage the project altogether.

Richard Hyland is an eclectic and imaginative law professor at Rutgers Law School, Camden, New Jersey. He has explored comparative legal systems and the cultures they reflect. The article reprinted here traces connections between the language of a culture and its legal system as well as its system of legal education. He contrasts France, Germany, and the United States, and he draws some radical conclusions about the lessons of such a comparative enterprise.

As we go deeper into hermeneutics, keep in mind that the culture we have in common, reflected in our language and our system of legal education, is just one part of the equipment we each have as individuals when we engage in interpretation, when we find meaning.

❧ Babel: a she'ur ❧

Richard Hyland

Unserem Packmeister sind nun doch noch Bedenken gekommen.

The letter bearing the sentence surfaces again, long afterward, as we leaf through an old correspondence file. She slowly reads the sentence aloud, savoring the surprisingly literary quality of the prose from a German shipping firm, then asks whether it is possible to translate the sentence into English. I stare at it for a moment, and suddenly the little memory floods over me. One of the reasons translation is so time-consuming is that it causes the mind to wander.

We were moving again. We had spent days dragging empty boxes from the market, packing them with books and padding them with crumpled pages from the sports section. Finally, we loaded them into a rented VW van and drove them to the freight forwarder. A worker pointed to a place for the boxes on a wooden pallet in the middle of a gaping warehouse. The random-size boxes, however, piled high and tilting slightly, did not look stable. Yet the warehouser was confident: the pile would not topple. A month later, back in the U.S., we received the letter telling us that our belongings had been shipped, that everything was in order, except that the boxes of books had had to be adjusted on the pallet and strapped down with wide metal bands.

Unserem Packmeister sind . . . To our packing master are . . . It is not yet the close of business. I call a moving company and ask for the term used to designate the member of the moving team who is in charge of packing. *The packer,* I am told. Is there no name for a specially skilled packer who, because of years of dedicated service and accumulated expertise, is consulted about particularly difficult questions? *You mean a supervisor?* Is there then no word like *packing master* or *master packer? Hey, what's this all about?* I manage to extricate myself, offer thanks, and hang up. I then report the results of the conversation. We fall silent. Why, she asks, does the German language have the concept while English does not? And who is the subject of the our? To whom in the end does the master packer belong?

nun doch noch . . . now yet again . . . Adverbs, expletives, and other German particles are packed with meanings as randomly as our boxes were packed with books. Some of the meanings can be approximated in English, but others can be translated only by a gesture — a shrug, a frown, a slap on the knee. The particles mean so much separately that they are able to mean almost anything when strung together.

Bedenken gekommen . . . thoughts-about come . . . Not just thoughts but apprehensions — doubts of some kind. The real question is where do the misgivings come from: What is the point of this odd sentence structure according to which the master packer, the human actor, serves only as the place at which thoughts come to rest?

Of course, the words can be interpreted to make at least some sense in English. *Nun* may well be the key. It seems to invoke a sigh of relief — *now, coming to a conclusion after long reflection.*

Doch can be taken with *noch* to signify a contrast, to insist that the new conclusion is firm, despite the initial contrary opinion. And perhaps it would be best in English to camouflage somewhat the surprising implication from the sentence structure, namely that thoughts possess their own means of locomotion.

In the end, second thoughts did in fact occur to our master packer. If this is a translation, then I am a translator. And I suppose Gadamer would explain not only that I have thereby interpreted the original but also that my horizon and language have become fused with those of the text. Yet I do not experience the fusion. I experience my translation as a sad and sorry compromise, and one that, far from fusing anything, instead reveals the great distance separating the very different sentences involved in the drama. There is the original. There are the several possible word-for-word renderings. There is my own approximation, together with the numerous alternatives that I have rejected. And there are the various sentences that I might have written in American English in such a letter — if the thought had occurred to me and if, in such a situation, I had found it useful to write it down. *Our supervisor had second thoughts about the way your boxes were loaded on the pallet*, I might have written. Or, more likely, I would have been more direct. *We decided that it was necessary, before shipment, to secure your boxes to the pallet*. The fact is, however, that I probably would not have found it necessary to mention the thought at all.

The experience of translating produces in me not the pleasure of merger and comfort but rather the acute distress of things torn apart and a vain and frantic desire to hold them together. In the end, the text entreats *me* to be a master packer. And so I pack my translation, somewhat arbitrarily, with as much meaning as possible. But the translation is, after all, only a sentence, and I am only a packer. Much has found its way into the translation, but as rereading it continually reminds me, much more has been left out — enough, surely, for many other sentences. In contrast to the master packer, I do not feel that I have completed my job, that my horizon is at one with another's.

The notion of translation implies that there is some relationship between languages. The fact that there is difficulty indicates at least that there is no one-to-one correspondence between words in one language and those in another. Since the law is formulated in language, the difficulty of translation suggests a similar lack of continuity from one legal system to another. It might then be asked how exactly to characterize the relationship between one language and another, or between two different legal systems. At least in the West, the discussion about such questions traditionally implicates a Biblical text (Gen. 11: 1-9) that tells the story of the tower of Babel.

The object of this essay is to explore the lesson of this story for the appreciation of diversity, particularly the diversity of legal systems.

Of God

There is no way around it: reflection about the meaning of Babel requires recourse to the notion of God. One of the difficulties in thinking about Divinity is that the prevailing tradition offers little margin for error. According to Revelations (3:12), the names of God are literally inscribed in the faithful. As Fray Luis de Leon (*De los nombres de Cristo*) remarked, those names are the essence that God communicates to the fortunate — brief ciphers wherein God miraculously encapsulates all that human understanding can and may perceive of Godhood. Since, in this tradition, all names of God partake of Divinity, the stakes in theological discussion are high: any assertion may not only be challenged as incorrect, but also branded as blasphemy. Even English, despite its extravagantly rich resources, lacks the necessary vocabulary for a completely open discussion about the nature of God.

Hebrew offers a convenient distinction — one which might easily be incorporated into English — that serves to relax the tension in theological discussion. Hebrew distinguishes between those names used exclusively when addressing the Holy One and others that may be employed in both discussion and everyday conversation.

Though there is some dispute about whether Hebrew contains a single word for *God*, it does contain numerous names *of* God. There is a twelve-letter name, and there is also a forty-two letter name, both long since forgotten. There is the word that was spoken to Moses when he inquired of the name he was to tell to the Children of Israel. In fact, it is said that the Torah contains nothing other than the names of God. Seven of these names are distinguished by the fact that, once written, they may not be erased. The first of these, the ineffable Tetragrammaton, may no longer be pronounced — a prohibition that leads to some confusion, since the true pronunciation has been forgotten. Even in the days of the priests, it was spoken aloud only in the Temple, most notably by the High Priest, after ritual purification on the holiest of days, in a whisper muffled by song. The six remaining names are used today when directly addressing the Holy One and may not be uttered outside of prayer or blessing. When, even in study, reference is made to these names, their pronunciation is altered, slightly but perceptibly, in order to avoid sacrilege.

In discussion or conversation about God, use is made of other names — oblique references, really. One such name is *HaShem*, which means simply *The Name*. It refers not directly to God, but rather to the Holy Name. Names such as this create space between the signifier and the signified and are therefore sufficiently removed from the name of God that their inadvertent misuse must not necessarily be considered irreverent. That is why they are needed here.

Even once a name has been agreed upon, the preliminaries are not over. A form must be found in which to discuss such matters. Theological discussion almost necessarily assumes that there is a fundamental ordering to the universe and thus does not proceed as though it involved a typical question from the law or politics. The Talmudic tradition offers a form for this sort of disputation. It is called the *she'ur*. The word *she'ur* may well be derived from a Hebrew verb signifying to *measure* or *estimate*. On one level, it indicates the measured or circumscribed time available between religious services for such discussions. Yet the idea of measurement reveals something of the substantive goal as well, the desire to open the nature of Divine order to human understanding — to demonstrate that, at least to some extent, humanity can grasp something about infinity. The *she'ur* begins by revealing a puzzle — usually an apparent inconsistency between two texts of the Written or Oral Laws. Since it is assumed that both texts were transcribed from Divine dictation, and since it is further assumed that Divine texts do not contain inconsistencies, the problem is to resolve the dissonance and restore meaning to the Holy Text. At the same time, precisely because the topic is the infinite and the Divine, no *she'ur* claims to be absolutely right, and one need fear being absolutely wrong. It is clear from the outset that every suggestion will enrich the discussion and equally clear that none will ever close it.

Though the *she'ur* was developed as a form for discussing the *Chumash* (the Five Books or Torah) and the Talmudic texts, its usefulness is not limited to that context. It may be understood more broadly to offer form to a discussion about the relationship between harmony and diversity — to the investigation of the affinities between empirically existing activities once it is assumed that there is order in the cosmos. The question here, for example, involves the relationship between homogeneity and diversity with respect to the human languages — and with respect to the various systems of law. The name *HaShem* is meant to serve here as a convenient reference to the idea of reason in diversity. The *she'ur* is employed as a mode for its elaboration.

Of History

The story of the tower built at Babel is based on the assumption that humanity once shared a single language. It was the language of

Noah's family, for only Noah and his wife, together with their three sons and their wives, survived the Flood. According to the *Chumash*, all nations are descended from this family. After the death of Noah, as humankind journeyed from Ararat, the mountain of the East where the ark of Noah had come to rest, it came upon the plain of Shinar. As the group looked out onto the plain, everything about the place must have reminded them of death, for the bodies of those who had died in the Flood had washed down onto Shinar. Perhaps it was the very proximity of the plain to death, together with humanity's desire to conquer mortality, that convinced the group to settle there and to build a city and a tower. Because of the events that soon transpired, the city became known as Babel, which may be derived from *Bab-ilu* (*Gate of God* in Assyrian, perhaps signifying the portals through which the nations were to go out), and, at least by popular etymology, is related to *balal*, the Hebrew for *to mix up* or *confuse*. The tower to be built there was designed to reach to Heaven. After construction of the tower was well along, *HaShem* came down to examine it. Upon seeing the tower, the Holy One destroyed it, confounded the speech of the various nations so that they could no longer understand one another, and scattered them over the face of the earth.

Tradition has had much to say about the tower. It is said to have contained two sets of stairs. The eastern stairs were used by workers carrying bricks to the top, while the stairs to the west were used by those who returned for new bricks. The tower was tremendously tall, so much so that its top appeared to touch the sky. When the tower was destroyed, the bottom third of it sank into the ground, the top third was consumed by fire, and only the middle third remained. Yet what remained of the tower was so immense that one might have walked for three days without leaving its shadow. (Some of the traditional stories about the tower are collected in *The Torah Anthology [MeAm Lo'ez]*.)

From Rashi to Derrida (Des Tours de Babel, in *Difference in Translation* (Graham ed. 1985)), the scholars have unanimously interpreted the confusion of language as a well-deserved punishment, one particularly designed to prevent the completion of the tower. The diversity of language and the inevitability of mutual misunderstanding have been considered elements of a curse brought on by Divine annoyance at human pride, particularly at the vanity implicit in the conception of the tower — the belief that human beings might reach Heaven, and therefore immortality, without the journey through death.

Despite its persistence, there is something peculiarly unsatisfying about this interpretation of the story. The tower, of course, could never have reached Heaven. The Holy One had no reason for concern. Moreover, pride of accomplishment and the desire to postpone or transcend death are constant elements of the human condition and certainly not its least attractive ones. Furthermore, though *HaShem* is capable of rage (metaphorically understood), the Rambam demonstrated that not every human failing is capable of inducing Divine anger: an examination of the incidents of wrath in both the Torah and the prophetic writings reveals that only one very particular sin provokes the Holy One, and that is idolatry. And finally, the confusion of language involves much more than the simple creation of a barrier to communication. If all that *HaShem* had desired was to obstruct human discourse, that could have been achieved by hindering the human ear or by slowing the tongue. In other words, the building of the tower seems to provide little enough reason for punishment at all, let alone for a punishment of this particular type. The difficulty then becomes to discover a connection between the confusion of language and the building of the tower that can be reconciled with the all-encompassing wisdom of the Holy One.

Once the problem is posed in this manner, the story of Babel is so evocative that numerous resolutions suggest themselves. My own favorite interprets the story as a fable of post modernism. The first step in conceiving of the story in this way is to reexamine its status as history. In my view, none of the stories recounted at the beginning of the *Chumash* need be interpreted as history, at least not history as we are used to conceiving of it. Though the sages do not deny the historicity of these stories, a few of their sentences seem to point to the possibility of a nonhistorical reading. Woe unto them, remarked Rabbi Shimon bar Yochai in the *Zohar*, who see in the Torah merely worldly stories and history. To Rabbi Yaakov Culi, the few stories retold in the Torah are really mysteries, enshrouded in words that make them appear like history. For the nonhistorical reading, it is irrelevant whether the incidents described in those stories actually took place, whether a tower was actually built or human language actually confused as described in the Torah. Rather the stories present analysis in the *form* of history. To decipher this curious form, the story of Babel must be read in context.

The *Chumash* presents a code of laws — 613 commandments, 248 mandating some positive act, the remaining 365 enumerating the prohibitions — interspersed with what appears to be an historical narrative. The culmination of the narrative is the recounting of the single Divine revelation in human history, the appearance of the Holy One and the giving of the Law at Sinai. What precedes the giving of the Law is an account of the formation and education of the people chosen to receive it, which begins with the story of Abraham our Father. Before beginning the story of Abraham and his descendants, the *Chumash* focuses on three events — the stories of Eden, the Flood, and Babel.

The three stories may be read as the preface to a legal text, a reminder of the three preconditions that are necessary for a functioning legal system. These stories describe not the past but the present, each designating a necessary element of the whole. Each story illustrates one of the prerequisites by means of an *as though* analysis, what Hans Vaihinger (*The Philosophy of "As If"*) might have called a heuristic fiction. The very possibility of the law is rooted in these three aspects of the human condition, yet they seem so natural that they are virtually imperceptible until they have been problematized — scandalized really — by ascribing to them fictional origins: it is as though humanity had been Divinely created and then suffered a Fall, *as though* it had received a covenant from the Lord after a terrible destruction, *as though* an original common language had been fragmented. The challenge is to redeem the wisdom sealed in the metaphors.

In Eden, our first ancestors tasted of the forbidden fruit, and thereby gained the ability to distinguish between good and evil. The story of the Fall recognizes in human nature an attraction to evil as well as an understanding of good, together with the ability to distinguish between the two, and the insight that they are often intertwined. The story describes one aspect of the human condition that serves as a prerequisite for a functioning legal system, a feature so essential that it is difficult to conceive of a legal system without it. If human beings did not both recognize the good and yet, at the same time, desire evil, the notion of a legal prohibition backed by coercion would be incoherent. There is also something more to the story. The teller of the tale must have marveled at the human ability to appreciate the distinction between right and wrong. It may have seemed that the knowledge of good and evil results not from reasoned inquiry but rather from a quality innate in human nature. And yet human beings are clearly not predetermined to do good. The knowledge of good seems to be Divinely inspired, as though the human race initially had been Divinely created and subsequently had fallen from the perfect identification with Divine will that constituted grace.

Unfortunately, the knowledge of good and evil, unguided by morality, did not prove sufficient to overcome temptation. Beginning with Cain and Abel, what resulted was such human iniquity that the Holy One decided to drown the world. After the Flood, *HaShem* covenanted with Noah that the world would never again be destroyed by calamity. By making the promise, the

Lord demonstrated to Noah the nature of obligation and thereby initiated him and his family into the concept of duty. The sense of duty or morality is the second prerequisite of a legal system, for there can be law only if humanity struggles to comply with the demands of duty. The daily, heroic, and largely successful human struggle to overcome desire makes it seem as though humankind is attempting to fulfill promises made in exchange for the Lord's own covenant.

An understanding that right differs from wrong and a moral commitment to the good are still not sufficient for the establishment of a legal system, at least according to the author of the *Chumash*. The final requirement is an understanding of the necessity of particularity. The Divine Text expressed the requirement by portraying the fragmentation of a single original language. This account raises two difficulties. The first is to make sense of the claim that the various natural languages have a common origin. The second is to understand why the notion of particularity is a necessary prerequisite for a code of laws.

Of Language

As our ancestors were resolving to build the city and the tower of Babel, it is written that they also decided to make for themselves a name, in order to avoid being scattered over the face of the earth. Confronted by the splendid yet frightening multifariousness of existence, they wished to prevent their dispersion by gathering together, by reducing everything to a unique name, to a single understanding. They sought transcendence beyond the realm of diversity in a unique foundational principle. The idea of the single name influenced the conception of the tower. Finding no stones, we are told, they made bricks and burnt them thoroughly. The tower's foundation was thus a human construction. Yet the tower builders believed that, if they were to construct a tower, even on such foundations, on a plain encountered by chance, they would be able to dominate Creation and, from the top of the tower, enter into Eternity.

The story of the tower of Babel suggests how easily the human mind can be seduced by reductionism. The story expresses the frantic yet persistent hope that it is possible to escape uncertainty by glorifying the theory of the moment: if only the tower is tall enough, our ancestors thought, it can reach to Heaven. The story reminds us that human intuition seeks truth in unity, in mono-causal explanation, rather than in multiplicity. If humanity were possessed of but a single language, it would inevitably believe that there is but a single valid understanding. In the end, Babel reveals the limitation of the human imagination, its difficulty in conceiving of infinite possibility.

This is an important limitation, because the ability to conceive of possibility is the difference between Divine and human understanding. The Holy One understands the world as it is, both in its existence and in its potential. That is what Heidegger called original being (*das ursprüngliche Sein*). Humankind, on the other hand, tends to focus on the given and the finite and to reduce it to a single explanation. However great its comprehension, no human mind can ever discover more than an extremely limited number of the possible alternatives.

Hashem destroyed the tower and scrambled language not to punish those who had sought to reach Heaven, but rather to open the human mind to the appreciation of possibility. For this purpose it was necessary to establish at least some of those possibilities empirically and to permit them to flourish independently. The confusion of language, by making it difficult for one nation to communicate with the next, permitted each group to develop relatively autonomously the possibilities inherent in the language it received.

The development of a particular language over time is a cultural tradition. There is of course never homogeneity within a tradition. For one, languages are often composed of numerous competing dialects. Moreover, each cultural tradition is the expression of a debate — at times only an unvoiced tension — between the rulers and the ruled, between sexes and races and religions, majorities and minorities of all kinds. There is also constant Babel or confusion even within the same language. And, of course, history matters too. To begin with, the tradition is constantly reorganizing itself, emphasizing today what it yesterday rejected. Moreover, at some point, cultural developments that occurred much earlier may prove difficult to interpret, so that, like Middle English, they are no longer fully able to contribute to the contemporary discussion. Yet despite the internal conflict and confusion, each tradition shares a common understanding. In fact, what distinguishes one tradition from another are the terms in which the various conflicts are fought out.

From the standpoint of Babel, in other words, language is not transparent. If the various languages were merely neutral instrumentalities for the communication of thought, it would be impossible to explain their extraordinary multiplicity and diversity. The tradition is that seventy nations received languages at Babel. These languages ultimately differentiated themselves into what may have been as many as ten thousand languages, of which possibly five thousand survive today. The reason for the diversity is that each language is constituted by, expresses, and reproduces a particular intelligibility. In Heidegger's phrase, language is *die redende Gliederung*, speaking articulation. Since each language represents only one of the many possible understandings, the existence of thousands of languages confirms the possibility of at least so many lived articulations of meaning. In fact, the number of possibilities may well be endless. The mission confided by the Holy One to human hands is to discover, explore, and develop these endless possibilities. It is as though an original common language had once been fragmented.

Of Translation

The Babelian understanding of language irrevocably alters the notion and goal of translation. Translation as traditionally understood—the phrase-by-phrase rendering of a message from one language into another while *retaining the sense* (Samuel Johnson)—proves to be impossible. The problem is not that languages are totally incommensurable with each other. It is not that it is inherently impossible to express in one language the meaning of a word or phrase from another. Language determines not, as Benjamin Lee Whorf seems to have believed, what it is *possible* to see and understand, but rather what *easily* can be grasped and what, in contrast, requires more effort. If languages were impregnable fortresses, nothing could be learned from a foreign culture.

The principal problem is rather that languages communicate simultaneously on various levels. On one level, language is a tool by which human beings attempt to come to terms with their world, either by attempting to describe or represent the world that they perceive to be external to them or by seeking to express their inner awareness and conflicts. The question about whether language is adequate to the task, an issue about which Richard Rorty has expressed doubts, does not bar human beings from the attempt. Even on this level, no message can be comprehensively translated from one language into another without constant resort to asterisks and extensive explanatory notes.

This is not a problem that affects only a few well-known untranslatables, such as *Aufhebung* or the pair *langue/parole*. Even the English word *bread* does not have the same meaning as the French word *pain*. Though there are dozens of differences, the easiest to explain are found on the side of the signified. Not only are the breads referred to by the two words significantly different in form, texture, and taste, but also bread in America is usually bought pre-packaged, pre-sliced, and even pre-frozen and is rarely eaten with the main course, while French bread is bought fresh in bakeries shortly before it is to be consumed at the main meal. On the side of the signifier, the differences are just as stark. Though the two words share many connotations, such as the notion of *daily bread (pain quotidien)*, colloquial English has developed the metaphor to produce the idea of the *breadwinner* and even equates *bread* with *money*, while French tends to use *pain* in metaphors related to the shape of the loaf, such as *pain de viande* (meat loaf) and *pain de cacheter* (sealing wax), and colloquial French even arrives somehow at having *pain* mean a slap in the face. Moreover, the literary associations of the two words are completely diverse. *Pain* rhymes with *sain* (healthy), *pin* (pine tree), and *vin* (wine), while *bread* rhymes with *dead*, *head*, and *said*. Upon hearing the word bread, it is unlikely that anyone but those with a childhood in English will recall the verse *"A loaf of bread," the Walrus said,* and suddenly feel the tug from the far side of the looking glass.

Language as a tool — the use human beings make of word is not all there is to language. Languages, too, communicate. They speak through those who are attempting to use them in their own communication. As John Sallis notes, language is not primarily an articulation of meaning that we perform, but rather one that is always already performed for us, one we have already assumed inadvertently by virtue of our life in language. (Language and reversal, in *Martin Heidegger: in Europe and America* (Ballard & Scott eds. 1973)). The particular intelligibility that a language conveys may be at cross purposes with the intent of the individual speaker. If, as we are used to saying, language is a game, it is not a game that we play with language, but rather one that language plays with us. This is one of the senses in which one might say, with Heidegger, that it is actually language that speaks (*Denn eigentlich spricht die Sprache*).

The consequences for translation are considerable. The problem is not simply that the meaning of a particular word or phrase in one language cannot find an exact equivalent in another. The problem is rather that there is nothing identical across languages. Languages are simply not equivalents as media for communication. The different understandings implicit in the natural languages render every one of their words, phrases, and sentences untranslatable — unless the translation is accompanied by an absurdly compendious and extraordinarily subtle textual apparatus.

Thus, if there is a relationship at all among languages — and only then would translation even be conceivable — it arises only in terms of the whole that, together, the various languages may have constituted. If the Holy Name is in fact the organizing principle of the universe, and if all of the world's languages are fragments of the original language spoken at Babel, then each language represents a piece of a much larger jigsaw puzzle. No piece can reveal its meaning alone, but each may acquire coherency when examined together with some of the other pieces. One problem, of course, is that, by now, we have lost half the pieces, even assuming that we ever once had them all. As a result, whatever the whole may once have signified will remain forever concealed from us.

The absence of a direct relationship among languages provides reason for skepticism about Gadamer's confidence in translation. For Gadamer, translation is simply a particular kind of understanding. All understanding is interpretation, the fusion of the reader's language and horizon with the language and horizon of a text. Since translation involves a similar fusion, it too would be merely interpretation. It would represent both an extreme form of and a model for understanding. Gadamer's confidence would be warranted if the task were merely to understand what human beings do with words. But his method is unable to account for what is communicated by the language itself. Another and very different strategy is needed in order to reproduce in one language the understanding constituted by another. As Walter Benjamin was probably the first to note, translation could solve this problem only by importing from one language into another an entire fragment of the foreign culture, and not merely the thing meant. In this sense, successful translation not only enriches the target language but also reminds us of its limitations.

Of Law and Legal Education

The story of Babel is particularly important as the preface to a legal text. It emphasizes the particularity of any single code of laws. No code promulgated in a post-Babelian language—even if conceived in Divine inspiration—can be universal. Every law is a particular law. It is part of a particular language, embedded in a particular cultural tradition, and designed for a particular people. The laws codified in the *Chumash*—the 613 *mitzvos*, including the Ten Commandments—apply directly only to the people in whose language the code is written.

Like languages, legal systems express particular understandings. And as with languages, the particular understandings are constituted in conflict and debate, are what the debaters share. Thus, no matter how successful, no particular legal system can make a direct claim to universality—none can overcome the particularity of the language in which it is formulated. Each legal system articulates the meaning of law and justice in a particular way. Wisdom in the law is not located within any particular understanding, but results rather from grasping all of these articulations at once.

The understandings incorporated in the numerous particular systems of law and justice may be accessed in several ways, but it may be easiest to begin at what might be called the beginning: not a beginning buried in the past but rather the beginning all new jurists experience as they are initiated into their craft — the various and extraordinarily diverse systems of legal education. Intuition suggests that legal education will differ greatly between traditions that are geographically dispersed and culturally disparate. But even a common cultural heritage does not prevent difference. For this reason, in order to suggest the range of methods in legal education, it is especially important to consider legal education in countries whose traditions seem to be closely related. Those established in West Germany, France, and the United States will be examined here. Though the skills taught in the three systems may seem to overlap somewhat, there is something very different about the manner in which they are articulated. The focus here is on those differences. In order to avoid a much more extensive discussion, I ignore other related processes in the law, such as the manner in which cases are decided and the methods of legal scholarship.

The principal object of German legal education is to develop the skill of the *Fallosung* or case resolution, a particular method for finding a legal solution to a hypothetical fact situation. It is the skill required for success at the German state examination, which is given at the conclusion of law school and which alone determines a student's final grade and rank in class. The technique of the *Fallosung* is considered so important that upper-level German law students often abandon university instruction entirely for the year or two prior to their state exam and follow courses taught by one of the many private tutors, the *Repetitoren*, who relentlessly drill and develop the skills required.

Substantively, German legal education tends to center in the private law, especially the law of contracts, particularly of sales contracts. The focus there is on questions of remedy, specifically on the relationship between the remedies and defenses available under general contract law and those provided by sales law. The complex set of rules provided in the German Civil Code and in the relevant case law to govern these matters involves elaborate cross-references, repeated resort to the interaction of principle, exception, and exception to exception, and reliance on elusively subtle distinctions. For those to whom intricate elegance is a virtue, this structure must be counted, with the verb forms in classical Greek, among the sublime creations of the human imagination. Needless to say, this part of German law is *Professorenrecht*, a matter for specialists. The complexity of the field is what recommends it as a test for the student's mastery of legal technique.

Success in resolving the German hypothetical requires a thorough knowledge of the remedial scheme and a comprehensive and systematic examination of the relevance of the various remedial provisions to the facts at hand. If the claimant in the hypothetical has several potential opponents, the claims against each must be discussed separately. If the claimant has more than one type of claim (*Anspruch*) against a particular party, the claims must be examined in the appropriate order. Much of German academic discussion focuses on questions of organization, and there are competing views on these questions. In general, primary claims are to be reviewed before secondary claims (specific relief before damages, replevin or ejectment before contract claims) and the claimant's primary objective before a secondary one. For each type of claim, there may be more than one potentially relevant basis for the claim (*Anspruchsgrundlage*) — the specific provision in the code or a well-established principle from the case law that offers the particular remedy to the claimant. Each substantive discussion begins with a statement of the relevant *Anspruchsgrundlage*, and all of the conceivably relevant bases for the claim must be examined in order — special before general norms, contractual before extra-contractual provisions, property-based provisions before restitution. For each particular provision, there is also an established order for the review of the legal requirements (*Tarbestandsmerkmale*). In tort, for example, though there is debate about the appropriate scheme, and any one of two or three alternatives is acceptable, the discussion traditionally begins with the nature of the harm, and then proceeds through the type of right that was violated, the tortious act, causation between the tortious act and the violation of the right, causation between the violation of the right and the harm, breach of duty (*Rechtswidrigkeit*), and fault (*Verschulden*). (The technique of the *Fallosung* is described in Uwe Diederichsen, *Die BGB-Klausur* 80-88 (6th ed. 1984), and in Dieter Medicus, *Burgerliches Recht* 1-14 (14th ed. 1989).)

In short, greater emphasis is placed on the framework for the analysis than on the result. What is essential for success in the state examination is that the student subsume the facts correctly under the elaborated system of remedies. Of course, policy arguments may be raised in the answer, but only if they are incorporated into the appropriate phase of the discussion. In any case, nothing is to be mentioned that is not directly relevant to the question at hand. At the same time, no logically necessary step may be omitted. A serious error in construction may lead to failure even if the theories and policies are adequately examined. Most importantly, no step may be taken and no argument advanced unless it finds authority in a code provision or a well-established case-law principle.

Though there may be slightly more flexibility and openness to innovation outside of the private law, adherence to preconceived outlines is cherished throughout German legal education.

Exclusive focus on the logic of the *Anspruchsgrundlage* encourages the German student to develop extraordinary rigor and orderliness and to pay close attention to subtle distinctions between the various remedial provisions. This emphasis, however, is not without its limitations. It tends to avoid explicit and wide-ranging discussion of policy alternatives and leaves the skill of advocacy largely undeveloped. Moreover, by concentrating on the accepted view and the firmly established remedial provisions, and by emphasizing the virtues of predictability and certainty, the *Fallosung* acquires a somewhat conservative cast.

German legal education, as it analyzes and orders the remedial scheme, enunciates a moral and political understanding of the nature of justice and of freedom under law. It asserts that a people is free when it deliberates in a parliamentary manner and when the commands of the legislature are rigorously executed by the judiciary. The implication is that progress in the law should be left to the political process and fine-tuning to the highest courts. The role of the individual judge is not to provide a remedy merely because it may seem just to do so but rather to respect the will of the people as promulgated in legislative enactments. The common lawyer may experience the German method as somewhat inflexible in reaching a legal conclusion and inattentive to the constellation of possibilities offered by the law. Yet, at the same time, the vision implicit in German legal education expresses not only a belief or yearning that is widely shared both inside and outside of Germany, but also a thought that may represent an element of every complex legal system.

French legal education focuses on a different skill and embodies a distinct understanding of the nature of law. To begin with, the French law professor avoids the hypothetical as a teaching tool: French law students are virtually never asked to consider a complicated fact pattern, identify the issues, and resolve the dispute. Instead, the focus is on a particular kind of synthesis. French students are taught to develop an overview of a legal topic or of a court decision and to convey that overview not only convincingly but also in a specific form.

The keystone of the French synthetic method is the *plan*, the organizational structure for the *exposé* or presentation. French jurists have developed the *plan* into an art form, one they elaborate according to strict rules. One rule is the maxim of elegance: the topic headings of the plan, when taken together, must envelop the entire subject matter, and each element of the whole must in fact be subsumed under one of the topic headings. Second, the *exposé*, between its brief introduction and its even briefer conclusion, generally contains exactly two parts, each divided into exactly two subparts. (A *plan* may include three principal parts — in its classical form, virtually never more than that — only if it is impossible to subsume one of the three under one of the other two.) The role of the introduction is to present and justify the *plan*. It begins from a commonplace that a legally educated reader would surely accept and then presents the subject matter in such a manner that the structural divisions of the *plan* seem convincing, even obvious. Each of the two principal parts of the *exposé* must be of approximately equal length. Each of two corresponding subparts must also be of similar proportion. Parallel topic headings must be symmetrical in syntactic form. In sum, the successful expose, gains clarity and persuasiveness by following the canons of balance and harmony. (The technique of the *plan* is described in Jean-Pierre Gridel, *La dissertation et le cas pratique en droit privé* 21-45 (2d ed. 1986).) This rule of two parts and two subparts is followed rigorously by students in both oral presentations and written examinations, and with some variation, by doctoral candidates writing dissertations, by the authors of law-review articles, and even by specialists when drafting comprehensive treatises.

The binary structure of the *exposé*, may seem somewhat arbitrary and rigid, but, as with the rhyme scheme of a sonnet or the number of syllables in a *haiku*, the appearance is deceptive. The *plan* is essential to the French understanding of the nature of law. The insight underlying the French conception of the *plan* is that legal topics are best presented from the point of view of a fundamental tension or contradiction. Until a basic tension is discovered and the subject examined from that standpoint, any understanding is unsatisfying: the details will seem to have outflanked the author and the subject matter still to lie beyond the grasp. It is important to note that the French understanding does not represent a camouflaged metaphysical assertion about a supposed dialectical structure implicit in the law. There is nothing absolute or objective about the *plan* as the French conceive it. For any one subject, there could be as many *plans* as — or even more *plans* than — there are jurists.

The French conception of the *plan* is intoxicating to the point of addiction. No one who has successfully apprenticed in the French system deems a presentation successful, whether written or oral, unless it has been harmoniously organized into two parts, each with two subparts. From this perspective, any other organization of a legal discussion suggests only that the author has not yet fully mastered the material. The *plan* renders it uncommonly easy to see and retain the structure of the law and is capable of displaying the relationship among even the most far-flung topics. In the end, a persuasive *plan* is about as satisfying as intellectual things can be.

The single-minded French concentration on synthesis necessarily neglects much of what is otherwise interesting in the law. For example, French legal education fails to develop in its students a sensitivity to the facts or an understanding of the art of advocacy. It also produces an overly harmonious and unified vision of the law. It places the law student outside the law, at the point of synthesis, and removes all but the most accomplished jurists from active participation in legal change.

The vision implicit in French legal education is that the law is the organizing force in a society wrought with tension and contradiction. To organize contradiction, of course, does not mean to deny it. The law's task is to recognize the tension, to perceive how every legal question is divided against itself, to evaluate the contradictory views and present them in a balanced manner, and to offer, if only temporarily, an elegant and satisfying reconciliation of opposites. Law, in this perspective, both guarantees the realm of freedom and creates social unity and cohesiveness. It squares the circle, imposes order upon chaos. It is the center that holds against centrifugal force.

American legal education offers yet a different understanding. As are many other systems, it is principally the study of decided cases. But cases are not studied in America as they are studied elsewhere. In many other systems in which cases are read, the case serves almost exclusively to demonstrate to the law student how to apply the law to the facts, how to evaluate the comportment of individual parties by recourse to the norms available in the legal order. The object is to understand which party acted appropriately and which did not. In America, the study of cases may often fulfill a similar function, but the power of the case method lies elsewhere.

For one, cases are not generally taught alone. They are taught in pairs, triplets, or even entire series. The coupled cases may seem at first glance to provide differing solutions to the same set of facts. The task is then to reconcile the cases, to distinguish their facts in a convincing manner so that it becomes clear why each deserves the result the common law judge accorded to it. The challenge is to discover the perspective from which seemingly identical cases appear to be opposites.

In addition, the facts in reported cases are frequently used in American legal education as a challenge. The aspiration in many classrooms is for students to use the case to reconstruct the legal system. Legal norms are then not used to decide which of the two opposing parties acted properly. The answer to *that* question — this is one lesson from legal realism — is not an exclusively legal matter. Instead, American law teaching often uses a particular case as an occasion to evaluate the appropriateness of the legal rules. The object of such class discussion is to determine how the legal order should be structured so that it would resolve the case before the court in a satisfactory manner. The student learns to stand up in class and argue that, despite statute, regulation, and precedent, a rule is not what it ought to be. The goal is not merely for students to learn to spot the difficult issues, but also for them to learn that the difficulties must be resolved in a socially and politically responsible manner. For this reason, the case law method is neither rigorous nor formal. It is an impressionistic attempt to integrate statutory provisions, case law, policy considerations, jurisprudential theories, and notions of fairness and justice. What counts is what works, what convinces the socially and politically concerned listener.

The beauty — and the limitation — of American legal education is that it does so much with the rather limited resource of the appellate court opinion. Probably more than any other system of legal education, it encourages and develops the skill at drawing fine distinctions between the facts of similar cases and turning those distinctions into convincing legal arguments. It also teaches students not only to spot issues — to create them, really — but, at least to some extent, to advocate and achieve change. The case method can expand a student's imagination and creative potential in a way that may best be described as psychedelic. Of course, by concentrating on these skills very much to the exclusion of others, American law students often fail to achieve technical proficiency at manipulating code provisions and rarely gain a comprehensive overview of the relationship between the diverse fields of the law.

American law schools aspire to reorganize the past and prepare the future. The understanding of the law implicit in such a system is that the judge, the lawyer, and the individual litigant each has a role to play not only in vindicating, but in fact in creating individual rights. It is a vision of decentralized decision making, of a state in which every individual has direct access to a rule maker. It is the conception of the courtroom as a forum for democracy.

Of Legal Education and Cultural Projects

The diversity of meaning articulated in the various languages and systems of legal education suggests that every cultural tradition is distinct. Each pursues a particular goal, which it might be useful here to call a *cultural project*. The project is present in the language that is spoken, in the method of legal education, in the manner in which bread is baked — in short, in every aspect of life in. a particular tradition.

Everyone who has lived abroad is aware of this. Yet, because it smacks of stereotyping, it seems slightly immoral to recognize it. One of the reasons stereotyping is such a serious sin is that the admission of global distinction may suggest grounds for prejudice and discrimination. For this reason, comparativists of all kinds usually attempt to demonstrate that, contrary to appearances, everything is really the same everywhere. Whatever the reason, little attention has been paid to the particularities of cultural projects. But the lesson of Babel is difficult to grasp until an effort is made to understand the peculiarities — and the potential contributions — of each of the various cultural traditions. What follows is a preliminary and subjective speculation about how language is related to the law in the three cultural traditions whose methods of legal education were examined above.

One particular feature of the German language is the manner in which abstraction is generated. It is part of the genius of the language that abstraction never loses touch with the concrete. In German, abstractions are living metaphors. They almost universally consist of two or more easily recognizable elementary words that have been yoked together. The basic, concrete meanings are generally active and present. The word *aufheben* is a good example. It consists of a prepositional prefix (*auf* = *up*) and a basic verb (*heben* = *to lift*). Its primary meaning is simply *to lift* or *to pick up* (to pick up a pencil from the floor) and the word is used in daily conversation in that sense. When used more abstractly, as is also common, the verb gains two virtually contradictory meanings. It can mean *to preserve* (to put something away in order to save it) as well as *to cancel* or *to set aside* (to abrogate or repeal a statutory restriction). Hegel employed the word philosophically to incorporate all of these meanings at once. To him it signified the process of transcending a stage of development by preserving it at a higher level.

The poetic and philosophical quality of the German language derives to a considerable extent from this constant resonance of the concrete in the abstract. For example, Hegel and Heidegger repeatedly interrogated the individual elements of composite words to discern their contribution to the resulting abstract concept. Both used the hyphen as the surgical tool for their investigation. Hegel, for example, on the last page of the *Phenomenology*, discovered in *Er-innerung* (remembrance/internalization) not only an indication of Spirit's reimmersion into itself, but also the suggestion that history is the result of Spirit's own internal development. Heidegger transposed the technique mythopoeically to classical Greek, interpreting *Existenz* (existence) from the perspective of

Ek-sistenz (to cause to stand and be exposed to), and *aletheia* (truth) as *a-letheia* (recovered from forgetfulness). Thus, one of the German language's central preoccupations is to assure that the individual element has been carefully and meaningfully integrated into the whole. Even basic words, when properly arranged with other words, gain metaphysical significance. The implication is that the individual not only gains meaning through, but to a large extent is identified with, its role in the complex whole.

Of course, this is not to say that this feature is unique to the German language. English, for example, occasionally employs the technique as well (*overcome, headhunter*), though English characteristically distinguishes between abstractions, which have Latin roots, and words for the concrete, which are derived from Anglo-Saxon. (Of course, *trans-late* too is a composite, both to those who know Latin and to English speakers who are aware of other *trans*-words (*trans-gress*) and other *-late* words (*elated*), but the elements are much less apparent than they are in the corresponding German compounds.) Moreover, the generation of abstraction is only one of the German language's central linguistic features. Another peculiarity, for example, is the delay of the verb until the end of the sentence, which requires a discipline in speaker and listener and an ability to anticipate and postpone gratification. Only after these and other elements have been illuminated can the nature of the German project become entirely clear.

This preoccupation with the role of the part in the whole, though only one of its elements, is constitutive of the German cultural project as well. The individual, though of course respected in its own right, is largely identified by its particular role in the community. It is a trait of Germanic languages, shared to some extent by English, that common proper names suggest the identification of the individual with its social role—*Schmidt* (smith), *Müller* (miller), *Wagner* (wainwright), *Kramer* (shopkeeper), *Bauer* (peasant farmer). The intensity of the German concern with these issues is what makes it so difficult to translate a sentence such as *Unserem Packmeister sind . . . Bedenken gekommen.* The suggestion of expertise implicit in the notion of the *Packmeister* or master packer emphasizes the importance of the development of a socially relevant skill to the identity of the individual. Moreover, by referring to the *Packmeister* as *unser* (our), the shipping firm both confirmed that the packer was in its employ and suggested that the master packer is a cultural resource, the polity's master packer, a person specially skilled in the craft and therefore deserving of job security and social insurance, a craftsperson of whom the entire nation might be proud. Furthermore, as the sentence suggests, master packers themselves are, in the end, only conduits for the tradition. The second thoughts arose from the practice of the craft over centuries, and merely came to rest in the person of the master packer. And, of course, the master packers' awareness of their role in the tradition redefines in turn how they conceive of themselves.

At the same time, there can be little doubt that the thoroughness with which the German project is organized generates a highly energized tension with individual rights and a heightened concern for the individual. That concern—which is also implicit in the Hegelian and Heideggerian hyphen—helps explain the focus in German philosophy on the status and nature of human freedom.

The German focus on the role of the part in the whole, though only one of its contradictory moments, is of great consequence to German legal education. The focus suggests the importance to the individual of a reliable social division of labor, both because of the security it affords and the opportunity it provides for the cultivation of craft and the mastery of technique. German legal education is simply a further expression of the same understanding. One of the hallmarks of a stable division of labor is a careful delimitation of the various social roles. The legislature makes the laws, while the lawyer and judge assure technical proficiency in their application. It seems, therefore, that central features of German legal education run parallel to the fundaments of the German language.

One of the exquisite qualities of spoken and written French lies in the distinction and alternation between the indicative and subjunctive moods of its verbs. Verbs in the indicative mood often end with syllables pronounced as open (despite the orthography), while those of the subjunctive are usually and emphatically closed (*vient/vienne*). The French subjunctive appears chiefly in subordinate clauses, generally after principal verbs expressing personal feeling, such as desire, joy, and sadness. Thus, as a simple proposition, *she is coming (elle vient)* is in the indicative, but is placed in French in the subjunctive following statements such as *I wish that . . . (je veux qu'elle vienne)*. The subjunctive may also appear in relative clauses that indirectly express similar emotions, and even in principal clauses, namely in a few fixed idioms expressing a great personal commitment or excitement that coincides with a socially recognized injunction (*Vive la France! Sauve qui peut!* Run for your life!). Much of the concern in teaching French and the joy in learning it revolves around the mastery of the forms and distinctions involved in the use of the subjunctive. The poetic quality of the French language also derives in part from the interplay between the two moods. (*Vienne la nuit sonne l'heure/Les fours s'en vont je demeure*).

The French indicative describes the objective, the verifiable, the repeatable. The subjunctive invokes the subjective, the personal, the desired. To delimit the appropriate sphere for the pursuit of individual desire within the structure of social cohesion is the central concern. The opposition between the two moods legitimates a role for individual exuberance within the framework of social convention. From this perspective, the French project attempts to maintain sufficient room for the expression of individuality while maintaining a cohesive centralized order. Once again, legal education seems to be structured like the language, for this of course is also the object of the *plan*. The *plan* both recognizes the tension that may result from the assertion of individual interest and demonstrates the necessity of the law as the structure for social organization.

Of course, the alternation between indicative and subjunctive is not unique to French — in fact it is shared with the other Romance languages. Moreover, French has other characteristic features, such as the double negative (*ne . . . pas, ne . . . rien*), that must be explored before the French project can be thoroughly understood.

It would be useful to include here a short discussion of American English and of the American cultural project. A sense of the particularity of American English, however, is largely barred to me. One of the most direct lessons of the story of Babel, as Paul de Man has noted, is that the most alienated and uncomprehending relationship one can have with a language is usually the one native speakers have with their own. However, those I have consulted who speak English as a foreign language usually tend to note the same peculiarities. Spelling does not coincide with pronunciation (tough/though/through, read/read). Prepositions are employed in an apparently idiosyncratic manner (the alarm went *off*, to study *under*). Word formation often ignores etymology (hamburger/cheeseburger) (sandwich/fishwich). There are some rules that few master (the distinction between *that* and *which*, the proper use of the comma), other rules that tend to be honored chiefly in their breach (the prohibitions against the split infinitive and against ending a phrase with a preposition), elaborate rules that are seldom used (much about the various past tenses), and vast stretches with no enunciated rule and nothing to assist the foreigner who has not yet acquired a sense of the underlying enterprise. The stated rules seem to be of little importance, while the effective rules seem to be unstatable. In fact, idiomatic expressions are so prevalent that it is possible to master all the rules and still not speak the language fluently. The consensus is that it is a language of infinite imagination but little discipline, a restless language in constant innovation. ("We got the repeat," San Francisco 49ers running back Roger Craig announced to the press after his team won the Super Bowl for the second year in a row, "now we want the *three-peat*.")

Needless to say, there is much in common here with American legal education, especially its impromptu and unsystematic character, the joy with which principles and theories are created, employed, and forgotten. The pragmatic American mode of politics, the role of individual initiative, and all the rest seem intimately bound up in all of this. But it can only be seen clearly by someone who takes it up from the perspective of another tradition. (Indeed, what I suggest above about the particular understanding implicit in American legal education is not my own insight but comes rather from Michel Pecheux, who mentioned the idea in conversation shortly before his death.)

One lesson is that each system of legal education, like the language in which it is formulated, constitutes a part of a larger cultural project and represents a particular articulation of meaning. The even more far-reaching lesson from the story of Babel is that diversity deserves to be recognized, preserved, cultivated, and developed. The political and theoretical implications of this lesson are perhaps best observed from the point of view of postmodernity.

First, the story of Babel seems to confirm much of what postmodernity has to say about the implication of madness in understanding. The idea is that understanding is fundamentally constituted by the desire to escape from chaos. (The idea is discussed by William Corleu in *Community without Unity* (1989).) In the hope of domesticating chaos, understanding constructs polar oppositions and forces every element of existence to adhere to one or the other of two poles — male and female, white and black, right and left, sick and healthy, individual and collectivity. Understanding thus not only bears the trace of fear in its constitution, but is itself a kind of derangement.

This, in fact, is what the story of Babel is all about. The confusion of language resulted directly from the seemingly unavoidable tendency to think in terms of polar opposition. Certainly each of the cultural projects examined here, including their systems of legal education and their languages, attempt to conquer chaos in this manner. German legal education emphasizes the obedience of the judge to the will of the legislature in a way that reflects the concerns of the German cultural project about the importance of integrating the individual into the collectivity. French legal education emphasizes that the opposition between individual desire and legal order is to be expounded by binary opposition, and thereby mirrors the oppositions found in its language between subjunctive and indicative, subjective and objective, individual and collective. American legal education emphasizes the conflicting demands of judicial creativity and precedent — another version of the tension between individual and collectivity, which parallels the opposition in American English between idiomatic expressions and traditional rules.

Each cultural project and each system of legal education seems to attempt to escape from chaos by constructing its own set of polar oppositions, oppositions that can be ordered on many axes, including the relationship between individual and collectivity. The deconstructionists are justly worried about the power of these oppositions and are correct in suggesting that we try to defuse them. In this sense, *HaShem* was the original deconstructionist, for that was also *HaShem*'s concern. What *HaShem* noticed upon descending to Babel was that humankind recoiled in fright from the unknown, and that it was quick to try to protect itself by articulating meaning in terms of oppositions — Heaven and earth, life and death, unity and dispersion, naming and chaos. *HaShem* thereupon confused language and sent humankind out into the unknown that it most feared. By creating a multitude of languages, *HaShem* hoped to melt the dichotomies into diversity and to assist humanity in overcoming its reduction of meaning.

In sum, the understanding present in any one language or cultural project is plagued with the structure of opposition that deconstruction has taught us to notice and reject. Each of these understandings is therefore not only particular and limited, but in fact suffused with fear and madness, or rather constitutes one kind of madness in order to escape from another. That is why translation can be not only frustrating but literally maddening: it tends to lead the translator beyond the habitual bulwarks against insanity. Hölderlin's translations of Sophocles were some of the last lines he composed before he plunged into almost forty years of crazed silence.

A second concern of postmodernism is the problem of the unitary origin. As I understand it, one of the goals of postmodern politics is to demonstrate the importance of differential plurality and to create a society that takes advantage of the potential synergism of all types of difference. In this perspective, the postmodern philosophies of difference attempt to demonstrate that differences cannot be confined within an original unity or totality in which they might, in the end, be reconciled. Difference, we are told, is *anoriginal*. (The term is from Andrew Benjamin, who summarizes the argument in *Translation and the Nature of Philosophy* (1989).) The danger that postmodernity thereby seeks to avoid is the single totalizing structure that may be imposed upon, and thereby destroy, diversity.

Yet not all stories of origins have this problem. Accounts of origins are problematic only when they imply that it would be beneficial to reduce diversity to unity or to return to an original golden age. An example is the extraordinarily conservative and nostalgically romantic myth of return that inhabits Marx's thought and that seems to have led Heidegger to Nazism. But there is not the least suggestion in the story of Babel that humanity would be better off returning to the Noachian condition. Moreover, as the story makes clear, there was never any meaningful unity at the origin. The original language must have teemed with an incredible multitude of patterns and ideas. Otherwise its confusion could never have produced ten thousand human languages. What led to calamity was rather the human insistence on reducing that incredible wealth to one set of simple oppositions. Furthermore, it is clear that there is no way, starting from the natural languages that survive today, to piece together the original language. Language is and will remain for us always already disarticulated into difference. Any unity that might once have existed can never be resynthesized. Since the remaining languages can never be reduced to a single meaning, all that results from piecing them together is the understanding of how each represents the kind of intentionality that Walter Benjamin referred to as pure language (*die reine Sprache*). Thus, the story of Babel is not so much the story of an origin as the indication of a trace.

One last theoretical issue raised by the story of Babel concerns the status of diversity. This is a problem that is never really resolved in the garden variety philosophies of difference. These theories attempt to demonstrate the plausibility of a way of thinking that conceives of difference as primary. But the mere existence — or even the primacy — of difference cannot alone convince us that difference is good. Instead of a normative argument demonstrating the value of diversity, the philosophies of difference offer only a clutter of difference, what might better be called *indifference*. Though these philosophies may be read to imply that we should respect those who hold views that differ from our own, there is nothing in them to encourage us to devote our energy to examining with care articulations of meaning that we initially find unconvincing or strange. Theirs is a position at which one might arrive just as easily by indolence as by conviction.

It is in this sense that the story of Babel demonstrates how much more there is to diversity than the philosophers of difference have perceived. For the message of the story is not simply that difference is an unavoidable fact of life. It is rather that diversity expands the limits of intelligibility. The reason is as follows. Language does not simply take the world as it is, but rather constitutes intelligibility as it communicates. There is no intelligibility outside of language. This thought, which Heidegger took from Stefan George — No thing can be where the word is wanting (*Kein Ding sei wo das*

Wort gebricht) — suggests that every language, and every tradition, is entitled to profound respect. However limited and deranged, the understandings in the surviving natural languages are the sum total of intelligibility. If each language constitutes a different fragment, then each is a treasure. We are the shepherds and not the masters of language.

The potential wealth of diversity is at least threefold. First, since the articulations of meaning present in the particular languages and traditions are each limited, each will find much that is evidently and practically useful in the other cultural projects. And this is true whether or not there was ever a single original language of which the surviving languages may be fragments. Second, the interplay between diverse traditions offers one of the few opportunities for the creation of truly new ideas, ideas that arise outside the scope of any one tradition's particular experience. Finally, diversity is a prerequisite to serious self-reflection. Without the existence of diverse traditions, it would become literally impossible to assess the peculiar characteristics of any particular understanding. Human beings who know only one language have little alternative but to consider the articulation of meaning within that language to be absolute. There is little they can do to step outside that understanding in order to relativize it. The articulation of meaning in their language will permeate everything they think or write and render it difficult to avoid totalizing reductionism. Should they become aware that other and different perspectives exist, they are of course capable of tolerance. But wisdom is not simply tolerance, never merely a recognition of diversity, no matter how generous and humanitarian. Wisdom rather is a vision from diversity, an understanding constituted in fragmentation. The multiplicity of languages is its irreducible condition. It is a blessing and not a curse.

Of Blessings

Blessings are opportunities. They are no less so because their realization requires effort and often suffering. The study of a foreign language and the initiation into a foreign culture can be intriguing and delightful, but they also involve mindless memorization, incessant repetition, and a painful reorientation of thought. When pursued seriously, they may result in a throbbing loneliness, the constant companion of foreigners who isolate themselves from their compatriots long enough to master the essentials of a foreign language. And apprenticeship in a foreign legal system can be even more disorienting and disturbing than learning the foreign language in the first place.

No one who succeeds at the enterprise does so without a good reason. Some have had their lives shattered in their homelands, been scattered into exile, and have been subjected involuntarily to the destructive force of diversity. They are thankful for the hospitality their hosts show them, but equally frustrated by the incomprehension they encounter. They survive the experience chiefly by clinging to the possibility of return. For others, diversity is a constant reminder of incompleteness, of the wound left in the soul by the dismemberment that occurred at Babel. Their awareness of the impoverished character of any single articulation of understanding requires them to reach out to embrace foreign cultures. But even for them, diversity is no more than a scar over a wound that can never heal.

There is no perspective from which the disastrous consequences of the confusion of language can be denied. But a blessing is not distinguished from a curse by the intensity of pain thereby avoided or by the quality of comfort it affords. What makes of Babel a blessing is that it offers, though at terrible cost, the otherwise unavailable challenge of possibility.

Discussion Topics

1. Most of us lack the experience to evaluate the congruences that Hyland points out and explains. In each of his examples (French, German, and American culture), do language, legal system, and legal education coalesce in just the ways that he suggests? The links are presented with imagination and sophistication. But every generality about culture is contestable; no doubt Hyland's claims would cause vigorous debate among representatives of these cultures.

One question is how deep or superficial these characteristics are. Once a French legal scholar has parsed a problem in her distinctive style, would her arguments, evaluations, and conclusions be predictably different from those of an American if, say, she were serving as a judge on an international court? It is hard to judge whether the differences are merely matters of form or also matters of content. Would certain substantive conclusions be *unavailable* to a German judge facing, for example, an international commercial law claim because of his training and ways of thinking? Or would he arrive at the same range of possible solutions as a Chinese judge, but perhaps arrive by a different path?

2. Hyland stresses that American language, legal training, and legal practice all have a kind of malleability and adaptability that other cultural practices seem to lack. His description of French and German legal analysis makes these systems sound rigid. Perhaps this is fair description. Or perhaps the fact that Hyland himself is an American, trained for the most part in the U.S., creates an unconscious bias. Not surprisingly, he may have had opportunities to see American problem-solving at work and may not have had similar opportunities during his times in France and Germany.

Consider also whether he segues a bit too readily from one aspect of American culture to another. He notes that the American version of English is particularly flexible and expressive, with many more idioms than other languages. He then finds a similar flexibility in common law and the ways in which precedents are interpreted to adapt to new situations. Is the connection between these two modes of flexibility purely accidental? Are they the effects of a deeper orientation in American ways of thinking and dealing? Have Americans cornered the market on imaginative and fresh solutions to new problems? In this form, the claim is especially tendentious and suspect.

To be sure, Hyland attributes some distinctive virtues to other cultures. He starts the essay by alluding to the German preoccupation with craft and expertise. He points out elegance as a French virtue. Compared with success in problem-solving, are these pale virtues?

3. Hyland concludes his essay by talking of blessings. But the blessed in his discussion are exiles and refugees. He recognizes that these persons have lives of turmoil. But their blessing is that, in occupying more than one culture, they have a special perspective and a special gift of understanding. In a crucial sentence, he says that "diversity is a prerequisite to serious self-reflection," and his exiles and refugees are examples of such diversity. He also says that "the interplay between diverse traditions offers one of the few opportunities for the creation of truly new ideas."

These comments are initially seductive. Almost everyone who has spent time abroad knows how acquaintance with other cultures freshens one's attitudes and can make one analyze what one has always accepted. It is hard to question that we are all better off if we can understand the points of view of those who have different backgrounds, who are in various explicit and implicit ways *foreign.*

But Hyland is claiming more than this in two ways. He is, for one thing, making a strongly negative comment. One who has not experienced cultural diversity is, he seems to say, not capable of self-reflection. And "truly new ideas" are not likely to be generated within a culture unless that culture is engaged in a clash or confrontation with other cultures. Both of these claims are questionable. Self-reflection can be prompted by all kinds of experiences. There is no reason to think that *intra*-cultural rather than *inter*-cultural ones are less likely to cause such reflection. Similarly, there is often a lot of intellectual ferment and conflict within a given culture.

There is no reason to think that the political, social, ethical, scientific, and technological turmoil that characterizes any complex culture cannot produce "truly new ideas." Hyland, it seems, presupposes bland homogeneity within a culture — and that is almost always a caricature.

By the same token, Hyland may overestimate the wisdom made possible by diversity. Other things being equal, it is probably better to have familiarity with several cultures. But things are rarely equal. Intercultural comparisons may generate superficial and cheap generalities. The relevant kind of wisdom depends not on knowing several cultures but on knowing them *well*. How likely is it that someone new to a culture will understand its complexities and nuances in the way a native does?

The Task of Interpretation

Thomas Grey: The Hermeneutics File

In setting out to interpret a phrase, a passage, a novel, or a constitution, we usually take the cultural setting and our cultural tools for granted. We are aware that each of us faces the job of interpretation as an individual. We are also aware that, by the very nature of interpretation, we must cede some precedence to the writer, the creator of the text. Unlike clouds that come together accidentally to form letters in the sky, any particular text was created purposefully.

If the beginning of wisdom is to think about what the author had in mind, it is not the end. And this is where our individuality must necessarily concern us. The aims of the author may be neither fully accessible nor decisive. Who knows what Homer had in mind in *The Iliad*? For that matter, who knows whether there was such a person as Homer? The aims of Shakespeare or the writers of our Constitution are somewhat more accessible, but only somewhat. We can only guess what Shakespeare intended in some of his plays, and we have been arguing about that for four hundred years. We certainly know what the founders had in mind about the age of presidential candidates, but how much do we know about their meaning for "due process"? Of course, some scholars claim that we know a great deal and that what we know is more than sufficient. And others disagree.

There are questions about conclusiveness as well as accessibility. Even if we do know that the founders never considered the application of Fourth Amendment search-and-seizure laws to Internet communications, we may conclude that this knowledge about them is irrelevant. The Constitution must be applied to problems and distinctions that they never anticipated. This insight leads to the notion that the document's phrases have taken on a life of their own. The founders' thinking cannot, in some situations, be decisive. While they uttered the words of the document first, but they have been reuttered with various other intentions by judges for well over two hundred years, and the Constitution is the sum of all those readings.

At this point, the sensitive interpreter may wonder whether her own background, experiences, and expectations will color her interpretation. And she may well conclude the basic hermeneuticist point that that result is inevitable. But even that insight is hardly the end of wisdom. Self-awareness of her disposition and self-criticism must and should be part of her process of interpretation.

Thomas Grey, a long-time professor of legal philosophy and constitutional law at Stanford Law School, is the author of "The Hermeneutics File." We meet Professor McGarr, who is confronting his own individuality in the course of an unusual interpretive task. McGarr must decide whether a document left behind by his recently deceased colleague, Terry Conn, is or is not a legal will making him Terry's executor. Should he submit the document for probate? He is dealing with this job in light of a long series of conversations and disagreements with Terry about the nature of interpretation, and this discourse becomes highly relevant to the way he performs the task.

❧ The Hermeneutics File ❧

Thomas Grey

"Hermeneutics seems to me to be animated by this double motivation: willingness to suspect, willingness to listen; vow of rigor, vow of obedience."
—Paul Ricoeur, FREUD AND PHILOSOPHY 27 (1967)

"If the poet says, 'Go and catch a falling star,' or whatever it may be, he doesn't seriously issue an order."
—J.L. Austin

The following four memoranda, written by George McGarr in the immediate aftermath of Terence Conn's death, are here published for the first time. They cast new light on the papers of the late Professor Conn, papers which first came to public notice in Professor McGarr's article published soon after their discovery (The Legacy of Terence Conn, THE BULLETIN, *Vol. 53, No. 2; and also George McGarr,* Editing the Conn Papers, THE BULLETIN, *Vol. 54, No. 7). Professor Conn's "Draft #13 (Conning McGarr)" is reprinted after the first memorandum for the reader's convenience. The footnotes have been prepared by Marvin Subal, Esq., who wishes to acknowledge the indispensible assistance of Professor McGarr.*

I

To: Dean Peter Stutz
From: George McGarr
Re: Terry Conn's Papers

Peter, thanks for your help with the memorial service. I have been virtually in shock during the whole business, and I couldn't have gotten through it without you. Your remarks were just perfect, in contrast to some others — and I don't exempt my own. I have been in such a swirl of confusion, sorrow, and resentment that I couldn't strike the right tone, or any consistent tone. But to the business at hand.

The immediate problem, as I understand it, is the status of Terry's papers. Let me review where we stand. You are effectively the custodian of them, since they were in his law school office at the time of his death. Janet asked you to go through them, though she and Terry were never formally divorced, in light of the estrangement she didn't think she was the one to deal with them. You agreed, and the two of you also agreed that I should help.

Early in our search of his office, I found, in a file-folder marked "Hermeneutics," a poem entitled "Draft #13 (Conning McGarr)" which was apparently addressed to me. The poem was handwritten on a single piece of paper, which had been crumpled and then smoothed out. From a photocopy of it I have had a version of the poem typed up, which I append here. It quite accurately represents the position on the original paper of the written matter which is (apparently) extraneous to the poem itself: namely, the date in the upper left-hand corner of the page; and the words *"Cal. Prob. Code Ann. 53,* 102 (1)" in the lower left-hand corner.** (I should also mention, though it seems clearly extraneous, that on the back of the piece of paper containing the poem appear the words "the red bird," also in Terry's hand, and written casually at an angle across the page.)

As you recall, I immediately showed you the poem after I had read it, with the remark that it was a joke characteristic of Terry's

---

** The poem is reprinted at the end of this memorandum as it appeared in Professor McGarr's original report in these pages (THE BULLETIN, Vol. 53, No. 2, at 17). In his editorial comment accompanying the original publication, Professor McGarr explained his decision to include the words "Draft #13" as part of the title, while excluding the date and legal research notes as extraneous; the reader's attention is drawn to his distinctions between "writing" and "text," and between "poem-text" and "will-text." We had wished to include a photographic reproduction of the original as part of this study, but this has not proved possible.

less attractive side, a somewhat malicious last shot at me in our longstanding debates about interpretation. It seemed obvious to me at the time, and as I recall you agreed, that the document could not actually be a legal will. It wasn't witnessed; it wasn't even signed. We went on with our search, and found nothing that looked like a will. You then went to look through the papers at Terry's apartment, and called me to tell me that there was no will there either. Terry had told me, and Janet confirmed, that he had no living relatives; thus it seemed clear that he had died intestate, and she as his wife would take his entire estate.

As much out of curiosity as caution, I looked up the Probate Code section referred to at the bottom of the poem. Section 53 turned out to be the provision dealing with "holographic wills." I don't know if you are as weak on trust and estate law as I am, but I had barely been aware that there are special rules governing wills written by hand. What I thought I did know was that wills have to be formal documents, signed on each page, with two or three witnesses attesting, and so forth. Imagine my feelings as I found, reading section 53 and the summaries of cases in the Code Annotated, that Terry's poem arguably met the formal requirements for a valid holographic will.*** The poem was apparently written entirely in his hand, and was dated by him. A holographic will need not be witnessed, and the cases suggest that the phrase "I, Conn . . ." with which the poem begins might serve as an adequate signature.****

My immediate reaction was anger. What did Terry think he was doing, placing me in an ambiguous position, possibly as his executor, without even asking, in a document that was at the same time a tasteless joke at my expense? What should I ever make of his gnomic "instructions," which seemed designed to spread confusion rather than to communicate anything? The damned thing didn't even make the debater's point it seemed designed to make; when had I ever denied that a person who set out to write an uninterpretable (or, the same thing, infinitely interpretable) set of "instructions" could do just that? My point against Terry had always been that most legal instruments, like most utterances generally, are designed to convey a definite content, a meaning that can be

---

*** *See CAL. PROB. CODE § 53* (West 1956):

A holographic will is one that is entirely written, dated and signed by the hand of the testator himself. It is subject to no other form, and need not be witnessed. No address, date or other matter written, printed or stamped upon the document, which is not incorporated in the provisions which are in the handwriting of the decedent, shall be considered as any part of the will. Section 53 was amended in 1982, after Professor McGarr's memorandum was written, but the substance of its requirements remains the same. *CAL. PROB. CODE § 53* (West Supp. 1984).

**** *See, e.g., In re Bloch's Estate, 39 Cal. 2d 570, 248 P.2d 21 (1952)* (name written anywhere in will qualifies as signature if testator wrote it there with intent of authenticating instrument); *In re Button's Estate, 209 Cal. 325, 287 P. 964 (1930)* (words "Love from 'Muddy'" near end of letter, propounded as will, from deceased to former husband to whom she was known by that name, was valid signature).

rationally discerned by the process of interpretation. This is all I have ever said, and it always seemed to me that only Terry's perversity led him to deny so obvious a common sense truism. But I digress.

My next discovery was that my anger was premature. The cases construing section 53 clearly establish — and (as "Code Ann." suggests) Terry surely knew this***** — a principle that avoids the horror of making Terry's poem into a valid will. Even an instrument that has met the (undemanding) formal requirements for a holographic will is not accepted as such if it fails to manifest "testamentary intent," or *"animus testandi."* The courts have relied on this principle to reject a wide variety of dubious handwritten documents proffered as holographic wills.******

Now there surely can be no difficulty in concluding that Terry had no "testamentary intent" when he wrote this poem. First, of course, there are serious doubts whether it was even meant to be a final document: it is entitled a "draft"; it breaks off in mid-line and mid-sentence; and he had crumpled up the page. Further, the scrawled legal research at the bottom of the page and the evidently unrelated note on its reverse side are not the sort of thing a testator would be likely to write on a final version of a will.

But, overriding these considerations, surely it is clear from the basic content that Terry was not attempting to make a will at all. He was writing a poem, for my eyes, a poem that took the form of a will: a pseudo-will, a fictional will. Who writes an obscure poem to dispose of one's estate — including in Terry's case one's voluminous unpublished life's work? Who vaguely orders his property distributed to "friends" in "reasonable shares"?******* Terry had been a good lawyer, and he was always a master of language; he knew what he was doing, and what he was doing was writing an ironic poem, not a will. The point is confirmed by his leaving the poem in a file marked "Hermeneutics" — the topic of our many debates. In the same filing cabinet were file-folders marked "Personal-Miscellaneous" and "Personal-Financial" that contained practical documents among which a will might naturally have been lodged. Finally, the decisive

---

***** The annotated code contains summaries of the case law construing the statutory provision as well as the text itself; the statute itself could have been cited, and normally would be, without the explicit reference to the annotation.

****** *See, e.g., In re Henning's Estate, 186 Cal. 307, 199 P. 39 (1921)* (handwritten letter not a will because written in contemplation of matrimony not death); *In re Kenyon's Estate, 42 Cal. App. 2d, 109 P.2d 38 (1941)* (handwritten letter discussing politics and weather was not a will because it contained no evidence that decedent intended it to be such).

******* The intention of testator to make a testamentary disposition of his property . . . must be expressed in such terms that the court can determine his intention or wish without resort to conjecture. Both the thing given and the persons to whom it is given must . . . be set forth with such certainty that the court can give effect to such gift when the estate is to be distributed. 1 Bowe-Parker, PAGE ON WILLS 187-88 (1960).

point is the parenthesized title, in which I take some wry comfort; it says straight out that the document is meant only as a last poke at me.

I conclude, then, that we are not in possession of a will of Terry Conn's. I have told Janet this. She has asked me if I would sort out the papers in Terry's office. She wants them disposed of, one way or another, without her having to deal with them. I have told her, what I am sure you will approve, that the Law School will retain custody of them in Terry's locked office (to which I now have a key) for the time being.

* * *

Draft #13 (Conning McGarr)

I, Conn, sound as age allows,
Bequeath to friends in reasonable shares
My money and my goods. As for the rest,
My hoard (imagined, literary *res*)
Shall be arranged with care, substance preserved,   5
And put out in due time, plain as can be.

All this shall be done by George McGarr,
My colleague, friend, conscience of afternoons,
Who also shall respect this final wish:
That my inchoacies may never come,   10
My Scottish breadman, to harsh scrutiny,
Those of my writings that are incomplete,
Destroy.

The stacks of pages wait for you;
Do not see in them matter wanting form,   15
Pebbles for a Japanese gardener's hand,
But mind's fixed intercept of lexicon.
You said, through all our restless afternoons,
"To interpret is to find intent in words;"
Now, exegete, now that the words are mine,   20
Now, grave George, draw from them what I mean —
Who knows my currents better than the shore
Against whose sea-wall they have spent their surge?

If you can judge which of my works are done
Not seeking shape where I let fracture be   25
(Old seconder of motions to adjourn!)
Nor forcing me unfinished into view

(The literate insist, and what's to hide?)
Nor claiming bold emender's privilege
(Conn says to mean, so mean away his say)   30

Then can your last word close our long jaw-jaw
Conformant to your sober principles.
But take care. Traps are here. Words mean.
I mean. You, reading, want

II

To: Peter
From: George
Re: Terry's Papers

I have spent the last five days reading the papers in Terry's office — with an eagerness that goes beyond any duty to you or Janet. Terry and I talked two or three times a week for years about his ideas, and yet I had never seen a word he wrote, apart from those summaries of contract and evidence law he handed out to his students. Eventually I will make a complete inventory of his writings, but for now I thought I should at least fill you in.

Also, I want to respond to your suggestion about the handling of the poem. You raise the point that perhaps if it arguably meets the formal requirements for a valid will, we should at least file it with the Superior Court, pursuant to the Probate Code.******** I don't read you as disagreeing with my conclusion that there is no "testamentary intent" here, but you think that in our respective positions, yours as temporary custodian of the papers (and the "will"), and mine as putative executor or whatever, we should in all caution leave it to the court to determine the intent question. I see the point, but I don't agree. Let me postpone saying why until after I tell you something about Terry's papers.

There really is a "hoard" in there. First, Terry left behind a fair amount of regular legal scholarship. We know about the contracts and evidence summaries. There are earlier versions of them in piles of old class materials for those courses. In his files are exchanges of letters with the publishers to whom you, Jack Goldberg, and I showed our pirated version of the summaries, hoping they could pry these manuscripts out of his obsessive grip and publish them. This was Terry's response:

How did you vultures get a copy of my Evidence summary? Please send all copies in your possession to me at once. I write these summaries only so that I can tell my students to stop

---

******** Section 320 of the California Probate Code provides:

The custodian of a will, within 30 days after being informed that the maker thereof is dead, must deliver the same to the clerk of the superior court having jurisdiction of the estate, or to the executor named therein. Failure to do so makes such person responsible for all damages sustained by any one injured thereby.

bothering me with their complaints about not learning doctrine in my classes. I have not authorized their use for any other purpose, and I regard you as in possession, now knowing possession, of stolen property.

(I remember telling Terry how helpful I thought those summaries would be if published, lucid doctrinal statements that they were, and his saying to me, in his coldest way, that when they were ready for publication I would be the first to know.)

Terry also left behind what I take to be the two article-drafts he showed his then colleagues when he induced them to give him tenure about fifteen years ago. They seem to me clear and intelligent doctrinal pieces, well above the norm of such work, though not otherwise remarkable. (One of them deals with the parol evidence rule and documentary interpretation; "hermeneutics" surfaced in Terry's mind long ago.) These pieces seem to me finished works, but the typescripts are marked "draft" — as is every single bit of Terry's writing I have come upon. There is also a long fragment of an article on the hearsay rule, written after the first two doctrinal pieces. Then there follows a gap of more than seven years for which there are no writings, except the earliest versions of the contracts and evidence summaries.

Then, about seven years ago, begins the "imagined, literary *res.*" There are quite a few poems; how good they are I'm certainly not qualified to say. There are a lot of short stories of a "fable" sort, Borges-like or Kafka-esque — or like law school exam questions. (I'm not much more confident in making any judgment of quality here either, but I do find some of them very intriguing.) There is a long, curious essay comparing the lawyer's distinction between fact and law with the distinction between perception and imagination made by various poets and novelists — Coleridge, Shelley, Proust, and Wallace Stevens.

There is another quite long essay that I read more intently because it is on the very topic ("interpretation") that was our favorite subject of discussion in our afternoon walks around the campus. Terry examines the theories of several of the philosophers he got me to learn a little about, especially Wittgenstein and Derrida. He makes the curious remark about these two (both Jewish I think) that Derrida is a "Protestant" while Wittgenstein was a "good Catholic," a believer in tradition; Terry used to ascribe our differences to my Scottish Protestant and his Irish Catholic background, mixing hermeneutic theory with vulgar ethnic jokes. The piece breaks off without a conclusion. Reading it leaves me remembering Terry most vividly.

There is a 200-page typescript of a murder story. The murder is at a law school, and the suspects are various members of the faculty, an assemblage of actual well-known law teachers from different schools, thinly disguised and more or less subtly defamed (you and I are not included). There are two competing detectives, whose efforts are chronicled in alternating chapters. Seamus is a private eye turned law student late in life; he follows intuitions, breaks into apartments and offices, gets hit on the head, and drinks too much, all told a la Raymond Chandler. Jane Muffett is a young lady philosopher from Oxford, visiting the faculty; she has tea with colleagues, examines rare old books in the library, and ratiocinates in her office — told as if by Dorothy Sayers. The two avoid and loathe each other, but then are thrown together in a confrontation in which there is a kind of courtship by exchanged insults, as in a Hepburn-Tracy movie. The book ends (breaks off?) with them going off for a drink together, the murder left unsolved, clues dangling, erotic tension high. Is the murder story a kind of allegory of the love story? (He will make me into a literary critic yet!)

There is also a stack of notebooks written by Terry over the last six years, filled with quotes from his reading, aphorisms, short sketches (germs of stories and poems in several cases) and ideas for articles. These are especially interesting to me, echoing as they do so many of the things he said in our talks. (I myself intermittently kept a notebook recording things Terry said to me, frustrated as I was at never being able to see what he was writing.)

Finally, the longest typescript is a 603-page autobiography (all the typescripts are unprofessionally typed, presumably by Terry himself; his secretary tells me she never saw this material). The thing is titled, facetiously, in a handscrawled cover page, "The Tao of Terry."********* I have read every word of it. To me, this work best reveals Terry's powers. There is a lot of direct narrative of the events in his life (many of them I had never known about), and this is intertwined in the most absorbing way with his reflections, which are often expressed in imaginary colloquy with two interlocutors, addressed as "my saint" and "my sinner" — evidently Augustine and Rousseau. I know the device sounds impossibly grandiose, and I may have been carried away by my fascination with Terry, but I truly think this is an astonishing work.

I have described Terry's "hoard" in this much detail partly because you deserve to know right away what we have here. You stuck by Terry when many people wanted you to pressure him to resign. I recall with gratitude your stiff response when Grimmett said Terry didn't belong here "because he isn't publishing anything and whatever he's teaching, it isn't law."

********* This work is now scheduled to appear under the title CONN'S WAY (Multiversity Press, forthcoming).

But in addition, some sense of the material does seem relevant to the question whether we should file the poem with the court and leave it to the judge to decide if Terry intended it to be his will. It seems relevant in this sense—what if some damn-fool judge *did* decide the poem was a will? We would be stuck with Terry's crazy "instructions" (which of course are really only mock-instructions) to destroy all the writings that are "incomplete." The chances are, I assume, strongly against a judge making any such idiotic ruling, but why take the chance?

I am not suggesting that we evade the letter or spirit of the law. If we had found a real will that gave such instructions, we would of course have to file it, and face up to the grim possibilities. But clear as we are that this poem is not a will, we are under no legal or moral obligation to take the risk. The Code section that imposes an obligation to file the "will" of a deceased within 30 days after death********** simply doesn't apply to us; we have no "will," only a poem in the form of a will, a pretend-will, something completely outside the scope of the statutory requirement.

Nor are we putting ourselves or the University at any practical risk of liability by not filing. The only sanction for noncompliance with the statutory duty to file seems to be liability for damages to any person injured by the failure to file. Here, even if this were a will, no one would be injured by its suppression. Where there is no harm that can come from not filing, a long-shot risk of harm if we do file, and we are clear in our own minds that no will exists, I say we should not file.

III

To: Peter
From: George
Re: Terry's Will

When I said that there was no one who could be injured by suppression of the will, you were right that I had not considered Terry's "friends" who would get his (nonliterary) property in "reasonable shares" under his instructions. In my defense, I could not accept this as a serious disposition of property. Also, Terry seems to have had practically no money or goods. But all this becomes irrelevant, I believe; as you know, a much more momentous injury, in all but the legal sense, is now threatened if Terry's estate passes to Janet by intestacy.

After I sent the last memo to you, I met with Janet to tell her what was in Terry's office. When I mentioned the autobiography,

---

********** *See supra* note 7.

she immediately asked whether it said anything about her. Well, it does indeed; there are many pages that deal with Terry's marriage and breakup with Janet. Since these events coincided with Terry's intellectual rebirth, the story and the ideas are closely intertwined here; and these are among the most important and, to me, among the best parts of the book. I don't know why I had not thought before of the possibility that Janet might object to these passages; perhaps because in them Terry seems to be hard on himself and understanding of her.

When I told Janet she was in the book, she wanted to see it right away, and (as I told you) I gave her the key to the office, thinking that I could hardly deny her access to what we had agreed were *her* papers. In no more than twenty minutes, she came back, very angry, and told me that she wanted all his papers destroyed! There was no arguing with her in that state of mind, so I called to warn you, and resolved to wait until she had cooled down. As I recall it, you were to tell her that any final disposition of the papers had to wait at least until the university counsel ruled on whether we had to submit the "will" to the court.

In the meantime, I went back to Terry's office to think, and I write this having been at his desk ever since; many hours now. As I turned over in my mind what I might say to Janet to dissuade her, I could not escape the possibility that she might remain implacable. She is quite capable of taking an extreme position and passionately holding to it. After all, that is what she did with Terry. When she was splitting up with him, I once tried to suggest that he wasn't so bad, that his new line of work sounded interesting, and so on. She responded in perfect, complete sentences with a denunciation of him so total that I wrote it down at the time: "He will never do anything worthwhile. His talk about new work is dilettante bullshit. He will not do anything in literature or philosophy for the same reason he did not do anything in law: he is a drunk and a liar; and he drinks and lies because he is a coward." Perhaps to be expected when someone is going through a painful breakup. The startling thing is that when I spoke with her just after we had learned of Terry's death, and said something vague and soothing about him again, she gave me the same speech; it might have been word for word. No *de mortuis*.

Let me give another example (these are not the digressions they may seem, as Janet's character is a central point in all this). While she and Terry were breaking up, we were good friends and I spent considerable time with her as a kind of sounding board (a role which, curiously, Susan played more with Terry; even then, before her illness, Susan had a febrile quality that matched Terry's temperament). After the breakup, Janet and I talked almost every day here in my office, sometimes for hours. After about a month, all at once, she stopped coming by, and then very suddenly (perhaps you'll recall) arranged to take a year's leave away. During that year, I took up my talks with Terry again. After she returned, and I know it was because of those talks, she would scarcely speak to me at all, and, to my great regret, she has not been more than civil to me for all these years — implacable Janet.

Having said all that, let me repeat what I said on the phone. While her reaction is extreme and wrong, it is understandable. Terry did put her through hell. I think many of our colleagues, and sometimes even you, Peter, have missed what a fine person Janet is; she can be difficult and rigid, but she is absolutely straight, dependably honest, and a generous friend. Like anyone, she closes herself off when she feels disliked, and she has had every reason to feel disliked around here. I only hope she will now listen to reason and back off from this awful resolve of hers.

But it *is* an awful resolve, and with that in mind I have made myself reread Terry's will. In fact, I have really read it seriously for the first time. Because what I am going to say comes in the shadow of Janet's threat to destroy the papers, believe me that I am aware of the ironies that hedge me round on all sides. I have little hope of convincing the larger world of this, Peter, but I do want to convince you: while the desire to save Terry's work has made me look hard at his will, it has not dictated what I find there.

This rereading — this first careful reading — has led me to see "Conning McGarr" as Terry's intended will. Let me try to set down for you (and for myself) what seem to me the main considerations supporting this.

First, read the actual words of the poem itself, putting in the background, for a moment, the contextual aspects — its verse form, its title, the crumpled page, the other writing on the paper, the file Terry left it in, and its apparent inconsistency with Terry's own often-asserted views on interpretation. I will come back to each of these features to show how none of them negates his testamentary intent. But look at the words first; as Terry wrote, "Words mean."

While there are some obscurities in the poem, careful reading reveals a serious, coherent statement of Terry's wishes about the disposal of his legacy. Of course, some instructions are vague; particularly "friends" and "reasonable shares," but I think it fair to conclude that Terry did not much care what was done with his very limited property. Further, the most crucial instructions, those on which writings to publish and which to destroy, leave room for much interpretation: I am to destroy writings that are "incomplete" or "unfinished," yet I must judge the completeness of each work not by my own relatively classical sense of "shape," but with due regard for Terry's modernist tendency to leave deliberately frayed ends — to "let fracture be."

Yes, these are vague instructions, but as we tell our law students, or at least as we should, vagueness (unlike irony or ambiguity) has its legitimate and indeed essential uses in serious legal drafting; vague words, like those of the United States Constitution, can grant the people subject to them flexibility to deal intelligently with new and unforeseen situations. Terry did not want to tie my hands with mechanically precise instructions about his manuscripts; he did not know what state his papers would be in when he died, and he trusted me to make reasonable judgments subject to the basic considerations he set down. These were certainly not contentless. Indeed, I am not happy about his instructions, for I would like to publish even those works that by Terry's own standards *are* incomplete. But the instructions are intelligible, coherent, and manageable — my calling them "crazy" in the earlier memo to you was a result of my failure, shocked and upset as I was, to read carefully and think clearly.

Now let me turn to the features of the will, including the more contextual ones, that might be thought to undercut testamentary intent. First, Terry put it in a file marked "Hermeneutics," kept with other subject-matter files, rather than among his business and financial records. I think the placement of the will in such a file, especially as the only item in the file, was simply Terry's way of emphasizing to me that he wanted me to interpret the will in the light of our debates about interpretation, or "hermeneutics."

The fact that the paper had been crumpled does suggest that Terry may have doubted at one time whether to preserve this as a final version (we found no preliminary drafts). In the end, though, he carefully smoothed out the paper and preserved it; surely it is understandable that he did not take the trouble of recopying the whole document in the uncharacteristically small, neat handwriting that would be required to fit it on a legal-size sheet of paper. (I place no significance on the words "the red bird" written on the reverse side of the paper. Perhaps he mistakenly used the page as a piece of scrap paper when it was lying face down.)

The marginal note at the bottom, referring to the holographic will section of the California Probate Code, is an obvious signal that Terry knew the poem had the legal form of a valid will. (Incidentally, section 102, to which Terry also refers in the same note, provides in pertinent part: "Of two modes of interpreting a will, that is to be preferred which will prevent a total intestacy.")

What about the use of the word "Draft" in the title? The fact is that this term is appended to *every single one* of Terry's writings that I have found. Unless we are to assume that he meant them all to be considered incomplete, and thus to be destroyed — a conclusion his instructions negate by presuming that distinctions are to be drawn among his works — that word cannot be said to show a lack of intent to endorse the document as his final statement. His use of the word "Draft" is consistent with his admonition to me that writings of his that were left in what might strike me as open, unfinished form, may nevertheless be finished, as finished as they can be, by his standards — "let fracture be." As various remarks in his notebooks indicate, Terry was drawn to the view, apparently common among contemporary French writers, that the "work" (finished, closed, classical) should be replaced by the "text" (open, infinitely interpretable, fluid).********** "Draft" may sometimes be a good word for "text" in this sense.

Now let me deal with the two things that at first quickly led me to conclude that this poem could not possibly have been meant as a will. First, of course, is the verse form itself; let me put off discussing that until I deal with the second feature, the apparently ironic sense of the thing. The most striking indication of this to me was the title, "Conning McGarr"; but ironic intent seems equally obvious from the poem's express challenge to me to try and carry out the principles of interpretation I had supported in my debates with Terry over the years. The message seemed to be the mocking one that if I tried to meet this challenge, I would inevitably fail, thus giving final, posthumous victory to Terry. The only other reading would be that Terry had somehow come to believe that I was right, that objective interpretation was a realistic possibility, a matter of finding "intent in words," and that he was conceding this to me and asking me to do, on his behalf, what he had always insisted couldn't be done.

The second reading seemed to me an impossible one. The poem is dated several months before Terry's sudden death, and in our discussions after that date there had been no indication of any change in Terry's position, or any slackening in the vigor with which he opposed me. Thus, the indication in the poem that this was my best chance to implement my theory, and that if I did so I would close our debate "conformant to" my "sober principles," seemed to be meant as a jab at me, one presupposing the impossibility of the task.

But I now see how the ironic reading ignores the language of the poem. The instructions are entirely serious in tone. There is no indication of irony (apart from the affectionate irony of line 25, and

---

********** Professor McGarr informs me that the Conn notebooks refer to R. Barthes, *From Work to Text*, in IMAGE-MUSIC-TEXT 155 (1977).

the ironically casual disposition of Terry's largely nonexistent material wealth, in lines 2-3). Read it: is its tone not one of challenge and serious entreaty? I should not have needed the jolt of Janet's threat to see this; I only needed to read, carefully, with open mind and heart. Consider what was at stake here from Terry's point of view. He could be a funny man, sometimes oddly and inappropriately so (as in the silly title he jokingly gave his autobiography), but he was deadly serious about his ideas and his writing. Think of the long hours he slaved to build this "hoard." He and Janet never began divorce proceedings; he knew she was legally his wife and might still be when he died. He knew how she felt about him, and about his later work. Is it likely that he meant to leave the disposition of his papers to her unguided mercies? And who is more suited than I to be the natural editor of his work — no self-praise intended, only the reminder that he talked about his ideas more with me than with everyone else put together?

To accept this reading, must I assume that in his will Terry is somehow recanting his long held position about interpretation? The last several hours of reading and recollection have brought me to a kind of revelation on this point. As I read the long precatory part of the poem, it was as if I could hear myself talking, but in Terry's voice. The views are recognizably mine. He distinguishes (lines 13-16) between regarding texts as mere raw material for the interpreter's untrammeled creativity, and seeing them as the determinate expression of the author's intent through the public conventions of language — "mind's fixed intercept of lexicon." He then attributes the latter position to me in my own plainer speech (lines 17-18), and illustrates a point I often made in argument with him: that theories of the impossibility of objective interpretation (such as I have always attributed to Terry) are likely to have their genesis in the fact that in many interesting cases (Terry's will and his papers providing one) correct reading is very difficult. But these cases in which interpretation is difficult are to be contrasted with the easy ones — as when someone says "pass the salt" in an ordinary dinner table situation — by the presence of various identifiable factors. I was never able to summarize these factors quite as concisely as Terry has in the last lines of the poem: "Words mean. I mean. You, reading, want. . . ." To put it prosaically, there is, first, the problem of possible conflict between meaning as determined by public conventions of language, and meaning as determined by speaker's intent; and there is, second, the problem of distortions introduced by the interests of the reader or interpreter. Yet these are sources of difficulty — "traps" — not guarantors of impossibility.

How is this restatement of my views to be explained, if not as irony on the one hand, or (implausibly) as surrender on Terry's part to me on the other? The answer has come to me in reflection upon one strand of Terry's position, a strand he constantly reiterated to me, but which I have never before really come to terms with. Terry always resisted my describing our debate as one between an "objective" and a "subjective" theory of interpretation. He would say that these terms were familiar ways of talking about our differences, but they brought along a lot of metaphysical freight he didn't want to carry. (He would then quickly get too deep for me.)

More illuminating to me now is what Terry would say when I raised my favorite argument, which I got from the literary theorist Hirsch. People who deny that utterances have an objective meaning that is "in" them to be discovered by the interpreter are just as vehement as anyone else about condemning their critics for "misreading" or "misinterpreting" their writings — thus contradicting themselves. When I made this argument, Terry would say "there you go, misinterpreting me again" — and when I asked for something more than this cute paradox, he said things I never understood. Or when I understood him, as when he talked of words as counters and of statements as moves in a game, it seemed to me he was just talking about the need to take context into account in determining the speaker's or author's intent — something I had never denied. He got me to read Derrida on "inhabiting the structures we deconstruct." But to me, all of that was just sophism designed to allow the half-hearted skeptic to say something and then hedge: "I don't really mean what I say." Terry denied this, saying Derrida was not a "giggler" (his word for people who take skeptical positions, giggle in self-congratulation, and go on as before). Well, if these words were not meant simply as a hedge, were they not then just dressed-up public relations advice — to get the swing voters you have to speak their lingo? In a way that was true, Terry once said, but he added "we have met the swing voters and they are us." More cleverness without real answers, from my perspective.

Another aid he called in to try to explain things to me was Borges' story "Pierre Menard." He said: "when you say someone is misinterpreting, you speak as Cervantes; when I say it, I speak as Pierre Menard." I read the story, thought it clever but baffling, and still didn't grasp his point; it seemed that Borges, too, was talking about saying something in scare-quotes, and anyway, wasn't Pierre Menard an ironist? Yet Terry and his follow subjectivists could complain angrily and quite without irony that they were being misinterpreted.

Now, just in the last few hours, I believe that I finally understand what Terry meant. He could protest against misinterpretation, seriously and angrily — of course he could; I have heard him do it many times. How could anyone live in our world, constituted of language as it is, and *not* talk in these terms? In just the same way, he could ask me, seriously and sincerely, to interpret his words accurately, regarding them as "mind's fixed intercept of lexicon."

At the same time, he could protest against my views, which I always phrased in terms of the possibility of this very kind of interpretation. What he was arguing to me through our long afternoon debates was that these rhetorical structures, of "objective interpretation" or whatever, were by now wholly problematical, that I could no longer just assume their viability. On the other hand, he would not claim that these very rhetorical structures — the same ones that he used in his will — no longer existed, or could simply be bypassed or ignored. Queer dying anachronistic structures that they were, they remained the only ones around. He hoped some day they would be replaced, but that would be a historical and collective achievement, not the gesture or act of some individual like himself. He always resisted the notion that individuals could just opt out of cultural forms, imagining themselves to exist as individuals apart from their culture — he used to say that that was the great Protestant fallacy.

I remember him telling me that he and Janet had been married by an Anglo-Catholic Episcopal minister in a religious ceremony, though he was a renegade Catholic and she was an unbelieving Jew. None of the available forms really fitted their case; they thought the purely civil forms conveyed the wrong sense of marriage. He said he still thought of it more as a sacrament than as a legal status or contract. Of course he would have argued against all the minister's religious doctrines, just as he argued with what I said about interpretation. I think I am his minister in this case, and he is an unbeliever asking me to serve him in God's name. There are many ironies in such an invocation, but not the kind of self-contradiction that cancels the message and renders the whole thing a mockery.

Peter, reading back over these paragraphs I despair at how opaque they must seem. Terry, a master of language, had years to make this point to me, an intent listener, and yet I never got it until now. I will have to struggle hard in the days and years to come to make myself clearer. Terry could accept pretty insouciantly that being understood is not a matter of effort, good will, or skill in explaining; people either get points or they don't. I can't accept that; what can be said can be said clearly — that is the Tao of

George. But I see that I cannot now clearly explain "McGarr's epiphany" to you — what will I ever do if I have to explain this to a judge?

But I must continue and finish. What about the title "Conning McGarr"? What can that mean except that Terry is putting one over on me? The answer is not difficult to find, especially when I read a passage by the poet Yvor Winters that Terry copied into one of his notebooks: "Poetry is a medium by means of which one mind may to a greater or lesser extent take possession of another, almost in the sense in which the term *possession* is used in demonology." Terry wanted to use the poem to get his view across to me finally and forcibly, so that I could truly understand him in order to act for him; thus, "Conning McGarr." Argument alone had not worked; maybe poetry could do the job. And there, too, is the answer to the last interpretive objection: Why would he use verse to make a final disposition of his legacy? The answer is that he wanted to possess me, as I suppose every testator who gives other than mechanical instructions would like to possess his executor, and he thought verse the medium best suited to the task.

In truth, Terry's poem could not do what he wanted it to do, not on its own. I'm not an experienced reader of poetry, but I imagine those who are will find it somewhat prosaic, somewhat lacking in possessory magic. It does speak very clearly to me now, but only after the shock administered by Janet's threat. As a poem, it probably is a bit too lawyerly, a little professorial; but on the other hand, why not — one law professor talking to another?

IV

Dear Peter,

Thank you truly for the heartfelt words of thanks; they mean a lot to me. Thank you too for the words of concern. I *have* been working long hours on this business. But it has never seemed a chore, only a fascinating challenge. As you know, I've always worked long hours, and especially so in recent months with Benjamin at college and Susan away in the hospital. It's good therapy, among its other rewards.

Peter, thank you too for your forebearance in the face of "McGarr's epiphany." When you say that you respect and accept what I decide though you do not fully understand what I say, your honesty makes your thoughtfulness all the more welcome. I do remain convinced that Terry meant the poem to be his last will and testament. It is true that the exalted feeling of revelation I recorded in writing to you during that long night in his office has faded a little in the light of common day — as I suppose is inevitable. I guess I would describe its residue as a subtle change in my attitude, a difference of degree in the way I look at the questions Terry and I debated: a more pragmatic view of language, a stronger sense of its rhetorical dimension, an enhanced suspicion of Platonic meanings, a feeling that talk about finding "intent in words" states a dilemma rather than a goal in many cases. But these theoretical matters should be reserved for more extensive treatment in calmer times.

Let me proceed in our now-established mode: me writing, for our future reference, some things you already know. When I first told Janet I had decided that it *was* Terry's will — the first morning after my "tower experience" — she was angry and incredulous. "He really did con you." She insisted that she would go to court, contest the will; the money wouldn't matter to her even if there were any, but she would fight to have "that self-indulgent garbage" destroyed. She would also pursue her community property claims on the papers.

My inspiration at this point was to urge her to read something of Terry's other than the painful chapters in the autobiography. At first she just raged: when she wanted to read literature or philosophy she knew where to go for it, and it wasn't to a dilettante law professor fleeing from his mid-life crisis. Terry was — the same litany — a liar and a coward. None of us knew him as she did. And so on.

But when I narrowed my urgings to get her to read his legal writings, to my surprise she agreed. It turned out the two draft articles had been a sore point with her; he had always refused to show them to her claiming they "weren't him." I had photocopies made for her to take home, so she wouldn't have to stay in his office to read.

The next day, she had changed her tone considerably. She thought the articles were good; they reminded her of a Terry she had forgotten. She conceded that, if she had the papers in her charge, she would want the legal writings published, if possible, to let people know that there had once been a "real Terry Conn." It turns out that she had even come to doubt that he had ever written *anything*; she wasn't here when he got tenure. She thinks of him as a dreadful liar, and tended to distrust anything he said.

I gave her my familiar (to you) pitch on the "lying." In my experience, Terry never lied to get a concrete benefit for himself, never made up things that put him in a better light. I call him a confabulator; he would imagine a story to illustrate a point of his or challenge someone else's, but would lose control over its origin in his imagination, and would claim it really happened. When I put that to Janet, she admitted that was usually how it was, but said that he also lied about his drinking, "like all drinkers." She said a further interesting thing: the drinking had been worse before he started his new line of work seven years ago, though (as you and I know) it by no means stopped afterwards.

Janet and I talked a long time that day, not just about the papers but about Terry generally. We broke off with her still talking about having the "literary" writing destroyed, but saying it with much less conviction. The next night we went out to dinner and had another long talk, the upshot of which was that she would not object to publication of anything Terry wrote except the passages mentioning her in what she calls "his memoirs"; she did not want these published in her lifetime. If she could get a binding agreement to this effect, she would not contest the will.

I tried to press her further, pointing out that the passages put her basically in a good light, but she said she would feel violated if that material came out in print. It was hard enough for her to agree to their being preserved and possibly published after she died. But she had decided that it was superstitious to concern herself with what happened then; even if she ever had any children, she wouldn't object if they saw it — she just could not stand it for herself. In any case, she thinks I greatly overrate the likely interest in the "memoirs," and doesn't suppose there is any likelihood that there will be readers or a publisher for them after she dies, even if there is now — which she also doubts.

Peter, how can I insist on more than this from Janet? She has been honest and fair, and she has been much more open minded than I expected. (It has been hard for us to be in the position of bargaining adversaries, rather than as — what I feel we are — old friends renewing a relationship that had lapsed by an unhappy accident.)

What I propose to offer her is this agreement: She will promise not to oppose the will, and I will give her a veto over publication of the passages mentioning her, during her lifetime. The problem with this, of course, is the possible conflict with Terry's instructions. To me, there are two alternatives; keep the whole autobiography suppressed as long as she exercises her veto, or edit it to excise, temporarily, the passages mentioning her, for publication now. My own inclination would be to do the latter, on the grounds that now is "due time." On the other hand, I recognize the will's strictures against publication of any but complete works; and I would never argue that the autobiography minus the Janet passages was "complete." In a sense, what it comes down to is a choice of interpretive presumptions. Does the will absolutely prohibit publication of any but complete works? Or is this a principle to be accommodated with the principle of timely publication, at least in the special case of a work that one day will be available in complete form?

Of course I realize that these are not the only two alternatives. I *could* simply try to get the will probated and take Janet on, and if I won, the whole autobiography could be published now. (I should say I am inclined to think that though the book in a sense "breaks off," this is a case of "fracture" rather than one of "incompleteness" in the terms of the will.)

If I pressed the fight with Janet, I might win, but I could easily lose; I have not forgotten that my own first reaction was that it was crazy to think this poem could be a will. I see now that I was wrong, and maybe I could convince a judge (or a jury?), but maybe I couldn't. If I lost, the whole corpus would pass to Janet by intestacy. I do believe that in that case she would publish the legal writings, but after the bitterness of litigation, who knows what attitude she would take toward the literary writings? Her destroying or completely suppressing them is not out of the question.

Whether I can properly accept a compromise really turns on what the dominant intent of the will is: is it to get at least some of Terry's work out into the world, or is it to make sure that only finished work is seen? And I cannot put aside, even from the point of view of Terry's intent, the gruesome picture of Janet and me snarling over his remains in court.

There is one further consideration that cuts in favor of entering into a compromise with Janet now. If she has the security of a legal veto over the passages that bother her, I believe she might eventually come to see that publishing them would do her no harm. As long as she and I are talking to one another, there is a decent chance that her thoughts will keep moving in this direction; once we are adversaries in litigation though, that is unlikely. If I can involve Janet to some degree as a collaborator in the work of editing Terry's papers, perhaps her sense of him as only a source of pain will lessen; perhaps she will even come to care that he be presented to the world in his best light.

I mention this because, in a way, this process has already begun in the course of our talks. To get off the painful subject of the autobiography, I described to her some of my general problems in applying the will to the papers. What should I do with the fact that all of them are marked "draft"; and that none of them have clear-cut endings in the usual sense? I cannot simply mechanically invoke "let fracture be" to publish everything Terry wrote; *he* obviously thought there were choices to be made between finished and unfinished works. I am not to be cowed by "the insistent literate" to push works he would have regarded as "unfinished" into the world. Obviously I need (what I have already mentioned) an overall presumption in favor of publication on the one hand or suppression on the other.

During this conversation, Janet pointed out to me something that I had not noticed. You recall the scribbled note below the poem: "*Cal. Prob. Code Ann. 53*, 102(1)." In researching that note, I had paid little attention to section 102, startled as I was by section 53. Later I made some reference to section 102, which does state a presumption in favor of "that mode of interpretation which will prevent a total intestacy." Janet, the careful tax lawyer, asked me about the reference of the parenthesized "(1)": did the section have subsections?

This got me to take another look at section 102. There are no numbered subsections in it; it is made up of a single sentence, with two clauses divided by a semicolon, the *second* of which is the presumption against intestacy I quoted earlier. Perhaps "102(1)" was meant to refer specifically to the *first* clause, which reads: "The words of a will are to receive an interpretation which will give to every expression some effect, rather than one which will render any of the expressions inoperative."

What could Terry have meant by stressing this boilerplate interpretive maxim? It is certainly a principle of literary criticism that in a poem every word is supposed to count. So I went back over the text again, focusing on phrases I had passed over as obscure, or as mere rhetorical or rhythmic filler. There are a number of phrases whose full import escape me; for example, "plain as can be" in line 6. But the one phrase that had struck me before and still struck me as completely enigmatic was the address to me as "my Scottish breadman" in line 11. "Scottish," sure, but what is "breadman" about?

In our next talk, I described to Janet the line of thought her suggestion had triggered. Did she make anything of the "breadman" reference? We batted it around for a few minutes, but couldn't come up with much beyond an implication of homely simplicity in "bread." Then we got back to what by then we were calling our "settlement conference." Only a few minutes of that had gone by when she suddenly interrupted me to ask, "Max Brod?" When I asked her what she meant, she said, "The baker. Brod sounds like German for bread. He is calling you his Scottish Max Brod. Didn't Kafka leave his writings with Brod, and tell him to destroy them, but he didn't?"

Well, it is a little far-fetched, but I haven't been able to give a better sense to the word "breadman." Terry was a great reader of Kafka, and I would guess he knew the Max Brod story. It's the only plausible reading I've got for "breadman," and Terry has told me to find a reading for every word. If he did have Brod in mind, I would read the phrase as suggesting to me the same basic presumption in favor of publication that Brod exercised. Terry might have obliquely suggested such a presumption rather than explicitly stating it to create some doubt in my mind, and prevent me from running wild with it. After all, a reference to Brod *could* be a caution rather than a license, though the placement and tone suggest otherwise.

Janet says I am being much too finicky about this. She sees Terry as having been driven by two contradictory urges: One, a terrible fear of facing judgment (possibly augmented by some neurotic association between finishing work, publishing, and dying), which prevented him from submitting anything for publication during his lifetime; but second, a powerful egotism that could only be satisfied by the conspicuous publication of every word he ever uttered. She sees the poem, and to her it is just a poem, as the completely ambivalent expression of these incompatible urges, not as a rational scheme for mediating or compromising them.

She puts great weight on the appeal he makes to *my* interests in lines 23-31. Terry there recognized that he would be dead and gone when the poem was read, and Janet sees him as surrendering the final word to me — me not as his literal legal executor, but as the personification of his readership. This means that I should use his writings for my own purposes, in the way readers always have the last word in their dialogues with writers. Together with the earlier reference to Max Brod, she thinks that that passage expresses, consciously or unconsciously, the side of him that gives himself into the hands of his future readers hoping that they will make him into another Kafka, whose every surviving word will be read — while he can retain the fastidious modesty of a writer who never submitted a word for publication.

I can't see it that way myself. Perhaps if it were just a poem, that would be the most interesting reading, and for that reason, in some sense, the right reading. As a poet, Terry meant to be interesting. But to me, it is more than a poem; it is Terry's will. We owe him something more than the most interesting reading. I can't "mean away" his "say" in the name of intriguing and admittedly plausible suspicions about his unconscious wishes, or projections from his sense of aesthetic value. I have to stick closer to the words.

The only way to treat the will as a consistent set of instructions is to see it as creating a complex agency relation, McGarr Conned. Terry was addressing *me*, George McGarr, "grave George," the man of the "sober principles," the somewhat overconscientious "conscience of [his] afternoons." At the same time, he did want me to grasp his way of seeing things better than I had while he was alive; that was why he tried to possess me; that is the point of the title "Conning McGarr." But he didn't want me to *become* him (Pierre Menard decided not to *become* Cervantes). If I were to identify fully with him and his intentions, it would necessarily be with his limitations; then, neurotically paralyzed like him, I would never publish any of his work. He wanted me to "fuse my horizons" with his, not to narrow my own.

Even if Terry was in some sense the contradictory mess of a modern man Janet says he was, he wanted to be treated as better and more coherent, and he had a right to be so treated. I think the California [*236] Probate Code gives me my marching orders, in a provision Terry didn't cite, section 103 — a profound moral state-ment, if its word "will" is expanded beyond its technical legal sense: "All the parts of a will are to be construed in relation to each other, and so as, if possible, to form one consistent whole. . . ."

What do you think of all this?

George

Discussion Topics

1. Students occasionally check whether Terry Conn's posthumous cor-pus remains unpublished. You may be well advised not to spend much time on this yourself. Terry Conn and McGarr are fictional characters. Even though the article appeared in a law review, it is essentially a story but one designed to raise important issues about interpretation.

2. Consider the problem of author's intent. Conn was nothing if not complex. Therefore, it is probably a mistake to impose a simple either/or set of intentions: either he wanted it to be a will or he wanted it to be an exercise in hermeneutics. We do in fact know that his life was dominated by ambivalence about his writings. He saved them but did not publish them. It is reasonable that this ambivalence may survive his very life and may be foisted on McGarr. Thus, we may consider the possibility that he saw the document *both* as a goad for further hermeneutic reflection and, quite possibly, as a will that (if McGarr concluded accordingly) might finally result in his work seeing the light of day.

3. McGarr's reaction to Janet's intention to dispose of the writings is important. But there are at least two ways of looking at it. A simple way is to say that, because of Janet's threat, he decided to ride rough-shod over the nuances of interpretation and save the work at all cost. A more complex way is to say that this crisis forced him to think more deeply about the relevance of interpretation and consider new possibilities. The fact that the document can, with repeated readings, seem very much like a will supports the more complex interpretation.

4. The actual debate between McGarr and Conn is a vital part of the article. It is an attempt to capture the fundamental debate between scholars about judicial interpretation of controversial parts of the Constitution, a debate that I anticipated in my introductory comments above. One side argues that meaning is nothing but author's meaning and that the job of interpretation is always to determine the intentions the author had in creating the text. Proponents of this view rebut objections about accessibility and decisiveness (or relevance). McGarr is presented as a strong proponent of this view, advocating direct access to the author as the only appropriate means of interpretation. (Among constitutional scholars, this view is called *originalism* or *interpretivism*.)

On the other side of the debate are those who take problems of access and decisiveness seriously and concede the hermeneuticist's argument, that the interpreter and her perspective are irreducibly part of the process. Conn, of course, held this view.

Throughout the essay there are elusive phrases and metaphors that echo the terms of the debate. Here are some of them. Keep in mind that they bring together a lot of complex philosophy in an abstract and elliptical way.

a. McGarr insists that his method is objective and that Conn's is inexcusably subjective. Conn insists that interpretation is inevitably both objective and subjective and that it would be best to get beyond that (unhelpful) terminology.

b. Conn, who is not talking in religious doctrinal terms, refers to McGarr as a Protestant and himself as a Catholic. What he seems to mean is that the Protestant thinks he does not need the intermediate transmission of history and culture to be in touch with God but can do so directly—just as the judge can ostensibly be in touch with the aims of founders. The Catholic way of thinking inevitably is mindful of transmission through a historical institution, whether it is the Church or the precedents of the Supreme Court.

c. By the same token, Conn alludes to the short story by the Argentinian writer, Jorge Luis Borges, "Pierre Menard." In the story, Menard supposed that he could go back in time and occupy the mind of Cervantes, writing *Don Quixote* in exactly the way the original author did. Borges' point, and Conn's, is that any reader or interpreter is grounded in his own time and place. The attempt to occupy the mind and creative voice of someone in a different time, place, or culture is doomed and inevitably produces a pastiche.

d. Conn quotes the French philosopher, Jacques Derrida, saying "we inhabit the structures that we deconstruct." This statement is elusive. But it seems to pick up an important truth about anyone who is trying to do interpretation (as a judge or any reader must inevitably do) and who is also asking questions about the *nature* of interpretation. To inhabit a structure is to interpret, and we all do so by inhabiting a particular time and place in human history as well as a particular personal history. That's true of all of us. But some of us feel called upon to describe the process of interpretation and to point out our "situatedness" in the way that hermeneutic theory does indeed point it out. This description (or reflection on the nature of the process) is what Derrida seems to mean by "deconstructing."

Deeper into Hermeneutics: Notes for Further Reading

Three further aspects of hermeneutics will complete a preliminary introduction. The influence of this way of thinking, namely an emphasis on the particular experience and tools that each reader brings to the job of interpretation, has been familiar for quite a while in many areas of study. For most of the twentieth century, not only literary studies but also politics, history, anthropology, and sociology have talked about the unique perspective of each individual, whether as an actor or observer. This bundle of ideas has been a latecomer to the field of legal interpretation.

(1) Some of the leading scholars of constitutional law who have been influenced by hermeneutics give the impression that their insights are revolutionary and subversive. In one of the earliest (1982) and most influential articles in the field, Professor Sanford Levinson ascribes to Robert Coover, who draws implications from the philosopher Nietzsche, the view that "it is up to us, the living, to decide for our own reasons what we wish the Constitution to mean." He then observes that he has "increasingly found it impossible to imagine any other way of making sense of our own constitutional universe." In other words, he has "less and less confidence that [it] is a sensible enterprise" to guide students through a search for "principles and methods of correct [constitutional] interpretation."

These insights require some qualification. If by "principles and methods of correct interpretation" Levinson is referring to principles that will be accepted by all judges, yielding objective answers to new and hard questions, that quest has to be Quixotic. But if he means that judges who disagree (and know that they are likely to continue to disagree) are being misguided or foolish when they attempt to come up with principles and methods that, in the structure they "inhabit," *seem* to them correct, then he is giving up too easily on what remains a "sensible enterprise."

Levinson is much influenced by the work of Professor Stanley Fish, who has drawn lessons from his extensive work in English literature and applied them to law. Many of Fish's essays are collected in a rich and compelling book called *Doing What Comes Naturally*. Fish stresses that there is no clear distinction between discovering the answer to a legal question (or other interpretative question) and inventing or creating that answer. His notion is that, within the parameters defined by our time and place in culture, we re-appropriate the law (and other aspects of culture) as unique individuals. This is, we have seen, a basic tenet of the methods of hermeneutics. But it must not be forgotten how constrained the process of re-appropriation or re-invention can be. How much leeway do we have in interpreting the minimal constitutional age of presidents? We have more leeway, to be sure, in construing "due process" but we are still the hostages of the traditions we inherit.

(2) In studying law and literature, one has a tendency to elide the differences between the two kinds of interpretive tasks. The differences matter. A judge has an institutional role and derives from it a kind of authority and power that a literary interpreter never has. Fortunes, well-being, and even lives often depend on what a judge decides. Because of this, a judge's decision must have finality. Even if it can be faulted on moral or logical grounds, it still becomes the official decision and is enforced. In time, it may be changed, but for the time being it *is* law.

The interpretation of literature is not an institution in the same sense. Uncertainty and disagreement can and will persist indefinitely. There is no official interpretation of *Macbeth* or *Finnegan's Wake*. The economic and social development of the country do not depend on the existence of official answers to literary questions.

As a result, there are reasons why a judge may need to take comfort in the ideal of an objective method of decision and may wish to regard her personal background and ways of thinking as irrelevant to her job. But, if the insights of hermeneutics are correct, her attempts to "deconstruct the structures she inhabits," to get outside the interpretive frame that she carries with her, will always be incomplete. That's not the same thing as saying they will be ineffective or irrelevant. The better she knows herself, the more experiences and attitudes she brings to consciousness and self-awareness, the better judge she is likely to be.

(3) The study of hermeneutics has, especially outside the U.S., been dominated by two German philosophers, Hans-Georg Gadamer and Jürgen Habermas. Their work is challenging, but the essential elements are clear. Gadamer addresses directly the problem of relativity or subjectivity. We saw above that this problem leads Levinson to pessimism about principles and methods. Fish, in turn, embraces relativity when he talks about each interpreter's reinventions. But for Gadamer, the conscientious judge will never lose sight of the fact that he is part of a tradition of interpretation and owes both to his predecessors and to his contemporaries a duty to take the tradition seriously, to wrestle with the relevant judgments of those who have gone before. But there are no guarantees about

what he will conclude. He may decide that important parts of the tradition are indefensible. Thus, Gadamer's reliance on tradition is not inherently conservative.

Habermas proposes a different answer to the question of relativity and subjectivity. For him, the judge's job is not complete when she reinvents the constitution with the satisfaction of having solved a problem. The next step is for her to engage in a hypothetical dialogue, an ideal conversation, with those who would solve the problem differently. She must come up with arguments that effectively rebut these alternative views. To be sure, this exercise is within the judge's own thoughts. Again there are no guarantees and no expectation that different judges' views will ultimately coalesce. But Habermas, like Gadamer, puts all this forward not to solve the "problem" of interpretation but to shed light on the ways that we use and sometimes take for granted.

ꞔ Further Reading

Because interpretation has been the main preoccupation of many writers and scholars in the law and literature movement, any short bibliographic note can merely skim the surface of this corpus of works. The omission of many influential and important writings is inevitable.

(1) At the end of this chapter, I refer to the influence of two German scholars of hermeneutics, Hans-Georg Gadamer and Jürgen Habermas. Gadamer's most comprehensive work is *Truth and Method* (1975, originally published in German in 1960). A collection of papers and articles, *Philosophical Hermeneutics* (1976), is accessible and stimulating. *The Cambridge Companion to Gadamer*, edited by Robert J. Dostal, is an illuminating collection of analyses and critiques. Habermas' most influential work is probably *Between Facts and Norms: Contributions to a Discourse Theory of Law and Democracy* (1996; originally published in German in 1992). Two highly influential earlier books by Habermas are *Theory and Practice* (1973, originally published in German in 1971) and *Knowledge and Human Interests* (1971, originally published in German in 1968).

(2) The study of interpretation and the critique of objectivity has always been an important theme of the critical legal studies movement in American jurisprudence. Many of the best original articles in the CLS movement appeared in the January 1984 issue (volume 36, number 1 and 2) of *Stanford Law Review*. One the most influential founding member of CLS, Duncan Kennedy, published *A Critique of Adjudication (fin de siècle)* in 1997.

(3) Various legal philosophers in the analytical linguistic philosophy movement have focused on interpretation. Andrei Marmor's *Interpretation and Legal Theory* (1992) is a clear and systematic analysis of interpretation

and the role it plays in the work of such philosophers as H.L.A. Hart, Joseph Raz, and Ronald Dworkin. In 1995, Marmor edited *Law and Interpretation: Essays in Legal Philosophy*, a representative collection of the views on interpretation of many legal theorists in the analytical tradition. Also relevant and notable are Frederick Schauer's *Playing by the Rules* (1991) and Brian Bix's *Law, Language, and Legal Determinacy* (1993).

(4) Several other somewhat eclectic collections of articles are relevant to the issues in this chapter. *Legal Hermeneutics: History, Theory, and Practice*, edited by Gregory Leyh, appeared in 1992. Two law review symposia with several interesting articles are the April 1995 issue (volume 16) of *Cardozo Law Review* and the 2000 Symposium on Philosophical Hermeneutics and Critical Legal Theory (volume 76) of *Chicago-Kent Law Review*.

SEVEN

The Law of Literature

Cultural products are a social asset. The music, art, and literature of a society shape and reflect its values and give voice to common interests. No society has ever existed without culture, and a flourishing and growing society is often marked by a vibrant culture.

Individual cultural products have a dialectical relationship to society's values. Culture and values are always changing and evolving; there is always an avant garde. This means that almost invariably one segment of society will be culturally conservative, will enjoy and cherish the status quo and fear change. Another segment will challenge the prevailing norms and pleasures. So culture wars are as common as culture itself. The nature of art is to be inventive; the nature of many audiences is to rest content with what is familiar and therefore safe. Artists who do nothing but reproduce works that are familiar and expected in some sense betray their role.

The role of government with regard to art is therefore complex and much debated. On one hand, it is generally accepted in Western cultures that free expression is itself a positive value. It is both a means and an end, a means to the discovery of new ideas and methods and an end insofar as spontaneous expression is the mark of an autonomous person. On the other hand, ideas and methods can be politically unsettling and even subversive. A free society is defined by its critics as much as by its supporters; it must not only tolerate but encourage debate even when the criticisms, if carried to their conclusion, can be destabilizing.

This apparent paradox is often called the liberal dilemma. The dilemma is fairly transparent. A liberal government that values freedom and toleration must tolerate the expressions of those who are intolerant, must tolerate those who advocate values and systems that would put an end to freedom and toleration. If one believes that citizens understand and cherish equal freedom as a permanent but vulnerable social value, then one also believes that the challenge of the intolerant can be met. But if one is more pessimistic about human nature, then one sees liberal government as perpetually under siege and in jeopardy.

The constitutional response to this predicament in the U.S. has been, for the most part, to interpret the first amendment, which guarantees free expression, expansively. Repeatedly, courts and observers have affirmed their conviction that our society can meet and withstand challenges from within, that unpopular and offensive ideas have as much right to be expressed as any other kind. This view, sometimes called an "absolutist" view of the first amendment, has proponents on both ends of the political spectrum. On what is called "the right," libertarians argue that government should interfere as little as possible in the lives of persons regardless of their opinions. On the left, liberals argue that equality is likely to be achieved only if those who think of themselves as disadvantaged and weak can make their sometimes unpopular and even revolutionary views heard.

By the same token, the absolutist view of the first amendment is challenged by theorists across the political divide. Conservative writers fear that new ideas will unsettle morality, family values, or established economic and social patterns. In the interest of the status quo (or of restoring the status quo of fifty or a hundred years ago), they argue for censorship of some ideas. By the same token, writers on the political left sometimes argue that the value of free expression has been exaggerated as other interests and rights have been compromised. Some feminists and writers on race and ethnicity argue that when ideas are potentially a tool for discrimination or oppression, they should be suppressed.

Debates about the role of our government vis-à-vis free expression begin with the first amendment, but they do not end there. Courts do indeed define the scope of the first amendment, and thus they put some instances of expression outside the protected realm. But even within the protected realm, government has the right to decide how publicly enabled resources can be used. For users of the airwaves, the government can regulate content as long as it does so in a non-discriminatory way. Thus, the Federal Communications Commission (FCC) and other agencies have used their power to regulate the availability of television and radio stations to minority groups and recently to enforce rules about what they call "decency."

Government affects culture by using carrots as well as sticks. It not only tells writers and other culture-creators what they cannot do (at the risk of being sanctioned), but it also supports some of them as creators. The U.S. has traditionally been less engaged than other countries in supporting artists and writers; every European country, for example, gives over a much higher percentage of its budget to the arts than the U.S. ever has.

The European tradition, of course, predates the rise of modern states. The major supporters of artists and writers in medieval and renaissance Europe were the royal courts and local rulers.

Even the modest amount of support that the states and federal government give to the arts has long been controversial. Some critics see subsidizing the arts as a way for government to bias the marketplace of ideas, to promulgate some ideas in preference to others. Others question whether there are any neutral criteria of excellence or importance that grant-givers can use. Underlying these questions is the distinction between the kind of art and culture that most benefits society and the kind that the marketplace most readily supports. Is this a real and troublesome distinction? If so, does government have a role in identifying and supporting the first kind of art?

The three sections of this chapter address these issues. This first section discusses the scope of the first amendment as interpreted in case law. It also examines briefly other legal tools for regulating expression. The second section looks at the theory of the first amendment, controversies about its purposes, justification, and scope, and proposals for reform. The final section considers the government's role in affecting culture by creating incentives and channeling support.

Free Speech, Decency, and Obscenity

The constitutional guarantee of free expression in the first amendment has many justifications, but two of them predominate in most discussions. The first justification is political and stresses the importance of a marketplace of ideas. An important element of democratic theory is that persons as citizens should not only be able to choose their political representatives, but also that they should be able to express effectively their views about public issues. The theory rests on the pseudo-Darwinian assumption that when ideas about government compete in the market, the best ideas will trump other ideas; the fittest ideas will survive. Moreover, the theory claims that no other method is likely to uncover the best ideas, those ideas that will produce the best situation for the greatest number of persons. In essence, the theory, which dates from the eighteenth century, is a response to absolutist and arbitrary rule by monarchs and despots.

The second justification for the first amendment makes no such assumption about the triumph of better ideas. It is a psychological rather than a political claim. It holds that a fully realized or complete life involves not merely the opportunity to think for oneself and arrive at autonomous conclusions, but also the opportunity to express those thoughts and preferences. Living well and freely is possible only when the expression of ideas is unconstrained. This second justification is consistent, of course, with the possibility that bad, harmful, illogical, and coercive ideas may gain as much currency as good, beneficent, and rational ideas. As a private citizen, one may have to live in a community in which prejudice and narrow-mindedness are common. But the public role of government is to insure that the opportunity for expression of all ideas remains effective.

The second justification has strengths and limitations. Its strength lies in its realism. The on-going two-hundred year experiment of our Constitution has provided conflicting evidence of the success, in the "marketplace" of good ideas. There are certainly grounds for skepticism. We will see later in this chapter warnings that those with economic and political power have an unfair opportunity to get their ideas, proposals, and agendas accepted. The argument is that ideas succeed because of the resources behind them not because of their inherent good sense. But if the second justification recognizes the pitfalls of the free market metaphor, it retains faith in the power of our constitutional system to rein in the intolerant, to limit social coercion to the private sphere and prevent it from infecting public policy.

In any event, the first amendment has consistently been interpreted as ruling out governmental censorship of ideas simply on the basis of their content. This does not mean, of course, that free expression has no limits at all. One cannot park a sound-truck in one's front yard and broadcast a political speech to the neighborhood at 3 A.M. One cannot falsely shout, "Fire!," in a crowded theater. The first is a public nuisance; the second presents a clear public danger. The law can impose what are called "time, place, and manner" restrictions on speech in the overall public interest. These rules make no reference to content and must be reasonable. A time, place, and manner constraint that says that you can express any political sentiment, but may do so only in the early morning while whispering inside a closet, would not pass muster.

Also, certain kinds of expression are crimes. Saying that a car is brand-new when it is in fact used is fraudulent. Agreeing with another person that one of you will commit theft or homicide is a criminal conspiracy to commit that crime. Prosecution of such crimes is consistent with the first amendment because, once again, it is not regulation of speech by its ideational content. Similarly, one may take legal action in many instances when a confidentiality agreement is breached.

If we look at the first amendment from the standpoint of this book, the intersection of law and literature, we can find more relevance in the second interpretation of the amendment's justification than the first. Much literary expression is not overtly political, not a vehicle for sharing ideas about how society should be organized and governed. But literature is fundamentally the expression of all kinds of ideas about human experience and human nature in the form of stories, parables, poems, memoirs, meditations, and so on. As such, it is an expression of the writer's freedom and imagination.

When law has had to assess the limits of permissible literary expression under the first amendment, it has almost always been concerned with sexuality. The prosecutions of the publication of James Joyce's *Ulysses,* Pauline Réage's *The Story of O,* and D.H. Lawrence's *Lady Chatterley's Lover* are landmark cases. The legal term for impermissible expressions of sex is obscenity. (Pornography is the non-legal term for works that are designed primarily to appeal to sexual interest. There is no reason to think that all pornography is obscene by the Supreme Court's criterion or that all works that fit the definition of obscenity are necessarily pornographic.)

The Court has struggled to develop a criterion for obscenity. The standard put forward in *Miller v. California* (413 U.S. 15 (1973)) remains the working standard for the current Court. *Miller* held that a state could prohibit selling or exhibiting materials "which, taken as a whole, appeal to the prurient interest in sex, which portray sexual conduct in a patently offensive way, and which, taken as a whole, do not have serious literary, artistic, political, or scientific value." The determination of the first part of the test, whether the work appeals to the prurient interest in sex, is to be made from the standpoint of "the average person, applying contemporary community standards."

The *Miller* test was put forward by a five-justice majority on a Court split five to four. The dissenters and later commentators have raised questions about the coherence and intelligibility of many aspects. Consider the following questions.

(1) Is there a difference between a prurient and a non-prurient interest in sex? If so, how can that be specified? Is the term wholly relative insofar as A's interest is prurient in B's eyes if and only if B finds it offensive? Is there an objective standard that does not make reference to offensiveness to individuals?

(2) Given the fragmentation of society and of individual communities, can we identify the views of the average person in a community? By the same token, can we go beyond an individual's opinions to generalize about "contemporary community standards"? Given the existence of communities defined not by geography but by interest and by communicative linkages (e.g., in cyberspace), can we locate and define the relevant community?

(3) Are we likely to find agreement on what counts as a "patently offensive" depiction of sexual conduct? There are segments of many communities that find interracial or same-sex sexual conduct patently offensive even if it amounts to little more than holding hands in public. There are segments of communities, perhaps refugees from strict Islamic cultures, that find the baring of a female leg or even an ankle to be sexually provocative and offensive. And there are many persons who find it hard to be offended by any kind of sexual conduct, however unusual, that does not involve coercion.

(4) How do we determine whether a work, taken as a whole, has artistic, literary, or political value? It can be argued that works that offend many groups have enormous political value because they prompt political discussions that focus on ultimate questions about freedom and imagination. Moreover, who determines what constitutes literary or artistic value? For more than two thousand years, since the time of Socrates and Plato, such value has inhered in the power of a work to lead one to rethink one's experiences and opinions. (Plato feared the revolutionary impact of literature for that reason.) In an age in which art galleries and museums as well as publishers and libraries are likely to feature eclectic collections of works, some of them controversial, it is hard to imagine how one finds a bright-line standard of value.

Notwithstanding its difficulties, the *Miller* test has remained the law. More recent cases have alluded to it and used it, but it has not been challenged or changed. For example, in *Reno v. ACLU* (521 U.S. 844 (1997)), the Supreme Court found the Communications Decency Act of 1996 unconstitutional due to overbreadth, noting that it criminalized speech that would be protected as legitimate and not obscene by the *Miller* criteria. The last twenty years have been a quiet period with regard to first amendment challenges and cases of ostensible content regulation.

The power of government to regulate speech extends beyond the scope of the first amendment when it is dealing with allocation of a limited resource, for example, the airwaves. Regulation of the airwaves, specifically radio and basic (non-cable) television, by the Federal Communication Commission (the FCC) is carried out in "the public interest." The FCC has the power to limit what is expressed through these media as long as the limitations serve the public interest and even when the excluded material is protected by the first amendment. In the past, the FCC has tried to allocate licenses for radio and TV stations to insure diversity, to bring about political balance and fairness in campaign advertising, and to implement what it understood to be family-friendly programming in the early evening. Most recently and controversially, it has tried to police decency standards with regard to exposure of body parts and use of salty language. Its concern with decency has not extended to limitations on violence or cruelty.

Some commentators contend that the FCC has been arbitrary in its policing of indecency on broadcast television and radio and that, since 2004, its efforts have been unduly influenced by a few powerful groups lobbying for severe sanctions against controversial content. The FCC rules are arguably inequitable given the fact that cable television and satellite radio have no such constraints and are limited only through the understandings of the first amendment. The broadcast media have become directly competitive with these newer modes of transmission, and therefore, it is argued, the same rules should apply. Moreover, the writers contend that the societal effects of so-called "indecent" broadcasts are poorly established.

Justifications and Critiques of Free Expression

We have seen the complexity of first amendment politics. Supporters of so-called "absolute" first amendment rights flourish on both sides of the political spectrum. Libertarians who argue for minimal government intervention in citizens' lives are usually situated on the political right. Liberals "who defend the familiar ACLU position that all ideas, however popular or unpopular, offensive or inoffensive they may be, have an equal claim to be expressed" are generally seen as being on the left. Their positions with regard to free expression coincide.

By the same token, proponents of more restricted coverage for the first amendment appear across the political spectrum. Self-styled conservatives claim that advocates for abortion rights, homosexual social arrangements, and recognition of equal rights for men and women undermine what they call family values. They argue that the advocacy of unorthodox political systems, sexual practices, and social arrangements destroys society's fabric. They question whether those who would change (what they regard as) society's values should have an equal right to persuade others to share their views.

On the political left, many writers raise similar questions. The "political correctness" movement advocates limiting, at least in certain contexts, kinds of expression that various groups might find offensive and distasteful. Often, educational institutions have become crucibles for these disagreements. On one hand, it is said that if free expression and robust debate are to flourish anywhere, they should be pursued in schools and universities because they are essential to effective learning. On the other hand, it is said in rebuttal that students are a captive audience, that they cannot easily escape being an audience for others, and that therefore speakers must be especially respectful and self-censoring.

The influential radical feminist legal scholar, Catharine MacKinnon, argues that the right of free expression does not exist in a vacuum but must be seen in the context of other social and constitutional values. Among those she singles out the right of equal protection of the law, the right not to be the victim of discrimination. She identifies various forms of speech as discriminatory, in particular toward women. She points out that a fundamental theme of novels, movies, plays, advertising, and other cultural artifacts is that women are objects of sexual pursuit and appropriation. And she concludes that these instances of free expression reinforce the status of women as second-class and as prey.

MacKinnon would accord first amendment protection only to speech that is not discriminatory, thus balancing the two constitutional rights. MacKinnon and her late colleague, Andrea Dworkin, attempted to implement this principle by drafting an ordinance for the city of Indianapolis that defined pornography as a practice that discriminates against women. In the words of the ordinance, pornography is the graphic sexually explicit subordination of women, whether in pictures or in words, that also includes one or more of the following:

(1) Women are presented as sexual objects who enjoy pain or humiliation; or

(2) Women are presented as sexual objects who experience sexual pleasure in being raped; or

(3) Women are presented as sexual objects tied up or mutilated or bruised or physically hurt, or as dismembered or truncated or fragmented or severed into body parts; or

(4) Women are presented as being penetrated by objects or animals; or

(5) Women are presented in scenarios of degradation, injury, abasement, torture, shown as filthy or inferior, bleeding, bruised, or hurt in a context that makes these conditions sexual; or

(6) Women are presented as sexual objects for domination, conquest, violation, exploitation, or possession, or use, or through postures or positions of servility or submission or display. [Indianapolis Code, article 16-3(q)]

The ordinance was adopted in April 1984 and challenged in federal court. In *American Booksellers Association v. William Hudnut, Mayor of Indianapolis*, 771 F.2d 323 (7th Circuit, 1985), the circuit court affirmed a lower court decision that the ordinance was unconstitutional and in violation of the first amendment. Judge Frank Easterbrook points out that "it is unclear how Indianapolis would treat works from James Joyce's *Ulysses* to Homer's *Iliad*; both depict women as submissive objects for conquest and domination." He concludes that the ordinance impermissibly "discriminates on the ground of the content of the speech. . . . Speech treating women in the disapproved way — as submissive in matters sexual or as enjoying humiliation — is unlawful no matter how significantly the literary, artistic, or political qualities of the work taken as a whole. The state may not ordain preferred viewpoints in this way."

In the course of the opinion, Easterbrook also argues that "one of the things that separates our society from [totalitarian governments] is our absolute right to propagate opinions that the government finds wrong or even hateful." He concludes that the Indianapolis ordinance is "thought control. It establishes an 'approved' view of women, of how they may react to sexual encounters, or how the sexes may relate to each other. Those who espouse the approved view may use sexual images; those who do not, may not." The judge concedes that prevailing views about race and gender may contain harmful untruths and may not readily be corrected in the market place. But he notes that "a power to limit speech on the ground that truth has not yet prevailed and is not likely to prevail implies the power to declare truth. . . . [T]he government may not restrict speech on the ground that in a free exchange truth is not yet dominant."

Another aspect of MacKinnon's critique is the claim that pornography is not protected by the first amendment because it does not express ideas at all. She seems to use a simple physiological metaphor. Ideas are processed by the mind; expressive works that do not contain ideas are indistinguishable from acts. The latter work directly on the emotions or on vulnerable organs that are located elsewhere than the head. This claim treats a complex distinction as a simple one. On one hand, most works of fiction, most plays and movies, and most pieces of art affect the emotions. Unlike political or philosophical arguments, their significance generally extends beyond their ideational content. On the other hand, it seems arbitrary to say that any work of art does not express ideas at all, even if the idea is one that is crude and in violation of commonly shared values.

The debate between those who would limit free speech in the interest of other values and those who see free speech as serving its role only as an "absolute" right remains vigorous. In the following article, Professor Thomas Emerson presents an analysis of the absolutist theory and a reply to Professor MacKinnon.

❦ Pornography and the First Amendment: A Reply to Professor MacKinnon ❦

Thomas I. Emerson

Professor Catharine MacKinnon, in a recent article in this journal, powerfully and perceptively developed her thesis that pornography is "[c]entral to the institutionalization of male dominance" — Pornography, she urges, is "a political practice" that "causes attitudes and behaviors of violence and discrimination which define the treatment and status of half of the population." I am not sure that I would draw the line between Eros and dehumanization at the same point as Professor MacKinnon appears to. Moreover, all the evidence is not yet in as to the actual impact of pornography, and Professor MacKinnon may overstate its role in the subordination of women. Nevertheless, generally speaking, I accept Professor MacKinnon's basic position and proceed upon the premise that pornography plays a major part in establishing and maintaining male supremacy in our society.

My concern arises not from Professor MacKinnon's statement of the problem but from her proposals for a solution. Despite her opening remark that "pornography cannot be reformed or suppressed or banned," but "can only be changed," it is clear that Professor MacKinnon would deal with the problem by invoking the power of the government to suppress pornography. Her specific proposals are embodied in the Minneapolis and Indianapolis Ordinances, which she and Andrea Dworkin drafted and persuaded the city councils of those cities to adopt. The Minneapolis

Ordinance was vetoed by the Mayor as a violation of the first amendment, but the Indianapolis ordinance was signed into law and is now the subject of litigation in the federal courts. I will take the Indianapolis Ordinance as showing, in concrete terms, what an attempted suppression of pornography by government mandate would entail.

The Indianapolis Ordinance is based upon the theory that "pornography is a discriminatory practice based on sex which denies women equal opportunities in society." It creates administrative and judicial machinery empowering any woman to bring civil proceedings for a cease and desist order (that is, an injunction) to prohibit the "production, sale, exhibition, or distribution of pornography," and require the offender "to take further affirmative action as will effectuate the purposes" of the Ordinance.

The key provision of the Ordinance is the definition of pornography: "Pornography shall mean the graphic sexually explicit subordination of women, whether in pictures or in words," that also includes one or more ways in which "women are presented." The features that make material pornographic include not only presentations of women being subjected to violence, but also presentation of women as "sexual objects who enjoy pain or humiliation"; women as "sexual objects who experience sexual pleasure in being raped"; women "being penetrated by objects or animals"; women "in scenarios of degradation, injury, abasement. . . . shown as filthy or inferior, . . . or hurt in a context that makes these conditions sexual"; and women "presented as sexual objects for domination, conquest . . . exploitation, possession, or use, or through postures or positions of servility or submission or display."

The sweep of the Indianapolis Ordinance is breathtaking. It would subject to governmental ban virtually all depictions of rape, verbal or pictorial, and a substantial proportion of other presentations of sexual encounters. More specifically, it would outlaw such works of literature as the *Arabian Nights,* John Cleland's *Fanny Hill,* Henry Miller's *Tropic of Cancer,* William Faulkner's *Sanctuary,* and Norman Mailer's *Ancient Evenings,* to name but a few. The ban would extend from Greek mythology and Shakespeare to the millions of copies of "romance novels" now being sold in the supermarkets. It would embrace much of the world's art, from ancient carvings to Picasso, well-known films too numerous to mention, and a large amount of commercial advertising.

The scope of the Indianapolis Ordinance is not accidental. Nor could it be limited by more precise drafting without defeating the purpose of its authors. As Professor MacKinnon emphasizes, male domination has deep, pervasive and ancient roots in our society, so it is not surprising that our literature, art, entertainment and commercial practices are permeated by attitudes and behavior that create and reflect the inferior status of women. If the answer to the problem, as Professor MacKinnon describes it, is government suppression of sexual expression that contributes to female subordination, then the net of restraint has to be cast on a nearly limitless scale. Even narrowing the proscribed area to depictions of sexual activities involving violence would outlaw a large segment of the world's literature and art.

I. The Ban on Pornography and Traditional First Amendment Doctrine

If we test Professor MacKinnon's proposals against traditional first amendment doctrine, there is no way that her solution of the pornography problem can be sustained. Obviously, the founding fathers, whatever restrictions they might have found constitutionally permissible with respect to sexually explicit speech, could not have intended the first amendment to allow the government to prohibit all speech that supported male domination. On Professor MacKinnon's own analysis, the very idea could not have occurred to them as members of the dominant male hierarchy. Insofar as "original intention" is a guide to constitutional interpretation, then, it runs squarely counter to the position taken by the proponents of the Indianapolis Ordinance.

Nor can government suppression of pornography be justified under current first amendment doctrine. The core element in first amendment theory is that the impact of speech — whether considered good, bad or indifferent — cannot be invoked as a basis for government control of speech. Speech, or more generally expression, occupies a specially protected place in a democratic society. As Justice Holmes remarked long ago: "[I]f there is any principle of the Constitution that more imperatively calls for attachment than any other it is the principle of free thought — not free thought for those who agree with us but freedom for the thought that we hate."

The reason for the supremacy of freedom of expression in our constitutional hierarchy is that it is essential to the operation of the democratic process. The values served by a system of free expression — individual self-fulfillment, advancement of knowledge, participation in self-government, and promotion of consensus by nonviolent means — form the bedrock of our democratic existence.

It follows that, as a general proposition, speech cannot be prohibited, curtailed or interfered with by government authorities. The state must seek to achieve its social goals by methods other than the suppression of expression. Were it otherwise, the government could readily outlaw or regulate expression that hampered the effectiveness of government operations, urged basic reform in our society, opposed government policies abroad, or cast aspersions on fellow citizens. Clearly the suppression of pornographic speech, on the ground that it causes or reflects discrimination against women, would run afoul of this basic mandate of the first amendment.

The Supreme Court has, of course, made some exceptions to the constitutional protection afforded freedom of expression. But it has never countenanced any degree of control that would create as gaping a hole in our system of freedom of expression as would the attempted suppression of "pornography."

The exception that bears the closest resemblance to the proposed ban on pornography is found in the law concerning obscenity. In its obscenity decisions, the Supreme Court has ruled that the government may prohibit the dissemination of materials "which taken as a whole, appeal to the prurient interest in sex, which portray sexual conduct in a patently offensive way, and which, taken as a whole, do not have serious literary, artistic, political, or scientific value." The theory upon which the Supreme Court permits the suppression of obscenity, as thus defined, is the legal fiction that "obscenity is not within the area of constitutionally protected speech," in other words, that obscenity is not covered by the first amendment at all.

Since obscenity law thus rests upon a totally irrational premise — that obscene materials are not speech — it is difficult to make a rational projection as to how far the obscenity exception extends. As a practical matter, however, it is inconceivable that the Supreme Court would hold that the far broader area of "pornography" is simply outside the scope of first amendment protection. More importantly, as Professor MacKinnon points out, the social goals sought by the obscenity laws are essentially moral in nature; they do not extend to what Professor MacKinnon describes as a political process — discrimination against the female sex. The likelihood that the Supreme Court would permit the government to embark upon a venture to control speech in this area of politics, free from the restraints of the first amendment, is most remote.

A second exception to the general rule that expression is entitled to the full protection of the first amendment occurs in the case of expression by, or directed to, children. Thus in *New York v. Ferber*, the Supreme Court upheld a New York statute that prohibited the use of children in "a sexual performance" and in aid of that provision prohibited dissemination of materials depicting sexual performances by children. The validity of such a measure rests upon the proposition that children are not and cannot be full participants in the system of freedom of expression. That system presupposes a maturity of understanding and judgment that children do not possess. As a result, the Supreme Court has consistently applied different rules, in the area of expression and elsewhere, to children than to adults. It explicitly did so in the *Ferber* case, making it clear that the result would have been different were the statute not "limited to works that *visually* depict sexual conduct by children." Moreover, the Supreme Court has made it plain that the special rules pertaining to children cannot operate to infringe the first amendment rights of adults.

Other exceptions to full protection under the first amendment are based on doctrines pertaining to libel, clear and present danger, and regulation of the time, place and manner of expression. None of these theories justifies the relaxation of the traditional guarantees of the first amendment in the case of pornographic materials. Libel laws deal exclusively with the protection of reputation against false statements and are narrowly circumscribed. The clear and present danger exception is applicable only to advocacy that is "directed to inciting or producing imminent lawless action and is likely to incite or produce such action." Pornography is not "directed" toward producing "imminent lawless action," nor is there persuasive evidence that it is "likely" to do so, except possibly in a most aberrational case. Time, place and manner regulations are sanctioned primarily in situations where exercise of the right to freedom of expression creates a physical conflict with the exercise of other rights, such as the use of a public street for a demonstration in a way that interferes with normal traffic. In any event, anti-pornography measures are not concerned with time, place and manner but with content. In all these areas, first amendment theory requires that the exceptions be confined to narrow and concrete categories that have the least inhibiting effect upon the system of freedom of expression. Creation of a vast new exception that would remove from the protection of the first amendment all sexually explicit expression that tended to promote the subordination of women would, to the contrary, leave the system a shadow of its former self.

The nearest analogy to what is proposed in the Indianapolis Ordinance would be an official enactment prohibiting all expression that promoted or encouraged racism in our society. The laws, constitutional and statutory, that attempt to eradicate racism in our national life have never been carried to such a point. They deal with discriminatory acts, not the expression of discriminatory beliefs, opinions, ideas or attitudes. And it is hard to believe that the Supreme Court would permit their extension into such areas. One is not likely to find the Supreme Court enjoining performance of the *Merchant of Venice* or banning William B. Shockley from expounding his views on the inferiority of the Negro race. It is true that in *Beauharnais v. Illinois*, decided in 1952 by a five to four vote, the Supreme Court upheld a group libel law. At that time, however, first amendment doctrine was in its infancy and received scant attention in the majority opinion. In any event the major premise of *Beauharnais* — that libel laws are not within the coverage of the first amendment — was overruled in *New York Times v. Sullivan*. While *Beauharnais* was cited in Justice White's opinion in the *Ferber* case, somewhat ambiguously, the prevailing view is that group libel laws cannot be reconciled with modern first amendment doctrine. Nor, in practice, have such measures come to be relied upon as a solution to the problems of racism.

The Indianapolis Ordinance's banning of pornography not only fails to fit within any of the exceptions to protection under the first amendment, but also relies heavily upon the injunctive powers of the courts. This is a crippling form of "prior restraint" that seeks to suppress expression in advance of its publication or dissemination. As the Supreme Court has repeatedly held, "prior restraints on speech and publication are the most serious and least tolerable infringement on first amendment rights." Few prior restraints have been upheld by the Supreme Court, and none on the scale contemplated by the Indianapolis Ordinance.

Finally, it should be noted that the attempt to avoid first amendment difficulties in the Indianapolis Ordinance by asserting that pornography "is a discriminatory practice" cannot succeed. This device, which has been hailed as a new approach to the problem, is no more than a play on words. Pornography is speech or expression, as those terms are used in first amendment theory, and like most expression has an impact upon attitudes and behavior. The question is whether, because of this impact, pornography can be proscribed. It does not help to eliminate the intermediate step in the legal analysis and declare that pornography "is" discrimination.

II. The Dynamics of Suppressing Pornography

Professor MacKinnon argues the case for the suppression of pornography at a high level of abstraction. One must also take into account the dynamics at work in implementing a program such as she contemplates. The hazards to our system of freedom of expression are manifest.

Most important is the inhibiting atmosphere inevitably created by subjecting a broad area of expression to governmental intervention. Persons engaging in any form of communication touching on sexual matters face the prospect of being haled before a censorship board, involved in prolonged litigation, saddled with back-breaking legal fees, compelled to justify their exercise of first amendment rights to government officials, threatened with damage awards and subjected to other forms of "affirmative action" such as confis-cation of earnings — all of this occurring at countless locations scat-tered across the country. It is true that the Indianapolis Ordinance does not provide for criminal penalties, apart from the possibility of criminal contempt. There is nothing in the legal theory underlying the Ordinance, however, that would preclude the censorship of sexual materials through the apparatus of police investigations, criminal prosecutions and prison sentences. One can hardly expect a system of freedom of expression to flourish under these conditions.

Moreover, there is a strong likelihood that the powers conferred by the Indianapolis Ordinance would be diverted to reactionary political ends. It is often difficult to separate the pornographic elements of a communication from other ingredients. It is entirely possible that the more powerful interests in our society, possessing the requisite funds, could utilize the machinery of government censorship of pornography to harass or silence unwanted points of view. One can readily imagine the Moral Majority or similar groups invoking anti-pornography laws against feminist authors who seek to make male domination "graphic" and "sexually explicit." Such a development has taken place in the operation of the libel laws; more and more, the right to sue for libel has provided the basis for litigation designed to weaken or eliminate criticism from less powerful political opponents. Thus, censorship of por-nography, far from being a liberating force, could become a tool with which to harass feminist or other progressive movements.

Along the same lines, the suppression of pornography through governmental intervention encourages the intolerance syndrome throughout a society. Civil liberties are, as is often said, indivisible. The legal doctrines, governmental machinery and attitudes that suppress speech in one area also promote suppression in other areas. The censorship of pornography thus gives comfort to the forces of reaction and advances the cause of those who seek a closed society. The movement for gender equality has little to gain from such a climate of opinion.

One additional, overriding consideration must be faced: The elimination of pornography by governmental censorship is simply not workable, at least by any democratic process. The area of pro-hibition is so vast, the machinery of civil litigation so cumbersome, the hope of changing attitudes by government decree so quixotic, that nothing positive is likely to be accomplished. Rather, the results, in terms of selective enforcement, underground circulation of "violative materials," encouragement of organized crime, and the general discrediting of law enforcement, would be entirely negative. In the ensuing confusion, the original problem would remain unsolved.

III. The Rejection of Traditional First Amendment Theory

Professor MacKinnon, as I read her, rests her case not primarily on traditional first amendment theory but rather on an attack upon first amendment theory. Her position is that "[t]he theory of the first amendment under which most pornography is protected from governmental restriction proceeds from liberal assumptions which do not apply to the situation of women." Indeed, she goes beyond this and argues that the traditional approach is "worse than useless." She would, in other words, discard the first amendment, at least until it was modified to reflect "non-liberal" assumptions. Since there is no chance the Supreme Court is going to reject traditional first amendment theory, this seems to leave Professor MacKinnon without any remedy short of constitutional amendment — or revolution. In my judgment, Professor MacKinnon seriously overstates the case against traditional first amendment doctrine and thereby grossly underestimates, in fact neglects altogether, the role that the system of freedom of expression can play in dealing with the issue of pornography and gender equality.

Professor MacKinnon's critique of the "liberal assumptions" underlying first amendment theory rests upon four propositions. The first is that the first amendment "presumes the validity of the distinction between public and private," the former being "the sphere of social power" and the latter "the area of private right." She contends that this distinction "does not cut the same for women as for men" because the exercise of male power that results in the subordination of women, as in the case of pornography, often takes place in the home, and that women may therefore need a higher degree of governmental, or social, intervention in the "private" than in the "public" sphere.

The private-public distinction is not one between governmental controls of conduct inside or outside the home, but one between individual right and collective power. The making of this distinction is a basic problem in any society, liberal or otherwise. The first amendment, generally speaking, places speech within the realm of individual right and action within the realm of collective power. This does preclude governmental control of pornographic speech, but it also leaves open a vast area of governmental control over male domination in the form of action. And this control can be directed against conduct inside the home as well as outside. Legislation imposing penalties for spousal rape, now being enacted in a number of states, illustrates that no liberal public-private assumptions foreclose such governmental attempts to achieve equality between the sexes.

Professor MacKinnon's second criticism of liberal first amendment theory deals with the assumption that freedom of expression "helps discover truth," promotes "consensus," facilitates "progress," and "frees the mind to fulfill itself." She argues that, although securing these values may justify freedom of expression "in a non-hierarchial society," the theory is not adequate "in a society of gender inequality." In such a society, she urges, "the speech of the powerful impresses its view upon the world," providing "the appearance of consent" but making "protest inaudible as well as rare."

There can be little doubt that, in any society, the more powerful forces will engage in a greater volume of speech, on a more pervasive scale, and with a deeper impact than the less powerful groups. A fully balanced equality of speech among all groups and individuals is probably unattainable, at least without a degree of governmental intervention that would destroy the freedom of the system. What the system does guarantee is that the unorthodox, minority, dissenting and submerged elements of the society have a constitutional right to express their views and endeavor to gain adherents. The system is not designed only for a "non-hierarchal society," assuming such a social order exists. It is designed precisely to give a subordinated group, such as women, a way out of their "powerlessness" by some method other than force.

It should be added that Professor MacKinnon has surely overdrawn the picture in contending that, under the first amendment today, protest against the status of women is "inaudible as well as rare." Her own work, and that of the whole feminist movement, can scarcely be so described.

Professor MacKinnon's third criticism of traditional first amendment doctrine is that it fails to recognize the harm that can be caused by speech. She asserts that first amendment logic "has difficulty grasping harm that is not linearly caused in the 'John hit Mary' sense," and that first amendment doctrine assumes that "words and pictures can only be harmful if they produce harm in a form that is considered action." This is not correct; first amendment theory does recognize that speech may cause harm, as well as good, and it is quite capable of recognizing the kind of harm that Professor MacKinnon describes. The theory rests upon the proposition, however, that the values served by freedom of expression are so essential to a free society that speech requires special, near absolute, protection against government interference regardless of any harm that may be caused. It also rests upon the premise, as noted above, that the government possesses sufficient powers to deal with such harms through means other than the suppression of speech. Thus, again, a vast area is open for government measures to promote gender equality. But the superficially easy out — passing a law to prohibit speech — is not available under first amendment theory.

It is admittedly difficult to draw the line between speech and action in some situations. But obviously the whole concept of the first amendment — that speech is entitled to special protection — requires that it be done. Of course, in the overwhelming proportion of cases, including pornography, the classification of the conduct involved as speech is not open to question.

Professor MacKinnon's fourth criticism, which is closely related to the second, challenges the first amendment assumption that "socially, speech is free," and that the problem is to prevent the government from constraining it. In actuality, she contends, "whole segments of the population" are "systematically silenced *socially*, prior to government action." "For women," she concludes, "the urgent issue of freedom of speech is not primarily the avoidance of state intervention as such, but finding an affirmative means to get access to speech for those to whom it has been denied."

Insofar as the argument is that the speech of the most powerful forces in society "impresses its view upon the world," the answer is the same as above: Freedom of speech does not protect individuals or groups from being persuaded, even against their own interests, but it does guarantee that every individual or group has a right to try to persuade others. Granted the right exists, the question of actually obtaining access to the means of communication becomes a crucial one. There is nothing in the first amendment, however, that precludes "finding an affirmative means to get access" for the less powerful, and indeed the failure to do so is one of the major weaknesses in our system of freedom of expression. But that does not sanction government intervention to restrict the free speech rights of others or to take any similar form of action that would undermine the system as a whole. Nor can it be said, as a factual matter, that those who have wished to speak out for women's rights have been denied access to do so.

Taking all these factors into consideration, it would seem that proponents of equality for women in our society have more to gain from participating in the traditional system of freedom of expression than from abandoning it in favor of a form of relief that would destroy it.

IV. Conclusion

Any attempt to deal with the problem of pornography through governmental suppression would involve a dangerous evisceration of the first amendment. The damage to our system of free expression would extend far beyond the area of pornography. Moreover, such an effort would almost certainly prove unworkable.

This does not mean that nothing can be done to achieve gender equality. One course of action is to utilize the system of freedom of expression, as Professor MacKinnon has so eloquently done, and thereby raise the American level of consciousness. Another is to expand the right of access to the media of communication through measures that utilize the opportunities afforded by cable television, satellites, video-cassette recorders and other advances in the technology of communication. A third is to mobilize non-governmental economic power through organization, picketing, demonstrations. boycotts and other forms of pressure. Surely opponents of pornography would receive sympathy and support from broad sections of the public in such endeavors. Ultimately, as Professor MacKinnon has emphasized, the issue is one of increasing the economic, political and social power of women. There are many ways to do so — through enactment of anti-discrimination laws, litigation to assure pay equity, ratification of the Equal Rights Amendment, and numerous other measures that do not impair the operation of the first amendment.

The difficulties in turning around centuries of male supremacy are manifest, but progress has been made and, one hopes, will continue.

Emerson argues that the only antidote to harmful speech is more speech. One may be optimistic that sound and beneficial ideas have greater intrinsic appeal than harmful ideas or pessimistic that harmful ideas can be seductive and hard to dispel. But both the optimist and the pessimist often agree that the worst outcome would be to give the government the power to censor ideas. For the optimist, this would create an additional barrier to beneficial ideas. For the pessimist, this would create the possibility that government could be the promulgator of ideas that strengthen those in power to the detriment of everyone else.

Catharine MacKinnon, of course, disagrees and offers a curious mix of optimism and pessimism. On the one hand she is optimistic that a government entrusted with the power to distinguish discriminatory from non-discriminatory expression will use that power judiciously and will not suppress any speech that threatens it. On the other hand, she is pessimistic about the free market of ideas, about the power of nondiscriminatory speech to achieve its own victories in the long run.

Behind MacKinnon's approach lies an assumption that some other writers share. It is the conviction that imbalances of power in the realm of speech and expression cannot be self-correcting and indeed tend to get more severe. The remedy may not be as extreme as MacKinnon's, namely the explicit regulation of ideas. Power, it is sometimes suggested, can be reallocated by more subtle moves. Jack Balkin, who teaches law at Yale, has long drawn attention (as have MacKinnon and many others) to the fact that the speech of some groups can have the effect of silencing other groups. This can occur at the level of race and gender. MacKinnon's claim is that men have always had a monopoly in the promulgation of ideas, opinions, and attitudes; she says that women have, for the most part, been silenced and that this has been not an accidental but an intentional result. Similar claims can be made about culture, that the culture of minorities has been drowned out by the cultural influences of the majority. On a global scale, this has led many foreign leaders to express fear about American cultural hegemony. And the same phenomenon has been criticized with regard to industry. The view is that large tobacco and pharmaceutical companies and entertainment conglomerates have shaped the beliefs of citizens in their own interest with almost unlimited resources and power.

Balkin's argument, presented in the following selection, can be expressed as follows. We have always feared the government as a censor or dictator of beliefs and ideas, emphasizing the government's relative power. And we have assumed that the private sector is one in which effective voices are equitably distributed. For Balkin it is clear that the openness of discourse and the avenues of imagination and innovation are threatened by private concentrations of power as least as much as they are by public ones. Thus if we are to take the ideals and goals of the first amendment seriously, we must pay attention to regulation.

❧ Some Realism about Pluralism: Legal Realist Approaches to the First Amendment (part I) ❧

J. M. Balkin

A few years ago, in my home town of Kansas City, Missouri, I found myself in a very uncomfortable position politically. The local chapter of the Ku Klux Klan asked the local cable company, American Cablevision, if they could show what was essentially a racist propaganda series, "Race and Reason,"' on the public access channel. They were told that the public access channel was available only for locally produced shows, and they responded by asking if they could air a locally produced show saying basically the same things, called " 'Klansas City Live.' " American Cablevision was concerned about the reaction of the neighbors (they're located east of downtown Kansas City in an all black neighborhood), and they complained to the City Council. They asked if they could be let out of their franchise contract in which they were granted a monopoly in the city in exchange for providing a public access channel. After a very public and emotional debate, the City Council finally voted to abolish the public access channel and substitute a "community access" channel. This meant that American Cablevision had editorial discretion concerning whether or not to allow any particular speaker on the channel and what they could or could not say. Needless to say, the Klan was not permitted to broadcast under the new regime, and in fact American Cablevision began to exercise its new authority toward other groups who had participated in public access programming before the changeover. And, not too surprisingly, the City's decision led to litigation that was ultimately settled out of court in the Klan's favor.

Just before the City Council vote, the local board of the American Civil Liberties Union of Western Missouri asked me, along with a former colleague, Joan Mahoney, to write a memo to the City Council explaining why their action would violate the first amendment and expose them to liability. We did so, and the memo was a straightforward exposition of first amendment doctrine. What made me uncomfortable was that on the other side of this dispute were not the usual opponents of the ACLU nor was it a question of the Kansas City establishment versus the guardians of freedom and enlightenment. On the other side of this controversy was the Reverend Emmanuel Cleaver, a liberal city councilman who is one of the leaders of the black community in Kansas City.

And this situation got me thinking: The left in the United States used to be solidly united around the overriding importance of protecting speech from governmental interference — proclaiming the necessity of protecting the speech we hate every bit as much as the speech we love. It's not that way anymore. An important realignment of political beliefs and attitudes is occurring in the United States. It is a sea change that may prove to be something rich, but at least for now is certainly something strange. I am an ardent advocate of the freedoms guaranteed by the first amendment, yet all around me I see the American left abandoning its traditionally libertarian positions, often for reasons I sympathize with. This change in the conception of the principle of free speech is one of the subjects of this article.

Let me offer a set of recent examples of left arguments about free speech. At first glance they all appeared isolated, but I think they share an underlying logic. I present these arguments in what I believe to be their strongest versions, although I do not agree with them in all respects. Nevertheless, I believe that the general form of analysis they offer is very important indeed, even if I would reach different conclusions by employing it. That form of analysis is the other major subject of this article.

The first example of left arguments involves the newly expressed disappointment with the free speech principle when it is used to protect racist speech that promotes racial stereotypes and racial oppression. As Professor MacKinnon tells us, if we view first amendment values as a system, so that a victory for free speech anywhere is a victory for free speech everywhere, then the same view applies to racism — a victory for racism anywhere bolsters racism in society in general. And this is, of course, the argument for abolishing the public access channel in the Kansas City Cablevision case. Since we, the public of Kansas City, subsidize the cable channel, we are actually making it easier for racists to communicate their message. We thus make it easier for them to spread racist dogma, gain converts, and foster racial oppression and racial violence. One might respond that we subsidize streets and parks too, so does that mean we should close off access to public forums for racist speech? Yet I think that if we really wanted to take this line of reasoning all the way, we would say yes, that when the government grants access to racist groups to use streets and parks for racist speech, it is to that extent subsidizing racist speech. In fact, we might add, when the state declines to allow suits for intentional infliction of emotional distress or other forms of racial harassment, it is permitting racists to harm minorities. Indeed a number of legal scholars have begun to argue in precisely this way. In fact, as I shall argue later on, many mainstream scholars have used this type of argument before, and accepted it before, although not in the context of speech.

The second line of arguments involves the radical feminist critique of pornography, and in particular, the work of Catharine MacKinnon and Andrea Dworkin. MacKinnon and Dworkin have argued that the free speech defense of pornography is largely a sham because there is no real free speech for women in a country in which women are relegated to the particular gender roles that society gives them. Patriarchy is so embedded in the societal conception of free speech that it has become invisible, and what appears to be the speech of women in pornographic films, for example, is actually expression that is forced upon them by males. More generally, patriarchy constructs a world in which pornography looks indistinguishable from speech, and in which women's speech is not their own but is constructed for them. Hence, Dworkin suggests that rather than listening to the speech of women in a male-dominated society, we should listen to their silence. The silence of women is the trace or evidence of their oppression.

The third line of arguments is very familiar nowadays, and I think there is a wider consensus among left thinkers that these arguments represent a genuinely left position, or rather, more people on the left agree with these arguments than with the arguments about racist speech or pornography. This line of arguments critiques the "money as speech'" position taken in cases like *Buckley v. Valeo*. It argues that regulation of campaign finance is necessary because what passes for free speech is really more like unregulated economic power that is used to influence (and corrupt) the political process. In fact, this position even can become a liberal argument in the *Carolene Products*/John Hart Ely style—that the political process itself is flawed or defective when large sums of money can be used to influence legislators under the guise of freedom of association, or influence voters under the guise of freedom of speech.

The anti-Buckley argument usually stops short at the limited position of reform of campaign finance (especially the liberal version), but one can take it much further. One could argue that free speech in a situation of radically unequal economic power is not free speech at all because it is skewed by the preexisting distribution of property. That is to say, in our country the power of persons to put their messages across loudly and repeatedly because of their economic power and influence effectively silences other, excluded and marginalized voices. The long term effect of the unequal distribution of power and property is an unequal exposure of particular ideas, and the stifling and co-opting of more radical and imaginative ideas about politics and society. Under this analysis, the paradigmatic example of free speech in our society is not the speaker on the soapbox, or the reasoned exchange of views on the television talk show or in the legislative chamber; rather, it is the endless succession of candidates for the two major political parties who sound exactly alike, it is the endless bombardment of our minds with commercials about shampoo and deodorant, telling us how awful our bodies are and how we have to change them or decorate them in some way in order to become worthwhile people, dictating for us what we really want and do not want. It is the repeated urge to cultural conformity as explained to us through the latest fashion statements on "Dallas," "Dynasty," or even MTV. In short, the paradigmatic example of free speech in this country is the parroting of values created for us by those groups and persons who have sufficient money and clout to monopolize our attentions and ultimately our very imaginations.

These different criticisms of first amendment law seem widely separated and distant from each other. I suggest, however, that they all have something in common. They all involve techniques first used by the legal realists in the 1920s and 1930s to deconstruct the ideology of the sacred right of freedom of contract. The only difference is that now the attack, the assault on the citadel if you will, is directed at the sacred right of free speech.

The legal realist critique of freedom of contract argued that when the employer and the employee contracted for the employee to work sixty hours a week in a bakery, this was only formally a relationship of free contract. It was actually the very opposite of free exchange because of the preexisting economic status of the parties. In fact — and something like this actually appears in the preamble to the Wagner Act — the legal realists argued that only through the regulation of employment contracts could one approach a truly free exchange of labor. Note the similarity to the MacKinnon/Dworkin approach — among other things, MacKinnon and Dworkin argue that when a woman appears in a pornographic movie, this is not the woman's real speech. Rather, it is speech forced upon her through a system of patriarchy. More generally, the lack of protest by women and the particular gender roles that men and women have in society are not chosen, but rather are imposed through a psychosexual equivalent to a "lack of bargaining power'" created by the dominant male ideology. Just as the exchange between employer and employee looks free but is actually coerced, so the speech of women and of other groups is not free but is actually the result of social forces beyond their control. Just as the Wagner Act was necessary to counter economic inequalities, so the dismantling of the social forces of patriarchy through regulation of pornography is appropriate in order to vindicate women's true rights of free expression.

A second legal realist critique argued that to the extent one protected the right of freedom of contract, one actually infringed on some other right that might be equally valuable. One could not justify this result by claiming no infringement was taking place, or by invoking a distinction between public and private infringement or between government action and inaction. The government was ultimately responsible for the distribution of power and wealth in society when actors made use of its rules of contract, property, and tort, which in turn defined the economic system. Thus, no articulation and protection of rights could be politically neutral — any definition of rights necessarily defined the rights of others. No regime of contract, property, and tort was unregulated or free of governmental policy or government intervention — there were only different possible regimes and different choices about which persons to benefit at the expense of others. This is also the argument for regulation of racist speech: To the degree that the state protects the free speech rights of racists, the state affirms that the rights of minorities to be free from certain forms of racial oppression do not count. If the government is unwilling to allow common law causes of action for racial insult, that reluctance is in itself an admission that the state is responsible for the balance it strikes between speech rights and the perpetuation of racism — the state has chosen to value the expressive liberty of racists over the feelings of their victims. Put another way, this argument is really the familiar legal realist argument that the public/private distinction between direct state abridgement of rights and private abridgement collapses in particular contexts. This argument has simply been extended from the realm of contract and property rights to the realm of speech rights.

Finally, the legal realists argued that one could not disregard the effect of economic status on the exercise of economic rights, and that neither the existing distribution of economic power nor the effect of that distribution on economic bargains were pre-political. But the same thing might be said of the right of freedom of speech in two senses: First, the right of political participation is no less affected by differences in economic power than is the right of economic participation. There is nothing natural, or (in modern post-*Lochner* terms) nothing fair, about the results of a process in which some have vastly more political clout because of vastly more economic clout. This is the critique of *Buckley v. Valeo.*

Second, and perhaps more important, the very desires and beliefs of persons in society are no more natural, no less skewed, by the maldistribution of economic and political power. To dissolve the public/private distinction in this particular context is not only to make government responsible for the citizen's ability to speak; it is also to make the government responsible for the values imposed and implanted in each citizen. This argument is implicit in Dworkin's and MacKinnon's attack on pornography as sustaining or giving comfort to male hegemony. Yet this is the point at which the legal realist critique of governmental responsibility begins to devour itself and its liberal premises. For now the problem is how we are to know what set of values should be imposed if our values are themselves infected by preexisting social constructs. This critique attacks not only the old style liberal belief in neutrality as between different perspectives, but also the newer and more sophisticated liberal belief in an essentially non-preferential attitude of fairness towards competing groups, all of whom want to instill their values in the hearts and minds of others. A critique that emphasizes the state's responsibility for the production and reproduction of values is hardly new. It is implicated, for example, in the problems that modern liberal thinkers now face in trying to explain why creationist parents should not be able to prevent secular education of their children when that education conflicts with their religious beliefs.

My argument so far has been that recent left critiques of traditional liberal first amendment doctrine bear a striking similarity to the legal realist critique of the favored right of laissez-faire conservatives, free contract. In one sense, it was inevitable that the skeptical acid of legal realism eventually would leak out and consume sacred rights other than contract. The question is, why did it happen now, and what does the future hold for the heretofore blissful marriage of the left and the first amendment?

To answer these questions, we need to examine a bit of history. It is important to remember that for most of America's history, protecting free speech has helped marginalized or unpopular groups to gain political power and influence. The first amendment normally has been the friend of left wing values, whether it was French émigrés and Republicans in the 1790s, abolitionists in the 1840s, pacifists in the 1910s, organized labor in the 1920s and 1930s, or civil rights protesters in the 1950s and 1960s. We should remember too that during the ACLU's early years the organization represented mainly draft resisters and labor organizers, whom Roger Baldwin saw as, and intended to be, the main beneficiaries of his work. So the historical connections between left politics and free speech in this country are obvious. However, it is also important to remember that the alliances between particular conceptions of rights and a particular political agenda are always contextual, always situated in history. Everyone is familiar with positions that originally were espoused by radicals and later became mainstream or even conservative positions. The radical ideas of the day often become the orthodoxy of tomorrow, and, in the process, take on a quite different political valance. I refer to this phenomenon as "ideological drift." Although this drift can move either from right to left or left to right, the most common examples are comparatively liberal principles that later serve to buttress comparatively conservative interests.

For example, laissez-faire was a liberal argument before the Civil War, as liberals like Jefferson, Jackson, and Van Buren tried to avoid the granting of corporate charters and other special governmental benefits to monied interests in the Northeast. By the 1890s, as we all know, laissez-faire had become a conservative argument because by that time American business was developed sufficiently that it needed government assistance less than it needed to avoid governmental regulation. The primary interest of American business was not gaining special benefits, but rather avoiding redistributive regulation at the hands of voting majorities of the middle and lower classes — majorities created by the Jacksonian movement for universal manhood suffrage. Thus, ironically, the conservatives of the 1890s adopted the liberal laissez-faire argument of the previous era, and generally the left has been committed to various forms of redistributive social and economic regulation ever since.

A similar transformation, I suspect, is overtaking the principle of free speech today. Business interests and other conservative groups are finding that arguments for property rights and the social status quo can more and more easily be rephrased in the language of the first amendment by using the very same absolutist forms of argument offered by the left in previous generations. Here's a quick quiz: What do the Klan, conservative PACs, R.J. Reynolds Tobacco, and the conglomerate that owns the holding company that owns the manufacturer of your favorite brand of toothpaste all have in common? They can all justify their activities in the name of the first amendment. What was sauce for the liberal goose increasingly has become sauce for the more conservative gander.

This social transformation is not yet complete, and indeed, I suspect, it probably never will be as complete as the transformation of political views regarding laissez-faire between 1830 and 1890. For example, I can't imagine a social context that would change so radically that the left would find it in its best interests to abandon completely its commitment to protecting the speech of unpopular groups. What I do expect will happen, however, is that gradually the left no longer will find the first amendment its most effective tool for promoting a progressive agenda. That job will fall to other fundamental rights and interests, which occasionally will conflict with the absolutist interpretation of the first amendment that the left traditionally has favored.

These developments are quite serious, and they signal a profound upheaval in legal theory, which will at first be felt most strongly on the left, but, if previous history is any guide, will gradually affect the mainstream view of free expression in American law. The skeptical and deconstructive aspects of the legal realist critique of property and contract rights were quite disruptive in previous generations and took a great deal of time to be accepted. If, as Professors Peller and Singer tell us, we are all legal realists now, we have only recently become so with respect to the first amendment.

The rest of this Article discusses some of the theoretical issues that face us as the legal realist critique of rights is assimilated into first amendment law. I raise these issues not because I have clear-cut solutions in every case, but rather to make the reader think about first amendment problems in different ways. It is important to understand that this project has both a conservative and a transformative purpose. When one offers a new perspective, one should always remember that some objects remain unchanged even when viewed from widely different angles. So it is with free speech. The application of legal realist methods to the first amendment may confirm that the balance of expressive liberties and other social interests should remain unchanged in many situations. On the other hand, a different perspective may reveal previously unrecognized unities in seemingly conflicting legal doctrines or goals. Conversely, new perspectives may show us that two situations we thought were indistinguishable in principle are, in fact, quite different. In any event, in our efforts to reconceptualize the problems of modern first amendment law, we should always keep in mind why the principle of free speech is important to us — because it protects dissent, egalitarian participation in public and private forms of social power, individual conscience, and individual autonomy. As the legal realists would no doubt remind us, these concepts themselves are fuzzy, and their exact contours cannot be determined in the abstract. Thus, ironically, fleshing out a theory of the first amendment is the only way we can truly come to understand what the first amendment means to us.

The goal of this Article, then is not to call for a total transformation of first amendment jurisprudence. Rather, it seeks to shake up the analytic picture a bit in order to stimulate more creative arguments and reconceptualizations. Indeed, the actual modifications to doctrine that this Article suggests — higher scrutiny of content-neutral regulations, greater guarantees of access to the mass media, greater judicial restraint in challenges to campaign finance reform, and a reinterpretation of the captive audience doctrine to permit regulation of face-to-face racial and sexual harassment and harassment in the workplace — do not depart greatly from arguments often made about the first amendment. My suggestions do not, however, fit easily within the libertarian theory of the first amendment traditionally offered by left-liberals. That is why I have moved to a different approach — to preserve what I believe is good about current first amendment protections, while justifying reforms I feel are equally important.

This approach, too, is in the spirit of legal realism. For the legal realists, although arguing that demarcations of property and contract rights were in no sense natural or required by the concepts of property and contract themselves, were not arguing for wholesale restructuring of the American economy. They were laying the theoretical groundwork to justify the reforms of the New Deal and the emergence of the regulatory and welfare state. Although their conservative opponents viewed them as communists, anarchists, or worse, they were nothing of the sort. From our perspective, we see them as preserving economic freedom by readjusting its contours and boundaries. Yet in order to do this, they had to foresake a libertarian conception of economic freedom that had been adopted by liberals of a century before and to which conservatives now fiercely clung.

Thus, I offer a legal realist approach not only as someone interested in theory, but also as someone who identifies and sympathizes with the goals of progressive politics. From what I have said above, it seems clear to me that more conservative forces soon will overtake and appropriate the libertarian approach to first amendment law that progressives have used so effectively in the past. Of course, this would not be the first time such an appropriation has occurred. The most recent example is the appropriation of the anti-discrimination principle by the right as a means of combating affirmative action. Just as an easy-to-apply principle of neutrality in racial distinctions at first served, and later thwarted, the forces of change, so the libertarian conception of the first amendment will soon become co-opted.

Events are rapidly overtaking us. The paradigmatic first amendment cases of the 1930s, 40s, and 50s concerned attempts by state and federal governments to punish seditious speech and unpopular dissent. These are situations for which the libertarian conception of free speech was well-designed. Yet the paradigmatic free speech issues of the 1970s, 80s, and 90s are quite different. They are questions of how to provide effective media access for unpopular groups, how to check the spread of corruption and manipulation of the political process, and how to balance the interests of free expression against a national commitment to eradicating racial and sexual discrimination. Finally, they raise questions of how to protect the expressive rights of unpopular groups from abridgement through manipulation of government taxing and spending programs—products of the very regulatory and welfare state that New Deal liberals fought to establish.

If progressive scholars cling to libertarianism because we cannot think of any other way to conceptualize first amendment problems, because we have no other voice in which to speak, we shall meet the same fate as progressives of the late 19th century, victims of what Clinton Rossiter called the "Great Train Robbery of Intellectual History," in which laissez-faire conservatives appropriated the words and symbols of Jeffersonian liberalism—liberty, opportunity, progress, and individualism—and gave them an economic and decidedly reactionary reinterpretation. As one who believes that language structures and determines thought, I think it is imperative that progressive scholars begin to experiment with new ways of talking about the problems of free expression. We must find our own voice, we must find a new voice, before it is too late. Otherwise we shall find the progressive tools of an earlier era turned against progress, and the goals of a more humane and egalitarian society thwarted in the name of the first amendment.

We can find two levels in Balkin's argument. The first is hard to dispute. What Balkin calls the "maldistribution of power" and resources is pervasive and likely to endure. Every generation has its opinion-shapers, whether they are Oprah or Fox News. An optimist can hope for balance, can hope that the average person is exposed to enough conflict in ideas so that she is forced to make up her own mind. A pessimist can conclude that people seek out voices that confirm their own preconceptions rather than risk exposure to new ideas. One might note that Rush Limbaugh's audience does not much overlap Jon Stewart's. But the more profound problem is that many points of view are altogether unheard. Balkin's question is how aggressive government should be in trying to correct inequities of power in the realm of ideas and in controlling the hegemony of the media.

His proposal runs three risks. One risk is that there is a fine line, if there is any line at all, between controlling the sources of ideas and controlling the ideas themselves. The second is that there are always controversial and uneasy trade-offs between freedom and equality. The attempt to balance or equalize access to ideas and points of view is likely to be seen, with some justice, as a limitation on freedom. And the third risk is that it is hard to know what equality and balance mean in this context. Do all points of views have an equal claim to be heard? Are there benign and malignant points of views? If so, how are they to be sorted out? And, among benign points of view, are some more benign and important than others?

The second level of analysis is Balkin's "legal realist" analogy of the first amendment to economic freedoms. He suggests that just as economic freedom came to be held hostage by big business conglomerates, so too has free expression come to be the trump card of big media (and other business) interests. He implies that just as we curtailed, by way of antitrust laws and other laws against unfair competition, the right of economic exploitation, we need to limit free expression in similar ways.

His analogy echoes some aspects of MacKinnon's argument. Like MacKinnon, he suggests that particular freedoms are not absolute but must be balanced against other rights and values. Just as economic freedom led to infringement of individual welfare, free expression, according to MacKinnon, reinforces discrimination. Like MacKinnon, Balkin has a theory of capture. Economic freedom is captured by those with power and control over markets and resources; expression of ideas is captured by those who have power to control the media. But unlike MacKinnon, Balkin's theory is evolutionary and describes a process of first amendment interpretation that must be sensitive to the vicissitudes of history. MacKinnon's theory is largely ahistorical; white men have always dominated the discourse of ideas and have left their discriminatory imprint from time immemorial.

There are reasons to question Balkin's analogy and the lessons he draws from it. The inherent problems spawned by unlimited economic power are arguably not comparable to the problems of unlimited free expression. In fact, Balkin's worries, unlike MacKinnon's, are best explained not by an analogy between abuse of economic power and abuse of expressive power. Rather, the problem remains what it was more than a century ago, abuse of economic power. The remedy remains economic. The purposes behind antitrust laws and similar laws remains relevant. The power of expression can only be affected indirectly. Thus, the remedy Balkin needs, as opposed to the one that MacKinnon seeks, is achieved not by the regulation of ideas but by cautious control of the resources used to promulgate ideas. And the test must be that interference is justified only when the use of these resources threatens to become a monopoly of ideas, threatens to starve discourse.

Literature and Culture: Support and Incentives

Government has almost always been in the business of supporting culture. Since ancient times, governments have believed that their mission goes beyond sustenance, shelter, and security. They have characteristically been the main support of culture. Of course, these efforts have been self-reinforcing. Individuals who are shaped by a culture tend to support it. But in most societies, the culture is rich enough to produce not just adherence but debate and conflict. Cultural expression of ideas gives rise to differing points of view about society and relationships. Culture is inevitably political, and politics is almost always an arena of controversy.

The history of the United States as a supporter of culture has been unique among western countries. While France, Germany, and England, for example, have long had traditions of support for literature and the arts, U.S. involvement dates from the so-called Great Society programs of the mid-1960s when the National Endowments of the Arts and of Humanities came into being. One observer has calculated that France spends $32 per person to support the arts and Germany $27, while the annual outlays of the endowments in the U.S. amount to about thirty-eight cents. Nonetheless, the influence has been significant, in large part because endowment funds have triggered matching grants. Compared with the 1960s, we now have four times as many orchestras and eight times as many theaters.

Is government support of the arts consistent with democracy? Critics of government support argue that government support inevitably involves subsidizing some ideas and not others and that this violates the democratic spirit of government neutrality toward ideas. They question whether government resources should be used to promote some kinds of work and not others. Others rebut this argument by saying that support of certain writers or artists in no way inhibits the ability of others to reach an audience. They claim that the goal is a stimulating mix of ideas and styles, and they add that democracy flourishes only when the mix is rich enough to stimulate individuals to choose cultural works for themselves.

Aside from the question of democratic values, critics also question whether the recipients of government grants really add to the realm of ideas or merely reinforce the biases of those who choose the recipients. They criticize the so-called elitist culture as one that tries to replicate and empower itself and may be out of step with the cultural climate as a whole. They see no reason why government should enable this process. The administrators of these programs, of course, counter that their efforts enrich the culture as a whole.

In the following excerpt, Professor Owen Fiss of Yale Law School addresses whether government should support the arts and what criteria should be used to allocate resources.

❧ *from* State Activism and State Censorship ❧

Owen M. Fiss

Recent political debates prompted by the Supreme Court's flag burning decisions have once more demonstrated the depth of the nation's commitment to freedom of speech. Although the Court's determination to treat flag burning as an act of political expression, and thus to protect it from state interference, provoked a strong, hostile response from both the President and members of Congress, leading some to call for a constitutional amendment, the campaign to reverse the Court on this issue quickly faded. There was a sense in the body politic that the First Amendment is not simply a technical legal rule, to be amended whenever it produces inconvenient results, but rather an organizing principle of society, central to our self-understanding as a nation and foundational to a vast network of highly cherished social practices and institutions. It can be amended only at the risk of changing the very nature of society. The principle of freedom that the First Amendment embodies is derived from the democratic nature of our society and reflects the belief that robust public debate is an essential precondition for collective self-determination.

That principle has received its most forceful expression in cases involving criminal prosecutions of outspoken critics of the established order for breaching the peace, inciting a riot, conspiring to overthrow the government, seditious libel, or distributing obscene material. At first, the Court erred on the side of the censor, allowing convictions on such charges to stand, but over the last sixty years the Court has placed increasingly stringent limitations on these exercises of state power. The recent flag burning decisions are but an example of this tendency. The state is sometimes allowed to arrest and prosecute speakers — freedom of speech is not absolute — but the Court has developed an elaborate body of doctrine to make certain that criminal interdiction of speech is a most extraordinary occurrence.

In recent years we have come to understand that the state does not act just as policeman, but also as educator, employer, landlord, librarian, broadcaster, banker, and patron of the arts. The twentieth century has witnessed an enormous growth of state power and, even more, a proliferation of the ways in which this power has come to be exercised. In speaking of the rise of the activist state in America, we refer not simply to the quantitative growth of state intervention, but more importantly to the changes in the ways that the state has intervened: a movement from negative to affirmative modalities. This development has been of considerable importance politically and socially and, at the same time, has created new challenges for the First Amendment. Is it an infringement of freedom of speech for a public library to exclude certain radical books? Or for a public school to offer a course on evolution but not creationism? Or for a state-owned television station to promote the development of nuclear power and not provide an opportunity for environmental groups to voice their opposition?

In grappling with these questions the Supreme Court has acknowledged that the First Amendment applies to the affirmative as well as the negative modes of exercising state power, but it has encountered great difficulty in specifying exactly *how* it applies. Stated in the most general terms, the question is whether the Court should apply a double standard — should the Court be more lax in its review of these affirmative exercises of power than it is when it reviews the enforcement of the criminal law? This is the question I wish to address, and to do so I will focus on the constitutional and political controversy concerning Robert

Mapplethorpe and the National Endowment for the Arts (NEA). That controversy was spurred by a number of public statements by Senator Jesse Helms of North Carolina objecting to the use of public funds to support the show. Although it did not reach the Supreme Court, for more than a year the Mapplethorpe controversy was a matter of national importance. It was in the newspapers almost on a daily basis, resulted in one criminal prosecution, the appointment of a presidential commission and several rounds of legislation, and raised complex issues that every modern democracy must confront in adjusting to the changes in the way state power is exercised.

Robert Mapplethorpe was a successful New York photographer. He was gay and in March 1989 died of AIDS. At that time, he was forty-two years old. Shortly before his death, a retrospective exhibition of his photographs was organized by the Institute for Contemporary Art of the University of Pennsylvania. That exhibition consists of 175 photographs and the subjects of the photographs vary widely. A number of the photographs are portraits of Mapplethorpe himself and of celebrity friends such as Andy Warhol; others portray flowers (lilies or tulips), which are presented in almost sculptural form, as if hewn from cold, inanimate stone. There are also two photographs of children of some of Mapplethorpe's friends: one is of a naked boy, sitting on the back of a chair; another is of a young girl, with her dress raised. She is not wearing undergarments. Still another group of photographs consists of shots of the male body, often heads, but sometimes the naked torso or its various parts. They too appear sculptural. One photograph in this group, entitled "Man in Polyester Suit," is of a black man dressed in an inexpensive suit of clothing with his penis exposed. His head is cropped. A final group of photographs — perhaps the most provocative — depicts homosexual relationships and homosexual activity. In one, two men are kissing ("Larry and Bobby Kissing") and in another, entitled "Embrace," two young men, one black, the other white, both wearing jeans, naked to their waists, are affectionately embracing one another. In addition, a number of photographs, part of the so-called "x, y, z series," include depictions of sexual activity that could be considered sadomasochistic. Starting in the early part of 1989 and continuing through the fall of 1990, the show was exhibited in various museums throughout the country. In one locality — Cincinnati, Ohio — a museum and its director were prosecuted for violating a local criminal statute that prohibits the pandering of obscenity. The director faced a fine of up to $ 2,000 and a one year jail sentence if convicted; the museum faced a $ 10,000 fine. The indictment was filed in the spring of 1990, soon after the opening of the show there, and later that fall, after a highly publicized trial lasting several weeks, the jury voted to acquit. As with any jury decision, it is impossible to know exactly what that verdict turned on—a dislike of the prosecutor? a failure of proof? a belief that pictures are constitutionally protected? a concern for the reputation of Cincinnati? It seems relatively clear, however, that the prosecution could not have survived under established First Amendment doctrine and that the jury would have been reversed if it had decided differently.

In the obscenity context, the Court's strategy has been to limit state censorship by propounding a constitutional definition of obscenity, which then is used to demarcate the outer boundary of state power: Material that does not fall within the narrow parameters of the constitutional definition of obscenity is protected. This strategy, first announced in 1957 in *Roth v. United States,* evolved through the sixties in cases like the one involving "Fanny Hill," and then received its most recent statement in 1973 in *Miller v. California.* According to *Miller,* a conviction for distributing or publishing allegedly obscene material will be allowed to stand if, and only if, the material, taken as a whole, (1) appeals to a prurient interest in sex, (2) depicts sexual activity in a patently offensive way, and (3) is without serious aesthetic, political, or scientific value.

In applying this test, the challenged work must be viewed as a whole, and from that perspective, it is doubtful that the Mapplethorpe exhibition could properly be regarded as either appealing to a prurient interest in sex or depicting sex in a patently offensive way. On these issues there might be some room for disagreement, but the situation is quite different when it comes to applying the third prong of the *Miller* test, which calls for an inquiry into the social value of the work and is meant to exclude from the ambit of constitutional protection the trivial or worthless, that is, literary or artistic material with no conceivable connection to the promotion of First Amendment values. Clearly, Mapplethorpe's work is not of that variety.

As a matter of aesthetics alone, the Mapplethorpe exhibit is a considerable achievement. His photographs are heartless; the flowers and bodies seem devoid of life—as I said, they appear almost sculptural—but they present an aesthetic vision that is original and in many respects stunning. The fact that a number of the most respected museums in the country ran the exhibition understandably made the work's aesthetic accomplishment the principal line of defense in the Cincinnati trial, and the testimony of leading figures from the national art establishment supported this aesthetic assessment. It is important, however, to understand that there is also a political dimension to Mapplethorpe's work and it too calls for protection under the *Miller* test, even more than does its aesthetic value. The political significance of the exhibition derives from its revelatory power: it brings into view the lives and practices of the gay community, a group long marginalized in American society that today is being ravaged by the AIDS epidemic. The show can be seen as a response to the angry protest of the gay community: "Silence = Death."

The Mapplethorpe photographs bear witness to the life of the gay community, boldly affirming its understanding of the erotic, portraying the full range of the community's sexual practices, some intimate, some quite brutal. The intimate encounters — the kiss, for example — might be grudgingly accepted by the casual museum-goer, while the scenes characterized as sadomasochistic in the "x, y, z series" force the same viewer to confront, and thus to critically reflect upon, the limits of his or her tolerance. Some of the shots in this series — for example, a picture of "a naked man with a bullwhip protruding from his posterior," as Senator Helms described it — shock conventional sensibilities in much the same way as burning a flag does. Like the confrontational tactics of gay political groups such as "ACT UP" and "Queer Nation," these photographs call on the viewer to recognize the gay community and its needs, a call made all the more urgent by the AIDS crisis which, many charge, has been allowed to continue unabated because it afflicts a group whose suffering has often been dismissed by an unsympathetic public as insignificant or, worse, as deserved. One of the most striking photographs in the exhibition, perhaps emblematic of the entire show, is a 1988 self-portrait of Mapplethorpe, taken in the year before his death, in which only his face and his right hand are luminous, as though set in a sea of blackness. His face appears worn, his eyes distant and still, his right hand is clenched, grasping a staff crowned with a skull, which, like Mapplethorpe himself, stares out at the viewer.

Seen in this way, the Mapplethorpe exhibition is, to use the *Miller* test, endowed with serious political value and on this basis alone, I venture to say, ultimately would have been protected from a criminal obscenity prosecution. But the other type of state response occasioned by the show — a loss of federal subsidies — appears more difficult to cabin. For most of our history, art in America has depended financially on the market and private charity, but for about the last twenty-five years the federal government, through the National Endowment for the Arts, has played an increasingly important role in financially supporting or subsidizing artistic activity. The appropriation for the NEA [National Endowment for the Arts] for fiscal year 1990 was approximately $144 million. The Institute of Contemporary Art of the University of

Pennsylvania had received some $30,000 in NEA funds to assemble the Mapplethorpe retrospective. The question posed, in circumstances where the exhibition is protected from an obscenity prosecution, is whether it would have been constitutionally permissible for the government to deny that grant.

The controversy over funding the Mapplethorpe show began in June 1989 when Senator Helms learned that the show was about to open in the Corcoran Gallery of Art, a highly respected private museum in Washington, D.C. Senator Helms denounced Mapplethorpe's work as "filth" and "trash" and publicly objected to the use of federal funds to underwrite it. The curator of the Corcoran Gallery, presumably acting out of fear for the impact of the controversy on the NEA or on future applications to the NEA by the Corcoran, responded by canceling the plans for the exhibition.

The Corcoran's decision to cancel the show angered the artistic community, and, not surprisingly, did not satisfy or quiet the congressional critics. In the appropriations statute enacted that fall, Congress excluded from the NEA appropriations an amount equal to what the Institute of Contemporary Art had received for assembling the Mapplethorpe exhibition. That statute also required that the NEA give thirty days notice if it again intended to make a grant to the Institute. The concern was not, however, only with the Mapplethorpe exhibition. Helms and his followers hoped to generalize these sanctions so that in the future the funds appropriated by Congress could not be used to support work like Mapplethorpe's.

Defining the category of artistic work that would be ineligible for NEA funds proved to be an arduous task, taxing the imagination of the lawyers and the negotiating skills of the politicians, and the result was the so-called Helms amendment. It provided:

> None of the funds . . . may be used to promote, disseminate, or produce materials which in the judgment of the National Endowment for the Arts . . . may be considered obscene, including but not limited to, depictions of sadomasochism, homoeroticism, the sexual exploitation of children, or individuals engaged in sex acts and which, when taken as a whole, do not have serious literary, artistic, political, or scientific value.
>
> Although the Helms amendment borrowed the language of the *Miller* test, the statute swept more broadly, prohibiting funding for projects that do not fall within *Miller*'s narrow definition of obscenity. Indeed, Senator Helms aspired to a rule prohibiting the government from funding all "indecent" art.

The Helms amendment applied to funds appropriated by Congress in the summer of 1989, and, of necessity, expired when the period (fiscal year 1990) covered by it had come to an end.

However, the controversy stemming from the funding of the Mapplethorpe show persisted and took on additional significance in the summer of 1990, when Congress took up the question of reauthorizing the NEA and making appropriations for it. The result, a statute passed in November 1990, just after the jury verdict in Cincinnati and shortly before congressional elections, did not reenact the original Helms amendment, but made changes in the statutory framework of the NEA that present an equally serious, but perhaps less visible, threat to artistic freedom.

On one level, the new statute appears to soften the censorial force of the Helms amendment. The statute still decrees that "obscenity . . . shall not be funded," but the determination of obscenity is left to the courts, and the standard articulated in the statute adopts the three-pronged *Miller* test. However, the new statute compounds the sanctions for an obscenity conviction by providing that if NEA funds are used to produce a work later decided by a court to be obscene, the funds will have to be repaid and the artist or recipient will be ineligible for further funding until full repayment is made. This provision is a matter of some concern, since an increase in sanctions increases the deterrent effect of state obscenity laws, thereby enhancing the risk that someone might be discouraged from engaging in conduct that is constitutionally protected.

Even more worrisome are the provisions in the 1990 statute consolidating the power of the NEA chairperson over grantmaking. In the past, applications for grants were reviewed by panels of experts, usually peers of the applicant consisting of museum professionals or artists involved in the same discipline. These panels were deemed "advisory," but in practice they dominated the process — approval by a panel usually insured receipt of a grant. The new statute anticipates a change in that procedure, vesting final authority for selection in the chairperson. Although the precise method by which that change will be effectuated is not specified, a commission appointed by President Bush in the midst of the controversy engendered by the Helms amendment points the way. Its report, issued in September 1990, should be read as part of the legislative history. The commission assumes that the chairperson will continue to use peer-review panels, but in order to concentrate responsibility for the selection in his or her hands, it recommends that the peer-review panels be asked to provide the chairperson with many more recommended applicants than can be funded. The chairperson will then pick and choose.

What standards will be used in making this choice? On this issue the 1990 statute is explicit. It directs the chairperson to ensure that "artistic excellence and artistic merit are the criteria by which applications are judged, taking into consideration general standards of decency and respect for the diverse beliefs and values of the American public. . . ." In directing the chairperson to attend to "general standards of decency," the 1990 statute, in effect, transforms the Helms amendment into an internal operating principle of the NEA. The chairperson is freed from the *Miller* standards and is able to deny funding to a project like Mapplethorpe's even though it is not within the constitutional definition of obscenity and thus not amenable to criminal prosecution. The chairperson could conclude that the project offends "general standards of decency," even though it has, within the meaning of the Supreme Court's standards, serious aesthetic or political value.

In the middle of December 1990, Chairperson John E. Frohnmayer sought to reassure an NEA advisory body (the National Council on the Arts) on this issue, since it had just adopted a resolution opposing the promulgation of explicit decency standards. He said, "I am not going to be a decency czar here." Weeks later he approved grants to two controversial performance artists — Karen Finley and Holly Hughes — whose applications had previously been deferred. But in light of the overall structure of the statute, as well as the position of the present administration on these issues and Frohnmayer's previous performance — especially the extraordinary measures he used to implement the Helms amendment, even against the advice of the same advisory body — his disclaimer rings hollow and his approval of the Finley and Hughes applications should not be taken as a bold reversal of policy. The risk remains great that, in the end, Helms will have his way, and grants will be denied by the Endowment for projects like Mapplethorpe's on grounds of indecency, even though they cannot constitutionally be prosecuted criminally for obscenity.

Most commentators and perhaps a majority of the justices would not see this double standard as posing a First Amendment problem of any sort, but my inclination is just the opposite. My analysis proceeds on the assumption that government subsidies are not gifts or bonuses for acts that would have occurred without them. Subsidies are not, I assume, redundant, but rather generally have a productive value: they bring into existence art, performances, or exhibitions that would not have existed but for the subsidies. They do this either by providing artists with an income, by defraying costs associated with a show, or by creating incentives for artists or the distributors of art. The NEA grant to the Institute for Contemporary Art for the Mapplethorpe exhibition encouraged or made possible the Mapplethorpe exhibition, and the denial of a subsidy would have had the effect of withdrawing that exhibition from public view or limiting its availability. A denial of a grant does not have the brutal consequences for the individual that might, on the worst of days, attend a criminal prosecution for obscenity, when the artist languishes in prison. From the perspective of the public, however, its effect is similar: It keeps art from us.

Of course, even without the government grant the artistic endeavor may survive and be made available to the public. Alternative sources of funds might be found, as might have occurred in the case of the Mapplethorpe show itself if the original grant had been denied the Institute of Contemporary Art. In that sense, the ban effectuated by a denial of grants, even federal ones, is not absolute and universalistic. To borrow a term from Harry Kalven, it is a "partial sanction." I believe the same might well be said of the criminal prosecution. An artist or museum director might decide to suffer the sanction of the criminal law (for example, pay the fine or spend some time in jail) rather than remain silent. Or, as became evident in the case of Mapplethorpe, the criminal sanction might be limited in its geographic reach. The Mapplethorpe exhibition provoked an obscenity prosecution in Cincinnati, but not in Philadelphia or Hartford (where it was shown previously) or in Boston (where it moved subsequently). In the American federal system, the administration of the criminal law is largely the responsibility of states and localities, all of which have jurisdictions of limited scope.

It is thus appropriate to assume that the effect of a denial of a grant is roughly equivalent to that of a criminal prosecution, in that each tends to silence the artist or, in the case of exhibitions, make the artist's work unavailable to the general, museum-going public. But a complication is introduced when it comes time to define the constitutional wrong. In the criminal context, the wrong can be defined in purely quantitative terms, that is, in terms of the overall quantity or amount of speech available to the public. Indeed, our reaction to the obscenity prosecution is largely shaped by the common assumption that the more speech the better; the function of the three-pronged definition of obscenity is to keep that silencing effect to an absolute minimum. In the case of subsidies, however, an additional element is needed to define the wrong, because the presence of scarcity transforms the decisional process into an allocative one.

The amount of money to be dispensed by government will always be exceeded by the number of applicants, and thus of necessity a competition will arise among the applicants for the grants. A grant given to one is necessarily denied to another. Giving a grant for the Mapplethorpe exhibition enhances the availability of his work to the public, but that money is simultaneously being denied to another artist, thereby silencing him or her or limiting the availability of that artist's work. Conversely, while denying a grant for the Mapplethorpe show might have impaired the availability of his work to the public, one must also assume that the funds withheld would not have lain idle but would have been allocated to some other artist, allowing that artist's work to flourish. This means that the silencing produced by the denial of the subsidy is of a different nature than that produced by a criminal prosecution. The difference arises from the fact that silencing is a necessary concomitant of every allocative decision. Does one artist's expression have greater claim to scarce state subsidies than another's?

At this point, the temptation is great to retreat from the concern with effect and, in contrast to the criminal context, to define the constitutional wrong in purely procedural terms. While the wrong in the criminal context consists of the silencing effect, which the constitutional definition of obscenity tries to keep to a minimum, the wrong in the allocative context is not the silencing effect but rather the reason or criterion upon which the allocation in question was based. Under this view, the First Amendment would be reduced to a rule requiring that the choice among applicants not be made on the basis of a forbidden criterion.

To support this view, an analogy might be drawn to that body of constitutional doctrine concerning the treatment of women and racial minorities under conditions of scarcity, say, in employment. In that context, the Court has abandoned the approach it had taken in the late 1960's and early 1970's, and beginning with *Washington v. Davis* in 1976, has taken the position that the constitutional wrong consists not of the effect (denial of employment) but the use of a forbidden criterion (race or sex). I have great difficulty with this shift in the Court's approach to equal protection or discrimination issues, and even more so with the notion of transferring it to free speech.

While in the discrimination context it might be possible to construct a finite and rather well-understood list of forbidden criteria (race, religion, national origin, sex, etc.), in the free speech context no such list readily suggests itself. What are the criteria prohibited by the First Amendment? In a library case, Justice Brennan grappled with a similar problem and, in an effort to honor the general norm of content-neutrality, used two notions to define the forbidden criterion: disagreement with an idea and a desire to suppress that idea. He said that a library's decision to remove a book from its collection cannot be based on a disagreement with the ideas presented in that book and a desire to limit access to those ideas. But, as is the case with any allocative decision, the acquisition and removal decisions of a library must reflect some judgment as to what ideas to make available to the readers, and what not to make available. It is not at all clear why the First Amendment would prohibit that judgment from being based on agreement or disagreement with those ideas, or any other reaction to the content of the material. In the allocative context, content neutrality makes little sense, for a choice must be made among competing ideas, and for that purpose the official entrusted with that decision must look to content. Surely, books should be purchased, or artistic awards granted, on the basis of content.

Moreover, even if the forbidden criteria could be identified with some specificity, a First Amendment approach that looks to the underlying criterion in judging the validity of allocative decisions would be extremely difficult to administer, the more so under the 1990 NEA statute. Such an approach entails an inquiry into the grounds or basis of a decision, and, as we know from the discrimination context, often the real reason for an allocative decision cannot be authoritatively ascertained. Imagine that a peer-review panel provides Frohnmayer with a list of a dozen applicants under circumstances where only one can be funded. The Chairperson chooses the one, and then justifies his decision on grounds of "artistic excellence." How can a court be certain that this is the real reason for his decision and that he is not basing it on some (still to be defined) forbidden criterion or, to use a phrase of Brennan's from the library case, that he is not impelled by an "unconstitutional motivation"? Granted, the legal system might create presumptions or devise various rules regarding the burden of proof to cope with this problem, but all these devices will invariably reflect some understanding of effect or impact. Similarly, the legal system will have to fall back on notions of effect, as it has done in the discrimination context after *Washington v. Davis*, to cope with the problems of multi-member decisional agencies (one official bases his or her decision on the forbidden criterion while the others do not) or mixed motives (the allocative decision is only partially based on the forbidden criterion).

It is also hard to understand the theoretical basis of an approach looking to the criterion of decision. In the discrimination context, the criterion approach rests upon considerations of individual fairness — it is arbitrary to judge someone on the basis of a criterion (such as race or gender) that has no discernible connection to productivity and over which the individual has no control. I, for one, believe it is a mistake to reduce the constitutional ideal of equality to considerations of individual unfairness, but however appropriate such a reduction might be in the discrimination context, it seems particularly inappropriate in the speech context. The First Amendment is a guarantee of collective self-determination, a method for making certain that the people know all that they must to exercise their sovereign prerogative, and for that reason, the focus should be on the condition of public discourse, not the process by which that condition was created. Keeping ideas and information from the public, not the unfair treatment of the speaker, is the gist of the constitutional wrong, and from that perspective a concern with the basis for an act that keeps ideas from the public makes little theoretical sense. As Justice Rehnquist put it in the library case, though only to score a debater's point, "If Justice Brennan truly recognizes a constitutional right to receive information, it is difficult to see why the reason for the denial makes any difference."

In the discrimination context, some have defended the criterion approach on the ground that it maintains a measure of state neutrality: if a judgment is based on some meritocratic criterion, such as performance on standardized tests, the state can achieve a measure of neutrality on issues of race even though it must make a choice among applicants for a job. A similar thought might account for the use of the criterion approach in the religion context in order to maintain the separation of church and state, and might have some sway in the speech area too, where state neutrality is also assumed to be a good. We want the state to be neutral between competing viewpoints, or competing conceptions of the good life, and it might be assumed that neutrality could be achieved by having allocative decisions based on some meritocratic criterion such as "artistic excellence."

This assumption, however, is unfounded. The ideal of neutrality in the speech context not only requires that the state refrain from choosing among viewpoints, but also that it not structure public discourse in such a way as to favor one viewpoint over another. The state must act as a high-minded parliamentarian, making certain that all viewpoints are fully and fairly heard. In the allocative context, the state's decision will necessarily have an impact on which viewpoints are heard by the public, and the state's obligation of neutrality requires that it make certain that the public debate is as rich and varied as possible. The use of a meritocratic criterion cannot insure the discharge of this duty, for it disregards the impact of that decision on public debate; as we learned in the discrimination context, a seemingly neutral criterion does not insure a neutral impact. A meritocratic criterion, such as a standardized test, may still have a discriminatory effect, because it may especially disadvantage minorities. Similarly, in the speech context, the use of a meritocratic criterion, such as "artistic excellence," for determining who is heard may silence viewpoints, or skew the debate, depending, of course, first, on the specific content given the (rather broadranging) notion of "artistic excellence" and, second, on the condition and needs of public discourse.

For these reasons, the judiciary should not adopt a criterion approach in judging allocations or other affirmative exercises of state power. Rather, it should keep the focus on effects, specifically the effect the exercise of state power has on public debate. In a case like Mapplethorpe's, the denial of a grant would impoverish public debate because it would reinforce the prevailing orthodoxy on an issue of great public importance, the status of the gay community, and the basis for that denial, whether it be aesthetics, taste, or ideology, is of no constitutional significance. The constitutional wrong of an obscenity prosecution arises from the effect such an exercise of state power has upon public discourse, and although there is an analytic difference in the subsidy situation, arising from the scarcity factor, the focus should remain on the effect of the government action. The difference between the two situations requires not an abandonment of the concern with effect, but a more refined conception of effect and the introduction of a more qualitative perspective in the allocative context: A court must determine what effect a challenged allocative decision would have upon public debate. To use the now talismanic phrase, a court must ascertain whether the allocative decision would contribute to a debate on national issues that is "uninhibited, robust, and wide-open," or whether its effect would be just the opposite.

Such a judgment requires a sense of the public agenda, a grasp of the issues that are now before the public and what might plausibly be brought before it, and then an appraisal of the state of public discourse, not to decide who is right or who is wrong, but to see whether all the positions on the issue are being fully and fairly presented so that the people can make a meaningful choice. These kinds of judgments must be context specific and perhaps for that very reason seem extremely arduous. The allure of the criterion approach is that it renders these kinds of judgments unnecessary. They are, however, required by the grandest aspirations of the Constitution and are not beyond our reach. In fact, they are analogous to the judgments made by the great teachers of the universities of this nation every day of the week as they structure discussion in their classes, and, turning to the case at hand, are implicit in our assessment of the Mapplethorpe controversy: the special egregiousness of the denial of NEA funding in such a case arises from the fact that it would perpetuate and reinforce the orthodoxy that tends to marginalize the gay community. Even those on the side of censorship in this controversy would acknowledge this effect; in fact, they may wish it to occur.

The effects approach calls for judgments that have analogues throughout the law, not just in discrimination cases, but also in such widely disparate areas as antitrust, when a judge determines the parameters of a relevant market, and torts, when a judge evaluates the frontiers of scientific possibility in order to adjudicate a state-of-the-art defense. Admittedly, we may have a special reluctance for allowing these judgments in the speech area for fear that the judicial power will become an instrument for constricting rather than broadening public understanding, or even worse, for favoring one viewpoint over another. In assessing the significance of this risk, however, two considerations must be kept in mind.

First, the courts will not make these judgments in a vacuum, but will be subject to intense scrutiny of the critical community that attends to matters judicial, in this instance, not just lawyers and the press, but also the leaders of the art world. The Mapplethorpe controversy has been remarkable in its capacity to mobilize the art community and to spur countless museums and theaters across the country into action. If judicial review of a funding decision were required, members of this community might participate in the judicial proceedings, as they did in the Cincinnati trial, to help the court appreciate the political and aesthetic significance of the work denied funding. Or, they might mobilize the public, as they did in response to the Helms amendment, to make certain that the judiciary does not shirk its duty or become an instrument of censorship while reviewing NEA practices under the effects standard. The courts may be less responsive to such criticism than institutions that are politically accountable, but they are not immune to it.

Second, a rejection of the effects approach, and a willingness to judge allocations on the basis of the decisional criteria, would invite the very same risk, namely, that courts will become an instrument for perpetuating an orthodoxy, but it would do so in an even more flagrant manner. The evidentiary difficulties of sorting out the real reason for a decision and impeaching the stated reason will tilt the process in favor of the NEA, and almost invariably lead to the endorsement of its decisions.

Even under the effects approach, state officials are likely to continue using meritocratic criteria, such as "artistic excellence," to allocate grants. The funding agency will select what it understands to be the best or most worthy recipient. The agency will, however, come to understand that its standards of excellence will have to be either interpreted or modified in light of the constitutional commitment to robust public debate. When a criterion such as "artistic excellence" is used in such a way as to have the consequence of keeping from public view art that presents ideas and positions otherwise absent from public discourse, and thus to constrain public debate, it will have to be qualified in order to fulfill the purposes of the First Amendment.

Considerations of merit will also have a role to play when it comes time for the judiciary to review a denial of a grant. As in the early discrimination cases, where the Court looked to effects, judgments of artistic merit emerge as a justification or defense for a course of conduct that produces the undesirable effect (the perpetuation of an orthodoxy). As a defense, considerations of artistic merit fix the outer limits on the state's duty to avoid the production of that effect, and the precise location of that limitation depends on the gravity of the effect produced and the urgency of the justification for what the state has done. The duty to attend to effects does not mean in the speech area, any more than it did in race, an end to merit. What it does mean is either a reexamination of the notions of merit that underlie funding decisions or, alas, a sacrifice of some of the values that might be furthered by notions of merit that do not incorporate, or, in fact, are antagonistic to, the constitutional goal of producing a public debate that is worthy of our democratic aspirations.

In determining whether there would in fact be such a sacrifice, and what its magnitude might be, it is important to understand how art typically performs its educative function: not by advancing a single viewpoint, in the way that a commercial advertisement or political propaganda might, but by leading the viewer to contemplate a familiar subject from a new perspective or by bringing the unfamiliar into focus. The best art leads us to ponder, reconsider, suspend conventional wisdom, and reject unreflective assumptions and expectations. Subjectively, art provokes an attitude of inquisitiveness; objectively, it reveals aspects of an experience or subject matter — in the case of Mapplethorpe, sexuality — that we have previously misperceived or ignored. The best art is art that enriches public discourse, not in the manner Stalin made familiar, but by opening our eyes and thereby transforming our understanding of the world.

The Mapplethorpe exhibition was not by any means a simple and straightforward celebration of homosexuality or gay life, nor is that the basis for its special claim for public support. The Mapplethorpe exhibition brought the gay community into focus, but only to complicate our understanding of it. Certainly, the photographs are defiant affirmations of gay sexuality, but they are also something more. Their manner of presenting their subject though classically simple composition and immaculately clear, precise renderings of sensuous surfaces, recalling fashion photography, has the effect of making the activities depicted appear staged or theatrical, as if the participants were merely performing for others, or as if their self-awareness depended on how they appear in others' eyes. These images suggest a parallel between, on the one hand, a theatrical sexuality that may have as much to do with posing, and even pain, as with emotion, and, on the other hand, the social position of gay people in contemporary America, simultaneously marginalized and subjected to intense and derisive public scrutiny. Walking through the exhibit, one is led to wonder whether social marginalization has been internalized in homosexual practice — whether homosexual self-understanding has been marred and distorted by public loathing and opprobrium. These photographs do not constitute a propagandistic endorsement of homosexuality, or anything else, but invite us — all of us — to reconsider our understanding of, and attitude toward, homosexual orientation and practice. In the case of the Mapplethorpe photographs, there is no sacrifice of artistic or democratic values. They are, at once, great art and a great lecture, an inspired contribution to a public debate that aspires to be "uninhibited, robust, and wide-open."

There is, of course, a danger the government might respond to judicial review of decisions denying grants to such controversial and provocative works by withdrawing from the field altogether. The state might abandon the subsidy program, or at least seriously cut back on it, in which case speech would be a loser to an even greater extent than when the government denies a grant to some controversial artist. The Mapplethorpe controversy did indeed result in diminution of the NEA appropriation in the 1989 funding statute, and it provoked some to call for an end to government funding for the arts. In the criminal context, there is no comparable risk because a state retreat — no prosecution or repeal of the obscenity statute — is assumed under standard doctrine to promote speech values.

It seems to me, however, that this difference between the criminal and allocative contexts requires a measure of caution, not a difference in standards or general approach. The reduction of the overall level of spending is a contingency, not a necessity. The judiciary should not assume that it will materialize, and in fact it should do all that it can to prevent that from happening, always keeping open the possibility that, in the worst of all possible worlds, it might have to freeze the level of spending or even mandate an increase in levels of spending to protect First Amendment values. The First Amendment commands that Congress make no law abridging the freedom of speech, but as in the case of the heckler's veto, where a speaker is left to the mercy of an angry mob, a decision of the state not to act — to go out of the funding business altogether — might itself be a form of action prohibited by the First Amendment. The broad discretion allowed the legislature in making budgetary decisions cannot be used in a way that interferes with the attainment of constitutional goals, or, more concretely, with the judiciary's efforts to further these goals by reviewing the programs established by the legislature and the way they have been administered by the executive.

In the school desegregation area, strong judicial intervention created a risk that the school boards would close their schools rather than integrate. It is remarkable, however, that over a thirty year period, involving thousands and thousands of court desegregation orders, that risk materialized only on two or three occasions, and in each instance, the judiciary somehow found that it had the power to order that the schools be reopened. This power was not defeated by sloganistic assertions that "there is no constitutional right to a public education" (which have recurred in the art context in slightly different form); this power of the judiciary has recently been affirmed by the Supreme Court in the Kansas City school case, in which a federal court ordered the state to raise taxes to finance the court's desegregation plan.

As a purely ideological matter, the argument in favor of a double standard, sharply differentiating between subsidies and criminal prosecutions, and applying a distinctly more relaxed standard to the former, has many roots, but perhaps none is more important today than the capitalist ethos that transforms money into power and gives to each productive agent prerogatives over the property or money he or she has earned. Capitalism contemplates private ownership of the means of production and, even more crucially, a sharply differentiated incentive structure. The best get paid the most. For this incentive structure to work as promised, the rewards distributed for efficient production must be secured from the rapacious greed of the less well paid and, even more, must empower those who are fortunate enough to receive these rewards. The private property system presupposed by capitalism is intended to provide to each individual, with respect to the money he or she has earned, a sense of entitlement as well as a sense of security. You may use your money in the way you wish, spend it on the goods you want, give it to anyone you wish, or deny it to those you do not like, approve of, or admire.

There is no reason in the world why the sense of entitlement associated with private property should extend to the money in the public treasury, which is not earned but rather collected and held for public purposes. But in this triumphant moment of capitalism, the norms of that economic system cannot easily be confined. Money is money, and what is worse, we tend to think of the state in much the same way as we would an individual entrepreneur, confusing Uncle Sam and Donald Trump. We personify the state and accord it the privileges of a productive agent, thinking that the decision of the government to support activities should be wholly discretionary and that government should not be obliged to support activities it does not like, approve of, or admire.

What is needed here by way of remedy is a sense of limits. One can readily appreciate the marvels of capitalism as an economic system, as a way of providing for the efficient delivery of goods and services, without believing that each and every decision of social life—say of the political domain or of the family—should be dominated by the norms of that economic system. It would be sad if the First Amendment became captured by the economic system and if we thus allowed free speech to be compromised by our desire to protect private property. The revenues collected by the state constitute a public resource, to be used for public purposes, and I can think of no higher purpose for these funds than the preservation of democracy, bringing before the public viewpoints and options that otherwise might be slighted or ignored. Government subsidies, whether they be for the arts or education, should not be used to reinforce the prevailing orthodoxy, but rather to further the sovereignty of the people by provoking and stirring public debate, so that we may live as we do because we want to, not because the familiar is all we know or can imagine.

How might one apply Fiss' suggestions? His arguments express a broadly shared sentiment. But there will always, one suspects, be tension between the goal of enriching public discourse and feeding the pool of ideas, on one hand, and wishing to limit access to ideas that undermine shared values. We deny public subsidies to discriminatory organizations such as the neo-Nazis and the Ku Klux Klan. To what extent would Fiss' criteria ask us to give more deference to those whose messages are ones of hate? Can we reconcile neutrality with the notion that some ideas are deeply abhorrent to the values at the core of our system? How firmly can we adhere to the notion of neutrality? Some of us are uncertain when the matter is one of tolerating hate and intolerance. Others, like Catharine MacKinnon, would draw the line at any messages that reinforce gender discrimination. Still others would censor ideas and expressions that they deem indecent or offensive. And yet a system of free expression seems, by definition, to be dedicated to tolerating offense and entertaining what some regard as dangerous thoughts. The dilemmas are not easily resolved. They are, however, at the core of our laws and our sense of ourselves.

✍ Further Reading

The first amendment is a favorite topic of legal scholars. Most have defended a broad or absolutist reading of the amendment, agreeing with the sentiment that the Constitution permits no limitation of speech solely on the basis of content. Because first amendment jurisprudence changes slowly, books written over a broad period of time remain relevant. Among the most influential discussions of the first amendment are the following: Thomas Emerson, *Toward a General Theory of the First Amendment* (1963); Harry Kalven, Jr., *A Worthy Tradition: Freedom of Speech in America* (1988); C. Edwin Baker, *Human Liberty and Freedom of Speech* (1989); Lee C. Bollinger, *The Tolerant Society: Freedom of Speech and Extremist Speech in America* (1986); Frederick Schauer, *Free Speech: A Philosophical Enquiry* (1982); and Steven H. Shiffrin, *The First Amendment, Democracy, and Romance* (1993).

We saw that Catharine MacKinnon is a widely read and much noted critic of the first amendment and the social effects of an absolutist interpretation on the status of women. The most succinct account of her views is *Only Words* (1993). Her critiques are laid out at greater length and depth in *Feminism Unmodified* (1987) and *Toward a Feminist Theory of the State* (1989).

Although the debates over the government's role in funding speech and culture change significantly with the prevailing political winds, two older articles remain highly relevant, "Beyond Unconstitutional Conditions: Charting Spheres of Neutrality in Government-Funded Speech," by David Cole (67 N.Y.U. Law Review 675 (1992)) and "Law for Art's Sake in the Public Realm," by Barbara Hoffman (16 Columbia-VLA Journal of Law and Arts 39 (1991)). Among the more interesting recent articles that respond to current policies and rulings is David Greene, "Why Protect Political Art as 'Political Speech'?" (27 Hastings Communications and Entertainment Law Journal 359 (2004)).